AVID

READER

PRESS

ALSO BY HELEN CASTOR

Joan of Arc:
A History

She-Wolves:
The Women Who Ruled England
Before Elizabeth

Blood and Roses:
One Family's Struggle and Triumph
During the Tumultuous Wars of the Roses

THE

EAGLE

AND THE

HART

The Tragedy of Richard II and Henry IV

HELEN CASTOR

AVID READER PRESS

New York   London   Toronto   Sydney   New Delhi

AVID READER PRESS
An Imprint of Simon & Schuster, LLC
1230 Avenue of the Americas
New York, NY 10020

First Avid Reader Press hardcover edition October 2024

AVID READER PRESS and colophon are trademarks of Simon & Schuster, LLC

Simon & Schuster: Celebrating 100 Years of Publishing in 2024

For information about special discounts for bulk purchases,
please contact Simon & Schuster Special Sales
at 1-866-506-1949 or business@simonandschuster.com.

The Simon & Schuster Speakers Bureau can bring authors to your live event.
For more information or to book an event contact the Simon & Schuster Speakers Bureau
at 1-866-248-3049 or visit our website at www.simonspeakers.com.

Interior design by Ruth Lee-Mui
Maps on pages xii–xv by Neil Gower

Manufactured in the United States of America

1   3   5   7   9   10   8   6   4   2

Library of Congress Cataloging-in-Publication Data has been applied for.

ISBN 978-1-9821-3920-9
ISBN 978-1-9821-3922-3 (ebook)

For my mother, Gwyneth,

and in memory of my father, Grahame

The king must be thus made. For he must sit in a chair clothed in purple, crowned on his head, in his right hand a scepter, and in the left hand an apple of gold, for he is the greatest and highest in dignity above all other and most worthy. And that is signified by the crown, for the glory of the people is the dignity of the king.

William Caxton, *The Game and Play of the Chess*, 1474, translation of Jacopo da Cessole, *Liber de moribus hominum et officiis nobilium ac popularium super ludo scacchorum*, c.1300

Be not thyself. For how art thou a king
But by fair sequence and succession?

William Shakespeare,
The Tragedy of King Richard the Second,
act 2, scene 1

CONTENTS

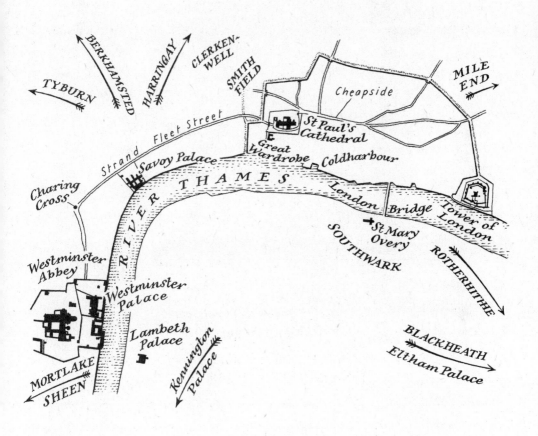

FAMILY TREE 1 – DESCENDANTS OF EDWARD III

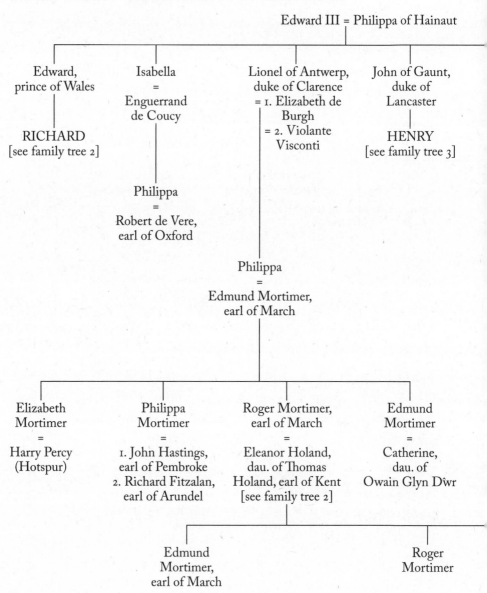

Edward III = Philippa of Hainaut

Edward, prince of Wales

RICHARD
[see family tree 2]

Isabella
=
Enguerrand de Coucy

Philippa
=
Robert de Vere, earl of Oxford

Lionel of Antwerp, duke of Clarence
= 1. Elizabeth de Burgh
= 2. Violante Visconti

John of Gaunt, duke of Lancaster

HENRY
[see family tree 3]

Philippa
=
Edmund Mortimer, earl of March

Elizabeth Mortimer
=
Harry Percy (Hotspur)

Philippa Mortimer
=
1. John Hastings, earl of Pembroke
2. Richard Fitzalan, earl of Arundel

Roger Mortimer, earl of March
=
Eleanor Holand, dau. of Thomas Holand, earl of Kent
[see family tree 2]

Edmund Mortimer
=
Catherine, dau. of Owain Glyn Dŵr

Edmund Mortimer, earl of March

Roger Mortimer

= married
---- extramarital relationship

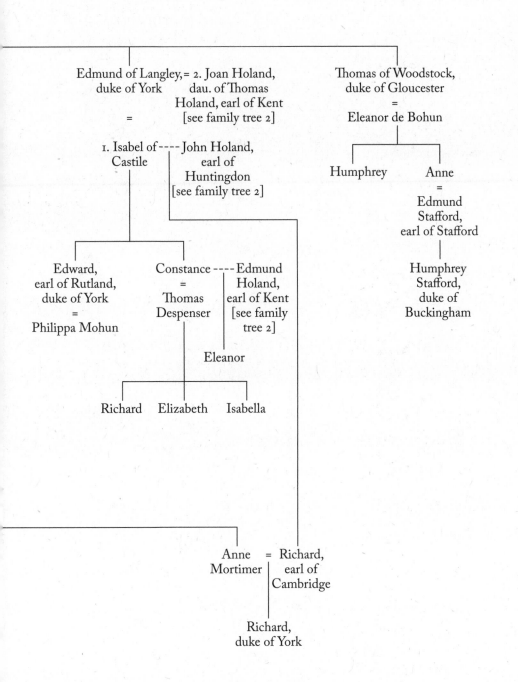

Edmund of Langley, = 2. Joan Holand,
duke of York   dau. of Thomas
               Holand, earl of Kent
          =   [see family tree 2]

Thomas of Woodstock,
duke of Gloucester
=
Eleanor de Bohun

1. Isabel of ---- John Holand,
   Castile   earl of
            Huntingdon
          [see family tree 2]

Humphrey   Anne
                 =
               Edmund
               Stafford,
           earl of Stafford

Edward,   Constance ---- Edmund
earl of Rutland,   =   Holand,
duke of York   Thomas   earl of Kent
     =   Despenser   [see family
Philippa Mohun   tree 2]

Humphrey
Stafford,
duke of
Buckingham

Eleanor

Richard   Elizabeth   Isabella

Anne   =   Richard,
Mortimer   earl of
          Cambridge

Richard,
duke of York

FAMILY TREE 2 – RICHARD AND THE HOLANDS

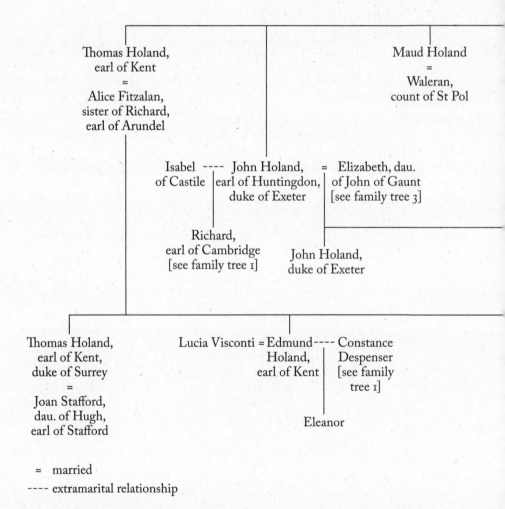

Thomas Holand,
earl of Kent
=
Alice Fitzalan,
sister of Richard,
earl of Arundel

Maud Holand
=
Waleran,
count of St Pol

Isabel ---- John Holand, = Elizabeth, dau.
of Castile earl of Huntingdon,   of John of Gaunt
           duke of Exeter   [see family tree 3]

Richard,
earl of Cambridge
[see family tree 1]

John Holand,
duke of Exeter

Thomas Holand,
earl of Kent,
duke of Surrey
=
Joan Stafford,
dau. of Hugh,
earl of Stafford

Lucia Visconti = Edmund ---- Constance
              Holand,   Despenser
              earl of Kent [see family
                            tree 1]

Eleanor

= married
---- extramarital relationship

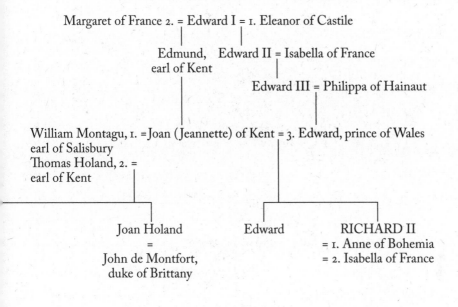

Margaret of France 2. = Edward I = 1. Eleanor of Castile

Edmund,   Edward II = Isabella of France
earl of Kent

Edward III = Philippa of Hainaut

William Montagu, 1. =Joan (Jeannette) of Kent = 3. Edward, prince of Wales
earl of Salisbury
Thomas Holand, 2. =
earl of Kent

Joan Holand   Edward   RICHARD II
=   = 1. Anne of Bohemia
John de Montfort,   = 2. Isabella of France
duke of Brittany

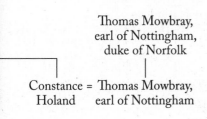

Thomas Mowbray,
earl of Nottingham,
duke of Norfolk

Constance = Thomas Mowbray,
Holand   earl of Nottingham

Eleanor Holand   Joan Holand   Margaret Holand
=   = 1. Edmund of Langley   = 1. John Beaufort,
Roger Mortimer,   [see family tree 1]   earl of Somerset
earl of March   = 2. William, Lord   [see family tree 3]
[see family tree 1]   Willoughby   = 2. Thomas of Lancaster,
                        = 3. Henry, Lord Scrope   duke of Clarence
                                                       [see family tree 3]

FAMILY TREE 3 – HENRY AND THE BEAUFORTS

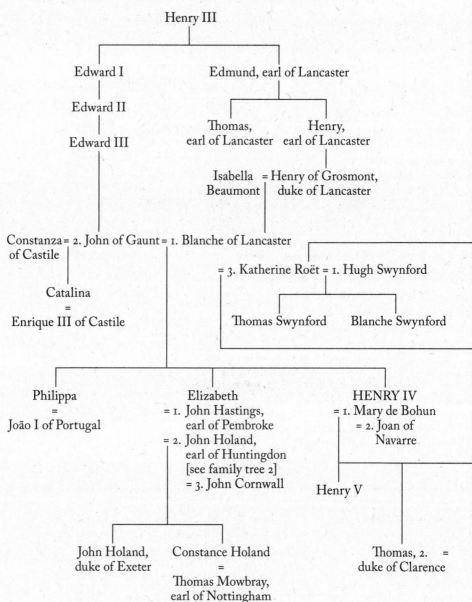

Henry III

Edward I   Edmund, earl of Lancaster

Edward II

Edward III   Thomas,   Henry,
     earl of Lancaster   earl of Lancaster

Isabella   = Henry of Grosmont,
Beaumont   duke of Lancaster

Constanza = 2. John of Gaunt = 1. Blanche of Lancaster
of Castile

= 3. Katherine Roët = 1. Hugh Swynford

Catalina
=
Enrique III of Castile

Thomas Swynford   Blanche Swynford

Philippa   Elizabeth   HENRY IV
=   = 1. John Hastings,   = 1. Mary de Bohun
João I of Portugal   earl of Pembroke   = 2. Joan of
     = 2. John Holand,   Navarre
       earl of Huntingdon
       [see family tree 2]
     = 3. John Cornwall

Henry V

John Holand,   Constance Holand   Thomas, 2.   =
duke of Exeter   =   duke of Clarence
      Thomas Mowbray,
      earl of Nottingham

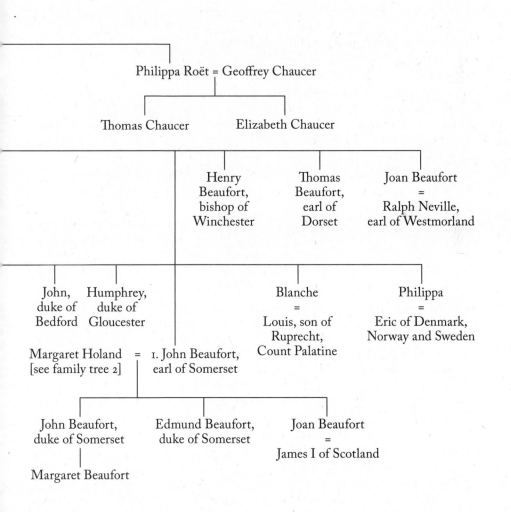

Philippa Roët = Geoffrey Chaucer

Thomas Chaucer   Elizabeth Chaucer

Henry   Thomas   Joan Beaufort
Beaufort,   Beaufort,   =
bishop of   earl of   Ralph Neville,
Winchester   Dorset   earl of Westmorland

John,   Humphrey,   Blanche   Philippa
duke of   duke of   =   =
Bedford   Gloucester   Louis, son of   Eric of Denmark,
                                        Ruprecht,   Norway and Sweden
Margaret Holand   =   1. John Beaufort,   Count Palatine
[see family tree 2]   earl of Somerset

John Beaufort,   Edmund Beaufort,   Joan Beaufort
duke of Somerset   duke of Somerset   =
                                                James I of Scotland
Margaret Beaufort

AUTHOR'S NOTE

All quotations from primary sources in the main body of the text are given in modernized form. I've occasionally made minor adjustments to published translations from non-English sources. In those cases, and often elsewhere, the original French or Latin is quoted in the notes.

Distances are given "as the crow flies," in rounded numbers.

Sums of money are mainly given in English pounds (£), shillings (s), and pence (d). There were twelve pence to the shilling, and twenty shillings to the pound. Some round numbers are given in marks—a mark being another unit of account (rather than coinage) valued at two-thirds of a pound (13s 4d).

For the names of people and places, I've sought to prioritize clarity and consistency for ease of comprehension. So, for example, England's territories in southwestern France—the extent of which shifted dramatically during different phases of the Anglo-French war—are called Aquitaine throughout, rather than Gascony or Guyenne, names with slightly more restricted (though still flexible) geographical connotations, which were also in contemporary usage. For individuals, I've settled on one identifying name, rather than changing designation over time as they acquired different noble titles. Sometimes, as in the case of Edward III's sons, that means their place of birth (so, Lionel of Antwerp, John of Gaunt [Ghent], Edmund of Langley, Thomas of Woodstock); for others, I've used a family name (such as Mowbray or de Vere) or a nickname (Hotspur, Boucicaut); and when none of those options is straightforwardly available, I've stuck with the first title acquired (for example, Edward, earl of Rutland, who subsequently gained and lost the dukedom of Aumale before eventually inheriting the dukedom of York). I've also used different linguistic forms, where possible, to offer a flavor of the multilingual world of late medieval Europe or to distinguish between different characters who share the same name. However, I've retained anglicized names where they're overwhelmingly familiar (for example, John, duke of Burgundy, rather than Jean, duke of Bourgogne).

Many of these characters will be familiar to anyone who knows Shakespeare's history plays—but, because of their changes of title over time, they don't all appear here under the names Shakespeare used. So, for example, my Thomas of Woodstock, Edmund of Langley, and Edward of Rutland are *Richard II*'s Gloucester, York, and Aumerle. Several characters also seem significantly older onstage than the true age of their historical selves, among them Shakespeare's Gaunt, and Henry himself in the *Henry IV* plays. For anyone in search of further information or clarification, I hope the "Directory of the Main Players in the Royal and Noble Families of England and France" at the back of the book will help.

Richard of Bordeaux and Henry of Bolingbroke were first cousins, born in 1367 just three months apart. They were ten years old when Richard became king of England. They were thirty-two when, in 1399, Henry overthrew him to become king in his place.

It was a shocking and intensely dangerous moment. The authority of the crown, contemporaries believed, was instituted by God to rule the kingdom and its people. England's sovereign was required to be both a warrior and a judge, to protect the realm from external attack and internal anarchy. To depose the king, therefore, was to risk everything—worldly security and immortal soul—by challenging the order of God's creation. Such devastatingly radical action could never be justified unless kingship became tyranny: rule by arbitrary will rather than law, threatening the interests of kingdom and people instead of defending them. Even then, could anyone but God rightfully remove a sovereign He had anointed?

Before Richard and Henry were born, that question had been answered in the affirmative only once in England in the 300 years since their ancestor William the Conqueror won his crown on the battlefield at Hastings. During the early decades of the fourteenth century, their great-grandfather Edward II had prioritized his favorites over the needs of his kingdom so consistently, to such appalling effect, that he undermined the rule of his own law. His wife led the resistance that, in 1327, put his son on the throne in his place.

But Richard's deposition in 1399 was the first in which the crown did not pass to an unequivocally legitimate heir. Richard had birthright on his side, and a profound belief in his own God-given majesty; beyond that, he lacked all qualities of leadership. Henry had everything Richard lacked, all the qualities of a sovereign, bar one: birthright. A king who was a tyrant was replaced by a king who was a usurper. In his attempt to preserve the kingdom, Henry had to undo the sacred authority of the crown and then try, somehow, to reconstruct it in his own image.

Richard and Henry are best known now through Shakespeare's history plays. *Richard II* and *Henry IV Parts I and II* (from which the chapter titles of this book are taken) span the years from 1398 to 1413. Shakespeare himself billed *Richard II* as a tragedy: containing some of his most hauntingly beautiful poetry, it forms a compelling psychological study of Richard as both sovereign and man. Most of the action, the course of historical events, happens offstage. The central drama lies instead in the play of the king's thoughts and emotions, the dismantling of his "self" as he is stripped of his power, then his crown, and finally his life. Richard's cousin is his nemesis, but Shakespeare offers no access into Henry's mind. We see only the weight of the choices that confront him, and the tough pragmatism of a politician and soldier seeking to save himself and the kingdom from tyranny. It is Richard who thinks out loud, who speaks truth to this new power, and has to face what it might mean to be a king unmade. This disequilibrium—with Richard at the tragic heart of the narrative, Henry as the means of his fall—continues in different form in the plays that bear Henry's name. There a figure scarcely recognizable as the dynamic Bolingbroke of *Richard II* has taken the throne as a gray man, worn almost into anonymity by rebellion and illness, who cedes center stage to his son Prince Hal, the future King Henry V, and Hal's (largely fictional) friend Falstaff.

When the plays were written in the second half of the 1590s, almost exactly 200 years after the moment at which *Richard II* opens, their contemporary relevance was immediate and controversial. The great historical cycle that they completed—alongside the three parts of *Henry VI* and *Richard III*, produced earlier in the decade—frames Richard's deposition and Henry's usurpation as the original sin for which England's punishment would be the darkness of civil war, a bloody conflict between the houses of Lancaster and York that ended only with the coming of the Tudors. In that reading, the aging Queen Elizabeth—by then in her sixties—embodied England's resurrection, its triumphant return to peace and prosperity. But *The Tragedy of King Richard the Second* also sets out the justification for Richard's fall;

its necessity, given the damage he was inflicting on his kingdom; and in the end its inevitability. The play depicts a capricious, childless monarch—an isolated figure surrounded by a cabal of self-interested courtiers, the succession to the throne unclear—who fails to recognize or even acknowledge the crown's duty to its subjects. And in the 1590s that description seemed, to the disaffected among Elizabeth's people, to describe England's present as well as its past.

Shakespeare's nuanced, lyrical treatment of the crisis of 1399 won popular attention and critical acclaim, but when the play was first printed in 1597, and then again twice in 1598, the provocative scene of the deposition itself was omitted from the text. In the year after that, another version of Richard and Henry's story became both a commercial sensation and a focus of intense political scrutiny. John Hayward's *The First Part of the Life and Reign of King Henry IV* appeared in February 1599, and "no book ever sold better," its publisher noted. Hayward dedicated his history in admiring terms to the earl of Essex, once Elizabeth's indulged favorite but now a bitterly disruptive malcontent within the regime. The queen was "mightily incensed with that book which was dedicated to my lord of Essex," reported the lawyer Francis Bacon, "being a story of the first year of King Henry the Fourth, thinking it a seditious prelude to put into the people's heads boldness and faction." In June 1599 the second edition was banned and burned as it came off the press, and in July 1600 Hayward himself was imprisoned in the Tower. The night before Essex finally took up arms in rebellion against Elizabeth in February 1601, his friends and servants arranged for a play about Richard and Henry—perhaps Shakespeare's *Richard II*, perhaps a dramatization of Hayward's book—to be performed at the Globe Theatre in London. They wanted to see it because they believed the earl would soon bring its drama "from the stage to the state," but the revolt collapsed within hours. By the end of the month Essex had lost his head, and six months later the queen was explicit about her identification with the dead king. "I am Richard II, know you not that?" she told the keeper of the archives stored in the Tower.[1]

Four hundred years on, after the reign of a second Queen Elizabeth, questions concerning specifically royal sovereignty—the rightful succession to the throne and the monarch's part in defending the kingdom's interests—lie in the realm of the politically symbolic and the passively structural. At first glance, it might seem unlikely that the crisis of 1399, so incendiary a subject in 1599, should resonate still. But the exercise of sovereign authority does not depend on the role or existence of a hereditary monarchy. The relationship between our rulers and the law, the interaction between their personalities, their principles (or lack of them), and the precedents and norms that shape our governments, remains central to the course of politics and the functioning of constitutions.

When I first began thinking about this book, I knew it would be a study of the psychology of power. Richard and Henry make a fascinating pair—so closely related by blood, such utterly different men—whose intertwined lives formed an extraordinary and fateful moment in England's history. But for a historian, thoughts and emotions aren't easy to interpret without the benefit of private letters, diaries, memoirs, or any other means of access behind the closed doors of a public life. At a distance of 600 years, drawing a psychological portrait is only made possible by joining scattered dots, rather than tracing a continuous line. I've set out to join dots from the surviving records of the lives of these two kings into a coherent representation of two very human beings: to investigate not only what they did, but why they did it, and how they came to be the men they were. The notes to the book show the contemporary sources from which I've worked. There's plenty of room within and between them for alternative perspectives, but in the pages that follow you'll find the Richard and the Henry I've come to see.

I also knew that, unlike some stories I've previously told, almost all of the book's protagonists would be male—not only because the world of the fourteenth century took it for granted that leaders must be men, but because the moment in which Richard and Henry lived was a moment of political masculinity in crisis, a moment at which the war that had shaped the experiences of the two generations before them began to fail. Still, I hope that the women in this history won't go unnoticed: many of them very young, some finding a kind of agency, personal or political, within a highly constrained existence, and almost all facing physical risk in childbirth just as much as their male contemporaries confronted danger on the battlefield.

What I didn't foresee was that, during the years I've spent in Richard and Henry's company, the conflict between them would come to feel so topical. To twenty-first-century eyes, the political world of the Middle Ages always combines the strange and the familiar. Fourteenth-century England was a remarkably centralized state with a complex bureaucracy, a sophisticated judicial system, and representative parliaments in which taxes were granted and statute law made—but it had no police force or standing army. The authority of the state relied instead on the private power of the aristocracy, the great landowners whose estates across the country gave them not only wealth but also control over people. England was a nation with its own distinct language, culture, and history—but its frontiers with its neighbors of France, Scotland, and Ireland were sites of constant conflict, wars shaped by feudal hierarchies and dynastic claims. All of these circumstances gave profound significance to perceptions of legitimacy in government: the relationship between principles of law and their practical enforcement, and the balance between individual interests and the common good.

And that, for me, is what makes the tragic history of Richard II and Henry IV so chillingly resonant. Theirs is a story about what happens when a ruler demands loyalty to himself as an individual, rather than duty to the established constitution. When he seeks to create his own reality rather than concede the force of verifiable truths. When he demands that his own will should trump the rule of law. When he recognizes no interests other than his own. It's a story about the terrifying unpredictability of unfolding political crises; about the interplay of conflicts within states and between them; about the ways in which authority can be bent, shaped, and broken. Its drama is rooted in family and dynasty, constitution and country, and its themes of power, legitimacy, and the limits of rule and resistance are as urgent now as they have ever been.

This is the story of how a nation was brought to the brink of catastrophe and disintegration—and, in the end, how it was brought back.

PART ONE

WAR

One

1367-1377

by my scepter's awe

Richard always knew he was special. From the moment of his earliest
memories, his life was set apart, his presence in the world shaped by his
God-given destiny.

But the world had taken a while to recognize his glory. When he was
born, on January 6, 1367, no one expected him to inherit the throne. He had
an older brother, Edward, a cherished toddler whose arrival two years before had been celebrated with a glittering ten-day tournament where, one
chronicler reported, more than 850 lords and knights had jousted by day and
partied by night. The bill for candle wax alone came to more than £400:
translated into an annual income, it was a sum for which many of the lords
present would have been grateful and of which their knightly companions
could only dream. Two years on, the same chronicler did not even mention
Richard's birth.[1]

His brother was not the only one ahead of him in the line of succession.
By the time Richard was born, their father, Edward, prince of Wales and
Aquitaine, had spent all thirty-six years of his life so far as a king-in-waiting.
A legend across Europe, he personified the chivalric virtues of honor and
sanctioned violence. At sixteen, he had been in the heat of the fighting at
Crécy when an English army inflicted a staggering defeat on the forces of
France. In the aftermath of that great day, he adopted the badge of an ostrich
feather in tribute to a brave opponent, the blind King John of Bohemia, who

had chosen to die a hero's death by charging sightless into the fray with his horse tied to those of the knights on either side of him. From then on, the Bohemian king's feathers appeared with the prince everywhere, picked out in white or silver on black pennons when he rode at the head of his retainers, and on rich black tapestries in the halls and chambers of his homes. At twenty-six, this "Black Prince" took command on the battlefield at Poitiers, capturing the French king and leading the English to a victory more overwhelming even than Crécy. At thirty-two, he was appointed to govern the vast territories of Aquitaine in southwestern France, a newly sovereign state under English rule according to the terms of the Anglo-French Treaty of Brétigny. Four years after that, when Richard was born in Aquitaine's capital, Bordeaux, the prince was about to move south on campaign, crossing the Pyrenees in the cold of winter to fight for England's ally King Pedro of Castile, against the illegitimate half brother who had usurped the Castilian throne. The result, at Nájera three months later, was another astounding triumph, hailed by one awestruck chronicler as "the greatest battle to be fought in our days."[2]

Richard's father was a hero. His grandfather was an icon. By January 1367, Edward III had worn the crown of England for forty years. He had become king at fourteen when his mother, the French-born Queen Isabella, and her lover Roger Mortimer, earl of March, had overthrown his father, Edward II, after years of first damagingly ineffectual, then dangerously tyrannical rule. The deposed king died, conveniently and without explanation, in the shadows of his prison, while Isabella and Mortimer took power in her son's name. A month short of his eighteenth birthday, Edward led a coup to take control of his own government, sending Mortimer to the gallows and his mother into lavishly funded retirement. From that point on he gathered his family, his nobles, and his realm around the lodestar of his sovereignty to become one of the most extraordinary monarchs England had ever seen. His pursuit of war with France both reached for glory—in asserting his claim, inherited through his mother, to be king of France as well as England—and defended England's shores by pushing the fight deep into French territory. He won his battles and learned from his mistakes, and his people believed without question that their fearsome and magnificent king had "most tenderly at heart his land of England," as his chancellor told a parliament held eight months before Richard's birth.[3]

These three royal Edwards—brother, princely father, and sovereign grandfather—stood between Richard and the throne. As the spare to the heir of the heir, the newborn's political future was, at best, indistinct. Meanwhile, the emotional landscape of his infancy was formed by a royal family that was both close-knit and unusually indulgent. Edward III had proved to be a doting royal patriarch. His early marriage to Philippa, daughter of the count of Hainaut, Holland, and Zeeland, had been a pragmatic alliance negotiated by his mother to secure military backing for her assault on his father's regime. Still, from its miserable start amid the wreckage of the family within which Edward had grown up, the young couple's relationship rapidly developed into one of deep affection and mutual support. Philippa traveled with her husband even on campaign, and by 1367 she had given birth twelve times. Three of these royal children died in infancy and three more in their teens, but one daughter and five sons survived, ranging in age from the thirty-six-year-old prince of Wales to the youngest, Thomas of Woodstock, who turned twelve the day after his nephew Richard's birth. Not only did the king and queen enjoy each other's company, but they kept their growing children close, along with an extended family of other young aristocrats, in a household that combined splendor, demonstrative warmth, and sparkling energy.

The marriages of a king's offspring were valuable commodities within the complex marketplace of international diplomacy. Royal brides—a rarefied kind of human freight, each delicately wrapped in her jeweled trousseau—were transported hundreds of miles over land and sea in bodily service to their country, to marry men they barely knew or had never met. The transaction might cement an enduring political relationship, or it could prove to be a fleeting aberration, a deal done in a moment of cynical manipulation or unwarranted hope—but, whether they found themselves cherished or isolated, these young women were unlikely to see home and family again. Edward knew as well as anyone his children's worth: initial negotiations to find a wife for his eldest son among the ruling families of Europe had begun just after the prince's first birthday.[4] But those discussions and many more came to nothing. In the end, the Black Prince did not marry until he was thirty-one. And his bride—to whom his vows were made privately, impulsively, without political consultation—was not a foreign princess but his cousin Joan, countess of Kent, a woman he had known since childhood, who had grown over the years into a luminous beauty with a scandalous reputation.

Their love match was not an act of defiance. In many ways, the marriage of Richard's parents was the culmination of Edward III's plan for his family's future, not a rebellion against it. The king's pursuit of a conventional set of matrimonial alliances had been jettisoned years earlier, after the unhappy outcome of the matches he arranged for his first two daughters. In 1347, the eldest, fourteen-year-old Isabella, had been jilted by her intended husband, Louis de Mâle, the sixteen-year-old count of Flanders. Much against his will, the young man had been forced into agreeing to the marriage after his father was killed fighting for the French at Crécy. With preparations for the wedding almost complete, Louis left his Flemish home to go hunting one morning and did not come back. By the time he resurfaced in Paris under French protection, his deserted bride and her double-crossed father had been left publicly humiliated. The following summer, the betrothal of Isabella's younger sister Joanna to Pedro of Castile promised better things. Her little fleet of ships packed with embroidered gowns, silver plate, and armed guards made landfall near Bordeaux, a staging post on her journey south, just as a terrifying epidemic was taking hold in the port. This apocalyptic disease, it turned out, had no respect for royal blood, nor for urgent prayers at the altar hung with heavy green silk that Joanna had brought from home. News of her death reached England at the same time as the plague itself.[5]

Over the next eighteen months, as the cataclysm that became known as the Black Death unfolded across Europe, almost half of England's people died. The political and psychological effects of living through horror that should have been unimaginable were profound and unpredictable. The war with France was barely interrupted: given that both sides claimed divine sanction for their cause, the intervention of heaven-sent mortality did not obviate the need for ongoing human slaughter. Edward's government also snapped into action to protect the economic structures on which the powerful depended, imposing a statutory maximum wage at the low rates to which landowners had been accustomed before death claimed half their workforce. But the king's experience of the plague had been devastatingly personal. See-ing one beloved daughter abandoned on the eve of her wedding had been a blow, both publicly and privately; just a year later he had agreed to part with another, sent on her way to become the queen of a distant country, only to lose her completely. His response, in this brutal world where God's purposes were harder than ever to construe, was to decide that his children would marry only in circumstances where the political benefits were under his own control, and where their consent was freely given.[6]

The results were varied but striking. In 1351 his eldest daughter flirted with the prospect of a new suitor in Aquitaine, to the point where five ships lay at anchor in Plymouth Harbour, laden and ready to take her to her wedding. This time, it was Isabella who changed her mind, returning to her adoring parents to spend the next decade living an elegant, extravagant, and remark-ably independent life as an unmarried royal daughter. When she finally took a husband, in 1365 at the advanced age of thirty-three, it was because she wanted to. Enguerrand de Coucy was a young French nobleman who had come to the English court as a hostage, one of the distinguished group of royally entertained prisoners who served as human security for the eventual payment of the French king's ransom. He proved to be human security in particularly winning and graceful form, and his new father-in-law gave him his freedom and the earldom of Bedford along with Isabella's hand.[7]

Her younger sisters Mary and Margaret married heirs to noble houses: Mary became the wife of John de Montfort, duke of Brittany, to whom she had been betrothed since birth, and Margaret the wife of John Hastings, earl of Pembroke. But both young men, who were almost exactly the same age as their teenage brides, had been brought up within the royal household as wards of the king and queen. For all the political gain they stood to confer, these were relationships founded in family, and familiarity, and it was to general grief that the marriages ended almost before they had begun when both girls died in a new outbreak of plague in 1361–62. Their brothers Lionel of Antwerp and John of Ghent—or, in the English spelling, Gaunt—also made matches that combined territorial advantage with personal compat-ibility. Lionel married Elizabeth de Burgh, heir to the earldom of Ulster, another of the noble children being raised within the royal family, while John's bride was Blanche, heir to the duke of Lancaster, the king's cousin and one of his greatest friends.[8]

Of all Edward's children, the one who benefited most from the king's permissive approach to their emotional lives was Richard's father, the prince of Wales. Given the pressing need to secure the succession, it was a rare thing for an heir to the throne to reach his thirties without having a wife picked for him. But if anyone in the royal family had been indulged in their marital choices even more than the prince, it was the woman he eventually decided to marry.

Richard's mother, Joan of Kent, was much loved by her royal relatives, to whom she was known as Jeannette; and her whole life had been marked by controversy.

Her father, Edmund, earl of Kent, was the younger half brother of Edward II. At first, he supported Isabella and Mortimer in their deposition of the king; then, duped into believing that his brother was still alive, he plotted against them and lost his head as a traitor. Only two years old when her father was executed in 1330, Jeannette was taken in by the young Edward III and Queen Philippa to be brought up with their newborn eldest son and the royal siblings who arrived at regular intervals as the years went on. In 1341, at the age of twelve, she was married to William Montagu, the equally young son and heir of the earl of Salisbury, one of Edward's trusted friends. Three years later, Jeannette's father-in-law died from wounds sustained in a tournament; and another three years after that, it became disconcertingly apparent that all was not well with the teenage couple who had become the new earl and countess.[9]

There had been warning signs: the suggestion of physical estrangement, for example, in the fact that the six years of their marriage had not produced any children. But in 1347, to the enthralled shock of aristocratic society, it was alleged that the marriage did not exist at all. The astonishing claim was made by Sir Thomas Holand, a knight of the king's household whose exploits in Edward's wars had so far cost him an eye and won him a fortune. Jeannette,

Holand said, had married him before she had ever been married to Salisbury. Back in 1340, they had made vows to each other and consummated their union. He, not the earl, was her lawful husband, and now he launched an appeal to the pope in the attempt to enforce his marital rights.[10]

Perhaps it was true, although the chronology of the story had its difficulties, requiring as it did a clandestine wedding and secret physical relationship between a twelve-year-old girl of royal blood and a twenty-five-year-old soldier trying to make his way in royal service. More likely, Holand and the countess—now thirty-two and nineteen—had concocted a tale that might enable her to discard an unhappy marriage in favor of a more recent liaison with a man of lower birth and much greater personal appeal. Either way, it was clear what Jeannette wanted; and the deciding factor that allowed her to swap one husband for another was the support of her cousin the king. Despite Salisbury's desperate efforts to contest the case with the backing of Jeannette's appalled mother, by the end of 1348—the year of the plague, in which King Edward lost his own daughter Joanna—the young countess was spending Christmas at court at the heart of the royal family. Attorneys rode back and forth to negotiate with the pope until, by the end of 1349, her old marriage to Salisbury was annulled and her new one to Thomas Holand publicly confirmed.

Over the next decade, Jeannette gave birth to a brood of Holand babies, three boys and two girls, of whom four survived: Thomas, John, Joan, and Maud. She also acquired a new title and estate, inheriting the earldom of Kent in her own right on the death of her brother in 1352. In December 1360, the security of her young family was shaken when her husband, now captain general of the king's forces in northern France, fell ill and died at Rouen. Jeannette, at home with the children in England, found herself a widow at the age of thirty-two. Then, less than six months later, her life was transformed beyond recognition: she married the heir to the throne, the Black Prince, hero of Crécy and Poitiers, the royal cousin she had known since they were infants.[11]

As the news began to spread, eyebrows were raised across Europe. "Many people were greatly surprised by this match," one chronicler noted mildly, choosing his words with palpable care. It was not just that England's heir had finally turned his back on the possibility of an international alliance, nor that according to the rules of the Church the couple were too closely related by both blood and spiritual ties: the prince was Jeannette's first cousin once removed, and had stood godfather to her eldest son. It was also the very fact that she was already a mother and had twice been a bride. Custom dictated that the wife of a future king should be young and thoroughly sheltered in her upbringing, as a public warranty that her children, when she married, would be legitimate heirs of the royal bloodline. But Jeannette—two years older than her new husband, and a widowed mother of four—was no unworldly adolescent. The scandal of her rival husbands had not been forgotten, and so much skepticism remained about the grounds on which her annulment had been granted that the less reverent of her contemporaries archly dubbed her the "Virgin of Kent."[12]

None of this concerned the happy couple, both of whom had become entirely used, over the years, to getting their own way. Nor did the king show any hint of disappointment or alarm. With Edward's help, the technical difficulties of consanguinity were swept aside. Hastily dispatched royal letters produced a papal dispensation for the marriage, which was formally celebrated at Windsor Castle in October 1361. The new princess of Wales dazzled in a gorgeous dress of red cloth of gold embroidered with birds. The earl of Salisbury did not attend.[13]

The groom and his beautiful bride might not yet be king and queen, but, as the heir to the throne and his wife, they alone in England held the exalted titles of prince and princess. Their unique status was matched by their magnificent style. In the year of their wedding, the prince bought jewels—rubies, diamonds, and thousands of pearls—that cost him more than £3,000. The equivalent bill for the following year came to more than £2,000, along with over £700 spent on richly embroidered clothes for the prince and princess and her two young daughters. These were breathtaking sums, matter-of-factly noted in between administrative and business expenses in the prince's accounts—but they were also business as usual, given that magnificence was the proper expression of God-given power. And the prince's power was increasing. In 1362 he was ceremonially invested by his father as ruler of the newly sovereign territories of English Aquitaine. The summer after that, his entire household—including the princess's children, the couple's retainers and servants, and the goldsmith and two embroiderers they had engaged as part of their essential staff—set sail for Bordeaux. There and across Aquitaine, they worked to establish both the authority and the irresistible grandeur of their new court.[14]

The prince and princess lived in "such sumptuous state that no other prince or lord in Christendom could match them," wrote Jean Froissart, a servant of Queen Philippa who visited Aquitaine three years later, at Christmas 1366. By then Jeannette—her husband's "dearest and truest heart, beloved companion"—had already given him a son and heir, his namesake Edward, the boy whose arrival was toasted with such extravagant celebrations at the start of 1365. Now she was about to give birth to their second child. The last weeks of her pregnancy, over Christmas and into the new year, were filled with anxiety. For the first time since their wedding, her husband was about to go to war. She "sorrowed so much," said one sympathetic observer, that "through grief" she went into labor. But if his mother's fear hastened Richard's arrival, it did so with auspicious results. The prince had time to meet his new son before he left for the fighting, and so did the baby's uncle John of Gaunt, who passed through Bordeaux a few days later on his way to join his brother on campaign.[15]

There were blessings from heaven too. January 6, the date of the little boy's birth, marked the celebration of Christ's baptism by Saint John the Baptist, whose head was kept in Aquitaine as a holy relic at the abbey of Saint-Jean-d'Angély, seventy-five miles north of Bordeaux. It was also the feast of the Epiphany, when three kings had brought gifts in tribute to the infant Christ, and remarkably—at any rate, as the story was told later back in England—three kings also stood around the font at this royal christening. Afterward, it proved difficult to be sure which three sovereigns they had been: the kings of Spain, Portugal, and Navarre, suggested an enthusiastic monk in Canterbury, although it was tricky to establish (not to say actively unlikely) that the rulers of Portugal and Navarre had in fact been there. By "Spain" the chronicler meant Castile, and that at least was possible, given that the baby's father was about to ride into battle to restore the deposed King Pedro to his throne. The one monarch who certainly stood godfather to the child was Jaume of Mallorca, a kingdom long since lost to the Aragonese—but the flimsiness of his title hardly mattered, not in the retrospective telling of the tale. The point was to note the presence of some latter-day magi when the child was given the name of Richard, the great lionhearted king of England, another second son who had spent much of his remarkable life in Aquitaine.[16]

At the time, it seemed reasonable to suppose that this new Richard's future might also lie in his birthplace, perhaps as a royal lieutenant governing Aquitaine on behalf of his father or brother, the two Edwards who would rule England in turn after the glorious reign of Edward III. This direct line of succession was celebrated in a glamorous public reunion when the prince returned to Bordeaux after his victory at Nájera. Welcomed into the city with processions, prayers, and hymns of praise, he dismounted his charger outside the towering cathedral to find his wife there to greet him with their firstborn son. He swept them into his arms, kissing them both, before walking hand in hand with his princess through cheering crowds to their magnificent home. The family appeared blessed; entitled in every sense of the word. But it was not long before signs began to emerge that, for the first time in the couple's charmed lives, God did not intend the world to bend to their will.[17]

In the year after Richard's first birthday, his father's health started to deteriorate. As the months wore on, it became unnervingly clear that this was a chronic illness, debilitating in its effects and not easily treated. At the same time, the challenges facing the prince's regime in Aquitaine were multiplying. His military triumph in Spain had left his treasury in major deficit, and Pedro of Castile, who had undertaken to cover the immense costs of the campaign, was unable to pay. By the end of 1368, his half brother and rival Enrique was back in Castile with French support. In March 1369, bereft now of help from the ailing and unpaid English prince, Pedro was defeated by an army under French command. Nine days later, he fell into the hands of his brother, who stabbed him to death.[18]

Left with nothing to show from his Spanish campaign except mounting debt, the Black Prince turned to taxation in Aquitaine to fill the hole in his regime's accounts. But his attempt to impose significant levies to be collected for an unprecedented five consecutive years provoked resistance from some of the principality's most powerful lords. Soon it became apparent that Castile was not the only place where the king of France was prepared to make trouble. Charles V—son of the captured king who had died in London in 1364—had inherited the Anglo-French Treaty of Brétigny as part of his father's legacy. But the agreement, while settled in theory, had not proved straightforward in its implementation. Both sides were required by its terms to surrender a measure of sovereignty: the English king would give up his claim to the throne of France, and the French king his claim to jurisdiction over Aquitaine. In practice, neither side had been willing to press ahead with these renunciations. Now King Charles made provocatively clear his readiness as "sovereign lord" of the nobles of Aquitaine to hear their complaints against the prince's financial demands. It was a pulled thread that, little by little, unraveled the already-fraying peace. The war that had never quite ended was formally resumed in 1369, and in the summer of 1370 the Black Prince again took the field at the head of his troops.[19]

This time, however, he was not mounted on a warhorse but carried on a litter. Illness compromised his command and dulled his charisma. He ground out a grim victory, retrieving the city of Limoges from the French in a short and brutal engagement in which hundreds lost their lives. But when he returned to his family at Angoulême there was no feasting or celebration, only news of terrible loss. A year earlier his beloved mother, Queen Philippa, had died in faraway England, and worse had now followed: his treasured heir, five-year-old Edward, was dead. The succession of Edward after Edward after Edward in a golden age for victorious England had been a phantasm, the illusory promise of a future that would never be—just like the sovereign principality of English Aquitaine, a state that was disintegrating day by day as its territories were engulfed by the resurgent French.

The Black Prince was a broken man. With his princess and their surviving son, Richard—uniquely precious now, as he passed his fourth birthday in January—the prince sailed home to England at the start of 1371. The voyage exacted such a physical toll that it was three months before he was strong enough to move on from Plymouth to rejoin his father at Windsor.

There, after an absence of eight years, the prince found everything changed. The king was almost sixty. With Queen Philippa's death, Edward III had lost the mainstay of his life, and the great lion of England was visibly diminished. His need for constant emotional support meant that his mistress Alice Perrers—a much younger woman of humble birth and relentlessly acquisitive ambition—exercised overwhelming influence at court. She was not alone. To the alarm of Edward's subjects beyond the palace walls of Windsor and Westminster, it was apparent that members of the royal household, led by the chamberlain, Lord Latimer, were taking advantage of their proximity to the vulnerable king to dip their hands into royal coffers. Edward's extraordinary political deftness was finally deserting him. It had been one thing to sustain popular support for war when there was a great deal to show for its appalling costs: victories in battle, and territorial and diplomatic gains, won by a warrior king who offered decisive, responsive leadership at home as well as in the field. It was quite another to persuade his people to underwrite campaigns that resulted only in an erosion of the territories they were designed to defend, while public funds disappeared into his courtiers' pockets.[20]

These were problems that Edward and his eldest son were in no position to address. The prince appeared briefly in London when his infirmities allowed, but much of his time was spent outside the capital, in painful seclusion with his wife and son at his manors of Berkhamsted to the north and Kennington to the south. His father's health, both physical and mental, was also beginning to decline. Several months after the prince's return to England, the once indomitable king was taken suddenly ill. He recovered enough to insist in the summer of 1372 that he should in person "go upon the sea . . . to resist and oppose the malice of his enemies"—in this case, a Castilian fleet blockading the harbor at English-held La Rochelle. But violent headwinds trapped Edward and his ships in the Channel. La Rochelle was forced to surrender on September 7, and five weeks after that, still immobilized off the English coast, the king had to accept that his campaign was dead in the unforgiving water. The shock and frustration did nothing to improve his judgment or his grasp on government. Month by disturbing month, the vacuum of royal leadership threatened to become a black hole.[21]

Only one man could step in. The king had had five sons, but his heir languished on his sickbed and the second was dead: Lionel of Antwerp had not long survived his glamorous second wedding in Milan in 1368 to Violante Visconti, daughter of the lord of Pavia—whether through misfortune or murder, nobody knew. The fourth royal son, Edmund of Langley, had already shown himself to be a military and political placeholder, not any kind of leader. The fifth and youngest by far, Thomas of Woodstock, was a frustrated teenager, yet to be blooded in battle, still without title or estates of his own. Born too late to have played a part in the Camelot his parents had created, he had come no nearer to practical experience of war than the deck of his father's marooned flagship as it failed to sail for La Rochelle. That left Edward's third-born son, John of Gaunt, now in his early thirties and already a devoted lieutenant to his father and eldest brother.[22]

Gaunt had spent the formative years of his education and military training in the household of the Black Prince, the brother he idolized. As an adolescent in the 1350s, the glory days of his father's wars, he won his spurs by witnessing campaigns and battles at first hand, at sea and on land, in the Channel, in France, and in Scotland. In 1359, at nineteen, he married Blanche, heir to the duchy of Lancaster, and captained soldiers for the first time in his father's last great invasion of France. A decade of war and diplomacy later, he was already a widower, after Blanche died in childbirth in 1368. But she left Gaunt the duchy they shared, and their three surviving children: two daughters and one son, Henry, who had been born at the Lincolnshire castle of Bolingbroke in April 1367, three months after his cousin Richard across the sea in Aquitaine.[23]

Back then, Gaunt had visited Richard, his newborn nephew, in Bordeaux on his way to fight in Spain—but, detained by the campaign, he did not lay eyes on his own son and heir until the baby was six months old. From the very first, the duke would show Henry that duty was the defining principle of their privileged life. It was Gaunt who took over the defense of Aquitaine when the Black Prince and his little family sailed for England in January 1371; Gaunt who, eight months later, sought to keep alive the hope of retrieving Castile from France's ally King Enrique by marrying the murdered Pedro's daughter and heir Constanza. In 1373–74—now, thanks to his new wife, styled king of Castile and León as well as duke of Lancaster—he commanded an English *chevauchée*, a brutal raiding march, across France from Calais to embattled Aquitaine; in 1375–76, he led the English delegation at an Anglo-French peace conference held at Bruges under the auspices of the pope. If his father and brother could no longer exercise these essential powers of the crown, it was his responsibility—as well as his honor, and his burning ambition—to step into the breach.[24]

But Gaunt's example also demonstrated that neither duty nor privilege could guarantee success. The duke might see himself as England's savior, but that was not a judgment the kingdom itself was prepared to endorse. His splendid isolation as the representative of his father's and brother's dimmed authority meant that he was left exposed, a lightning rod for blame, when his labors failed to restore the grandeur of their conquests. By 1376, the might of English Aquitaine had been reduced to a precarious coastal strip from Bordeaux to Bayonne. Gaunt's *chevauchée* had failed to bring the French to open battle, or to achieve anything else beyond a great deal of expenditure and human suffering. The Bruges conference, months of diplomatic sound and fury on the grandest scale, produced no more than a temporary truce, which was already being violently disputed on the ground before it had even been formally sealed. And Castile—the kingdom Gaunt impotently claimed the right to rule—had not been a party to the negotiations, leaving English ships off the Atlantic seaboard as much at the mercy of Enrique's marauding fleet as they had ever been.

It was not that Gaunt lacked ability as a politician or a soldier, but he was firefighting on so many fronts, with such limited resources, that even small victories were far beyond his reach. Meanwhile, those left behind in England, powerful and humble alike, had seen only the proud army that marched out of Calais with Gaunt in 1373, not the forces that reduced it to a straggling, starving rump by the time his men stumbled into Bordeaux in 1374; only the triumphal history that underpinned the English demands at Bruges, not the present realities that made inevitable their frustration. The explanation for these disasters, many of Gaunt's countrymen came to believe, was that the duke's efforts were spurred by personal ambition, not public duty. Through his second marriage he had already secured himself the paper crown of another country. Why would he not seek to be king in his own land?

The parliaments of 1371, 1372, and 1373, summoned to approve grants of taxation to fund the war and shore up the crown's rapidly deteriorating finances, had been tense affairs. The Commons—representatives of the lesser landowners and town oligarchs on whom the brunt of the tax burden fell—had been restive and relentlessly critical of the regime's financial management. But the parliament that met in April 1376 was angry. In this, the fiftieth year of Edward's glorious reign, his kingdom stood impoverished and under threat. Despite the pause in the fighting agreed to at Bruges, his government was asking yet again for taxes to pay for a failing war, while those who clustered around the aging king in the royal household did nothing but line their own pockets. The Commons—meeting separately as they usually did, in the chapter house of Westminster Abbey—for the first time elected one of their number, a resourceful and articulate knight named Peter de la Mare, to be their spokesman or "Speaker" in discussions with the lords. On their behalf, de la Mare demanded action against the courtiers whose financial crimes, he said, threatened to destroy the realm.[25]

This was not intended as an attack on Edward himself—nor on Gaunt, who, on behalf of his incapacitated father and brother, was presiding over the whole assembly—but on "certain intimates of the king and others of their faction," as the rolls of parliament cautiously put it. Criticism of royal ministers and favorites had long been a necessary feint in order to avoid a direct assault on the anointed sovereign. The king ruled by the will of God, and resistance to his authority always risked a charge of treason—although less so than it once did. It had been part of Edward's political genius that, back in 1352, he had seen the benefit for both crown and people of defining treason clearly by statute for the first time, thereby renouncing its possibilities as an unpredictable weapon in royal hands in favor of demonstrating his commitment to the security of his subjects under his law. In any event, in this case it was patently true that the king himself was not personally responsible for the current corruption of public finances other than by default. Through de la Mare, the Commons presented a lengthy list of those they deemed answerable, including both the royal mistress, Alice Perrers, and the chamberlain, Lord Latimer. The latter stood accused—probably correctly, and among other similarly creative offenses—of having embezzled the king's own money in order to lend it back to the government on extortionate terms.[26]

The Commons believed the remedy should involve the removal and punishment of these criminals and, in an appeal to the historical precedents of earlier political crises, the appointment of a standing council of three bishops, three earls, and three lords to supervise the workings of government on the king's behalf. Instinctively, Gaunt had no truck with such attempts—outrageous as they would be in any normal circumstances—to place formal constraints on the exercise of royal authority. But he was no fool, and in the end he recognized the urgent political need to defuse the current crisis by offering concessions in response to the scale and force of the Commons' demands. In late May, he persuaded his father to approve the establishment of a council exactly as the Commons had asked. More remarkably—given that two years earlier Edward had commissioned a brooch for his mistress bearing the motto *Sans départir*, "Never apart"—the increasingly frail king also agreed to banish Alice Perrers from court. Latimer and his associates were then charged with abuses of office by an evolving legal process known as impeachment, which allowed groups of complainants to present charges in which the crown had an interest, and which was now used for the first time by the Commons in parliament against ministers of the king. But by the time the guilty men were condemned, imprisoned, and fined, another blow had already fallen on the reeling kingdom.[27]

The prince of Wales, like the king himself, had been too unwell to do more than sit in state at the opening session of the parliament in late April. By the end of May, he was critically ill. After a visit from his heartbroken father at his manor of Kennington, the prince was brought back across the Thames to the palace of Westminster. There, on June 7, 1376, he made his will. His body, he said, should be buried in Canterbury Cathedral near the shrine of Saint Thomas Becket, and his coffin attended during the funeral ceremonies by knights wearing his coat of arms and his black badge with silver ostrich feathers. With his family at his bedside, he entrusted his wife and son to the care of his father and brother. At his urging, Edward and Gaunt solemnly swore that they would look after the boy and uphold his rights as heir to the throne. The next day, Trinity Sunday, the Black Prince died. He was not quite forty-six years old.[28]

"Never, so God help me, was such sore grief beheld as there was at his departing," wrote a herald who had served under his command. For once, there were no dissenting voices. "He was the very flower of chivalry, without peer in this world," noted his military surgeon John Arderne; "another Hector," offered the monastic chronicler Thomas Walsingham. "When he died, all the hope of the English died with him." But abandoning hope was an indulgence the beleaguered kingdom could not afford. The Commons, whose proceedings against the corrupt courtiers were temporarily halted by this royal tragedy, stood in need of the same reassurance as the dying prince himself: that, even if God did not intend Edward IV to follow Edward III, the rightful line of succession would still prevail. They petitioned the king "in great comfort of all the realm, to cause the noble child Richard of Bordeaux . . . to come into parliament, so that the lords and Commons of the realm could see and honour the said Richard as the true heir apparent of the realm." Their request was granted. A little more than two weeks after the Black Prince's death, the boy was led through the palace to the chamber where the lords and Commons were assembled. There the archbishop of Canterbury declared that, although his father was gone, "it was as if the same prince was still present and not absent, having left behind him such a noble and fine son who is his true image and very figure."[29]

In that moment, Richard stood alone for the first time on the political stage. He was nine and a half years old, and in the cocoon of his upbringing so far the fact that he was England's "true heir" was the one essential lesson he had learned. It was not clear to him what it might mean to be the image of his father, beyond their physical resemblance. For as long as Richard could remember, the prince had been an invalid, made short-tempered by pain and often too weak to function at all. Within the opulent isolation of a household arranged around his father's medical needs, Richard's education had been severely restricted. The Black Prince, as heir to the throne, had been brought up in close proximity to a father who had been only seventeen when he was born, a king in the prime of his life who threw his remarkable energies into the businesses of war, government, and magnificently staged fun, and insisted that his son should take part in all three from the earliest possible moment. But if the prince had learned to swim in the challenging waters of his future role by being thrown into the deep, Richard was barely paddling in the shallows. To him, the exploits of his father and grandfather were a mythic past, a hallowed tale bearing no relation to the limitations of his world at Kennington or Berkhamsted. Magnificence he understood, but of war and government—or even fun—he knew very little.

He did have a "governor" or tutor, Sir Simon Burley, a soldier and devoted retainer who had served the Black Prince in Aquitaine and Castile, and a proud and cultured man under whose guidance Richard was taught to ride well and to read in both of the languages he spoke, English and French, as well as a little Latin. But as his father's health failed, the overriding concern within the household was to protect Richard, not to push him. The prince's only son was precious because he was irreplaceable; all eyes were fixed on what he was, and would one day be, not on what he was doing or learning. And now that God had taken his father as well as his older brother, Richard stepped outside the bounds of his luxurious home to find that a parliament otherwise full of grievance and complaint fell silent in awe at his presence. The Commons made a formal request that he should become prince of Wales like his father before him, only to be told that parliament must not usurp the royal prerogative by directing matters that the king alone had the right to decide. All the same, their wish was soon granted. By the end of the year, Richard had been invested as the new prince and given his own royal household, with his tutor Simon Burley as its chamberlain.[30]

In practice, this was his parents' establishment rearranged with a new intensity of focus on their son. Burley—a man steeped in the pomp and protocol on which the Black Prince had insisted—still directed Richard's education and regulated access to him, all under the continuing supervision of the boy's mother, whose previous devotion to pleasure had given way to an anxious vigilance. Jeannette's gilded life, once a chivalric adventure in sunlit Aquitaine, had run out of her control. Since her return to England, grief at her husband's illness and the loss of their firstborn son had been compounded by fear of the danger that confronted the children of her previous marriage as a result of the renewal of war. Her sons Thomas and John Holland were serving as soldiers, and her daughter Joan Holand had married the duke of Brittany, widower of King Edward's daughter Mary, whose struggle to defend his duchy against French incursions more than once left his new duchess terrifyingly close to enemy lines. Now Jeannette mourned not only her husband but the future that had been hers for fifteen years. No longer a queen-in-waiting, she would be forever the dowager princess of Wales. Her one remaining task was to shield and nurture her youngest child, the boy chosen by God to wear the crown.[31]

In that mission, she had the support of her cousin and brother-in-law Gaunt. She had known him all his life, and had seen at first hand his uncompromising dedication to his royal duty and his veneration for his father and brother. When she and the Black Prince had sailed from Aquitaine for the last time, deep in mourning for their little son Edward, they had left arrangements for his funeral, along with the rule of the principality, in Gaunt's hands. Back in England, Gaunt and Jeannette had exchanged costly gifts at the start of every new year that followed. In 1372, the duke gave his "most honoured and beloved sister the princess of Aquitaine and Wales" a jeweled greyhound—one of his badges—fashioned in gold and studded with eight sapphires; she gave him an elaborate golden cup with a cover on which appeared one of hers, a white hind—a female deer—lying encircled by a crown. Now he became chief executor of her husband's will, and rededicated himself to the defense of his father's crown and his nephew's inheritance.[32]

In the weeks and months after the Black Prince's death, the sheer weight of responsibility on Gaunt's shoulders and his self-conscious pride in the standing of his dynasty combined to produce an increasingly strident defense of the rights of the crown, rather than the capacity to learn from encountering resistance that King Edward had shown in his prime. During the parliament of 1376—an assembly soon popularly known as the "Good Parliament" for its impeachment of the courtiers—Gaunt had recognized that compromise was necessary in the moment to neutralize the Commons' demands. Once the meeting ended in July, however, and the representatives of the realm returned to their homes, it became abundantly clear that the duke intended the concessions he had made to be temporary, not permanent, and reversed without delay. The council appointed to supervise the workings of government lapsed almost immediately. In October, Lord Latimer was formally pardoned for his crimes, and—this the initiative of the infatuated king himself—Alice Perrers was forgiven all debts she owed the crown and all indictments laid against her. Within weeks she was back at Edward's side.[33]

Gaunt also moved against those he deemed responsible for heaping humiliation on his father's throne. The Commons' Speaker, Peter de la Mare, was arrested and held without charge in Nottingham Castle. The duke brought pressure to bear on the London oligarchs and the bishops who, among the Commons and lords respectively, had backed the criticism of Edward's court. He launched a provocative attack on London's judicial privileges, and signaled his support for the controversial theologian John Wycliffe, who was making a case for confiscation by the government of the huge wealth of the Church. As a result, when another parliament was called to meet at Westminster in January 1377, it was a cowed and more compliant assembly. Under the leadership of Gaunt's own steward as Speaker, the Commons were finally persuaded to make a grant of taxation, not least because of ominous rumors that the French king was planning a naval assault on the south coast of England as soon as the ragged remains of the truce expired in April. Even so, they would agree only to a radical innovation: not the traditional levy on movable property, but a poll tax of four pence on every one of the king's subjects over the age of fourteen, a measure that served to shift the burden of payment away from the Commons' own purses and further down the social scale.[34]

This was crisis management, which left little time for Gaunt to educate the young heir to the throne in the colossal responsibilities that would soon be his. But Richard was coming to his own precocious conclusions about the nature of his royal being. On January 27, three weeks after his tenth birthday, he was brought into the Painted Chamber in the palace of Westminster to preside in his grandfather's place at the opening of the new parliament. In a block adjoining the palace's great hall to the south, the room was the king's state bedchamber, more than eighty feet long and twenty-five feet wide, its lofted ceiling over thirty feet high. Around its walls ran brightly painted murals layered in narrative ribbons: at the top, Old Testament stories

of the triumphs of virtuous kings, descending stage by stage into the dreadful
crimes and bloody punishment of biblical tyrants. Richard's grandfather, had
he been there, might have tried to explain to his grandson the meaning of
these complex tales picked out in brilliant pigment. Instead, the boy's gaze
was drawn to the largest image, the one directly behind the empty bed of
state: a monumental, shimmering image of the coronation of Edward the
Confessor, the king of England who, almost a century after his death in 1066,
had been recognized as a saint.[35]

Holding himself with the royal dignity his mother and tutor required,
Richard turned his attention from the holy king to the chancellor of England, the bishop of St. David's, who rose to address the representatives of
the realm. King Edward had sent Richard "to comfort and welcome you on
his behalf," the bishop declared, "in the same manner as the scripture says,
'Here is my beloved Son, here is He who is wished for by all men.'" They
were bound to do honor and reverence to the young prince "in the manner
the pagans, that is to say the three kings . . . did to the Son of God when
they offered him gold, myrrh and frankincense." It was insistent and unsub-
tle, this rhetorical identification of England with the Holy Land, England's
king with God, and England's heir with Christ: an attempt, made with a
desperation evident to any seasoned politician, at uniting a fractious and divided kingdom by appealing beyond current conflicts to an ideal of divinely
sanctioned sovereignty. But the bishop's audience was not composed wholly
of seasoned politicians. Seven months earlier, Richard had been hailed, in
another parliament, as England's true heir. Now he heard himself described
as England's messiah. To the ears of a boy who knew that three kings had
attended his baptism, the chancellor's words did not sound like metaphor.[36]

The reminders of his extraordinary status kept coming, in private as well
as in public. A few days later, Richard and his mother were at Kennington,
the luxurious home his father had built less than a mile across the river from
Westminster, just past the archbishop of Canterbury's palace at Lambeth
on the south bank of the Thames. There they were joined for Candlemas,
the feast that marked the end of the Christmas season, by great lords of
the realm including his uncles Gaunt and Langley and the earls of Warwick and Suffolk. While King Edward rested in the comfort of his manor

of Havering, northeast of the capital, it was clear that Richard's home had become, in effect, the royal court. That impression was reinforced on the evening of Sunday, February 1, when a party of more than a hundred London citizens arrived at the gates on horseback in a blaze of torchlight, trumpets blaring. They were mummers in masks and disguises, come to entertain the young prince: one dressed as an emperor, another as a pope attended by twenty-four cardinals, the rest as knights and esquires in matching outfits of crimson silk. Welcomed into the decorated hall, the players produced a bowl, a cup, and a ring, all three gilded and shining, and offered Richard a pair of dice, "which they so handled that the prince did always win when he cast them." In three throws, the gifts were his. It seemed a sign of the boy's future, a destiny confirmed, not least to the boy himself: everything Richard touched turned to gold.[37]

He was also starting to suspect that it was not only mummers who wore masks. He was not yet used to the presence of outsiders in his home, whether lords visiting on feast days or the handful of noble boys, including his cousin Henry of Bolingbroke, who were beginning to spend time in his household. But it was Henry's father, Gaunt, of whom Richard was most wary. As far as he could see, the authority of the crown—which he knew to belong to his grandfather the king, and then to himself as prince of Wales—was being impersonated, even appropriated, by his uncle. And the whispers that Gaunt's ambitions might reach further still had become louder since the Black Prince's death. In London, rumors were running wild that the duke might prove a predatory uncle like his ancestor and namesake, King John, who, almost two centuries earlier, had imprisoned and murdered his twelve-year-old nephew, Arthur, taking the throne for himself. Ten-year-old Richard spent no time listening to gossip on the capital's streets, but he was fascinated by his family's history; and on February 20, less than three weeks after Gaunt's visit at Candlemas, the Londoners' anger at the duke erupted so violently that its shock waves penetrated the royal sanctuary at Kennington. A raging mob attacked Gaunt's palace of the Savoy outside the city walls to the west, and the duke himself, who was at dinner with friends elsewhere, fled for refuge across the river to his sister-in-law. The princess not only offered him shelter but sent her most trusted knights—including

Simon Burley and Burley's friend Aubrey de Vere, who had served the Black Prince faithfully for more than a decade—into the city in a fraught attempt to appeal for calm.[38]

His mother had confidence in Gaunt; but, as the weeks crept by and the time of his own kingship drew nearer, Richard was less convinced of his uncle's benevolence.

Winter became spring and the ship of state sailed on, while the undertow beneath its hull grew stronger and more menacing. When the truce with France reached its formal end on April 1, all that proved possible for the two sides to agree on was the briefest of extensions, first until the beginning of May, then a few weeks more till midsummer, June 24. As a heavily armed French and Castilian fleet massed off the Normandy coast, Gaunt convened regular meetings of a war council, only to find their efforts impeded by the shortage of money and the miasmically demoralizing effect of mistrust between the regime he led and the people it ruled. Still, in late April there came an opportunity to assert the continuing greatness of the king's achievements in the annual celebration of the Order of the Garter, the chivalric brotherhood-in-arms Edward had founded in the wake of his victory at Crécy three decades earlier.[39]

The Order's statutes allowed only twenty-four of England's knights, the realm's bravest and best, to be installed as members at any given time. The Black Prince had been among those named at its foundation; so had his wife's previous two husbands, the earl of Salisbury and Sir Thomas Holand. Now it was the turn of Jeannette's youngest son. At Windsor Castle on April 22, the eve of the Garter feast, the fragile king was propped unsteadily on a cloth-of-gold throne to dub as knights a crowd of aristocratic young men. They included Edward's youngest legitimate son, twenty-two-year-old Thomas of Woodstock, whose bitterness that he had had to wait quite so long for knighthood was compounded by the fact that he was forced to share the moment with the teenage John Southray, his father's bastard son by Alice Perrers, the woman who had replaced his dead mother in the royal bed. Beside them were the earl of Salisbury's son and heir by the wife he had taken after the annulment of his marriage to Richard's mother; and Aubrey de Vere's nephew Robert, the fifteen-year-old earl of Oxford, who was married to the daughter of Richard's wayward aunt Isabella and her handsome husband, Enguerrand de Coucy.[40]

But at the head of the crowd stood two ten-year-old boys, the king's eldest grandsons, on whose narrow shoulders rested the future of the royal line: Gaunt's son Henry, and Richard himself. Of all the newly made knights, it was only Henry and Richard, in matching white robes lined with blue, who were admitted the next day to the elite company of the Garter. Over the last ten months Richard had become more practiced at taking part in public ceremonies, but he had done so alone, the focus of all eyes as the heir to his grandfather's throne. Two was not the number he preferred. Nor did he find the military tenor of the occasion entirely comfortable. Wearing little suits of bespoke armor, the cousins were too young to do more than spectate at the tournament that followed the investiture, but the prospect of fighting in the future—as opposed to the riding and hunting he was beginning to enjoy—was not one Richard relished. Still, the imagery was compelling: just as Gaunt had been the greatest lieutenant of his brother the Black Prince, Gaunt's son Henry would stand at Richard's right hand when the time came for them to take up their grandfather's legacy.

All the same, the fact that ten-year-olds were being invested with the Garter—the order of knighthood that had once been the Round Table of Edward's lost Camelot—showed how wide the gulf now yawned between the trappings of chivalry and the reality of war. In the weeks that followed the celebrations at Windsor, while the final days of the extended truce trickled away, Gaunt set plans in motion for the muster of 4,000 troops. They were to fight, their indentures said, under the supreme command of Prince Richard. At the age of ten Gaunt himself had been on board his father's ship during Edward's stunning victory over a Castilian fleet off the English coast near Winchelsea in Sussex, as one of many royal sons learning to fight in a war his father was triumphantly winning. More than a quarter of a century later, it was inconceivable that Richard would find himself anywhere near the front line. His name would serve to rally his men; his person would remain safely at home in the care of his mother.[41]

But on June 21, the plans Gaunt had made in his nephew's name were abruptly halted. That day at the palace of Sheen, westward along the Thames from London, Edward III suffered a devastating stroke. He died in the early evening. It was said that Alice Perrers stripped the rings from his fingers before she fled his chamber.[42]

The inevitable and unthinkable had happened. After a reign lasting half a century, England's people had lost the greatest—for most, the only— sovereign they had ever known. The shock was profound, and the challenge immense. The first and most pressing issue to be tackled was not the day-to-day administration of government; for a king too incapacitated to rule to be succeeded by a king too young meant that, one way or another, the lords would have to continue as improvised caretakers until Richard came of age. There would be time to decide exactly how. What mattered was that the center must hold. However great the danger from France, the war would have to wait. The urgent task was to bury the old king with honor, and confirm the unity and loyalty of the realm by crowning the new.

The surviving inhabitants of Rye, Hastings, and Lewes could have been forgiven for feeling less than sanguine about this order of priorities after their towns were sacked and burned to ashes by French raids along the south coast at the end of June. But by then the funeral arrangements were nearly complete. On Friday, July 3, an extraordinary cortège wound slowly along the south bank of the Thames, across London Bridge, and through the heart of the city to St. Paul's Cathedral. The coffin containing Edward's embalmed corpse was transported on an ornate carriage, a life-size wooden effigy of the dead king in full regalia lying above it under the shelter of a cloth-of-gold canopy, while hundreds of mourners dressed all in black carried torches behind the bier. Walking slowly at their head were the men who might otherwise have been commanding soldiers against England's enemies, if they had not been required to escort the sovereign on his journey to the grave: the king's three remaining sons, John of Gaunt, Edmund of Langley, and young Thomas of Woodstock, along with their adoptive brother, the duke of Brittany, and the earl of March, son-in-law of the dead Lionel of Antwerp. The next day, they continued their solemn progress through Ludgate and along Fleet Street, the main thoroughfare leading westward out of the city, to

Westminster Abbey, where a catafalque draped in starched black cloth under a canopied frame that blazed with candles waited to receive the coffin. There, on Sunday, July 5, Edward was laid to rest beside the shrine of Edward the Confessor, the abbey's founder, his royal predecessor and saintly namesake.[43]

Richard had no role to play in these somber ceremonies. His grandfather's funeral was a farewell to the past, but he was king of his country's future. And so, eleven days later, the soaring space of the abbey was transformed from a place of mourning to one of renewal. As tradition dictated, Richard was brought from Kennington to the Tower of London, the crown's great fortress—*his* great fortress—on the city's eastern edge. On July 15, he emerged, a small figure dressed in white, from the Tower's looming gates. He had always known his destiny. For the first time, he would be revealed in majesty to his realm. The procession was vast. There were representatives from many parts of his dominions, wearing white in his honor: lords and Londoners, knights and esquires, bodyguards and trumpeters, a cheering cacophony in the sunshine.[44]

As they rode along Cheapside, the great commercial street that transected London from east to west, Gaunt, riding at the front of the king's section of the cavalcade, had to force a path through the crowds. But for once—for Richard's sake—the antagonism between the duke and the city was set aside. The people gave way with noisy enthusiasm, their good humor lubricated by the wine that flowed for hours from the public conduits. Directly ahead of the king's charger, his sword was carried upright by his tutor Simon Burley, and one of the knights of his chamber walked beside him, holding the bridle to guide the horse so that Richard was free to show his royal face to his subjects and survey the tableaux they presented in tribute as he passed. In Cheapside stood a timber frame covered with painted canvas to form a tower—the City of Heaven itself, made manifest in London's streets—from the turrets of which four white-clad girls showered the king with decorative golden leaves and coins under the benevolent gaze of a golden angel, a mechanical figure so artfully constructed that, at Richard's arrival, it bent forward to offer him a crown.

When the parade left the city, winding past St. Paul's and following the curve of the river south to Westminster, the contrast with the scene that had unfolded on the same streets ten days earlier could not have been more stark. Then a dead king was carried through hushed crowds, his attendants all in black, the air heavy with grief. Now, to the sound of trumpets, flutes, and drums, came a king with his whole life ahead of him, his entourage all in white—a color, one chronicler explained, representing the purity of Richard's innocence. That night, while he rested in his palace, his capital gave itself over to partying, and the catharsis of hope.

The next day, Richard understood, would be the greatest he had yet known. The order of ceremonies that would confirm the sacred purpose for which God had chosen him began with mass in his chamber. Then he was dressed and brought in state to Westminster's hall, where he was met by the archbishop of Canterbury and other prelates in their rich vestments, come to escort him to the abbey along the striped red cloth that had been newly laid to cushion the royal feet across the flagstones. When the time approached, the procession assembled: at its head, the gaggle of clerics in their jewel-colored silks; then the bishops of Worcester and St. David's in their offices as treasurer and chancellor of England. Next came Gaunt bearing Curtana, the square-tipped sword of justice, and behind him the earls of March and Warwick with the second and third ceremonial swords of the realm, before Edmund of Langley and Thomas of Woodstock, each holding a rod with a dove at its tip. As Richard followed them into the open air where his people could see him, there was a flare of sunlight and a sudden wall of sound, and soon the cool of the abbey, its walls all vermilion and gold and painted saints under vaulted arches that reached toward heaven itself.[45]

It was intoxicating, the heady scent of incense in the nostrils, the rise and fall of liturgical song echoing on stone, the brilliant purple of the silk canopy carried high above his head on silvered lances with a golden bell shivering at each corner as he walked. Before the altar, the exquisitely worked pavement of onyx, porphyry, serpentine, and glass was blanketed in soft carpets and cushions so that he could prostrate himself in royal humility for the archbishop of Canterbury's blessing. Then he moved from the ground to the heights: to a seat on a stage specially constructed at the crossing of the choir and the transepts, raised so high that all those in the packed church could see the diminutive person of their king. The ancient regalia of England were displayed reverently before him by the earls of Arundel, Salisbury, and Suffolk. Next came the archbishop's voice. Would he swear to uphold the laws and customs of his predecessors? Would he bring peace to the Church and his people? Would he do justice to all, in mercy and truth? Would he keep and defend the laws that his people should justly and reasonably have chosen? He would, he swore. And the archbishop presented him to his subjects on all four sides of the stage, and told them of his oath. Would they obey him as their sovereign lord? The air filled with a shout of acclamation and assent.

There was more music, and more prayer, and he made his way down from the platform, negotiating the steps with care, to take his seat facing the altar on Edward the Confessor's throne, just as he had seen it on the wall of the Painted Chamber. This, he knew, would be the most sacred part of this sacred ceremony. The moment was so holy that his people must not witness it: four earls unfurled a shining cloth of gold to hide him from their view. The shirt he wore was pulled aside, and slowly, delicately, as the priests sang of the biblical consecration of Solomon's kingship, the archbishop poured holy oil in the shape of a cross on the palms of Richard's hands, on his head, his chest, his shoulders, and the soft inside of his elbows. Another pause, before the top of his head was touched with chrism, holy oil mixed with fragrant balm. It was done. He was—he would always be—God's anointed, forever set apart from other men.

Fine linen dried the pooling oil from his skin, and finer lawn was wrapped around his head to shield the place of unction from any pollution. Then, once he was robed in royal vestments, came the insignia of the office God had given him: crown, sword, scepter, ring, and spurs. His head, hands, and feet were too small to fit the priceless treasures that had once been the Confessor's, but for now there was help to hold the heavy crown, and his body would grow. What counted—the one thing, the only thing, that mattered—was his uniquely royal blood, and the consecration of his sovereignty under God.

The great hymn of praise Te Deum laudamus rang out. While the clergy gathered at the altar to sing mass, Richard sat, solemn and still, to receive the homage of the lords who held their titles from his crown: first Gaunt as duke of Lancaster and Edmund of Langley as earl of Cambridge; the duke of Brittany, for his English earldom of Richmond; then the earls of March, Arundel, Warwick, Suffolk, Stafford, and Salisbury. It was nearly over. Simon Burley was there to carry him from the abbey. The press of people was so intense that one of the Confessor's oversized slippers slid from his foot and was lost in the crush. On the way back into the precincts of the palace they passed a looming eagle on a marbled column, proud in its gold paint as wine poured between its talons. But Richard's work was not yet finished. There were loyal subjects waiting to be raised to the ranks of the nobility by his royal hand. In moments, Gaunt's friend Henry Percy became earl of Northumberland; John, Lord Mowbray, an orphan barely older than the king himself, earl of Nottingham; and the king's "most dear uncle" Thomas of Woodstock, mulish with resentment at being overlooked for so long, earl of Buckingham.[46]

Finally, there was breakfast. The hall was so full that Gaunt, as steward of England, had to patrol the doors on his warhorse to make sure the servants could reach the guests before the food was cold. As dish followed elaborate dish Richard sat, straight-backed in his dignity, at the highest table, bishops and abbots to his right and his left. And because his steward could not attend on him in person, the royal sword Curtana was held at Richard's side by the duke's son Henry, his face a mask of fierce concentration.

There was feasting and dancing until breakfast became dinner and the sun went down. The day had been long. It was time for the king to go to bed. And while he slept, the men who ruled his kingdom made their plans without him.

Two

1377-1381

measure our confines

Henry of Bolingbroke's childhood had little in common with the reverential quiet of his cousin's home at Kennington, a household choreographed around Richard's exceptional being under the princess's watchful eye. Henry's home was his father's bustling, vivid, restlessly magnificent establishment, in which he had to find his place among a tumble of siblings, half siblings, and stepsiblings; and he had no memory at all of his mother. Instead, he grew up surrounded by stories of her. His sisters Philippa and Elizabeth told him everything they could remember, while others in the household made sure Henry understood how noble her lineage had been, how impressive her person, and how deep her devotion to her family.

Blanche of Lancaster was the younger of the two daughters of Henry of Grosmont, duke of Lancaster, King Edward's gifted, charismatic best friend. The title of duke was new to England, but Edward saw no reason why his greatest lords should not have the same high rank as those of France. The second Englishman he promoted—after his own eldest son, who became duke of Cornwall at the age of six—had been Grosmont, whose earldom of Lancaster became a dukedom in 1351 in recognition of his royal blood, inherited from his great-grandfather Henry III, and his devoted service to the crown. This brilliant man had no son to inherit his title or his place at the king's right hand. That fortune would fall to the husbands of his daughters, who, as female heirs, would divide the Lancastrian estates equally between them. The older, Maud, made a dazzling marriage at the age of twelve to Queen Philippa's nephew the duke of Bavaria, but she died only ten years later, leaving no surviving children. The remaining hopes of the Lancastrian line lay with Blanche, who in 1359, at seventeen, had married John of Gaunt.[1]

Blanche was universally admired. She was tall and fair, like her father; "young and beautiful," wrote Jean Froissart, a member of the queen's household in the 1360s, ". . . vivacious, happy, fresh and charming, gentle and sincere, and modest in manner." The success of the young couple's relationship, like that of Gaunt's parents before them, was measured in the rapid expansion of their family. Their first child—Philippa, named after her royal grandmother—was born within a year of the wedding. Together they grieved for two boys, John and Edward, who died in infancy. But in 1364 Elizabeth survived; and three years later, while Gaunt was fighting in Castile, came the birth of a healthy son, Henry. By then, after the deaths of Blanche's father and sister in 1361 and 1362, her inheritance had made her husband duke of Lancaster, the richest nobleman in England by far, with lands—and therefore power—throughout swathes of the north and the midlands, south Wales, East Anglia, and Sussex. Gaunt might not be the heir to the kingdom, but, with his adored wife, he could look forward to his growing family's future as the central pillar of his father's regime.[2]

Henry was only seventeen months old when the shape of that future changed forever. In the short years of her marriage, Blanche had faced repeated physical danger in her confinements just as surely as her husband had on campaign. Her sixth labor would be her last. On September 12, 1368, at the age of twenty-six, she died, along with their child. Gaunt's grief was embodied in the superb alabaster tomb he commissioned at St. Paul's Cathedral from Henry Yeveley, England's greatest master mason, in which the duke intended one day to lie beside her; and it was given voice in the first long poem written by a prodigiously talented esquire of the king's household named Geoffrey Chaucer. The narrator of Chaucer's *Book of the Duchess* dreams of an encounter with a noble knight dressed all in black, who tells him of his lost love White, "my lady bright," a golden-haired beauty of such goodness, charm, and constancy that her death has left him half-mad with anguish:

"For I am sorrow and sorrow is I." Chaucer had known Gaunt for a decade and saw his suffering at first hand; but the duke had no time to give himself over to mourning. There were more losses to bear—his brother Lionel died a month after Blanche, and his beloved mother, Philippa, the following summer—and more battles to fight. The renewal of war with France, together with his father's age and his older brother's illness, urgently required Gaunt's presence in the field and at the negotiating table.[3]

Their father's preoccupations meant that, at not yet two, Henry was sent with his sisters to live in the household of their elderly, childless, and long-widowed great-aunt, Henry of Grosmont's sister Blanche, Lady Wake. But in these unfamiliar surroundings, the bereaved children could take comfort from the warm and reassuring care of their governess Katherine Roët, Geoffrey Chaucer's sister-in-law, a young gentlewoman who had served their mother as a lady-in-waiting. Katherine and her sister, Chaucer's wife, Philippa, were daughters of a knight of Hainaut who had come to England in Queen Philippa's retinue. In her teens, Katherine married Sir Hugh Swynford, a Lincolnshire landowner in Gaunt's service, and had a son and a daughter to whom the duke stood godfather. After the duchess's death, while Katherine's husband traveled with Gaunt on campaign, she remained in England to look after Blanche's small children as well as her own. Her generous intelligence, and the company of young Thomas and Blanche Swynford, enfolded Henry and his sisters within an approximation of family life until Gaunt returned from Aquitaine at the end of 1371.[4]

With him, the duke brought his children a stepmother. Pedro of Castile's daughters, Constanza and Isabel, were all that remained of the murdered king's claim to his kingdom. Hostages for their father's debts since the Nájera campaign, they had passed from the Black Prince's custody to Gaunt's when the duke took command in Aquitaine—and now Gaunt decided to make the recovery of Castile a personal ambition as well as a military imperative. By the time he sailed for England that autumn, seventeen-year-old Constanza had become the new duchess of Lancaster.[5]

When they arrived, accompanied by Constanza's sister Isabel and a small coterie of Castilian loyalists, the couple were formally recognized by England's royal council as king and queen of Castile and León. On February

10, 1372, Constanza rode into London, attended by a splendid entourage and watched by curious crowds. Her new home in the capital was her husband's palace of the Savoy on the riverfront between the city and Westminster, and there, over the next few months, she and Gaunt—now addressed by all as "my lord of Spain"—established a Castilian secretariat, which issued royal letters concerning their rights in their lost kingdom, each signed by Gaunt as "*Nos el Rey.*" In July, England's commitment to the claims of this court-in-exile was underlined by another wedding, when Isabel married Gaunt's brother Edmund of Langley. His characteristic passivity had left him still without a wife at the age of thirty-one, and therefore available as a husband who could neutralize any possibility that Isabel's stake in the Castilian succession might one day be leveraged against English interests.[6]

Gaunt's homecoming allowed his children to be welcomed back into the duke's own household. Henry, who turned five that April, could hardly remember his father, but Katherine Swynford's maternal presence helped ease the little boy and his sisters into their new environment. She too was adjusting to profound change, since her husband had died in Aquitaine before the duke's return. As the months went by, the Lancastrian establishment that moved between the Savoy and Gaunt's castles at Hertford, Tutbury, Leicester, and Kenilworth also became Katherine's family home. In 1372, her sister Philippa was appointed to attend on Duchess Constanza, bringing her own small children, Thomas and Elizabeth Chaucer, to join the fatherless Swynfords and the motherless Lancastrian siblings within a nursery that continued to grow. Constanza was already pregnant when she landed in England, and gave birth that summer to a daughter, Catalina. It was Katherine who took the happy news of the baby's arrival to Gaunt's father, the king.[7]

By the following year, all but the most myopic of observers could see that her devoted service to the Lancastrian children was not the only reason Katherine was receiving marks of the duke's favor. Gaunt's marriage to Constanza was a political project. Even allowing for the fourteen-year difference in their ages, their relationship was not a meeting of minds or temperaments. The duke paid his wife every respect in formal and material terms: he gave her jewels, silks, and furs for her new wardrobe, and at Easter 1373 a white enameled eagle made of gold, a badge elegantly gesturing both to King

Edward, who often wore eagles among his many devices, and to the emblem of John the Evangelist, one of Gaunt's own name saints. But Gaunt, like his father before him, could not readily do without the emotional and physical comfort he had found in his first marriage. Instead, he found it with Katherine. In 1373 she gave birth to a boy named John, and three more children quickly followed: two boys, Henry and Thomas, and a girl, Joan, all of whom were given the name of Beaufort, a French lordship that had once been part of the Lancastrian estates. It was an unusual situation: not the ubiquitous fact of a great man having a mistress, but the relationship being so closely embedded within his domestic arrangements. However, both Katherine and Constanza conducted themselves, always, with graceful and dignified restraint. Even during Gaunt's military and diplomatic absences—and even when in 1376 Constanza endured the loss of a baby boy, John, who died soon after his birth—the Lancastrian household remained close and functional, its hierarchy uncontested, and its grandeur unsurpassed among the nobility of England. If there were tensions below the surface—costs to be borne by the women who enabled Gaunt to combine political goals with personal gratification—they were not permitted to show.[8]

Henry's home was both tight-knit and many layered. He was his father's third surviving child, but the oldest and—it turned out as the years went on—only legitimate son. From the moment of his birth, Henry's rights as heir to the greatest noble estate in the kingdom had been clear and unchallenged, but he was surrounded by checks on any bloating of a youthful ego: two older sisters and soon three Beaufort half brothers, one of them a second Henry and another who, after the death of an infant John in each of Gaunt's marriages, was the only one of the duke's remaining sons to bear his name. All the same, the weight of expectation on the heir's shoulders was unmistakable.

From the age of seven, when by custom boys left the nursery to begin their formal education, Henry had a governor to oversee his tuition, appointed by his father from among the knights and esquires of the Lancastrian retinue. The household was multilingual—the English and French of English aristocratic culture reinforced by Katherine's roots in French-speaking Hainaut and supplemented by Constanza's Castilian Spanish—and as instinctively European in outlook as Gaunt's own experience and ambition. From 1376, when Henry turned nine, his governor was William de Mountendre, a knight from Aquitaine who, before moving into Gaunt's service, had fought under the command of his countryman the Captal de Buch, one of the heroes of King Edward's wars and a founding member of the Order of the Garter. The duke's aspirations for his son reflected those of chivalry itself in combining the cultural and intellectual with the military. Like his cousin Richard, Henry was taught to read in English, French, and Latin. Like Richard's, his schoolroom contained volumes of myth and chivalric romance, history and scripture. Like Richard, Henry learned to ride, and the principles of combat with sword and lance, and to sing and dance, and to master the manners of the court. Unlike Richard, the central focus of Henry's education was the range of his studies, not the reinforcement of his status; what he might learn to do, or set himself to achieve, given the resources and responsibilities of his inheritance. He was determined to try his developing skills in the lists as soon as his father allowed. Meanwhile, he was discovering a love of books and music, and enjoying the company of his friends and family, especially his younger half brother John Beaufort and John's half brother, Thomas Swynford, a boy almost exactly Henry's age.[9]

Gradually Gaunt began to create a household-within-a-household for his eldest son. Alongside his governor, Henry was assigned a financial officer of his own—his "receiver" Hugh Waterton, a Lincolnshire man who had fought in France with Gaunt in 1373—and a chaplain, Hugh Herley. There was a page and a valet; there were clerks, and servants in the kitchen and the stables. But from the summer of 1376, as his father cast a protective eye over the new heir to England's throne, Henry also began to spend more time with Richard. They stood together as new knights of the Garter at Windsor in April 1377, two small figures among the greatest lords and soldiers in the kingdom. Then came the death of Edward III, the grandfather they hardly knew, and Richard's transformation from England's heir to England's king. Henry found himself changed into the earl of Derby, one of the subsidiary titles passed down from the Lancastrian grandfather for whom he had been named. In the months after his disciplined performance as his father's deputy at the coronation feast, the little earl's presence at court was marked in the records of the royal wardrobe by the liveries he was given for his attendance on the king: gilded blue brocade for Christmas and blue silk at Easter; fur-trimmed gray for the winter cold, and russet with mottled green, the rich colors of the forest, when the season came to hunt.[10]

They both loved the excitement of the chase, learning to ride with hawks on their wrists and greyhounds at their heels. Otherwise, the two boys were finding that they had little in common, even apart from the suspicions Richard had already begun to harbor about the political intentions of Henry's father. On both sides, greater familiarity bred, if not contempt, then at least a profoundly wary distance. And, as the coronation began to recede into a golden memory, Richard's questions about his own sovereign authority in relation to Gaunt and the great men of the realm only grew.

It had not been possible to agree a plan for government before the old king died. No one had known how long Edward might live, and in the meantime anyone anticipating the sovereign's death in word or deed ran the risk of being branded a traitor. Besides, political developments were proving difficult enough to manage from moment to moment without trying to preempt an uncertain future, especially given the intensity of the resentment Gaunt stirred up among England's people. The rioters in London in February 1377 had nailed his coat of arms upside down—a visual allegation of treason—on the doors of St. Paul's Cathedral and Westminster Hall, and added notices declaring that he was the offspring of a Ghent butcher, swapped in the cradle for a dead royal baby. The duke's outraged response to these insults helped nothing. Those who had abused his arms and slighted his lineage should be sentenced to death unless he chose to reprieve them, he told the mayor and citizens in cold fury, and in reparation the city should set his escutcheon in a place of perpetual honor on a marble pillar in the middle of Cheapside. Neither demand was remotely realistic, but that fact did nothing to diminish the dangerous volatility of the politics from which they had sprung.[11]

For a few weeks in the summer of 1377, those politics were set aside. Edward's funeral and Richard's coronation allowed a moment of emotional release as mourning gave way to celebration, the past to the future. But all the problems posed by that future remained to be tackled—and as soon as the coronation was over, the lords met to thrash out an answer to the questions that now confronted them.

England's new king was ten years old. How should the kingdom be ruled until Richard grew old enough to rule for himself? In theory, the obvious solution to a royal minority was the appointment of a regent. It was a proposition reinforced by the closest precedent England's history had to offer, that of 1216, when Richard's great-great-great-grandfather Henry III had inherited the throne at the age of nine and the veteran warrior William Marshal had been named "guardian of the king and the kingdom." More than a century and a half later, the only possible candidate for that role was John of Gaunt, as the young king's oldest surviving uncle and the kingdom's preeminent magnate, a nobleman without rival in experience, status, wealth, and power. But the only possible candidate was also an impossible choice. The duke was too divisive a figure to lead England's people: too unpopular to be appointed, and too powerful for anyone else to be appointed in his place. In practice, there could be no regency.[12]

And Gaunt, it turned out, had no desire for the job. For all his undoubted ambition—and despite the fact that common report took it for granted that he had designs on his nephew's throne—he had never been anything but unswervingly loyal to his father, his brother, and his brother's son. He had had enough of the brickbats. Even Thomas Walsingham, one of the chroniclers most relentlessly hostile to the duke, was moved to note Gaunt's fear that "if anything bad happened to the king or the realm he would be blamed, and he would receive little or no thanks for the good things he had done." And so, shortly after the coronation, the duke took leave of the king and court to spend the summer with his family in the midlands, at his castle of Kenilworth. This was no petulant tantrum, even if, with an aggrieved insistence the Londoners recognized all too well, Gaunt complained in parliament that October of the ways in which "his person had been spoken of so malevolently, and accused of something which should rightfully be considered open treason, if it were true, which God forbid." But, once mollified by a formal declaration that neither lords nor Commons could possibly believe any such defamation, he continued to lend his considerable weight to the improvised regime that was beginning to govern in the young king's name.[13]

It was a fudge and a fiction, the plan to which England's political community resorted in the attempt to manage the inconvenient truth of Richard's age. In such troubled times, since Richard was the focus of the kingdom's loyalty, then Richard must be seen to rule. Officially, there would be no minority: officially, the king would exercise his authority as freely as his grandfather before him. But the official story could not be made real. In practice, government would be authorized by the crown, but not directed by the ten-year-old king. Instead, decisions would be taken by his leading subjects, their loyal "advice" given executive force until the king should be ready to steer the ship of state himself. An attempt was made to buttress public confidence in the nature of that advice by appointing a standing council to represent the estates of the realm, like the one temporarily instituted by the Good Parliament in the previous year, and made up this time of three bishops, two earls, two lords, and two gentlemen. But the council was window dressing, just as much as the role of Richard himself. The inescapable reality was that the realm could not be governed, nor the war pursued, without the support and participation of the most powerful men in the kingdom, Gaunt—however unpopular he might be—first among them.[14]

There was a great deal for them to do. During the golden age of the old king's reign, England's defense strategy had been the fact of the war itself. For as long as English forces were winning victories on French soil—capturing the vital bridgehead of Calais, launching devastating raids across the French kingdom, pushing outward the boundaries of English Aquitaine—there had been little need to think about the protection of the realm beyond continuing to fight. But now the momentum of the conflict was entirely reversed. The French and Castilian ships that burned their way along the Sussex coast within days of Richard's accession were a terrifying harbinger of what might be to come, and in the autumn of 1377 both the outer fortifications of Calais and what remained of English lands and loyalties in Aquitaine were damaged by French attacks.[15]

Danger threatened on every front, and every front needed money on a scale that far outstripped the crown's regular income. The only option was to summon parliaments—four in the first three years of the reign—in the attempt to secure grants of taxation for the urgent defense of the realm. The military results, however, were underwhelming at best. In 1377–78, naval expeditions under the command of Gaunt's youngest brother, Thomas of Woodstock, and Richard Fitzalan, the new earl of Arundel, succeeded in taking control of the ports of Brest in Brittany and Cherbourg in Normandy. These bridgeheads would be valuable outposts for the defense of English interests in the Channel and the sea route south to Aquitaine, but only if they could be retained in English hands—and their ongoing occupation would require yet more soldiers and yet more funds. As time went on, even these expensive victories proved difficult to match. During the summer of 1378, in between missions to keep order in the north on the frontier with Scotland, Gaunt himself led a fleet that tried and failed to capture the Breton port of Saint-Malo, a damp squib of an operation for which the duke yet again took the blame. There was trouble too in Ireland, where Gaelic resistance was threatening English rule, and in the spring of 1380 Edmund Mortimer—the earl of March and also of Ulster, thanks to his marriage to the daughter and heir of Gaunt's dead brother Lionel—was sent across the Irish Sea with 1,000 troops, more men than had been committed to military operations there for decades. Only a few months after that, the Franco-Castilian fleet brought the war back to England's shores, sacking the port of Winchelsea and pillaging its way up the Thames estuary to within striking distance of London.[16]

The unimpressed spectators of these efforts included not only the Commons in successive parliaments but the young king himself, from within his royal household. There Richard was watched over still by his mother, and by Simon Burley and Aubrey de Vere, the dedicated guardians of his royal person and his father's memory. He was also beginning to enjoy some company his own age: the young noblemen among his attendants included Ralph Stafford, son and heir of the earl of Stafford; Thomas Mowbray, younger brother of the earl of Nottingham; and Richard's cousin by marriage, Aubrey de Vere's nephew Robert, earl of Oxford. For the young king, all three were more welcome companions than his cousin Henry, but it was Robert de Vere in particular—a glamorous five years older, and a courtly sophisticate where Henry was sociable and sincere—who was capturing his attention. Beyond this close and attentive circle, the rhetoric of his rule remained as pleasing as ever. In October 1377, when he sat in state at the first parliament of his reign, he heard himself described by the Commons as "a sacred and anointed person." The men who had charge of his education, they humbly requested, should be "the most virtuous, honest and worthy of the kingdom," because it would be through their young king's nobility and virtue that "the whole realm might be saved and preserved." But as he passed his eleventh and twelfth birthdays Richard could not help but notice how little influence he had on the government conducted in his name. His authority, it seemed, was everywhere invoked and never consulted.[17]

In the parliament of January 1380 that opened ten days after he turned thirteen, there were gestures at last toward the future of his prerogative power. The Commons were so incensed by the relentless weight of the government's financial demands and the lack of positive military results that they demanded the dismissal of the standing council that had been in place, in various different iterations, since Richard's accession to the throne two and a half years before. Their request was made, the Commons said, bearing in mind that the king was "now of great discretion and fine stature." He was almost as old, they added, as Edward III had been when he was crowned, a moment at which that great king had been formally advised only by "the customary five principal officers of his kingdom"—the chancellor, the treasurer, the keeper of the privy seal, and the chamberlain and steward of the royal household. What the Commons did not point out, in this careful appeal to the past, was that after his coronation it had taken the teenage Edward III three years and a meticulously orchestrated coup to seize control of his own government. Still, their request was granted and the formal council dismissed, a move that changed nothing about the need for the lords to continue running the regime but made its day-to-day workings even more difficult for the Commons to see. Meanwhile, their encomium to his maturity only encouraged Richard to believe that his people were waiting impatiently for his rule, and that the powerful men of his kingdom were standing in his way.[18]

For now, the governmental occasions that required his presence concerned not policy or strategy but the ritual theater of kingship. Mostly—as at the opening of his parliaments—he sat enthroned and silent, a passive embodiment of sovereignty. From time to time, however, he had a fleeting chance to experience the exercise of power. In June 1380, he was called to preside over the uncommon spectacle of a trial by battle, a judicial duel held within specially built wooden lists on the stone pavement outside Westminster Hall. It was a complex case brought to a brutally simple end: an accusation of treason against an esquire named Thomas Catterton, who had been in command of the fortress of Saint-Sauveur in Normandy when it was surrendered to the French after a year-long siege in 1375. His opponent, Sir John Annesley, claimed that the lordship was part of his wife's inheritance, and that Catterton was guilty of treason for "selling" it to the enemy. Annesley had tried and failed to obtain satisfaction through a process of impeachment in the Good Parliament of 1376, but without written evidence or witnesses to support his allegation, he was left to defend its truth in combat under the jurisdiction of the court of Chivalry.[19]

This military court was overseen by the constable of England—an office currently held by the king's youngest uncle, Thomas of Woodstock—but Richard's was the deciding authority as the duel played out in a devastating combination of tragedy and farce. In front of the king and his lords, and surrounded by a raucous crowd, the two men fought with lances, then swords, then knives, to a point of physical exhaustion. At last, Annesley disarmed Catterton and knocked him to the ground. Then, to press home his advantage, Annesley tried to throw himself onto his prostrate opponent to pin him in place, but his vision was blurred by pouring sweat under his helmet, and he missed. Now both men were down, one beside the other. Using his last reserves of strength, the much larger Catterton rolled himself on top of Annesley. This was stalemate: Catterton scarcely conscious, Annesley barely able to move. It was time for the king to intervene. Richard stopped the fight, ordering his attendants to lift the combatants, but Annesley—realizing that Catterton was almost out cold—implored the king "to grant him the favor of being placed again on the ground where he was before, with the esquire on top of him," "insisting that he was all right and would win if the esquire was again replaced." So earnest were his requests that Richard was persuaded to agree, but before it could be done Catterton fell in a faint from the chair on which he had been propped. He was stripped of his armor and his clothes, and doused in water and wine, but could not be revived enough to fight again. The king gave his formal judgment in Annesley's favor. As a proven traitor, Catterton's life was forfeit. He escaped execution only by dying the following day.

For thirteen-year-old Richard, this was kingship: a moment when he sat center stage, attended by his nobles and admired by his people, the source of all authority and the arbiter of all action. Holding the power of life and death in his hands, he had spoken to decide when the duel should end, who had won, and who lost. But such moments were rare. More often, as in his parliaments, he sat but did not speak while the great men of his realm argued over and around him. And time and again he heard the Commons talk not simply of their loyalty to his person and their obedience to his crown, but of their bitter complaints about the faults of his lords and ministers.

While Richard waited for public recognition that he was no longer a child, Henry was getting married.

1380 had been a year of weddings. In April, Gaunt and Henry joined the king and court at Windsor Castle for the marriage of Richard's half sister Maud Holand, who, like Gaunt's sister Isabella before her, had fallen in love with a French nobleman held in honorable captivity in England. When the relationship was discovered, scandal quickly gave way to pragmatism: the council, hoping to acquire a valuable ally in northern France, agreed that the count of St. Pol should be freed and the young couple allowed to become man and wife. Then, only weeks later, the Lancastrian family gathered at Kenilworth Castle for a very different ceremony: the union of Henry's teenage sister, Elizabeth, and the seven-year-old earl of Pembroke, son of the earl who had grown up in the royal household with Gaunt and his siblings. This, clearly, was no romance, and it would be years before the groom was ready to be a husband in anything but name, but in the meantime Elizabeth, like Henry, began to make regular appearances at court—the new countess of Pembroke and the young earl of Derby pursuing their political and chivalric education under Richard's regal eye.[20]

Next, it was Henry's turn. His was the marriage that would determine the future of the Lancastrian dynasty—and, in Gaunt's choice of a wife for his son, there were parallels with the duke's own history. Like Blanche of

Lancaster, Mary de Bohun was the younger of two sisters who, because they had no brother, would share a great noble patrimony. Her father, the earl of Hereford, Essex, and Northampton, had died in 1373, and now, at the age of eleven, she was one of the most eligible heiresses in the country.

The match, however, set Gaunt and Henry on a collision course with Gaunt's brother Thomas of Woodstock, who was already married to Mary's sister, Eleanor. For Woodstock, the Bohun estates represented a political lifeline. As an overlooked youngest son, Woodstock had lacked not only opportunities and attention but the resources that would give him real power: land and money and the relationships of lordship and service that could be built upon them. His marriage in 1374, when he was nineteen and Eleanor eight, was his chance. With it came a grant of Bohun properties, topped up by an annual cash sum from the Exchequer, as well as the expectation that Woodstock would take full possession of his wife's inheritance when she came of age. And that, Woodstock was determined, should mean all of the Bohun lands, not just half, since he planned that Eleanor's younger sister, Mary, should enter a convent rather than acquiring a husband of her own.[21]

Back then, Gaunt had welcomed Eleanor graciously into the family, presenting his little sister-in-law with a wedding gift of an ornate silver-gilt cup and pitcher he had once been given by his brother the Black Prince. In the years that followed, Woodstock did everything he could to capitalize on his new position. Earl of Buckingham since his promotion at his nephew's coronation, he began to assert himself as a military leader, first at sea in 1377–78, and now, in 1380, at the head of a new land campaign, the first major English incursion into French territory since Gaunt's forced march of 1373–74. Before leaving with his troops, he secured permanent control of his wife's half of the Bohun inheritance—Eleanor having just turned fourteen, the age at which her husband could take formal possession of her property—and obtained a royal grant of the custody of Mary's share during her minority.[22]

But everything he could do was not enough. In July 1380, just a week after Woodstock and his forces landed at Calais, Gaunt paid the enormous sum of 5,000 marks—or rather deducted it from money he was owed by the crown—for a grant of the right to choose Mary's husband, "for marrying her to his son Henry, earl of Derby," as the wording of the grant helpfully explained. With the support of the girls' widowed mother, Mary was removed from Eleanor's household at Pleshey Castle in Essex, and on February 5, 1381—with Woodstock still away on campaign—she and Henry were married. The ceremony precipitated no immediate change in their lives: Mary remained with her mother and Henry with his father. But already there were hopeful signs for their future together. Mary was a quiet girl, as bookish and musical as Henry, and raised in a deeply cultured home. In any case, both accepted the responsibilities, and the tensions, that lay ahead in this merging of dynasties. Woodstock and Gaunt had never been close, but now their interests were structurally at odds; and Woodstock, who had been struggling for years to acquire a territorial endowment even a fraction as powerful as his brother's, had every reason to resent the fact that he would have to spar with his nephew Henry, already the heir to Gaunt's vast lands, over the division of an estate he had hoped to hold in its entirety.[23]

For the time being, though, the relentless pressure of the war meant that neither brother had the luxury of time to indulge their private quarrel. Woodstock's expedition to France was designed to help England's ally John de Montfort recover control of his duchy of Brittany, as an extended bridgehead on the Atlantic coast from which military aid could finally be sent to what remained of English Aquitaine. But the project was no more successful than Gaunt's *chevauchée* seven years earlier. The Breton duke's long-standing alliance with England, underpinned though it was by his English upbringing and his two English marriages, did not survive the sudden death of Charles V of France in September 1380 and the accession of the eleven-year-old dauphin as King Charles VI. The change of regime at the French court offered de Montfort a new opportunity to secure his possession of Brittany on the basis of concord rather than conflict with the French crown. As a result, by January 1381, Woodstock was discovering just how punishing a continental campaign could be. At the head of a starving, dysentery-ravaged army, his soldiers freezing in the bitter cold, their morale broken, he found himself betrayed by the ally he had come to support. And, like Gaunt before him, he arrived home to learn that his compatriots saw only his failure as a leader, not the intractable difficulties—of geography, politics, finance, resistance—that formed the vicious spiral within which the realm's war effort was caught.[24]

Gaunt, meanwhile, had gone north. In theory, hostilities between England and France's old ally Scotland had been suspended in 1369 by a fifteen-year truce, but since then clashes between the frontier families of Percy, on the English side, and Douglas, on the Scottish, had begun to escalate into alarming violence. As the only magnate with the territorial power in the north that might allow him to enforce peace, Gaunt was appointed the king's lieutenant in the Scottish marches in 1379. In October 1380, after witnessing his daughter Elizabeth's marriage and arranging Henry's betrothal, the duke led a large contingent of troops to the border. His show of strength was enough to induce the Scots to confirm a temporary truce that would last until the following summer. And so, after Henry's wedding, Gaunt rode north again in the spring of 1381 to resume negotiations, leaving his dutiful son at court in the company of his cousin the king.[25]

Richard had seen nothing of the unspooling realities of a failing war. Instead, he sat in successive parliaments watching the incredulity of the Commons grow. Each new assembly demanded to see detailed accounts of what had happened to the previous tax, and to be assured that the next would be spent wisely, with guarantees of how long the revenues could be made to last before more would be required, only to discover that such promises were worthless because the hemorrhage of cash could not be stemmed.

In response to these desperate pleas for funds from an administration they did not trust, the Commons resorted twice more to the innovation of a poll tax, which served as a mark of dissent at the scale of the crown's financial demands, and an attempted solution to their own conviction that they, the lesser landowners and greater townsmen, had so far been shouldering an unfair share of the burden. They had seen the economic gains made by their social inferiors in the years after the Black Death, when the demographic certainties on which their own prosperity had always depended were so abruptly and cruelly reversed: with half the population dead, labor was no longer a cheap and endlessly renewable resource. Together they had tried to enforce Edward III's hastily enacted law fixing wages at pre-plague levels, and to impose landlords' rights over their tenants to the full. But in the end they had to break ranks to secure the services of laborers, servants, and artisans who suddenly found themselves able to demand higher wages, better conditions, shorter hours. And if customary terms of employment and service had changed, why should customary taxes remain the same? In 1379, when the Commons returned to the idea of the flat-rate tax they had granted for the first time in the last parliament of the old king's reign, they gestured to its regressive nature with an elaborate scale of tariffs requiring the rich to pay more than the poor. But in November 1380, confronted with the impera-tive to keep Woodstock's army in the field in Brittany at a cost they deemed "quite outrageous and altogether beyond them," they agreed that every one of the king's subjects over the age of fifteen—both male and female, all but the truly destitute—should pay the sum of twelve pence, three times the amount per head that had been levied only three years before.[26]

To a great many of the king's subjects—especially those in the south and east, where economic opportunities were most abundant, government enforcement of repressive statutes most immediate, and the danger of enemy raids most intense—the issues appeared quite different. Workingmen and -women in the countryside and in the towns could see the opportunities for greater prosperity and greater freedom that, after the devastation of the plague, should have been theirs for the taking. For some time, they had also been able to see exactly who stood in their way: the wealthy and powerful who, having failed in their duty to defend the realm, did nothing but swap the hats they wore while they lined their own pockets as corrupt ministers, self-interested members of parliament, oppressive landlords, harsh magis-trates. And now the tripling of an already egregiously inequitable tax set this tinderbox of thwarted hopes and frustrated expectations alight.[27]

At first, resistance took the form of evasion. When the returns of the new poll tax were set beside those of 1377, a third of England's population appeared to have vanished into thin air. But the warning went unheeded. In March 1381, commissions of inquiry were dispatched into the shires with sweeping powers to identify every individual missing from the returns, "so that no lay person should be allowed to escape in any way." At the end of May, a commissioner named John Bampton arrived at Brentwood in Essex, twenty miles northeast of London, accompanied by two sergeants at arms, elite military servants of the crown. From there he summoned the inhabitants of neighboring villages, only to be met with their outright refusal either to name names or to proffer more money, on the grounds that they had already paid the tax and would give no more. Bampton threatened them with mass arrest, but their courage held, not least because they knew they had crossed a terrifying line: there was no safe way of backing down from such overt defiance. "The commons rose against the royal officers and would not be arrested," reported a chronicler with detailed knowledge of the day's events. Instead, they threatened to kill the three men, who fled back to London to save their own skins.[28]

This volatile compound of anger and fear fueled a revolt that spread like wildfire in the early summer's heat. After the confrontation at Brentwood, violence flared across Essex and Kent as the rebels attacked the structures and personnel of what they believed to be an irretrievably corrupted political system: buildings were looted and burned, documents reduced to ash, blood brutally spilled. By the second week in June, the men of Kent had found a leader, Walter Tyler, known as Wat; "a tiler of houses and an evil, malevolent man," wrote the chronicler Jean Froissart with appalled contempt. Forceful and fearless though he was, Tyler could hardly have been more different from the blue-blooded knights Froissart idolized—which, for Tyler's adherents, was entirely the point, given the years they had spent watching blue-blooded knights trample their interests underfoot. Armed with longbows, knives, axes, and any other makeshift weapons they could find, thousands of Kentishmen followed Tyler along the old Roman road to London, gathering recruits as they went, while insurgents from Essex and Hertfordshire made for the capital from the east and north. On Wednesday, June 12, the Kentish contingent reached Blackheath, an expanse of open upland overlooking Greenwich and the river, five miles southeast of the city. From there they launched raids farther along the south bank of the Thames, tearing down the Marshalsea prison in Southwark, and sacking Lambeth Palace, the London home of the archbishop of Canterbury, Simon Sudbury, who had held office as the new chancellor of England since the previous year's dismissal of the standing council. But their purpose was more than destruction. They wanted to speak to the king.[29]

The king's household, meanwhile, was humming with barely suppressed panic. That day, when news reached the capital of the rebels' approach, Richard was moved under guard from the palace of Westminster to the greater safety of the Tower, the royal fortress at the southeastern corner of London's city walls. With him were the chancellor, Archbishop Sudbury, and the treasurer, Robert Hales, as well as the earls of Salisbury, Arundel, and Warwick, all of them experienced politicians and—the archbishop apart—soldiers. To this small group fell the minute-by-minute calculation of how best to set about protecting their sovereign and suppressing the insurrection. For comfort and reassurance, the king could also look to his mother, who had only just reached the city after the narrowest of escapes from Tyler's men on the road from Canterbury; his grown-up half brothers Thomas and John Holand; his friend Robert de Vere; and, on one of his periodic visits to court, his cousin Henry of Bolingbroke. Henry's father, Gaunt, meanwhile, was 300 miles away at Berwick on the Scottish border, powerless to intervene in defense of the king or the kingdom, his property or his family. The safety of his son would now, it seemed, stand or fall with the safety of his royal nephew.[30]

But already there were signs that the two boys' fates might be dramatically different if they fell into the rebels' hands. Gaunt was as hated as he had ever been, resented for his thin-skinned pretensions and blamed, along with others who had taken leading roles in the regime, for the mounting failures and oppressions of the last years. In Essex, estates belonging to the controller of the duke's household had been targeted for attack, and the Kentishmen had forced everyone they met on the road to swear an oath "that they would accept no king called John." There could be no confidence about the continued well-being of Gaunt's son if he were to be discovered in the Tower. But Richard was different. Even as they pledged themselves to the destruction of government as they knew it, the rebels swore an oath of loyalty not just to their cause, but to their king. Tyler's men had a password to identify their own: "With whom hold you?" they asked. "With King Richard and the true commons," came the answer. "And those who did not know how to reply or would not do so," noted a London chronicler, "were beheaded and put to death."[31]

As a result, Richard and his chief counselors stood in radically different relation to the rebels' demand for a meeting when a go-between—a knight,

Sir John Newton, who had been taken hostage by Tyler's men in Kent—arrived at the Tower that Wednesday afternoon. "Most dread lord," Newton said, "... you need have no fear for your person, for they will do you no harm, and they hold and will always hold you their king." All those gathered around Richard in the Tower knew that the same guarantee did not extend to them, the "traitors" from whom the rebels had declared their intention to save him.[32] But refusing to leave the fortress was not an option. Something had to be done, some action taken. In the absence of a standing army on English soil, the enforcement of public order depended on the divinely ordained hierarchy of landed power and social deference of which the crown was the keystone, with chains of command and obedience reaching across the realm, into the smallest local community. Now, throughout the south and east, those chains had been broken. The commons proposed a new order: themselves, and their king. They had surrounded the capital, and they required an answer.

The rebels wanted Richard to come to their encampment at Blackheath, but that, the king's advisers agreed, was too dangerous to contemplate. Instead, he would meet them at Rotherhithe, on the south bank of the river between Blackheath and the Tower. The next morning, Thursday, June 13, the feast of Corpus Christi, Richard heard mass in the Tower's chapel, then boarded his royal barge with his chancellor and treasurer, his earls and his bodyguard huddled closely around him. So far, his experience of kingship had been one of frustration and resentment: a performance of enforced passivity, moments of ritualized theater punctuating his own exclusion from a failing government conducted in his name. His people had seen it. They objected. He would go to them, and at last he would speak.[33]

But when the barge approached the appointed place, there stood waiting not a deputation but a growing mass of men, hundreds upon hundreds of the rebels streaming down the hill to meet their king. It was not what his counselors had anticipated. They had refused to go to Blackheath; instead, Blackheath had come to them. At the sight of the royal party, a great cry went up, noise filling the sky, and a spokesman came forward to the bank with a shouted request for the king to step ashore so that his subjects could tell him their grievances. Richard replied that "he would do so willingly," the London chronicler reported, but his alarmed advisers would not contemplate entrusting him, or themselves, to the chaos. The barge remained on the river and the king on the barge, until the oars shifted in the water and the craft began to move away. It was the turn of the men on the Rotherhithe landing to stand in shock. Today, it seemed, the king would not hear their complaints.[34]

There were other ways of expressing them. Soon the Kentish rebels were pressing westward along the river and then north over London Bridge, while the Essex insurgents streamed into the city through Aldgate, half a mile north of the Tower. The mob headed west along Cheapside, past St. Paul's, and out again through Ludgate onto Fleet Street, until acrid air began to catch at throats and lungs. Gaunt's palace of the Savoy was on fire. So focused was the rebels' anger—so clear their determination, Thomas Walsingham reported, "to show the whole community of the realm that they were doing nothing out of greed"—that there was no looting of the duke's jewels and silver plate, his fine furnishings and exquisite tapestries, the costly materials of a royal life. There was only obliteration: of his possessions, hacked and broken and burned or cast into the Thames, and of the administrative records in which, year by year, his authority over people and property had been so carefully inscribed.[35]

Throughout the night, flames rose across the city. The prisons of Newgate, Westminster, and the Fleet were broken open, prisoners scattering into the disorder on the streets. Lawyers and officials were dragged from beds and hiding places and killed without ceremony or remorse. From the heights of the Tower the king and his counselors watched as the capital was overrun. They saw another contingent setting up camp immediately to the east of the fortress, just outside the city walls. In effect, they were under siege. Confrontation was coming: the question was of what kind. London's mayor, a wealthy merchant named William Walworth, argued for a military strike at midnight, launched from inside the Tower and the households of the city's elite. The rebels, poorly armed as they were, could be killed like flies, he said, when they were drunk and sleeping. But the stakes were too high to risk a plan where failure would mean catastrophe. Rather than that, suggested the earl of Salisbury, the king should pacify them with fair words, inducing them to disperse by agreeing to grant what they asked for; only then could control be regained. And so the message was sent. The king would meet his loyal subjects early on Friday at Mile End, an open field a little more than two miles northeast of the city walls.[36]

It took courage: courage to command that the gates of the Tower should be unlocked, and courage to ride out into the bright morning of a frighteningly changed world. This was royal performance in deadly earnest. Beside Richard were the experienced soldiers Salisbury and Warwick, and his young friend de Vere, but it was the fourteen-year-old king on whom all eyes rested. And when the cavalcade reached Mile End, where crowds had by now assembled, it was the fourteen-year-old king who spoke: "Good people, I am your king and your lord. What do you need? What do you wish to say?"[37]

The men before him were a long way from an organized host. It was mainly the Essex contingents who had gathered there. Unlike the Kentish rebels, they had no Tyler to speak for them, and many of their comrades were still sleeping or stirring in the city. All the same, they knew why they had come, and what they wanted from their king. They wanted the abolition of serfdom, the state of unfreedom by which the lives of some men and women were bound to a particular manor and their labor owed to its lord, with no right of access to the common law and the jurisdiction of the king's courts. There were relatively few serfs in the southern counties—and none, by custom, in Kent—but it was precisely their close proximity to greater rights that made the burdens of this subordinated status intolerable. Next, the rebels wanted a general pardon for themselves; and last, they wanted the king to concede that they should "take and deal with all the traitors against him and the law."[38]

The tactical plan drawn up in the Tower was that Richard should agree—and the rebels' demands were such that agreeing did not, to Richard, seem difficult. Putting an end to the specific rights that lords exercised over their unfree tenants would serve to extend the reach of his direct royal jurisdiction over every one of his subjects. And if some of those responsible for the failings of a government that he had been prevented from leading were to be held accountable—as the Commons in his parliaments had repeatedly asked they should be—might that not be desirable? He raised his voice again: "I grant this to you." They should return peacefully to their communities, he said; and with them he would send royal banners and letters under his great seal to confirm what he had done. His words were met with a roar of approval. It was finished. While the clerks in his train began work on the documents to be handed over to nominees from each village, the crowd began to disperse, and the king and his attendants made ready to return to the city. But as they drew near the walls, it became appallingly clear what "dealing with the traitors" might mean. The rebels now believed they acted with the full authority of the crown, and nothing was finished. Tyler's men had taken the Tower.[39]

It should not have been possible. The Tower was the greatest stronghold in the country. But even the greatest stronghold could fall if its doors were unlocked from the inside. And the men who sought to enter were armed not only with the sympathies of London's rank and file, including soldiers of the Tower's garrison, but with news of the king's endorsement of the demands made by the Essex rebels at Mile End—news that had raced back along the road to the city faster than the king himself. Once past the gates, Tyler's men showed the same discipline that had shaped the attack on the Savoy. Their purpose was neither plunder nor indiscriminate violence. When they burst into the royal apartments, some were in an ebullient mood, stretching out on the king's bed and asking the king's mother for a kiss; Jeannette's scandalous past had not been forgotten. But they were on a hunt, from which the princess was only a diversion. When they found their quarry, their temper became instantly darker.[40]

The chancellor and the treasurer—Archbishop Sudbury of Canterbury and Robert Hales, the English prior of the military order of St. John of Jerusalem—had been prominent on the list of "traitors" the rebels were determined to punish. When the two terrified men were found praying in the chapel, they were dragged out to Tower Hill, where their heads were hacked from their bodies. The corpses were abandoned where they fell. The severed heads, with Sudbury's red miter nailed to his skull, were paraded on poles through the city streets, all the way to Westminster and back again to London Bridge. There, like the remains of traitors executed by the crown, they were set on spikes, a ghastly warning for the people to see. The exhilaration of the killings ignited a frenzy of violence. As the light faded, xenophobic rage propelled the mob through the city streets toward the Flemish quarter, where clothworkers from the Low Countries had settled and built their lives—lives that were now taken "without judgment and without cause," railed a monk of Westminster, until mutilated bodies lay heaped in the streets.[41]

Meanwhile, three other men had been murdered in the storming of the Tower: a royal sergeant at arms, a lawyer, and a physician—a friar named William Appleton—who was known to have found favor with Gaunt. But one more had survived against the odds. Henry had not accompanied Richard to Mile End; he was too young to be either useful or put at risk in the confrontation with the rebels. He was learning to fight in the choreographed violence of the lists, but nothing could have prepared him for the invasion of a fortress that should have been impregnable. Given the summary execution of a doctor in holy orders whose only crime was to have treated Henry's father, it seemed certain that death had come for Henry too. And it would have done, had it not been for a rebel named John Ferrour, a Kentish smallholder with business interests in Southwark, who had participated in the destruction of the Savoy—but now, recognizing Gaunt's young heir, took pity on him and saved his life.[42]

For the first time, Henry was experiencing the visceral shock of uncontrolled violence and mortal danger. For Richard, the flood of adrenaline came instead from the knowledge that, confronted with this anarchy and bloodshed, he alone was untouchable. At Mile End he had had a taste of the potential of his power, but the conflict was not over. That night at the Great Wardrobe—a royal residence and storehouse in the west of the city where Richard and the earls took refuge, along with others, including his mother and Henry, who had escaped from the Tower—preparations were made for a second meeting with the rebels. This time, the king would meet Wat Tyler and the men of Kent at Smithfield, the "smooth field" that lay outside the city walls to the northwest.

The next morning, Richard and his attendants rode along Fleet Street and the Strand, past the blackened shell of the Savoy, to Westminster Abbey. He heard mass, and prayed, and left an offering, before turning back east and then north to the appointed place where thousands of his people were waiting for his arrival, some of them carrying the royal banners that had been distributed the day before. At their head was Tyler, an imposing figure on a small horse. He rode forward to greet his king, a slight boy on a huge charger; but Tyler was unintimidated by the presence of his sovereign. As John Ball, a radical preacher who had become a leading voice in the revolt, liked to remind his comrades in arms, "When Adam delved and Eve span, who was then the gentleman?"[43]

"Brother," Tyler began as he took Richard's hand and shook it vigorously, "be of good comfort and joy, for you shall have, within the next fortnight, forty thousand more commons than you have here now, and we shall be good companions." Such insolent familiarity was not what Richard had expected from this encounter with his subjects. Did he and they not agree on his own exceptional status? He was struggling too to understand why his royal intervention at Mile End had not already settled the matter. He drew himself up. "Why will you not go back to your own places?" But Tyler had not been at Mile End, and he was not satisfied by what had happened there. The commons, he said, required the abolition of serfdom, as the men of Essex had made clear. But he and the rebels of Kent—who were already free men—wanted a more root-and-branch leveling of the structures of society. There should be only one bishop and one archbishop in the whole of England, with the property of the Church returned parish by parish to the people. And the private jurisdiction exercised by lords within their manors should end. Instead, the only law and the only lordship in the kingdom should be that of the king.[44]

That last proposal, at least, was music to Richard's ears—and in any case the plan, just as it had been at Mile End, was for him to agree. Tyler, he declared, should have everything he asked, insofar as it accorded with the regality of the crown. And now he and his men should go home. For a minute, there was silence. Was the revolt at an end? In the last thirty-six hours, Tyler and his followers had torched the Savoy, taken the Tower, killed the chancellor and treasurer of England, and forced concessions from their sovereign. Even if the upstart man believed he could escape reprisals, was it plausible that he would immediately return to Kent, and obscurity?

Certainly he appeared in no hurry to leave. Muttered asides among members of the king's retinue grew louder and more heated. Words were exchanged, and within minutes insults became a scuffle between Tyler and London's bullish mayor, William Walworth. Weapons were drawn, blades glinting in the sun, and suddenly Tyler was tumbling from his horse, blood streaming from his wounds. In horror and confusion the rebels saw their leader fall, not knowing what had happened or what they might now face. Some drew their longbows, notching arrows to the strings. Walworth galloped back to the city in urgent search of reinforcements while panic gripped the men who remained around the king. But one person recognized a moment in which a unique protagonist might act. Without looking back, Richard spurred the flanks of his horse, calling, "Sirs, what do you need? You have no other captain but me. I am your king! Be at peace!"[45]

It was extraordinary even that they were seeing him in the flesh, let alone that he should ride toward them, offering himself as their leader, calling them to rally around him in the open field at Clerkenwell a few hundred yards farther north. And so in their bewilderment they obeyed this sacrosanct boy, confident in his majesty, and moved away from the scene of Tyler's final stand to a place where they soon found themselves surrounded not only by the knights and esquires of the king's bodyguard but by the armed men Walworth had swiftly summoned. All their momentum, their clarity of purpose, was gone. By the time they began to disperse—some scattering in small groups, some escorted by royal servants on their way through the capital—Wat Tyler's severed head had already replaced those of the chancellor and treasurer on public display. His sightless eyes stared from a spike on London Bridge while the men who had followed him trudged the long road back to their homes.[46]

In the next days and weeks, as the regime set about restoring control and suppressing farther-flung disturbances, an uneasy peace settled on the southeast of England. After his dramatic role in the last days of the London rising, the young king remained in public view while his government mustered forces at Blackheath, riding out each day on his warhorse to inspect the troops with the royal standard carried before him. "He enjoyed being seen in the army," reported Thomas Walsingham, "and being recognised by his men as their lord." Then, when commissions were sent into the shires to bring to trial those who had rebelled, Richard made a royal progress into Essex and neighboring Hertfordshire in support of his judges. There he was shocked to discover some of his subjects still resisting the proposition that the revolt had been definitively ended by his own courageous leadership at Smithfield. When the last of the diehards had been rounded up, Richard lent the full force of his majesty to the judicial efforts in both counties of Sir Robert Tresilian, the new chief justice of the court of King's Bench after the killing of the previous incumbent, Sir John Cavendish, by rebels in Suffolk.[47]

It was not as easy as Tresilian would have liked to ensure that those arrested were charged with the most heinous crimes. Treason, as defined in Edward III's statute of 1352, included offenses against the person of the sovereign and members of his family, with specific mention too of the murder of the chancellor, treasurer, and chief justices in the course of their duties. But in terms of violent insurrection, the act spoke only of "levying war against our lord the king in his realm." Could that definition be used of a revolt that had explicitly proclaimed its loyalty to the king? Of all the royal judges, Tresilian in particular was determined to punish the rebels as traitors wherever he could. "He went everywhere and spared no one, so causing a great slaughter," wrote one chronicler. "Gibbets rose where none had been before," added another, "since existing ones were too few for the bodies of the condemned." And many of those hanged under Tresilian's hawkish eye—a dozen in Chelmsford alone—were pulled down from the gallows before they were dead, for disemboweling and decapitation. Their quartered corpses were exhibited on city gates across the country as a grim demonstration of the penalties for treason.[48]

For Richard, there was satisfaction in seeing justice done to those who had dared to raise arms against his peace. He had no interest in the rebels' grievances beyond their interaction with his own authority, and obedience to his crown was the sacred duty of all his subjects. But that fact raised a further question. What of the grants he had made at Mile End and Smithfield? His lords thought them insubstantial and without consequence, words said in the heat of a violent moment, to be retracted without further discussion. That was not how Richard wished any royal declaration to be treated—and the abolition of serfdom would extend his own royal jurisdiction over England's people. He saw no reason why his decision should not stand.

Richard's unhappiness at the setting aside of his edict emerged into public view when parliament met that November. Every parliament began with a speech explaining why it had been called, a steer from the government about what the representatives of the realm were expected to do. But this time the reasons given for the summoning of the assembly pointed in several directions at once. England's new treasurer, Sir Hugh Segrave—a trusted servant of the Black Prince, who had been the steward of Richard's household for the past four years—rose to speak on his sovereign's behalf. The king, he said, intended to restore peace to the realm in the wake of the "great turmoil and tumult" caused by the rebels and their terrible offenses against God and the crown—even though, he noted pointedly, they had "portrayed their said misdeeds in another light by saying that they wished to have no king except King Richard." King Richard himself, Segrave continued, wanted not only to punish the malefactors but to root out the causes of the revolt so that such an uprising might never happen again. As his faithful subjects knew, the king had been constrained by the rebels to grant freedom to the serfs of his kingdom, "knowing full well that he should not do so in good faith and according to the law of the land, but he did it for the best, to stop and put an end to their clamour and malice." Since then, on his council's advice, Richard had revoked the grant. Now, however, he wished to know the will of his lords and Commons, "and whether it seems to you that he acted well in that repeal and pleased you, or not"—because if, after all, they *did* wish to free the serfs, the king would agree to their request.[49]

It was a speech in which the rebels were traitors and at the same time loyal to their king; in which Richard had been both wrong to grant the letters of manumission and—potentially, pending his parliament's agreement—right. That this dissonance reflected the young king's arguments with his council, rather than any wider debate among the landed classes, became abundantly clear once the lords and Commons gave their response five days later. They said "with one voice" that the repeal of the letters had been right and just, because the serfs could not be freed without the assent of those who had the chief interest in the matter—in other words, themselves as manorial lords—"and they had never agreed to it, either voluntarily or otherwise, nor would they ever do so, even if it were their dying day." Given such a trenchant answer, the young king had little choice but to acquiesce in royal silence, while his parliament embarked on a familiar litany of complaint about his government's failure either to manage his finances or to defend his realm.[50]

Just five months after his moment in the sun at Smithfield, the bold decision he had taken that day had been overturned. The Commons in parliament—as opposed to the true commons of England, who had looked to him as their king even in revolt—seemed to Richard to be blocking his path to power just as much as the lords who did not think him capable of ruling his own kingdom. And, now that more poll taxes had been rendered politically impossible, the Commons' anger over the government's ongoing need for money found a new target: the size and extravagance of the royal household, and its failure to pay for the vast supplies it commandeered as it moved around the kingdom. Richard's household was his home, his sanctum, the place where his majesty was made real. Now, however, a parliamentary commission was appointed to review and reform its administration and personnel, a body led by the unwelcome figure of his uncle Gaunt and the earls of Arundel, Warwick, Stafford, Suffolk, and Salisbury.[51]

It was not only his household that would operate under an intrusive new kind of supervision. Two new senior officers—the combative earl of Arundel and Sir Michael de la Pole, a veteran soldier-turned-diplomat who had fought under both the Black Prince and Gaunt—were appointed "to accompany the person of the king and belong to his household, to advise and govern his person." As he passed his fifteenth birthday on January 6, 1382, the king himself saw little need for the ongoing government of his person. The events of the previous summer had demonstrated to his own satisfaction that he was revered by his people, and that his courage and judgment could match the fêted examples of his father and grandfather. But it remained difficult for him to see exactly how he might escape the restrictions of a minority that could not formally end because it did not formally exist.[52]

The sole consolation was that he, like his cousin Henry a year earlier, was about to take an undeniable step toward independent adulthood. Richard was getting married.

Three

1381–1384

be rul'd by me

Not everyone was impressed. She was "not so much a gift as a purchase," wrote a monk of Westminster acidly, "since the king of England laid out no small sum for such a tiny scrap of flesh." It was true that she came with only the promise of a dowry which her cash-strapped family stood no realistic chance of supplying, and that in return her new husband's government dispatched the eye-watering total of £7,500 in loans which stood no realistic chance of being repaid. To Richard, however, money seemed a petty irrelevance compared to the priceless treasure of his bride's pedigree. Anne of Bohemia was the granddaughter of the blind king whose ostrich-feather badge Richard's father had adopted in honor of his heroic self-sacrifice at Crécy. Her father, Charles, had been not only king of Bohemia but, even more magnificently, Holy Roman Emperor; and although his heir, Anne's half brother Wenzel, had not yet been crowned by the pope, the young man already held the title of king of the Romans, the elected successor to the imperial throne.[1]

Grandeur no longer went hand in hand with fiscal liquidity, now that Bohemia's lucrative mines were beginning to run out of the silver that had funded the splendid rebuilding of Prague during Charles's pomp. The emperor had also granted substantial territories to his younger sons and his nephews, leaving Wenzel—who, at twenty, showed no sign of his father's talents—with a fraction of the resources that had supported Charles's rule. But Richard was delighted by the glory of an imperial alliance, while for the men who ran his government the appeal of the match lay in diplomatic rather than financial calculations. New tensions were pulling at the intricate web of European politics, ever since a chaotic papal election in 1378 had produced two rival popes: Urban VI in Rome, a rebarbative Italian intent on reducing the power of the French-dominated college of cardinals, and Clement VII in Avignon, the "antipope" installed by the same cardinals once they realized how egregious a mistake their first selection had been. Now kingdoms, states, and cities were lining up on either side of the schism. France and its allies, including Castile and Scotland, declared for Clement, while those who sought to resist any increase in French influence—among them England, Flanders, and the territories of the Holy Roman Empire—affirmed their allegiance to Urban. In such circumstances, the Roman papacy had every interest in promoting a closer relationship between the English and Bohemian kings.[2]

Previous suggestions that Richard might marry daughters of the kings of France, Navarre, or Scotland had foundered as soon as they surfaced in the turbulent waters of the Anglo-French war. The one offer that had been pursued with any seriousness was the hand of Caterina Visconti, daughter of the lord of Milan. Envoys including Michael de la Pole and Simon Burley's brother John had traveled to Italy in 1379 to negotiate the match but soon found themselves summoned from Milan to Rome to discuss Pope Urban's plan that Italian interests should instead be linked with those of England and the Empire through a marriage agreement between London and Prague. The proposition was intriguing enough that de la Pole and Burley moved north from the Holy See across the Alps to Bohemia for immediate talks with Wenzel and his advisers. After they returned to England in the spring of 1380—later than they would have been, had they not been kidnapped by bandits on the road and forced to pay large ransoms for their release—it took two more embassies, one led by Simon Burley himself, before a treaty was finally concluded in the spring of 1381.[3]

All that remained was the arrival of the bride. Anne's progress was so stately that she reached Dover only on December 18, almost four months after her departure from Prague. She had barely set foot on land when a storm blew up, the waves crashing into the harbor with such violence that her ship was broken into pieces. It was "a portent that astonished everybody, and was interpreted by many," Thomas Walsingham noted uncertainly, "as a sign of God's favor." Another month elapsed before her new capital was ready to welcome her with crowds and pageants, the city decked out as a New Jerusalem, just as it had been to greet Richard himself before his coronation. At last, at Westminster on January 20, 1382, the marriage was solemnized, and two days later the fifteen-year-old queen returned to the abbey to be crowned. After the ceremonies a tournament was held at Smithfield, the site of Richard's triumph over Wat Tyler seven months before. The newlyweds, wrapped in fur-lined robes, took their place in the specially built stands to watch the knights of the court compete in their honor. They made a glamorous couple, Anne fine boned and elegant, Richard tall and fair, and universally agreed to be growing into a beautiful young man. But in the lists it was his fourteen-year-old cousin Henry who shone: a shorter, more compact figure with a sportsman's grace, displaying his courage and his physical prowess in armor that shimmered with a thousand gilded sequins.[4]

For Henry's father, it was a moment of consolation, of hope that this new year might be better than the last. Gaunt's experience of the revolt had been bruising. His gorgeous home at the Savoy was a heap of ash and rubble, and he made no plans to rebuild it. While the mob was burning it down, he had been stranded 300 miles away on diplomatic duty at the Scottish border. From that distance, it was impossible to distinguish horrifying news from terrifying rumor, and word had spread that a rebel army was marauding northward in search of the duke they saw as a traitor. Gaunt sought shelter under the roof of his erstwhile ally Henry Percy, the new earl of Northumberland, but Percy, in fear, closed the gates of Alnwick Castle against him, and the duke was driven to seek refuge instead in Edinburgh under the protection of the king of Scots. His duchess, Constanza, was turned away by the frightened keeper of his own castle of Pontefract in Yorkshire; she had no choice but to ride another twenty miles north by torchlight until she reached the Lancastrian fortress at Knaresborough, and safety. His mistress Katherine Swynford fled into hiding. When the danger was over, the duke's relief at reuniting his family was overshadowed by the knowledge of how desperately near his son had come to death at the rebels' hands inside the walls of the Tower.[5]

The trauma left marks. For years, behind Gaunt's back, people had talked of his pride in his sinful life and the brazenness of his adultery with Katherine, that "she-devil and enchantress," as one scandalized chronicler called her. But the shock of the close call his family had faced at last convinced the duke of the need to seek spiritual absolution by giving up his mistress. On his way south after the rebels' defeat, he greeted his forbearing wife in public with notable tenderness and warmth. Three months later, with characteristic dignity, Katherine left the Lancastrian household. Her ostensible charges, the duke's daughters Philippa and Elizabeth, were twenty-one and seventeen, too old to need a governess any longer. The move was discreet and effected without drama. Katherine was established in luxury in two homes in Lincolnshire, one the moated manor house at Kettlethorpe she had long ago shared with her late husband, the other a town house in Lincoln itself, nestled close to the towering cathedral. From now on, Gaunt was determined that his domestic conduct should be beyond the reproach of either God or his own censorious countrymen.[6]

It soon became apparent, however, that he was full of rage as well as repentance. His anger found a target in the earl of Northumberland, whose refusal to offer him shelter he denounced repeatedly at court in the months after the revolt. In August, when the lords of the council gathered in the presence of the young king at Reading and Westminster, there were rancorous altercations between the former friends, Gaunt unbending and icy, Northumberland vehement in his self-justification. On October 9, when the council met again at Berkhamsted, twenty-five miles northwest of London, Northumberland threw down a glove, demanding that Gaunt should either withdraw his accusations or defend them in combat—a challenge the duke could not with honor refuse. Richard had already relished one chance to preside over a trial by battle, but his anxious counselors knew that a duel between two of England's greatest noblemen would unleash far more dangerous problems than it could hope to solve. Instead, they referred the case for a full hearing a few weeks later in the parliament that had already been summoned to deal with the aftermath of the revolt.[7]

The chronicler of Westminster Abbey, watching in alarm as Gaunt and Northumberland approached the capital with large companies of armed men, feared the quarrel might reignite the summer's violence and thereby "destroy the whole of England." The conflict was lent a particular intensity not only by the Londoners' ongoing hostility to Gaunt—while Northumberland and his retinue were noisily welcomed inside the walls of the heavily guarded city, Gaunt and his men were shut out—but by the fact that Richard's simmering suspicion of his uncle was beginning to generate reciprocal suspicion in the duke himself. Northumberland had clearly believed it possible, when rumors raced north in June, that Gaunt had been denounced as a traitor by the young king as well as by the rebels. Now Gaunt's demand that the earl should be punished for "forcing" him to flee into Scotland seemed rooted in a need for public vindication, for an unequivocal demonstration that he *did* enjoy—had always enjoyed—his nephew's trust.

He did not get what he wanted. In public, Richard could say nothing other than that—*of course*—his uncle enjoyed his utmost confidence. But Northumberland was furiously insisting that he too was a loyal servant of the crown who had done his best in appallingly difficult circumstances. The complexity of the dispute, and the political need to find a workable solution, gave the fourteen-year-old king a moment in which he could wield his authority over both men in the presence of all the lords of his realm. With the main business of the parliament adjourned until the hearing had taken place, Gaunt and Northumberland were each given a day to make their case against the other before the king and assembled peers. While their adversary spoke, each was required to listen in silence. Gaunt was not used to being told that he must sit still and keep quiet, but he had no grounds on which to resist this display of his nephew's sovereignty. And when judgment came, it was not the wholesale victory for which he had hoped. Blame for the offending message in which Northumberland had denied Gaunt refuge at Alnwick was pinned not on the earl but on the men who had delivered it, two Percy associates who found themselves committed to the Tower for supposedly exceeding their instructions. Northumberland himself knelt to ask forgiveness from both Richard and Gaunt, but his apology dwelt almost entirely on his insubordination in arguing with Gaunt in front of the king, and scarcely at all on the substance of the duke's original complaint.[8]

Stiffly, Gaunt accepted this partial submission, along with a ritual exchange of the kiss of peace. Two days later, on November 11, the duke was officially reconciled with the citizens of London, riding into the capital at the head of his imposing retinue to be met by the mayor and aldermen on his way to hear mass at St. Paul's for the soul of his dead wife, Blanche. In public, what the relieved chronicler at Westminster called the "proper courses of harmony and peace" had been restored. On November 13, the postponed business of parliament finally got under way with the opening speech of the treasurer, Sir Hugh Segrave, about the causes and consequences of the revolt. But those consequences had left Gaunt licking his wounds. Meanwhile, Richard's satisfaction at sitting in judgment over his uncle lasted only a few days, until the Commons rejected his royal suggestion that they should endorse his abolition of serfdom, and began to renew their complaints about the extravagance of his household.

Both uncle and nephew had reason to be glad of the break when the parliamentary session was adjourned again on December 13, to make way for Christmas and the imminent arrival of Richard's bride. Gaunt led the splendid deputation that greeted Anne when she landed at Dover after her long journey from Prague. A proud father, he bought his daughter Elizabeth a velvet saddle embroidered with lions so that she could ride with fitting magnificence in the wedding procession, and watched Henry acquit himself with glittering distinction at the tournament held to celebrate the royal marriage. But the events of the summer had been seismic in their effects. As the aftershocks eased, unnerving shifts began to show in the structures of politics. Richard was absorbing his first tastes of his sovereign power: both its glorious potential, and the ways in which that potential was still constrained. And when parliament reconvened on January 27, 1382, five days after the new queen's coronation, Gaunt began to discover the limitations of the influence he could now bring to bear on the direction of his nephew's government.[9]

In the cold light of a January morning, the reassembled lords and Commons had to face the unpalatable fact that England's treasury was empty and its war policy in chaos. Thomas of Woodstock's campaign in Brittany had been an ignominious failure. The poll tax intended to pay for it had precipitated popular rebellion on an unprecedented scale. As a result, the Commons had already declared before December's adjournment that they did not dare to grant any further taxation, instead asking the lords to "consider the wars, wisely and considerably to reduce them if it can be done, for the relief of the king and the kingdom." But in practice there was no way to reduce the wars without making peace, and viable terms for anything more than a temporary truce remained far out of reach.[10]

Gaunt, however, had a new proposal for their urgent consideration. As so often in England's war with France, the duke's eyes were fixed on Spain, his political perspective shaped by duty and ambition so closely intertwined that they were indistinguishable one from the other. For Gaunt, it was a simple fact that, through his marriage to Constanza, he was the rightful ruler of Castile. It was also unarguably true that England desperately needed to curb or control the fearsome naval power of Castile, currently deployed in the Channel and along the Atlantic seaboard in support of its ally France. And one of these circumstances offered the possibility of an elegant solution to the other: install Gaunt as king and the Castilian fleet would abandon France to serve England instead.[11]

That had always been his strategy, which over the past year—frantically preoccupied as he had been with his responsibilities in England—the duke had delegated to his brother Edmund of Langley. The opportunity Langley had been enlisted to exploit was the death in 1379 of Gaunt's old enemy Enrique of Castile and the succession of his son Juan, a young man of uncertain physical health and faltering political will. Gaunt had pushed to take advantage of this disruption in Castilian politics through an English alliance with the neighboring kingdom of Portugal, a realm with its own large fleet and its own Atlantic coastline, and in the summer of 1381 Langley had set sail for Lisbon with 3,000 troops. The plan was for these soldiers to join Portugal's forces in an invasion of Castile to depose Juan and place Gaunt and Constanza on the throne.

The plan did not work. By the time the English contingent arrived in July, Portugal's navy had already been destroyed in a disastrous engagement with the Castilian fleet. The English troops had no horses, which the Portuguese had undertaken to provide, but nothing had been done; it was winter before enough animals were requisitioned. By then the year was too far gone to launch a campaign, given the difficulties of bad weather and scarce supplies. Funds were running out, and discipline among the restive soldiers breaking down. In December, Langley wrote dejectedly home to his elder brother to report that all would be lost without urgent reinforcements of money and men.[12]

So far, the campaign had failed to meet a single one of its objectives, but when he stood to speak in parliament on January 27, Gaunt refused to contemplate letting the moment slip away. Though Gaunt did not say so, Langley had always been a less than ideal deputy. Evidently, the duke himself now needed to take personal command of the Portuguese campaign. He had heard the Commons insist that they could grant no new taxes, but surely a loan would be acceptable? £60,000, he calculated, would give him 4,000 troops for the six months it should take to bring the venture to a successful conclusion. He promised to repay the money within three years in cash or some other form of service to the kingdom, and meanwhile he would be not only recovering his own rights in Castile and protecting the Englishmen who were already in Portugal but defending England and the safety of the seas, he declared, "to the great destruction of our enemies."[13]

It was, he believed, an unanswerable case. Parliament thought otherwise. Over the next four weeks, there was "great disputation and altercation" among the lords, noted the clerk whose task it was to record the proceedings: some agreed with Gaunt, but others insisted that the removal of such a force from England would leave the still-volatile country at the mercy of another uprising. Even worse, the Commons saw no benefit in his request for a loan rather than a subsidy. The money would have to be found either way, which meant taxation now, whether or not it was repaid later. And the citizens of London, whose suspicion of Gaunt sprang eternal, were profoundly disturbed at the possibility that the duke might yet again (as they saw it) be corralling the resources of the kingdom to fund the pursuit of his personal ambition.

No resolution had been reached by the time London's mayor and aldermen, along with 600 members of the city guilds, visited the king at Kennington on February 23 to receive confirmation of their civic privileges. Five years before, when Richard was prince of Wales, London had sent mummers with dice and golden gifts to entertain him. This visit was altogether weightier: a formal ratification of the direct relationship between the young king and his capital, a city that had witnessed his bravery and the force of his sovereignty during the revolt the previous summer. Now they took the opportunity to assert their loyalty in sharply pointed terms, petitioning "that they might have only one king, declaring that they wished to be the subjects of one man alone." Eight months earlier, these wealthy elites had had no sympathy with the rebels except in this single matter. Now the echoes of the Kentishmen's oath that they would have "no king called John" were much too close for Gaunt's comfort. The next morning, the duke left London in unsettled haste, riding twenty miles north to his castle at Hertford. The day after that, the Commons at Westminster made their final offer: not a grant of taxation to fund a campaign in Castile but a four-year extension of the customs duties on wool exports, a modest amount that they specified should be used only for the defense of the realm. It was a blunt demonstration that Gaunt could no longer count on a decisive say in the military pursuit of what he believed to be his country's interests.[14]

The Londoners' petition struck as close to home for Richard as it had for his uncle. With the opening of each of his parliaments he had found himself forcibly reminded that there *were*, in fact, two kings in his kingdom, when "my lord of Spain"—as Gaunt was addressed at court—took his seat among England's peers as "the king of Castile and León and duke of Lancaster."[15] Now the inhabitants of Richard's capital were looking to him for leadership, just as the rebels had in the summer; yet here was an explicit reminder that—bafflingly, enragingly—Gaunt and the other lords, however divided they might be among themselves, still blocked his royal path.

Within the magnificent ceremonial and hierarchy of Richard's household, his growing authority was pleasingly acknowledged. His mother was in her mid-fifties and no longer well. After the shock of her traumatic encounter with the rebels in the Tower, the dowager princess was happy to step back from a controlling stake in her son's life, secure in the knowledge that the men to whom she had entrusted his education were serving him as faithfully as they had once served her husband. Simon Burley and Aubrey de Vere had been joined as senior household officers by Michael de la Pole, one of the two men appointed in parliament in November 1381 to "advise and govern the king's person." At the time, this formal supervision had been unwelcome, but in practice de la Pole's collaboration with Burley and de Vere was proving seamless and sympathetic. All three were of Richard's father's generation, in their forties or early fifties, and all had fought under the Black Prince's imperious command; all three had also been closely involved in negotiating Richard's marriage to Anne. The king had every confidence that their quasi-paternal presence served not to restrict but to express his authority—as did the quiet devotion of his queen, and the courtly companionship of the young aristocrats among his attendants, fifteen-year-old Ralph Stafford, sixteen-year-old Thomas Mowbray, and twenty-year-old Robert de Vere.[16]

Outside the royal household, however, it was a different story. The great nobles, with their lands and their retinues, were supposed to be his servants, but it seemed to Richard that their lands and retinues gave them the means to exercise power that should have been his. In late December 1381—while Richard was absorbing the discovery that his leadership during the revolt had changed nothing about his position in government—the sudden death of Edmund Mortimer, the twenty-nine-year-old earl of March, offered the king an unexpected chance to take control of the second-largest noble estate in the country. The earl's son and heir was only seven, which meant that by law the rich Mortimer lands passed into the keeping of the crown until the boy should come of age. Richard's grandfather Edward III had treated this right of royal custody as a partnership with his nobles' families, maintaining continuity in the management of their estates until the heir reached adulthood. But for Richard, who did not see the nobles as his partners, the Mortimer inheritance was a prize to be exploited. From January 1382, he set about dismissing the officers who had previously administered the dead earl's estates, and replacing them with knights, esquires, and clerks of his own household. Through these new appointments, the revenues and military resources of the earldom—including the formidable Mortimer castles in the marches of Richard's principality of Wales—would fall directly under the young king's personal command.[17]

In practical detail, Richard's scheme had its flaws. The responsibilities he handed to one of the knights of his chamber as "steward of all the lands late of the inheritance of Edmund Mortimer"—estates that ranged right across England, Wales, and Ireland—were patently too much for a single man to manage, let alone one with no previous knowledge of the earldom's administration. But as a statement of royal intent it was unmistakable, certainly from the ringside seat of the new chancellor, Lord Scrope, to whom Richard's instructions were sent for authorization under the great seal. As the months went on and the royal letters piled up, Scrope at first resisted, then refused to comply. He was a veteran soldier and an able public servant, widely respected for his intelligence and integrity, who had been a trusted friend of the dead earl. He knew that taking the Mortimer estates away from the experienced officials who represented the earl's family would not only damage the prospects of the Mortimer heir but set an alarming precedent in the eyes of all landowners who looked to the crown for security. He also knew that siphoning off the Mortimer revenues into the young king's household would do nothing to relieve the crippling burden of debt and the relentless military expenses with which, year on year, the government was struggling. It was not simple to defy royal orders, but the king was young, and the fault must lie, Scrope concluded, with the private ambitions of those who surrounded him. "He said," reported Thomas Walsingham, "that those men, who knew of the debts which the king owed, were not being loyal to the king, but were concerned only to satisfy their own greed rather than what was in the best interests of the realm."[18]

To Richard, this distinction between the king's will and the interests of the realm made no sense. The realm was *his* realm. What could it need other than what its king wanted? Scrope argued that, as England's chancellor, his hands were tied by his responsibilities: he could not do as the king asked because the king was still a child and Scrope might later face his adult sovereign's wrath for obeying adolescent orders that had harmed both crown and realm. But what was meant as counsel was heard as insult. At fourteen, had Richard not been man enough—king enough—to confront the rebels at Mile End and Smithfield? Now he was fifteen, and his chancellor was attempting to invoke the authority of his own crown against him. He would not brook this defiance. In fury, he demanded Scrope's resignation. Scrope tried to stand his ground, but Richard was implacable. When Scrope finally gave the great seal back into the king's hands, he protested his enduring loyalty but said that he would never agree to hold office under him again.[19]

Given that within the space of thirteen months one chancellor had been brutally murdered and then another unceremoniously sacked by the teenage king, it briefly seemed possible that no one would agree to hold this particular office again. Scrope stood down on July 11, 1382, and it was September 20 before a replacement—Robert Braybrooke, the king's former secretary, now bishop of London—was found and installed. During these weeks of vacancy, "the king did whatever he liked," Walsingham noted waspishly—although that was not how Richard saw it, stewing as he still was over Scrope's insubordination and the restrictions on his authority it represented. That summer, he and his queen went traveling westward from the capital, spending two weeks in August at Woodstock in Oxfordshire and two more at Bristol in September. In principle, government moved with the king, but these were not normal circumstances—a royal minority-that-was-not-a-minority could never be that—and it was precisely the ambiguities of practice rather than principle that had caused the rift with Scrope.[20]

During the summer and early autumn, Gaunt too was on the move, attempting to exorcise his own fears and frustrations by touring his estates in the midlands and the north with Henry at his side. Physical distance only served to emphasize the political fractures that separated both the king and the duke from the administration at Westminster—and in the absence of Richard and Gaunt it was far from clear who else might offer decisive direction to the regime. Edmund of Langley had achieved less than nothing in Portugal, while Gaunt's youngest brother, Thomas of Woodstock, remained resentfully on the political periphery. Now twenty-seven, Woodstock had so far had a brief and bitterly unsuccessful taste of military command in France, and his young wife, Eleanor, had given him two children as well as the benefit of her inheritance; but still he enjoyed neither the landed estate nor the voice as a royal counselor he believed to be his birthright.[21]

Beyond the obvious figures of the king's uncles, it was hard to see where leadership might come from. Some lords were ruled out of political contention by personal tragedy. In February 1382, William Ufford, earl of Suffolk, collapsed and died on the steps of Westminster Hall while parliament was sitting. He left no direct heir. Six months later, William Montagu, earl of Salisbury—the dowager princess's former husband, whose father had died four decades earlier from injuries sustained in a tournament—accidentally killed his only son in a tilting match. He was left wrestling with his grief and the destruction of his dynastic hopes, and entangled too in an acrimonious legal dispute with his brother John, the steward of the king's household, which caused a permanent rift within the family.[22]

There were other peers with plausible military and political records. Thomas Beauchamp, earl of Warwick, and his brother-in-law Hugh Stafford, earl of Stafford, the father of Richard's young companion Ralph, had served as captains under the command of Edward III, the Black Prince, and John of Gaunt from the late 1350s onward. They had known victory under forceful royal leadership—an experience not shared by Richard Fitzalan, earl of Arundel, who had come to military prominence only after inheriting his title and estates in 1376 and, like Thomas of Woodstock, had therefore fought in later campaigns that proved less than triumphant. Either way, all now seemed mired in impotent dissatisfaction. Clarity and cohesion about the regime's objectives could not be achieved while money was so short, fear of renewed popular unrest so strong, and political trust so brittle.[23]

Even at the height of the revolt in June 1381, one well-informed London chronicler alleged that none of the small group of lords with the king inside the Tower, including Warwick and Arundel, "could or would give him any counsel."[24] By that point it was already brutally clear—with smoke from Gaunt's burning palace hanging heavy in the air—that any move by one of the king's subjects to take the reins of government might incur frightening consequences in terms of immediate danger or subsequent blame. Then the young king himself had appeared in his majesty before the rebels. Now the drifting inertia of the battered regime offered another opportunity ripe with potential for Richard to assert himself, had he had plans for the future of his kingdom and its people, or any interest in making them.

He had neither. What Richard wanted was to take the power of his crown away from his presumptuous nobles into his own sovereign hands. Beyond that, there was no sign of what he wanted to *do*, but only of what he did not, which included stepping into the arena where his realm was in most desperate need of direction: the theater of war.

The drain on England's resources was inexorable: the beleaguered garrisons at Calais, Brest, and Cherbourg; the forces stretched thin in Aquitaine, on the Scottish border, in Ireland; the threadbare defenses of England's coasts. But escape from an untenable status quo would require a strategy—and it was no longer clear how, where, or by whom such decisions might effectively be reached. By the late summer of 1382, the one certainty was the need to call a new parliament, without which there could be no hope of funding any action at all.

When the assembly met at Westminster in October, Gaunt tried once more to persuade the representatives of the realm that the "way of Portugal" remained the best route to the defeat of Castile and then France. By now, he was insisting that his expedition could be financed with a reduced parliamentary loan of only £43,000, a bargain price that he again solemnly undertook to repay into the kingdom's coffers. This time, he succeeded in convincing the lords to support his proposal, despite the alarmingly inconvenient fact—unmentioned in public at Westminster—that the exhausted Portuguese regime had finally made peace with Castile two months earlier, leaving Edmund of Langley's diminished, mutinous forces struggling to secure their passage home.[25]

But the "way of Portugal" was not the only path laid out for parliament to consider. "God has shown us two noble ways," explained the bishop of Hereford, "along which, by reason and with His grace, we may escape all perils and arrive at great honour." The other, he said, lay through Flanders, where the great industrial towns of Ghent, Ypres, and Bruges were in revolt against their lord, Louis de Mâle, the man who had long ago jilted the king's aunt Isabella. Louis had turned for help to his son-in-law, Philip, duke of Burgundy, one of the powerful uncles of the young king of France. In response, the Flemish rebels were asking for military support from England; "and that path," the bishop continued, "is most noble and broad enough to cause the enemy more trouble than they have known for a long while, if we have the means to keep it open."[26]

For the Commons, the idea of exerting pressure on France from the north via Flanders, rather than from the south via Castile, had much to recommend it. The Flemish towns were vital to English economic interests: it was in Ghent, Ypres, and Bruges that fine English wool, exported in lucrative bulk, was manufactured into luxury cloth for sale across the Continent. Any interruption to this crucial trading relationship—let alone the future prospect of Flanders passing into the control of France, whenever Count Louis should be succeeded by his only child, the duchess of Burgundy—was a source of intense alarm to the wealthy merchants and lesser landowners who sat as MPs.[27]

As fortune would have it, any campaign in support of the Flemish rebels would also attract an unexpected subsidy. The Roman pope Urban VI had declared that war waged by his faithful supporters against adherents of his rival in Avignon, wherever in Europe the conflict might be, should have the status of a crusade. In theory, this prescription should have applied to Gaunt's proposed assault on Castile, a kingdom loyal to the "antipope" Clement VII, more than it did to any intervention in the civil unrest within Urbanist Flanders. But the "way of Flanders" was aimed beyond Louis de Mâle at Clementist France, and the crusading potential of the plan was given insistent substance in the autumn of 1382 by the dramatic intervention of Henry Despenser, bishop of Norwich.[28]

Despenser, like many well-born younger sons, had been ordained into the Church at the behest of his family, but for years it had been clear that he would have preferred the life of a soldier. When the revolt of 1381 reached Norfolk, the flamboyant bishop had taken up his sword and hurled himself into battle against the insurgents, "gnashing his teeth like a wild boar," Thomas Walsingham reported admiringly. Now, a little more than a year later, he announced that he would take personal command of a crusade into Flanders, with full authority from Pope Urban to grant indulgences—that is, remission of the time a soul would spend in purgatory as punishment for sin—to all those who either volunteered for the army themselves or paid the wages of a professional soldier to fight in their place.[29]

The plan came as music to the Commons' ears: a military offensive recognizably focused on England's immediate geopolitical interests, pursued by a charismatic leader who had the incalculable advantage of not being John of Gaunt, at a cost that would not, for once, fall entirely on their shoulders as taxpayers. In these encouraging circumstances they were willing to contribute their share, offering up a standard grant of taxation—reckoned by established precedent at one-fifteenth of the value of movable property belonging to those in the countryside, and one-tenth for those who lived in the towns—for the defense of the realm. Exactly how the defense of the realm might best be defined was the bone of contention over which parliament was wrangling, but the Commons made it explicitly clear which side they were backing. Before the assembly dispersed, they submitted a petition to the king in fulsome support of the bishop's crusade, which, they argued, "might greatly alleviate the expense of your said wars, and enable greater exploits and a speedy conclusion."

It was a measure of how lacking in functional leadership the regime had become that the dilemma of whether to strike at France via the north or the south had ever been aired beyond the walls of the royal council chamber, let alone that the strategic decision should effectively have fallen to the Commons in parliament. But three weeks after the parliament ended, events unfolding across the Channel gave the projected campaign a new urgency. French troops tore into Flanders, burning towns and villages into submission as they went. On November 27 at Rozebeke, fourteen miles south of Ghent, the invading army obliterated the massed ranks of the rebel forces. Thousands upon thousands lost their lives, hacked to death where they fell or smothered in the Flemish mud. By the middle of December, when the visitors finally turned for home, only the city of Ghent was left holding out in fragile defiance. Suddenly French-controlled Flanders was not a threat but a frightening reality.[30]

This was Richard's chance. In the face of fresh danger, would the king step forward to lead his kingdom? Going to war was no small thing, but he did not yet have to be ready for the technicalities of military command. France's thirteen-year-old king, Charles VI, a boy almost two years younger than Richard, had taken the field beside his generals when France's army rode triumphantly into battle at Rozebeke. Even if he was not yet a warrior like his father and grandfather, England's monarch too could be a figurehead for his troops, a focus for their loyalty and service, an icon like the image on his royal seal of a king on a warhorse brandishing the naked blade of a sword in defense of his people. But Richard much preferred the image on the seal's other face: the king magnificently enthroned as judge and lawgiver, orb and scepter balanced in his sovereign hands. He had never been interested in fighting, nor in putting his sacred person at risk in the unpredictable heat of battle, and he did not intend to start now.

If the king would not assert himself, however, the gray area in government left by the issue of his age meant that the proposal could still be made on his behalf. By now, even Gaunt saw the need to put his Portuguese proposals temporarily aside to tackle the crisis in Flanders with all the resources England could muster. The danger to English interests was immediate and overwhelming: not only were English shipping and the crucial stronghold of Calais under threat, but France's total embargo on trade with England had been extended at a stroke into Flanders, to devastating economic effect. England's people were so determined to resist that when Bishop Despenser took his crusading vows in a theatrically staged ceremony at St. Paul's four days before Christmas, Londoners streamed into the cathedral to offer him their service. For Gaunt, and others among the lords, it was deeply regrettable that the "way of Flanders" had become so closely identified with a freelance crusade led by a grandstanding priest, but Despenser was a loose cannon who could surely be shoved aside without too much difficulty by seasoned military leaders in the name of the crown.

In January 1383, therefore, a specially summoned council of lords and knights declared that the king would lead an army to relieve the besieged town of Ghent and end the French occupation of Flanders, a plan that was presented for approval to a newly summoned parliament a month later. Richard had just turned sixteen, the age at which his father had fought so heroically at Crécy, and as Chancellor Braybrooke told the assembly "it is plainly the case that every loyal liegeman of the king would more eagerly and ardently desire to labor beside his liege lord . . . than beside any other person in the world." The idea might have been irresistibly compelling but for one fundamental flaw that could not be concealed. As one chronicler laconically put it, "*Rex laborare noluit*": the king did not want to go.[31]

And if the king did not want to go, the Commons would provide no more money for a full-scale campaign. They had already granted a tax for Bishop Despenser's war chest that had been collected but not yet disbursed, and Gaunt and the lords dared not ask directly for more, hoping instead that the prospect of the monarch leading his people into battle might win broad-based support and loosen taxpayers' purse strings. But the Commons did not trust Gaunt's public conversion to the "way of Flanders," and they were not about to fall for the patently tall tale that Richard was itching for the fight. A freelance crusade led by a grandstanding priest might be eccentric, but it was cheap and already under way. The Commons formulated their "no" to the lords with respectful care. It would be too dangerous, they said, for the king or his uncles to leave the kingdom while the northern frontier remained so unstable and the Anglo-Scottish truce so close to expiring. Fortunately, noted the Speaker, Bishop Despenser had already offered to mount the campaign in the service of both God and king without requiring any further funds, and it was the Commons' considered advice that his "great and noble proposal . . . should be warmly and readily accepted." Gaunt was so angry at this obstruction of his plans that he walked out. The other nobles were not much happier, but there was little they could do.[32]

Bishop Despenser took delivery of the tax revenues from the Exchequer, mustered his eager volunteers, and sailed for Calais in the middle of May. As armies went, they were a more than usually haphazard bunch—the promise of salvation not being an entirely predictable recruiting tool—which, together with the bishop's idiosyncratic generalship, had persuaded the French that their arrival need not be treated as a serious threat. As a result, the crusaders, marching behind banners bearing the pope's crossed keys and the Despenser family arms, swept easily from Calais through Gravelines to Dunkirk, where, on May 25, they inflicted a dramatic defeat on ad hoc forces hastily assembled by local French garrisons and a bastard son of the count of Flanders.[33]

In triumph, they moved on to besiege the great town of Ypres—but there for the first time they met determined resistance. Their assaults failed. Supplies ran scarce. Disease broke out, and discipline broke down. As they struggled, argued, and eventually abandoned the siege, the French were making good their misjudgment, gathering a huge army that marched north from Arras in late August under the command of King Charles and his royal uncles. They were accompanied by John de Montfort, duke of Brittany—once Edward III's loyal son-in-law and still the husband of Richard's sister Joan Holand—who was now fighting for France against the English for the very first time. By the end of the first week in September, they had taken back Dunkirk, leaving Despenser and the tattered remains of his forces pinned down at Gravelines.

Gaunt had spent much of the summer in the north as the Commons had asked, to negotiate a new truce with the Scots. He was back on his midland estates that August when news arrived of the bishop's desperate retreat from Ypres. Enraging and wearyingly predictable though the unfolding disaster was, the duke did not hesitate. He and his youngest brother, Thomas of Woodstock, summoned their retainers and wrote to the king, telling Richard the time had come for him to go to the defense of the Englishmen who stood in such terrible danger only a few miles from Calais.[34]

Richard too had been traveling that summer, descending in state with his queen and his lavish entourage upon long-suffering monastic houses from East Anglia through the midlands into Yorkshire. For two weeks after the arrival of his uncles' letter he did nothing but continue on his royal way. Then on September 11, at Daventry in Northamptonshire, he received a message directly from Bishop Despenser. Dunkirk had fallen to the French king, who stood with his soldiers at the very gates of Gravelines. It was too much: if that impudent boy was in the field just ten miles from the English jewel of Calais, then the king of England would be too. His temper up, Richard took horse for London—riding through the dark "as though he were going to kill the king of France that very night," said Thomas Walsingham, watching him commandeer the abbot of St. Albans's palfrey en route—until at last he reached Westminster. It was too much: he needed sleep. When he met his councillors the next day, he was exhausted. Surely there was no sense in exposing England's sovereign to jeopardy when there was so little time to raise the necessary troops? His uncles would go instead, and Despenser would hold out until they got there.[35]

But they did not, because the bishop did not. While Gaunt and

Woodstock struggled to round up soldiers and enough ships to carry them, Despenser was discovering that his disillusioned captains were no longer willing to wait for rescue. The duke of Brittany—who, along with the duke of Burgundy, believed French interests would be best served by expelling this irritant English army at speed—made a deal with the soldiers behind the bishop's back: the surrender of Gravelines in return for a cash payment. Despenser had no choice but to turn tail for home. He was met with incredulous recrimination. Parliament opened on October 27, eight months almost to the day since the start of the assembly that had committed the campaign into the bishop's hands. Now he was impeached for its failure. The lords were incensed because they had known all along that putting an episcopal amateur in charge of an army was a stupid mistake. The Commons were incensed because they had believed—or had badly wanted to believe—in the bishop's promises and their trust had been betrayed. Although Despenser had lost none of his self-assurance, his lengthy arguments that he was to blame for nothing persuaded no one. As a churchman, he was personally immune from punishment by secular law, but the temporal assets of his bishopric were confiscated. He was sent back to administer his diocese in obscurity.[36]

And while the sorry saga of the Flanders crusade limped to its sorry end, England's young king had shown no sign of taking the threat to his country's interests seriously at all.

The regime pieced together to nurse England through Richard's minority had always been a patchworked simulacrum of personal rule. Now it was falling apart. After years of attritional reverses, of revolt at home and defeat abroad, the great lords of the realm were no longer capable of the approximation of unity that could produce a coherent policy in the king's name and then convince the Commons in parliament to fund it. The only lasting solution would be the reality of personal rule: the king must raise his banner to rally his subjects. But the nature of the crises threatening to engulf the kingdom meant that the banner required was a military standard, and, barring momentary rushes of blood to the head, that was something Richard was not willing to do.

The king's vision of his personal rule was entirely different. The real world, for Richard, did not lie outside his household, but within it. As he traveled between his palaces of Windsor and Westminster, Kennington, Eltham, and Sheen, the people and possessions that moved with and around him, their deference and luxury, were his citadel, the only setting within which he believed his sovereignty to be fully acknowledged. As he grew older, the protective cocoon of his childhood was evolving into something more rarefied and more assertive.

Like his parents before him, Richard was spending thousands of pounds on silks, brocades, furs and cloth of gold, on silver plate, pearls, and jewels. Gifts for his queen bought in the summer of 1382 from a London goldsmith included a band for a headdress finely worked in gold with a ruby and two sapphires, and three rings, each set with four pearls around a great diamond; together, their price would have kept a knight in comfort for a year, but by Richard's standards they were little more than trinkets. He was already planning to remodel the royal accommodation at Sheen, his riverside home ten miles west of London, to include a bathhouse lined with 2,000 painted tiles and plumbed with hot and cold water through newly installed bronze taps. He took pride in the fine falcons and goshawks that filled the royal mews at Charing Cross, half a mile north of the palace of Westminster; and, though it was obvious by now that he was neither a fighter nor a scholar, the elaborate courtliness he cultivated in his surroundings echoed the sophistication of the chivalric romances—the *Roman de la Rose* and the Arthurian tales of Gawain and Percival—that he kept, beautifully bound in leather, in his chamber.[37]

It was calm inside his household: an expression of majesty that was serene because unchallenged. Simon Burley had been at his side to defend his rights since before Richard could remember. His queen was applying her unshakable faith and her calm intelligence—Anne could read in Latin, German, and Czech and was learning English—to her new role as his devoted consort. She was already anxious that she had not yet given her husband an heir: she lacked nothing, she would soon write in formal Latin to her brother in Prague, "save that we write in grief that still we are not rejoicing in our childbed." God willing, she added, that happy day would not be far away.[38] But in the meantime it was becoming apparent that, while the king expected constant support from all those around him, it was Robert de Vere, the young earl of Oxford, on whom his own eyes were fixed, the one person to whom he looked without expecting anything in return.

The difficulty came when Richard was required to step outside this perfect world. There he found complaints about his spending, usually from the Commons in parliament, and about his choice of attendants, usually from the lords. "If it please you, most redoubtable lord," the Commons asked pointedly in February 1383, ". . . that your household be so managed that it would please you to live within the revenues of your kingdom." "There arose a great quarrel between the king and the lords," a monk at Westminster reported from the next assembly eight months later, "for it seemed to them that the king was following bad advice, and on this account would not admit good governance into his circle."

Richard found it unacceptable—beyond infuriating—to face such criticism, given that the crown was his, and the right to rule being kept out of his hands. But in the spring of 1383 he made a breakthrough. When Robert Braybrooke resigned as chancellor after an undistinguished tenure of only six months, Richard appointed Michael de la Pole in his place. The chancellor held the great seal by which orders made on the authority of the crown were publicly authenticated and put into operation. In the clouded circumstances of Richard's not-quite-minority, the administrative offices of both the great seal and the privy seal—once, long ago, the monarch's personal seal, but by now another institutionalized mechanism within the public processes of government—remained subject to the collective scrutiny of the council. In the summer of 1382, that supervision had resulted in Chancellor Scrope's resistance to the king's plans to take control of the Mortimer inheritance, and his own thwarted rage. Richard was determined it would not happen again. He knew de la Pole to be his loyal servant. Now he could seal documents privately with his own royal signet, and his chancellor, armed with the great seal, would set his instructions in motion exactly as he wished.[39]

What he wished was to reward his loyal servants. None of them, Richard believed, had yet received the largesse that would adequately reflect their service to him, or his own glory. Simon Burley and Aubrey de Vere were younger sons, in Burley's case from a minor gentry family, and Michael de la Pole the heir of a merchant financier who had lost much of his self-made fortune in his dealings with Richard's royal grandfather. None of the three could easily afford to maintain themselves among the leading men of the realm out of their own pockets. In part, Richard wanted the style of his attendants to match his own. The wardrobe Burley was amassing included furs of miniver and ermine, a cloth-of-gold tabard embroidered with roses on a red ground lined with green silk, and a white leather coat with fifty-four gold buttons; he "excelled all lords," one chronicler said, "in the equipment of his horses and worldly show."[40]

But it was also a question of the power they would be capable of deploying on the king's behalf once they held lands and offices to match the trust Richard placed in them. He had made Simon Burley master of the royal falcons, but it was people, rather than birds, that Richard wanted him to control. In December 1383, pressure from the lords had finally succeeded in forcing a transfer of custody of the Mortimer inheritance from the king to a group of trustees headed by the earls of Arundel and Warwick, noblemen who, like the earl of March, held great estates in the borderlands of Wales. After almost two years, this final frustration of Richard's attempt to harness the resources of the Mortimer earldom prompted him to look in another direction. On January 5, 1384, the day before his seventeenth birthday, the king used his signet to appoint Simon Burley constable of Dover Castle and warden of the Cinque Ports for life, with an accompanying fee of £300 a year. Now southeast England could not be defended without Burley's command. Richard was also determined that his old tutor should have the private power to match this public office. Over the next months, he set in motion a scheme through which Burley bent the law to breaking point in order to take possession of estates in Kent, directly between Dover and London, which Edward III had set aside in trust for religious bequests in his will.[41]

And while Burley and de la Pole were establishing their grip on power outside the royal household, Richard was also concerned to reward those of his friends who, in theory, already stood among the leading men of his realm. Robert de Vere's earldom of Oxford was an ancient noble title, but poorly endowed with lands and income. What estates the family did possess were almost all held for life by his widowed mother, who was still only in her thirties. The benefits to de Vere of his marriage in his early teens to the king's even younger cousin Philippa de Coucy had therefore included her future inheritance from her parents, Richard's aunt Isabella and Enguerrand de Coucy, the French nobleman who had been created earl of Bedford by Edward III. But with the renewal of war, Philippa's father had returned to France and renounced his English allegiance, which meant that after her mother's death in 1379 all the de Coucy estates in England passed into the possession of the crown. In the autumn of 1382, "in consideration of their not having land or other maintenance," Richard granted some of these properties to the young couple in terms which made clear that the legal claim to them was Philippa's.[42]

A year later, however—only days after the alarming end of Bishop Despenser's campaign in Flanders—Richard felt moved to adjust the terms of the grant. If his cousin and her husband had no children, the king said, and if Philippa died, then de Vere should simply keep the estates for himself. There seemed little question about where—and with whom—Richard's priorities lay.

Four

1384-1386

the blood is hot

The more experienced figures within the royal household were well aware of the sheer scale of the challenges facing the kingdom. Michael de la Pole was an intelligent man who had spent years in military service, fighting both on land and at sea. He understood the inexorable realities of the war, and in October 1383 his first address to parliament as chancellor offered an eloquent exposition of the compound threat with which England was now confronted: from the Scots in the north—"bearing in mind that they can enter our realm at any time on dry land, without impediment of sea or fresh water," he pointed out grimly—as well as from France, Castile, and now France's "recently gained land of Flanders."[1]

In response to these challenges, Richard's greatest subjects were still willing to put their shoulders to the wheel. When the French offered a ceasefire and fresh negotiations at a high-level peace conference, Gaunt left parliament early to lead the English delegation, taking with him both his sixteen-year-old son, Henry, and the king's brother John Holand, who was now in his early thirties and rising to prominence in the duke's service. By the time they returned in February 1384 with a potential treaty drafted and an eight-month truce sealed, the importance of the duke's diplomatic efforts had been emphatically underlined by the sudden death of Louis of Flanders, whose territories passed directly into the duke of Burgundy's hands. Gaunt had barely reached English soil before he was on the move again with his brothers Langley and Woodstock, leading troops north in an unsuccessful attempt to subdue Scottish attacks on English strongholds in the marches.[2]

But under these relentless pressures, the persistent fractures in Richard's government were turning into open wounds. In the glory days of the reign of his grandfather, King Edward and his nobles had been constantly together, in the council chamber, on the battlefield, at the tournaments and feasts that simultaneously displayed the magnificence of his kingship and celebrated their bond as brothers-in-arms. As their God-given leader, Edward in his leonine prime was first among equals, among lords who shared his ambitions and fought alongside him to achieve them. When all the representatives of his realm met from time to time in parliament, it was to ratify funding for wars they supported and to petition for redress of their grievances, redress that they knew (if the grievances were reasonable, and always at the king's pleasure) would be forthcoming. Those assemblies were one part of a complex political mechanism driven by constant communication—public and private, individual and collective, local and central—underpinned by a common understanding of the fundamental interests of the realm.

Under Richard, everything was different. The king was separated from his lords by age and experience, or lack of it; by instinct and inclination; by physical distance. Shut away in splendor as he was, he showed no sign of wanting the kind of interaction with his nobles that might facilitate consultation through informal discussion, let alone encourage his court to become a place of united purpose or chivalric camaraderie. If his lords had access to him only in formal settings, then only in formal settings did they have the opportunity to speak directly to him, to advise, persuade, or remonstrate. More and more often, because of the encircling wars and the desperate need for money they entailed, king and nobles met in parliaments. And parliaments were therefore the setting in which confrontations that should have happened behind closed doors—if at all—began to erupt.

Of the two men appointed to "advise and govern" the king back in 1381, one, Michael de la Pole, had become a household insider. The other, Richard Fitzalan, earl of Arundel, had not. Arundel had found it difficult to establish a place for himself anywhere within the increasingly fragmented regime. In some ways, his was a career that had been out of joint from the start. His father had been one of Edward III's right-hand men, strong-minded, influential, and spectacularly wealthy—and among the many marks of favor the old earl had received was unwavering royal support when he decided to repudiate his wife, a bride to whom he had been married in childhood. In 1345, nearly twenty-five years on from their wedding, the union was annulled and their three teenage children declared illegitimate. Richard, the eldest son and heir of the earl's new marriage, therefore grew up dogged by the shadow of scandal and the bitter claims of a disinherited older half brother. He was already thirty by the time his father died in 1376 and, with title, estates, and political agency at last in his hands, he was eager to go to war, not least to protect his rich lands along the southeast coast and his lucrative stake in the Flemish wool trade. But the campaigns of the late 1370s achieved little, and every year brought fresh struggles and new frustration. During the summer of 1383, Arundel had offered to go to Flanders as the king's lieutenant to take command of the faltering siege of Ypres, but Bishop Despenser had been allowed to wave the proposal away. And when parliament convened yet again in the spring of 1384—this time to consider the possibility that England might be forced to accept permanent losses of territory and sovereignty in the search for peace with France—the earl's discontent spilled over.[3]

In front of the king and the entire assembly, gathered this time in the great hall of the episcopal palace at Salisbury, Arundel took the floor. A lack of prudent rule, he declared, would bring any kingdom to the brink of destruction, and that was the condition in which England now stood. For a long time, he said, the realm had been so badly governed that it was "almost in a state of decay"—and if something were not urgently done, it would be swallowed completely by "the dark abyss into which it has fallen." Perhaps he intended his words as a rallying cry, an attempt to offer the kind of leadership in which he had so far been thwarted; but they were heard as barbed accusation. The young king's face was ashen and contorted with rage. First his nobles had kept him from ruling his kingdom, and now, it seemed, they held him responsible for its plight. "If you are blaming me, if you say it is my fault that the realm is badly governed, you lie in your teeth. Go to hell!" For a second, no one breathed. Then Gaunt rose to his feet and, speaking slowly into the deafening silence, began the work of placating his nephew's wrath.[4]

Privately, Gaunt had little sympathy or respect for Arundel. The two men had fallen out on campaign in Brittany six years earlier, when the duke blamed the earl for their joint failure to capture the port of Saint-Malo; and if Arundel was criticizing the conduct of policy during the seven years of Richard's reign so far, then it was Gaunt—whatever Richard himself might think—who was first in the firing line. But impatience with Arundel did not mean that Gaunt saw eye to eye with the furious king. Nor, by some way, was Richard's public outburst the most dramatic or violent incident of the parliament. One morning during the session, a friar named John Latimer celebrated mass privately for the king and his attendants in the chamber where Robert de Vere was staying. Afterward, Latimer approached Richard and handed him a document containing extraordinary and explosive allegations: that Gaunt was plotting to kill him and seize the kingdom for himself.[5]

The accusation found its mark because it was so intensely familiar. It was what the London mob had believed in 1377 when Gaunt had sought refuge with Richard's mother at Kennington. It was what the rebels had believed in 1381 when they confronted Richard at Mile End and Smithfield. Now Richard did not hesitate: Gaunt must die for his treachery. It took the king's attendants some minutes to persuade him that his uncle had the right to a hearing. It took Gaunt many minutes more, when he was ushered into his nephew's presence, to convince him that the charges were baseless. In Walsingham's account of his words, the duke sounded exhausted: "Ah my lord, why do you trust such informers? Why do you think such things of me? Am I not your uncle? Am I not your protector? Am I not the chief man in the realm after you? What could induce me to betray or kill you, when I would gain nothing from your death? Would your enemies make me more powerful in their land than I have become in your land, on my native soil? Or, if I were to aspire to rule the kingdom, is it to be believed that after—God forbid— your murder, the lords of this realm would placidly support me, as a traitor to my lord and country?"

At length, Richard allowed himself to be assured of his uncle's loyalty, and Gaunt asked that the friar should be kept in custody until charges could be brought against him for his dangerous lies. Responsibility for the prisoner was entrusted to Gaunt's protégé John Holand, the king's brother. With another of the duke's knights, Holand questioned Latimer under torture. They strung him up by his neck and his genitals, and weighed down his stomach with a stone so heavy that his back broke. He died in agony. The monastic chroniclers, keeping notes on these startling events, were disconcerted that such eminent men had dirtied their own hands with this punishing interrogation; but the friar had likely been mad, nothing more than that, and in public all was well again between the king and his uncle. Still, Gaunt's men had their suspicions about how Latimer and his insane ravings had come to be in Robert de Vere's room in the first place, and what that might mean about the attitude of the king's closest friends toward the duke's role in his government. And of this drama behind the scenes—even of the intemperate exchange between Richard and Arundel in the assembly itself—the clerks whose task it was to produce the official transcript of parliamentary proceedings tactfully recorded nothing.

Instead, they concentrated on the discussion of the peace proposals Gaunt had brought back from his conference with the French, a debate that resembled nothing so much as an ostentatiously deferential game of pass the parcel. As Chancellor de la Pole explained to the Commons, the king could of course conclude a treaty simply on his own sovereign authority, but his care for his people, who had contributed so much to the war for so long, meant that he wished to hear their advice on the matter before taking a final decision. No, no, the Commons replied: their humble request was that the king, with the advice of his council, should do whatever seemed best, and that his poor subjects should be discharged from giving any further answer. The question was put to them again, in words of one syllable: Did they want peace or war with France? Well, they said, an honorable peace was greatly to be desired, although they were unhappy—as they thought the king himself must be—at the suggestion that he might be required to do homage to the king of France for Calais and Aquitaine, rather than holding those lands in full sovereignty. But, came the implacable reply, peace could not be had on any other terms, so what would they do to achieve a settlement "if it were *they* who were king of the realm, or placed as the king now is?" This time, the Commons tried resorting to the human shield of their more powerful colleagues. They would say exactly what the lords had already said before them: that all things considered—and with a plea that they should not be asked again—they would probably, in the king's position, agree more readily to peace than war. Further than that, they would not go.[6]

The paralysis of the regime could hardly have been more clearly demonstrated. Richard had no interest in fighting, and in any case was entirely preoccupied with subverting the curbs he believed his nobles were placing on his authority, rather than countering threats from beyond the borders of his kingdom. But if the king himself would not take the decision to give up his claim to sovereignty over his French possessions—a concession that represented the one plausible route to a lasting peace—no one else could do it for him, or at least not without fear that he might later cry treachery. The one possible safeguard might be unanimous action by the lords and Commons together, but Gaunt—who had not stopped moving for months in the effort to contain the threats his nephew was ignoring—could not command the support he needed among the nobles to push through the settlement he had taken such pains to negotiate. And the Commons, their fingers burned by the debacle of Despenser's crusade, were not willing to take responsibility for any decision the costs of which, political and financial, might fall on their heads. Before they dispersed, they granted the smallest amount of tax possible—a half-fifteenth, to be collected only if a peace agreement were not found and if the clergy also made a contribution—and Gaunt and his brother Woodstock were dispatched once again to another round of negotiations with the French. But, given the failure of the last set of draft proposals, there was nowhere for the talks to go except in ever smaller circles. All that could be achieved this time was a seven-month truce. When parliament met again at Westminster in November 1384, Michael de la Pole's opening address invoked a now familiar litany of perils that were pressing ever closer: "the French with their great resources of manpower, the Castilians with their fleet of galleys, the Flemish with their many large ships, and the Scots who can enter the realm of England on foot at will."[7]

The profoundly disturbing possibility was that peace might no longer be an option, "surrounded as the kingdom was by deadly enemies all in league with one another," noted de la Pole, as a matter of fact rather than rhetoric. In his desperate search for some form of practicable consensus, the chancellor had no choice but to play the one card remaining in his hand, tattered and dog-eared though it already was. King Richard himself, he insisted, was now—despite all previous appearances—"wholly and most readily desirous of involving himself in labors and troubles for the defence of the realm." As a result, all his subjects were duty bound to contribute to the military campaign that their sovereign would soon be leading in person. The situation was frightening enough for the Commons to comply, granting a tax of two full fifteenths and tenths in place of the half to which they had agreed in the spring, although their skepticism was showing: they asked Chancellor de la Pole to repeat his declaration that the king himself would command his troops, and then stipulated that the second installment of the tax should be canceled if he failed to do so. But the urgency of the cumulative threat could not be mistaken. Before parliament was dissolved on December 14, news arrived that the Scots had taken the frontier fortress of Berwick-upon-Tweed. And this time Richard had been volunteered for the front not by the nobles he hated, but by de la Pole, his trusted chancellor. One question remained: Where, and against whom, should the king of England lift his sword at last?[8]

Across the Channel, the French were making plans. Their alliance with the resurgent Scots, along with the duke of Burgundy's new-minted possession of Flanders, gave them the means and the opportunity to prepare an invasion of England from north or south, or even both simultaneously. For decades, English soldiers had fought across scorched earth in the kingdom of France. It was time for French troops to do the same in England.

Reports reached London in February 1385 of a French fleet massing in the Flemish harbor at Sluys. A great council was summoned to Waltham Abbey, a little more than ten miles north of the capital, to decide how England could best be protected. By now, Gaunt's weariness had turned to anger. He had tried to make peace. His efforts had been rejected. And so, if not peace, then war. Attack, as Gaunt's royal father had always known, was the best form of defense. An English invasion of France would prevent a French invasion of England. The towns to be sacked and the fields to be burned would belong to King Charles, not King Richard. It would take huge sums of money, hundreds of ships, and thousands of men, but it was the best, the only workable strategy. Gaunt's brothers Langley and Woodstock stood with him. But the other lords and councillors could see only the financial and logistical impossibility of mounting a continental campaign after years of recrimination and failure. Instead, England would have to batten down the hatches and prepare to guard its coast against the coming assault. At this, Gaunt lost his temper, declaring that he and his men would offer their swords in the king's service only if Richard led them across the sea to France. With his brothers beside him, he turned on his heel and walked out.[9]

It was a high-handed ultimatum born of utter frustration, and a political rift that, if not quickly repaired, might prove a fatal breach in England's defenses. But the eighteen-year-old king and his friends had no patience for these interminable military debates, tedious discussions that paled into insignificance against the outrage of Gaunt's insolence. In full view of his peers, the duke had made clear that his obedience to his sovereign was conditional, that he would serve only insofar as Richard complied with the strategy he, Gaunt, supported. Such disloyalty, such treachery, could not stand. Nine months earlier, allegations emanating from within Robert de Vere's chamber had sought to convict the duke of plotting the king's murder, but the attempt to frame him had failed. His removal, it seemed, would require direct action.

Word reached the duke that, at jousts to be held in Westminster Hall on St. Valentine's Day, he would be assassinated on the orders of men within the royal household. He stayed away. Ten days later, he arrived at the riverside palace of Sheen, closely guarded by his own men-at-arms, to confront Richard in person. Wearing a breastplate under his costly robes, he upbraided his nephew for colluding in a plot against his life, a plot for which he blamed de Vere and young Thomas Mowbray, who had grown up in Richard's household and was now, after the death of his elder brother, earl of Nottingham. Even Gaunt could not point a finger directly at the king, but this public accusation of royal complicity—its unspoken implications clear—was shocking enough.[10]

Confronted with these charges, Richard was evasive and emollient. Of course—*of course*—he intended his uncle no harm, and would attend to any injustice. Wholly unconvinced, Gaunt withdrew from court to the safety of his own castle at Hertford. He would not stay, he told the king, in the company of those who wished to kill him. It took an intervention by Richard's mother, laboriously shuttling the twenty-five miles between Sheen and Hertford, to negotiate a formal reconciliation between king and duke at Westminster on March 6. At fifty-seven, Jeannette had been almost immobilized by ill-health and excess weight, but she was determined to travel as far as it took to make peace between the brother-in-law she had always trusted and her beloved son.[11]

The formality of the reconciliation, however, did not make it sincere. A week later, on March 13, 1385, Richard used his signet to grant Robert de Vere the castle of Queenborough on the Isle of Sheppey off the north Kent coast. Queenborough was a formidable new fortress built in the 1360s by Richard's grandfather King Edward, named in honor of his grandmother Queen Philippa, and designed to play a key part in guarding the Thames estuary and the river Medway. Richard had already given the castle at Dover into Simon Burley's hands; now he was entrusting de Vere with responsibility for another stronghold on the Kent coast at exactly the moment when the royal household, and de Vere in particular, seemed intent on attacking the king's uncle rather than defending the kingdom against its French enemies. Not only that, but the grant itself suggested that Richard was inclined to see himself and de Vere as a pair united against the world. Very unusually, de Vere was to hold the castle during both of their lives, rather than just his own; if he died first, it would revert to the crown, but if the king died first, de Vere and his heirs could keep it. Like the Kent estates Burley had acquired, Queenborough had been left in trust by Edward III, but Richard made clear that he would tolerate no interference with his gift, however dubious its legality. In the text of the grant itself, he called down an extraordinary triple curse in the name of God, the royal saint Edward the Confessor, and himself as king on anyone who dared attempt to contravene his order.[12]

There were further alarming outbursts of Richard's erratic temper. Shortly after his public rapprochement with Gaunt, the archbishop of Canterbury, William Courtenay, ventured to speak in a council meeting of the lords' concern about the men around the king who had embroiled him in such a reprehensible conspiracy against his noble uncle. Richard responded by hurling abuse and threatening to confiscate the rich possessions of the see of Canterbury as a punishment for questioning the authority of the crown. Later that day, out on the Thames, the royal barge happened to cross paths with another in which the archbishop was traveling. At the sight of Courtenay, the king drew his sword and had to be restrained from lunging wildly at him over the side of the boat. It seemed possible that government in England was on the point of disintegration.[13]

To no one's surprise, the French proved unwilling to pause their preparations for war while Richard tried to kill his uncle and assault his archbishop. In the name of King Charles, the French royal council led by the duke of Burgundy had narrowed down their strategy: lacking as they did a bridgehead on the English coast, they would land an army safely in Scotland and combine forces with their Scots allies to invade England by land from the north. An advance guard of French troops, arms, and artillery under the command of their admiral Jean de Vienne sailed from Flanders to Scotland in late May, with arrangements in motion for a larger army to follow in August. News of their arrival in Edinburgh came as a shock in London, where the council was urgently convened at the beginning of June. The current Anglo-Scots truce would expire on July 15, 1385. If, as soon as possible after that date, an English army could take the fight north of the border before the main French forces landed, a chance remained that the invasion could be forestalled.[14]

There was no other option. Faced with the existential threat of a French and Scottish horde pouring over the northern frontier, Chancellor de la Pole must deliver on his promise that Richard would lead his people into battle, and the lords of England must put aside their differences and follow him. After the years of inertia and indecision, of argument about faraway Flanders and farther-away Castile, there was relief in action, and in military strategy of the most straightforward kind. Every nobleman in England would summon his knights and retainers. Their king would raise his banner, and they would march north against their enemies.

In a triumph of necessity over experience, the greatest army the country had seen in forty years gathered at breakneck speed in support of the young king. And de la Pole was as good as his word: when the lords and their troops assembled under a hot sun at York in mid-July, just six weeks after the decision to fight had been taken, Richard was there. He had resisted campaigning on the Continent—had resisted campaigning at all—but if he had to ride with soldiers, better to do it in a form that was as much as possible like transporting his court to war. Richard enjoyed grandeur, and this was magnificent: every one of his most powerful subjects arrayed behind his royal standard. All told, counting men-at-arms and archers, servants, and auxiliaries, his army numbered more than 20,000 men, the population of a city moving north in battle order.[15]

The armorial colors of England's great men blazed from pennants and banners, surcoats and horse trappings. Gaunt, of course, commanded the largest retinue, which included his eighteen-year-old son, Henry, ready to fight in the field instead of the lists for the first time. Gaunt's brothers Langley and Woodstock were there, alongside the earls of Arundel, Warwick, Stafford, Salisbury, and Northumberland. The king's circle was represented in force: Robert de Vere, earl of Oxford; Thomas Mowbray, earl of Nottingham; the earl of Stafford's heir, Ralph; and their mentors within Richard's household, the experienced soldiers Michael de la Pole, Simon Burley, and Aubrey de Vere. There too was Salisbury's estranged brother John Montagu, the steward of Richard's household, beside the king's brothers Thomas and John Holand. By the time they crossed the border in the first week of August, Richard had decided to augment the brilliance of his host by scattering new honors on the most eminent of his servants. His uncle Edmund of Langley became duke of York, and Thomas of Woodstock duke of Gloucester. Michael de la Pole was given the vacant earldom of Suffolk, and Simon Burley became earl of Huntingdon. Robert de Vere was marked out with a new distinction, becoming marquis of Dublin, the first time promotion to that rank—which stood in order of precedence between an earl and a duke—had been bestowed by an English king.

At last, Richard had summoned his kingdom to war, and his people had responded to his call. In scale and spectacle, his first military expedition rivaled the most impressive of his grandfather's campaigns. But in unity and comradeship, it came nowhere near. Even aside from the febrile figure of the king himself, tension and mistrust radiated through his army: between Gaunt and his alleged would-be assassins, de Vere and Mowbray; between

Gaunt and the earl of Northumberland, over the events that had taken place four years earlier in the borderlands into which they were now marching; between the earl of Salisbury and the brother with whom he was locked in litigation; between the choleric earl of Arundel and almost everyone around him. But in Yorkshire, even before the expedition reached Scotland, the most disruptive member of these divided forces turned out to be the king's half brother John Holand.

Some kinds of disruption were more covert than others. One scandalous matter in which Holand was implicated could not be spoken of openly. It concerned the fact that, not far away from the army's Yorkshire camp, at Conisbrough Castle near Doncaster, Edmund of Langley's thirty-year-old wife, Isabel of Castile, was giving birth for the first time in ten years. During that decade, Isabel had endured a great deal in her husband's company. She and their young son Edward had accompanied Langley on his disastrous mission to Portugal; the plan had been for Edward to marry the little daughter of the Portuguese king, but the betrothal had not outlasted the failure of the campaign. There had been no more children since the birth of their daughter, Constance, in 1375, and it seemed obvious that the couple had little in common. But if Isabel found her unimpressive husband dull, the same could not be said of John Holand, whose character was as forceful as her own. And now the arrival of her new baby boy—named Richard after his godfather the king, but greeted with no celebration or fanfare by Langley himself—suggested that the closeness between John and Isabel had gone beyond the merely temperamental.[16]

Whispered gossip about the domestic tribulations of one of the king's royal uncles was hardly likely to be conducive to harmony and discipline, but Holand's hotheadedness proved to be a problem of another order altogether. On July 16, just outside York, a fracas broke out in which an esquire in his service was killed by an archer from the retinue of the king's friend Ralph Stafford. In his anger and upset, Holand went looking for the perpetrator. When he encountered Stafford instead, he lashed out and killed him. The enormity of what he had done did not take long to hit home. He fled into sanctuary at Beverley, thirty miles east, in the hope of saving his own skin, while waves of shock ricocheted through the army he left behind. Among those reeling in grief and horror were Ralph Stafford's father, the earl, and his maternal uncle the earl of Warwick. The young man had been a favorite of both the king and the queen, and Richard, distraught in his rage, gave the earl of Stafford his royal word that his half brother should not escape the penalty for murder.[17]

The blow was too much for the dowager princess. When her sons marched north Jeannette had been left at Wallingford Castle, forty-five miles west of London, under the protection of a handpicked bodyguard. Now, when news reached her that one of her sons was in hiding from the law that another had sworn to uphold, she sent messengers begging Richard to have pity on his brother for her sake. The king's response came that he could have no mercy. A few days later—"overwhelmed by grief," Thomas Walsingham reported—Jeannette died. She left a will, dictated the day before her death, in which she asked to be buried not in Canterbury Cathedral with the Black Prince, but at Stamford in Lincolnshire beside the tomb of John Holand's father, her previous husband Thomas.[18]

Richard's mother was dead, his friend murdered, his brother a murderer, and two of his earls bereaved. His army pressed on, only to discover that they could not locate their enemy. Wraithlike, the Scots and the French had melted away before them, leaving the English unable to force a battle but constantly at risk of raids from the soldiers they could not see. They arrived in Edinburgh on August 11 to find the town deserted by its inhabitants except for the garrison holding the castle that towered above them on its rock. As they had done all along their way, the English burned everything the Scots had abandoned. But as flames rose from homes and churches, Richard's glorious expedition was beginning to collapse. Feeding so many troops required logistical support they did not have, and the retreating Scots had made sure to leave nothing they could forage. Disease was taking hold in their ranks. Gaunt argued that they should nevertheless advance across the Firth of Forth, the great river estuary that separated Edinburgh from the lands to the north. The weather was good, he said, and God was with them; having come so far, they should either engage the enemy or destroy as much of the country as they could before reinforcements from France had the chance to set foot on Scottish soil.[19]

But Richard was not enjoying his first experience of war. He had had enough, and the tirade he launched at his uncle was vitriolic. The campaign had done nothing to alter his enduring conviction that the heart of the issue was not strategic advantage or effective defense, but himself: his own authority, his own wishes, his own well-being. Gaunt, he opined, was a poor general offering ruinously poor advice, whose instincts and priorities were consistently wrong. In Walsingham's version of his words, it was entirely clear what Richard believed his uncle's central preoccupation should be: "You are always concerned for your own purse and totally unconcerned for me. And now, typically, you want to force me to cross the Scottish sea so that I may die with my men from hunger and destitution, and become prey for my enemies." Gaunt, he declared, could go on if he wanted. "My men and I will go home." "But I too am your man," the duke countered. "There is no sign of that!" came the petulant response.[20]

If the king was refusing to take a step further, the decision was already made: the campaign was over, with not a single military objective accomplished. By August 20, the army had arrived back at Newcastle, where its contingents dispersed. Gaunt and Henry—whose own first experience of war had been eye-opening, if not quite in the way he had expected—rode to the duke's northern estates and stayed there. Richard returned to the comforts of his palace at Westminster. While the English made their way south, the French and Scots—freed now from the need to keep within tracking distance of the invaders—swept across the frontier into Cumberland and Westmorland, plundering and torching everything in their path, before laying siege to the walled town of Carlisle. The earl of Northumberland, left in lonely command of the border, frantically rallied soldiers to rush to its rescue.[21]

In the end, Richard's kingdom was saved not by English efforts but by the troubles of his enemy. Ever since their arrival, bad blood had festered between Jean de Vienne's knights and the Scottish troops of King Robert II. The French found their hosts uncouth and uncultured, the country poor and primitive, the food inedible, and the lack of wine almost insupportable. The Scots objected to their guests' presumption of their own superiority in all things, but especially their insistence that they knew best when it came to the question of how to fight in Scotland. The formalities of siege warfare, with all the attendant risks to besiegers as well as besieged of being pinned for weeks in one place, made little sense to the Scots, who knew the value of unpredictable, fast-moving raids across the open territory of the marches. Before the English had even begun their trek north, the French had attacked and destroyed the dilapidated Northumbrian castle of Wark, but only at the cost of heavy casualties, while the Scots—who thought the assault a stupid idea—stood and watched them struggle. Now they were forced to abandon the siege of Carlisle when the earl of Northumberland's troops marched into view.[22]

Meanwhile, it was gradually becoming clear that the second, much larger contingent of the French army, for which de Vienne's men had supposedly been the advance guard, was not coming to Scotland after all. They were still in Flanders, where, in July, the rebels of Ghent had managed to seize the river port of Damme and fortify it with a large garrison. Damme lay only six miles from Sluys, the harbor where the French forces were preparing to embark on their voyage, and four miles in the other direction from the great commercial center of Bruges. The immediate danger to the duke of Burgundy's grasp on the region was too great for the French to ignore. The troops mustered at Sluys were summarily diverted to a ferocious assault on Damme in the attempt to take it back. Success did not come until the very end of August, by which time it was too late in the year, in terms of weather, supplies, and cash flow, to set sail for their planned invasion of England's far north. Stranded in Scotland, de Vienne and his resentful, demoralized men were left to find their way home as best they could.

In England, disaster had been averted, but recriminations were only just beginning. Enormous sums had been spent, but no battle had been fought, and nothing achieved beyond the reprieve the men of Ghent had furnished. There was no choice but to call another parliament to consider the two impossible questions from which England could not seem to escape: how best to prosecute the ongoing war, and how to find the money to pay for it.[23]

When the assembly met at Westminster on October 23, 1385, the representatives of Richard's realm—both the lords, reassembling for the first time since Newcastle, and the Commons, waiting to hear how the crown might account this time for the spending of their taxes—were in an uncooperative mood. It did not help that Richard's priority, out of all the pressing matters facing his kingdom, was to secure parliamentary ratification of the promotions to noble titles he had so graciously bestowed on the way to Edinburgh. "For the lord king was lately engaged in discussing regality," recorded the clerks, ". . . and just as the sky is rendered bright and clear by the stars, so not only kingdoms but kingly diadems reflect the light of dignity, and as he who is laden with honours becomes more noble and potent, so it follows that he is made more virtuous . . ." It was a lofty description of the function of ennoblement, but Richard's subjects had more practical concerns. Given the alarming state of the realm, was the service of these particular men worthy of this extraordinary recognition? And such eminent titles required substantive backing with land and income. The crown was in debt and the Exchequer empty of cash, so where were these resources to come from?[24]

The royal blood of the king's uncles made their cases difficult to contest. Langley was confirmed as duke of York, and Woodstock as duke of Gloucester, each with an annual grant of £1,000 from the revenues of the Exchequer until estates to that value could be assigned to them. But Richard was far more concerned with the promotion of his household men, whose cases precipitated ugly controversy. Simon Burley's elevation to the earldom of Huntingdon could not be forced through at all. Michael de la Pole was eventually recognized as earl of Suffolk, but only with a cobbled-together estate, and eyebrows derisively raised about his mercantile origins. The thorniest case was that of Robert de Vere. Three years earlier, the first of the grants he had received from the king had acknowledged that de Vere and his wife had no "land or other maintenance to support their estate." Now Richard insisted not only that he should be raised above all the other earls with the unprecedented title of marquis of Dublin, but that the whole lordship of Ireland should be given into his hands. De Vere was only twenty-three, and his "magnificent deeds," which the king claimed to be rewarding, were not obvious to anyone else. English rule in Ireland was intrinsically important to the crown and perennially difficult to maintain, but de Vere showed no obvious sign of interest in the job except for the income he might draw from it. So far, his most notable public attributes seemed to consist of the king's intense attachment to his company, and the opportunity he thereby had to drip venom into the royal ear.[25]

It took until December 1, six weeks into the parliament, for agreement to be reached. At last, de Vere stood defiantly before the entire assembly while Richard buckled a sword at his hip and placed a gold coronet on his head in token of his new status. To the king's anger, the investiture had been delayed by ill-tempered debate over the fraught issue of royal spending and the need for financial retrenchment, traces of which found their way into the tight-lipped formal record. When the Commons asked that the personnel and finances of the royal household should be inspected and reviewed each year, Richard's response was bald: "The king will do as he chooses."[26]

In saying so, he was not without allies. As in previous moments of financial crisis, and despite all his differences with the king, Gaunt proved a doughty defender of the royal prerogative, if this time through tightly gritted teeth. Among the raft of petitions from the Commons was a request that recent crown grants should be revoked, in the attempt to ensure proper use of the king's own revenue before he demanded money from his impoverished people; but Gaunt's opposition was weighty enough to shoot the proposal down. Yet the calls for restraint to be imposed on a king who had so far acknowledged no need to check his expenditure kept coming. What emerged from the tense negotiations were significant concessions. No more grants of any kind would be made from crown revenues for an entire year. Meanwhile, a newly appointed committee of two bishops and two lords would launch a wholesale investigation into the state of the royal finances.[27]

With these safeguards in place, the Commons were prepared to turn their attention to the encircling military threats and the inescapable need for another grant of taxation. Chancellor de la Pole had run through the usual arguments—that attack was the best form of defense, that the king was willing to go to war in person—and it could hardly be denied that the south coast, the Channel, and the Scottish border required urgent attention and reinforcement. But after the failures of the Flanders crusade and the royal campaign in Scotland—after everything that had transpired over the past three years—the proposition that now won the backing of both lords and Commons was a new iteration of Gaunt's "way of Portugal."[28]

Much had changed since the remnants of Langley's ill-fated contingent had limped back to England in 1382. In the following year, King Fernando of Portugal had died, leaving his young daughter Beatriz—who was now, as a result of the Portuguese peace treaty with Castile, married to the Castilian king—to inherit his throne. But Juan of Castile, it turned out, intended to annex his child-bride's kingdom rather than upholding its autonomy as he had promised. When his troops invaded, Portuguese resistance was led by Fernando's illegitimate half brother, João, with such success that he was proclaimed king by his supporters and crowned in Lisbon Cathedral in April 1385. Four months later at Aljubarrota, João's forces inflicted an overwhelming defeat on the Castilian army. Shortly after that, he wrote to Gaunt to urge him to seize the moment: now, finally, a renewed Anglo-Portuguese alliance could depose their Castilian enemy and put Gaunt on the throne in Juan's place.[29]

It was another whiplash-inducing shift in military perspective, but it offered a genuine opportunity: the tantalizing possibility that Franco-Castilian domination of the Channel and the Atlantic seaboard, so recently reinforced by French control of the Flemish ports, could be overturned at last in favor of the naval power of England and Portugal. For Gaunt, it was a chance after fourteen long years to make real the paper crown his marriage had brought him, or at the very least to enforce substantial recognition for the hereditary rights of his wife and their daughter within the Castilian kingdom. It was a chance too, after enduring the constant accusations and blame, the frustration of his plans and outright threats to his safety, to be master of his own destiny on campaign.

When Gaunt rose in parliament to make his case—claiming not only that he could break Castile's alliance with France, but that his expedition would draw fire away from the Scottish border and from Aquitaine—his arguments fell on newly sympathetic ears. The "way of Flanders" had closed. The summer's royal campaign to Scotland had failed. None of the plans that had so far been preferred to Gaunt's proposals had worked. Now Castile was vulnerable, and Portugal poised to strike. The duke had proved his tenacity and his devotion to duty over and over again. Some of those assembled in parliament believed in his capabilities, while others—those less keen on the long shadow he cast at home—were simply looking to usher him out of English politics by any means possible. The result was a parliamentary grant of one and a half fifteenths and tenths, to be paid into the hands of specially appointed treasurers who would ensure the money was used only for the purposes of the war.[30]

Among those most enthused by Gaunt's imminent absence was the king himself. The prospect of his uncle's departure helped persuade Richard to concede to the financial reforms and constraints that had been negotiated during the difficult discussions with the Commons. The king's acquiescence in turn reassured Gaunt that the realm as a whole, and his own dynastic interests within it, would be protected after he left for Castile. But Gaunt was not abandoning his duchy into the hands of his officers; he was entrusting it into the hands of his son. At eighteen, Henry was attending parliament for the first time, summoned to join the lords as earl of Derby. He had had his first taste of diplomacy on his father's mission to France in the winter of 1383–84, and of war during the past summer in Scotland. His passage into adulthood had been marked in his personal life as well as in public. In 1384, his wife, Mary, had turned fourteen, a milestone that enabled the young couple to take possession of her estates and set up a household together at last. And in December 1385, when Gaunt started to recruit soldiers and requisition ships for his newly approved expedition to Castile, the duke also set about preparing Henry to take immediate custody of everything he would one day inherit.[31]

It was not the only family business Gaunt had to settle. John Holand was family too, and had been in the duke's service for several years before the horrifying events of the summer. From the autumn of 1385, when Holand was formally charged with the murder of Ralph Stafford and his property confiscated, Gaunt worked furiously behind the scenes to broker a settlement that might pacify the king while also somehow assuaging the furious grief of Stafford's father and uncle, thereby allowing Holand to resume at least an altered version of his life. In the process, the duke found another form of responsibility for the younger man added to his ledger: that of a father. Gaunt's twenty-one-year-old daughter, Elizabeth, had been married for five years to the earl of Pembroke, who had just passed his thirteenth birthday, but because the earl was still a child the couple did not yet live together. Elizabeth had inherited her mother's elegant charisma, along with a headstrong streak entirely unlike Blanche—and by the time it became widely known that she and Holand had caught each other's eye, she was already pregnant. Something would have to be done.[32]

The process of freeing her from her existing marriage was simpler than it might have been. Marriages were made by the consent of the two parties, followed by consummation of the relationship. But in the absence of consummation, consent could be relatively straightforward to revoke for a bride with access to Elizabeth's father's resources—and Gaunt was clearly inclined to accommodate his daughter's predicament rather than to condemn it. While the duke's secretaries busied themselves with undoing administrative knots, in early 1386 Holand took his first steps toward rehabilitation. On February 2, the feast of the Purification of the Virgin Mary, he attended court at Windsor Castle for a public ceremony of penance and absolution. Flanked on one side by William Courtenay, the archbishop of Canterbury, and on the other by Robert Braybrooke, the bishop of London, Holand entered the presence of the enthroned king. Three times, as he approached Richard, he knelt to beg with tears and outstretched arms that he might be forgiven his offense. When the assembled lords, led by the earls of Stafford and Warwick, added their voices to his petition for mercy, the king gave his assent. Holand was pardoned. In the weeks that followed, he began preparations to join Gaunt's expedition to Castile as the constable of his army. Richard, it seemed, had forgotten his grief for his dead friend enough to enjoy the drama and his own role in conferring his sovereign grace upon his errant brother. The earl of Stafford, whose words of forgiveness had clearly stuck in his throat, left court on pilgrimage, first to the Virgin's shrine at Walsingham in Norfolk, and then to the Holy Land. He died before he reached Jerusalem.[33]

Meanwhile, other gestures were being made toward other kinds of peace. On February 3, the day after Holand's atonement, Richard bestowed a gift of £1,000 a year on a newcomer to the English court, Leo of Lusignan, king of Armenia, a monarch who had lost his kingdom to the Mamluk sultan a decade earlier and was now roving around western Europe in the hope of drumming up support for a crusade to win it back. An end to the war between England and France, Leo reckoned, would be a boon to his cause, and he therefore offered himself to Charles VI as an intermediary between the courts of Paris and London. It was an unusual embassy: Leo knew no Latin or English and spoke only halting French, but when he arrived at the palace of Eltham at Christmas 1385, Richard was delighted by the advent of this king from the east bearing a message of peace. He welcomed the visitor with spectacular hospitality. Wearing his richest robes, he accompanied Leo to Westminster Abbey at dusk one evening to show him England's crown and royal regalia, the gold and jewels blazing in the candlelight. The young king seemed entranced by this experience of sovereign-to-sovereign diplomacy, and when the royal council agreed to a new round of talks to be held near Calais in March 1386, Richard declared his intention to meet his French counterpart in person if agreement could be reached.[34]

Others were less convinced by either the Armenian king's charm or his proposals. Thomas Walsingham spoke for many when he called him a grifter. On January 25, three days after the council meeting, Richard had a heated argument with the earl of Arundel, who had consistently rejected any available terms for peace as unacceptable, even shameful—a discussion that ended with the king losing his temper so extravagantly that he punched the earl to the ground. Equally startling, in terms of his relationship with the wider realm, was the fact that Richard's lavish gift to Leo broke the year-long parliamentary prohibition on royal grants only two months after it had been imposed. But parliament was no longer in session. Gaunt was wholly focused on Castile, and in any case the duke was opposed in principle to restrictions on the royal prerogative. If the king was intent on breaking his word, who else could restrain him? For a second time, after his charter placing Queenborough Castle in the hands of Robert de Vere eleven months earlier, Richard's only acknowledgment of questions about his right to make the grant was a curse on anyone who might stand in its way, in the name of God, the Confessor, and himself.[35]

It did not pay to dwell on these manifestations of the king's unpredictability, not when there were peace talks in motion. But within weeks the
flimsiness of the Armenian king's mission had been exposed. De la Pole
led a delegation to the spring negotiations, but, despite his best efforts, the
conference was scuppered by the English refusal to cancel Gaunt's imminent
military expedition against France's ally Castile. The duke, de la Pole knew,
would not give up a campaign that had become his life's ambition, and Richard was so eager to see the back of his uncle that he gave Gaunt an elaborate
farewell at court, presenting him with a golden crown and hailing him as
sovereign of Spain, as if he had always welcomed his uncle's claims to regality
and no threats had ever passed between them.[36]

By the end of March 1386, Gaunt's preparations were intensifying. The
duke and his entourage rode almost 200 miles to the southwestern port of
Plymouth, where his troops and ships were gathering. There, on June 24,
his daughter Elizabeth married John Holand. The unconventional order
in which the ceremony and the bride's pregnancy had come about went
tactfully unremarked by almost all the chroniclers, and the newlyweds were
getting ready to sail together on her father's voyage. With them would go
Gaunt's wife, Constanza, and their thirteen-year-old daughter, Catalina, as
well as the duke's eldest daughter, Philippa, still unmarried at the advanced
age of twenty-six, and a large and splendid household fit for a king-in-
waiting.[37]

Throughout these hectic weeks, the duke was shadowed by his eldest
son. Henry had been at Gaunt's side for most of the five years since his
narrow escape from death in the Tower at the hands of the rebels. At nineteen, everything in his life was about to change. He was soon to become a
father himself: fifteen-year-old Mary was pregnant with their first baby. At
the same time, he was losing the company of the father who had been his
protector, his mentor, and his guide. With the fleet would go his sisters, the
companions of his childhood. If all went well, Henry might never see any
of them again. Gaunt would be king of Castile, and Philippa and Catalina
would find powerful husbands there or in Portugal. If all went badly, they
might not meet again for less happy reasons. Henry's family was risking their
lives for a crown, but it was a crown he would never wear. His one certainty

was that the defense of Lancastrian interests in England, and his father's part in defending England itself, now fell to him.[38]

On June 30, twelve immense Portuguese transport ships, escorted by six galleys of war, appeared in Plymouth Sound to join the vast English fleet already assembled in the harbor. Only the wait for a favorable wind remained. On July 8, Henry and Gaunt were dining together on board the duke's flagship when the water shifted beneath the hull and a cry went up. The time had come. They said their goodbyes, and Henry headed back to shore. As the light began to fade, the mass of sails made for the haze of the horizon until, at last, they disappeared from view.[39]

Five

1386-1387

am I not king?

In the autumn light, masts jostled and danced along the skyline. "Never, since God created the world, were there seen so many great ships together," reported an awestruck Jean Froissart, and—here at Sluys, at least—it was true: a thousand vessels already, and more on the way. The greatest fleet was required for the greatest army, thousands upon thousands of men-at-arms and archers, for now camped with their horses and equipment in the flat fields that stretched around the Flemish city of Lille. The French king's loyal subjects had answered his call to arms in such overwhelming numbers that their embarkation had had to be postponed for a month while commissioners were dispatched across Europe in search of yet more ships to carry them.[1]

Their goal was nothing less than the end of the war. After almost fifty years of fighting, after the terrible reverses at Crécy and Poitiers, the loss of Calais, the concessions at Brétigny, after humiliation and defeat, at last the kingdom of France would have its revenge. The previous year's plan to invade England from the north via Scotland had been thwarted by the need to rescue Damme from the Flemish rebels, and since then another peace conference had failed. The time had come. Accompanied by his noble uncles, the dukes of Burgundy, Berry, and Bourbon, King Charles would lead his host across the North Sea directly onto the beaches of eastern England. At the age of just seventeen, he would succeed where his father and grandfather had failed: he would wreak havoc and destruction on English soil, and impose a final peace at sword point upon his upstart enemy.[2]

At first, it had seemed impossible that the English king's uncle of Lancaster, whose muster at Plymouth in the spring and early summer had fueled fear and anxiety in Paris, would simply sail away to Castile, leaving England at the mercy of whatever was to come. But in July the impossible had happened; and since then, preparations for the impending assault had gathered speed and intensity. Carpenters in Normandy constructed sections of a huge wooden fort to be carried across the sea for assembly on the Suffolk shore, its twenty-foot walls and thirty-foot towers designed to shield the troops over the dangerous days it would take to complete the landings. Barges laden with food and matériel converged on Sluys, and more taxes were levied in France to sustain the necessary flow of funds. Now, at the end of September, all activity was concentrated on the new date set for the launch of this French armada, four weeks away.

During the spring and early summer, the English had been equally uncertain about the exact shape of the danger they might be facing. Not yet knowing that the French planned to sail from Sluys across the North Sea to East Anglia, the royal council moved to counter what they guessed—piecing together fragments of information from scouts at sea and spies in France and Flanders—would prove to be an immediate cross-Channel attack on England's south coast. Efforts were made to reinforce defenses in the ports of Kent, and orders issued that the priceless shrine of Saint Thomas Becket should be taken for safekeeping from Canterbury Cathedral to Dover Castle (even if, in the event, the horrified monks refused to hand over their sacred treasure).[3]

Meanwhile, the king's eyes were fixed firmly in the opposite direction. It was a year since he had given Robert de Vere the castle of Queenborough on the Kent coast, where Richard's subjects were now bracing themselves for the sight of a French fleet on the horizon. The obvious conclusion should have been that de Vere would take charge of defensive measures at Queenborough, just as Simon Burley was doing at Dover. Instead, he and the king were spending their time at Windsor and Sheen, absorbed in pursuing the possibilities of de Vere's creation as marquis of Dublin, and the grant of the lordship of Ireland that had accompanied it. The parliament in which de Vere had received those marks of royal favor in December 1385 had also declared that no further grants should be made from crown revenues for the next year, but it was abundantly clear that Richard was not willing to stick to either the letter or the spirit of the agreement. His eye-catchingly wasteful gift of £1,000 a year to Leo of Armenia in February 1386 was followed on March 23 by a grant to de Vere of the ransom of Jean de Blois, a claimant to the duchy of Brittany who had been in English custody for decades. The sum involved was huge, an anticipated £45,000, and was supposedly intended to pay for a military expedition to shore up English rule in Ireland. But de Vere was not even proposing to lead the campaign in person; and in late June—at the same time as people on the Kent coast were being told to leave their homes with all the food they could carry to seek refuge in the walled ports of Dover, Rye, and Sandwich—Richard was riding west toward Bristol, fondly keeping de Vere company while he prepared to dispatch his newly recruited troops across the Irish Sea.[4]

By the first week in August, the sheer scale of what the French were preparing to unleash in the east had become horrifyingly apparent. The expected assault on the south coast had not materialized; instead, the latest reconnaissance from Sluys indicated that England now faced a full-blown invasion. The threat was stark. So too was the difficulty of meeting it. Gaunt's fleet was gone, along with the tax that had been granted to send him on his way. The government was juggling expensive short-term loans from Italian bankers in London, but the money was nowhere near enough to underwrite either wholesale defense or preemptive attack. The king was persuaded to return from the west country to preside over a meeting of his lords at Oxford, but all they could agree was that nothing could be done without more taxation, which would require the assent of parliament. The representatives of the realm were summoned to meet at the beginning of October. In the meantime, the country would have to patch together what resistance it could.[5]

During September, the council at Westminster sent orders streaming into the shires. Local officials were to muster all able-bodied Englishmen between the ages of sixteen and sixty, and to find ways to fortify harbors and river crossings along the eastern coast. Royal sergeants were riding from port to port to requisition English merchant ships and charter foreign vessels, and this hurled-together fleet was gathering in the Thames. The musters from counties that lay inland and to the west were summoned to protect London. The capital had known its share of violence in recent decades, in its own tumultuous politics and during the frightening summer of 1381, but panic was growing at the gravest risk in living memory that the city might face an enemy siege—a grim prospect that was given official credibility on September 13, when the mayor ordered householders within London's walls to stockpile enough food to last for three months. Over the next fortnight, the lords and newly elected knights and burgesses of the Commons converged on Westminster. There they would stand ready to defend the capital while attending parliament, which the council hoped would provide the funds to pay for these urgent attempts to save the kingdom.[6]

On October 1, when Chancellor de la Pole rose to put his case at the opening session, he found himself confronted with the greatest challenge of what had been a remorselessly difficult three years in office. Time and again, he had been forced to ask the representatives of the realm for money to tackle imminent threats to England's security; time and again, the money had been spent and the threats had intensified. The only rhetoric left to him was by now laughably threadbare, but he tried it all the same. King Richard, he said, showing great courage and *entirely* of his own accord, had decided to lead a mission across the sea to strike at England's foes. If they had heard it alleged that the king did not want to campaign in person, they should know that their sovereign was utterly determined to prove such slander false, and that, in actual fact, he was more involved in the direction of his own government than he had ever been before.[7]

Clearly, the chancellor was protesting too much—and if his claims were excessive, so too were his demands. Over the last three years he had repeatedly struggled to secure a levy of even one fifteenth and tenth whenever he sought parliamentary taxation on his royal master's behalf. Now he was requesting four times that amount: a breathtaking £155,000, more than any previous parliament in England's history had ever been asked to supply in a single grant. It was a devastating double blow: the king's subjects were facing invasion on an unprecedented scale and financial exactions of unprecedented size, while bitter experience gave them no reason to hope that handing over the money would do anything to guarantee the kingdom's safety.[8]

The result was uproar. The men who sat listening to de la Pole were frightened, and they were angry. For the first time in decades, John of Gaunt was not there to take either the lead or the blame, and criticism could not, of course, be directed at the crown. In any case, as the chancellor's speech had only served to emphasize, it remained far from obvious to outside observers how actively Richard himself was involved in shaping the policies of the regime. Instead, their anger was concentrated on the man who stood before them. De la Pole had presided over the disasters of the last three years. If England were somehow to be saved, de la Pole would have to go.

Together, lords and Commons addressed a petition to the king demanding the dismissal of both the chancellor and the treasurer. Their plan was clear: following the precedent of the "Good Parliament" in 1376, the king's ministers should be removed from their posts, and de la Pole impeached. "They had matters to resolve with Michael de la Pole which they could not pursue while he held the office of chancellor," reported one chronicler ominously. Ten years earlier, Edward III had been too old to take personal charge of restoring the competence of his government. Now his grandson was nineteen, by any normal measure old enough to lead his kingdom—but Richard was not a normal king. For his subjects, there was comfort, and political safety, in the familiar idea that he was still too young to take responsibility for the catastrophic emergency England was facing. It was de la Pole's fault; and removing de la Pole, they had to believe, would be the first step toward rescue.[9]

Richard did not agree. Ever since he could remember, he had been told he was too young for the crown he wore. It had been a ruse, an excuse for his nobles to stand in his place, to wield power that should have been his alone. For years, his uncle Gaunt had been the loudest voice in his parliaments and councils while interminable arguments raged about the endless war. But Gaunt was gone at last. This time, the king would formulate his own reply, without gloss or filter. And in Richard's world, the imminent invasion and the empty treasury were a sideshow. What mattered was that his subjects had dared to demand the removal and impeachment of his chancellor, a man who stood at the heart of his royal household and who represented his own personal authority. For Richard, this was not an argument over policy or strategy, but a full-blown assault on his divinely ordained kingship.

He could barely control his rage. From his chambers at Westminster, his words, dripping with contempt, were carried back to parliament exactly as he had uttered them. His lords and Commons should not speak about matters that lay beyond their remit. They must proceed at once with the business for which they had been summoned—and they should do so in the knowledge that, at their request, he would not dismiss even a scullion from his kitchen. Then Richard turned his back on Westminster and the assembly that sat there, riding with his household to his palace at Eltham, eight miles away on the other side of the Thames.[10]

The lords and Commons received his message in incredulous silence. Finally, the fractured mechanism of government had juddered to a halt. For years, parliamentary meetings had been the only setting in which the lords of England could reliably address their king and, in discussion with the Commons about grants of taxation, affect the direction of policy. Now Richard had angrily rejected even this limited channel of public communication. With it, he had jettisoned their attempt to tackle the looming danger in which England currently stood. And with every passing hour the threat of French sails on the horizon grew closer. Surely his decision could not hold? Lords and Commons together sent a message to Eltham: they could not and would not proceed with any part of parliament's business until the king returned to join them.[11]

But Richard was not about to take instruction from his own subjects. The messenger returned to Westminster: the king would not come to parliament. Parliament must come to him, in the shape of forty knights, the most experienced political heavyweights the Commons could find to represent their views. It was an unnerving command. Richard was discarding all norms, all precedents. It seemed he no longer wished to give audience of any kind to his lords; instead, he wanted to receive the leaders of the Commons. The question was why. Rumors began to spread, and with them, fear.

The king's friends were already suspected of having planned to assassinate Richard's uncle, the most powerful magnate in the country. If Gaunt could be a target, why not the Commons, if they were members of a parliament that would not bend to the king's will? The stories were credible enough to stop the delegates in their tracks. If they risked going to their deaths, they would not go at all.

Days passed in tense stalemate. Thanks to the previous month's frantic activity, almost 150 vessels lay at anchor in the Thames and almost 10,000 men in camps in the countryside north of London, all of them waiting not only for orders but for pay. In the circumstances, it was no surprise that discipline in the ranks was collapsing before the enemy was even in sight. Many deserted; others turned to robbery on the roads or looting nearby villages. But south of the river at Eltham, the king's attention still lay elsewhere. On October 13, the feast of the saint-king Edward the Confessor, Richard promoted Robert de Vere from marquis of Dublin to duke of Ireland, a newly created title and the first dukedom ever bestowed by an English king on a man with no royal blood in his veins. At twenty-four, de Vere now outranked every nobleman in England except for Richard's three uncles.[12]

The eldest of those uncles was not there to object, but the youngest had had enough. Thomas of Woodstock, duke of Gloucester, was thirty-one. In the course of his thwarted career so far, he had been too young to fight in the glory days of the war, too far down the pecking order to receive the same material rewards as his brothers, and—marooned between royal generations as he was—too old to join the young noblemen in the household of his nephew the king. England was facing greater danger than at any point in Woodstock's lifetime, and to the injuries caused by Richard's failures of leadership the king had added the insult of de Vere's worthless elevation. If Richard wanted a deputation from parliament, then Woodstock would provide one.

With him came the earl of Arundel's brother. As an aristocratic younger son, Thomas of Arundel had been destined for the Church from birth; at thirty-three, he had already held office as bishop of Ely for more than a decade. Intelligent, educated, and pragmatic, he was by temperament far less abrasive than his older brother. His was a more measured voice than Woodstock's, but neither man, by this stage, was in a mood to indulge the royal tantrum. They arrived at Eltham with authority from the lords and Commons to deliver an ultimatum. If the king would not come back to Westminster, then the representatives of the realm would go home. In that case, clearly, no taxes would be granted. But Richard, for his part, was in no mood to negotiate over the limits of his sovereign autonomy. His people, he retorted in fury, clearly meant to rise up in rebellion against him. In that case, he would have no choice but to turn for support to his cousin the king of France, "and rather submit ourselves to him than succumb to our own subjects."[13]

Whatever the duke and the bishop had expected to hear, it was not this. This was dumbfounding. Charles of France had already moved north from the encampment at Lille at the head of his vast army. Intelligence reaching London suggested that the embarkation of the fleet at Sluys was set for the end of October, less than two weeks away. The armada was coming. And, at this of all possible moments, England's king was choosing to suggest that— of all possible things—he might look to France for help against the people of his own kingdom. It was more than dumbfounding; it was bordering on delusional.[14]

Perhaps there were ways of attempting to understand his thinking. The political circumstances of the French king were the twin of his own. Richard was nineteen, Charles seventeen. Richard had inherited his throne at ten, Charles at eleven. Charles, like Richard, was not yet in command of a government that had been dominated for years by his royal uncles. If kingship were understood as a purely personal state, as the enactment of the rights of a unique individual, there might be reason to imagine that the French sovereign might sympathize with the frustrations of his English counterpart.

But, if those were Richard's thoughts, Richard had a lot to learn. Sovereignty did not concern the rights of the king alone. To the listening ears of Thomas of Woodstock and Bishop Arundel, his response was an appalling indication of his failure to understand his responsibilities as head of the body politic. The king should act to protect his realm. Instead, he was not only repudiating wise advice, but actively threatening all of his subjects who sought to offer it. The duke and bishop had no time for this adolescent narcissism. Instead, they pointed out the stupidity of his attempt at intimidation. The king of France was his enemy, they said tersely, and more likely to take his throne than offer him help. His father and grandfather had labored all their lives to prosecute this war, and his people had paid a heavy price in both casualties and cash. It was his duty to honor those sacrifices. Not only that, but they had a warning of their own. Sixty years earlier, Richard's great-grandfather Edward II had been deposed when his determination to rule by his own will rather than by law and precedent began to threaten the security of his subjects. That previous example, they said—naming no names, but their meaning acidly clear—was one Richard should take care to remember.[15]

It was the nearest he had ever come to a slap in the face. Overbearing though his uncle Gaunt could be, Richard knew he would never have allowed such an outrage to stand. But Gaunt was not there to intervene. And it was true: in 1326 Edward II had been overthrown by his wife, then forced to abdicate in favor of their son. A few months later, he had died behind the walls of his prison, a murky end that Richard was beginning to see as a royal martyrdom worthy of sainthood. It was not, however, an end he wished to emulate. Thankfully, his devoted wife was dutiful and loyal, and they did not yet have a child in whose name his possession of the crown could be challenged. But if his uncle Woodstock were to stir up this parliament against him, with London surrounded by soldiers, and without Gaunt's presence as a shield, he might find himself backed into a deeply unpleasant corner. Better to make a tactical retreat than to lose the war. Sullenly, the king told his unwelcome visitors that he would come back to Westminster within the next three days.[16]

Richard was not the only one intensely aware of Gaunt's absence. When parliament reconvened, the stony-faced king sat surrounded by his nobles: not only Woodstock and Bishop Arundel, who had seen him at Eltham, but all the other lords, temporal and spiritual, who had waited three weeks for his return. Among them was the bishop's belligerent brother, the earl of Arundel; beside him, Thomas Beauchamp, earl of Warwick, still mourning the death of his nephew Ralph Stafford, and Thomas Holand, earl of Kent, brother of the man who had killed him. Edmund of Langley, who as duke of York was technically the senior lay peer there, shrank as he always did from making his presence felt. Also silent, for different reasons, was Gaunt's nineteen-year-old son, Henry, earl of Derby. Henry had arrived at Westminster just in time for the beginning of the parliament on October 1. Before that, he had been at the Lancastrian castle of Monmouth in the Welsh borders where, on September 16, his young wife, Mary, had given birth to their first child. Over the course of little more than two months, he had said goodbye to his father and welcomed his own son, another Henry, into the world. When he reached the capital to witness the political implosion for which he had been forced to leave his week-old baby, his responsibilities to family and country weighed heavy on his shoulders.[17]

With the king's resistance broken, parliament moved fast. On October 23 and 24, Chancellor de la Pole was formally removed from office and replaced by Bishop Arundel. Articles of impeachment against de la Pole had already been prepared, and the Commons now presented them to the king and lords. The charges fell into two categories. The first related to his public duties as chancellor: he had not implemented the financial reforms agreed upon at the previous parliament, nor used the taxes granted there as intended for the defense of the seas. The second listed the ways in which he had enriched himself privately while in office through favor from the crown. De la Pole defended himself with some heat and considerable justification: How could any fault be his alone? He had striven to serve both king and realm, and had done nothing—including accepting rewards—without the knowledge of the king and other councillors. Reluctantly, the lords had to concede that he was not solely responsible for the failure to enforce the last parliament's edicts; but the crisis required a scapegoat. And so, on the charges of peculation, de la Pole was found guilty, fined, and imprisoned at Corfe Castle in Dorset.[18]

The arguments had taken days. By the beginning of November, word came that the king of France had reached Bruges, while his troops waited on the plain between Damme and Sluys for orders to board ship. At Westminster, with de la Pole finally gone, attention turned to the reorganization of government: Should a tax be granted for the purposes of defense, and if so on what terms? This time, the arguments took weeks. At least the weather was bad—winds and heavy rain that would surely, it had to be hoped, delay French plans—and by November 8 a letter had arrived from Leo of Armenia, once more proposing mediation between England and France. But this was political debate conducted on the brink. Parliament's conclusion, to which the king was forced to consent on November 19, was that a derisorily small subsidy—just half a fifteenth and tenth, with another half to follow if required—should be accompanied by a wholesale takeover of the regime.[19]

Extravagance, corruption, and mismanagement lay at the heart of England's problems; on that, lords and Commons were agreed. A fourteen-strong council was therefore appointed to oversee every aspect of the royal administration: the royal household, the royal courts, royal officials, royal income, royal grants, royal gifts, royal taxes, royal spending, the royal jewels. The councillors included the archbishops of Canterbury and York; the royal dukes Edmund of Langley and Thomas of Woodstock; the new chancellor, Bishop Arundel, along with the new treasurer and keeper of the privy seal; Lord Scrope, who, four years earlier, had refused to comply with Richard's plans to take control of the Mortimer inheritance; and—relishing his chance to get his hands at last on the levers of power—the earl of Arundel. They were to hold office for a year. All this was done, according to the official parliamentary transcript, by the king's "royal authority, certain knowledge, good grace, and free will."[20]

That was not how Richard saw it. At the closing of the assembly on November 28, the king "made open protest by his own mouth," the same transcript recorded, "that he willed that nothing done in the parliament should harm him or his crown, and that his prerogative and the liberties of his crown should be saved and kept." But his will had been rendered impotent, his prerogative useless. At the age of nineteen, only weeks from his twentieth birthday, he found himself more explicitly excluded from control of his own government than he had been when he inherited the throne at ten. And this time, wary of the debacle of the previous year's toothless financial reforms, parliament was determined there should be no room to flout or undermine the councillors' work. The statute giving legal force to their authority decreed that anyone who resisted the exercise of their powers—or anyone advising, encouraging, or inciting the king to countermand their orders—should forfeit his movable property, his freedom, and, for a second offense, his life.[21]

Panic, barely suppressed, had suffused every moment of the discussions in parliament. But when the newly appointed councillors set about their task, they did so in an atmosphere of deliriously sudden liberation. A few days before the end of the session, extraordinary news reached Westminster: the French were not coming after all. The launch of the armada had been scuppered by its own size. The time that had passed in assembling so many hundreds of vessels and thousands of men had taken with it all hope of clear skies and calm water. Headwinds pinned the fleet in the harbor; torrential rain spoiled supplies and dented morale. There had been jubilation in the camp at the end of October when, at last, November 9 was announced as the prospective date for departure. It took a full week to bring the soldiers and horses aboard, until on November 8, King Charles reviewed his waterborne forces from his flagship, his painted badge of a winged white hart with a golden crown around its neck shining brightly even under the gray skies. But setting sail remained impossible while the wind failed to turn, and the troops could not wait forever in their cramped and increasingly unsanitary quarters. The weather was getting worse and the days shorter. Food and money were running out. By November 16, it was clear there was no option but to defer the invasion and try again in the spring.[22]

In London a week later, it was as if the sun had burst through lowering clouds. To the new council, the miracle of England's deliverance could only mean that God was smiling on their work. The earl of Arundel seized his moment with energy and zeal. Appointed admiral of England on December 10, he immediately began to requisition ships and recruit men for a naval counter-expedition in the new year. Others among the lords, those who had not been named to the council, left Westminster with relief. Henry rejoined his wife and baby son; within weeks of his return, Mary was pregnant for a second time. The king himself—accompanied by his self-effacing queen, acutely aware that after almost five years of marriage she had not yet given her husband an heir—also rode west from the capital to Windsor Castle. There they were joined for the Christmas festivities by Michael de la Pole. Richard had ordered his release almost as soon as his imprisonment had begun, and now the former chancellor was ostentatiously welcomed back to the king's side.[23]

It was a gesture of intent. For three years, de la Pole had been the means through which Richard had found a way to assert himself in government. He knew that if he sent instructions sealed with the signet he wore on his finger directly to his chancellor, his orders would be carried out as he wished. Since de la Pole's appointment in the summer of 1383, the number of such signet letters, expressions of Richard's personal wishes and desires, had grown so rapidly that by the summer of 1386 more royal grants under the great seal of England were authorized by the king's signet than by any other means. But now, with the great seal resting in the uncooperative hands of Bishop Arundel and decision-making committed to the council, that avenue had abruptly closed. From now on, Richard's method of evading his opponents' control would need to go beyond the administrative. And in his fury at the outrageous humiliations his subjects were heaping upon him, he was not prepared to lend the cover of his royal presence to the council's attempt to govern without him. In February 1387, once the Christmas season was over, the king and his household rode north and kept moving, as the weeks and months went by, through Leicestershire, Nottinghamshire, Yorkshire, Lincolnshire, Warwickshire, Staffordshire, and Cheshire. Richard was determined to give the regime in Westminster no chance to overhaul his personal entourage, the tiny atoll within a hostile sea where his prerogative still ruled. By now, he was certain, more than ever before, that anyone who was not with him was by definition his enemy.[24]

That was a lesson learned the hard way by his childhood companion Thomas Mowbray, earl of Nottingham. In July 1384, only a couple of months after the king's explosive confrontation with the earl of Arundel at the Salisbury parliament, Mowbray had married Arundel's daughter. Although Richard attended the wedding celebrations, the match had been arranged without his formal permission, and from then on his affection for Mowbray noticeably cooled. At the beginning of 1387, after watching the autumn's crisis unravel in parliament, the young earl did not accompany the king on his flight to the midlands and the north. Instead, he joined his father-in-law's newly planned naval expedition. In March, Arundel's little fleet, with Mowbray and his men on board, ambushed a returning convoy of French and Flemish ships that had sailed from Sluys to La Rochelle to collect cargo. The result was a triumph: a dozen ships sunk or burned and dozens more captured, along with 8,000 barrels of wine, which, sold off at rock-bottom prices back in England, did much to lubricate an upsurge of goodwill toward Arundel and the council. Not, however, from the king. When Mowbray next saw Richard he was met with a clenched jaw and a blank stare. The friendship was over.[25]

The opposite was true of Robert de Vere, to whom Richard's devotion only grew. In the king's eyes, the new duke of Ireland could do no wrong. If de Vere said black was white, Jean Froissart reported, Richard would not contradict him. In the summer of 1387, the extent of this indulgence enabled the duke to rearrange his personal life in a way that shocked even a political community that viewed his presence at the king's side with deep suspicion. After ten years of childless marriage to Richard's cousin Philippa de Coucy, de Vere had tired of his young wife. With the king's approval, he sent to the papal court to request an annulment. Then, in anticipation of the success of his suit, he took a new bride named Agnes Lancecrona, one of the ladies-in-waiting who had come to England with Queen Anne from her home in Bohemia.[26]

It was an insult to the royal family to which the king seemed utterly indifferent. But Philippa was not without support. Thomas of Woodstock, for one, was apoplectic at this disparaging treatment of his niece. Others were more scandalized by speculation that de Vere's marital dramas might be a smoke screen for the true nature of his relationship with the infatuated king. Froissart described Richard as dazzled to the point of blindness by a man who was "his whole heart," while Thomas Walsingham, deftly combining lofty disapproval with salacious gossip, noted rumors of an "obscene intimacy" between the king and the duke. On balance it seemed more likely that de Vere, who had outraged his own mother with his callous treatment of his wife, was an egotistical opportunist exploiting the king's affection to get what he wanted.[27]

Certainly, though, Richard's tastes and the culture of his court raised misgivings in the minds of contemporaries who associated the virtues of manhood with the military pursuits at which his father and grandfather had excelled. Most of the men around the king "were knights of Venus rather than of Mars," wrote Walsingham contemptuously, "showing more prowess in the bedroom than on the battlefield." And while his father and grandfather had also loved magnificence, Richard's style was more remote and altogether more effete than theirs had ever been. At his own insistence the king's sacred person—always sumptuously dressed and sparkling with jewels—could be approached only with elaborate shows of deference, with a delicacy in relation to his body that was a world away from the uncompromising physicality of war. The costly buildings taking shape under his direction at the palaces of Eltham and Sheen were designed with a striking emphasis on hygiene as well as splendor, their accommodation equipped with elegant bathhouses and their bedchambers with individual latrines. So fastidious were the king's habits that he had taken to carrying in his hand a specially hemmed piece of the finest linen in case he needed to dab or blow his nose, an accessory so new that there was not yet a word to describe it. His preoccupation with distance and purity seemed all-consuming; so much so that it was not clear how often he might ever allow touch of an intimate kind, whether from his queen—who was seeking the intercession of the Virgin and her mother, Saint Anne, in her continuing struggle to conceive—or from anyone else.[28]

Refined to the point of fragility though his persona might appear, Richard had lost none of his preoccupation with power. That summer, as his household kept moving from town to town and manor to manor through the midlands and the northwest, the question with which he was grappling was how to strike back against the coup that had ousted him from his rightful place in government. The offices and castles in Kent that he had granted to de Vere and Simon Burley were no use now, not when they lay out of reach on the other side of London, where the council ruled. The king would have to look elsewhere for support.

He knew that the practical power of the lords, their military muscle, was rooted in the regions where they held their estates. The nobles retained local landholders—knights and gentlemen—in their service by paying them an annuity, and this formalized retinue became the heart of an "affinity": a wider network of connections who all, in more or less direct ways, looked to their lord for protection, influence, and leadership. In return, their lord could call on them for service of all kinds in peace and, when necessary, war. But the king had no need of an affinity, because the whole kingdom was his. His law governed and protected every one of his subjects, and his lordship represented the interests of the "common weal," the realm as a whole. And so, in peace and in war, he could harness the power of these noble affinities by calling on their lords, his closest advisers and the greatest supporters of his crown. That, at least, was the theory.[29]

It was not Richard's experience of his own rule. His experience was that his lords were the greatest adversaries of his crown, who had exploited the power their affinities gave them to strip him of the authority that should have been his. And since they had leveraged their regional influence against him, why should he not make use of a territorial power base of his own? The estates of de Vere's earldom of Oxford lay in Essex, Suffolk, and Cambridgeshire; even if most of them were still held by his mother, it was a place to start. In August, Richard sent a royal sergeant at arms into those counties to retain men into the exclusive service of the crown, giving them badges in the shape of silver and gilt crowns to wear as a display of their allegiance, just as the nobles' retainers did, and making them swear that, "forsaking all other lords, they would stand by him as their true king." It was a striking echo of the oaths of loyalty sworn by the rebels of Essex and Kent six years earlier, when they had called on Richard to be their captain against the lords they saw as traitors. But the plan did not work as the king wished. De Vere, who had spent those six years constantly at Richard's side rather than anywhere near his family's estates, could command no personal loyalty there. Thomas of Woodstock, on the other hand, had already made his home in Essex for a decade, at Pleshey Castle, the chief seat of his wife's inheritance. It did not take long before the unfortunate sergeant at arms found himself arrested and imprisoned.[30]

More fertile ground was offered by Richard's travels around the midlands and the north. The earldom of Chester—stretching from Cheshire in northwest England across into the north Welsh county of Flintshire, lands dominated by the two great castles of Flint, looking over the Dee estuary, and Chester itself, farther upriver—had been among the estates that belonged to Richard's father as heir to the throne. Because Richard did not yet have a son, he still held these titles and properties as earl of Chester and prince of Wales along with his crown. The county of Cheshire in particular had a remarkable depth of military experience and expertise on which the Black Prince had drawn heavily for his campaigns overseas in the 1360s. It was also one of only three palatinates in the kingdom; that is, a territory where the king's writ did not run. Instead, its lord had the right to exercise judicial authority within its borders in the king's name and on his behalf. In Cheshire, therefore, Richard was both king and lord—but now, with the crown's powers in the hands of the council, it seemed disconcertingly possible that he might enjoy more freedom of action as earl of Chester than he did as England's king. On that basis, if de Vere's estates in the eastern counties would not serve as a recruiting ground, Cheshire might offer a viable alternative. As he traveled through the northwest, Richard was taking local knights and gentlemen into his service, and doing what he could to establish de Vere as the commander of this nascent army, appointing him justice of both Chester and north Wales, and giving him the keeping of the stronghold of Flint Castle.[31]

There might be other ways of fighting besides the purely military. Covertly, without attracting attention in the capital, Richard made contact with the French court. If at last he could meet King Charles face-to-face to negotiate a truce, he would be free from the pressure to lead an army against France, free from the need to call parliaments to pay for the war, free to rule as he wished without scrutiny or supervision. And since he preferred to be not a warrior but a judge—a king like Solomon, distinguished by his magnificence and his wisdom—perhaps the law could be his weapon. In July 1387, as the end of the council's year-long term of office in November came more closely into view, Richard sent letters under his signet summoning the six judges of the courts of King's Bench and Common Pleas to attend on him at Shrewsbury on the Welsh border, near de Vere's new power base in the northwest.[32]

The judges arrived at the beginning of August to find the king sitting in state with Anne, his queen, and the band of loyalists who had accompanied him on his six-month odyssey: Robert de Vere, his closest friend, and Simon Burley and Michael de la Pole, his closest advisers; Alexander Neville, the archbishop of York, who had been appointed to the council by parliament but had immediately thrown over his responsibilities to travel with the king;

and Nicholas Brembre, a wool merchant and former mayor of London who had made it his business in recent years to extend serious lines of credit to the royal household. But of them all, the key figure in this meeting would be Robert Tresilian, the chief justice of King's Bench, who had been so energetic in condemning the rebels of 1381 as traitors. Richard had found a new use for his legal talents. Tresilian swore the judges to secrecy, then asked them a series of questions about the ways in which the king's authority was currently constrained.[33]

Drafted under Tresilian's exacting eye, the questions moved step-by-step through the actions of the parliament that had left Richard hamstrung and sidelined within his own government. Their inexorable progression left little room for doubt about the responses they required, or the likely consequences if the frightened judges did not comply. Was the appointment of the council by parliamentary statute "derogatory to the regality and prerogative of the lord king?" Yes, the judges said, because it was done against the king's will. What penalty should be faced by those who had wanted the statute drawn up and incited the king to agree? Death, came the reply. How should the men be punished who had compelled the king to consent to the passing of the statute, and hindered him from exercising his regality and prerogative? They should be punished—here their answers were phrased with meticulous care—"as though they were traitors." Still the questions kept coming. Yes, the judges agreed: it was the king's right to direct parliament's business and dissolve it at will, and anyone resisting his use of those powers should be punished as a traitor. Anyone seeking to impeach royal officials without the king's permission should be punished as a traitor. And as for those in parliament who had cited precedents from the reign of the king's great-grandfather, precedents pointing to the fact that in 1311 Edward II had also been subjected to the supervision of a noble council, they too should be punished as traitors.

Richard's exchange with Woodstock and Bishop Arundel in October 1386 had been dumbfounding. Ten months later, the implications of these legal arguments were terrifying. Treason was the worst of all crimes, carrying the worst of all punishments for members of the political class: not only death for the traitor himself, but the destruction of his name and his line through the permanent forfeiture of his estates. The offense had been closely defined by the statute of 1352 as a set of provisions clustered around the central charge of plotting the king's death or making war against him; but, in their desperation to bind the king into their plans, the parliament of 1386 had come close to suggesting that resisting the council's authority might be regarded as equivalent to treason. By establishing the council through a parliamentary statute, they had also tried to ensure that Richard could not undo their actions without again consulting the representatives of his realm. But now, step-by-step, he had mirrored their legal moves in the opposite direction. Where they had appealed to the collective embodiment of the kingdom, he asserted the singular will of the king. And, with a form of words that delicately sidestepped the statute of 1352, his judges had delivered the definition of treasonable acts into Richard's own hands. Who could decide whether the king had been hindered in the exercise of his prerogative, or induced to agree to something against his will, except the king himself?

In effect, Richard's questions to the judges were a declaration of war. If this was how he saw the relationship between his will and the law—that, essentially, they were one and the same—then there could be no peaceful way forward, no lessons learned, no new understanding between the king and the great lords who had led the criticism of his ministers and royal household. Instead, he was laying the ground for a countercoup to destroy his enemies when the council's term of office came to an end on November 19. For the moment, the plan was secret: at Richard's command, the judges swore again not to reveal his questions or their own answers. But one of the justices, Roger Fulthorp, had failed to come to Shrewsbury. All six, including the missing man, were summoned to appear again before the king at Nottingham Castle on August 25. There Fulthorp, like the others, put his seal to the judges' answers, but his alarm at their substance was such that when he returned to Westminster he confessed everything to Richard's brother Thomas Holand, earl of Kent—who was married to a sister of the Arundels—and the earl of Northumberland. The earls went straight to the council.[34]

For the lords of the council, the news brought fear and consternation. A year earlier, they had begun their work of retrenchment as they meant to go on, by handing over one of Richard's diadems as collateral for a loan of £4,000 from the mayor and citizens of London. Since then, they had had reason to feel pleased with their achievements. Royal expenditure and royal debts had been reduced, and efforts made to improve the administration of justice. In May, the earl of Arundel, fresh from his triumph over the Franco-Flemish fleet, had put to sea again to relieve the besieged English garrison in the Breton port of Brest; only a month later, French plans for the postponed and already much diminished invasion were finally canceled as a result of poisonous infighting among the magnates who surrounded the young King Charles. But it was suddenly clear to everyone at Westminster that King Richard's recent travels had not simply been evasive meandering. He believed that his enemies had usurped his crown as well as pawning his jewels. Now he was bent on revenge.[35]

Six

1387–1389

come I appellant

By the first week of November 1387, the king was advancing on London. In the city the familiar low thrum of panic had returned in fluttering nerves and stilted conversations, but this time the danger lay inside, not outside, the kingdom. One of Richard's messengers to the royal court in Paris had been intercepted at Calais, from where rumors were swirling that the king had done a deal with his French counterpart to surrender the town in return for military support against his own subjects, just as he had threatened in his barbed conversation with Woodstock and Bishop Arundel twelve months earlier. Richard himself—given that no such deal had in fact yet been made—was planning to raise forces in the capital through his loyal servant Nicholas Brembre, the former mayor who had been a controversial player in the city's turbulent politics for the last fifteen years. The council's statutory year in office would end on November 19, less than three weeks away. It appeared that the king was intending to reimpose his personal rule with an iron fist.[1]

At Westminster, the lords of the council and the noblemen who had backed them had urgent decisions to make. When Richard arrived, should they submit to him as their sovereign and hope to weather the storm, whatever form it might take? Perhaps—despite the judges' answers at Shrewsbury and Nottingham—the king could still be persuaded of the loyalty of his greatest subjects, whose only concern had been for the security of his kingdom. To hope so was to take a dangerous chance, but the alternative might be more dangerous still. If they did not submit to him as their sovereign, would that make them traitors by every definition of the term?

The chancellor, Bishop Arundel, with fellow members of the council— Edmund of Langley, Lord Scrope, the archbishop of Canterbury—and other lords including the earl of Northumberland and Richard's oldest brother, Thomas Holand, decided to run the risk of staying in place. They were faithful servants of the crown. The king was young. Now that the threat of French invasion was past and the administration at Westminster reformed, they had to believe that wise counsel could guide the king back from the brink and that the unity of the realm could be restored.

But three of England's greatest noblemen—Thomas of Woodstock and the earls of Arundel and Warwick—saw no hope of safety for themselves or prosperity for the realm in Richard's return. Woodstock and Arundel had been the most vociferous critics of Richard's household regime. Warwick's nephew Ralph Stafford had been killed by John Holand, the younger of the king's brothers, only for Richard to break his promise that the murderer would be punished for his crime. In recent months, all three lords had learned that, on his travels, the king was retaining local landowners into his service as though he were a magnate himself, in regions that encroached directly on their own local power: Woodstock in Essex, Arundel in north Wales, and Warwick in the west midlands. They had witnessed Richard's temper, his solipsism, his lack of judgment; they believed he would not listen to anyone other than the household men who currently surrounded him. They would take the risk of refusing to submit. By the time the royal party crossed London Bridge on November 10, Woodstock and Warwick had already ridden away with their retinues on the great road north from Smithfield. The earl of Arundel left with a heavily armed guard for his fortress at Reigate in Surrey, twenty miles south, and locked himself in.[2]

This was uncharted territory. For all Brembre's assurances to the king that the people of London would rise in arms in his support, the city's unnerved leaders could think only of their own self-preservation. They welcomed Richard and his household with due civic dignity but no sign of a militia in the making. At Westminster the formal reunion between king and council was tense, and became more so when Richard heard that Woodstock, Arundel, and Warwick were missing. The king had banked on troops responding to his call when he reclaimed his capital. Instead, it seemed possible that three lords he loathed might raise an army against him.

So far, the three rebels had not yet joined forces; perhaps one could be picked off before they had a chance to coordinate their position. On November 12, forty-eight hours after his arrival in London, with just a week of the council's year in office left to run, Richard sent the earl of Northumberland to Reigate to bring the earl of Arundel back. Finding the castle fortified against him, Northumberland—one of the lords still hoping against hope to find a path toward peace—retreated rather than risk blows being struck. But Arundel knew it would not be Richard's last attempt to arrest him. That night, when a herald arrived at the castle gate bearing messages from Woodstock and Warwick, the earl seized his moment, riding with his retainers twenty-five miles through the darkness to meet them at the manor of Harringay, just north of the capital. There, in a forested park belonging to the bishop of London that lay conveniently close to the highway, armed men were gathering behind all three lords' banners. The next day, November 13, their growing forces marched another seven miles north, to make camp around the village of Waltham Cross.[3]

On Thursday, November 14, a jittery meeting convened in the palace of Westminster. At Richard's side, as always, sat the languorous figure of Robert de Vere, and around them the king's older advisers: Michael de la Pole and Simon Burley, Chief Justice Tresilian, Nicholas Brembre, and Archbishop Neville. With them were Bishop Arundel and the other lords of the council, men who knew that, in this treacherous landscape, there were few steady footholds left. The question before them—what to do about Woodstock, Arundel, and Warwick—was simple to formulate; the answer, anything but. Some of those close to the king, especially the combative Archbishop Neville, pressed loudly for a military solution. The dissidents, he said, should be crushed in battle. It was left to Bishop Arundel and his allies to point out that victory in combat could not be guaranteed, and that, even if it could, no good would come to the king from slaughtering his own subjects.

Richard had never been a soldier, and his hatred for the rebel lords was shot through with fear. At last, he allowed himself to be persuaded by the councillors' arguments for negotiation rather than war. The king needed time to regroup without finding himself trapped by the forces mustering north of London. The only way forward was to compel Woodstock, Arundel, and Warwick to show their hands. It was agreed: Richard would offer them an audience and ask to hear their demands. The councillors, led by Arundel's brother the bishop and Woodstock's brother Langley, left Westminster for Waltham Cross to parley as best they could.[4]

There Woodstock, Arundel, and Warwick presented the manifesto they had hastily assembled to justify their actions. They protested their loyalty to the crown but declared that the king was surrounded by traitors. Everything, failure abroad and division at home, was the fault of de Vere, de la Pole, Tresilian, Brembre, and Archbishop Neville. They themselves had gathered in arms, the three lords said, to bring these false and wicked men to justice. It was a message they wanted all the king's subjects to hear. As the councillors rode back to Westminster to arrange the meeting with Richard, the lords repeated their accusations in a public letter to the citizens of London. Right, authority, allegiance, and treason: all were now bitterly contested terms, and all now hung in the balance.

On Sunday, November 17, Richard took his seat on the marble throne in Westminster's cavernous hall. He stared blankly ahead as Woodstock, Arundel, and Warwick stalked through the east door. Three times before the lords reached the king, they dropped to their knees in obeisance. Richard was not impressed. His message—delivered by Bishop Arundel—was of their outrageous presumption in taking up arms and his own heroic restraint in not crushing them without mercy, "although he could easily have done so, if he had not been concerned for your welfare and that of the men in your forces. For no one can doubt that, if he had assembled an army, he would have had many more men than you." Instead, the bishop explained, their patient and merciful king, who preferred peace to the shedding of blood, had called them into his sovereign presence to explain their actions. The words were carefully chosen; all the same, the young Solomon of whom the bishop spoke could not restrain himself: "Did you think you could frighten me? Do I not have soldiers who, had I wished, would have rounded you up like cattle and slaughtered you?" In the moment there could be little question that he did in fact wish, but it was not the king who had 300 men-at-arms stationed directly outside the hall. The three lords waited for the royal temper to bluster to a halt.[5]

When their turn came to speak, they announced that they had come in arms only because they feared for their lives at the hands of the five traitors who were constantly at the king's side. The lords presented their "appeal of treason"—allegations of treason formally laid by private subjects of the king— and threw down their gauntlets, declaring that they would prove the truth of the charges in combat with the men they had named. But none of the five was there to answer the challenge. Lord Scrope, one of the councillors trying to find a political route out of the crisis, asked that they should instead be detained and everyone's safety guaranteed until a parliament could gather to hear the case according to the law. To all of this, Richard—calmer now— graciously gave his word. He would summon parliament to meet in three months' time, on February 3, 1388. On that day both sides would appear to receive his justice, and in the meantime neither would cause harm to the other.

The skirmish, it appeared, was over. Woodstock and the two earls had laid their charges against the king's friends, and agreed to a hearing in parliament. Richard had railed at them in fury, but in the wake of his outburst and their acknowledgment of his authority his mood had lifted. He rose from his throne, magnificent in his robes, and invited the three lords to drink wine in his chamber before they left. If his behavior was bewildering, it seemed at least that Bishop Arundel's painstaking mediation had done its work. Whatever he had pressed the judges to say at Shrewsbury and Nottingham, the king had now—two days before the formal end of the council's statutory powers—committed himself to participating in a parliament, and renounced the possibility of arbitrary action until then.

But the king lied. Richard had no intention of seeing the men of his household named as traitors in his own parliament. As soon as Woodstock, Arundel, and Warwick were gone from Westminster, the five men they had accused of treason scattered: some into hiding, some to raise an army in Richard's name. Judge Tresilian and Archbishop Neville disappeared from public view. Heavily disguised, de la Pole made for Calais, where his brother Edmund was in charge of the castle; but even had Edmund been sympathetic to his cause—which was by no means a foregone conclusion, given the rumors that Richard planned to hand Calais over to the French—his commanding officer, without whose approval he would not act, was Warwick's brother Sir William Beauchamp. De la Pole found no recruits or refuge there. Simon Burley headed to the south coast, where he held the castle at Dover and the wardenship of the Cinque Ports, but he had made himself so unpopular during the defensive fiascos of the previous three years that he could not muster forces there either. De Vere rode north. In Cheshire at least, and Lancashire and north Wales—the lands of Richard's earldom of Chester and principality of Wales, where the king had been retaining men into his service over the past nine months—he might find troops willing to take the field. Richard himself retreated from the capital twenty miles west along the Thames valley, to the safety of Windsor Castle. He was still hoping that the citizens of London would fight under his banner, but when their mayor was summoned to the royal presence a few days later, the frightened man made his excuses: they were not men-at-arms, he said, but merchants and craftsmen, who could do no more than defend their city's walls.[6]

It was a damning indictment of Richard's position that his opponents were not facing the same difficulty. After meeting the king, Woodstock, Arundel, and Warwick withdrew their forces another fifty miles north to the town of Huntingdon, a vantage point from which they could move quickly in whatever direction danger threatened. There they were joined by two more noblemen and their retinues, neither of whom had previously served on the council or spoken out against the king and his friends. One was Arundel's son-in-law Thomas Mowbray, earl of Nottingham, the young man who had been comprehensively displaced in Richard's affections by Robert de Vere.

Alongside Mowbray rode a second young lord, with men-at-arms and archers recruited from his absent father's duchy: Richard's cousin Henry.

Henry had spent the summer of 1387 at the Lancastrian castle of Kenilworth with his pregnant wife and baby son, only to find the happiness of his little family overtaken by political crisis. His opinion of his royal cousin had not improved as they grew to adulthood. During the Scottish campaign of 1385, Henry had seen at first hand the peevish superficiality of Richard's engagement with the demands of war. In the autumn of 1386, he had sat in a parliament that Richard treated with hostility and contempt while the country stood on the brink of invasion. Since then, he had tracked with growing concern Richard's attempts to piece together some sort of regional power base beyond the royal household. From his midland seat at Kenilworth, Henry was acutely aware that the king was taking local men into his service during his recent peregrinations; he understood the threat this royal retaining represented in its encroachment on his father's political heartlands in the north midlands and northwest, and especially on Gaunt's palatinate of Lancashire, the neighbor and twin of Richard's own in Cheshire.[7]

In the early autumn, Henry moved his family to London, where seventeen-year-old Mary gave birth to their second child, another boy, on September 29. He wanted to be close to Westminster to observe whatever might unfold when the council's year in office came to an end in November, a prospect rendered even more unsettling by the news from Shrewsbury and Nottingham that, behind closed doors, Richard had redefined the law of treason as a weapon in royal hands. If that were allowed to stand, Henry knew worse would follow, not only for his own family—a profound responsibility entrusted to him by his father, intensified now by the arrival of his two small boys—but for the entire kingdom. The question was how it could best be resisted.[8]

From his London lodgings, Henry witnessed the brinkmanship of Richard's return to the capital and the defiance of Woodstock, Warwick, and Arundel. His relationship with the rebel lords was not simple. Woodstock was Henry's family twice over—his uncle by blood and his brother-in-law by marriage—but the fact of their wives' shared inheritance was a source of tension between them, given the range and scale of Woodstock's unfulfilled ambitions. Arundel was Mary's maternal uncle, but Henry's father had never been impressed by the earl's belligerent self-assertion. Still, they were experienced men who had spent the last year trying to address military and financial crises with which Richard had shown himself to be utterly unconcerned—and any doubts in Henry's mind about the rebels' political judgment paled into insignificance beside his antipathy to the king's friends. It was bad enough that Robert de Vere had so carelessly discarded Henry's cousin Philippa de Coucy that summer, but three years before, de Vere and Thomas Mowbray had plotted to kill Gaunt. If Mowbray had changed his spots since then—a transformation on which Henry was keeping a close eye—de Vere had shown no remorse whatsoever.

Before mid-November Henry made no public move, although those close to his household knew that he and Mary had named their newborn son Thomas: in the circumstances, it was a striking decision to choose the forename shared by Woodstock, Warwick, and Bishop Arundel, rather than that of the king or either of the baby's grandfathers. Henry was close at hand when the three rebel lords made their appeal in Westminster Hall. He heard Richard's promise to take both accusers and accused under his protection until the case could be heard in parliament in February. Then he watched Richard break his word.

What his cousin was doing was wrong, Henry knew. There was an imperative, now, not only to protect his father's duchy, but to safeguard his sovereign grandfather's legacy, the compact between crown and realm that would preserve England against attack from outside its borders and tyranny within. Edward III had rebuilt the kingdom after the devastating conflicts of the reign of Edward II, conflicts in which resistance to the king and his predatory favorites had been led for years by Henry's Lancastrian forebear, his mother's great-uncle Thomas, earl of Lancaster—another namesake for Henry's baby son—who had been beheaded on Edward's orders in 1322. There were many in England who saw Thomas of Lancaster as a martyr, even a saint, and it was a history Henry knew intimately: the terrifying risks of taking up arms against the crown, and the terrifying reasons it might sometimes prove necessary. His father was 700 miles away. The decision was his. A week after Woodstock, Arundel, and Warwick confronted Richard in Westminster Hall, Henry sent Mary and the children back to the safety of Kenilworth. He summoned his men, and rode north.[9]

When he reached Huntingdon, he found the lords arguing. Woodstock and Arundel wanted to march on London to capture the king. Their patience—never a deep well—was exhausted. They had tried listening to

Arundel's brother the bishop, tried listening to Richard's promises; but the king's word, they now knew, was worthless. They saw no point in continuing to believe that he might reform his behavior, or in trying to mitigate the risks of their own position. Warwick vehemently disagreed. Richard, he said, came from an illustrious line of kings, and at his coronation all the lords of the realm had sworn a sacred oath of allegiance. To break that oath would be dishonorable treachery. They should strive instead to defeat the traitor de Vere and the forces he was currently raising in Cheshire and north Wales.[10]

To the newcomers, twenty-year-old Henry and twenty-one-year-old Mowbray, it was obvious that Warwick was right. They had raised their banners in the cause of loyal resistance. They clung to the rhetoric—and, behind the rhetoric, the stubborn insistence—that if de Vere and the other household men could be removed, then Richard's government could be refashioned with Richard himself still at its head. Apart from anything else, what was the alternative? The queen had not given birth in almost six years of marriage. In the absence of a direct heir, the removal of the king might precipitate not just civil war, but anarchy; and if they failed in the attempt to depose him, their lives would be forfeit and their dynasties destroyed.

For now, the cooler heads prevailed. The five lords sent public letters around the country addressed to the sheriff of every county, just as Woodstock, Arundel, and Warwick previously had to the citizens of London, declaring themselves to be "obedient and loyal lieges of our most redoubtable lord king" seeking only to remove traitors from his side. But even the cooler heads knew they would have to fight. Henry had spent his formative years training in the lists, and he had been to war once before—even if, two years ago in Scotland, the English had failed in the end to track down the enemy. The same could not be allowed to happen again.[11]

De Vere was their prime target and chief military threat. From Huntingdon the rebel lords marched west in the attempt to intercept him on the road from Cheshire, splitting their troops across three locations to shut down his route south to the king and capital. The pincer movement worked. A harried de Vere and his forces—by now more than 3,000 men—made a dash for the crossing of the Thames at Radcot Bridge in Oxfordshire. When they got there on December 20 in thick fog, they found Henry and his troops waiting. This would be Henry's first taste of the military command for which his father had sought to prepare him, in a conflict his father had strenuously sought to avoid. It was de Vere's first taste of command too—but, whatever his talents were, they did not include those of a soldier, and it took only minutes for the rout to begin. Many of his men drowned in the Thames marshes as they tried to run; others surrendered and were sent packing, stripped of their arms and possessions. De Vere himself fled, ditching his expensive armor to make his escape. Their target was lost, but still: Henry had joined the resistance, and he had won.[12]

On Christmas Day the rebel lords partied at Oxford in masks and costumes and overwhelming relief. The respite was short. By December 27, they had marched their forces to Clerkenwell, the field outside the walls of the capital where, six and a half years earlier, Richard's moment in the sun with the rebels who had looked to him for leadership had finally ended. Now it was winter, and the king had shut himself inside the Tower. At first, he declared his intention simply to wait; if he refused to engage with the lords and their army, surely, eventually they would go away? But slowly, with Bishop Arundel, Edmund of Langley, and London's nervous mayor acting as go-betweens, Richard was brought to see the limitations of his plan: the lords' agenda commanded substantial support within the city, and they had no intention of leaving. On December 28, the Tower gates were opened to admit them to the king's presence. Six and a half years earlier, Henry had almost died inside the fortress. This time, surrounded by his loyal retainers, he knew he could protect himself—but the stakes could scarcely have been higher, or the outcome less certain.[13]

The lords had come armed with incriminating paper and parchment: intercepted letters from France offering Richard and de Vere safe-conduct to Boulogne, and Richard's own letters, found in de Vere's abandoned baggage train at Radcot Bridge, insisting that the king's "heart was set on living and dying with him." But de Vere was gone. Dressed as a servant, he had scrambled into Richard's presence for a fleeting farewell before escaping, via his castle at Queenborough, to the Continent. De la Pole had followed him; after returning empty-handed from Calais to Westminster, he made for Hull, his family's hometown, and there took ship for Dordrecht in Holland.

Alexander Neville had disappeared into his northern archdiocese. Judge Tresilian was nowhere to be found. Brembre's hopes of influence within the city of London had proved vain and hollow. The truth was that Richard was in no position to negotiate.[14]

Instead, it was the rebel lords who wrangled over their next step. For their own safety, and that of the kingdom, could the king be allowed to remain on the throne? The question was the same one they had confronted in principle at Huntingdon, but now it was immediate and real. Woodstock and Arundel were convinced that Richard was irredeemable; that, at not quite twenty-one, he had conclusively shown the danger he posed to his people. There was an alarming amount of evidence to support their position. Time and again, the king had proved that he understood his kingship as a matter of rights, but not responsibilities; that he saw any attempt to constrain his will as unlawful, even treasonable; that he would not learn from either adverse experience or unpalatable advice; that his word could not be trusted. The duke and earl were so forceful in their arguments that on December 29, within the walls of the Tower, a provisional decision was reached that Richard should be deposed. Almost exactly six decades after the crown had been forcibly removed from Edward II's anointed head, his great-grandson found himself facing the same extraordinary and terrible fate.[15]

But if the question was the same as it had been at Huntingdon, so were the objections. If the lords failed to carry the country with them, they would lose their lives, their estates, and their families' future. If they succeeded, what then? Without a head, the body politic could not function. Back in 1327, Edward II had had a son to whom the crown could pass without dispute about the legitimacy of his right to inherit, but Richard had no sons or royal brothers standing next in line. Woodstock had an answer: as the king's uncle, son of the great Edward III, the senior royal peer there present and, at almost thirty-three, a man of both experience and untapped potential, he himself was the obvious choice. Not obvious, however, to Henry, whose father was Woodstock's older brother—a senior hereditary claim that Henry had no intention of letting Woodstock wave away in Gaunt's absence.

Any attempt to argue instead for a Lancastrian succession could look to the authority of the great Edward III himself. Back in the last year of the old king's reign, during the troubled months after the Black Prince's death, Edward had sealed a document setting out his wishes for the descent of his crown. It should, he said, pass in the male line; in other words, for as long as Richard remained childless, his next heir should be John of Gaunt, since the dead Lionel of Antwerp—the older brother of both Gaunt and Woodstock—had left only a daughter, Philippa. But the document had never been made public, and it was far from clear that the king had the right to dispose of the throne by will rather than precedent. Richard had shown no sign of accepting his grandfather's prescription, which in any case risked undermining the English claim to the throne of France, relying as that did on inheritance through the female line from Edward's French mother. So far, Richard had seemed to incline toward the claim of Philippa's son Roger Mortimer, the new earl of March, not least because at thirteen he did not yet stand among the lords whose influence in government the king resented. But a thirteen-year-old boy was not an answer to England's current woes. Gaunt was no better prospect, even had he not been 700 miles away; more than once in the last decade, rumors that the duke coveted the crown for himself had helped incite the king's subjects to violence. Woodstock's claim, meanwhile, convinced no one but himself.[16]

By January 1, it was apparent that the problem had no solution. Richard's crown was replaced on his head without anyone outside the Tower knowing there had been a brief interregnum. The rebel lords turned to deal with the undesirables around the king who—obviously, necessarily, given that there was no other option now but to believe it—had been responsible for the errors in his government. A month remained until the parliament Richard had called to hear the appeal of treason against his five friends, a process the lords would now control to ensure that justice was done. Brembre, the only one of the five who had not disappeared from London, was taken into custody along with twelve knights and clerks of the king's household, among them Simon Burley. Others were expelled from court, and key officers replaced; the ports were sealed, and orders given to collect evidence against the accused. On February 1, the six judges who had answered the king's questions at Nottingham were arrested and replaced by nominees of the new regime. When parliament assembled and the trials began, the lords would be ready.[17]

The realization that he was powerless to prevent these rebellious subjects invading the sanctum of his household and threatening his sovereignty had left Richard deeply disturbed. At first, he had been confused and tearful. Then he tried to bargain with his former friend Mowbray and his cousin Henry, seeking to detach them from their alignment with the older lords who had initiated this insult to his crown. But Richard had never before found common ground with Henry; and now, since he did not acknowledge the gravity of his own actions, he could not answer the gravity of Henry's concerns. By February 3, 1388, when parliament opened in the White Chamber of the palace of Westminster, Richard had accepted the inevitable. He had always reveled in the magnificent theatricality of kingship. Now he had no choice but to take part in a performance over which he had no control at all.[18]

As he sat enthroned, motionless and silent, Henry, Mowbray, Woodstock, Arundel, and Warwick entered the chamber arm in arm, five abreast, dressed identically in cloth of gold. Together they knelt before him; together they declared for all to hear that they had never sought or plotted his death. Woodstock then spoke alone, insisting that, despite rumor to the contrary, he had never intended to make himself king in Richard's place. If they were protesting a little too much, that was part of the point: this was a public moment in which they could disavow any suggestion of treasonable behavior and simultaneously remind the king of the stakes for which he was playing.

The tactic worked exactly as planned. Sticking to his script, Richard announced that he considered his uncle "guilty of nothing." That formality dispatched, the assembly could move on to the trials of the men whom the five "Lords Appellant" (as they were now described in the parliamentary record) had accused of treason. Not that their cases were simple, in either process or substance: step-by-step, the logic of this conflict had pushed so far beyond the bounds of the law as it stood that at each stage, on each side, there seemed no option but to press further. In seeking to unravel the actions of the parliament of 1386, Richard had seized the definition of treason into his own hands, taking his aim at anyone who compelled or incited the king to act against his own will. In seeking to counter him, the Appellants seized it back in the name of the king-in-parliament—the sovereign attended and advised by the representatives of his realm—arguing that the men around Richard had ensnared and then manipulated his will in order to use the royal prerogative for themselves. The Statute of Treason of 1352 had been left so far behind that established legal mechanisms were no use in prosecuting these charges—a difficulty that was sidestepped by blunt assertion rather than reasoning when the Appellants declared that so high a crime committed by peers of the realm could only be judged "by the procedures of parliament and not by the civil law or the common law of the land." But no such procedures existed, or at least not in any prescribed form. In practice, parliament would be making up the rules as it went along.[19]

It took two hours for the clerk to read out the appeal of treason in full. De Vere, de la Pole, and Neville, with the support of Tresilian and Brembre, had taken advantage of "the tender age of our lord the king and the innocence of his royal person" to turn Richard against his people and usurp his authority, "so that they alone had the government of the realm." They had enriched themselves at the king's expense and to the impoverishment of his kingdom. They had interfered in the provision of justice. They had caused the conflict between the king and his loyal subjects in the parliament of 1386. Everything the king had said and done since then to the detriment of the realm—the whole narrative spelled out in detail, point by devastating point—had been at their instigation.[20]

When the recitation of all thirty-nine articles was finished, de Vere, de la Pole, Neville, and Tresilian were summoned to answer the charges. Given that the four men were not already in custody, there was no chance that they would come when called; but it was crucial that due process should be publicly observed, even—or especially—when that process was being invented from moment to moment. The proclamation was made first within the White Chamber itself, then in the great hall of the palace, then at the palace gates. It was repeated the next day, and the day after that. They did not appear. The common law did not allow verdicts to be returned in the absence of the accused, but this trial was in parliament's hands, and on February 13, after a week's deliberation, they were found guilty on all counts. Enough of the offenses were judged to be treasonable—fourteen out of thirty-nine, including the appropriation of the king's power, the questions to the judges, the conspiracy with France, and the raising of de Vere's army in the north-west—for them to be convicted as traitors. All would forfeit their property. Neville's life would be spared because he was a priest; the others would be drawn on a hurdle to the gallows and there hanged until they were dead.[21]

Or at least they would be, just as soon as they could be found. For now, Nicholas Brembre was the only one of the accused to face his trial in person. On February 17, when he was brought from the Tower to the White Chamber, he declared his intention to prove his innocence in combat "as a knight ought to do." That, he was told, was not allowed; trial by battle obtained only in cases where there were no witnesses. The next day, Richard attempted to speak in his support, but the five Appellants—standing together as they did through-out the hearings—threw down their gauntlets to affirm Brembre's guilt. Other lords joined them, and the Commons added their voices to the clamor that drowned out the royal intervention. A committee of twelve noblemen led by Edmund of Langley, who had so far been a hand-wringing bystander to his younger brother's self-assertion, was appointed to review the charges. When they returned the next morning to say that in Brembre's case they could find no justification for a death sentence, anger began to build in the assembly, until an urgent message caught the Appellants' attention. As they spun on their heels and left, word raced around the room: Judge Tresilian had been found hiding in a house abutting the palace. When Woodstock, Arundel, Warwick, Mow-bray, and Henry hauled him into the chamber he was almost unrecognizable, bushily bearded, unkempt, and oddly dressed in an attempt at disguise. He tried to claim the protection of sanctuary, since he had been discovered within the purview of Westminster Abbey, but the Appellants were not about to be deflected from their purpose by the sheltering arm of the Church. Tresilian the judge was now Tresilian the traitor. Without further ceremony he was lashed to a hurdle and dragged almost two miles northwest to the crossroads at Tyburn where London's great gallows stood. There he was stripped of his clothes and hanged.[22]

Brembre's conviction took a little longer. Casting about in their search for evidence to clinch the case against him, the Appellants summoned Lon-don's mayor and aldermen to appear at the hearing on the day after Tresilian's death. The uneasy officials would say no more than that if the treasons described in the charges had in fact taken place, they "supposed he was more aware of them than not." It was enough. Brembre died at Tyburn that afternoon. By now every clause of the appeal had been publicly vindicated, but the trials did not stop. With parliament in session and the Commons in full cry against the king's friends, it was easy to harness the more familiar process of impeachment, and in March and April six more men were accused of treason. Two of them—Tresilian's legal clerk John Blake and an associate of Brembre's named Thomas Usk—sought to answer the charges by saying that everything they had done was at the king's command. That, the lords replied, only made their guilt "more apparent rather than excused," not—*of course*—because the king himself bore any blame, but because Blake and Usk had known him to be under the control of the traitors who had already been condemned. Blake was hanged. The Londoner Usk was first strung up on the gallows and then cut down and decapitated, his head set on a spike on Newgate near his family's home at the western entrance to the city.[23]

The other four newly accused men were knights of the chamber, all of them favored household servants of the king, but the most prominent name was that of Simon Burley. His closeness to the absent Michael de la Pole, the royal grants he had received, his high-handed style, and the dubious legality of some of his property acquisitions made him an obvious target. At the same time, his record of loyal service as a soldier under the Black Prince's command and as the king's boyhood tutor could not be denied. And in dealing with his case, the first major cracks began to appear in the Appellants' carefully constructed theater of unity. The distress of the king and queen was obvious: despite Richard's puppet status in proceedings, he sought to declare Burley's innocence, and Anne—whom Burley had escorted to her marriage in England from her home in Bohemia—knelt before the lords to beg for his life. Even the ineffectual Edmund of Langley was roused to action, almost coming to blows with his brother Woodstock in front of the whole parliament in Burley's defense.[24]

The most significant interventions, however, came from an unexpected quarter. Henry and Mowbray had been late to join the Appellant rebellion; three months later, they were the first to break ranks. Mowbray had spent his teenage years in Richard's household, where Burley had been a constant presence. Henry's personal connection came through Burley's nephew Sir Richard, one of Gaunt's most trusted retainers, who had left England with the duke to fight in Castile. Now both Mowbray and Henry spoke up to say that Burley should not die. But Woodstock, Arundel, and Warwick, with the support of the Commons, were not about to give ground to their junior partners. Richard insisted at least that the man who had carried him in his arms at his coronation should be spared the indignities of drawing and hanging that usually accompanied a traitor's execution. On May 5, Burley was allowed to walk from Westminster eastward through the city with his hands tied behind his back, to lay his head on the block on Tower Hill. His three fellow knights of the chamber died a week later.

Henry had joined the resistance, and he had won; and now the movement he had helped to lead was running beyond his control. He had always known that the work of what one chronicler named the "Merciless Parliament" would be bloody. The question was how—and whether—it would stop. The fundamental dilemma with which the Appellants had wrestled in the Tower still remained, in newly mutated form. Richard's favorites had been removed from around his throne. How should the kingdom be governed now that they were gone? Even if the condemned men had been solely responsible for the oppressions of Richard's rule, as the Appellants' rhetoric implausibly had it, there could be no doubt that the king had been a coerced and unwilling participant in their fall. If his power were restored, would he take revenge on the lords who had destroyed his servants and companions? Or must he somehow be kept under permanent restraint?

The second option seemed hardly plausible because hardly justifiable: that was not how sovereignty worked. Even the Appellants' own charges against Simon Burley, in seeking to argue that he and the other traitors had "enslaved" Richard, declared that "the king ought to be of a freer condition than any other in his realm." Instead, the lords and the parliament they led tried to bind Richard into the future they wanted. In order to renew "the good peace and firm unity" of his kingdom, the king was required to grant a general pardon to all of his subjects "for every kind of treason, insurrection, felony, trespass, conspiracy, confederacy . . . and any other actions whatsoever committed before this time." The Appellants were expressly indemnified against any reprisals for what they had done. At the same time, because it was disquietingly clear how far they had ended up taking the law into their own hands, the clock was turned back on the definition of treason to the statute of 1352. Everything that had happened during the present parliament was correct, and could never be contested; but none of it must set a precedent. On June 3 in Westminster Abbey, Richard swore again the oath he had taken at his coronation, including the promise that he would uphold the laws and customs of his realm, and his subjects swore again their fealty to him, as well as a new oath to uphold the actions of the parliament. Then the archbishop of Canterbury and all the bishops pronounced sentence of excommunication upon anyone who might dare to break their oaths or the peace and tranquility of the kingdom. All the powers of God and man had been invoked in the attempt to set in stone the outcome of the parliament, and simultaneously to set aside the means by which it had been achieved.[25]

It remained to be seen if that was how the future worked. For now, there was other business to attend to. The Commons had grudgingly granted a tax of half a fifteenth and tenth to fund another naval campaign under Arundel's command, for which the earl was already gathering ships and men. Arundel's brother the bishop—who, as chancellor, had managed to steer a nerve-wracking course between the king and the Appellants and, like all the spiritual peers, had taken no part in imposing death sentences on the convicted traitors—was rewarded with the archbishopric of York of which Alexander Neville had just been deprived. The five Appellants were granted £20,000 between them for their costs "in saving the king and the whole kingdom," and in July, Woodstock finally secured the landed income he had always believed he was owed as duke of Gloucester, when estates forfeited by de Vere and de la Pole and others to the value of £2,000 a year were given into his keeping. Meanwhile, the ranks of the nobility had been reinforced by a promotion that seemed to reach across the bloodstained divide of the previous weeks. In April, the king's brother John Holand had returned early, accompanied by his wife, Henry's sister Elizabeth, from his service on Gaunt's campaign. On June 2, he was given the earldom of Huntingdon, the title that, in 1385, Richard had tried and failed to bestow on Simon Burley.[26]

The day before Holand's installation, the king presided at a banquet attended by all his lords. The day after came the ceremony of renewal and reconciliation at the abbey. Then, as soon as he could, Richard left Westminster to spend the summer hunting.[27]

The events of the Merciless Parliament had been a vivid shock to the political system, a bout of judicial bloodletting within government on a scale unknown since the aftermath of Edward II's deposition sixty years earlier. Among the lords, the violence had given rise to growing unease, which had made itself felt not only in the arguments over the execution of Simon Burley, but in a subsequent decision to commute the death sentences passed on the judges who had redefined the law of treason at Shrewsbury and Nottingham—men who claimed they had acted only in fear of their lives—to permanent exile in Ireland.[28]

But for Richard, the experience was one of deep trauma. For as long as he could remember, he had been cocooned by his royal household, shielded, empowered, and armed by the constant attendance of men whose loyalty he trusted implicitly, and whose service had begun to give his authority substance in a wider world that he believed had been criminally slow to acknowledge his majesty. Now they had been stripped from him. He had lost the fatherly support of Burley and de la Pole, and the exhilarating company of de Vere. His friends and his servants had been brutally killed, or driven from his kingdom, and his own sovereignty had been threatened, undermined, disregarded.

He had been saved by the fact of being—as he had always known he was—irreplaceable. If he had had a child, everything might have been fatally different, just as it had been for his martyred great-grandfather Edward II, a king abandoned by his people and murdered, on the orders of his faithless wife, in the name of their son. As it was, the presence of his devoted, obedient queen was his only remaining emotional ballast. That, and the certain knowledge that he was chosen by God, unique in his destiny, whatever tests were set in his path. If the ritual of oath taking in the abbey had seemed like a bitter charade, a repetition-as-farce of the sacred rite that had endorsed his kingship, it was also a reminder of the moment when the touch of holy oil had changed him forever, never to be undone.

In recent years, he had been quick to anger, letting his frustration at outrageous constraints on his autonomy spill over, even to the point of lashing out physically at those who dared criticize their anointed king. But the constraints of the present were so appalling that he had been forced to bite his lip. He had refused to sit in the parliament chamber when Burley was condemned, leaving his presumptuous uncle Woodstock to preside in his stead. Otherwise, he had had no choice but to perform the role prescribed by his rebellious subjects. He would need to find new sources of loyal support, and new reserves of patience, before he could put the traitors in their place. For now, he left government in their hands and withdrew.[29]

He was not the only one who needed time. In the autumn of 1387, Henry had believed himself bound to act, driven by the need to protect both his father's duchy and England as a whole from Richard's assaults on the relationship between the crown and its people. But, young though he was, Henry had learned enough at his father's knee to be always wary, always cautious; and although he had dutifully played his choreographed part in the Appellants' public interventions, he had no illusions about his allies' instincts and motivations. Mowbray, he knew, had only left the king's camp when it became clear that he was being edged into the all-consuming shadow of de Vere, and before then had had no compunction about involving himself in his rival's plans to assassinate Henry's father. Woodstock's conviction that this was his chance, at last, to take the place in government he had always deserved had already led him to suggest that the crown should rest on his own head. Henry's months as an Appellant had been a baptism of political fire that had burned hotter and consumed more than he had intended. It was hardly surprising that, once the nerve-shattering tension of the parliament was over, he fell ill during the summer with an infection so severe that the pocks of his rash had to be lanced with a gilded needle.[30]

At least he was now in more regular contact with his father, who, since the autumn of 1387, had been installed with his household at the Franciscan

monastery in Bayonne at the southwestern tip of the English duchy of Aquitaine. Fifteen months earlier, Gaunt's campaign in Castile had begun well.
When he landed in Galicia, on the northwestern edge of the Iberian Peninsula, the province and its holy city of Santiago de Compostela proved willing
to accept the presence of his army and his claim to the Castilian crown, even
if only as a matter of realpolitik rather than partisan commitment. In February 1387, his alliance with João of Portugal was confirmed when the king took
Gaunt's daughter Philippa as his wife and queen. But by then the English
expedition was already running into trouble. Juan of Castile's strategy was to
pin down the English in Galicia, refuse to give battle, and wait for the spring,
when he hoped his French allies would send reinforcements to his aid. For
Gaunt's troops, the wait meant disaster. In the rocky Galician landscape,
winter was harsh. As lack of food and plunging temperatures hit hard, the
army was overwhelmed by epidemic disease. By March, half of the duke's
soldiers were dead.[31]

Meanwhile, tensions were mounting with the Portuguese over tactics
and the unrelenting scarcity of supplies, fractious arguments given a bitter
edge by the same kind of antagonisms that had hobbled the Franco-Scots
coalition against England. The English thought the Portuguese hotheaded,
garrulous, and uncultured; the Portuguese found the English to be patron-
izing, arrogant fools. Despite the efforts of Gaunt and King João, who remained on constructively civil terms, by early May their armies were barely
capable of functioning in tandem. At the same time, it was becoming alarmingly apparent that the other provinces of Castile and León, unlike remote
and phlegmatic Galicia, were determined to resist the duke's incursions.
Whatever loyalties to Duchess Constanza's dynasty still persisted, they were
not enough to open city gates across the kingdom to English men-at-arms.

Companies of French troops were on their way south to join the fight,
but Juan of Castile showed no greater inclination as the weeks went by to
meet Gaunt in the field, and when the cold of early spring gave way to the
heat of early summer, starvation and sickness again took hold in the English
and Portuguese ranks. Among the dead this time were two of Gaunt's closest aides: his son-in-law Sir Thomas Morieux, husband of Blanche, an illegitimate daughter he had fathered just before his first marriage; and Simon

Burley's nephew Sir Richard, who had served the duke faithfully for two decades. When Gaunt made a deal with Juan of Castile for safe-conducts to allow the ill and wounded to attempt the hazardous journey home, he had to defend his decision to the Portuguese king, his new son-in-law, who came to remonstrate with him on the road. The soldiers who were leaving, Gaunt said, were "not traitors, but men conquered by hardship." Then the duke— who, at forty-seven, had spent more than thirty years fighting battles of one kind or another—bent over his horse's neck and wept.

Only weeks later, he reached the inevitable conclusion: his hopes of becoming king of Castile could not succeed. A profitable and permanent settlement was the best option of the few that remained. If Gaunt's goals could not be achieved, then João of Portugal had nothing to gain from fighting on—and King Juan, it turned out, was equally anxious to see the back of the English for good. A treaty was quickly drafted. Fourteen-year-old Catalina, Gaunt and Constanza's only child, would marry Enrique, Juan's seven-year-old son and heir. In time they would become king and queen, uniting the rival claims to the throne and bringing reconciliation to Castile and its people. In return for giving up their rights to Castile in favor of the young couple, Gaunt and Constanza would receive a vast lump sum of £100,000, as well as a lavish pension of more than £6,000 a year for the rest of their lives. While the surviving soldiers of the English army were left to find their own passage home, Gaunt and his wife sailed for Bayonne at the end of September, determined to stay as close as they could to Castile until the settlement was confirmed.[32]

It took nine months before the treaty was finally ratified in July 1388. In September, Catalina and Enrique were married in the cathedral of Palencia, between the great cities of Valladolid and Burgos. A month later, the first installment of Gaunt's financial compensation arrived in Bayonne on pack mules laden with boxes of silver and gold. In return, the duke dispatched to Juan of Castile the golden crown Richard had given him before he left England.

Gaunt's presence in Aquitaine brought him back into closer communication with Henry and the regime at Westminster. Still, at a distance of hundreds of miles, he could not intervene publicly in the violent drama in which his son was caught up, and he did not try. In the summer of 1388, however, after the end of the Merciless Parliament, Woodstock and Arundel attempted to fold the absent duke into their angry repudiation of Richard's covert attempts during the previous autumn to negotiate for peace with France. They planned to coordinate a seaborne assault via Brittany with a land campaign in the south—to be led, they proposed, by Gaunt. But Arundel's naval expedition, launched in June, was thwarted yet again by the double-dealing of the Breton duke John de Montfort, and Gaunt, it rapidly became clear, had no interest in further fighting. A truce with France would allow him to ensure the success of his newly negotiated settlement in Castile—the terms of which in any case required him and King Juan to work for peace between England and France—while at the same time shoring up English rule in what remained of English Aquitaine. Meanwhile, Arundel and Woodstock were discovering how limited the funds available for the war effort still were, despite their removal of the hated de la Pole. They had run out of money even before the Scots invaded northern England, only a fortnight after Arundel had sailed away.

More ships were urgently mobilized in an attempt to find and recall the earl and his fleet, without success. At the beginning of August, French galleys raided the south coast, while more Scots troops poured over the northern borders. In Gaunt's absence, English forces there were led by Sir Henry Percy, eldest son of the earl of Northumberland and, at twenty-four, already so daring a soldier that the Scots had nicknamed him "Hotspur." On August 5, Hotspur led his men out of the city of Newcastle, marching at speed almost thirty miles northwest to Otterburn by the river Rede, where reports placed the Scottish army under the earls of Douglas, Moray, and Dunbar. At twilight, when they reached the Scottish camp after long hours on the road, he unleashed a surprise attack. It was a typically bold decision that, on this occasion, proved a risk too far. Douglas, who had not even had time to put on his armor, died in the bloody mêlée, but Hotspur's men soon found themselves engulfed in more chaos than the troops they had ambushed. As darkness fell, the English were routed and Hotspur himself captured. By the time the news reached Westminster, confidence in Woodstock and Arundel's leadership was crumbling.[33]

Seven months earlier, the Appellants had commanded overwhelming support for taking a stand against the king's friends, against their mismanagement of the kingdom's defenses and revenues, and against Richard's manipulation of the law in their interests. By September 1388, when financial necessity compelled the meeting of yet another parliament, everything had changed. Woodstock and Arundel had helped themselves to thousands of pounds of public money and conducted a seaborne campaign that achieved nothing other than to distract their attention from the threat of the Scots in the north. Richard's questions to his judges back in the summer of 1387 had rewritten the law of treason in such a way that the security of every one of his subjects was threatened—but in 1388 it was the Appellants, not the king, who had held show trials leading to the gallows and the block on the basis of their own expanded definition of treasonable acts. The extent of that violence had fractured the Appellant coalition. It remained to be seen how much support within the wider political community the regime could still muster.

When the new parliament opened at Cambridge on September 10, it was a tense and prickly affair, willing to grant only a single fifteenth and tenth for defense in the north, rather than for the renewed continental campaign Woodstock and Arundel wanted. Otherwise, the Commons were preoccupied with the lords' distribution of livery badges to retain men into their service—the means by which the Appellants had raised their forces, which the king himself had tried to emulate, and on which the Commons now requested a ban. No matter that many of the Commons themselves were retained in noble service in exactly this way; their concern, which had surfaced before at moments of political tension, was the resulting potential for local corruption and intimidation, because, as the Westminster chronicler put it, "those who wear the badges on account of their lords' power are puffed up with such stubborn pride that they do not hesitate to commit widespread extortion." Richard, presiding again in his newly impassive persona, saw an opportunity to drive a subtle wedge between his noble opponents and the community they claimed to lead. He offered, "out of a desire for tranquility in the realm," to set an example to his greatest subjects by abandoning the use of his own badges, wholly ineffective as they had so far been. Still the lords would not agree, but a compromise was reached—some greater regulation of the practice, as a provisional measure until the issue should be considered again—before the parliament dispersed.[34]

The principle of divide and rule, however, was one that was beginning to serve Richard well. The controversy over Simon Burley's death had already detached the two younger Appellants from their older colleagues' side. Henry was keeping a watchful distance from Westminster, from time to time appearing at court or council meetings, but for the most part staying at Kenilworth Castle with his wife and children; not long after the Cambridge parliament, Mary knew that she was pregnant again. Now that Robert de Vere was safely displaced—to Utrecht, last time news came—Thomas Mowbray was drifting back toward the king's presence, a development that Richard was doing nothing to discourage. The earl of Warwick, who at fifty was the oldest of the Appellants, had been formally named to the council put in place by the Merciless Parliament, but as the year went on he turned the focus of his attention back to his local interests in the midlands. It was Arundel and Woodstock who remained exposed at the head of government, pressing for a war that no one else now wanted to pursue, facing the fallout of their own defensive failures, and realizing little by little that they had no exit strategy.[35]

The French, meanwhile, had embarked in September on what proved to be a disastrous campaign against the duchy of Guelders, military action driven entirely by the territorial interests in the Low Countries of Charles VI's uncle the duke of Burgundy. For his part, the young French king— who had once declared he preferred armor to treasure and a helmet to the crown—was as war obsessed as ever, but the embarrassing disintegration of yet another glorious expedition provoked him into listening at last to those at his court who resented the overbearing influence in government of his powerful uncles. On November 3, 1388, exactly a month before his twentieth birthday and eight years almost to the day since his coronation, Charles sat in majesty in the hall of the archbishop's palace at Reims and announced that he was ready to rule his kingdom in person. His uncles had been loyal and devoted guardians, but the time for guardianship was past. His minority was over, and their service in that capacity was no longer required. The stunned royal dukes found themselves summarily dismissed. Across the Channel, the king of England, who had always been conscious of the remarkable parallels between his own situation and that of the young French king, was paying close attention.[36]

At the palace of Westminster six months later, on May 3, 1389, Richard took his royal seat in the Marcolf Chamber, a room so called because its walls were painted with scenes from the popular tale of Solomon and Marcolf, a series of entertainingly instructive dialogues between the wise king and a quick-witted peasant. Dialogue, however, was not what Richard had in mind. Once all his nobles were assembled, he raised his voice to speak. He was, he said, of full age. He had had tutors before, but the need for them was past. For twelve years both his person and his kingdom had been in the control of others; now he would rule England himself as his predecessors had done. He began at once by dismissing Archbishop Arundel from office as chancellor, along with the treasurer and the keeper of the privy seal. From now on, all royal appointments—councillors, officers, members of the royal household—would be in his own hands. It was a remarkable move. A boy king who had never had a formal minority had become a twenty-two-year-old monarch rescuing himself from a crisis of his own making by declaring that his minority was finally at an end.[37]

It worked. His punch-drunk kingdom was eager—desperate—for some return to what might pass for normality. By pronouncing himself newly of age, Richard was distancing himself, rhetorically at least, from everything that had happened in the preceding years. He committed himself publicly, in proclamations made county by county, "to rule with deliberation of the council more prosperously than heretofore, to the greater peace of the people and fuller exhibition of justice," and promised to uphold the pardons he had previously granted, "no man being hereafter impeached for any act so pardoned." There were some for whom the restoration of royal authority by willed amnesia was profoundly unnerving, but—whatever Woodstock, Arundel, and Warwick might privately think—Richard's people chose to believe him.[38]

Of the two remaining Appellants, Mowbray threw himself into support for the king's reconstituted regime. But after three years of brutal experience in the front line of politics, Henry took another step back. Mary gave birth to their third child, a boy they named John after Henry's father, at Kenilworth on June 20, 1389, two days after a three-year truce with France was finally sealed at Leulinghem outside Calais. Then in November, Gaunt himself, who had left for Castile in 1386 as one of the most divisive figures in the realm, returned to England as an elder statesman, his hands clean of the dirty war that had taken place in his absence. When the duke made his way inland from Plymouth to Reading to attend a council meeting for the first time in three years, Richard came to meet him on the road, greeting him with a kiss of peace before taking the Lancastrian livery collar of interlinked silver-gilt *S*s from Gaunt's neck to place around his own as a sign of welcome. The duke's reunion with Henry was more private, more heartfelt, and, given the events of the last three years, even more complex. No one could be sure what Richard now intended, but one thing at least was clear. With Gaunt back to take care of his dynasty and his country, his heir was no longer required to stand guard.[39]

There was a world to explore, and this was an opportune time for exploration: a chance to put some greater distance between himself and the royal cousin with whom he had so recently been locked in bloody conflict. At twenty-two, and already the father of three young sons to continue the Lancastrian line, Henry found himself free to leave England's shores.

PART TWO
PEACE

Seven

1389-1393

this little world

For a knight like Henry who had good reason to go wandering, there were new challenges to pursue on the Continent as the war between England and France sputtered to a halt. The French king had grown into a young man of febrile physical energy, as enthused by the tournament as Henry was himself. From the moment he announced the start of his personal rule in November 1388, Charles had seized every opportunity for his court to throw itself into chivalric entertainments of the expansive and breathtakingly expensive kind in which he delighted. At the beginning of May 1389—in the same week as Henry sat in the Marcolf Chamber to hear Richard declare the end of his own minority—it seemed as though Camelot had risen again at Saint-Denis, five miles north of Paris. To mark the knighting of the king's young cousin Louis of Anjou, brave knights and esquires jousted for three days in lists specially constructed outside the great abbey that belonged to France's patron saint. By night they feasted and danced in a vast wooden hall purpose-built by the royal carpenters, hung inside with rich tapestries and cloth of gold that shimmered in the candlelight.[1]

Since negotiations for an Anglo-French truce were already in motion, invitations to the festivities were sent to London; but, since negotiations were not yet concluded, neither Henry nor any other English knight made the journey across the Channel. The only members of the English nobility to attend were already in France. Richard's beautiful sister Maud Holand, wife of the count of St. Pol, was first among the ladies dressed in jeweled green gowns who led the competitors in procession to the tournament and then joined the heralds in judging their prowess. More controversial was the presence of Robert de Vere, the dispossessed duke of Ireland, who, along with Michael de la Pole and Alexander Neville, had now shifted his place of exile from the Low Countries to Paris under the protection of the French crown, much to the English king's relief and gratitude.[2]

In the celebrations at Saint-Denis, King Charles and the new generation of nobles who surrounded him laid public claim to the military glories of France's past. A month later, however, the three-year truce sealed at Leulinghem brought the war between France and England to an official standstill. The military glory of the battlefield would have to wait. Instead, for the first time in decades, the greatest knights of the two kingdoms would have the chance to meet formally in the martial games that were the stuff of their shared chivalric culture—a degree of mutual understanding that had been emphasized in recent years by the discovery, at close quarters, of their differences with their respective allies in Scotland and Spain. In Castile in 1387, despite the hardships of the campaign, English and French captains had taken advantage of fleeting local truces to renew old acquaintances and to stage impromptu jousts. Now it was time for a spectacular contest.[3]

In the autumn of 1389, three French knights led by Jean Le Meingre, nicknamed "Boucicaut," a young nobleman almost exactly Henry's age, sent out heralds across Europe challenging all comers to meet them in jousts of peace and war—that is, with the deadly points of their lances capped or uncapped—at Saint-Inglevert, between English Calais and French Boulogne on the northern French coast. Boucicaut's reputation went before him. He had first gone to war as a boy of twelve in the service of the duke of Bourbon, the French king's maternal uncle. He was sixteen when he fought in Flanders at the battle of Rozebeke in 1382; eighteen when he campaigned in Prussia with the military order of Teutonic Knights against the pagan Lithuanians. Since then, he had not only confronted the English in France and Spain, but traveled to the great cities of Venice and Constantinople, to the courts of the Ottoman sultan and the king of Hungary, and to the Holy Land as a pilgrim. He was one of the brightest stars of European chivalry, and in the spring of 1390 more than a hundred English knights responded to his call.[4]

Among them were John Holand, the new earl of Huntingdon, and Thomas Mowbray, earl of Nottingham, but the brightest star of the English contingent was Henry of Bolingbroke, earl of Derby. In his retinue rode his seventeen-year-old half brother, John Beaufort—known to the French, in respectful recognition of his parentage, as "the Bastard of Lancaster"—and twenty-five-year-old "Harry Hotspur," Henry Percy, heir to the earl of Northumberland, who had been ransomed from his captivity in Scotland during the previous summer. But for all Hotspur's military fame, at the tournament it was Henry who shone.

Boucicaut and his companions were offering to face each challenger five times in the lists they set up in a wide meadow outside Saint-Inglevert's abbey, but Gaunt had written to the young knight to negotiate a special test for Henry. Boucicaut was so valiant a champion, the duke said, that he wished his son to learn from him. In Henry's case, would he graciously agree to run ten courses rather than five? It was an elegant rhetorical move, displaying the chivalric virtues of humility and courtesy by acknowledging Boucicaut's renown while simultaneously marking Henry out from the crowd as a challenger of special status.[5]

Gaunt was well aware of his son's abilities. All the same, there could be no cast-iron guarantee of Henry's safety in combat with a man of Boucicaut's caliber. On March 21, 1390, the three French champions began their month-long residence in their splendid pavilions at Saint-Inglevert, attended by an eager company of knights and squires, heralds and minstrels. On the lower branches of a great elm in front of the camp hung a horn and six wooden shields, two for each champion, one representing the joust of peace, the other the joust of war. Henry and his friends, like all the contenders, were required to blow the horn to summon their opponents, then strike the relevant shield of the man they wished to fight. It was the challengers' decision whether or not to use sharpened lances, and Boucicaut's specially adopted motto— "What you will"—gestured at their right to choose, with his own stylish compound of courtesy and cool self-assurance. In such gallant company, who could opt for blunted arms without showing himself a coward?[6]

In the first days of fighting, blows were struck and blood drawn. John Holand, who had been first of the English knights to arrive, had a bruising encounter with Boucicaut that won him admiring attention, although not as much as the French champions themselves, whose courage, skill, and stamina in running course after course after course—taking on even more bouts to cover for one another whenever the hits they sustained required some hours of rest or medical attention—left onlookers open-mouthed in wonder. But, as Gaunt had intended, among the challengers it was Henry, one of the last to fight, who made his name. Boucicaut was only a few months older but vastly more experienced on the battlefield, an athlete who trained so hard for strength and speed that, despite his small stature, it was said he could vault onto his warhorse in full armor without putting his foot in the stirrup. In the lists, Henry faced him twice as many times as any other knight, their coursers' hooves thudding into the earth, lances braced for the shuddering impact, razor-sharp steel striking sparks from helmet, shield, and breastplate. He emerged unhurt, unbeaten, and unrivaled, the French agreed, in his bravery and the largesse of the gifts he lavished on his hosts.[7]

For Henry himself, the meeting was a revelation. He had jousted many times in England at court entertainments or celebrations in his father's household. He had been to war in Scotland as part of the fractured, fractious English army of 1385, and had commanded troops in England during the desperate conflict with Richard in 1387. Through it all, his talent for friendship and leadership had been evident. Among his small and close-knit company now were not only John Beaufort and Harry Percy but Henry's childhood companion and almost-stepbrother Thomas Swynford, as well as a formidable soldier named Thomas Rempston who had served on his father's campaign in Castile. But Saint-Inglevert was a taste of a different world: a brotherhood-in-arms resilient and capacious enough to contain the rivalries of knights and the enmities of kingdoms, a collective culture in which honor—the greatest prize of all—had to be earned, not simply demanded as a birthright. As Boucicaut's admiring biographer would later note, "it is deeds, not words, that make the man."[8]

And Henry, like Boucicaut, was not willing to rest on laurels he had already won. The two young men spent time together at the dinner table in

Boucicaut's pavilion, time in which their mutual respect in the lists became friendship, and a determination to dedicate their sword arms together to the service of God. Crusading was the dream of all good Christian knights, even if in recent years it had been co-opted as a weapon for the schismatic popes in Rome and Avignon to aim at each other. As Henry knew all too well after the ignominious end of Bishop Despenser's efforts in Flanders, there was little glory to be found in the technicalities of Pope Urban's "crusades." But Boucicaut, young as he was, had already taken the field against the infidel, and Henry was intent on matching him. Now that their own countries were no longer at war, the new friends planned to fight the enemies of Christ wherever they threatened the frontiers of Christian Europe. The duke of Bourbon was preparing a campaign to defend the Mediterranean against the Muslim pirates of the North African coast by wresting control of their base at the port of Mahdia, a little more than a hundred miles southeast of Tunis, from the Hafsid caliphate. Boucicaut proposed to join the duke's forces, and Henry decided to go with him.[9]

He returned to England for two weeks to gather a company of 120 men-at-arms and archers, then sailed back to Calais on May 9, sending ahead to Paris to request a safe-conduct for his journey south to meet Bourbon's fleet at Marseilles. But King Charles was not keen to see either of the heroes of Saint-Inglevert commit themselves to his uncle's crusade. He had a magnificent plan of his own to lead a French army into Italy to pursue the hereditary claim of his cousin Louis of Anjou to the kingdom of Naples, reinstall Pope Clement in place of the usurper Urban in Rome, and establish France as the dominant power throughout the Italian peninsula. He had no wish meanwhile to see his champion Boucicaut disappear over the horizon to Africa, nor—with the ink so recently dry on the Anglo-French truce—to allow the son of John of Gaunt to ride unsupervised at the head of an armed retinue through the heartlands of his kingdom.

Rapid recalculation was required. So be it: if Henry could not reach the southern frontier of Christendom to fight against Islam in the heat of North Africa, he would sail east to join the Teutonic Knights in the damp of Lithuania. The Teutonic Knights—the German military brotherhood of St. Mary's Hospital, Jerusalem—had been founded in Acre around 1190, in emulation of the monastic orders of Knights Hospitaller and Knights Templar established in the wake of the First Crusade almost a hundred years earlier. Over the following decades, the German knights' field of operation had begun to shift from the Holy Land to the Baltic, and the campaign there to convert the pagan Prussians to Christianity. By the end of the thirteenth century, their base at Acre had fallen to the Mamluk sultan; instead, they controlled the newly Christian lordship of Prussia, from where they declared a crusade of conversion, of Christianization at the point of a sword, against the pagans of Lithuania. It was a crusade in which, during the fourteenth century, knights from all over Christian Europe flocked to participate. For Henry, a voyage to Prussia—which had been in his thoughts in any case, as a second expedition after Bourbon's campaign against the Berber corsairs— was a chance to follow in the footsteps not only of his friend Boucicaut but of a distinguished line of English knights who had fought there, from Hotspur in 1383 all the way back to his own Lancastrian grandfather Henry of Grosmont in 1351–52.[10]

Now he brought forward his plans. After a thwarted month in Calais, he returned to England in early June, moving north via the Lancastrian castles at Hertford, Leicester, and Bolingbroke to spend time with his father and his wife and sons on his way to the eastern port of Boston in Lincolnshire. There two great ships were being prepared, loaded with everything Henry and his military household would need for three weeks at sea before their landing on the Baltic coast: hardware for cooking, riding, and fighting; coffers of clothes and coin; vast stores of food, from salted meat and fish to aniseed and almonds, verjuice and sugar syrup; barrels of ale and Gascon wine; cages full of live chickens; and a tapestry, altar, and hammock for Henry's newly wainscoted cabin.[11]

Thanks to the gold his father had brought back from Castile, there was no need to worry about funds for this extraordinary enterprise. The Lancastrians now stood among the very richest noble houses in Europe. Time spent with his family also offered a reminder that other anxieties were no longer required. His eldest son, Henry, was almost four, and Thomas almost three, while John had just turned one. Mary was pregnant again, and would give birth for a fourth time in the autumn. Gaunt—in fine health at the age of fifty—was back in England, with no intention of leaving. The dynasty was in safe hands, and his boys represented its future. Should the worst somehow happen, Henry was replaceable. That meant he was at liberty to test himself, to push beyond his known horizons to discover what he might achieve with a sword in his hand and friends at his side.

His brother John Beaufort was not with him. The Bastard of Lancaster, as opposed to the heir, was no threat to the kingdom of France, and unlike Henry he had been given permission to make his way to Marseilles to join Bourbon's North African crusade. But other close friends joined Henry at Boston: Thomas Swynford and Thomas Rempston, both fresh from the triumph at Saint-Inglevert, the latter named his standard-bearer; his chamberlain Hugh Waterton, along with Waterton's older brother, John, and younger cousin Robert; his chaplain Hugh Herley; and Sir Thomas Erpingham, a veteran of the French war and of Gaunt's Castilian campaign, who now moved from the duke's service into Henry's household. Erpingham and Hugh Waterton were senior figures, more than ten years older than Henry, and had known him since he was a child, but they were not there to supervise or instruct. Instead, they were traveling under his command and putting their talents and experience at his disposal. Altogether, it was a superbly equipped retinue of more than seventy knights, esquires, valets, grooms, officers, and musicians who boarded the two vessels at Boston. The ships were piloted by a team of lodesmen under the highly paid command of two skilled captains from Danzig, the port belonging to the Teutonic Knights for which they were headed. On July 19, 1390, under a blue sky, Henry and his men set sail at last for the adventures of war.[12]

Richard was congratulating himself on war averted. In January 1390, a parliament had met for the first time since the sealing of the truce with France and his own declaration that he had reached his majority. Given recent history, it was a remarkable assembly—calm, conciliatory, and constructive—in which Richard seemed intent on signaling his commitment to a fresh start in his own government. Although the king "had always had the good will to govern his people in quiet, peace and tranquility, right and justice," said the bishop of Winchester as chancellor in his opening speech, "he now had a greater and better intent and firm purpose to govern his said people and his land well, as well as he could." As Richard looked on benignly, the chancellor, treasurer, and members of the council he had appointed the previous May then offered their resignation, and asked that if anyone wished to accuse them of committing any offense in the discharge of their offices they should speak now, here, to the king in parliament. The Commons requested time to think, and when they returned said they had no complaint but wanted to thank the councillors for their praiseworthy service. After this ritualized performance, and to general acclaim, Richard reappointed them to their posts before adding his uncles—the previously absent Gaunt and the previously estranged Woodstock—to their number.[13]

The same unfamiliar lack of contention greeted other nominations and promotions the king chose to make as the parliament went on. In late February, Richard's brother, Gaunt's son-in-law John Holand, was named chamberlain of the royal household. A few days later, Edward, the seventeen-year-old son and heir of the king's loyally ineffective uncle Langley, was created earl of Rutland. On March 2, Rutland's title was formally confirmed, along with the grant of an estate worth more than £500 a year, and on the same day Richard made Gaunt duke of Aquitaine for the term of his life. Such reinforcement of the standing and influence of the king's blood relatives, as opposed to his friends of the last decade, appeared to be an uncontroversial good that his parliament was happy to endorse. Meanwhile, formidable challenges lay ahead if a permanent peace with France were to be negotiated during this time of truce—challenges to which the status of Aquitaine, whether in Gaunt's hands or Richard's, would be central—but for the moment the Commons were pleased not to be confronted with a demand for direct taxation. Instead, they renewed their grant to the king of the revenues from customs duties, and agreed to remit to the consideration of the king and council their ongoing concern about the threat to law and order posed by the nobles' distribution of livery badges.[14]

In May, once the parliament was over, the king and council did produce an ordinance that sought to restrict the circumstances in which lords could give their retainers liveries of clothing to wear, and also made stern noises about the grievous harm done by those in noble retinues who attempted to exert undue influence on the operation of royal justice. It was a gesture, a promise kept; but the reality was that—given the complexity of local disputes, the adversarial processes of the courts, and the necessary involvement of local landowners in enforcing the king's law—the difference between justice properly supported and justice improperly overborne often lay in the eye of the beholder. Gentlemen who complained vociferously about the powerful backing their opponents could invoke in any conflict wasted no time in the search for equally powerful intervention of their own. The lords had no intention of abdicating their authority over their retainers and the wider local networks that formed their affinities; and while those retinues and affinities remained in existence, the gentry would continue to find places within them by offering service in return for the many benefits of "good lordship."[15]

In theory, the king's unique authority made him the "good lord of all good lords," the man who stood at the apex of every hierarchy, formal and informal, public and private, with all the resources of his kingdom at his command. But back in the dark days of 1387 and 1388 Richard had found himself constrained and defeated by the military power of five of his greatest nobles. In that moment, he had discovered that, with the exception of the men of his earldom of Chester, he could not simply summon up a retinue of his own at will, out of thin air. Attempting to sprinkle crown-shaped badges across the regions of his realm had done nothing to activate a ready-made army looking only to their king for leadership. Since then, he had lost the advisers he could trust without question. Not only had Simon Burley been taken from him in the most public and brutal way but news reached London that Michael de la Pole, by then in his early sixties, had died in exile in Paris in September 1389. Richard was biding his time on the question of de Vere's return to England, and his current companions—the turncoat Thomas Mowbray, the volatile John Holand, and the teenage Edward of Rutland—were poor replacements for the man whose company he valued above all others. But one project on which he could immediately embark was that of creating a retinue of the kind he had lacked in 1387: followers who, whatever the future might hold, would stand ready whenever he might call on them.[16]

For the mark of the new livery he planned to distribute, the image the

king chose was a white hart. It seemed appropriate in multiple ways: a graceful echo of the white hind that had been his mother's badge, and a nod—as
a "rich" (that is, noble) "hart"—to his own name. If there were parallels with
the winged stag that was already an emblem of his brother-in-sovereignty
the king of France, that too was fitting. Charles's white hart, like Richard's,
wore a golden crown around its neck, but it sprang into the sky—as it had in
a royal dream, Froissart explained—with its feathered wings lifted in flight.
Richard's hart, by contrast, sat serene and still, a golden chain falling from
the crown that formed its collar, its fine-boned head and majestic antlers
elegantly raised. In the purity of its luminous hide and the patience of its
submission to both crown and chain, it spoke of Christ-like holiness, and
devotion to divinely ordained authority as manifested both in heaven and
on earth.[17]

This new sign of Richard's kingship was put to public use for the first
time in October 1390 at the English court's answer to the recent flowering
of chivalry in France. Detailed reports had reached London of the lavish
entertainments at Saint-Denis in May 1389, and the celebrations that accompanied the coronation three months later of Charles's new young queen,
Isabeau of Bavaria. The following spring, John Holand and Thomas Mowbray returned from Saint-Inglevert with tales of the glory won by those who
had responded to Boucicaut's challenge. Richard's England would not be
outdone. That summer, heralds carried a royal proclamation to France, the
Low Countries, Germany, and Scotland: an invitation to a great contest of
arms in London, where brave knights would joust and feast and King Richard would bestow prizes on the most worthy.[18]

Richard had no intention of taking up arms himself. He was well aware
that in Paris a year earlier, at the tournament that followed the French
queen's coronation, the knights who wore the royal device of the golden
sun—including the exiled Robert de Vere—had been led into the lists by
twenty-year-old King Charles. To precisely no one's surprise, the king was
then awarded the prize for the first day's combat—but, as the chronicler
at the abbey of Saint-Denis noted, reactions to this show of prowess were
far from unanimous. While some applauded Charles's valor and his willingness to engage in chivalric camaraderie, others thought his participation

unworthy of his sovereign dignity. That criticism was not one Richard proposed to incur. The majesty of his throne was inviolable, the security of his royal person paramount. His kingship was not constituted by his actions; it lay in his very being. He would sit in splendor while his champions fought, and they would display their allegiance to his crown by bearing his white hart on their shields.[19]

The lists were built on the great open ground of Smithfield, where Wat Tyler had died and Richard had taken command of his rebellious people. This, however, was an entirely different expression of his kingship. On Sunday, October 10, a gorgeous procession made its way west from the Tower through London's streets. First came the warhorses, armed for the tourney, each ridden at walking pace by a squire; then, on their palfreys, the ladies of the court in matching gowns, each leading a steel-clad knight by a silver chain; and everywhere, on horse harness and coat armor and rich folds of drapery, were Richard's white harts, glittering with gold thread. The king himself, with Queen Anne at his side, took his lofty place in the decorated stands to receive them.[20]

The honors that day, as judged at the feast that night, went to the two combatants closest in blood to the king: Richard's half brother John Holand for the English champions, and his brother-in-law the count of St. Pol for the challengers. The next day, Richard appeared among his lords wearing superb armor as a sign of his leadership of the defending knights. This time, the prize was awarded to the newly arrived count of Ostrevant, son of the duke of Bavaria, who had jousted at Queen Isabeau's coronation in Paris a year earlier and now made an ideal witness to the grandeur of England's response. On Wednesday, October 13, when the fighting was done, the king celebrated the feast of England's royal saint Edward the Confessor by appearing at mass in Westminster Abbey, sitting in the choir surrounded by his chaplains near the Confessor's holy shrine, his jeweled crown glimmering on his royal head. That evening, when his guests gathered for another sumptuous meal, the king and queen again sat enthroned in their crowns, a solemn embodiment of majesty, "to demonstrate his excellent kingship to these foreigners," one chronicler noted.[21]

It was a demonstration that seemed to be paying off. When his sister and her husband had arrived from Paris, their splendid entourage included not only heralds, minstrels, and 200 horsemen but King Charles's private secretary, carrying newly generous terms for a permanent peace that might be discussed by the two sovereigns in person, the French proposed, at a conference to be arranged for the following year. It seemed to Richard that Charles, like him, understood the futility of continuing a conflict that neither side could win, as well as the royal freedom to be gained by escape from the endless pressure to launch military campaigns that cost fortunes and achieved nothing. His uncle Gaunt, who hosted an opulent dinner at the end of the week's festivities, supported these efforts to end the war. His uncle Woodstock and the earl of Arundel did not; but that, pleasingly, mattered little.[22]

Behind closed doors, however, what mattered most to Richard was the future of his beloved de Vere. In 1389 the young man had been welcomed by King Charles as a novel presence at the French court, but as Froissart archly remarked, "Nowadays is there nothing of which one does not tire?" Royal boredom was nudged along its path by Enguerrand de Coucy, whose political influence and military distinction were matched only by his rage at his faithless former son-in-law, whose mistreatment of his daughter he could not forgive. By the end of 1390, de Vere found himself left with no choice but to move on from France to seek shelter farther north, in the duchy of Brabant. With Alexander Neville trailing in his wake, he took up residence near the great cloth-making city of Louvain, fifteen miles east of Brussels. Richard knew that for the moment he could take no direct action to rescue his friend, but in the spring of 1391, de Vere's mother quietly crossed the Channel to pay her son a visit, bringing counsel from England and gifts to sustain him in his banishment. That March, Richard himself commissioned a handbook of geomancy, the practice of divination using a system of sixteen "figures" formed from the random placement of dots on parchment or paper—a science, many believed, founded on the same essential mathematical and cosmological principles as astronomy and astrology. The exquisitely illuminated volume was made, its preface explained, "for the consolation and by the special request" of the king, who was already adept enough in geomantic methods not to require the inclusion within the manuscript of any basic instructions. He kept to himself the questions he hoped to answer, but the compiler of the volume deferentially noted his own cryptic wish for the return of "the innocent exile." Richard, it seemed, was playing a long game, looking to couple the military strength of a new retinue with the power of arcane knowledge. As the preface pointed out, "*Vir sapiens dominabitur astris*": "the wise man will be master of the stars."[23]

Barely three years since the horrors of the Merciless Parliament, he had reason to feel satisfied with his achievements. De Vere, if not yet home, was at least safe in Brabant, and in London he, Richard, had reconstructed the magnificent theater of his kingship, freshly adorned with his badge of the white hart. He knew he could rely on the quiet encouragement of his queen and the powerful backing of his uncle Gaunt. The Appellants' unholy confederacy had disintegrated, and the war with France—the catalyst of so much discord in his realm, so much illegitimate dissent—was nearly over. He had a great deal still to do, but the authority that should always have been his was close at hand, almost there for the taking.

On October 20, 1390, a week after Richard's jousts at Smithfield had come to their lavish conclusion, Henry and his tired men arrived back in Königsberg, a prosperous port belonging to the Teutonic Knights that lay seventy-five miles eastward along the Baltic coast from Danzig. During the previous two months, they had fought doggedly through grueling terrain farther to the north and east—the dense forests and boggy marshes of Samogitia, the "wilderness" of Lithuania—to join the Order's forces in a siege of the city of Vilnius. There was cognitive dissonance of a kind involved in this *reyse* (as the Prussian campaigns were known), since the Lithuanian king, whose brother and lieutenant was installed in command of Vilnius, had finally converted to Christianity four years earlier when he married the reigning queen of Catholic Poland. But the momentum of more than a century of war on this frontier of the Christian world could not be halted so easily, and, whatever their king and his brother now professed, the people of Samogitia still held to their pagan beliefs. Henry and his band of military pilgrims faced no crisis of conscience as they hurled themselves into the fight.[24]

There were losses to be borne—one of Henry's knights was killed and two more captured, including his standard-bearer Thomas Rempston—and by the time the advancing autumn forced the Order and its fellow crusaders to turn back, the stone-built citadel of Vilnius still stood against them. But prisoners and plunder had been taken, bravery displayed, and honor won, in exploits that grew as the tale was told and retold on its long journey west. By the time news of the campaign reached Westminster, the abbey's chronicler was convinced not only that Vilnius had fallen, but that the first standard had been raised on its walls by Henry's own hand. Henry himself was happy to reward the English man-at-arms who, in fact rather than breathless report, had succeeded in planting a flag on the city's outer fortifications, and to return to Königsberg before the waterlogged wilderness became impassable once again.[25]

Exhaustion and a damp chill in the bones were mixed with adrenaline-fueled exhilaration, the physical knowledge of battles fought in a noble cause; and winter comforts were the Englishmen's reward. They faced weeks of waiting to discover whether another brief campaign would be possible in the new year, if the ground were frozen hard enough to allow the movement of men and horses, but the snow not too deep and the cold not life-threatening. For now, they settled into warm lodgings stocked with excellent food and wine, and wrapped themselves in furs of squirrel, marten, and beaver, all bankrolled by Gaunt's Castilian treasure.[26]

At the beginning of November, while diplomatic work continued in the attempt to retrieve the captured men, good news arrived from England: on October 3, while Henry was camped in the mud outside Vilnius, Mary had given birth to their fourth son, named Humphrey after her late father. A household already in high spirits threw itself into celebration. Henry and his friends spent their days jousting, hunting, and hawking, their evenings feasting and gambling at dice—his favorite game—while musicians played and acrobats tumbled. They had won the respect of their hosts, whose Grand Master presented Henry with a gift of some fine falcons and sent his own physician to attend him when he was briefly unwell. Meanwhile, Henry took care to demonstrate the Christian purpose of their mission by worshiping at Königsberg's new brick-built cathedral, giving alms to the needy, and providing for a number of Lithuanian women and children he had bought or captured and brought to the city for conversion to the true faith.[27]

In January 1391, once the cheer of Christmas was over, it became clear that the weather would not permit a winter *reyse*. Henry and his men were going home. On February 9, they left Königsberg, carts and horses corralled into a grand baggage train, for Danzig, the biggest port under the Knights' control. There they rented a comfortable town house while two ships were prepared and two German skippers recruited, this time with pilots from Boston to guide them into the English coast. They sailed on March 31, a week after Henry had marked his twenty-fourth birthday. When they landed safely at Hull at the end of April, he rode twenty-five miles north to the great Augustinian priory of Bridlington to offer thanks at the tomb of John of Thwing, Bridlington's prior until his death eleven years earlier, a man of such holiness that miracles were regularly reported at his grave. At last, on May 13, Henry arrived at Bolingbroke Castle to be reunited with Mary and his boys, and to meet his new son for the first time.[28]

In his nine months away, he had missed the grandest chivalric gathering his country had seen in decades, the Smithfield festival of arms at which he might have been expected to excel but which Richard had conspicuously chosen to stage in his absence. The reason for that absence, however, had elevated his reputation into another league. This fine young man, the grandson of a great king and the heir to a great duchy, had proved himself not only a brave and skillful competitor in the lists but a leader of men in defense of Christendom, a devout and honorable crusader whose name, one chronicler wrote, was now "on everyone's lips." On his return he took the politic decision to associate himself with the new style of his cousin's court, ordering a red velvet "pair of plates"—an armored jacket—and a matching pair of sleeves all embroidered with the white harts of Richard's livery. But this display of sartorial loyalty was quickly subsumed within a spectacular new wardrobe to match his growing fame. As the months went by, Henry jousted in exquisite Milanese armor and dressed, when the contests were done, in robes of fur-lined taffeta, satin, brocade, and velvet. Every outfit was richly jeweled and gorgeously embellished, and across the fabric of gowns, belts, and sleeves trailed forget-me-nots, intricately worked flowers and silver-gilt leaves in visual representation of his motto, *Souvenez-Vous de Moi*: Remember Me.[29]

Gaunt had not won the crown he wanted, but it was clear that he could rejoice in his dynasty's future as a political force on the European stage, embodied in his daughters, the queens of Portugal and Castile, and in the charismatic person of his son. Crusading in Prussia, Boucicaut's biographer said, was the desire of "all those valiant knights who hope to improve their standing," and in the spring of 1391 a key part of such knights' ambition was to rival the achievements of the Lancastrian heir. While Henry settled back into life at home in England, the English nobles heading in the other direction included the lords Clifford, Beaumont, Bourchier, Despenser, and Fitzwalter. A year earlier, Clifford and Beaumont had jousted alongside Henry at Saint-Inglevert against Boucicaut, whom they encountered again at Königsberg, preparing to fight in the summer *reyse*. The most prominent figure to request leave from the king to travel to Prussia, however, was Henry's uncle and brother-in-law Thomas of Woodstock, duke of Gloucester.[30]

Woodstock's was a flamboyantly public departure, a statement of his own noble purpose made by a profoundly unsatisfied man. While a residual current of popular opinion still looked to him as a champion of good government, Gaunt's return from Castile in 1389 had put paid to any lingering hope Woodstock might have had that his leadership of the resistance to Richard in 1386–88 might somehow result in a permanently enhanced role in his nephew's regime. Over the last two years his military reputation had been eclipsed by another nephew, Henry, with whom he was still in dispute about the division of their wives' inheritance, while every birth that took place in the family's next generation displaced him further in the line of royal succession: by the end of the summer of 1391, Mary was pregnant again, as was the wife of the young earl of March, heir to the bloodline of Lionel of Antwerp. For Woodstock, in the short term at least, campaigning with the Teutonic Knights appeared to be a plan with few drawbacks, if it allowed him to leave the country while enhancing his good name. He announced his intention at a council meeting in September, and received the king's license to travel east for the winter *reyse*.[31]

Before he left England the duke presented Westminster Abbey with a set of vestments of red cloth of gold and black velvet embroidered with the monogram "TA"—his own initial and that of his wife, Eleanor ("Alianora")—as well as their badge of a swan, inherited from her father, worked in gleaming pearls. But the gift did nothing to secure the success of the voyage. Autumn storms broke up his little fleet and several ships foundered, along with the men, horses, and costly supplies they carried. The duke himself tried to reach safety on the coasts of Denmark and Norway before turning back in desperation toward Scotland. Finally, just before Christmas, he made landfall at Bamburgh in Northumberland. An expedition begun with elaborate fanfare had ended in loss, embarrassment, and renewed frustration.[32]

His uncle's failure only served to emphasize Henry's success: his easy charisma, his ability to combine friendship with command, and the capacity to make his own luck through intelligent preparation and skillful execution that every successful leader required. Now he wanted more: more experience of war, and of companionship in arms; more exposure to new landscapes and cultures; more purpose in the service of God. And it was also clear—at least, if his father's current rapprochement with Richard was anything to go by—that an extended absence from England offered the best chance of patching up his strained relationship with his cousin. Already in the winter of 1391 Henry was planning a return to Prussia. He and Mary spent Christmas at Hertford with Gaunt and their growing family. Then, at their home at Peterborough in the spring of 1392, Mary gave birth to their first daughter, named Blanche after the mother he had barely known. At the christening the baby's two oldest brothers, five-year-old Henry and four-year-old Thomas, solemnly wore their new silver-gilt collars of linked *S*s, the livery of their Lancastrian grandfather. But preparations for their father's departure were soon under way at the Norfolk port of King's Lynn: three ships this time, with carpenters at work building cabins for the distinguished passengers, and the crane on the dock in constant motion as barrel upon barrel of provisions were winched on board. On July 24, Henry and his men sailed again for Danzig—only to find, when they reached Königsberg at the beginning of September, that a treaty had derailed the season's campaigning.[33]

Henry was not inclined simply to retrace his steps. Turning back would allow him neither to serve his faith nor to keep his distance from Richard. If he could not fight, he would continue as a pilgrim traveling in peace. He sent home his armor and most of his military retinue, and turned south with a smaller group of companions, officers, and servants including his chamberlain

Hugh Waterton, his chaplain Hugh Herley, and the distinguished knight Thomas Erpingham. Instead of a return to the forests and swamps of Samogitia, this would be a tour of discovery and diplomacy through the Continent and the Mediterranean. Their journey would range over 2,000 miles by land and sea to a city in which even the illustrious crusading kings of England—the lionhearted Richard I, and Henry's own great-great-grandfather Edward I— had never set foot. He was going to Jerusalem.[34]

First there were the courts of Europe, where Henry's name and fame— advertised by freshly painted arms displayed outside his lodgings whenever the small convoy stopped on the road—secured them a princely welcome. In Prague, they were entertained by Wenzel, king of Bohemia, the half brother of the English queen. In Austria as guests of the Habsburg duke, Henry took the opportunity to cross the Danube to meet another of Anne's brothers, Sigismund, king of Hungary. From Vienna they took the road southwest, their baggage carts rumbling with difficulty through the steep and icy grandeur of the eastern Alps, to reach Venice, the maritime superpower of the eastern Mediterranean, at the beginning of December. There Henry was received in sumptuous state by the doge and senate, and given the use of a galley for his onward journey. While the hull was fitted with the necessary cabins and stores of food, paid for with a transfer of funds arranged by Gaunt through the Florentine bank of the Alberti family, the travelers explored the glittering city, a breathtaking metropolis on the freezing lagoon, and made offerings beneath the shimmering domes of St. Mark's Basilica.

Just before Christmas, everything was ready. During another month at sea along the Adriatic coast and into the eastern Mediterranean, they put into port every week or so, at Corfu, Rhodes, and elsewhere, to buy wine, bread, olive oil, herbs, eggs, and fresh fish. It was late January before they reached the Holy Land, where the ruling Mamluk sultanate tolerated both a permanent Christian presence and the visits of Christian pilgrims. In Jerusalem, for the first time in his life, Henry's name opened no doors at the highest political level. But the friars of Mount Zion, where the apostles had shared the Last Supper and received the gift of the Holy Spirit, recognized his standing. To them he presented a set of antiphonaries, volumes of liturgical music gloriously illuminated by the Sienese painter Andrea di Bartolo, which he had bought on his journey through Italy. Otherwise, like the rest of the faithful, Henry and his friends made their way on foot to the sacred sites of Christ's passion, among them the Church of the Holy Sepulchre, built around Christ's tomb in the very place of the crucifixion and the resurrection, and outside the city the Mount of Olives, where the risen savior had ascended in glory to heaven. There was a tariff of indulgences—of time in purgatory remitted—simply for the act of setting foot in those hallowed places, just as surely as there was for wielding a sword against the pagan and the infidel. But even these calculations of spiritual benefit were overwhelmed by the sheer intensity of spiritual experience, of intimately familiar objects of devotion made suddenly real in soil and sky and stone.[35]

The galley waited at the port of Jaffa for their return voyage. They sailed via Cyprus and Rhodes to Venice, arriving in plenty of time to celebrate Easter and to buy furs, rich fabric, and goldsmiths' work to be packed into coffers for the journey home. From there they rode to Padua, Verona, Milan, and Turin, over the alpine pass of Mont Cenis where snow lay on the high ground even in May, and on into France for a brief, dazzling visit to Paris before Calais and the crossing to Dover. All along the way their encounters with princes and dignitaries continued, from the king of Cyprus and the Grand Master of the Knights Hospitaller in Rhodes to Gian Galeazzo Visconti, lord of Milan, who took Henry to Pavia to show him the tombs of Saint Augustine, the philosopher Boethius, and his own uncle Lionel of Antwerp. In Paris he was welcomed by the dukes of Berry and Burgundy, the most powerful noblemen in France, who knew his father well. If these were glamorous hosts, Henry was a glamorous visitor. Gian Galeazzo's young cousin Lucia Visconti would later say—albeit in the context of accepting another marriage proposal—that if she could have been certain of becoming Henry's wife, she would have waited for him "to the very end of her life, even if she knew she would die three days after the wedding."[36]

Henry reached London on July 5, 1393, almost a year after his ships had slipped away from the Norfolk coast. He had served God as a crusader in the Lithuanian wilderness and as a pilgrim in the holiest places on earth. With some of his closest friends, men whose company he loved and whose judgment he trusted, he had journeyed through unfamiliar lands, breathed different air, seen extraordinary wonders. He had done so as the heir to a great dynasty, meeting princes and rulers across Europe. Though his personal relationship with his own king was strained, his loyalty to the English crown—a crown to which, while Richard remained childless, Henry and his father stood in close proximity—could not be doubted. He was a loving husband to a noble wife who had given him five healthy children, four of them boys, to continue the Lancastrian line. He had wealth, power, honor, and renown, and in his baggage train he brought home an Italian parrot for Mary, an ostrich from Bohemia, and a cheetah trained for the hunt, a present from the king of Cyprus, which traveled on board ship in a specially built cabin and overland in a cage drawn by two horses.[37]

By the beginning of September, he was back with his family at Peterborough, enfolded in the music, books, prayers, and warmth with which he and Mary filled their home. Only a few weeks later, they knew that she was pregnant again. It seemed that Henry was a man who had everything.[38]

Eight

1391-1394

to be a make-peace

Others did not enjoy such blessings. In the summer of 1390, while Henry was away in Prussia and Lithuania, harvests in England had been poor for the first time in years, and that winter scarcity of grain and high prices pressed hard on people all across the country. "You might see babies and children on the roads and in their houses crying and clamouring with hunger," wrote the chronicler Henry Knighton, "and begging for bread, and their mothers with none to break for them." In the west and the north, food shortages were compounded by a calamitous outbreak of plague; but in London the mayor and citizens set to work to mitigate suffering by using funds available to the city government to buy foodstuffs to sell at fixed prices to those in need. "And those who could not then afford the money could pledge to pay within the following year," Knighton reported, "and thus they were relieved, and no one perished of hunger."[1]

The politics of the capital could never be described as serene, but they were quieter now than during the knife-edge tensions of the 1380s. After the frightening events of 1386–88—compounded by the Londoners' refusal to rise against the Appellants as Richard had demanded, and their subsequent entanglement in the trial and execution of Nicholas Brembre—the mood in the city was cautious and watchful. The truce with France had eased fears about the security of the realm and the costs of defense, but confidence in the king's restored independence and in his displays of magnanimity remained brittle. The delicacy of the détente between Richard and his subjects had been apparent in the parliament that met in November 1390, an assembly that was almost eerily uneventful by the standards of the last decade, apart from a further renewal of the grant of customs duties to the crown and a curious, stiffly worded petition: the lords and Commons humbly begged the king that his regality and prerogative should "be forever saved and preserved," and that anything "done or attempted to the contrary" should be "redressed and amended." A year later, in November 1391, another parliament made another version of the same entreaty, with the added stipulation that any statute or ordinance to the contrary, including those made in the time of the king's deposed great-grandfather, Edward II, should be annulled. On both occasions, Richard was graciously pleased to agree to requests that could hardly have dovetailed more closely with his own priorities had he drafted them himself and had them proposed in parliament as a put-up job—which, seasoned observers concluded, was exactly what had happened.[2]

But if the king was preoccupied with performative restatements of his own sovereignty, the mayor and citizens of London had more immediately practical concerns. For decades the crown had looked to the merchants of the capital, both as individuals and as a civic body, as a source of loans to ease governmental cash flow, especially at times when parliamentary taxes had been granted but not yet collected. By 1391, however, circumstances appeared to the Londoners to have changed. The king was no longer fighting an expensive war. Not only had his costs decreased, but in the autumn of 1390 he had found the money for the most spectacular chivalric entertainments yet seen in the capital since he came to the throne. Meanwhile, the city of London was spending significant amounts in the attempt to stop its poorest inhabitants dying of starvation. By the beginning of 1392, it was clear that during the previous twelve months neither the city nor a single one of its merchants had proved willing to furnish the king with a loan of any kind.[3]

Richard was well aware that his capital city had lent substantial sums to his enemies while they were in control of his government: £4,000 to the council imposed on him in 1386, and £5,000 to the Appellants' regime during the Merciless Parliament of 1388. Since then, all of his own requests for a corporate loan had been refused, while lending by individual Londoners had tailed away to nothing. If this seemed like rank disloyalty, insult was added to injury by a case heard in the court of Chancery in December 1391, in which one William Mildenhall of London acknowledged that he had failed to report his late father to the authorities for saying that the king was unfit to govern, and—reports of Richard's luxurious taste in bathrooms having apparently reached the ears of his subjects—that he should stay in his latrine for the rest of his days. Mildenhall was allowed to go free in exchange for a promise, on pain of a large fine, that he would declare to the king and council any such unlawful and abusive words he might hear in future. But Richard's public forgiveness did not mean that he would forget. Nor would he tolerate disobedience of more physically disruptive kinds. Just before Christmas, he issued an order to the mayor and sheriffs that the city's inhabitants should not bear arms or assemble illegally, since he had heard that those who "lurk and run about in divers places within the city and suburbs committing assaults, mayhems, robberies, manslaughters etc" were preventing London's officials from doing their duty, "which the king will not and ought not to endure." In the painstaking process of rebuilding his rightful authority, he would keep a close eye on both talk and action in his recalcitrant capital.[4]

In the meantime, Richard had come to a momentous decision: he was ready to raise the question of de Vere's return. His opportunity came during a five-day meeting of his great council in February 1392, nearly a year after Richard had commissioned his handbook of geomancy and four years almost to the day since de Vere and Archbishop Neville had been found guilty of treason in their absence by the Merciless Parliament. His councillors—the lords spiritual and temporal, including the former Appellants Woodstock, Arundel, Mowbray, and, in the interval between his expeditions abroad, Henry—had no warning of the question the king intended to lay before them. Instead, they were there to talk about the war: to consider the state of negotiations with France, four months before the three-year truce of 1389 was due to expire. In that time, little progress had been made toward a permanent peace. The personal meeting between the two kings mooted by the French in 1390 had not taken place; the memories of Richard's secret communications with France in 1387 were still raw enough for the English lords to fear what their king might agree to, if such a royal summit were to happen behind closed doors. But now, with the end of the truce looming, Gaunt was about to lead an English delegation to an Anglo-French conference at Amiens, and the lords had gathered to decide the outline of England's negotiating position.[5]

On the fourth day of the council's discussions, they discovered that Richard's mind was elsewhere. He presented a formal proposal: the sentences given in 1388 against Robert de Vere and Alexander Neville should be quashed, and the two men recalled to England. But whatever prognostication Richard had used to decide on the timing of his intervention had failed. It was met with shocked silence, then outright refusal. Led by Gaunt, the lords were not ready to contemplate the reversal of those judgments. Who knew what fresh division de Vere might provoke if restored to Richard's side, or what the consequences might be of revisiting an explosive legal process on which the door had been comprehensively closed?[6]

Faced with their resistance, the king kept his temper under control. In four years Richard had learned a great deal. Instead, an exchange of oaths was negotiated. The king gave his word that he would not harm any of his subjects who might previously have caused him displeasure, and that it was "not his intention" to restore to his realm anyone sentenced to forfeiture in parliament. In return, his lords swore that, as his loyal subjects, they would do nothing by force except uphold the law at his command. Richard's composure was striking; and those who were tempted to recall previous instances of royal promises broken, or to wonder why basic principles of government should need restating in such novel form, had only to remember the bloodshed of 1388 to be reassured that this was progress.

The chronicler at Westminster Abbey summarized the agreement in rather more dramatic terms. The king, he said, graciously accepted that the exile of his friends "should preclude any hope of return"; the lords undertook to "support the king against any attackers and enemies whatsoever, outside the realm or within it," and recognized his "power to rule his kingdom as he pleased for all time to come." The king himself was left privately meditating on the incongruity between his right to rule as he pleased and this forced renunciation—however carefully worded—of his plan to be reunited with de Vere. But at least now, with the publicly committed backing of his lords, he could test the extent of his publicly confirmed power. And the target on which he fixed his sights was the unruly, disloyal, and tight-pursed city of London.

Fractious exchanges between the king and his capital had continued in the new year over the extent of London's legal privileges. A flash point in January 1392 was the right of arrest within the boundaries of the city: the mayor argued that, by established custom, no one should be taken into custody by royal officials without the agreement of the mayor or his representatives. This was a restriction on royal authority that Richard was not prepared to accept, and on January 20, in demonstration of his command over every one of London's citizens, the mayor himself was ordered to appear before the king's council every day for a week or forfeit a bond of £1,000. But in February the Londoners once again rebuffed a royal attempt to raise money in the city. Then, only a few weeks later, a riot broke out on Fleet Street, the thoroughfare leading into the city from the west, when a servant of the bishop of Salisbury, the current treasurer of England, snatched a loaf from the basket of a passing baker and hit him in the head when he protested. It was hardly surprising that this display of aggressive entitlement on the part of the treasurer's man should provoke rage in the people of a recently starving city, but the violence gave Richard the excuse for which he had been looking to demonstrate the irresistible power of his crown. London's leaders were shrewd and practical men, well used to sparring in defense of their own interests and those of their city; still, they were utterly unprepared for what they were about to face.[7]

The king showed his hand little by little, at each stage without explanation or warning. On May 13, he ordered that the court of Common Pleas, where his justices heard civil cases between his subjects, should move from its traditional place in Westminster Hall to the city of York, 175 miles north—a massive, unforeseen, and shocking dislocation of long-established judicial process for which Richard offered no justification other than unspecified "urgent causes affecting the king and the estate of the realm." Four days later, London's mayor, in alarm, ordered his aldermen to extract new oaths of allegiance from the city's inhabitants as proof of their loyalty to the crown, but it was too little, too late. Before the end of the month, the judges, clerks, and records of Common Pleas were followed on the road north by the Chancery—the king's secretariat and court of equity—and the Exchequer, his financial administration. Even apart from the blow dealt to London's commercial interests by the sudden disappearance from its streets of hundreds of officials and crowds of litigants, the removal of these key parts of government raised immediate questions about the city's future as England's capital.[8]

Richard himself was on his way to Nottingham Castle, his fortress at the heart of his kingdom, and summoned London's mayor, sheriffs, aldermen, and other leading citizens to appear before him there on June 25, on pain of death. But when they arrived, the terrified men—a hundred miles away from their own city and its people—were given no hearing. Instead, the king declared that they must answer for the "intolerable damages and perils" caused by "notable and evident defaults which he had notoriously and openly found" in their rule of the capital. The mayor and sheriffs were dismissed from office and taken into custody. Richard appointed one of his knights as a temporary warden in the mayor's place, and named a commission led by Langley, Woodstock, John Holand, and Thomas Mowbray to investigate London's failings. Their terms of reference were set by a statute of 1354 allowing for the correction by royal authority of errors in the city's government, a piece of legislation that, it soon became clear, Richard had examined in careful detail. Step by implacable step, as his commissioners completed their inquiry during July, the statute's full penalties were invoked. The mayor, sheriffs, and aldermen were found guilty, fined, and replaced by men appointed directly by the king. The liberties and income of the city were taken into the king's hands. Then a corporate fine was imposed on London in the almost inconceivable sum of £100,000.[9]

It had taken Richard just ten weeks to eviscerate the political structures of England's greatest city. London had lost its customary privileges, its administrative independence, and its financial resources, and all the while the "notable and evident defaults" that ostensibly justified such draconian royal intervention were asserted but never specified. The Londoners were left unable to defend themselves against charges they could not pin down, or even to respond at all without risking self-entrapment. The city found itself without recourse and without friends. The great lords who sat on the royal council and the commission of inquiry had just pledged their obedience to Richard as part of the deal by which de Vere's return to England had been blocked. Chancellor Arundel's archiepiscopal city of York was a direct beneficiary of the king's sanctions against the capital, and Gaunt's antagonistic relationship with London's citizens by now stretched back two decades. Royal mercy was their only hope. And so—knowing Richard as they did, and with guidance from their new warden—the Londoners set about choreographing a magnificent performance of their loyalty.

The date was set for August 21, when, by careful prearrangement, Richard would come to London to see "whether my people have learned to recognise their king." That morning, Richard and Anne rode in procession from their palace at Sheen eastward along the south side of the Thames to Wandsworth. There they were met by representatives of the various companies of the city's trades and crafts, a thronging crowd dressed in their finest liveries, and at their head the warden and aldermen—Richard's own appointees—who gave him a sword and the keys to the city in token of London's submission to his grace. At the gate of London Bridge the royal couple were presented with two fine coursers for the king and a palfrey for the queen, each horse bearing a gilded saddle and trappings of cloth of gold. The streets, when they crossed the river into the city, were hung with richly colored silks, and the Cheapside conduit ran with wine, while singing angels descended from a castle hanging in the air to bestow golden crowns upon them. Richard and his queen had each made a ceremonial entry into London before, at the time of their coronations, but now the repeated ritual reached its apotheosis, with the king's arrival figured as the second coming of Christ into the holy city, the New Jerusalem. At Temple Bar, the westernmost boundary of the city, Saint John the Baptist himself appeared in a painted wilderness surrounded by ingeniously costumed beasts. "Behold," he declared at Richard's approach, "the Lamb of God!"[10]

That evening the enthroned king received the leading Londoners in Westminster Hall, where his queen, the archbishop of Canterbury, and the bishop of London begged on their behalf for his forgiveness. The next night, after another round of ceremonies, the royal couple were welcomed to a feast in the city itself. Amid the gifts and prayers and music, Richard was gratified and gracious, while Anne, as always, played her part as intercessor in the cause of peace to gentle perfection. Along with a delicate process of negotiation behind the scenes, it was enough to win the city a pardon, but a pardon strictly on terms of Richard's making: a reduced fine of £10,000—a fortune still, but a reprieve compared to the previous threat of ten times that amount—and a restoration of London's liberties "until the king shall otherwise ordain." The capital's future now explicitly depended not on law or custom, but on the will of the king. That autumn there was relief in the election of a new mayor and sheriffs, and a royal order that the Chancery, Exchequer, and court of Common Pleas should return to Westminster for the start of the new term in January. It was obvious, all the same, that Richard's benevolence depended on his capital's continuing adherence to its new script. At Christmas the Londoners provided mummers for the extravagant royal entertainments at Eltham Palace, along with exotic gifts to the king and queen of a dromedary and a pelican. The following summer, at Richard's instruction and the city's expense, newly commissioned statues of the royal couple were placed above the gate on London Bridge, each figure holding a gilded scepter.[11]

London's capitulation was commemorated in literature as well as public art. In 1393, while the statues were being prepared, a Carmelite friar and theologian named Richard Maidstone, one of Gaunt's confessors, presented the king with a panegyric of the pageants in more than 500 lines of Latin verse. His stately couplets showed the city surrendering to a young sovereign as beautiful as Absalom and as wise as Solomon, "whose power is to be feared / and also to be loved, and equally revered." The result of that power, in this loyal vision, was the king's peace, a peace to be achieved through his people's perpetual obedience. For Richard, there was deep satisfaction in the double triumph portrayed in Maidstone's lines: the glorious performance of his divinely ordained sovereignty, given unarguable political substance by the subjection of his capital to his will.[12]

But if Maidstone was Richard's official rapporteur, the verdict of another poet with a front-row view of the king's dealings with London was much less sanguine. A friend of Geoffrey Chaucer, John Gower lived and worked in the city. He had already written long poems in Latin and French by the late 1380s, when his first major composition in English was inspired by a personal encounter with Richard. The prologue of the *Confessio Amantis*, finished in 1390, described a journey on the Thames during which Gower's boat crossed paths with the royal barge; invited on board, the poet was instructed to write "some new thing" for the king's pleasure and edification. By 1393, however, after the terrifying upheavals Richard had precipitated in London's government and the lives of its inhabitants, Gower no longer wished to present his work as

A book for King Richard's sake,
To whom belongeth my allegiance
With all my heart's obedience
In all that ever a liege man
Unto his king may do or can.

He revised his prologue to remove all mention of the royal conversation on the river, instead calling the *Confessio* simply "A book for England's sake, / The year sixteenth of King Richard. / What shall befall hereafterward / God knows. . . ." The tales of love it contained sought to elucidate the ways in which the world could be saved from division and restored to peace, but the peace to which Gower had devoted his poem was the concord of unity, not the order secured through fear by which his city now found itself gripped. And his new text came with a new dedication:

This book, upon amendment
To stand at his commandment,
With whom my heart is of accord,
I send unto my own lord,
Which of Lancaster is Henry named:
The high God him hath proclaimed
Full of knighthood and all grace.

Henry had not been in England in the summer of 1392, either to be appointed with his uncles to the commission of inquiry into London's government or to witness the city's submission; but a year later, when he returned from his pilgrimage to Jerusalem and his fêted travels across Europe, he acknowledged Gower's tribute by granting the poet a Lancastrian livery collar of Ss.[13]

Richard, meanwhile, was not thinking about poetry. He was preoccupied instead by the fact that the return for which he had longed above all others could not now take place. Only a few weeks before his triumphal entry into the capital, news had reached England that Robert de Vere was dead, killed by a boar in a hunting accident at the age of just thirty. The man whose presence the king required was gone forever. Richard would not give his subjects the satisfaction of seeing him grieve. In public, he honored his friend's memory with cool formality. In parliament in January 1393, the king declared that, since de Vere had been "called to God," his forfeited estates should be restored to his uncle Aubrey as the next heir to the earldom of Oxford; and a knight who had gone with him into exile "for the whole life of the said Robert" was granted a royal pardon. But without de Vere, Richard's future had changed. There would be no going back to the household, the court, or the regime he had built in the 1380s. The project of reconstructing his rightful authority would remain Richard's alone.[14]

Across the Channel, the king of France was struggling with existential challenges of a dramatically different kind. On August 5, 1392, while London was anxiously rehearsing its pageants, twenty-three-year-old Charles rode out of the northwestern French city of Le Mans ahead of an army assembled, amid mounting tensions within his regime, to strike against the duke of Brittany. During the previous few weeks, the king had been unwell with intermittent fevers, little sleep, and less appetite. Now, dressed for protection in a padded black velvet jacket despite the oppressive heat, he was sweating and agitated. Behind him an accidental clash of a weapon on armor made a sudden clang, and he started in the saddle, turning with his sword already in his hand. In seconds, two pages lay dead and he turned again, lashing out at anyone within reach, shouting that traitors were attacking him, blood vivid on his blade as it glinted in the sun. It dawned on his horrified attendants that the king recognized no one. Four of them were killed and several wounded before his sword broke and he could at last be restrained, his eyes rolling in his head. By the time he was carried back to Le Mans, strapped into a litter, he had lapsed into unconsciousness.[15]

For the kingdom of France, this was chaos descending from a clear blue sky. Six months earlier almost to the day, Queen Isabeau had given her husband a son, but an infant heir was no reassurance to the realm when the king hovered between life and death. By the time it became apparent a few days later that Charles would survive—although he remained physically weak and mentally fragile—his uncles of Burgundy and Berry had already set about reestablishing their control of his government. It was inevitable, they thought, that news of the king's illness would give heart to France's enemies, but reliable sources reported instead that the king of England was distressed by Charles's misfortune. For Richard, the disempowerment of a monarch he had always seen more as a counterpart than an adversary was no cause for celebration. Not only that, but it meant the further postponement of his vision of peace between the two kingdoms made face-to-face by sovereign equals. The conference Gaunt had attended at Amiens in March 1392 had achieved no more than a seventeen-month extension of the Anglo-French truce so that more talks could be arranged. Perhaps when Charles was fully recovered, the summit of kings that Richard had imagined for so long might still come to pass. For now, there was no choice: the two kings' royal uncles would continue the search for a settlement.[16]

Delegations from England and France assembled in splendor at Leulinghem in April 1393. Leulinghem itself was not splendid: a ruined village in the bleak flatlands south of Calais that had been scoured and scarred by decades of fighting. Its significance depended on its thatched church that the tides of war had left stranded, straddling the border between English-held territory and French. Via its two doors, the two sides could enter the building simultaneously and then negotiate in person without either party having to leave the lands ruled by their own king, thereby avoiding the disputes over diplomatic precedence that could so quickly derail such conferences or even prevent them happening altogether. What the place entirely lacked was magnificence, but that could be made up in other ways. On the plains on either side of the church, pavilions of extraordinary size and luxury were constructed. That belonging to the duke of Burgundy, the monk of Saint-Denis reported, was like a town, surrounded by wooden towers and crenellated walls; that of the duke of Lancaster, said Thomas Walsingham, contained a chapel, arcades, courts, and markets.[17]

There was parity too in the composition of the embassies, with two dukes on either side. Burgundy was joined by his older brother Berry, and Gaunt by his younger brother Woodstock. In between sessions at Leulinghem, the French retreated west to Boulogne and the English northwest to Calais while the two kings waited for news, Richard across the Channel at Canterbury, and Charles—still recovering not only from his illness the previous summer but also from a narrow escape in January when costumes had caught fire at a court masque—forty-five miles south at Abbeville. It was clear that there was a will to peace at the highest levels. Equally clear were the obstacles that remained. The general principle was accepted by both regimes: Charles would cede possession of the duchy of Aquitaine to Richard, and in return Richard would recognize Charles's sovereignty over it. The devil, as always, was in the detail. Would the king of England as duke of Aquitaine have to do homage in person—that is, swear loyalty and service as a vassal—to the king of France? If so, would he be subject, as duke of Aquitaine, to the jurisdiction of the French king's courts? Would he be required, as duke of Aquitaine, to do military service in the French king's wars? If the answer to those questions was also yes, then he might face the impossibility as king of England of being summoned to serve in a war against himself. But if the answer was no, would that make the French king's theoretical sovereignty over Aquitaine meaningless in practice?[18]

In England, the intractability of these questions had given rise to further problems behind the diplomatic scenes. Richard's desire to end the war himself through a personal agreement with Charles had never won widespread support in his own realm, given that mistrust of the king's motives in his dealings with France had not wholly disappeared. At the same time, Gaunt's role in the negotiations was not straightforward either. One obvious

answer to the question of Aquitaine was for the duchy to remain permanently in the hands of Gaunt and his heirs, who could perform homage to
the French king without immediately compromising the authority of the
English crown. But for Gaunt, as the crown's principal representative, to
put forward a solution involving such enormous benefit to his own family, as he had done during the previous round of negotiations in 1392, did
nothing to increase support for the proposal or confidence in the process.
Beyond even that was the feeling in large parts of the country that concessions of any kind, when England had invested so much in the war and had
not been defeated in the field, were shameful, damaging, and unnecessary.
And that view had been given inconveniently prominent voice by Thomas
of Woodstock, at least until the decision to include him in the embassy of
1393 silenced his public interventions.[19]

Still, when the conference opened with scrupulously observed ceremony
in Leulinghem's little church it was apparent that the cause of peace had
real momentum. By now, fifty-three-year-old Gaunt and fifty-one-year-old
Burgundy had had enough of the attritional damage caused by a war that
had started before they were born. Their own interests would be served by a
settlement, which would allow Gaunt to consolidate his hold on Aquitaine,
and Burgundy on his territories in the Low Countries; but those personal
ambitions dovetailed seamlessly with the sincere conviction that neither
England nor France stood to gain by continuing the fight. There were pressing reminders too of the Christian duty to unite against the infidel, a duty
rendered increasingly urgent by the advance of the Ottoman Turks into the
Balkans. A devastatingly bloody battle on the field of Kosovo in 1389 had
destroyed the principalities of Serbia as a bulwark against Islam, and the
kingdom of Hungary and the waters of the Adriatic lay vulnerable to attack.
The call to crusade was represented within the French delegation by Leo
of Armenia and a visionary known as Robert the Hermit, while at Gaunt's
request the church in which they met was hung with tapestries depicting
scenes of Christ's passion, to focus their minds on the divine grace they
sought. Over the previous year, Gaunt, Burgundy, and Berry had developed
a working relationship of mutual respect, founded on the understanding that
their royal nephews wanted a lasting peace. By June, an extension of the truce

was in place and a way forward identified. A permanent accord, it seemed, was within reach.[20]

The protocol did not solve everything, but it laid out a road map toward a final agreement. Its starting point was a remarkably generous drawing of Aquitaine's borders to include almost all of the vast territories the English had held at the Treaty of Brétigny back in 1360, with a cash payment to compensate for the rest. In return, the English would abandon any claim to sovereignty over the duchy, and hold it instead in liege homage from the crown of France. Lawyers from the two sides would meet in August to thrash out the thorny technical details of what such homage might mean in terms of jurisdiction and military service. Next, the four dukes would reconvene at Leulinghem in late September to review any outstanding issues. The two kings would then meet face-to-face in February 1394 to resolve the last few questions, including the legal status of the outpost of Calais, and whether it should be Gaunt or Richard himself who would be required to perform homage in person.[21]

A skeptical eye could see that the most difficult problems had simply been kicked down the road for the lawyers to solve, but still: this was greater progress toward peace than had been made in more than three decades, since the Treaty of Brétigny itself. The proposals seemed tantalizingly close to a triumph, a vindication of the delicate alliance that Gaunt and Richard had managed to sustain since the duke's return in 1389. Woodstock remained as suspicious and hostile as ever. "You French have so many deceptive words that are difficult for us to understand," he told Robert the Hermit, "that when you want war it's war, and when you want peace it's peace." But even Woodstock, compromised as he was by his own participation, put his seal to the protocol and swore to uphold its terms. Resistance, it turned out, would come from elsewhere.[22]

Unrest in the northwest of England, especially in Lancashire and Cheshire, had begun that spring before the delegations at Leulinghem had even met. The men of Cheshire in particular had a long tradition of military service under Richard's father and grandfather, and of direct action where their own concerns were at stake. Their leaders now were military veterans from both counties: Sir Thomas Talbot, Sir John Massy, and Sir Nicholas Clifton, three knights who had made their careers in the war and were fundamentally opposed to its end, as both a dereliction of England's interests and a threat to their own. John Holand was sent north in the attempt to contain the disturbances, but by June the region was in full-blown revolt.[23]

With thousands of men gathering in arms, the waves of this resistance joined crosscurrents of other grievances. The rebels, said Thomas Walsingham, nailed manifestos to the doors of parish churches, blaming Gaunt, Woodstock, and Gaunt's son Henry for giving away the king's title to the kingdom of France for their own private advantage. As an allegation, it was not simple to construe. Richard, by this analysis, was absolved of any responsibility for what was happening, which—while always a politic line for critics of royal government to take—was barely plausible here, given how obvious it had been for years that the king had no desire to pursue the war. But the bonds between Richard and his palatinate of Chester ran deep. Men of Cheshire had come out to fight for him under de Vere's command in 1387, and they remained acutely sensitive to the possibility of encroachment on his royal rights—or their own. According to Walsingham's report, the rebels also declared that the three lords had removed dominion over the county of Chester from the king, and now wanted to do away with their ancient liberties.[24]

It made a tangled kind of sense. Gaunt was England's chief representative in the negotiations for peace with France, the outcome of which promised to leave the duchy of Aquitaine permanently in his own possession. At the same time, he was lord of the palatinate of Lancashire, Cheshire's neighbor to the north, where the three knights who led the revolt had failed to find a place within the duke's overwhelmingly powerful local retinue. Over the previous few years, Talbot and Clifton had instead offered their service to the king, as Richard sought to find local retainers of his own, and Massy to the Holands, but even so they had found it near impossible to bypass Gaunt's dominance within the region in pursuit of their personal affairs. For them, rejection of the peace proposals, opposition to Gaunt, and loyalty to the crown formed a coherent defense of their own future and that of the kingdom they served.[25]

Woodstock's skepticism about the peace process, meanwhile, won him no credibility with the rebels. Not only had he undermined his own stance by joining Gaunt in sealing the agreement at Leulinghem, but he had led the attacks on Richard back in 1386–88, a conflict in which he had taken the office of chief justice of Chester and north Wales from de Vere, and he had held on to it ever since. Henry, the third name on Walsingham's list, seemed the least likely of all. In the early summer of 1393, he was still traveling home from Jerusalem and had nothing to do with the discussions at Leulinghem. But as Gaunt's son he stood to inherit both Aquitaine, should Richard's grant of the duchy be made hereditary, and the powers of the palatinate in Lancashire. And six years earlier it had been Henry who routed de Vere and his Cheshiremen at Radcot Bridge.[26]

The tangled motives behind the revolt made for a tangled response. In the early weeks of the disturbances, Richard's reluctance to crack down on men whose loyalty to himself was intense and personal became so obvious that in the first week of May, with the conference now in session at Leulinghem, he was forced to issue an extraordinary proclamation from Westminster explicitly denying that he supported the rebellion in any way. The very fact that he did so only served to focus attention on the possibility that—however deeply he wished to be rid of the war—he was nevertheless enjoying this demonstration of popular resentment toward his uncles, and of devotion to his crown.[27]

It was Gaunt, when he returned to England on June 20, who rode north with royal judges at his side and armed men at his back to suppress the disorder, which he did over the course of the next three months with patience and care rather than an iron fist. He made concerted efforts to rebut the accusations against him, Walsingham reported, and to respond to the rebels' grievances, issuing many pardons and offering to train the poorest of the insurgents as soldiers to serve for generous pay in Aquitaine. He was helped by Henry, who turned his horse northward to join his father as soon as he reached London from Dover on July 5, and discovered what had been happening in his absence.

Woodstock, however, despite his responsibilities as chief justice in the palatinate, left his brother and nephew to deal with Cheshire. And the underlying fragility of the regime was further exposed by the disturbing presence there of the earl of Arundel, who held massive estates in the northern Welsh marches and in neighboring Shropshire. Unlike Woodstock, Arundel had played no part in Richard's reconstituted government since 1389. In 1390, at the age of forty-four, he had taken as his second wife Philippa Mortimer, the fourteen-year-old sister of the young earl of March, and was fined a year later for doing so without the king's permission. Otherwise, he had kept his head down and his thoughts to himself, beyond the certainty that his opposition to the idea of a peace settlement had not changed. His brother Archbishop Arundel, who had been dismissed by Richard from his post as chancellor in 1389, was reappointed to the same office in September 1391, his intellect and political acumen too valuable for the administration to lose; but the archbishop's official presence at Richard's right hand did nothing to ease the estrangement between the earl and the king. Now, with the northwest in uproar, Arundel and his armed retinue installed themselves on the very border of Cheshire in his castle of Holt, just seven miles south of Chester itself. Then the earl and his men did nothing. Was Arundel protecting his own lands while refusing to help subdue the rebels—or might he be contemplating the possibility of joining them?[28]

Gaunt scarcely had time to wonder. As he and Henry struggled to restore order in England's northwest, the peace process in France was slipping through his fingers. Before the duke had even left Calais, the French king was losing his grip on reality once more. This time, his illness grew so severe that he no longer knew who he was, denying that he was king, even that his name was Charles, and rebuffing his heavily pregnant queen as though she were a stranger. His condition was kept secret for as long as possible, subterfuge that allowed the lawyers from both sides to meet in August as envisaged by the protocol, but their examination of the key issues of homage and jurisdiction yielded nothing beyond a restatement of the historical precedents that had helped precipitate the entire war in the first place. By September, when the four royal dukes were due to reconvene at Leulinghem, Burgundy and Berry were forced to send a message to England to halt negotiations until the king should recover, whenever that might prove to be.[29]

Tantalizingly close to a triumph, it turned out, was not close enough.

The protocol had stalled. The intractable questions that had stymied every previous attempt at a permanent settlement were no nearer resolution. Such progress as Gaunt had made at Leulinghem had already come at the cost of rebellion in England. If the representatives of the realm would give his proposals their public backing, perhaps there was still a chance of success; if they would not, then taxation would be needed to pay for the renewal of war. Either way, Richard had no choice but to call a parliament to meet at Westminster in January 1394. And as so often before in his reign, parliament was a place where simmering tensions might boil over in public.

Gaunt and Arundel had not confronted each other in Cheshire, but they did so now. Before the assembly's formal discussions had even begun, Gaunt angrily denounced Arundel for sitting out the rebellion at Holt. Arundel responded by seeking an audience with the king and senior nobles including his brother the archbishop and Gaunt's brother Woodstock, but not Gaunt himself. It rapidly became apparent that the earl had not gained in tact or diplomacy during his time in the political wilderness. The king, he declared, treated Gaunt with undue favor, to the detriment of the crown. He spent too much time in close company with his uncle, and publicly wore the Lancastrian livery collar of Ss—the elegant gesture of support that Richard had first made after Gaunt returned from Castile—which, Arundel argued, could only detract from his honor as king. He should not have given Gaunt the duchy of Aquitaine, or so much money to campaign in Spain, or allowed him to negotiate the present terms for peace; and all the while, Arundel said, the duke bullied meetings of council and parliament so much that others did not dare speak their minds.[30]

Back in 1384, when Arundel had spoken his mind in another parliament, Richard had told him to go to hell. In ten years the king had changed, even if the earl had not. With icy self-control, Richard answered the charges one by one. It was his choice, he said, to have not only Gaunt but all three of his uncles attend upon him, and to wear their liveries as a sign of the great love that existed between them. Everything granted to Gaunt, both titles and money, had been expressly endorsed by parliament. The duke had done nothing at the peace conference that had not been approved by the king and his councillors, of whom Arundel was one; and it was the duty of everyone in council or parliament to say what they thought, no matter what they heard from the duke.[31]

By the time the king finished, it was abundantly clear that, whatever Arundel had imagined he might achieve, he had failed. The full extent of his failure, however, emerged only when, at Richard's command, the exchange was rehearsed in front of the lords gathered in parliament, Gaunt and Henry sitting among them. All agreed that Arundel's accusations were baseless and that Gaunt's honor was secure in every respect. Did the earl wish to say anything more concerning the duke? He did not. But the choice, he discovered, was not his to make. The king and lords decreed that he must apologize to Gaunt and beg forgiveness, his words scripted for him and delivered through clenched teeth. The humiliation was such that Arundel decided to remove himself, securing the king's permission never to attend parliament again, and covering his back as best he could by suing for pardon for any unspecified offenses he might have committed, up to and including "treasons and insurrections."

Parliamentary unity was simple to achieve when closing ranks against the friendless earl, but much less so when discussing the war. The lords and Commons did not, of course, support the revolt in Cheshire and Lancashire. The rebel leader Thomas Talbot had finally been arrested in the autumn of 1393 but subsequently managed to escape from custody, and now, in response to a petition from Gaunt and Woodstock, he was declared a notorious traitor who should be convicted without trial if he failed to surrender himself to the authorities. But when it came to discussing Gaunt's proposals for peace, it emerged that both lords and Commons shared Talbot's concerns about the sovereignty of the English crown. They would agree to the settlement, they said, so long as the king's homage for Aquitaine did not commit him to serve the French king; so long as the terms were modified to ensure that no exercise of French jurisdiction could ever succeed in confiscating the duchy; and so long as the English claim to the crown of France, which had justified the war for more than half a century, could be reactivated in response to any French infringement of the treaty in future.[32]

The tone of the formal transcript was punctiliously deferential, but the Westminster chronicler's unofficial summary of the debate made it clear that feelings were running high. The Commons did not want to pay for a failing war, but nor would they accept a peace that compromised the grounds on which the war had been fought for so long. It would be absurd for Richard to become the sworn liegeman of the French crown, they believed, since "every single Englishman under the lordship of the king of England would find himself under the heel of the king of France, held in the yoke of slavery from then on." Any lesser man suggesting such terms, the monk continued, would have been branded a traitor on the spot, and rightly so; "but the duke of Lancaster does as he likes, and nobody brands him." Once again, Gaunt stood suspected of betraying the interests of the realm for his own personal gain, an old narrative reemerging in spite of the present reality that he was fulfilling the wishes of the twenty-seven-year-old king, and the brute fact that an exchange of sovereignty for territory was the only possible basis on which a deal could be struck.[33]

After all Gaunt's efforts during two long years of intensive diplomacy, the stipulations attached to the "consent" provided by parliament—stipulations that rendered any acknowledgment of French sovereignty over Aquitaine so provisional as to be worthless—left the peace proposals dead in the water. But still, after all his efforts, the duke was not ready to give up. Within days of the parliament's end on March 6, he received the king's authorization to return yet again to Leulinghem, this time with Langley rather than Woodstock in his company. More weeks passed in conference with the dukes of Berry and Burgundy, their presence made possible by King Charles's recent return to a fragile kind of sanity. Gaunt did not falter when news arrived from home at the end of March that his wife, Constanza, had died at the age of just thirty-nine. With preparations in motion for a magnificent funeral worthy of her royal blood, he remained at the negotiating table throughout April and into May, hoping against hope that something could be salvaged from the rubble of the treaty. In the end, all he could get was time: a four-year extension to the truce, during which he promised to join Burgundy in an Anglo-French crusade to be fought in the Balkans or the Baltic. The agreement was sealed by the four dukes at Leulinghem on May 27, 1394, and ratified by the king at Eltham on June 5.[34]

The moment was gone. The losses continued. Two days later, at the palace of Sheen to the west of the capital, Queen Anne died, almost exactly four weeks after her twenty-eighth birthday. She had been Richard's constant companion for nearly half their lifetimes, a quiet, composed presence offering unquestioned and unquestioning loyalty. By June 10, the king was back at Westminster, summoning the lords temporal and spiritual to appear in London on July 29 in preparation for a funeral of unparalleled grandeur to be held on August 3. Henry had been in the north since early April to continue the work of mopping up disturbances in the aftermath of the rebellion, leaving his pregnant wife and children at home in Peterborough. Not long after the arrival of his royal cousin's letter, he too received news. Mary had given birth to a girl, their second daughter, but after six pregnancies in eight years her luck had run out. The baby was healthy; Mary was dead. She was twenty-four years old.[35]

For Henry, Richard, Gaunt, and England, nothing would be the same again.

Nine

1394-1395

an immortal title

For Gaunt, the loss of his wife was a matter of regret. Their partnership of twenty-three years, one of respect and dignified collaboration, had achieved many of its aims. He and Constanza had not succeeded in recapturing her father's throne, but their bloodline would rule in Castile once their daughter Catalina gave her young husband, King Enrique, an heir. It was also thanks to Constanza's claims in the peninsula that his own bloodline would one day rule in Portugal, where his daughter Philippa had already given birth to four healthy sons. Since their return to England in 1389, the duchess had kept her grand household mainly in the midlands, at the Lancastrian castles of Tutbury and Leicester, while Gaunt had been busy at Westminster, Leulinghem, and elsewhere. Now the duke was determined that the dignity of her birthright should be reflected in the rites that took her to the grave. He spent a huge sum, more than £600, on a ceremony held on July 5 at the beautiful Church of the Annunciation in the outer precinct of Leicester Castle, where the first duke of Lancaster, the great Henry of Grosmont, lay buried before the high altar. And behind the scenes of this formal mourning Gaunt could lean on the emotional support of Katherine Swynford, the mother of his Beaufort children, who, over the dozen years that had passed since his public renunciation of their relationship, had remained a discreetly sustaining presence in his life from the distance of her home in Lincoln.[1]

For Henry, everything was different. The loss of his wife had shattered his world. It was Mary who had made the home to which he could return from his travels. For the last two years she had chosen to live with the children at Peterborough, a smaller, more domestic place than the imposing castles of the duchy of Lancaster. From time to time when Henry was away he would send her gifts, sometimes fine fabric, damask and brocade—although her taste and style were much less extravagant than his—and sometimes a consignment of pears and apples, or oysters and mussels. Now, for Henry and the children, that home no longer existed. Their four boys and two girls— young Henry at seven, Thomas six, John just turned five, Humphrey not yet four, Blanche two, and newborn Philippa—still had their devoted nurses and attendants. But like Henry himself when his own mother died, they moved into the care of another household, that of their grandmother, Mary's mother, Joan, dowager countess of Hereford, at Bytham in Lincolnshire, within easy reach of their grandfather Gaunt's castle at Leicester. Mary was laid to rest in the Church of the Annunciation there on the day after Constanza's funeral, her own burial simpler and quieter, as her life had been. Then, in his grief, Henry had only three weeks to ready himself for the gathering in state of the peers of the realm in London for the funeral of Queen Anne at Westminster Abbey.[2]

That royal ceremony, said Thomas Walsingham, "was all the more famous because of its cost, so that it surpassed all others of our time." But sheer expense was not the only reason for its notoriety. For all the meticulous planning, the two months of elaborate preparation, and despite the example of Anne's own quiet piety, the service itself descended into violent farce.[3]

Richard had demanded that all his lords and their wives should gather in the capital several days before the funeral in order that they should be present to escort the queen's embalmed body from the palace of Sheen, where she had died, on its last slow journey along the south bank of the Thames, across London Bridge into the city to rest for a night in St. Paul's Cathedral, and then on, westward through Ludgate to the abbey. When the procession assembled on July 29, however, the earl of Arundel was not there. When he did eventually arrive, it was to seek permission to leave again almost immediately. In parliament seven months earlier, the king had controlled his anger at Arundel's insubordination. Now his fury was unleashed. At the hour appointed for the funeral to begin on August 3, when king and earl came face-to-face in the abbey church, Richard seized a staff of office from one of his attendants and swung it at Arundel's head. The earl fell to the floor, blood streaming across the flagstones. In that moment, Walsingham believed, the king wanted to kill him. As it was, the queen's obsequies were delayed while Arundel was removed to the Tower, the pavement was hurriedly cleaned, and the shaken priests performed the rites necessary to remove the pollution of bloodshed from the consecrated space. When they finally began to sing the Office of the Dead, the air was thick with tension. Night fell before the ceremony was done.

Everything was unsettled, jittery, under strain. After being held in custody for a week behind the Tower's massive walls, Arundel was brought into Richard's presence in a side room at the archbishop of Canterbury's palace of Lambeth, across the Thames from Westminster. There the earl—once again finding himself forced to speak from a prepared script—took an oath guaranteeing his good behavior toward the king and promising not to make riots or gather forces against him. Assembled in the little chamber with Richard and the archbishop were a group of lords and knights led by the earl's brother Archbishop Arundel and his brother-in-law the earl of March, his son-in-law Thomas Mowbray, and their fellow former Appellant the earl of Warwick, as well as Aubrey de Vere, uncle of the king's dead favorite. The ten men were there to stand surety for Arundel's future conduct on pain of a collective fine in the immense amount of £40,000. Once the oaths were sworn, the earl was allowed to go free.[4]

But the unease only grew. The last time Richard physically assaulted Arundel had been at the beginning of 1386, not long before the eruption of the crisis that had engulfed the kingdom for the next two years. True, it was clearer than ever that the earl was an unhelpfully disruptive political presence, but only three months earlier he had sought and received a royal pardon for any offenses he might have committed before that date. There was no escaping the fact that one of the most senior noblemen in the kingdom had been arrested, imprisoned, and placed under a bond of good behavior that left a group of other lords under ongoing threat of a swingeing financial penalty, not because he had broken the law, but because his failure to comply with royal instructions concerning attendance at the queen's funeral had offended the king.[5]

Gaunt held no brief for Arundel, but he too had reason to feel anxious about Richard's state of mind. The duke was deep in preparations for an expedition to Aquitaine made necessary by resistance there to his own tenure of the duchy. Revolt had been simmering since the spring, fueled by fear that the peace negotiations would leave Aquitaine permanently in the hands of Gaunt and his heirs rather than, as had been the case for the last 200 years, in direct relationship with the English crown. In the absence of any such treaty, and with preliminaries for the proposed Anglo-French crusade not yet far advanced, the four-year truce of May 1394 gave Gaunt a chance to return to the duchy in the attempt to reassure doubters and subdue dissent. By late August, arrangements were well in hand for the muster of men and ships, but at his Yorkshire castle of Pontefract the duke found himself preoccupied with events elsewhere. With him as his guests were his brothers Langley and Woodstock, and Langley's elder son, Edward, earl of Rutland, all of whom had witnessed Richard's volatile behavior at the queen's funeral three weeks earlier. Now rumors reached the gathering that someone—of low birth, they had heard, but name unknown—had, in Richard's presence, explicitly questioned Gaunt's loyalty. The duke was uncomfortably aware that he had failed to secure the permanent peace Richard wanted. Did he need to fear the kind of conspiracies emanating from within the royal household that had threatened his life a decade before?[6]

He decided to confront the rumours head-on, writing to his nephew to emphasize the affection and allegiance of all those present with him at Pontefract, and protesting his own fidelity in thought and deed, "of which I believe and truly hope, my lord, that you have always had such proof by experience of all my dealings with you, that you would not believe any such utterances." For now, there was little more he could do. His arrangements were made: his retainers were mustering for a year's service in Aquitaine, and during his absence, as had been the case when he was in Castile, Henry would watch over his interests at home. Meanwhile, there were further safeguards in the fact that Langley would have new authority in England and that Woodstock and Rutland would be constantly at the king's side, because

Richard, for only the second time in his reign, was also leaving his king-dom.[7]

It seemed that the king had been energized by the drama of his be-reavement and its violent aftermath. Not long before Anne's death he had conceived a plan to go to his lordship of Ireland, a place where no English king had set foot since his great-great-great-great-grandfather John almost two centuries earlier. Richard had once envisaged Ireland as a dominion that would give his beloved de Vere a unique place within his nobility, one that would outshine even the overbearing presence of his royal uncles. That strat-egy had disintegrated in the wreckage of 1387–88, its collapse made permanent by his favorite's death. But if Ireland could not be his gift to de Vere, Richard would make it the stage for a new expression of his own sovereignty. He had never wanted to fight in France, where the greatest achievement to which he could aspire—far out of reach though it had always been—was a pale imita-tion of the victories won by his father and grandfather. He *had* wanted to seal a lasting peace with France for the good of Christendom but had been thwarted by the complexities of the conflict and the illness of the French king. Instead, he would embark on an expedition that was all his: a campaign to impose the personal authority of his crown on a perennially disordered land.

The decision that he would cross the sea to Ireland was already public knowledge by June 16, little more than a week after the queen's death. On July 1, the sheriffs were ordered to muster troops by August 3, the very day of her funeral. As soon as the earl of Arundel had been dealt with at Lam-beth on August 10, the king began his journey west, moving via Oxford and Gloucester into south Wales, where he took ship at Milford Haven on Sep-tember 30. With him were a group of noblemen too young to have fought in his grandfather's wars: Thomas Mowbray, earl of Nottingham; Roger Mortimer, earl of March; Thomas Holand, son and heir of Richard's oldest brother, the earl of Kent; and Edmund of Langley's son Edward, earl of Rut-land. Thomas of Woodstock followed not far behind the royal party. It was a bolt from the blue, this sudden initiative, but at least—unlike the promotion of de Vere—it promised engagement with the needs of the king's dominions; and Langley himself remained to watch over the administration in England during Richard's absence.[8]

Gaunt sailed for Aquitaine a month later. As he had done in 1386, Henry
rode with his father to Plymouth to say their farewells. On his way back to
London he stopped at Glastonbury Abbey to visit the fabled tomb of King
Arthur and Queen Guinevere. His own adventures as a wandering knight
were still fresh in his memory and in his correspondence: that November he
received letters from the king of Hungary, and in January 1395 he sent horses
and greyhounds as a gift to Gian Galeazzo Visconti in Milan. His mourning outfits in fur-trimmed black were as superb as ever, and when he moved
between his rented home in the capital and his father's castles at Hertford,
Leicester, Kenilworth, and Tutbury he kept his books and his harp with him
as he had always done. He visited his children at Bytham when he could,
and as the older boys' education progressed they too spent time at the great
Lancastrian strongholds in the midlands. At Leicester in March his eldest
son was briefly unwell, and Henry sent urgently from London for news.
Otherwise, with his uncle Langley in the strangely empty chambers of the
palace of Westminster, he watched and waited.[9]

Richard had not been to sea since he was four years old, when he had made
the long journey from Aquitaine in the care of his mother and ailing father.
At twenty-seven, he seemed delighted with the novel experience. "We had
the most smooth and easy passage," he wrote happily to his councillors at
home, "with complete good health, without any turbulence or disturbance in
the air or any roughness of the sea, thanks be to God, so much so that our
passage lasted no longer than a day and a night, and we arrived at our city of
Waterford in our land of Ireland where our citizens there received us most
honourably and very joyfully."[10]

The last time he had led troops out of England, over the land border
with Scotland in 1385, he had been a teenage monarch hemmed in by an
older generation of powerful nobles. Even then Ireland had been in his
mind, when he named de Vere marquis of Dublin on his journey north.
Now the man he had loved was dead, but at least his young captains on
this Irish voyage were more congenial company than their predecessors had
been. Twenty-one-year-old Rutland had already been picked out for royal

approval four years earlier when he was appointed admiral of England and
constable of the Tower of London at the age of seventeen. The rapprochement between Richard and Mowbray, who was older than the king by only a
matter of months, had also gathered pace; the earl had been captain of Calais
since 1391, and in the spring of 1394 he replaced Woodstock as chief justice of
Chester in the wake of the revolt there. For Roger Mortimer, earl of March,
and his brother-in-law Thomas Holand, both just twenty, this was the first
time they had taken on major responsibilities in the service of the crown;
in Mortimer's case, it was also his first visit to a land in which he held vast
estates, and where his father had died during his childhood. When thirty-
nine-year-old Thomas of Woodstock landed at Waterford two weeks after
the arrival of the king's fleet, he found himself less an éminence grise than an
older odd man out among the peers who now surrounded his royal nephew.[11]

There was further gratification for Richard in the composition of his
forces. Among the soldiers who marched behind the royal banners were not
only the armed retinues maintained and led by his nobles, but a substantial
contingent retained directly by the king himself. Richard had not forgotten the hard lessons of 1387–88, when it had proved impossible to recruit
an army from a standing start to counter the Appellants' military resources.
Since then, his adoption of the sign of the white hart had not been merely
for chivalric display. In 1392, when bestowing the honor of knighthood on a
Venetian citizen, the king had written to the doge to explain that he had also
given the man "our badge of a hart couchant, which is borne by the knights
who stay at our side." Quietly, in the years since 1391, he had been building
up a network of men from across the country to whom he granted annuities
for life to serve him in peace and war. With him when he landed at Waterford were forty-eight "king's knights," each at the head of their own men, of
whom nine were attached to his chamber within the royal household and
thirty-nine retained in his service by life indentures in exactly the same way
as they might have been by any other magnate. No longer, as he surveyed his
troops, did the king feel his sovereign authority to be overborne by noblemen seeking to impose their counsel through the deployment of military
resources that should always have been his to command. Now he had the
reassuring capacity to flex military muscle of his own.[12]

That did not mean Richard himself intended to fight. The appeal of this Irish campaign included the fact that, unlike the decades of war with France and its allies, it was not a head-to-head confrontation with the claims of a rival king. The expedition's purpose, as Richard had told the duke of Burgundy in a letter written from Haverfordwest not long before he boarded ship, was both "to punish and correct our rebels there, and to enact good governance and establish just rule over our faithful lieges of our foresaid land." His royal presence in Ireland had been requested as early as 1385 by the bishops, lords, and Commons of the Anglo-Irish parliament, who warned that they were rapidly losing ground to the incursions of the Gaelic Irish, and that, "the conquest appearing so imminent upon the land, they cannot nor know how to find or think of a remedy except the coming of the lord king in person." But nine years later, when Richard finally arrived, it became apparent that he did not share their view that his task was to restore Anglo-Irish overlordship exactly as it had existed before.[13]

Anglo-Norman conquerors and colonists had taken possession of all but the far north and west of Ireland during the late twelfth and early thirteenth centuries. Over the past eight decades, however, a Gaelic resurgence—helped by a Scots invasion under Robert Bruce's brother Edward in 1315, and later by the English crown's overwhelming preoccupation with the war in France— had pushed the limits of English rule back again toward the eastern seaboard. The administration in Dublin and the parliaments regularly held in Dublin and Kilkenny were populated exclusively by the Anglo-Irish, but throughout the island the "English of Ireland," as they called themselves, both fought and came to accommodations with the Gaelic Irish, who were simultaneously fighting and coming to accommodations among themselves.[14]

These shape-shifting identities and conflicts were not easy for English incomers to understand. The policy of successive royal lieutenants— especially that of Lionel of Antwerp in the 1360s, who acquired the earldom of Ulster through his marriage to the heiress Elizabeth de Burgh—had been an attempt to reinforce the English of Ireland as a colonial elite, separate from and superior to the Gaelic population in terms of both culture and jurisdiction. The English crown had therefore always sought to draw clear lines of demarcation between three groups: the "faithful English" of Ireland,

"English rebels" who had compromised their allegiance by adopting Gaelic customs and alliances, and the "wild Irish," "our enemies."

But Richard was not persuaded that such categorizations were either useful or necessary. In 1381, facing rebellion in England born in part at least of the legal distinction between the free and unfree among his subjects, he had believed that the solution lay in the unique force of his own sovereignty. His personal intervention had quelled the revolt, and—had his lords not sabotaged his plan—all the people of England would have been brought into the same direct relationship with his crown. Now, as his army began to move north from Waterford, it was becoming clear that, in his mind, establishing "just rule" over the people of Ireland also depended fundamentally on his sovereign presence. He saw no reason why all of Ireland's powerful men— Gaelic chiefs just as much as the Anglo-Irish lords themselves—should not bow the knee directly before him. Two years earlier, the principle of collective surrender to his sovereignty had succeeded in restoring order to London. Once established as the source of peace in Ireland, a dominion that had been divided and disrupted for so long, it would surely serve him well on his return to the long-term project of reasserting his royal authority throughout his kingdom of England.

The first steps were military ones. His authority would be enforced by his troops under the operational command of his noble captains, who had Irish interests of their own to pursue. In Ireland the earl of March was earl of Ulster, a title inherited from his maternal grandfather Lionel of Antwerp, but its territories in the north long lost to the powerful Ó Néills, Niall Mór and his son Niall Óg. Richard had given his cousin Rutland the new title of earl of Cork in the southwestern province of Munster, power base of the Ó Briains and the family of Mac Carthaigh Mór, while Thomas Mowbray had a hereditary claim to the southeastern lordship of Carlow in Leinster, a region dominated by the formidable Art Caomhánach Mac Murchadha.[15]

It was in Leinster that the campaign began. While the English fleet blockaded the coast, the king's forces pinned Mac Murchadha into the hills south of Dublin within a ring of heavily garrisoned strongholds, from Carlow and Kilkenny in the west to Wicklow and Wexford in the east. Mowbray led a series of punishing raids on the chief's lands and tenants, burning villages, seizing cattle, and one night almost catching Mac Murchadha and his wife in bed at their home in the woods near Leighlin. As they fled into the darkness, Mowbray's soldiers ransacked and torched the house while Richard looked on in satisfaction. It took only days for Mac Murchadha to recognize the impossibility of holding out and the advantages of giving in. The English king, he realized, was seeking not his destruction but his submission. And submission in the form of liege homage would create a relationship of mutual obligation: royal justice and protection in return for Mac Murchadha's service to his sovereign lord.

Before the king and his entourage moved north to Dublin at the beginning of November, Mac Murchadha and other Irish captains appeared before Richard, bareheaded and unarmed, to offer him their swords. He graciously accepted their oaths of obedience, and let Mac Murchadha go free while the precise conditions of this surrender were negotiated. When the king wrote to his council in Westminster with the news, he sounded almost rapturous at the transformative power with which his sovereignty had taken effect: "... we seem to have conquered and imposed peace upon the whole land of Leinster, between divine providence and the ordinance that we have thought to make there, which land and country right up to our city of Dublin, woods, meadows, pastures, arable lands and rivers, are the most beautiful, plenteous and delightful that man could find anywhere, we believe." While Richard celebrated Christmas in style in his Irish capital, Mowbray remained in Leinster to agree on terms with Mac Murchadha. By January 7, 1395, it was done. Mac Murchadha and his men swore fealty to the king forever. They would give up the lands they had occupied in Leinster, and in return—as well as a hereditary grant of eighty marks a year for Mac Murchadha himself—they would retain in perpetuity whatever lands farther west they could retrieve from those who continued to rebel against the crown, fighting as they would be now in the king's service and at his wages. Face-to-face in a field east of Carlow, Mowbray and Mac Murchadha put their seals to the indenture.[16]

But as the weeks went on, there was much less fighting and many fewer lands to be won than the agreement had anticipated. The same calculations that had induced Mac Murchadha to come in, and the encouragement of his example, produced a flood of further submissions. The most important was that of Niall Mór Ó Néill, who performed homage to Richard for himself as "prince of the Irish of Ulster" and on behalf of his son Niall Óg, the "captain of his nation," at Drogheda, north of Dublin, on January 19. Between then and the beginning of May, a total of eighty Irish leaders came forward to acknowledge Richard's sovereignty, including Brian Ó Briain and Tadgh Mac Carthaigh Mór of Munster, brought in by the Anglo-Irish earls of Ormond and Desmond respectively. At each one of this stream of ceremonies, the chiefs took their solemn oaths of allegiance in Irish, kneeling before the king with their hands palm to palm between his, before their words were translated into English for the benefit of the sovereign and his attendants. Some lesser men, in expiation of past offenses against the crown, prostrated themselves further: at Kilkenny on April 21, Art Ó Diomusaigh threw himself at Richard's feet, a cord bound around his neck, to beg the royal forgiveness. "Most excellent and serene lord," the Irish called him, "your magnificence," "your royal majesty"; and the growing file of official documents recorded that the king admitted them all to his "illustrious grace."[17]

It seemed to Richard to be exactly the triumph he had foreseen, a still greater iteration of the peace that he had imposed in London, and a proper recognition of his own royal might. "We think that by the grace of God we shall shortly have complete obedience in all our land," he wrote to his council from Dublin in late January. The firsthand account of the campaign given at Westminster at the end of the month by Thomas of Woodstock, who had been sent back to England for the purpose, was enough to persuade parliament to grant a fifteenth and tenth to support the king's efforts, even if behind closed doors Woodstock was less than impressed either with Ireland itself ("a very poor and uninhabitable country") or with his own allotted role as errand boy.[18]

It was certainly true that the submissions of the Gaelic Irish were reframing the political landscape in ways that might make possible a settlement of the conflicts of the previous century and more. If all of Ireland's powerful men, English absentees, Anglo-Irish lords, and Gaelic chiefs, now explicitly recognized the supreme authority of the English crown, then royal lordship and royal justice—if exercised with care and insight, and consistently enforced—could in theory impose lasting resolutions on the mass of

competing claims to Irish lands and the governance of Ireland's people. But
the complexity of the task was already unnervingly apparent, especially given
that the king himself could not stay in Ireland forever. That much was clear
from the letters sent in February 1395 by his lords spiritual and temporal at
Westminster to congratulate him on his victory and to request his return,
"provided that your deputies left in your absence to govern your said land do
their utmost diligence and duty to treat your people there in the good and
rightful way of justice."[19]

The Gaelic lords' contention that they now stood in exactly the same
relation to Richard as his English and Anglo-Irish subjects, and could call
on his authority in exactly the same way, was obvious in every word they
addressed to him. A stream of Irish letters followed in the wake of the ceremonies of submission, petitioning humbly and anxiously for Richard's
protection against their enemies, compensation for past wrongs, and confirmation of title to their lands, rights, and possessions, many of which were
contested by the English of Ireland or those who had sailed with the king
from England. "If in anything I have sinned against your majesty I intend to
make satisfaction according to my power," wrote Niall Mór Ó Néill, "asking
most humbly that you should graciously receive me into your royal protection, and be to me a shield and helmet of justice between my lord the earl of
Ulster and me." The offer of such protection was, of course, one of the principal incentives that had led the Irish chiefs to submit in the first place. Their
humility and anxiety, on the other hand, seemed to their rivals to be a great
deal less than sincere. "The people are so false that no man can trust them,"
wrote Janico Dartasso, a Navarrese esquire who had been in the service of the
English crown for fifteen years and retained by Richard for two. He had been
granted land in Ireland by the king, which, "if it were near London, would
easily be worth 1000 marks a year, but by my faith I have had such trouble to
guard it that I would not wish to lead such a life any longer, not for a quarter
of the country."[20]

Dartasso's problem was that the formal oaths of loyalty and homage
by which the English set such store carried no weight within the political
culture of the Gaelic Irish, a crucial point that the English had missed entirely. The chiefs therefore saw no difficulty and no dishonor in manipulating

Richard's theater of submission to serve their own interests, while continuing to pursue those interests by any means necessary. And Richard, for his part, remained fixated on the performance of obedience, rather than the substance of the relationship supposedly so created. Despite the indenture sealed with Mowbray, for example, Art Mac Murdchadha received not a single install-ment of the annuity he had been promised from the Dublin exchequer. It was a gap between appearance and reality to which the king, exulting at the speed and majesty of his own success, seemed oblivious. By late April, he had returned south to his fleet at Waterford. The last submissions he received in person, those of three chiefs from Connacht, were taken on May 1 on board his flagship, the *Trinity*. Richard sailed for home two weeks later, leaving as his royal lieutenant the earl of March and Ulster, England's greatest Anglo-Irish lord, a young man who had just marked his twenty-first birthday, and whose responsibilities on behalf of his departed king now included the ad-judication of his own bitter territorial dispute with the Ó Néills. As the months passed, a settlement was not forthcoming.[21]

Even before he took ship at Waterford, Richard's thoughts were turning back to England. Ahead of him, for the first time in thirteen years, lay the reality of life without the constant presence of his queen. On April 9, he sent instructions from Kilkenny that the palace of Sheen, where they had spent so much time, on which he had lavished so much money, and where Anne had died ten months earlier, should be pulled down, and all its fabric—glass, tiles, stone, timber, and ironwork—carefully put into storage for reuse at the new palace he was planning to build two miles farther west at Isleworth. The demolition of Sheen was a manifestation of the king's grief, wrote the chronicler at Evesham Abbey, "nor, for a whole year after the queen's death, would he enter any place that he knew she had previously been, except a church." It was a dramatic conceit rendered technically plausible by Rich-ard's absence on his Irish campaign from August to May, although the king showed no sign of avoiding any of the usual royal residences in the weeks before and after his travels.[22]

In fact, rather than debilitating sorrow, Richard was continuing to display the buoyant energy that had characterized his time in Ireland. As well as his architectural ambitions, he was preoccupied with the design of the magnificent tomb that would house Anne's body at Westminster Abbey, in which he intended one day to lie beside her. The site was already chosen: the queen had been laid to rest within the arcade of pillars that surrounded the jeweled shrine of Saint Edward the Confessor, in the bay immediately next to that occupied by the king's grandfather Edward III. From Ireland, Richard approved the contracts for the master masons who would build the ornate marble table-chest, and the coppersmiths who would fashion gilded metal images of the king and queen. Richard had no intention of dying in the near future; nevertheless, the effigies would capture the couple in the same moment, smooth skinned and clear-eyed, their right hands clasped, their left hands holding scepters. Heraldic beasts would sit at their feet, two lions for the king, an eagle and a leopard for the queen, while eight golden angels and twelve golden saints of Richard's choosing would keep watch around them. The commission also gave the king the chance to oversee the composition of their paired epitaphs. Anne, the Latin couplets announced, had been a paragon of female virtue, pious and beautiful; she calmed quarrels and helped the poor, the pregnant, the sick, and the needy. But Richard's encomium took pride of place: "Prudent and pure, here lies Richard, by right the Second, overcome by fate. . . . He was truthful in speech and full of reason; his body tall, his mind prudent like Homer. A friend of the Church, he subdued the mighty, and cut down anyone who violated the rights of the crown." It was a startling description of his own kingship, utterly distinct from the martial triumphs commemorated on his grandfather's tomb a few feet away. Edward III's epitaph, set in brass on a monument built after the end of his long reign, recalled him as the leader of his people, "the glory of the English," "an invincible leopard, powerful in war." But Richard was unwilling to wait for the judgment of posterity. He knew how he should be remembered: as faultlessly *right*, a lone figure of ineffable virtue and wisdom, his weapons trained not on external enemies but on anyone who dared challenge his God-given sovereignty.[23]

Meanwhile, those among his mighty subjects who had been left to run his government in Westminster had been ordered to set about the task of finding him a new wife to replace the one whose remains now rested in the abbey. By February 1395, they had identified a target: Yolande, the young daughter of the king of Aragon. She was already promised to the French king's cousin the teenage duke of Anjou, but such betrothals could always be unmade if the political will was there. An Anglo-Aragonese alliance would reinforce the interests that Gaunt had established in Castile and Portugal, and strengthen England's hand over the fate of neighboring Aquitaine whenever peace negotiations resumed with France. From Ireland, Richard approved the choice, and in early March an English embassy set out for Barcelona to negotiate the match. When news of their mission reached the royal court in Paris, there was consternation at the prospect that the benefits of Aragon's support—and potentially a claim to its throne, given that Yolande had no brothers—might be lost to France and gained by England. Within days French envoys arrived in London asking for permission to travel to Ireland to put a counteroffer to the king. At the head of government in Richard's absence, Edmund of Langley tied himself in anxious knots trying to work out whether his nephew ("your majesty," "your royal highness," "dread lord") would want to see them or not, and how best to avoid the royal anger if he guessed the wrong way.[24]

When the French delegation finally sailed for Waterford in late April, it became apparent that Richard was keenly interested in the proposal they brought. The dukes of Berry and Burgundy and their royal nephew's council now suggested, in the interests of peace between the two kingdoms, that the next queen of England should be French. The initial form of the plan was unworkable, since the three cousins of King Charles named as potential brides were not of sufficient status to be plausible matches for King Richard. But the principle of a matrimonial alliance with his French counterpart was one the king was more than willing to consider, and within weeks the proposal had improved. Not long after Richard's return to Westminster at the end of May, another French embassy arrived in the capital, this time led by the visionary Robert the Hermit, who brought an impassioned letter from Charles—"good brother, let us be God's helpers and hold firm in the vocation to which God has called us in our youth, that is, in the sweet peace for which Christendom longs so much"—along with an offer of the hand in marriage of the king's eldest daughter, Isabella.[25]

Her royal blood made her a worthy candidate to be Richard's wife, but there were drawbacks. Isabella was five. It would be another decade before the twenty-eight-year-old king could hope that she might give him a child, and in the meantime, England had no heir apparent. In private, the late Queen Anne had been acutely conscious of her failure to give birth. In the last year of her life, she had bought medical preparations including a compound known as *trifera magna*, made from opium mixed with cinnamon, cloves, galangal, spikenard, and other sweet-smelling plants, which was thought to be of "great utility to women and makes them fruitful." But her husband appeared unconcerned. Richard had been publicly matter-of-fact at the beginning of 1394 in granting Thomas Mowbray the right to use a heraldic crest that would have belonged to "our first-born son, if we had begotten one." And by now, the existence of such an heir would have been actively inconvenient to Richard in some directly practical ways. Precedent dictated that the king's eldest son should become prince of Wales and earl of Chester, but Richard's recruitment of his prized new military retinue depended, politically and financially, on his own possession of those estates.[26]

Not only that, but the king seemed to sit more comfortably on his throne while the identity of its next incumbent remained unclear. Happy though he was to design his own superb tomb, Richard had no wish to contemplate the reality of his end in any more detail than his epitaph's splendidly vague suggestion that he would one day be "overcome by fate." In the meantime, he knew all too well that arguments over the succession had saved him from the threat of deposition during the bleak winter of 1387–88. Nor did either of the forebears for whom he showed special reverence offer any encouragement to become a father. Edward the Confessor, the Anglo-Saxon king and peace-loving saint beside whose shrine Richard's own tomb would nestle, had had no children. Instead, Edward had designated as his successor Duke William of Normandy, who established the glorious line of English monarchs from which Richard himself was descended. The king's veneration for the Confessor had intensified in recent years to the extent that he had begun to display the saint's coat of arms—a flowering cross surrounded by five martlets, all in gold on a ground of blue—side by side with his own, including on banners at the head of his forces in Ireland. Now, in the summer of 1395, he began to impale those arms with his own, half and half on a single escutcheon. Reverence, it seemed, was evolving into identification. At the same time, he was campaigning more earnestly than ever for the canonization of his great-grandfather Edward II, a king who had fathered an heir but might well have wished, in the end, that he had not. It was in the name of their son that Edward's queen, another Isabella of France, had overthrown and murdered him. Freshly painted white harts circled the pillars beside the deposed king's tomb in the abbey church at Gloucester, and two royal messengers had just delivered an account of the miracles that had occurred there to the pope in Rome, in the hope of securing recognition of his sainthood.[27]

But for all his belief in Edward's holiness, Richard had no desire to join him in martyrdom. Marrying a wife who was still in the nursery would mean he ran no risk of discord with this new Isabella. Instead, in symbol and in practice, the match could lay to rest the conflicts caused by the old Isabella: the decades of war precipitated by the claim to the French throne she had bequeathed to her son Edward III, and the damage she had done to the crown in England.[28] Certainly there was no sign that his childlessness gave Richard a moment's pause. More than ever, the king saw the existence of competing claims to be his heir—and his own consequent room for maneuvers between his cousin March, his uncle Gaunt, and cousin Henry, perhaps even his newly favored cousin Rutland—as a source of strength in the exercise of his royal authority, rather than any kind of weakness.

Not everyone agreed that peace with France secured by the king's marriage to a small child was in England's best interests. When the royal council met at Eltham Palace in July 1395, Thomas of Woodstock was the leading dissident. He had never wanted a permanent end to the war, and the insulting way he had been sidelined on campaign in Ireland in favor of March and Rutland, men half his age, had done nothing to convince him of the value of his nephew's alternative military priorities. As for the succession, he could be under no illusion about his own vanishing chances of wearing the crown, but that did not mean he wanted to see his brothers' descendants prioritized over his own. Jean Froissart, arriving in England that summer for the first time in almost thirty years, heard that Woodstock had offered his twelve-year-old daughter, Anne, as a bride for the king, since she had royal blood in her veins and was mature enough to give him children. But Richard waved the proposition away. They were too closely related, he said, and besides, it was good that the French king's daughter was so young. He could guide her, and bring her up in English ways, and meanwhile he himself had plenty of time to wait for her to grow.[29]

Still, he had no intention of selling himself short as a royal bridegroom. A full-blown peace agreement to accompany the marriage would depend on the French offering substantially more in relation to the contested issues of sovereignty and homage than Gaunt's proposals from Leulinghem, which had already been rejected in parliament. As a result, the English embassy that arrived in Paris at the end of July was notable in two distinct respects. First, unlike the Leulinghem delegation, it was not led by any of the king's uncles. Gaunt was still in Aquitaine, and Langley and Woodstock remained in England. Instead, the chief envoys were Richard's new protégé Rutland and his reconciled friend Mowbray—much younger men, and much more clearly the king's personal proxies. Also remarkable were the terms the two earls had been instructed to offer. Richard would accept Isabella as his bride if she came with a dowry of two million gold francs—more than £330,000—although this startling figure could be reduced by up to half at his ambassadors' discretion. Then came an even more staggering list of the concessions in return for which England would now accept a permanent peace. Richard demanded possession in full sovereignty of all the territories held by his grandfather in 1360 at the Treaty of Brétigny. In addition, he required that the duchy of Normandy and the counties of Anjou and Maine—territories England had lost to France almost two centuries before—should be settled on his eldest son or sons by Isabella. The French were to send military assistance for the conquest of Scotland, should he wish to give that kingdom to another future son. They were to pay all arrears from the ransom of the French king's royal grandfather, and to repay all costs incurred by the king of England since the start of the war more than half a century earlier. The pope in Rome, unrecognized by the French since the schism with Avignon in 1378, was to be included in the terms of the treaty. Finally, the royal arms of England were to incorporate the fleurs-de-lis of France, as they did now, forever.[30]

Richard had personally charged his ambassadors with these orders even before his council had gathered at Eltham. Their scope was extraordinary; so extraordinary as to be divorced from any possible reality. Perhaps, like the dowry, the king intended them as a maximal opening bid from which his representatives could bargain their way to a more expansive agreement than the failed proposals of the previous year; but if so, unlike the dowry, he gave no explicit instructions to that effect. In the event, it hardly seemed to matter. Rutland and Mowbray and their entourage arrived in Paris with great pomp. They were given magnificent lodgings and lavishly entertained, and, as the weeks of August went by, their king's enthusiasm for the match with little Isabella was warmly reciprocated. In response to the bizarre extravagance of their king's demands, however, the earls were met with nothing more than elegantly raised eyebrows.[31]

It was a start, at least. For the moment, Richard had other projects to occupy his imagination. He had decided to commission a full-length portrait of himself, a dazzling icon of sovereignty enthroned, to adorn the back of his royal seat in the choir of Westminster Abbey. Together with the gilded figure the coppersmiths were currently preparing for his tomb, there would soon be two life-size images of himself permanently installed in the holiest part of this holy church, one immediately in front of the high altar, the other immediately behind it, next to the Confessor's shrine. As these works of art took shape, they were recognizably a pair: the same heavy-lidded eyes, long nose, and pursed lips in the soft oval of his face; the same slight, double-pointed beard on his small, rounded chin. In the light of the abbey's torches and candles, the portrait, like the effigy, blazed with gold: on a ground of stamped gilt the king sat in majesty, his crown, orb, and scepter shimmering in gilded gesso, his initial *R* powdered across the brocaded fabric of his robe, and over it a cloak of rich red velvet, lined with the same soft ermine that draped across his shoulders. The figure appeared alone, but in form it mirrored the depiction of the Confessor newly crowned by his archbishops on the wall of the Painted Chamber in the adjoining palace of Westminster. And Richard's vision for the sacred space of the Confessor's church continued to grow. Another large painting above a door in the mezzanine gallery of the south transept imprinted the king's presence further into the fabric of the abbey: a white hart lying on a golden ground, its elegant neck encircled by a crown on a gilded chain, its great antlers filling the pointed arch above its head. The image was carefully placed to catch the light and the eye; anyone lifting their gaze as they turned from the high altar, or beside the Confessor's shrine, or passing through the ambulatory on the outer side of Richard's newly constructed tomb, or processing into the choir from the north would see the king's emblem glowing as if from heaven.[32]

Just fifty yards from the abbey, meanwhile, teams of masons, carpenters, and laborers were at work in the palace's great hall. Its vast space had remained structurally unchanged since it was first built 300 years earlier, but in January 1394 Richard had decided that this public stage for the exercise of his kingship should be entirely remodeled. On his orders the Norman pillars that ran the length of the hall were being removed, the walls heightened and resurfaced, the windows enlarged, and a new wooden roof installed that could span the hall's entire breadth—almost seventy feet—without support from the ground. It was a breathtaking feat of engineering and craftsmanship, unprecedented in its ambition; but the king was concerned above all with the decorative scheme that would mark the space as his own. Already, ten years earlier, he had commissioned statues of all thirteen kings of England from the Confessor to Richard himself, an imposing roll call of his royal lineage, to stand in niches along the north and south walls. Now the stringcourse, the line of stone where the walls met the base of the windows and the lowest timbers of the newly vaulted roof, would be studded with finely sculpted white harts. The stone corbel supporting the base of each vault would bear either Richard's royal arms or those of the Confessor, alternating around the hall; then looking down from each projecting hammer beam would be an angel, carved in oak, wings outspread, holding the king's coat of arms in its heavenly hands.[33]

Progress was inevitably slow, but as he constructed the grandeur of his future, Richard was also finding ways to reckon with the past. In October 1395, while his ambassadors set out again for Paris to pursue the question of the royal marriage, the king dispatched a messenger to Louvain. He wanted de Vere's body brought home. In late November, the royal household made its way to Colne Priory in Essex, where the earls of Oxford had been buried since the twelfth century, and where almost £300 had been newly spent in preparation for the ceremony that would lay the royal favorite to rest. Among the king's entourage was de Vere's mother, come to see her only child interred, as well as the archbishop of Canterbury and a distinguished crowd of bishops, abbots, and priors. But very few nobles were there, Walsingham reported, "since the hatred they felt for the dead man had not yet dissipated."[34]

By the light of hundreds of candles, Richard had the cypress coffin opened so that he could see de Vere's face once more and touch his embalmed fingers. It had been seven years and eleven months since their last, frantic farewell, and the king had forgotten nothing.

Ten

1395–1396

conclude and be agreed

While Richard was in Ireland and Gaunt in Aquitaine, Henry found himself in limbo. He was at Westminster in late January 1395 when parliament met without the absent king; he heard his uncle Woodstock's report of the Irish campaign, and put his seal to the letter sent by the assembled lords requesting Richard's return. But other than that—and unlike his young cousins Rutland and March or his erstwhile associate Mowbray—he had no formal responsibilities within government, no grants of royal office or military command.[1]

It was a glaring omission. Perhaps the king was simply taking account of the scale of his cousin's duties as Gaunt's lieutenant within the duchy of Lancaster—but, given the name Henry had made for himself across Europe as a brave leader of men, it was difficult to read Richard's refusal to find a use for his skills as anything other than a lack of royal trust, even a measure of royal hostility. Ever since Gaunt's return from Castile six years before, Henry had been sheltered by the closeness of his father's alignment with the king in the search for a permanent peace with France; but that quest had failed, and in Gaunt's renewed absence there were reasons to feel that portents for the Lancastrian future might be darkening. In Ireland, Richard had enjoyed the freedom to exercise his sovereign authority without his uncle's advice or participation for the first time in five years. On his return, the alacrity with which he seized the opportunity to send his chosen envoys to Paris with his own outlandish proposals for peace suggested that he was relishing his new independence.

Men who had built careers by serving both Gaunt and the king were beginning to find those two loyalties pulling them in different directions. John Holand, Richard's brother and Gaunt's son-in-law, had left England back in January 1394 on a diplomatic mission to Hungary, sent to discuss plans for a crusade against the Turks as part of what seemed likely, then, to be an imminent settlement between England and France. He returned a year later to a changed world, in which all Gaunt's efforts at Leulinghem had produced only a truce, along with the unrest in Aquitaine that the duke had been forced to leave England to suppress. Holand lost no time in sailing for Ireland to join the king for the final weeks of the campaign there. Holand's deputy as chamberlain of the royal household since 1393, William Scrope, eldest son of the aging Lord Scrope who had served as chancellor in the early 1380s, was an experienced soldier and administrator with a long history in Gaunt's service in both England and Aquitaine. But he too accompanied Richard to Ireland, and then traveled with Rutland and Mowbray to Paris to negotiate for the king's marriage.[2]

To Lancastrian eyes, the new choices confronting these influential men were not the only disconcerting features of the shifting political landscape. The revolt in the northwest in 1393 had served as a warning that Gaunt's power in the palatinate of Lancashire, overwhelming though it might be, was not invulnerable, and that Richard's growing retinue in Cheshire and its neighboring counties might make the king a rival, even a threat, to his uncle's lordship in the region. For the moment, Gaunt himself was not there to keep an eye on the continuing attempt to bring the rebel leader Thomas Talbot to justice, but Henry could hardly miss the remarkable fact that Talbot succeeded in escaping from custody for a second time early in 1395, on this occasion from the Tower, where the king's brother Thomas Holand was constable.[3]

Meanwhile, Richard's ongoing preoccupation with the canonization of Edward II also had unnerving resonances for the Lancastrian dynasty. King Edward's principal political opponent had been his cousin Thomas, earl of Lancaster, until the earl's execution as a traitor in 1322—a death that gave rise to a popular cult venerating him as a saint. When Edward was deposed, the Lancastrian estates and title had been restored with honor to the Lancastrian line. But if Edward, rather than Lancaster, were now to be formally recognized as a holy martyr, and his removal from the throne as unjust, then—far-fetched though the prospect of reversing seventy years of political reality might seem—the argument might follow that the earl's conviction for treason should be reinstated and the Lancastrian estates and title forfeited once more to the king.[4]

For now, all Henry could do was shoulder the responsibilities Gaunt had left him, and use what voice he had in defense of his father and his family's interests. In June, he was at Mary's graveside in Leicester to mark the first anniversary of her death, but in the following month he rode to the palace of Eltham, southeast of the city of London, to attend a meeting of the council summoned by his cousin the king. Under consideration there, as well as the proposal for Richard's French marriage, was the revolt in Aquitaine, which his father was currently attempting to contain. The plan to circumvent the need for the English king to do homage to the king of France by granting Aquitaine to Gaunt and his heirs had had much to commend it from Richard's point of view as well as Gaunt's; but—quite apart from the opposition the idea had provoked in England—it was obvious now that the king and his uncle had failed to take sufficient notice of the vehement objections of the people of Aquitaine themselves. Their security, their legal status, and their prosperity, they believed, depended on their direct relationship with the English crown, a relationship that defended them not only against the threat of French incursions but also against what they saw as an inevitable erosion of their liberties and privileges, should the duchy ever become a private lordship. After Gaunt's arrival there in January 1395 it had taken more than three months, and a series of behind-the-scenes deals with leading figures in the duchy, before he was allowed to enter the city of Bordeaux on March 13. A week later, a temporizing agreement had been reached: Gaunt would be recognized as duke of Aquitaine just as soon as King Richard defined the nature of his title.[5]

However, when delegates from the duchy arrived at Eltham that summer to consult on the matter—their visit observed from the fringes of the royal household by Jean Froissart, in England to gather material for his chronicle—it became apparent how little had been resolved. Richard had expected the men from Bordeaux, the city of his birth, to be overawed by the grandeur of his moated palace with its spectacular views across the Thames to his capital, and by the ceremony and magnificence of his court. But when they were ushered into his presence on July 22 the envoys were undaunted and focused only on their mission. Their position, cogently and forcefully argued, was that Aquitaine was irrevocably annexed to the crown of England, and could not be given away by the king. In support of their case they produced documents under the weighty authority of England's great seal: a letter of Edward III publicly affirming the duchy's established status, and an assurance given by Richard himself, during an earlier stage of Gaunt's negotiations in Bordeaux, that Aquitaine's privileges would always be maintained. These royal undertakings, they declared, were patently incompatible with the king's grant of the duchy to Gaunt.[6]

They were met with silence. All eyes turned to the king. But Richard was faced with a dilemma. He wanted peace with France, along with the freedom it would bring in the exercise of his kingship. He therefore wanted the interminable arguments over homage for Aquitaine—a place he had left at the age of four and showed no inclination to revisit—to be over once and for all. On the other hand, the people of the duchy were resisting his command to accept Gaunt as their duke on the grounds that they were determined to be ruled only by Richard himself. They would live and die, they had announced in Bordeaux a year earlier, in their resolve never to obey anyone else. Back then, the king had responded angrily to the head-spinning claim that the duchy's obedience to him justified its refusal to abide by his orders. Since then, however, his reiteration of those orders had produced no greater compliance. And the argument they were making—that, as his loyal subjects, their allegiance was owed uniquely and directly to his sovereign authority— might be inconvenient in Aquitaine, but it remained at the heart of his own conception of his rule in England and Ireland. Besides all of which, Rutland and Mowbray were about to leave for Paris with the demand that, in return for his marriage to the French king's daughter, he should hold Aquitaine in full sovereignty with no homage to be done; and if the French were to agree, this whole infuriating wrangle would simply disappear.[7]

For now, in the expectant presence of the lords of his council, the king said nothing. After a few moments, the chancellor, Archbishop Arundel, suggested that the crown's lawyers should offer an opinion on the case. When the clerks returned from their deliberations, their view was clear: legally, Aquitaine was annexed to the crown, and the grant to Gaunt should therefore be revoked. The one allowable exception would be a grant to the heir to the throne, as in the case of the king's father, the Black Prince; but—as everyone present knew—Richard was not about to designate Gaunt as his heir, and even if he did, Aquitaine would not accept as duke an heir presumptive who would be displaced in the line of succession by any child of the king's future marriage.[8]

Silence fell again. Given the tortuous complexity of the issue, and in the absence of any indication of the king's thinking, speaking up was not a simple proposition. The bishops turned to Woodstock and Langley. Perhaps the king's uncles might offer some advice, since they were the lords closest to the crown? But the dukes demurred: Surely this was a matter that required discussion by the whole council? It took a few moments more before Woodstock could be prevailed upon to speak. Afterward, Froissart was told that he had been blunt. It was a serious matter, the duke said, to undo a grant that had been made by a sovereign with the unanimous consent of his counselors. After all, the king was not master of his inheritance if he could not do what he wished with it. Far-fetched though it seemed to hear of Woodstock arguing for the inviolability of his nephew's royal will—albeit with the essential caveat of the agreement of his lords—Froissart's informant believed that the duke had his own reasons for wanting the grant to stand, since he hoped to expand his own room for maneuvers within English politics by keeping his powerful older brother far away in Aquitaine. The terse official minutes of the meeting recorded much less: only that Woodstock stipulated the need for adequate proof of the duchy's privileges, and the right of the two Lancastrian knights who were there as Gaunt's representatives to be given a further hearing. But both the official minutes and Froissart's account noted that, after Woodstock, Henry too spoke up in support of his father's claim to the duchy.[9]

While the rest of the lords began to murmur among themselves, Wood-stock stalked out of the chamber. He had said his piece, and had no further patience for a discussion that promised little in the way of resolution. Henry followed him. They sat down to dine in the great hall, where Langley soon joined them. The three men made an odd trio: Woodstock bristling with frustration at the ineffectual meeting and the fact that, at forty, his voice still did not carry the weight in government he had always believed it should; Henry, at twenty-eight, acutely aware of his exclusion from his cousin's royal favor and of his need, despite that disadvantage, to represent his father as best he could; and Langley who, at fifty-four, had recently taken as his sec-ond wife the beautiful teenage daughter of the king's brother Thomas Hol-and, earl of Kent. To Froissart's well-informed source, the delights of this new marriage seemed to have rendered the duke even more hopelessly dis-tracted than usual.[10]

As it turned out, their meal marked the end of the council's active de-liberations on the question of Aquitaine. Woodstock rode back to London that afternoon. Henry and the other lords stayed for three more days, and Langley longer than that; but the envoys from Bordeaux could secure no an-swer beyond a safe-conduct to stay in England as long as they pleased. The royal judgment, it seemed, would be some time in coming. For now, Richard was much more interested in pursuing his marriage to the little daughter of the French king, and—having graciously granted the visiting Froissart a personal audience—in making sure that the chronicler knew what a triumph his campaign in Ireland had been. The relationship between Gaunt and the duchy of Aquitaine remained in suspended animation, but neither side had yet lost—and that meant, at least, that life could go on as it had before.[11]

Gaunt and his household left Bordeaux in September, sailing for Brit-tany to visit its duke, John de Montfort, with whom he had grown up and who had once, long ago, been married to his sister Mary. After the death of de Montfort's second wife, Richard's sister Joan Holand, the duke had married another Joan, daughter of the king of Navarre, by whom he now had five young children. The two men took the opportunity presented by their reunion to negotiate a personal alliance and another prospective wed-ding, agreeing that Gaunt's nine-year-old grandson, Henry's eldest son and namesake, would marry de Montfort's four-year-old daughter, Marie. Back in England, Henry himself was waiting anxiously for his father's return. Christmas had passed by the time Gaunt at last made landfall at Dover, and it was January 1 before father and son were reunited at Canterbury. There was relief, but also concern; the year in Aquitaine had been taxing, and the duke's health was no longer as resilient as it had once been. Concern politically too: when Gaunt rode to the palace of Langley, northwest of London, to pay his respects at court, Richard received him with cool formality. It was the week of the king's twenty-ninth birthday; it had taken time, but finally— as Woodstock had recently told him he should be—Richard was master of his own inheritance. In his kingdom of England, in his lordship of Ireland, and in his dealings with the kingdom of France, he now made his own royal decisions without reference to his uncle. The moment had come, perhaps, for Gaunt to spend more time with his family.[12]

That, at least, was the choice Gaunt made. When he left Langley, he rode to Lincoln. There, in the glorious light and space of the cathedral, he married Katherine Swynford. To observers who knew him only in public, and many more besides, it was an astonishing decision: that the greatest of the king's subjects, a duke who had hoped to be a king himself, a man whose daughters were queens, should stoop to marry his mistress, the daughter of a mere knight, a woman who had given him four children conceived in adultery. Froissart relished the gossip. The great ladies of England, he said, were horrified by Katherine's elevation, especially since they would now be required to cede precedence to her as the greatest among them. The chronicler's credibility as a witness was undermined somewhat by the fact that he added Henry's dead wife to the names of these outraged noblewomen; on the other hand, it was not hard to believe that the perennially thin-skinned Thomas of Woodstock, the lone man on Froissart's list, might balk at calling Katherine Swynford his sister. But those close to Gaunt—including Henry, to whom the new duchess of Lancaster had been part of his family for as long as he could remember—were well aware of Katherine's intelligence, her grace and dignity, and recognized how much sustenance this enduring relationship could bring to a man whose life had been driven relentlessly by duty as well as ambition. Even Froissart acknowledged that Gaunt's decision to marry Katherine was propelled by love not just for her but for their children, all four of whom were grown to young adulthood. John, Henry, Thomas, and Joan Beaufort had been born out of wedlock, but their parents' belated marriage meant that, if Church and state could be brought to agree, they might one day be recognized among their father's legitimate offspring.[13]

Domesticity had not been Gaunt's original plan for this stage in his life. If the agreement he had made with the duke of Burgundy at Leulinghem two years earlier had come to fruition, both men should now have been riding east at the head of an Anglo-French host to confront the Ottoman forces on the frontiers of Hungary. But, even aside from the issue of Gaunt's deteriorating health, there had been no pause in their political responsibilities on either side of the Channel. The dukes had therefore entrusted the defense of Christendom to their sons. Burgundy's deputy was his heir, twenty-four-year-old John, count of Nevers; Gaunt's was his eldest son by Katherine, John Beaufort, who at twenty-three had already jousted alongside Henry at Saint-Inglevert, fought against the corsairs of North Africa under the duke of Bourbon, and followed in Henry's footsteps on a *reyse* in Lithuania in 1394. Beaufort accompanied his father when Gaunt sailed for Aquitaine later that year, before traveling on toward Hungary with a detachment of Lancastrian troops when the duke returned home—albeit that the difference in status between the heir of Burgundy and the Bastard of Lancaster, as well as the disparity in the size of their forces, meant that he was serving not on an Anglo-French crusade but within an unmistakably Burgundian-French army.[14]

Still, Henry envied his brother. Now that their father was safely back in England, he was chafing against the confines of his life, lacking as it did either the comforts of the home he had created with Mary or any wider sense of immediate purpose. When a message arrived from the count of Ostrevant, heir to the county of Holland, with an invitation to join his attempt to annex the neighboring territories of Friesland, Henry badly wanted to go. But Gaunt refused to let him leave; it was too uncertain and dangerous, the duke said. He meant the campaign in the Low Countries, but a different kind of dangerous uncertainty was already in play in England. For the first time in his nineteen-year reign, Richard stood alone and free at the helm of the ship of state. Should treacherous waters lie ahead, Gaunt wanted Henry close by his side.[15]

When Gaunt returned from Aquitaine in late December 1395, Rutland, Mowbray, and Scrope were preparing to depart for Paris for the third time. Their task was simple, or at least as simple as any with which ambassadors between the two kingdoms had been confronted in the fifty-five years since the war began. Richard's astonishing demands of the previous summer had been gracefully sidestepped, never to be spoken of again, which meant that a permanent peace was no longer under discussion. Gaunt's solution, hammered out around the negotiating table at Leulinghem in 1393, had not worked, and there was no other settlement to be found. Instead, Richard now wanted three things. He wanted to be certain that the war would not start again in the immediately foreseeable future. He wanted the French king's daughter as his queen. And—given the current scale of his spending on his court and his personal retinue—he wanted cash.

These goals, at least, were achievable. His marriage was his own to negotiate, along with the size of the dowry his bride might bring in her train. And if a permanent peace was impossible, then war would instead have to be deferred by another truce, to begin once the current ceasefire expired in 1398. That too left the terms of the agreement in the king's hands since, as a renewal of the existing status quo, a truce could be arranged behind closed doors without public scrutiny or parliamentary endorsement. When they reached Paris in January 1396, Richard's envoys set to work to close the deal.

His initial stipulation that Isabella should come with a dowry of two million francs had to be revised substantially downward. In the end, the amount was set at 800,000 francs—a little more than £130,000—which Richard would receive over the course of five years: 300,000 on the day of the wedding (up from the 200,000 originally proposed by the French), and the rest in annual installments of 100,000. Meanwhile, the length of the truce to which he was committing his kingdom was revised substantially upward, from five years to twenty and then, in the end, twenty-eight. This new term would run from 1398, meaning that hostilities would be suspended until 1426. The agreement was sealed on March 9. Three days later, six-year-old Isabella was brought in state to the exquisite Sainte-Chapelle in her father's palace on the Île de la Cité. There she was married by proxy, with Mowbray standing in for the king, as a formal commitment by both sides to the wedding that would take place when she and Richard finally met. At the lavish banquet after the ceremony she was given the seat of honor as the new queen of England. The deal was done.[16]

Richard had what he wanted, but there were reasons to suppose that his subjects would not all be equally pleased. Negotiating for peace with Gaunt in 1393, the French had been willing to hand back almost all of the duchy of Aquitaine as it had stood at the Treaty of Brétigny in 1360, an area three times the size of the coastal strip between Bordeaux and Bayonne that currently lay under English control. Now—as was noted with satisfaction in Paris—they had secured a truce that would last for a generation without addressing any of the central issues of sovereignty and homage or giving up a single square foot of territory beyond what the English already held. It remained to be seen what response this fait accompli would elicit once the news became more widely known in England, but for now the truce—as opposed to the royal marriage—was not announced in public. The few who were privy to the detail of the discussions were also aware that the king's instructions to his envoys had contained one unsettling clause. In haggling over the down payment on the dowry, Richard had said that he would be willing to accept the smaller sum proposed by the French if they would undertake to provide him with assistance, should he need it, against any of his subjects. That bargain was not struck because the envoys secured the greater amount; but the request could only be a disconcerting echo of the king's explosive retort to the criticism delivered by his uncle Woodstock and the then Bishop Arundel ten years earlier, at the crisis-ridden parliament of 1386, when he had talked of seeking French support against his own people. Richard did not specify which of his subjects he had in mind—but what might he mean, given the order that prevailed in his kingdom?[17]

For now, the only objections to the settlement emanated from behind the gates of Thomas of Woodstock's castle at Pleshey in Essex. It seemed that the duke saw himself as a torchbearer for the old ways; not just a soldier holding out against the sybaritic culture of his nephew's court, but a steadfast defender of the cause to which his revered father and eldest brother had devoted their lives, and of the glorious achievements to which they had led the realm. It was a cause to which Gaunt had once been equally committed, before he abandoned the past to support the king's headlong pursuit of peace. Knowing there was no hope of persuading his oldest brother to change course, Woodstock shifted his attention to the more biddable Langley, but their private conversations did nothing to coax Langley into swimming against the tide. Instead, Woodstock nursed his resentment at Pleshey, while with every passing month his estrangement from his nephew's regime became more obvious in Westminster and beyond.[18]

In Paris, the dukes of Burgundy and Berry were so concerned about the disruptive potential of Woodstock's opposition to the deal that, early in 1396, they sent another embassy across the Channel to investigate at first hand. Robert the Hermit, whose charismatic voice in support of the unification of Christendom against the Turks had won him a key role in French diplomacy, spent five days with Richard at Eltham before riding to Pleshey, where he was welcomed by Woodstock with grandeur, but no perceptible warmth. Dressed in the gray habit he had adopted when his calling began, the Frenchman urged the duke to commit himself to the truce. "The war has gone on too long," he declared, "and God wants it to end." He knew this to be true because a vision—which he recounted blow by blow for the duke's benefit—had told him so three years earlier, when he and the ship in which he was sailing were miraculously saved from a storm at sea. His heaven-sent task was to bring this message to the kings of France and England, and that he had done, to extraordinary effect; but Woodstock was no more impressed by the Hermit's perorations than he had been at Leulinghem. He would of course support an honorable peace, the duke said, but this deal unjustly rewarded the French for their treachery in overturning the Treaty of Brétigny by reasserting French sovereignty over Aquitaine almost three decades before. If King Richard were to persist with the truce, he would in effect be disinheriting the crown of England, and depriving the kings who would come after him of lands that should by right be theirs.[19]

As Woodstock well knew it would, every word of the conversation reached the ears of his nephew at Eltham. There Richard confided in his brother-in-law the count of St. Pol, who had traveled with the Hermit from

Paris. Surely it was easy to see how strongly his own royal will bent toward peace, and how much he was supported by his brothers Thomas and John Holand and his uncles Gaunt and Langley, all four lords there present by his side. His uncle Woodstock, on the other hand, was nothing but a danger to him, seeking constantly to rouse the people of London and the whole realm against his plans. What could be done before all was lost? St. Pol—at forty, a veteran of Anglo-French politics in both war and peace—was reassuring. For now, he said, Woodstock should be handled with kid gloves. But once the king was married and his French queen installed in England, then everything would be different. Then Richard could deal with those who dared to challenge him. And he could be sure that the king of France would send whatever help he needed.[20]

The message was a comfort, and meanwhile, however fraught the tension between Eltham and Pleshey, there was a wedding to organize. For a fleeting moment it seemed possible that the Anglo-French détente would produce not one royal wedding but three, since two further marriages were briefly under discussion: that of twenty-three-year-old Rutland to five-year-old Jeanne, second daughter of the French king, and that of her one-year-old sister, Michelle, to Gaunt's grandson Henry. In the end, neither proposal came to anything, although the turning of the marital merry-go-round was enough to dissolve young Henry's recent betrothal to the daughter of the duke of Brittany. Still, one wedding was enough, especially given the ongoing uncertainty over the health of the little bride's father. Back in January, negotiations had been delayed for weeks when Charles lapsed again into the mania and extravagant delusions that robbed him of his reason, but since February the prayers of his subjects had been answered and, for the time being at least, his wits were restored. In Paris there had also been fears that the disparity in age between Richard and Isabella might mean that the English king would leave his new queen in the care of her parents until she reached her twelfth birthday, the canonical age for marriage, and that during the intervening years he might renege on the treaty. But Richard was so eager to conclude the alliance and take his wife into his own keeping that in June he asked the duke of Burgundy to meet him at Calais to discuss the wedding arrangements in person.[21]

It had the flavor of a dress rehearsal: the first time since childhood that the king had set foot in his French territories, and his first encounter with the blood royal of France. Richard was determined that Philip of Burgundy should return to the French court with a dazzling description of the splendors of England. On August 14, when the duke and his entourage arrived at Guînes, the southern frontier of the Calais Pale, Richard sent an imposing cavalcade to meet them. At its head rode the royal uncles—Gaunt all poise and dignity, Woodstock maintaining a mutinous silence—and the king's personal envoys, Rutland and Mowbray, along with several bishops and, behind them, 500 English knights and esquires, their banners and armor shining in the sun. With trumpets sounding, this noble escort brought Burgundy to Calais, where the leading townsmen in matching liveries lined the streets in his honor. In the market square stood a vast wooden hall, specially built for the occasion and decorated as if it were a temple, with archers and men-at-arms deployed around its walls. There Richard—who seemed thrilled by this exhibition of his wealth and power—welcomed the duke with regal courtesy.[22]

The next day came a mass, celebrated by Archbishop Arundel in the Calais church of Saint Nicholas, at which the king sat enthroned, his scepter in his hand and his crown on his head; then a magnificent feast, served in the great hall that glittered with cloth of gold in the candlelight. Richard's delight in these ceremonies was as evident as his uncle Woodstock's displeasure. Woodstock had been required to accompany the royal party across the Channel along with his duchess and their children, only to see the places of honor beside the duke of Burgundy at the king's table go to Gaunt's mistress-turned-wife, Katherine Swynford, and, despite the irregular circumstances of her birth, their seventeen-year-old daughter, Joan Beaufort. The fact that, as duchess of Lancaster, Katherine was technically the greatest lady in England until the arrival of Richard's new bride did nothing to diminish Woodstock's resentment.[23]

And with personal slights came political alarm. For Woodstock, it was enraging enough to see his nephew's rapturous enthusiasm for treating with the enemy; but after the banquet, and an exchange of precious gifts, Richard's conversations with Burgundy precipitated an impromptu royal decision of exactly the kind his lords had always feared, should he ever take personal

charge of an Anglo-French summit. Amid the talk of the truce and the wedding, Burgundy raised the subject of the papal schism between Avignon and
Rome, now almost two decades old. Until recently France had been trying
to depose the Roman pope by force in alliance with Gian Galeazzo Visconti,
the aggressively expansionist duke of Milan. But in a change of strategy led
by the dukes of Burgundy and Berry, France was now seeking to resolve the
schism by means of the so-called "path of abdication"—that is, by persuading
the rival popes to resign so that a single new election could take place. Whatever the theoretical force of the suggestion, it had already become clear over
the previous year that in practice neither pope was prepared to step down.
But Richard had never been concerned with diplomatic detail, and his part
in the peace of Christendom was at stake. Without hesitation or consultation, he agreed on the spot to join the French in pursuing their proposal—
this despite the fact that, after almost two decades of international argument,
the Church in England was unlikely to be swayed from its support for the
Roman papacy by sudden royal diktat.

At least the evident unfeasibility of the plan meant that the king's uni-
lateral declaration made minimal political waves.[24] For now, all attention was
focused elsewhere: on the elaborate ceremonies that would soon join the
royal houses of England and France in holy matrimony. By the time Burgundy turned his richly caparisoned horse back toward the border, formal
agreements were in place for an encounter at which Richard would meet his
fellow sovereign Charles of France face-to-face at last.

It was a wedding on the scale of a military campaign: the costs immense and
the logistics overwhelming. By early October, after a brief return to England,
Richard and his greatest nobles moved en masse to Calais—all except Edmund of Langley, who was left behind again to watch over the realm, and the
earls of Arundel and Warwick, whose company was not required by the king.
From the opposite direction the French royal party was gathering a little
more than twenty miles away at Saint-Omer, and the royal dukes—Gaunt
and Woodstock, Berry and Burgundy—led delegations back and forth as the
final passages of intricate choreography were put in place.[25]

There were many details to consider. The two sovereigns could encounter each other only on a meticulously equal footing. In the no-man's-land between Guînes and Ardres two palisaded encampments had therefore been constructed, each containing 120 pavilions, and at the entrance to each a single magnificent tent, which on the French side was vast and square and on the English tall and round. The midpoint between the two was precisely measured and marked with a stake so that, when they met for the first time, neither king would walk an inch farther than the other. The demands of security required just as much thought as the issue of precedence. It was agreed that each monarch would be escorted by exactly 400 knights and esquires, every man armed only with a single sword or dagger, and an exhaustive set of rules was proclaimed by heralds in the surrounding towns to restrict movement, trade, and the carriage of arms for the duration of the conference. There could be no surprises and no improvisation, principles rendered all the more essential by the fragility of King Charles, who would be supported through the diplomatic rituals not only by the dukes of Burgundy and Berry but by his brother, the duke of Orléans, and their maternal uncle, the genial duke of Bourbon, as well as the duke of Brittany and the count of St. Pol. Attending Richard alongside Gaunt and Woodstock were the king's special representatives, Rutland and Mowbray, and his brother John Holand, earl of Huntingdon. Gaunt was accompanied by his son and ten-year-old grandson; but Henry was afforded so limited a role in the proceedings that Froissart, chronicling the details of this great occasion, believed he had stayed at home in England with his uncle Langley.[26]

It was not the first snub that had come Henry's way at his cousin's court, and he accepted it with no outward sign of bitterness. Instead, the Englishman whose antipathy to the whole occasion drew whispered comment behind perfumed hands was Thomas of Woodstock. As the momentous hour of the royal meeting drew closer, the duke was going through the required ceremonial motions with a barely concealed lack of grace. In public, he objected to nothing. Nor, as the French noted tetchily, did he reject the gifts and expressions of esteem they lavished on him in the hope of tempering his private resistance. But word reached Froissart of an infuriated duke of Burgundy muttering to his aides that there would never, he believed, be a

permanent settlement between France and England for as long as Woodstock drew breath.[27]

Yet on October 27, 1396, when the time finally came for this summit of
sovereigns to begin, the ceremonies unfolded without a single misstep. The
royal camps rose like a mirage from the bleak flatlands, miniature twin towns
built of richly colored fabric, humming with activity. Richard had imagined
the scene for more than a decade: the kings of England and France joined
in peace and friendship to the glory of God and the joy of all Christendom. Now, at twenty-nine, he was triumphant at the fulfillment of his plans,
resplendent in red velvet and jewels, full of regal bonhomie as he arrived
in procession with his splendid entourage to greet his new father-in-law.
Charles, at twenty-seven, was a less robust figure, lucid for now but looking to his uncles for direction, his own red velvet gown shorter and plainer
than Richard's flowing robe. Both kings wore a gleaming livery collar of
Charles's golden broom-cods, the seed pods of the broom plant; both wore a
gold-and-enamel brooch, studded with pearls, of Richard's white hart. Surrounded by their kneeling attendants, they clasped hands and exchanged
a kiss of peace. The royal dukes served goblets of spiced wine, Gaunt and
Woodstock to Charles, Burgundy and Berry to Richard. Gifts of gold vessels
were offered and received. Together, the two kings agreed, they would found
a church in the place where they stood, dedicated to the Virgin in her role
as peacemaker. They walked hand in hand to the magnificent French pavilion where they sat on matching thrones, side by side under a cloth-of-gold
canopy, to preside over private deliberations with their noble advisers; they
walked arm in arm to the English tent where they ate and drank together.
By the time they returned to their royal lodgings at Guînes and Ardres, the
first day's diplomatic dance had been executed with immaculate precision.

They met again the next morning, with the same ritual, at the same spot,
Richard this time in red and white velvet, and Charles—the English could
not help noticing—in the same outfit as the day before. (The monarchs had
agreed to dress simply, explained the chronicler of Saint-Denis, since the
peace was built on affection, not luxurious clothes. It was an elegant gloss
on the challenge, behind the scenes, of presenting a king of precariously
sound mind on such an elaborately formal stage.) Once again, the kings

exchanged compliments and exclamations of regard and amity; once again, they sat in conference on their golden thrones. Once again, every conversation and change of location was punctuated by the giving of breathtaking gifts: pouches of jewels, golden collars sparkling with rubies and sapphires and pearls, basins and ewers of solid gold. Out of this display of sovereign harmony came confirmation under oath of their diplomatic accord. The dukes of both royal houses would meet again soon to continue negotiations for a treaty to end the war forever, but meanwhile the two realms were at peace; and, for the three decades of the truce, each king solemnly swore to support the other against all comers.[28]

That night an apocalyptic storm swept the plain. In the darkness the wind and rain were so violent that much of the French camp and a few English tents were flattened, and the fine wool and silk that lined them ripped into pieces. Though it briefly seemed as though God wanted to unleash a second flood, noted the monk of Saint-Denis, those who feared a bad omen soon realized it was a sign of the devil's rage at his failure to prevent the making of peace between the two kingdoms. But the devastation was not the only surprise of the summit's third day—a Sunday, left free for worship, rest, and unscheduled tent reconstruction. At Ardres, a messenger arrived from Italy with an urgent letter for King Charles. French strategy in the peninsula had changed dramatically along with French policy on the papal schism. The dukes of Burgundy and Berry had turned their backs on the alliance with Gian Galeazzo Visconti of Milan in favor of expansionist plans of their own: they would send an army to defend the city-states that Visconti was trying to conquer, and thereby conquer the lands of Milan for France. They had already sealed a treaty to that effect with the republic of Florence; now the messenger brought word that the maritime republic of Genoa had ceded sovereignty over its territories to King Charles in return for protection by French troops.

The news had nothing to do with English interests, except that England had always feared such an enlargement of French territorial power. But that was before the king of England and the king of France were joined in peace and concord. Had Richard not sworn the day before to assist his father-in-law against all comers? Already at Calais Richard had committed himself, without consulting his Church or his counselors, to France's "way of abdication." Now his backing for France's war in Italy was instantaneous and enthusiastic. In public, he rewarded the messenger who brought word of Genoa's submission. In private, he promised to send English forces to Italy under the command of Rutland and Mowbray to join the French campaign.[29]

There was no time for England's shocked lords to dwell on new and alarmingly implausible military commitments 500 miles away. On Monday, October 30, the last day of the summit—with Richard in ankle-length blue and gold—the king's new wife was brought to meet him at last. The little girl was dressed in a matching royal robe of blue velvet powdered with gold fleurs-de-lis, a diadem of gold and pearls on her head. She played her part with focused concentration, curtsying twice to her new husband and crying only when she was embraced by her father, uncle, and great-uncles before being handed over to the English ladies led, as precedence dictated, by the duchess of Lancaster. Though no one dared mention it, for the six-year-old queen, it seemed some small good fortune that, in her former life as Katherine Swynford, the duchess had long experience of caring for children other than her own. After a banquet in the circular English pavilion, at which the French king was the honored guest of his elated son-in-law, the dukes of Berry and Burgundy rode with the English court back to Calais. There they remained until November 4, when Richard and Isabella were married by Archbishop Arundel before the high altar of the church of Saint Nicholas in the heart of the walled town. Then the queen and her trousseau—her dolls carefully packed among the jewels and embroidered gowns—were gathered up for the short voyage to her new home.[30]

It had been the dazzling success of which Richard had dreamed. Putting this ceremonial army into the field had cost England more than £25,000 in gifts, logistics, and supplies, but on his wedding day the king had taken receipt of 300,000 francs—almost £50,000—as the first installment of his wife's dowry, with more to come year by year. Isabella's arrival in England was marked by more celebrations and yet more expensive presents; her seventh birthday on November 9 was followed two weeks later by the pageantry of her entry into London and then the festivities for Christmas and the New

Year. On January 5, 1397, the little queen was crowned in Westminster Abbey, a smaller figure even than her husband had been at his coronation long ago. The next day, the king and court marked the feast of the Epiphany and the thirtieth anniversary of his own birth.[31]

Richard had everything he wanted. For thirty years to come, England and France would be at peace. His treasury was full of French gold. His new wife represented the reconciliation of the two kingdoms, and her royal blood was the twin of his own—but still, she was a child, and he alone embodied the sacred authority of his crown. The scale of his achievement was expressed in yet another artistic commission: an exquisite altarpiece, a little more than a foot tall, painted on hinged panels of oak so that it could be carried with the king everywhere for use in his personal devotions. On the outside blazed the royal arms impaled with those of the Confessor, and opposite them Richard's white hart, radiantly and much more delicately rendered than the monumental image on the wall of Westminster Abbey, its golden antlers shimmering against a luminescent gold ground. The tableau inside was more striking still. On the left panel Saint John the Baptist and the royal saints of England, Edmund the Martyr and Edward the Confessor, presented the kneeling figure of Richard himself to the Christ child on the right, tenderly held by his virgin mother before a crowd of angels in celestial blue. As he had been in the field between Guînes and Ardres, this painted Richard was decked in harts and broom-cods—but here he was joined by the host of heaven, every angel wearing a golden broom-cod collar and a gold-and-enamel hart as though Richard's newly peaceful England, by divine mandate, extended into paradise.[32]

Richard had always known he was special. Now the world reflected what he knew, and he would at last be free to rule as he pleased.

PART THREE

VENGEANCE

Eleven

1396-1397

on ancient malice

In January 1397, while the little queen settled into her new surroundings, Richard was looking forward to the opening of a new parliament. It was three years almost to the day since the king had last presided in person over a meeting of the representatives of his realm. In that time, he had triumphed in Ireland and made a lucrative peace with France that would last for a genera-tion. This parliament, he was sure, would be unlike any he had experienced before. England was safe, and the decades-long arguments about the causes and costs of a war that had seemed never-ending were over. Where once he had met criticism, resistance, treachery, and loss, he would instead find gratitude and glory, his sovereignty unconstrained. All was well when he sat in state at the assembly's opening on January 22 and when, the following day, the Commons elected as their Speaker Sir John Bushy, a Lincolnshire knight in his early forties who had built a profitable career in Lancastrian service on his smooth-tongued political competence. The way forward was clear: Richard would inform his loyal subjects of the decisions he had taken during his conference with his royal father-in-law of France, and they would offer him their support.[1]

His loyal subjects had no idea what was coming. When they gathered in the refectory of Westminster Abbey on January 24, the nonplussed Com-mons discovered that their king had promised to send an English army to Italy to help the king of France fight the duke of Milan. Not only that, but he wanted them to fund it. The demand seemed incomprehensible. Precedent required them to make a grant of taxation if the money could be shown to be necessary for the defense of the realm, but "necessity" had proved difficult enough to define even in the context of England's long war with France. There were no English interests directly at stake in Lombardy, and it was far from clear to Richard's subjects that supporting an extension of French power in the Italian peninsula would be of any conceivable benefit to England, let alone one worth paying for. Members of the king's council dutifully did what they could to explain and persuade: not only Rutland and Mowbray, the prospective commanders of the expedition, but Archbishop Arundel, newly promoted to the see of Canterbury, and the bishop of Exeter, who had replaced him as chancellor. Nothing worked. When the king heard of their resistance, he insisted on addressing the Commons himself. [2]

It was immediately obvious to the more experienced among his listeners why it had been a good idea in previous parliaments for the chancellor to speak on the king's behalf. To Richard, his own reasoning was self-evidently right. The war with France, he said, had caused terrible destruction. The best way to reinforce peace with his fellow sovereign of France was therefore to go to war by his side. If he, Richard, were to help Charles now, Charles would be more likely to help him in return. Besides, the two of them were such valiant and worthy Christian princes that they were honor bound to destroy tyrants wherever they found them. And he wished to be free, he declared, "to command his people, to send them to help his friends, and to dispose of his own goods at his will, where and whensoever he chose." The Commons listened, perplexed and anxious, to this gracious explanation, which from their perspective had no bearing on the case. Of course they would not seek to prevent the king from keeping his promise to his father-in-law by sending such an expedition. All they were saying—with the utmost respect—was that his decision and its costs were nothing to do with them. [3]

By the time the formal minutes of the session were written up by the clerks, it was judged politic not to record that a request for taxation had ever been made—an editorial choice that left the intensity of the exchanges unexplained in the parliamentary record, and a whole week of the assembly's discussions obscured. The fiction that the king had always intended simply to *inform* the Commons of his Italian plans, rather than to enlist their financial support, served for the moment to paper over the differences between Richard's view of the realm's interests and that of his subjects. But there could be no mistaking that the king was profoundly displeased.[4]

Days later, his frustration erupted into full-blown rage. Word had reached him, he told the lords on Friday, February 2, that the Commons had been debating matters "contrary to his regality and estate and his royal liberty." In particular, he had heard that a bill submitted for their consideration was proposing a reduction in "the great and excessive costs of the king's household," and alleging that too many bishops and ladies were resident there. He wished the Commons to know that they had no right to claim control over his person, his household, or anyone he chose to have in his company. By so doing, they had committed a great offense against his royal majesty, and he required them to name the man who had produced the bill in the first place.[5]

There were layers to Richard's reaction. Hearing that the Commons had been dabbling in such presumptuous criticism offered him an opportunity, certainly: an outlet for his anger about their refusal to pay for a military campaign to which he had already given his royal commitment. But it was also a trigger in its own right. His memories of the years of struggle to assert his authority as king were dominated not only by arguments about funding for war, but by his experience of repeated parliamentary criticism of his household, onslaughts that had culminated in the humiliation of the Merciless Parliament and the loss of the men on whom he had most depended, from his tutor Simon Burley to his adored de Vere. Slowly, patiently, he had fought his way back. He had rebuilt his royal establishment and left Woodstock, Arundel, and Warwick out in the cold. Yet now, again, the old refrain. This time, he had no intention of letting it stand.

For his subjects, there was alarm mingled with wearying familiarity as they scrambled for a strategy to contain the sudden crisis. It was true that the cost of the royal household had risen significantly—from £16,000 in 1389, the year the king had declared his own majority, to £26,000 in the last year—as Richard began to live in ever more extravagant style and to recruit his knights of the white hart. It was also true that, when seats within the English Church became vacant, the king was promoting clerics from within his household. The chancellor Edmund Stafford, bishop of Exeter since 1395, was one; since then, appointments had included Richard's confessor John Burghill as bishop of Llandaff; Robert Waldby, the new archbishop of York; and Thomas Merks, named bishop of Carlisle less than three weeks before the opening of parliament. These men, who showed no sign of visiting their dioceses, now sat among the lords spiritual of the realm. Meanwhile, if there were too many ladies in Richard's household, it was because his court had always been designed for display rather than the demands of war. But everyone in parliament knew the dangers of unleashing the royal wrath, and none of these facts was troubling enough to risk such an extreme confrontation.[6]

On Saturday, February 3, the Commons—led by their Speaker, John Bushy, and knowing from long experience what might succeed in placating the king—prostrated themselves before him. They offered up the name of the man who had put forward the bill about the royal household, a clerk named Thomas Haxey, and declared that they themselves had never intended to offend or to infringe upon the king's majesty. They surrendered themselves to his grace, implored his understanding, and begged his forgiveness. Meanwhile, the lords were preparing to make a scapegoat of the unfortunate clerk—whose bill, when presented for their detailed inspection, was hardly a wholesale assault on Richard's prerogative. Haxey's entirely accurate observations about the cost and character of the royal household had been designed to make the argument that bishops should attend to their spiritual duties by living in their dioceses, while the second half of his petition explicitly sought to defend the king's authority against the assertion of papal rights over the English clergy. But what counted in the attempt to appease Richard's anger was submission, not factual analysis. On Monday, February 5, the lords declared that anyone found to have incited the Commons, or anyone else, to seek reform of "the king's person, his rule or regality," should be held to be a traitor. In a full meeting of parliament two days later, a verdict of treason was returned in Haxey's case, and Haxey himself was condemned to death. But as soon as Gaunt, as steward of England, had pronounced the sentence, Archbishop Arundel stepped forward with the assembled prelates to pray for the king's mercy. The choreographed capitulation, it turned out, was enough. The king agreed to a stay of execution, and the reprieved clerk was handed into the archbishop's custody.[7]

For Richard, this performance of his sovereignty was a salve after the previous fortnight's bruising encounter with political reality—and, along with Haxey's reprieve, there was another act of grace he now deigned to bestow. Some months earlier, his uncle Gaunt, the man who had once presumed to command his government, had come to him in humble supplication, asking for a mark of favor that only Richard could provide. Gaunt, at fifty-six, was no longer quite the towering figure he had once been. He was weary and—having done everything he could for England's future—he was focusing his attention on the future of his family. Since he had made Katherine Swynford his wife in January 1396, he had been working to regularize the position of their four children, on the grounds that the illegitimacy of their birth could be overridden by their parents' marriage. He started with the Church, petitioning the pope in Rome to recognize their legitimacy in canon law, a request that was granted on September 1, 1396. But the pope could not intervene in English law to give the Beauforts the rights of inheritance they would have had if their parents had been married when they were born. That was a matter for the king, and, amid the excitement of his own wedding, Richard was graciously pleased to agree. His cousins' legitimation had been noted on the agenda for the parliament to meet in the new year, for which royal writs of summons were issued on November 30, shortly after the king had returned to London with his new queen.[8]

Just days later, devastating news reached Westminster: the military expedition against the Ottoman Turks that John Beaufort had joined in the summer had ended in bloody catastrophe. On September 25, outside the fortress of Nicopolis on the lower Danube, amid arguments over strategy and precedence between French and Hungarian commanders, the French cavalry had charged headlong into battle only to find themselves overwhelmed by the forces of Sultan Bayezid. The admiral of France, Jean de Vienne, had died defending the standard, and his noble companions, including Henry's friend Boucicaut and the duke of Burgundy's son and heir, were taken prisoner. The disaster left in tatters the crusading vision that had helped propel the Anglo-French peace. Behind the walls of his castle at Pleshey, Thomas of

Woodstock could not resist some mirthless celebration. But John Beaufort, to the relief of his parents and siblings, escaped the battlefield with his life, his freedom, and his reputation. In parliament on February 6, 1397—the day before Thomas Haxey's condemnation and royal reprieve—all four Beauforts were proclaimed by royal charter to be legitimate in English law "as if born in wedlock." Then, four days later, John was raised to the peerage as earl of Somerset in recognition of the honor he had brought to himself, the king, and the realm through the bravery and distinction of his service overseas.[9]

Gaunt's pride in his children and the closeness that had always existed within his blended family were now matched by the standing of the young Beauforts among the nobles of England. But the drafting of these grants was significant for the king as well as for his cousins. They, and their father Gaunt, stood in his debt; their status depended on his royal prerogative. And Richard took particular care over the terms in which that prerogative was expressed. Back in 1385, when he had scattered ennoblements like confetti on the occasion of his army's march into Scotland, the language of his charters had been ornamental. ("We believe our royal crown to glitter with many gems and shimmer with precious stones, insofar as virtuous and active men, especially those excelling in counsel, are summoned to high office . . .") This time, it was forensically assertive. In proclaiming the legitimacy of the Beauforts, the rolls of parliament recorded in their habitual French that he was acting as "*entier emperour*"—with fully imperial authority—within his realm of England.[10]

Richard's subjects already knew that he was gratified by more exalted forms of address than the ones to which his English predecessors had been accustomed; for some years the novel phrases "your majesty" and "your royal highness" had been in regular use at his court, rather than simply "the lord king." But this was not just a matter of royal gratification. The vocabulary of imperial majesty—an explicit claim to sovereignty that recognized no possibility of an earthly superior—was familiar in England through its use by the rulers of the Holy Roman Empire, including Richard's former father-in-law, and by his new father-in-law of France, whose throne descended from the Emperor Charlemagne. Now, for the first time, Richard was adopting the title to describe his own rule. In removing at a wave of his royal hand the "defect of birth" that afflicted his cousins, he had also bound Gaunt's family—and the parliament in which the grant had been made—into this new formulation of his sovereign power.

The articulation of an authority that sought to reach beyond the conventional relationship between the king and his realm was not the only way in which the landscape of Richard's new peacetime politics seemed to share disconcerting features with the battle-scarred terrain his subjects had hoped to leave behind. The king might be dismissing the notion that he had ever expected a grant of taxation to fund his Italian war, but those attending the assembly knew that such a request had, in fact, been made. Thomas Haxey's life had been spared, but it remained the case that an Englishman had been sentenced to die as a traitor for offering a suggestion about ways of reducing the costs of the royal household. And before parliament was dissolved on February 12—five days after Haxey's trial, two after John Beaufort's creation as earl of Somerset—the troubling echoes of the conflicts of a decade earlier were amplified by a direct reminder of the events of 1387–88. At Richard's demand, the lords and Commons agreed that the surviving judges who had been exiled to Ireland by the Merciless Parliament should at last be allowed to return home.[11]

There was no explicit mention of the menacing redefinition of the law of treason for which the judges had been banished in the first place. All the same, the implication that—"contrary to the oath that he had sworn," as Thomas Walsingham pointed out—Richard could revisit the trials of 1388 and amend their verdicts was enough to send a chill down the spines of the five former Appellants, the men who had laid charges of treason against the king's closest friends. After all this time, did Richard harbor thoughts of revenge? Mowbray could reassure himself that he at least was comfortably placed, his loyal service and his standing in Richard's affections manifestly restored. Henry had no signs of personal royal favor on which to rely, but he was shielded by his father's eminence and the might of his inheritance to come. For the three older lords, however, their relationships with the king and with their fellow peers offered few guarantees.

In recent years the earl of Warwick had removed himself from the political front line, but now judgment was given against him in response to a parliamentary petition presented by the king's confessor, the newly appointed bishop of Llandaff, over a dispute concerning a manor within the earl's lordship of Gower in south Wales. Warwick was forced to submit himself to Richard's grace and fined for his actions. His former allies Woodstock and Arundel, meanwhile, sat silently by, or silently enough that their names were barely mentioned in the parliamentary record. On February 10, they were conspicuous by their absence among the senior noblemen invited into the king's chamber to witness his charter bestowing the earldom of Somerset on John Beaufort.[12]

As February gave way to March, these three lords, Woodstock, Arundel, and Warwick, faced a particularly fraught version of a question the realm as a whole was slowly beginning to confront. The entirety of Richard's reign so far had been shaped by the pressures of war with France. Freed from those constraints—free to rule his kingdom as he pleased—what might the king choose to do?

He would not, it transpired, be sending an army to Italy. In Paris, King Charles had lapsed once more into distraction and incoherence. There would be no campaign in Lombardy for English forces to join. After the enraging debacle of the discussions in parliament, and having insisted on his right to dispatch soldiers whenever and wherever he wished, Richard was not inclined to speak of the matter again.[13]

The Anglo-French pact to seek an end to the papal schism, on the other hand, was still theoretically in force, and ambassadors from the two kingdoms were going through the diplomatic motions in pursuit of the "path of abdication." But since, in practice, abdication was a proposal that neither pope would entertain, the dead end that lay ahead was obvious to all. If the pontiffs in Rome and Avignon refused to step down, then any move to name a new "unity" candidate would result only in the existence of three popes rather than two. It was so clear that the conflict would continue that in March the king's brother John Holand even toyed with the idea of fighting in Italy as the Roman pontiff's champion, accepting an appointment as gonfalonier—standard-bearer—of the holy Roman Church and captain general of the papal forces "for the extermination of schismatics and rebels and usurpers of cities and lands of the pope." That too was an expedition that never left England's shores.

As well as his papal title, Holand's portfolio of nominal offices included the captaincy of Brest, the Breton port that had been in English hands ever since its capture in a naval campaign commanded by Thomas of Woodstock twenty years earlier. With hostilities suspended, Richard set in motion negotiations to tie up this loose end of the war by selling Brest back to the duke of Brittany for 120,000 francs, a bargain made in March for completion in the summer. The king also sent Rutland, Mowbray, and Scrope to Paris to arrange the next stage of talks for a permanent peace, as agreed at the wedding summit, only to find that the French felt no urgency about moving on from a thirty-year truce that had cost them not a single territorial concession. But Richard was unconcerned. His attention was diverted by events elsewhere on the Continent. He had decided to become Holy Roman Emperor.[14]

Richard's former brother-in-law Wenzel had always struggled to follow in his father's magnificent footsteps as ruler of the confederation of German states that made up the Empire. Never formally crowned by the pope, Wenzel had barely left his kingdom of Bohemia in the two decades of his reign so far, preferring to apply himself to hunting and drinking rather than the needs of his people or the interests of the Empire as a whole. By 1395, Bohemia had imploded into civil war, and some of the imperial electors in Germany were contemplating an attempt to depose him. Wenzel had no children; his brother Sigismund of Hungary would have been the prime candidate to replace him had it not been for the disastrous defeat at Nicopolis in 1396. In their search for a stalking horse, the gaze of the rebel electors turned west to a ruler who had more than a passing interest in the magnification of his own sovereignty. Why, their representatives asked Richard, should the imperial crown not pass to a king who had made peace in his own realm, a king who, in his majesty, was the equal of his former father-in-law in Prague and his present father-in-law in Paris?[15]

As they had hoped, Richard took very little persuading. In the whole history of Christendom there had been only one English pope, back in the 1150s. A century later, the younger brother of Richard's great-great-great-grandfather Henry III had been crowned king of Germany in Cologne during another disputed imperial election. But there had never been an English emperor recognized in Rome. Wise heads with long experience of continental politics—Richard's uncle Gaunt, for example—might have pointed out the reason for that fact: England's position, surrounded by the sea on the edge of Europe, offered many strategic advantages, but the ability to intervene decisively in the affairs of the Empire was not one of them. Wise heads might therefore have suggested that the rebel electors were proposing Richard's candidacy for tactical reasons, as a front for their own machinations. But Gaunt's advice no longer weighed in his nephew's thinking, while the noblemen Richard had gathered around him in recent years had been chosen precisely because they would tell him only what he wanted to hear.

By March 1397, Richard was in private communication with Ruprecht, Count Palatine, leader of the resistance to Wenzel. In April, through their intermediaries, the two came to an initial agreement: the count would swear homage to the English king, and in return for his service would receive £1,000 a year from the English exchequer. In June, Richard's envoys Rutland and Mowbray moved from France to Germany to make a similar arrangement with Ruprecht's son and heir, this time with an annual grant of 1,000 marks. On July 7, in a deal coordinated between the palace of Westminster and the castle of Godesburg, another elector, the archbishop of Cologne, also promised his allegiance to Richard in return for a pension of £1,000. Richard's enthusiasm for the project was reflected in the sheer scale of these grants, multiple iterations of his gift to Leo of Armenia that had provoked such controversy when the storm clouds were gathering in 1386. The difference now was that the kingdom was no longer at war, and the Exchequer flush with cash from the little queen's dowry. As the king had so sharply reminded the Commons, he was free "to dispose of his own goods at his will, where and whensoever he chose." And what he wanted was to become "*entier emperour*" outside the realm as well as within it, by adding the imperial diadem to the English crown.[16]

The plan was moving fast. What was needed, Richard believed, if his majesty were to transcend the limits of his kingdom, was greater certainty that peace in England was permanent and that his subjects lived in a state of perfect obedience to his authority. It was already apparent that those who had offended could seek redemption by submitting to the king's will, and that in return the king might choose to be merciful. In May, he pardoned the clerk Thomas Haxey, freeing him from the sentence of a traitor's death that had been pronounced against him in parliament. A month before that, Richard had also granted a pardon to Thomas Talbot, the leader of the Cheshire rebellion in 1393—even if Gaunt, who had asked in January that justice should finally be done in Talbot's case, had every reason to suspect that the king had never intended to punish a man who wore the badge of the white hart.[17]

But it was also becoming clear that Richard might choose to demonstrate the awesome power of his crown through retribution rather than forgiveness. In May, the sixty-year-old earl of Warwick, fresh from humiliation in parliament over his dispute with the king's confessor, started to discover how much greater his losses might yet become. His valuable Welsh lordship of Gower had been given into his father's possession by Edward III in 1353 after a legal battle with Thomas Mowbray's grandfather, but in 1396 Mowbray—once Warwick's ally in opposition to the king, now absolved through his devoted service to Richard—had reopened the case. Since landholding conferred power as well as wealth, such property disputes at the highest level were always political, not simply judicial; and when the verdict was handed down in the court of King's Bench at the end of May 1397, Mowbray's victory was total. Warwick was forced to surrender Gower, and to put seventeen of his manors across the midlands in trust as a guarantee that he would pay his rival more than £5,000 in compensation for the years of his family's occupation.[18]

It was a devastating blow to Warwick's resources and authority, and to the prospects of his fifteen-year-old son and heir. Not only that, but Mowbray's acquisition of Gower formed one element of a wider reshaping of the structures of power within the kingdom. In a series of grants over the winter of 1396 and the spring and summer of 1397, Richard placed key fortresses around the coast in the hands of Rutland and Scrope, his other trusted proxies. To Scrope, he gave command of the great royal castles in Wales and at Queenborough in Kent, the stronghold that had once been Robert de Vere's; to Rutland, Carisbrooke Castle on the Isle of Wight, and Dover and the Cinque

Ports—formerly held by Simon Burley—to go with his constableship of the Tower of London. The ranks of the nobility were also being refreshed as an older generation gave way to the new. Richard's oldest half brother died in April 1397, to be succeeded as earl of Kent by his twenty-three-year-old son, another Thomas Holand, who had already served the king on campaign in Ireland. The elderly earl of Salisbury, who had once, long ago, been married to Richard's mother, died in June; his successor, his forty-seven-year-old nephew, John Montagu, was desperate to seize his own belated chance to win the king's favor. Meanwhile, Richard was quietly continuing to build up his personal retinue. By the summer of 1397, across the country more knights and esquires than ever before were wearing his badge of the white hart.[19]

But reinforcing the means by which he could impose his royal will was only one part of his campaign to become emperor as well as king, both inside and outside his kingdom. His attempts to assert his sovereignty had always been propelled by rage at the lords he believed had stood in his way—rage compounded by his grief for de Vere, the only man whose interests had ever mattered to him as much as his own—and by his fear that he might face such resistance again. All elements of this volatile compound were now in play. Even as he sought to demonstrate his mastery of his own realm to the watching eyes of Europe, the glorious freedom in the exercise of his rule that he had anticipated after the sealing of the truce with France had not materialized quite as he expected. His capacity to calibrate threat had never been calm and judicious, but in these circumstances it seemed to be operating on a finer hair trigger than ever before. And at the beginning of July came fresh crisis, precipitated when disorder broke out on the streets of his capital, a city he believed he had brought to heel four years earlier.

It was not the Londoners themselves who were rioting, but that did not make the disorder any less disturbing for a king who had staked his authority on peace secured through obedience. The violence was the work of soldiers from the newly disbanded garrison of Brest, men who had poured into London after scrambling to find passage home to England when the port was relinquished to the duke of Brittany. The money the duke had paid for its return was safely in the hands of the king's officers, but none of it in the soldiers' pockets. Under John Holand's administration their pay had already fallen into arrears. Now the war was over and their jobs were gone. They came in search of compensation from the government that had betrayed them, rampaging through London and Westminster for several days until they were corralled out of the city into billets hastily found for them in surrounding villages.[20]

In Richard's eyes, however, neither John Holand's absentee captaincy nor his own deal to surrender the port was to blame for this uprising. There was malign influence at work: the malign influence of men who had always wanted to destroy him. The capture of Brest all those years ago had been the greatest—the only—military victory his uncle Woodstock had ever won, in a brief moment when England's naval operations had been directed by Arundel and Warwick as admirals of England. Their opposition to peace—their objection to the truce itself and their disgust at Richard's failure to insist on any territorial concessions from the French in return—was well known on both sides of the Channel. If anyone was stirring up the returning soldiers to rebel against their sovereign, it must be these three lords. Woodstock's castle of Pleshey lay only thirty miles northeast of the capital. Within its walls, what further conspiracies was the duke fomenting against his nephew's throne, just as he had with Arundel and Warwick a decade earlier?[21]

This time, Richard was determined to strike before the lords could show their hand. He would have to move carefully if their schemes were to be frustrated. He began with an invitation. Would his uncle Woodstock and the earls of Arundel and Warwick join him for a banquet at John Holand's riverfront mansion at Coldharbour, just west of London Bridge, on July 10? It was careful, but not careful enough. From Pleshey Woodstock sent his excuses, claiming illness. Arundel—unconvinced by this sudden access of royal hospitality—did not move from his castle at Reigate, twenty miles south of the capital, where the king had tried and failed to arrest him almost exactly ten years before. Only Warwick arrived at the appointed hour. Richard greeted him warmly, an urbane and courteous host, offering commiserations and reassurances over his loss of the lordship of Gower. The meal was served and eaten. Then, at a gesture from the king, Warwick was seized by the royal guards and bundled away downriver to the Tower.[22]

Other means would be required to complete the task. Richard sent

Archbishop Arundel to Reigate to bring his older brother in. The archbishop was uneasy, but it would be worse—he believed, he *knew*—if Arundel tried to defy the king's summons. If Richard had suspicions that the earl was plotting against him, noncompliance would only serve to confirm them. Submission would give the king what he wanted, and when the moment had passed—when the German electors had observed how masterfully Richard ruled his kingdom—Arundel would be free again. Had not the archbishop saved Thomas Haxey from a death sentence? Besides, Richard had sworn by John the Baptist, one of the saints to whom he was particularly devoted, that the earl would not be harmed. It took some hours of persuasion before the gates of Reigate swung open and Arundel surrendered to the armed escort sent to take him to the Isle of Wight. There a cell waited for him in Carisbrooke Castle, one of the fortresses in Rutland's keeping.[23]

That left Thomas of Woodstock, who, Richard believed, was already fortifying his position at Pleshey. With four earls at his side—Rutland, Mowbray, and John and Thomas Holand—the king mustered troops from the royal household and the city of London, as many men-at-arms and archers as could be gathered in the space of a few hours, and rode through the night into Essex. He had never been a soldier. All his life his uncle had berated him for his softness, his unwillingness to fight. This display of power would be his vindication. He had to be prepared for what he might face. But at dawn, when the royal party approached Pleshey's gatehouse, Woodstock emerged to meet his nephew without armor or weapons, pale with illness, attended only by his household servants and his chaplains. His "excuse" was real, his "conspiracy" nothing more than rumor and speculation. Whether because he was unwell or because resistance was so obviously futile, the duke showed none of the haughty aggression that had marked his public life. With dignity, he said goodbye to his duchess, Eleanor, telling her to declare her loyalty to the king. Then he mounted his horse and, under close guard, rode south to the coast. His prison, the most secure of all, was to be Calais, under the authority of Mowbray as captain of the garrison.

It was Thursday, July 12, by the time Richard settled back into the royal apartments at Westminster. The news of the arrests spread in shock waves along the roads from London, from Reigate, from Pleshey. Currents met, mingled, intensified. If the three lords who had led the opposition to the king a decade earlier—acts for which they had been expressly and explicitly pardoned—had been detained without warning or explanation, what might that mean for anyone who had followed them then, or since? By Friday, July 13, panic was rising in and around the capital. Richard sent a message north to Cheshire commanding Robert Leigh, the sheriff there, to raise a force of 2,000 archers with the utmost urgency. On the same day he ordered the sheriffs in London and every county across the kingdom to proclaim that Woodstock, Arundel, and Warwick had been taken into custody "for the peace and safety of the people," that order must be maintained, and that any of the king's subjects gathering without royal permission were to be treated as traitors.[24]

Forty-eight hours later, the proclamation was reissued in amended form: despite rumors on the streets, the king's subjects should know that the three lords had *not* been arrested because of their "assemblies and ridings" in the past. There was no cause for alarm, and no intention to indict members of their households and retinues, then or now. The crimes against the king and the kingdom for which they *had* been detained would be explained when parliament next met—which, it was announced three days later, would be at Westminster in mid-September. Three days after that, on Saturday, July 21, Richard sent another embassy to pursue his imperial negotiations in Cologne, led this time by the bishop of Carlisle, one of the prelates to whose presence in the king's household Thomas Haxey had objected so strongly. Rutland and Mowbray, until now the king's personal envoys on the Continent, were needed in England.

This was what Richard was choosing to do.

Henry and Gaunt were not with the king when the arrests took place, nor were they among the eight lords with whose support Richard claimed to have acted when he issued his first proclamation on July 13. As always, there was the key triumvirate of Rutland, Mowbray, and Scrope, with Rutland first in order of precedence and described—as he had been for some time by virtue of his proposed marriage to the little queen's younger sister—as "the king's brother." They were joined by the king's half brother John Holand and nephew Thomas Holand; by the ambitious new earl of Salisbury; and by Thomas, Lord Despenser, the young husband of Rutland's sister, Constance. The last name on the list was a Lancastrian link in the chain: Gaunt's son John Beaufort, earl of Somerset, who—thanks to his recently elevated status—had just married Thomas Holand's twelve-year-old sister, Margaret.[25]

Beaufort's place in Richard's inner circle was new: a reflection of his dependence on the king for the legitimation of his birth and his promotion to the peerage. But his formal part in the detention of Woodstock, Arundel, and Warwick did not mark a breach with his half brother or their father. By God's will, the crown lay on Richard's head. The twentieth anniversary of his accession to the throne had just passed, and during those two decades Gaunt had done everything he could to defend the king and the realm as well as the interests of his own dynasty. In all that time, Woodstock and Arundel had been nothing but divisive and disruptive. If a reckoning was coming, this time the house of Lancaster would take shelter while the storm raged. Ten years earlier, in his father's absence, Henry had done what was necessary to defend the rule of law from Richard's claim that any resistance to his will was treason. But when Woodstock and Arundel had gone too far—when Simon Burley's head was hacked from his body on Tower Hill—Henry had stepped back, and Mowbray with him. That, it seemed, was the line in the sand, the decision that mattered to Richard. Warwick had jumped the other way, and he was paying the price. If Richard wanted to bring the three lords down, Gaunt and Henry would not take a lead, but where the king led they would follow.

Richard knew he needed their support. In the week leading up to the arrests, there had been notable royal gestures of esteem and reassurance. Henry's movements that spring, bereft as he was of a real home or driving purpose, had been leisurely; desultory, even. He had spent Easter with his father and stepmother at Tutbury Castle in Staffordshire, and then paid a visit to his daughters, five-year-old Blanche and two-year-old Philippa, who were being cared for at the Herefordshire home of his chamberlain Hugh Waterton. After that he spent time in London and with Gaunt at Hertford Castle, twenty miles north of the capital. But on July 6, with three servants and two chaplains, Henry moved into the king's household. There was no fanfare, no sense of a prodigal returning or an outcast readmitted to the fold, just a quiet repositioning, unnoticeable to anyone who, like Woodstock, was not there to see. That same day Richard confirmed Gaunt's title as duke of Aquitaine; not a new grant, but a reinforcement of existing authority. This sotto voce expression of royal affection also embraced the younger members of Gaunt's family, the children whose future the duke was so anxious to secure. John Beaufort had been a king's knight, wearing the badge of the white hart, since 1392. Now, also on July 6, Richard brought Beaufort's youngest brother, twenty-year-old Thomas, formally into his service, retaining him for life as a king's esquire with a generous grant at the Exchequer of 100 marks a year.[26]

An understanding had been reached. And so, in the tense, chaotic days after the king made his move against the three lords, Gaunt and Henry took their places beside him. By July 15, when Richard's second proclamation sought to quell the fears that were engulfing London, the king declared that Woodstock, Arundel, and Warwick had been detained with the agreement not only of the eight noblemen named two days earlier, but also of Gaunt, Henry, and Rutland's father, Langley. This was the legitimation Richard needed. If Woodstock's arrest was publicly endorsed by the duke's two royal brothers and by Henry, his nephew and brother-in-law who had been his ally ten years earlier, then the king must surely have just cause. All the same, it was with grim resolve—and taking care to obtain Richard's explicit approval for their actions—that Gaunt and Henry summoned their armed retainers to join them at Nottingham Castle, where the king had called his council to meet at the beginning of August.[27]

The location was not an accident. In part, there were the practicalities of making sure the resources of the realm were at the king's immediate disposal. Richard was wasting no time in raising money as well as men; while troops were beginning to assemble from every direction, his sergeants at arms were riding across the country to demand that his loyal subjects make loans to the crown. The fortress at Nottingham, immense on its rock near the crossing of the river Trent in the center of his kingdom, provided both vantage point and rendezvous for these military and financial operations. And although the fact was left unspoken, it was also the place where, exactly ten years before, the judges of the royal courts had declared in response to Richard's questions that anyone who resisted the king's will was a traitor. On the same spot in the summer of 1392, the mayor and sheriffs of London had knelt before the king to find themselves dismissed from their offices and taken into custody. Rather than Westminster, where he had so often felt constrained and silenced, Nottingham was the stage on which Richard had played out his sovereignty in its most imperious form. Now it was the setting in which he would charge Woodstock, Arundel, and Warwick with their treachery.[28]

Only one piece of the puzzle had not fallen into place. The unspecified new crimes of which the three lords stood accused in the proclamations made after their arrest—by implication, the conspiracy that Richard had been convinced his uncle Woodstock was hatching—seemed in the cold light of day to have melted away, untraceable and unrecoverable. But the king was not about to let this absence of evidence deflect him from his certainty about their guilt. The events of a decade earlier offered a way forward that, for the moment, required no specific allegations. In 1387, Woodstock, Arundel, and Warwick had laid an appeal of treason against the king's friends. In 1397, the king's friends would lay an appeal of treason against them.

On August 5, Richard sat crowned in majesty, surrounded by his court, in the great hall of Nottingham Castle. Kneeling before him, in the gesture of supplication Richard increasingly required from his faithful subjects, were the eight lords who had publicly supported the arrests. Edward of Rutland, Thomas Holand, Thomas Despenser, and John Beaufort, all in their twenties, had been scarcely more than children during the crisis to which this was a sudden, shocking sequel. Of the men in their forties, John Holand and William Scrope had been overseas in 1387—Holand with his father-in-law, Gaunt, in Castile and Scrope serving as captain of the captured port of Cherbourg—while John Montagu of Salisbury had not then come into his inheritance even from his father, let alone his uncle the earl. The only one who had taken part in that bloody conflict was thirty-one-year-old Thomas Mowbray, and he had done so as an Appellant in opposition to the king. Since then, he had worked hard to regain Richard's trust as a courtier in England, a soldier in Ireland, and a diplomat in France. The logic of that service had led him here, to a role reprised as if in a hall of mirrors: an Appellant again, but this time as Richard's mouthpiece, not his critic. And the cause in which he was speaking was still obscure. The bill of appeal that he and the other lords presented—a bill addressed to the king, dictated by the king—declared only that Woodstock, Arundel, and Warwick were traitors. Their lives and estates hung in the balance, but the details of their treason would not be publicly revealed until the case was brought before parliament.[29]

The only one of the Appellants of 1387 not acting in this political drama, the only one who was neither accuser nor accused, was Henry. He and Gaunt watched in silence as the charges of treason were laid. But this was a process in which neutrality was not an option. Woodstock, Arundel, and Warwick, locked in their far-flung prisons, had no voice at Nottingham. If Henry were to speak up for them, he would share their fate. Instead, standing beside his father while his brother knelt before Richard's throne with the rest of the new Appellants, Henry knew that the future of his children and of his dynasty depended on his compliance.

With the ceremonies concluded and the appeal of treason made, there was work to be done before parliament met. The king had declared his need for more men and more money. Loans were starting to roll into the Exchequer at Westminster, sums large and small from individuals and communities across England, including 10,000 marks from the city of London, where the new mayor, Richard Whittington, was the king's personal choice after the previous incumbent died in office in June. A mercer who over the years had supplied first Robert de Vere and then Richard himself with thousands of pounds' worth of cloths of gold, silk, and velvet, Whittington had already lent £600 of his own money to the king in March. Now he petitioned that the city's liberties—which had been restored only at the royal pleasure after the king's punitive intervention in London's government in 1392—should be regranted in perpetuity in return for this massive corporate contribution to the royal coffers. Richard, flush with his success in compelling his capital's ongoing loyalty, was pleased to agree.[30]

He was also summoning to his side the men who wore the white hart, the network of knights and esquires under his direct command that he had so signally lacked in 1387. By royal proclamation, all the king's retainers were called to muster in arms on September 15 at Kingston-upon-Thames, ten miles southwest of London, ready to ride with him to Westminster before the opening of parliament two days later. The sheriff of Cheshire—himself newly retained by Richard—was ordered to recruit another 300 archers on top of the 2,000 he was already assembling, the whole force to serve as a royal bodyguard. The lords publicly named as having consented to the arrests were also to bring troops to parliament "for the comfort of the king," including a major mobilization of the Lancastrian retinue: 300 men-at-arms and 600 archers for Gaunt, and 200 men-at-arms and 400 archers for Henry. In the meantime, care was taken to suppress all dissent and prevent any disruption to the king's plans. The sheriffs were to imprison anyone who dared speak up for Woodstock, Arundel, and Warwick in the counties where their estates, and therefore their greatest support, were concentrated. In late August, Mowbray was dispatched across the Channel to take personal charge of Woodstock in his prison at Calais, while Rutland remained in England to supervise the keeping of Warwick in the Tower and Arundel at Carisbrooke.[31]

By now, preparations were moving so fast there was barely time to think. On Saturday, September 15, the king and his forces rode over London Bridge and through the heart of the city. The air was thick with dread. This was turning out to be a military occupation of his own capital. The Lancastrian troops were already in place. On Sunday, September 16, Henry held a banquet at the house he had rented in Fleet Street, just outside the city walls to the west, a lavish occasion at which Richard was the guest of honor. There too were Henry's older sons. It was young Henry's eleventh birthday; Thomas was two weeks away from turning ten. In their new gowns, eyes like saucers, they watched the entertainments, the guards, the genuflection to their father's cousin the king. Both boys had been born while the crisis of 1386–88 was unfolding. It was their world and their inheritance that Henry was desperate to protect.[32]

The next morning, parliament would meet, and the trials would begin.

Nothing was normal. Because the king's masons and carpenters were still at work in the vast space of Westminster Hall, Richard had ordered the building of a huge marquee in the courtyard between the palace and the abbey in which the representatives of his realm could gather—but when the lords and Commons arrived on Monday, September 17, they found that this temporary structure had taken a sinister turn. Hundreds of the king's Cheshire archers were standing guard around the insubstantial sides of the tent, their bows held ready in their hands. It was an unambiguously intimidating setting: a weaponized version of the royal pavilion at the wedding summit, or the wooden hall into which Richard had welcomed the duke of Burgundy on his state visit to Calais. Only two months earlier, this royal bodyguard on the scale of a private army had not existed. Why the king might feel the need to deploy it to encircle his loyal subjects on the soil of his own kingdom was a question that hovered over the assembly, unspoken and unsettling, while Richard made his entrance and took his seat on the elevated throne.[33]

The beginnings of an answer came when the chancellor, the bishop of Exeter, rose to speak, taking as his theme a verse from Ezekiel: "One king shall rule them all." Parliament, he said, had been summoned for the salvation and correction of the realm. The key to that salvation was the supreme authority of the king, who should, in any well-governed kingdom, compel his subjects to obey his laws. The royal rights vested in the king by his coronation were integral to his crown; so much so that the one thing *not* within his power was the capacity to hand over that power to anyone else within his kingdom, whether by law, or by oath, or by any other means.[34]

It was a dizzyingly theoretical opening, but as the speech went on—the bishop talking now of the need to correct any reduction in the crown's prerogatives—the meaning behind his words came swimming into view. Despite all the proclamations, all the royal protestations and reassurances, the new crimes for which Woodstock, Arundel, and Warwick had supposedly been arrested did not exist. Instead, the king was turning the clock back to the events of 1386–88 when the three lords had forced him to cede control of his government, and had justified their actions with laws and oaths and pardons. Richard intended to unpick history, and to rewrite it.

The overwhelming presence of the king's archers, white harts on their breasts, arrows at their fingertips, served to focus the minds of everyone listening, in case anyone were tempted to express an unwisely independent opinion on the question of the limits of the king's sovereignty. But Richard was taking aim at their security under the law as well as their physical safety. Out of affection for his people, the chancellor announced, "so that they should have greater courage and will to do good," the king would grant a general pardon to all his subjects—all, that is, apart from the three arrested lords, and another fifty people whom Richard would not yet name. Who might be on that list, and why? What crimes might he deem unforgivable? And who would risk displeasing him until they knew for sure? There were a number of those present, Gaunt and Henry included, who were aware by now of what lay ahead, who knew what Woodstock, Arundel, and Warwick would face, and had signed off on the process out of concern for their own interests, or those of the kingdom, or a combination of the two. But this was just the first session; and the deal, it seemed, was getting worse all the time.

Proceedings began in earnest the next day. Richard was determined to exploit every legal precedent at his disposal. As a result, Woodstock, Arundel, and Warwick would not only be appealed of treason like de Vere; they would also, like Simon Burley, be impeached by the Commons. As their Speaker, the Commons had once again chosen John Bushy, the Lancastrian knight whose skillfully subservient handling of Thomas Haxey's case in the previous parliament had attracted the king's favorable attention. In preparing to corral his new colleagues through the impeachments Richard required, Bushy had consulted closely with two other parliamentary veterans: Henry Green, a capable political operator with more than two decades' experience in Lancastrian service, and William Bagot, a forcefully ambitious and politically flexible man who had built his career by working simultaneously for Warwick, Mowbray, Henry, and Gaunt. The detailed charges were ready. The silence was heavy as Bushy rose to present them for the first time.[35]

Back in 1386, he declared, the traitors Woodstock and Arundel had imposed a governing council on the king as a means of usurping his royal authority. They had sent Arundel's brother—then a bishop, now the archbishop of Canterbury—to tell him his life was in danger if he did not comply. They had suborned Warwick to their cause, and together raised an army at Harringay with which they had forced the king to summon the Merciless Parliament of 1388, during which Simon Burley had been condemned and executed. As a result, all the statutes and pardons associated with that illegal council and parliament, up to and including the special pardon that had been granted to the earl of Arundel in 1394, should be revoked and annulled.[36]

The assembly was quiet when Bushy returned to his seat. It was a narrative that took some unraveling. First, there was the visceral shock—to everyone, but most of all the archbishop himself—that Archbishop Arundel, one of the most able politicians at the heart of Richard's rebuilt regime, who had hoped to save his brother from the worst of the king's vengeance, was instead being swept up in the purge. Yes, in 1386 he had joined Woodstock in the first confrontation with the king at Eltham; yes, he had replaced Michael de la Pole as England's chancellor, serving under the authority of the council. But from that point on he had remained at Richard's side, attempting to steer a path out of the crisis. He was at Richard's side still, sitting next to the throne while Bushy spoke, turning in horror to protest, to defend himself, only to be silenced by a wave of the king's hand. He would have his chance, Richard said, but for now his response was not required.[37]

At the same time, all those listening were beginning to realize quite how sinuously this tale of Woodstock and Arundel's treachery skirted the moments when either of the two younger Appellants, Henry and Mowbray, might have been denounced as traitors alongside them. Neither Henry nor Mowbray had been part of the council of 1386. They had not mustered their forces at Harringay, but at Huntingdon two weeks later. And during the Merciless Parliament they had tried to save Burley from the headsman's block. Everyone present knew that they had also fought de Vere and his troops at Radcot Bridge, and then stood arm in arm with the three accused, dressed in identical cloth of gold, to make the appeal of treason against Richard's friends. But it would take a brave man to point out those parts of their story, given their present standing in a different parliament, in a very different world.[38]

How different became clear when Bushy's proposal was put to the lords. Should the statutes and pardons that had underpinned these terrible crimes be annulled? Each peer, whether spiritual or temporal, was required to offer his answer individually, starting with those of lowest rank. The mechanism was blatant in its intent, and brutally effective: those who were forced to speak first, their voices shaking, had least power to resist. Their response was unanimous until the very last, when Archbishop Arundel took his turn. It was a grave matter, he said, to revoke actions taken by the exalted authority of the king himself. But the king's will had changed, and the archbishop's influence was gone. When parliament reconvened on Thursday, September 20, he was nowhere to be seen. Instead, charges of impeachment were laid against him. Both judgment and sentencing were deferred for the king's consideration, but the verdict could hardly be in doubt. It was already obvious that one of the most influential men in England had been summarily excised from public life, as if with the fine blade of a paring knife.[39]

A blunter instrument would be used for his brother. On Friday, September 21, the new Appellants made their formal appearance before the king and the lords: Rutland, Mowbray, the two Holands, Salisbury, Despenser, Scrope, and John Beaufort, all in matching robes of red silk banded with white and powdered with letters of gold. At every step, the parliamentary theater devised by Woodstock, Arundel, and Warwick in 1388 to remove their opponents was being restaged for the purpose of their own destruction, as if to emphasize that there existed no political weapon, no means of resistance, that did not ultimately belong to the king. This new appeal of treason echoed the narrative laid out in the Commons' impeachment, with additional incriminating (and exonerating) detail; in particular, that the three lords had threatened Richard with the loss of his crown using the precedent of Edward II's deposition, and had stepped back from the brink only when Henry and Mowbray had intervened in the king's defense.[40]

Once the charges had been read, the constable of the Tower—Gaunt's son-in-law Ralph, Lord Neville, Joan Beaufort's new husband, who had been hurriedly appointed to the post that morning to avoid Rutland having to play two roles at once—was ordered to produce the earl of Arundel to answer them. Arundel's entire career had been defined by his belligerence, his impolitic truculence, and the rashness of his temper, but he had always been brave, and he came to face his accusers with blistering defiance.

To Gaunt himself—physically frailer than he once was, but still steward of England as well as the most senior peer of the realm—fell the responsibility of conducting the trial. The duke and the earl had no love for each other, and if Gaunt had any doubts about Arundel's fate he did not let them show. He ordered Neville to remove the prisoner's scarlet hood and his belt. Now, the duke said, Arundel should account for his crimes. What crimes? came the earl's response. He could not deny his actions, but they had been taken for the good of the king and the kingdom. If he had sought royal pardons for them later, he told Gaunt with palpable contempt, it was only as a shield against the malevolence of his enemies, "of whom you are one, and one who has more need of a pardon than I." For the Commons, John Bushy spoke up to demand that the case should proceed, and the eight Appellants—including Arundel's son-in-law Mowbray and his sister's son Thomas Holand—threw down their gloves in token of their willingness to defend their accusations in combat. If he were at liberty, the earl replied, and if the king would allow it, he would gladly fight to prove his innocence. As it was, he claimed the protection of the charter of pardon the king had freely given him. "Traitor," said Gaunt, "that pardon is revoked." "You are all liars," Arundel retorted bitterly. "I am no traitor."[41]

Henry rose to his feet. His participation was required as the price of his own future, and the future of his children. He and his father had made their choice, and Richard had guaranteed his safety. Richard had also, once, guaranteed Arundel's safety, but that was a thought on which it did not pay to dwell. Henry turned to the earl. "Did you not say to me at Huntingdon, where we first gathered in revolt, that before doing anything else it would be better to seize the king?" There was an admission, as well as an accusation, in his words, but Arundel filled the silence. "You, earl of Derby, you are lying in your teeth. I never thought of anything concerning our lord king except what was in his interests and to his honor."[42]

The moment passed. Henry's evidence had done its work; and as the king himself began to talk of the death of Simon Burley, it was clear that the verdict would not be far behind. At a nod from Richard, Gaunt stood to pronounce it. Arundel was a traitor. His lands were forfeit. He was condemned to be drawn to a place of execution, there to be hanged, disemboweled, beheaded, and quartered—albeit that by the king's grace, in recognition of his noble birth, he would be spared all but the beheading.

Mowbray and the Holands stepped forward with a detachment of the king's Cheshire archers to escort the earl from the hall. With his hands bound behind his back like Burley before him, Arundel walked through staring crowds in the city streets to Tower Hill. He made confession of his sins—although not of the treason he continued to deny—and stared, impassive, into the faces of his son-in-law and his nephew. He tested the edge of the executioner's sword with his finger. "It is sharp enough. Do what you must." It took one stroke to sever his head from his body.

When Thomas Mowbray watched his wife's father die, he knew his service to the king was not yet done. He was captain of the town and garrison of Calais, responsible for the detention there of Thomas of Woodstock, and, once Arundel's life had ended on the scaffold, he had been instructed to produce his prisoner for trial at the next session of parliament. But when the assembly gathered again on Monday, September 24, Mowbray appeared alone. "I cannot bring before you Thomas of Woodstock, duke of Gloucester," he said, "because the duke is dead."[43]

There had been rumors, whispers carried on the winds that brought ships from Calais into harbors all along the south coast—and if Mowbray knew, then so did the king and those around him in the palace of Westminster. But to hear it said out loud—a publicly acknowledged fact, offered without explanation—changed everything. Unwell though he had been before his arrest, Woodstock was only forty-two, a man still in the prime of his life, and for twenty years it had been impossible to imagine English politics without his bullish presence. Suddenly he was gone; suddenly and conveniently. The executed earl of Arundel had been a great nobleman, son of one of Edward III's wealthiest and most powerful lieutenants, but Woodstock was a royal duke, son of Edward III himself. Giving him the chance to address the representatives of the realm in his own defense—in England's defense, as he would have put it—was a risk that could not have been avoided, had he stood trial in person. But the dead could say only what the living would let them. And Woodstock, it was now announced, had made a confession before dying to William Rickhill, one of the king's justices who had been sent to Calais for the purpose. In a document written in his own hand, the duke acknowledged that he had done wrong; that he had overborne the king's authority, and debated the possibility of his deposition, "wherefore I beseech to him, notwithstanding my unkindness, I beseech him ever more of his mercy and of his grace, as lowly as any creature may beseech it unto his liege lord."

Woodstock was—somehow—dead. In public that fact remained unexplained, but in the absence of any indication of curiosity from the king, no one dared ask questions. Still, he had confessed, and he was guilty. As a traitor, therefore, his lands were forfeit. No heir of his body should ever bear the royal arms or stand in line to inherit the crown. The dead man stood condemned, and the proceedings moved on. By the end of Tuesday, the verdict against the duke was matched by another against Archbishop Arundel. Because he was a priest, the archbishop would be spared a traitor's death, but the estates of his see were surrendered into the king's hands, and the archbishop himself was exiled from England until the king should otherwise ordain.[44]

On Friday it was Warwick's turn. When Ralph Neville brought him into parliament, it was obvious that the deaths of his former allies had left the earl a desperate man. He had never intended treachery against the king's majesty, he said, but could not deny that he had ridden with Woodstock and Arundel. "Would that I had never laid eyes on them!" Weeping in terror, he accepted his guilt and begged for Richard's mercy. His pleas made a pitiful spectacle, by which the king was so gratified that, once sentence of death had been pronounced, Richard declared he would spare Warwick's life. The earl was handed over to William Scrope to be taken to the Isle of Man, where he would spend the rest of his days as a prisoner.

In barely more than a week, Richard had destroyed his enemies. Next, he intended to reward his friends. He began that Tuesday by declaring that, "for the great love and affection he had for the county of Cheshire and its people," he was annexing Arundel's forfeited estates in north Wales and Shropshire to his own earldom of Chester to create a new principality within his kingdom, a vast power bloc to be held in perpetuity by the king or—should he have one—his eldest son. Ten years before, Richard had railed at his inability to put a royal army into the field that could face down the retinues of his magnates. Now, as hundreds of archers from his newly minted principality surrounded his parliament and muscled their way through London's streets, he sat easier on his throne knowing he could outmatch the territorial resources and the military might of his greatest subjects.[45]

Plenty more lands remained to be distributed. During the week, in the privacy of the royal chambers within the palace, document after document was sealed with the privy seal, parceling out the traitors' manors, lordships, and castles into the hands of the men who had accused them, the men who stood closest to the king. To Edward of Rutland went the castle of Clun in Shropshire, and estates in Yorkshire and Hertfordshire; to young Thomas Holand, Warwick Castle and other valuable manors in Warwickshire; to John Holand, Arundel Castle with lands in Sussex, Devon, and Cornwall; to Thomas Mowbray, Lewes Castle in Sussex and Castle Acre in Norfolk, with lands there and in Worcestershire and Buckinghamshire; to John Beaufort, manors in Staffordshire, Northamptonshire, Wiltshire, and Norfolk; to William Scrope, lands in Wales, Essex, and Durham; to Thomas Despenser, estates in Worcestershire and Gloucestershire. The knights who had managed the impeachments in the Commons shared in the plunder: the lands and goods received by John Bushy, William Bagot, and Henry Green included the barge the earl of Warwick kept on the Thames, and household furnishings and kitchen utensils from Arundel's London home.[46]

Possession would make these forfeitures permanent, but it would be backed up to the greatest degree possible by the law. In between the trials, a new statute decreed that anyone seeking to overturn any act of this parliament would be guilty of treason. It was a bold verdict, sweeping into the future with terrible power. But at the same time, loopholes were woven into its fabric, exemptions that spared men on whom the sunlight of the king's grace now shone. The male heirs of Woodstock, Arundel, and Warwick, the lords and Commons agreed, should be barred forever from the councils and parliaments of the realm. But their daughters and their daughters' offspring—Thomas Mowbray's sons, for example—should not be affected by this proscription. Then too there was the question of the members of the council of 1386 other than the three condemned traitors. Several were dead, but those still living included Rutland's father, Edmund of Langley, and William Scrope's elderly father, Richard, Lord Scrope. They, the king announced, were loyal and innocent men who were in no way responsible for the "evil purpose and intent" of the council on which they had served.[47]

From the perspective of logic and legal principle, it was bewildering. In 1386–88 Woodstock, Arundel, and Warwick had been guilty of treason so outrageous, so damaging to the king's regality, that the royal pardons they had subsequently received were null and void. Meanwhile, others who had acted with them were the king's faithful subjects whose allegiance to the crown was unquestionable. But in practice no one was bewildered; in practice, the outcome was chillingly clear. The naming of traitors lay in Richard's hands. And so on Saturday, September 29, the king made another parliamentary proclamation. Henry of Bolingbroke and Thomas Mowbray were his loyal liegemen, who had acted out of honor and duty to restrain the treasonable purposes of Woodstock and Arundel, and should come to no harm for what they had done. It was a queasy kind of reassurance, requiring as it did explicit acknowledgment of their past association with the dead men, but in the circumstances it was a great deal better than no reassurance at all.[48]

Still there was no time to pause, to take stock, to calculate or plan. Richard had always enjoyed bestowing titles on his faithful servants. Now, even as he destroyed the unworthy, he would raise up the deserving. Since his coronation two decades earlier, England had known only four dukes: his uncles Gaunt, Langley, and Woodstock, and fleetingly his friend de Vere. De Vere was long dead and Woodstock newly so, but more candidates could be found among the living to "reinforce and strengthen the royal scepter," noted the parliamentary record. These would be no decorative promotions. In conjunction with the wholesale distribution of the traitors' lands, this was a seismic reshaping of the political landscape.[49]

The list was long, and the names familiar. Rutland, already the heir to his father's duchy of York, became in his own right duke of Aumale. The Holands, John and Thomas, became dukes of Exeter and Surrey, and Thomas Mowbray duke of Norfolk. There were lesser titles too. John Beaufort, after just seven months as earl of Somerset, became marquis of Dorset. Thomas Despenser received the earldom of Gloucester, and William Scrope the earldom of Wiltshire. Ralph Neville, Gaunt's son-in-law, became earl of Westmorland, and the earl of Northumberland's brother, Thomas Percy, who had acted as the lay representative of the clergy in this most compliant of parliaments, earl of Worcester. But the greatest of them all—by birth, if not by royal favor—was the king's cousin Henry of Bolingbroke, earl of Derby, heir to the duchy of Lancaster. By Richard's fiat, Henry was named duke of Hereford.

There had never been so many new peerages created all at one time, and this unprecedented multiplication of once-rarefied titles did not convince the king's subjects. "The common people," said Walsingham, "derisively nicknamed them not dukes but *duketti*—that is, 'the little dukes.'" But Richard was more than satisfied with his fortnight's work. He had redesigned the political geography of his kingdom to his own specification. He had done so without a breath of criticism or resistance in parliament. There was more business to attend to, but for the time being it could wait. At the end of Saturday's ceremonies, he adjourned the assembly to meet again in four months, not at Westminster but—in demonstration of his new world order—140 miles away in Shrewsbury, on the edge of his principality of Chester.

On Sunday, September 20, the lords and prelates, one by one in their new order of precedence, knelt at the Confessor's shrine in Westminster Abbey under the silent gaze of the painted white hart in the south transept gallery, to swear a sacred oath: on pain of a traitor's death, they would uphold every one of the judgments and statutes made in the last two weeks. Then the bishops pronounced a sentence of excommunication upon anyone who might dare to break his word. If the taking of oaths in the abbey at the end of the Merciless Parliament had seemed to Richard a mockery of the holy vows made by the king and his subjects at his coronation, that wrong had finally been put right. True peace, at last, was restored.[50]

All that remained was a great feast that evening, over which Richard presided in sumptuous state. England's court dazzled. The prize for the most graceful dancer was awarded to Henry's beautiful sister Elizabeth, the new duchess of Exeter. Nobody spoke the name of their dead uncle Woodstock. In the days and weeks that followed, English envoys traveled to Rome to make arrangements for the replacement of the banished Thomas Arundel as archbishop of Canterbury, and to pursue the king's plans for his election as Holy Roman Emperor. Richard himself wrote to the duke of Bavaria to tell his fellow prince of his triumph. He had been beset by traitors, he said: noblemen within his family and household whom he had treated with affection, generosity, and clemency, but whose malice had proved obstinate and damnable. By God's providence, therefore, he had raised his royal hand to destroy them and disinherit their heirs, and in so doing had brought everlasting peace to his people.[51]

"Future generations," he wrote, "however young they may be, must learn what it is to offend the royal majesty. For he is a child of death, who offends the king."

Twelve

1397-1398

to stand upon my kingdom

Henry's new title was only hours old when one of his retainers was ambushed and murdered near his rented London home. Fleet Street was a road so busy that violent altercations regularly broke out among the crowds jostling outside the fine houses that studded its route. In this case, however, the killer was a knight from Richard's principality of Chester, Sir John Haukeston, against whom the dead Lancastrian, a man named William Laken, had been pursuing a legal dispute through the courts. Haukeston had been lying in wait for Laken with a crowd of supporters for the best part of forty-eight hours in various places on the road and river between London and Westminster. During the evening of Saturday, September 29, they found him. Haukeston dealt Laken a blow from behind with his sword, deep into his body through his right leg. Laken died instantly.[1]

Three months earlier, as earl of Derby, Henry would have felt confident of his ability to secure some sort of justice for the man's family, despite Haukeston's service to the king. Now, as duke of Hereford in a brutally changed world, it was hard to be so sure. He and his father had participated in the trials of Woodstock, Arundel, and Warwick, but since its improvised beginnings Richard's assault on his enemies had moved faster and further than they had ever anticipated. Henry remained an outsider among the tight-knit group of lavishly rewarded noblemen who surrounded the throne, while the capital was still in the grip of the king's heavily armed bodyguard, who swaggered through the streets and acted as though the fact of the king's favor made them untouchable.

For now, Henry kept an impassive public face. His first public act as duke—other than taking his turn to swear the oath at the Confessor's shrine on Sunday, September 30—was to host a banquet the next day in honor of Thomas Mowbray's long-dead father, who had been killed by the Turks on his way to the Holy Land when Mowbray was an infant. His bones had been retrieved from Constantinople for reburial at the Carmelite friary that lay between Fleet Street and the Thames—and, after the requiem mass had been sung, the court gathered in its finery in the friary's hall to eat and drink at Henry's expense, the king and his seven-year-old queen sitting under canopies of state that had been specially made for the occasion on Henry's orders.[2]

Amid the rictus smiles and elaborate courtesies, the new duke of Hereford was not the only one feeling ill at ease. Richard's satisfaction at the destruction of Woodstock and Arundel had not brought him rest. In the palace of Westminster his Cheshire archers kept watch outside his chamber day and night, but they could not shield him from his thoughts. Within days of Arundel's corpse being laid to rest in the Augustinian friary just inside the northern edge of the city, people began to flock to the church, drawn by rumors of miracles taking place at a grave within which the earl's severed head was said to have spontaneously rejoined itself to his body. But rumor also had it that Richard was haunted by nightmares, fear-filled dreams in which Arundel's ghost appeared before him. Ten days after the execution—whether to quiet his own disturbed mind or to stamp out the first flickers of a martyr's cult—the king sent Gaunt, Rutland, Mowbray, and Thomas Holand to inspect the earl's remains, and to ensure that the burial site was paved over and left unmarked.[3]

The more troublesome ghost turned out to be Woodstock's. No cause had yet been announced for the duke's death in his Calais prison, and Richard showed no interest in providing one. Instead, he ordered prayers for Woodstock's soul, and gave directions that his body should be handed over to his distraught widow, thirty-one-year-old Eleanor, for burial among his ancestors in Westminster Abbey. Two weeks later, the king changed his mind, requiring Eleanor instead to deliver the corpse to Bermondsey Priory on the south bank of the Thames, where the grave would attract less attention. In Essex, her traumatized children—sixteen-year-old Humphrey and his three younger sisters—had to watch the king's officers rifling through the contents of their elegant home at Pleshey, making an exhaustive inventory of the gorgeous tapestries and embroidered silk bed hangings, their father's remarkable library and his rich clothes and armor, all of which were now forfeit to the crown. But the duke's sudden absence was not just agonizing for his frightened family. For as long as it remained publicly unexplained, Woodstock's death would be as politically provocative as his life had once been.[4]

Henry had ample reason to be disturbed by his uncle's fall. Even aside from their personal relationship, the destruction of the son of a king on charges of treason had few precedents in English history. It was almost seventy years since Edward II's brother Edmund of Kent had been executed in the tangled aftermath of Edward's deposition—and the specter of that calamitous reign was present in more ways than one. Woodstock's forfeiture of his title as duke of Gloucester had paved the way for Richard to revive the ancient earldom of Gloucester for Rutland's young brother-in-law Thomas Despenser. Despenser was the great-grandson of Edward II's favorite Hugh Despenser, who had held the Welsh lands of the earldom of Gloucester until his execution in 1326. For Richard to promote Despenser in this way gestured again at the alarming possibility that he might one day seek to reverse all the political consequences of Edward's deposition. Another English delegation had been in Rome since the summer to argue yet again that the dead king should be made a saint, but—as Richard had just demonstrated—he did not need the pope's permission to rewrite history within his own realm. Did he intend to revisit the moment in 1322 when the Lancastrian estates and title had been forfeited to the crown? Gaunt was less and less robust, and his protective presence would not be there forever. For now, Henry accompanied his father to attend the king at Windsor Castle in the early weeks of October, and then rode west through Gloucestershire to visit his own estates in Herefordshire and south Wales, lordships that would be the first to feel the pressure if the new earl of Gloucester began to flex his political muscles in the region.[5]

But the man whose fears for the future began to overwhelm him was Thomas Mowbray. Like Henry, Mowbray had just been declared blameless for his part in the events of 1387–88. Unlike Henry, he could look for encouragement to his years of restored closeness to the king. But the fate of Woodstock and Arundel had demonstrated that pardons in whatever form or iteration offered no reliable protection against future royal vengeance— and, with Richard, closeness did not ever mean safety. In fact, it had left Mowbray trapped in a new dilemma. The rumors racing around the capital were unanimous: as captain of Calais, he was responsible for Woodstock's death, which had been the result not of illness or accident, but murder. And what made Mowbray's position terrifying was that the rumors were true.

That October, shortly after the end of the parliament, Mowbray and his retinue rode out of London toward Westminster, down Fleet Street and on, past the site where Gaunt's palace of the Savoy had once stood. The noises of the road—of horses and men and the clatter of the street—offered cover for a private conversation, and Mowbray called forward his chief steward, William Bagot, from the entourage behind him. Bagot was a forceful man, experienced and savvy. His ability to get results both inside and outside the letter of the law had recommended him to several powerful masters, including the king, for whom he had just managed the impeachments in parliament alongside John Bushy and Henry Green. But he had served Mowbray loyally for years, and now Mowbray took the chance of confiding in him. Did Bagot know anything, Mowbray asked, about how the duke of Gloucester died? Bagot's reply was blunt: "No, but the people say that you murdered him." In response, Mowbray unleashed a tirade tinged with unmistakable panic. Yes, the king had sent him to Calais in August with orders that Woodstock should die, but at that point, he said, he had *saved* the duke's life for more than three weeks. He had never been more afraid than when he returned to Richard's presence to confess that his prisoner was still breathing, only to find himself dispatched back across the Channel in the company of a guard handpicked by the king to get the job done. Mowbray swore, as he would answer before God on the dreadful day of judgment, that he had never wanted Woodstock put to death; but in the end he had been unable to stop the murder, out of fear of the king and in order to save his own life.[6]

His terror was both clear and comprehensible. He had banked on his participation in the arrests of Woodstock, Arundel, and Warwick to save him from sharing their fate—but what had happened after their arrests seemed to have brought that fate closer. He had simultaneously agreed to serve as Richard's patsy for the murder of a royal duke, and angered the king by not complying promptly enough. Should he simply trust Richard to protect him, when there was nothing simple about trusting Richard at all? Or should he look for some way to protect himself, before the king had the chance to dispose of his chosen scapegoat?

By the first week in December, holding his nerve proved too much to bear. Bagot knew his secret, but Bagot was also working for the king. How much longer would he keep his mouth shut? Mowbray needed support and advice from an ally who shared at least some of his vulnerability. Henry had been staying with the king's household near Oxford for a couple of nights on his way back from south Wales. When he moved on toward London, Mowbray caught up with him—suddenly and unexpectedly, as Henry later told the story—on the road near Brentford, ten miles west of the capital. "We are about to be undone," Mowbray said. "Because of Radcot Bridge."[7]

Henry was stunned. Not at the idea that they were in danger—that much had been clear since the arrests of Woodstock, Arundel, and Warwick back in July—but because he had no reason to trust Mowbray. How could this be so, he asked, choosing his words with the utmost care, "since the king has given us grace, and declared in parliament that we have been true and loyal?" That meant nothing, Mowbray replied. "He will do with us what he has done with the others. He wants to wipe that slate clean." But it would be astonishing, Henry said, if the king were to go back on his public word. "This is an astonishing world," came Mowbray's response, "and a false one." Henry should know that there had been plots laid at court. Had it not been for himself, Rutland, John Holand, and Thomas Percy—lords who had sworn, he said, never to agree to the destruction of one of their peers without just cause—Henry and Gaunt would have been arrested or murdered at Windsor that October. The conspirators were the ambitious newcomers: young Thomas Holand, Scrope, Salisbury, and Despenser, men who had set their sights on all who stood in their way. They wanted to turn back time to the forfeiture of the Lancastrian estates in 1322, estates that would be rich pick-ings for a redistribution of power more far-reaching even than the one that had just taken place. ("God forbid!" Henry exclaimed.) And they would not stop, Mowbray insisted. Even if they did not succeed now, with the king's help they would still be trying "to kill us in our houses ten years hence."

Mowbray had hoped for an ally. Instead, he had handed over his quan-dary to Henry. Should he believe Mowbray, keep quiet, and plan for his own defense? Or might Mowbray be in league with Richard, attempting to trap him into betraying his own disloyalty? Within Richard's vertiginous hall of mirrors, Henry could see no safe response. The best of a set of bad options was to tell his father. During a tense Christmas at Leicester Castle, Gaunt—to whom the experience of plots against his life was devastatingly, exhaustingly familiar—argued that their only hope of safety lay in dragging the whole mess into the light. That way they could not be accused of con-spiracy, not even a conspiracy of silence; and the king, whatever his private intentions, would surely be forced to reiterate his public support for his uncle and cousin. In the new year Gaunt left Leicester to inform Richard, who had spent Christmas twenty miles away at Coventry, of what Mowbray had said. Henry rode north to pray at the shrine of John of Bridlington where he had once, long ago, given thanks on his safe return from Prussia. Those had been simpler days: fighting in defense of his faith with his friends by his side before coming home, laden with gifts, to the happiness of his family. Now he found himself sending to his London goldsmith for a gilded chain on which to wear a "medicinal stone" for dipping into drinks as a prophylactic, an antidote to neutralize the threat of poison.[8]

The drawback to Gaunt's plan was that it left Mowbray out in the cold. He had never been the steadiest or most principled of politicians, and now his panic reached new heights. Whether or not he had been telling the truth about his previous attempts to resist court conspiracies against Henry and Gaunt in October, his attempt to confide in Henry had backfired to the point where the Lancastrians suddenly represented the most immediate threat to his safety. He tried to set an ambush to have Gaunt killed on the road to Shrewsbury for the reopening of parliament. When that failed, he fled into hiding. It was a head-spinning reversal: the man who, with Rutland,

had for years been Richard's personal proxy was on the run, his future hanging by a fraying thread. His disappearance left both stage and script to his
new enemy, but Henry was taking no chances. Arriving in Shropshire in late
January to give an account of himself to the king, he brought with him an
armed retinue of Lancastrian knights, esquires, and archers.[9]

When the representatives of the realm assembled at Shrewsbury Abbey
in the last week of January, there was no sense of relief after the drama that
had played out at Westminster. If anything, the subliminal hum of tension
was louder, the prickles of fear sharper under the skin. A parliament had
not been held in Shrewsbury for more than a century; it seemed the king
had chosen such unfamiliar surroundings, near the interlocking borders
of Shropshire, Cheshire, and north Wales, so that his lords and Commons
would meet not only under the watch of his Cheshire archers but in the
looming shadow of Richard's new principality of Chester itself. And as the
meeting started it became obvious how little had been settled by the show
trials in September. Richard had used parliament to wipe out past parliamentary judgments. How could he be certain that a future parliament would
not do the same in the opposite direction?[10]

In his search for the security that still eluded him, the enforced declara-
tions and oaths began again. The Merciless Parliament was annulled in its
entirety "as a thing done without authority, and against the will and liberty of
the king and the right of his crown." Then the judges' answers to Richard's
questions of 1387 were read into the parliamentary record, and their redefinition of the law of treason confirmed as correct by the king's lawyers and
justices. By what means, Richard demanded, could these decisions be made
irrevocable forever? The lords tried to point out that they had already sworn
never to reverse the actions of the present parliament, but Richard required
them to swear the same oath again, this time on a cross brought all the way
from Canterbury. The king's lawyers expressed the view that the authority
of parliament itself provided "the greatest security there could be," while the
bishops attempted gingerly to explain that Richard's own arguments about
the royal prerogative, as well as the constitutional position of the crown,
made it impossible for him to restrict the freedom of his successors as king.
No matter, he said. He himself would give the question further thought,

and in the meantime he would ask the pope to excommunicate anyone who contravened his new statutes.[11]

Then, at Richard's invitation, the floor was Henry's. By the king's order, Henry said, "and not through malice, enmity or for any other reason," he had come to recount his conversation with Thomas Mowbray on the road to London, a conversation in which Mowbray had uttered "many untrue words, to the slander of the person of our lord the king." Henry told the whole story from Mowbray's opening—"We are undone"—to the allegation that Thomas Holand, Scrope, Salisbury, and Despenser were plotting to destroy Gaunt and Henry and other lords with the approval of the king. The room, when he finished, was alive with apprehension. It was clear that Mowbray was in deep trouble; it was equally clear that the mention of Radcot Bridge risked implicating Henry too. Not only that, but the pretense of unity that had sustained the trials of Woodstock, Arundel, and Warwick was fractured beyond repair. Henry and Mowbray—who had acted with the three lords in 1387, then helped destroy them in 1397—were locked in public conflict from which neither looked likely to emerge unscathed.[12]

Richard, meanwhile, seemed to relish their plight. He kept Henry waiting overnight for a formal response. The next day, Thursday, January 31, the king declared his decision in parliament. There would be no rush to judgment in the matters Henry had brought to his attention. Instead, he would take the advice of a newly established commission to which the authority of parliament would be delegated, a panel to include Gaunt, Langley, Rutland, the two Holands, John Beaufort, Salisbury, Despenser, and Scrope, as well as the Percy earls of Northumberland and Worcester, the earl of March— who had recently returned from Ireland—and several of the king's knights, including the increasingly indispensable John Bushy and Henry Green. And if the commission could speak with the authority of parliament, then parliament itself was no longer needed: at the end of the day's business, the assembly would be dissolved.

The lives of Henry, duke of Hereford, and Thomas Mowbray, duke of Norfolk, were at a crossroads. The king's behavior was becoming increasingly, ominously capricious. At the same time, it was more than ever apparent how much he had learned from the desperate drama of the late 1380s.

Then Richard had found himself without support among his magnates and defeated in his own parliament. Now, whatever might happen to Henry and Mowbray—just as had been the case with Woodstock, Arundel, and Warwick—their peers would be complicit in their fate.

For those who cared to see, England's ship of state was careening at speed into unknown waters. There were some who did not choose to look: not only Richard's favored Cheshiremen, but those among the *duketti*—Mowbray now excepted—who were enjoying the territorial spoils of the treason trials. But the rest of the king's frightened subjects could find no steady foothold from which to take their bearings. The everlasting peace that Richard had claimed as his gift to his people was revealing itself as a process of perpetual revolution in which no one could be sure they were safe. On the last day of parliament, after the Commons had meekly approved a grant to the king of the subsidy on wool exports—usually given for a term of years—for the rest of his life, Richard responded by proclaiming another general pardon. It was a reward, he said, for "the great tenderness and diligence his people have shown for the salvation of his royal estate and the right of his crown." But the reward was not for everyone. At Westminster four months earlier, he had pardoned all of his subjects apart from fifty people he still refused to name. This time, he excluded from his grace those who had followed Woodstock, Arundel, and Warwick into rebellion in 1387. When the lords had first been arrested, the king had promised their retainers and servants that they faced no danger. Now he offered a five-month amnesty during which they could sue for individual forgiveness. It was a policy of deliberately designed judicial insecurity, constructed around an impossible calculation: Was it better to remain silent in fear, and thereby hope to avoid royal attention, or admit some sort of guilt in return for absolution from a king who had already demonstrated in the most public way that his pardons could, if he chose, be revoked at any time?[13]

A special committee of the royal council had been appointed in September, during the last week of the Westminster session of parliament, to hear such petitions for the king's grace. The chancellor, the treasurer, and the keeper of the privy seal—all three offices currently held by bishops within the king's household—and the king's knights John Bushy, William Bagot, and Henry Green would assess the applications, compile lists of names, and place the fines paid for the pardons into a special bag "to the king's use" that would bypass the normal Exchequer accounts. Over weeks and months, the lists grew longer and the bags heavier as hundreds of frightened men came forward, not knowing for sure whether the charters of pardon they received in return for their cash and confessions would save or damn them.[14]

Whatever arrangement they came to, it was becoming more and more obvious that only a fool would stake any part of his future on the king's word. Of the loans Richard had extracted from his subjects after the arrests of Woodstock, Arundel, and Warwick, just two—those made by the treasurer of Calais and Mayor Whittington of London—were repaid by Easter 1398, the date on which they were due. Less well-placed men could only hazard a despairing guess at when, if ever, their money might be returned. But what option was there other than folly, when the king's word underpinned all law and all justice, in the present as well as the future? Even Bushy, Bagot, and Green were careful to secure pardons from their own committee for their actions in 1387–88—actions which they left discreetly unspecified—before taking the double precaution of having the documents formally copied into the records of the royal Chancery.

Meanwhile, the king's methods for keeping his subjects at his mercy became ever more elaborate. If his people wanted general pardons, why should he not require general confessions? That summer, proctors were appointed to represent London and the sixteen counties nearest the city in the south and east, the part of the country most closely implicated in the events of 1387–88 and farthest away from the king's new principality of Chester in the northwest. At Richard's demand, these proctors—in the capital's case, the new archbishop of Canterbury and the bishop of London alongside Mayor Whittington and his two sheriffs—put their seals to documents acknowledging unspecified collective offenses against the king's majesty, and declaring their "burning desire" for his grace. These admissions of guilt were known as "blank charters," since they gave Richard carte blanche to impose more fines at will, or simply to hold a perpetual threat of further punishment over his subjects' heads as a way of enforcing their obedience. He had experimented with such documents as early as the autumn of 1396, when he required the monks of Canterbury to submit "*lettres à la blanche chartre*" to the crown after Thomas Arundel became their archbishop—but their wholesale application to half his kingdom was unprecedented, and chillingly unpredictable in its implications.[15]

"No man knew what it meant," one bewildered Londoner wrote of these blank charters—a paralyzing uncertainty in the face of the king's demands that gripped the political hierarchy right to the very top. Henry had secured another pardon from Richard three days before parliament reopened at Shrewsbury, and another on the session's last day, kneeling at his cousin's feet to beg renewed forgiveness in front of all the representatives of the realm. But the very fact that Henry was seeking repeated public statements of his pardon—just as Richard was requiring repeated public oaths of allegiance from his subjects—served to erode even further the idea that promises of any kind could be trusted.[16]

Henry himself knew that, however many times he knelt before the throne, he would still have to wait for the verdict of Richard's freshly established parliamentary commission on his dangerous dispute with Thomas Mowbray. If they believed Henry's account of the conversation, then Mowbray would be judged a traitor for slandering the king. If they did not, what punishment might Henry face? At least the commission included his brother and father—but at fifty-seven, after a lifetime immersed in national and international politics, Gaunt was struggling to respond to a world in which he had lost any kind of control. Attempting to protect his son and his duchy required him to uphold and demonstrate his loyalty to his nephew's kingship, in circumstances where his nephew's kingship represented the principal threat to his son and his duchy. It was a process that necessitated minute-by-minute decisions of increasing complexity, and no reliable outcome.

Gaunt was already amassing a file of legal documents, the need for which would once have been impossible to imagine. Before the end of the Shrewsbury parliament, just as Gaunt and Henry had feared, Thomas Despenser, the new earl of Gloucester, had been given permission to sue for recovery of the lands of his ancestor Hugh Despenser, Edward II's favorite, whose forfeiture for treason in 1326 was now formally annulled. In return, Despenser swore on the cross of Canterbury that he would never prosecute his restored rights to properties currently held by ten other lords, including Gaunt and Henry. But even if Despenser's word could be believed, it remained the case that one judgment from the moment of Edward II's deposition had been undone. Might the Lancastrian estates—forfeited by Thomas of Lancaster in 1322 and restored when Edward fell in 1326–27—be the next target?[17]

The chance was not worth taking. On February 20, Gaunt secured a charter from Richard declaring that the king would never pursue any claim "which he could have" to the Lancastrian lands dating back to the time of Edward II. That "could" was exactly what Gaunt feared and Mowbray had alleged Richard and his new favorites were planning—and the fact that Gaunt felt the need to extract this royal promise was not even the most extraordinary evidence to emerge that Mowbray might have been right. Less than a fortnight later, William Bagot—whose incisive political brain and sharp eye for the main chance were helping him rise in Richard's service at breakneck speed—put his seal to two documents. One promised on pain of £1,000 that Bagot would not try to disinherit Gaunt or his wife and children; the other declared that if he were ever to kill Gaunt or his wife and children, he should be put to death without further judicial process. And with that, armed with a freshly issued pardon from the king, Bagot went straight back to his place at Richard's side.[18]

Perhaps Bagot had been conspiring with his new friends at court against his former masters Gaunt and Henry; perhaps he was seeking to put public distance between himself and plots in which he was not personally involved. Either way, it was staggering, unthinkable in any normal circumstances, that one of the king's most trusted knights should have to provide a written legal undertaking not to murder the king's uncle. Finding himself through the looking glass, Gaunt had no choice but to carry on. He had to travel north for talks about the Anglo-Scottish truce to which he was already committed, but he succeeded at least in keeping Henry out of custody in the weeks leading up to the hearing of his case. Mowbray—realizing he had nowhere to run—had given himself up once parliament closed, protesting his own innocence and calling Henry a traitor. He was held under lock and key until the commissioners finally met in Richard's presence, without Gaunt, at Bristol on March 19. But their task was impossible. Between the indecipherability of their increasingly autocratic king's wishes and the alarmingly unstable rabbit hole into which the dispute between Mowbray and Henry might lead, no procedure was clear, no decision watertight.[19]

Step-by-step, moment by moment, over the last eight months the norms, precedents, and safeguards of political life had been hacked away. The crown had once been the fount of justice and order, the king's law a framework within which disputes could be resolved and the peace of the realm maintained. Those days were over. Three of England's greatest nobles had been destroyed, one executed, one imprisoned, one murdered, for offenses that had already been pardoned. Richard's authority was volatile, threatening, and apparently impossible to resist. The commissioners' response was to refer the argument to a higher power. Henry and Mowbray were each accusing the other of treason. If neither claim could be independently verified, they said, the case should be tried by combat. The two dukes would be required to stake everything not on law and judgment but a duel, a chivalric game turned to deadly reality.

They were almost exactly the same age—Mowbray just a few months older—and both were accomplished fighters. Henry had won the admiration of Europe in the lists and on the battlefield, but for all his prowess he could not be sure the contest would go his way. In the decade since the Merciless Parliament he had been cautious and he had been careful, and still he found himself faced with the risk of catastrophic loss. At least now, after years of silent compliance, he had a limited kind of agency, choices to make in his own defense. Before buckling on his armor, he opted for a differently dangerous gambit. Trial by combat came into play when neither witness nor written evidence could be found to settle the truth of an accusation. His conversation with Mowbray about plots and royal vengeance had been heard by no one else; those implicated in its substance would never testify, and would hardly have incriminated themselves in writing. If the king's commissioners required proof of Mowbray's guilt, so be it: Henry would present new allegations for which proof could be supplied.

His opportunity came a few weeks later, at Windsor on April 29, when the king and council—this time including Gaunt, newly returned from Scotland—met to hear the case under the jurisdiction of the court of Chivalry. Richard sat surrounded by his lords on a dais in the castle's courtyard as Henry and Mowbray were brought in. Were they willing to make up their quarrel, and to receive in return his royal grace? Their honor would not allow it, they said. If it occurred to Henry to mention the two pardons he had already received since bringing the dispute to the king's attention, he did not say so. Instead, one of the knights of his retinue stepped forward to place Henry's charges against Mowbray on the record before their sovereign and their peers. First: as captain of Calais, Mowbray had received huge sums of money from the crown but had not paid the garrison as he should, so that Calais was in danger of being lost. Second: he was the cause of all the treasons committed in the kingdom for the last eighteen years. Third: he was responsible for the murder of Thomas of Woodstock, duke of Gloucester.[20]

For a moment, there was silence. Woodstock's death had been announced but never explained. For seven months, no public questions had been asked about the fate of Richard's imprisoned uncle—and now Henry had chosen to break this *omertà* in the most incendiary way. His calculation was twofold. There would be witnesses to what had happened to Woodstock at Calais, which was therefore susceptible of proof, unlike the "he said/he said" back-and-forth of his own dealings with Mowbray. Knowing this, Richard might shut down the investigation by declaring Mowbray's guilt. What else was a scapegoat for?

His calculation, however, was wrong. Richard had every interest in Mowbray being on trial—as he already was—but no interest in declaring him guilty of a heinous crime in which he would immediately then implicate Richard himself. And Mowbray, who was still hoping to escape with his life, had no interest in addressing the accusation if Richard had no interest in pursuing it. One of Mowbray's knights rose to speak on his behalf. Henry was a liar. He, not Mowbray, was disloyal to the crown. That, clearly, was the rebuttal prepared for Henry's account of their conversation at Brentford on the road to London. Did Mowbray wish to speak further in his own defense? He had received gold from the king for Calais, he said, and had spent it there, so that the town was well guarded and no complaint had been made. He had to acknowledge that he had once sent men to kill Gaunt, there sitting beside the king; but "my lord forgave me, and peace was made between us, for which I thank him."[21]

That was all. No one but Henry had mentioned Woodstock's name. The word "murder" hung in the air while the meeting moved on. As the laws of chivalry required, Henry threw down his glove, and Mowbray picked it up. The date was made: a duel, to be fought at Coventry in September.

Henry's life was running off the road. Since Mary's death four years earlier, he had been in unhappy stasis: his father's deputy and a loving father to his own children, but shut out of office and influence by Richard, and refused permission to adventure abroad by Gaunt. In recent weeks, there had been small signs of hope that new avenues might be opening to him. The evaporation of Richard's plans for English troops to fight alongside the French in Italy meant the way had become clear for Henry to explore the possibility of a marriage to Lucia Visconti, cousin of his friend Gian Galeazzo, duke of Milan, a young woman he had met on his journey back from the Holy Land in 1393 and whom the duke now offered as a bride. But everything depended on his fight with Mowbray. Even if he won, Richard's dangerous volatility made it difficult to see what lay ahead. Without victory, there was no future at all.[22]

He had five long months to wait, months that seemed at times like torture. He moved restlessly around the Lancastrian estates, from the north to the south and then back to the midlands, sometimes in the company of his father and always with loyal friends who had served him for years: Thomas Rempston, who had been retrieved by Lancastrian diplomacy from his Lithuanian captivity after the *reyse* of 1391; Thomas Erpingham, the senior Lancastrian knight who had been at Henry's side ever since that campaign; Hugh Waterton, in whose home Henry's little daughters were being raised; Waterton's cousin Robert, who would be his squire and second when the duel took place. As he traveled through the duchy's lands, he sought new recruits for his retinue, granting annuities and distributing livery collars of forget-me-nots. He was also equipping himself for the combat to come.

At Henry's request, Gian Galeazzo Visconti sent him a suit of the finest Milanese armor, along with four expert Lombard armorers to ensure that the engraved and burnished steel fitted him exactly, to tiny fractions of an inch.[23]

Richard too was corresponding with allies on the Continent. His attention was no longer principally focused on Paris. Ever since the triumph of his marriage and the subsequent collapse of the proposed Italian campaign, he had lost interest in other practical manifestations of his treaty with France. Instead, he remained fixed on the glorious vision of himself as Holy Roman Emperor. The English king had "set his hopes on the Empire," the pope in Rome told the Milanese ambassador, "although truly it is impossible for him to win it." Not that Richard showed any sign of recognizing that obvious geopolitical conclusion. In the autumn of 1397 he had distributed pensions to a handful of German knights, and in the spring of 1398 he confirmed the £1,000 annuity to be paid from the English exchequer to the new Count Palatine after the recent death of his father. In May, Richard arranged for the archdeacon of Cologne to visit Rome in pursuit of his claims to the imperial title. There the archdeacon would join the bishop of Lichfield, William Scrope's cousin Richard, who had been at the papal curia for months already to lobby for Edward II's still-elusive sainthood. The king also responded to the Byzantine emperor Manuel II Palaeologus, with whose court at Constantinople embassies had been exchanged during the previous year, and who had now requested military assistance against the Turks. He could not yet send troops or money, Richard told the emperor, because his treasury had been drained by the need to deal with the malevolence of some of his magnates; but "at length, by the aid of God's grace, we have by our own valor trodden on the necks of the proud and haughty, and with a strong hand have ground them down, not to the bark only, but even to the root." As a result, he declared, "we have restored to our subjects peace . . . which by God's blessing shall endure for ever."[24]

A glance around his kingdom, however, was enough to suggest that with each passing day Richard's grandiloquent claims bore less and less resemblance to reality. A stream of knights and esquires presented themselves to apply for pardons before the council committee, and others were individually summoned to account to the king for their past service to Woodstock,

Arundel, or Warwick. Yet Richard did not seem reassured that treachery had been expunged from his realm. From March 1398, letters carried in and out of England's ports were routinely intercepted and read by the king's agents, while Rutland and Thomas Holand, the new dukes of Aumale and Surrey, were commissioned to hunt for traitors, wherever in the kingdom they might be, and to punish them as they deserved. Paranoia, the ongoing search for enemies within, was becoming the standard operational mode of Richard's state.[25]

And paranoia fed hungrily on its own effects, since the king's assault on those he perceived as his enemies was beginning to precipitate new forms of resistance. On March 31, Palm Sunday, several hundred men rose in revolt in Oxfordshire, near the site of the Appellants' victory over de Vere's Cheshire-men at Radcot Bridge a decade before. One of the rebel leaders in the vil-lage of Witney, where the earl of Arundel had taken up position before the battle, called himself by the name of Arundel's young son and heir. Another, a man named Henry Roper from Bampton, a village just three miles from the bridge itself, rallied his followers with his axe in his hand. "Arise all men and go with us," he cried, "or else truly and by God you shall be dead!" It was part intimidation, part warning. The king, who had once promised that no harm would come to those involved in the events of 1387–88, was now forcing his subjects to pay for pardons that were not worth the parchment on which they were written. The people of Oxfordshire had noticed the threat. The re-volt was put down and Roper found guilty of treason; he was hanged, drawn and quartered, and sections of his dismembered body dispatched to cities in the south, east, and midlands for display as a grisly deterrent. But rumblings of unrest continued, and as spring turned to summer the council kept a wary eye on potential troublemakers in the shires.[26]

The king's response was only to double down. At Nottingham in June, he added another four months to the deadline by which those who had served Woodstock, Arundel, or Warwick were required to compound with the council for pardon. At the same time, he distributed financial rewards to the Cheshiremen who had fought at Radcot Bridge, all the while recruiting more retainers to wear his badge of the white hart. Together with the blank charters extracted over the summer from London and the sixteen counties of the southeast—a part of his kingdom in which he was spending less and less time—it seemed clear that Richard now divided his subjects into two categories: his favored servants on whom he lavished boundless rewards; and the rest, whose suspect loyalty he intended to compel with endless punishments.[27]

Still, much depended—for everyone attempting to gauge the king's intentions as well as for the combatants themselves—on the outcome of the trial to be held at Coventry. Spectators were arriving from across Europe. The duke of Brittany was already in the country, visiting Richard's court to negotiate a formal alliance; it was agreed that his herald should act as an honorable and neutral umpire for the duel. The count of St. Pol came from Paris. The dukes of Burgundy, Orléans, and Guelders sent their heralds, as did Henry's brother-in-law the king of Portugal. Knights and squires traveled from Scotland, France, and Germany. By Sunday, September 15, great crowds had gathered at Coventry, where part of the butchered remains of the Oxfordshire rebel Henry Roper could still be seen above the city gate. The king had taken up residence two and a half miles away at Baginton Castle, the home of William Bagot. Henry had been staying at his father's nearby castle of Kenilworth but now moved into the city itself, as did his opponent, Mowbray. The challenge was set for the next morning at nine.[28]

In the early autumn light, the protagonists assembled in the splendidly decorated lists. In the royal stand, Richard sat surrounded by his bishops and lords under the vigilant gaze of his Cheshire archers, Gaunt grim and drawn beside him. This, for Richard, was kingship: a moment when he sat center stage, the source of all authority and arbiter of all action. The masters of ceremonies were Rutland and Thomas Holand as constable and marshal of England, offices that had formerly belonged by hereditary right to Woodstock and Mowbray but had now, like so much else, been abruptly reassigned. Both men were dressed in liveries of red silk embroidered with silver garters, the emblem of England's chivalry. From his elegant pavilion sewn with red flowers, Henry, the challenger, stepped forward in his Milanese armor, a silver shield on his arm bearing the red cross of Saint George, to declare his opponent "a false and disloyal traitor to God, the king, his kingdom, and myself." Mowbray, in German armor, swore to prove before God that he lied.

Their sharpened lances were measured to check they were of equal length for a fair fight; their tents were cleared away, and both men mounted their horses. At a word from the Breton herald, Henry spurred his charger forward to take his place for battle. Richard had first sat in judgment at a trial by combat when he was thirteen years old, the same age at which Henry had first jousted before the court. But not like this. Silence fell.[29]

Then Richard rose to his feet and told them to stop.

The "coronation portrait" Richard commissioned in the mid-1390s, to be placed in the choir of Westminster Abbey.

The gilded bronze effigies of Richard and his first wife, Anne of Bohemia, on their tomb in Westminster Abbey. Commissioning the tomb after Anne's death in 1394 allowed Richard to write his own epitaph, in which he compared himself to Homer.

Richard's emblem of the white hart filling an archway in the gallery above Westminster Abbey's south transept, which can be seen from multiple angles at floor level below.

Charles VI, the mentally fragile king of France who became Richard's father-in-law in 1396. This illumination is by the Boucicaut Master, an artist so called because he also made a Book of Hours for Henry's friend in chivalry, the French knight Jean II Le Meingre, known as Boucicaut.

The left interior panel of the *Wilton Diptych*, a portable altarpiece commissioned by Richard around the time of his marriage to the six-year-old Isabella of France. The king is presented to the Virgin and Child (on the right panel) by the saint-kings Edmund the Martyr and Edward the Confessor, and Saint John the Baptist.

The right interior panel of the *Diptych*, in which Richard's homage is received by the infant Christ in his mother's arms. The angels surrounding them wear Richard's badge of the white hart and the French king's collar of golden broom-cods.

Folio from a handbook of geomancy, a method of divination using "figures" of dots, commissioned by Richard in 1391. Hints in the text suggest that Richard was seeking information about the return of his favorite, Robert de Vere, who had fled into exile in 1387 after his defeat by Henry's forces at the battle of Radcot Bridge.

Westminster Hall, built at the end of the eleventh century and seen here in 1925, is one of the few parts of the medieval palace to have survived a catastrophic fire in 1834. It was remodeled on Richard's orders during the 1390s with a superbly engineered hammer beam roof.

On each hammer beam is an angel, finely carved in oak, holding the royal arms of England. At the first parliament held in the hall after the work was finished in 1399, Richard was formally deposed and Henry acclaimed as king.

The alabaster effigies of Henry and his queen, Joan of Navarre, on the tomb Joan commissioned to mark their resting place in Canterbury Cathedral. Haunted by what he had done to take and keep the throne, Henry himself had not requested an elaborate funeral or monument.

Thirteen

1398–1399

the hollow crown

After a second, silence became noise. All was confusion: bewildered faces in the stands, the baffled crowd straining for a view, the constable and marshal, every certainty gone, turning to the king for new instruction. At a gesture from Richard, Henry and Mowbray gave up their lances and dismounted their chargers. The horses were led away while the lords of the council pressed urgently around the king. Ever since the arrests of Woodstock, Arundel, and Warwick, the sense that Richard was improvising from moment to moment had been growing. Now, in an adrenalized instant, everything for which Henry had spent five fearful, angry months preparing had vanished into the September air.[1]

If he could not fight for his life, there was nothing to do but wait, unmoving in his superb armor, the people massed behind the barriers watching and waiting too—anxious, joking, curious, bored—for some denouement to the interrupted drama they had come to see. An hour went by, then another. At last, the Breton herald came to the front of the stand to call for quiet. Beside him stood John Bushy, the king's fixer, carrying in his hand the scroll of a newly written proclamation. In the sudden hush, Bushy began to read. Both dukes, he said, had bravely defended their honor by appearing armed in the lists. However, the matter was so grave, and the need to avoid further conflict so great, that the king now ordered their banishment from the realm, Henry for ten years and Mowbray for the rest of his life. Mowbray must go to Prussia, Bohemia, or Hungary, or as a pilgrim to the Holy Land. Henry could choose his place of exile, so long as they did not meet or communicate with each other, or with the already-expelled Archbishop Arundel. They had a month to organize their affairs, and then, on pain of a traitor's death, they must leave England.[2]

Without warning, after five months, one unprecedented royal judgment had flipped into another. Among the crowd there was uproar, "so much noise that they could not hear one another speak," wrote one eyewitness; not just confusion, now, but shock, even in a political world that was learning to take nothing for granted. For Richard, testing out the power of his reconfigured royal authority, it seemed an ingenious solution. No blood had been spilled, no dangerous truths aired, no victory awarded to either Henry or Mowbray, yet both would be removed from his kingdom. But questions remained. If Henry and Mowbray had both defended their honor, what exactly were they guilty of?

A number of allegations against Mowbray were included in the formal record when Richard's decree was noted in the rolls of parliament. The duke had been insufficiently active as an appellant against Woodstock, Arundel, and Warwick, and had argued against undoing the acts of the Merciless Parliament of 1388, "wicked and unlawful" though they were. In April 1398, he had also made a new confession—presumably, though no detail was supplied, his admission that he had tried to assassinate Gaunt—which "might be the cause of great trouble in the realm." And then, as Henry had claimed, there were irregularities in the financial management of Calais. Until these unspecified sums were repaid, Mowbray's lands would be sequestrated by the crown, except for an allowance of £1,000 a year with which the duke could support himself in exile.[3]

In Henry's case, there was nothing. No charge, no accusation, only a verdict given for "the peace and tranquility of the king, his kingdom and his subjects." But the order, once made, was shored up with both threats and reassurance. Any attempt to alter or overturn his decision, Richard declared, would be an act of treason. He took Henry's eldest son, who had turned twelve on the day of the abandoned duel, into his own keeping at court, whether as ward or hostage no one could tell. Of all the children, young

Henry had the longest memories of their mother and the home they had lost at Peterborough. Now he would have a new home with the king who had banished his father from England for the next ten years of his life. But Richard did explicitly confirm, in royal letters given under his privy seal, that the older Henry would be allowed to take possession of any inheritance— Gaunt's duchy of Lancaster, say—that might fall to him during his exile.[4]

It had to be done. Henry made arrangements for the care of his younger children. His second son, ten-year-old Thomas, would travel with him as a vestige of familial comfort, and an unspoken acknowledgment that it might not be wise to leave every one of his heirs within Richard's unpredictable reach. His third, nine-year-old John, would stay in London with a tutor, while seven-year-old Humphrey would remain with little Blanche and Philippa in the household of Henry's friend and chamberlain Hugh Waterton. Waterton was one of the experienced Lancastrian retainers to whom Henry also left the management of his estates, under what he hoped would be the protective supervision of his cousin Rutland and other powerful figures in Richard's inner circle. Once everything was organized he took leave of the king at Eltham, and of his father, with whom he had spent as much time as he could in the preceding weeks. It was a difficult parting. They had said uncertain goodbyes before, when Gaunt had left for Castile and Henry for Prussia, but this time Gaunt's failing health made it almost impossible to imagine that they would meet again. On October 13, with loyal servants including the wise Thomas Erpingham and the formidable Thomas Rempston, Henry took a ship from Dover to Calais. Six days later, Mowbray sailed from Lowestoft to Dordrecht, aiming for Venice and from there to Jerusalem. The two dukes' exile had begun.[5]

On his father's advice, Henry made for Paris. The French court was as opulent and as fractious as ever, but the greatest lords around the fragile king had reason to welcome Henry with honor: the royal uncles Burgundy and Berry because of their hard-won friendship with Gaunt, and the king's brother Louis of Orléans as the son-in-law of Henry's ally Gian Galeazzo Visconti. There were many luxurious aristocratic mansions in the French capital, of which one, the Hôtel de Clisson in the northeast of the city near the royal Hôtel de St. Pol, was given over to Henry and his household. As they settled in, he felt the relief of his own liberation from the fear-filled need to genuflect to Richard's every wish, a demand that had come to define political life in England. Instead, at thirty-one, he had another chance to revel in the glamour of the greatest capital west of Constantinople, and to revive his own reputation as one of Europe's most skillful and honorable knights.[6]

At the same time, he found himself in a fresh form of limbo. The unhappy circumstances of his exile made it difficult to pursue his dreams of chivalric adventure. With Mowbray heading to the Holy Land, Henry was in principle free to join the ongoing crusade against the Turks in Hungary, where Boucicaut—who had returned to France in February 1398 with other noblemen ransomed after the disaster at Nicopolis—was hoping to lead an expedition to avenge that defeat. But when Henry was sent to England to consult his father, Gaunt told him to stay closer to home, either in Paris or with his sisters in Castile and Portugal, where his physical safety could be guaranteed and lines of communication more easily maintained. Henry's brother John Beaufort had been lucky to return unhurt from Hungary. Gaunt was not inclined to let his heir take unnecessary risks.[7]

The ambiguity of Henry's position also meant that negotiations for his marriage to Lucia Visconti had come to a halt. How could he ask an Italian noblewoman to leave her home for him, if it would be ten years before he could give her a new one? But there was no interruption to Gian Galeazzo's friendship, and in the meantime Henry's French hosts suggested an alternative bride, one already at home in Henry's temporarily adopted city. The duke of Berry's twenty-three-year-old daughter, Marie, had previously been married to the count of Eu, a friend of Boucicaut who had been captured alongside him at Nicopolis and died in Turkish custody a few months later. The proposal that the young widow might marry the French court's English visitor won the support of Louis of Orléans, who invited the pair to spend time at his castle of Asnières in Normandy in January 1399, an occasion on which Orléans's duchess, Gian Galeazzo's daughter Valentina, made Henry a gift of a rich and valuable diamond.[8]

All the same, there was a palpable sense that Henry had exchanged one kind of stasis for another. As heir to the greatest noble estate in England, his future should have been glitteringly assured. Instead, it remained unreadable.

If his father could preside over Lancastrian interests at home for ten more years until Henry was able to return, their situation might still be salvaged. But at Christmas news came from Leicester that Gaunt was seriously ill. His political strength had been waning for some time. Despite his presence beside the king at Coventry, he had been unable to prevent Henry's banishment. Meanwhile, the growing political and military power of Richard's new principality of Chester was encroaching on Gaunt's spheres of influence in the north and the midlands. Now it seemed that, at fifty-eight, his physical resilience was spent. Three hundred miles away, Henry knew he had to prepare himself for devastating loss, but he was powerless either to go to his father or to shield the inheritance Richard had promised would be his. Back in October, less than two weeks after Henry had sailed into exile, Sir John Haukeston, the Cheshire knight who had murdered his servant William Laken on Fleet Street a year earlier, had been pardoned by the king. Without Henry there to watch over his lands and his people, how many more times would justice be denied?[9]

For Richard, stasis was an aspiration: the perfect stillness of perfect authority. His kingship had always been primarily concerned with *being*, not doing; with making sure that his subjects bowed to his sovereignty and reflected it back to him in terms that made clear its divine origin and its irresistible presence in the world. If the imperial electors in Germany could be convinced to hail him as their emperor, his majesty would soon be recognized on the greatest possible stage. Beyond that goal he had no further aim: no battles he wanted to fight for his God or his crown, no plan to ameliorate the lives of his people. He had sought peace with France as a way of subverting criticism at home, and as an opportunity to associate the glory of his throne with that of the "most Christian king" who ruled in Paris. He had sailed to Ireland to see the "wild Irish" kneel before him, tamed, as he had felt sure they would be, by their encounter with his royal person. Now the men who had opposed him in England had been executed, or exiled, or otherwise put at his mercy. This was the "everlasting peace" he intended to bestow upon his subjects as the awestruck witnesses of his greatness.[10]

Its maintenance required not only constant vigilance, but an ongoing capacity to strike down his enemies. The proceedings of the last parliament had given him the power to root out traitors wherever he found them, and his permanent personal bodyguard of 300 Cheshire archers, with 300 more in reserve, stood ready to protect him from physical harm. While the Cheshiremen made clear the fate that would befall anyone who resisted—"wherever the king went, night and day, they stood guard over him, armed as if for war, committing adulteries, murders, and countless other crimes," wrote the chronicler Adam Usk—Richard could rest easy in his royal bed. So easy, in fact, that the familiarity between the king and his lowborn archers, as well as their violent behavior, attracted outraged attention. "Dickon, sleep soundly while we wake, and dread nought while we live," another chronicler reported them saying. The king, Usk noted, would hear no word of complaint against them.[11]

As a result, those who objected dared do no more than murmur behind their hands. Others, feeling the direction of the wind, turned to praise their sovereign. "Once, the sun was hidden behind a cloud," wrote a monk at Kirkstall Abbey in Yorkshire, ". . . but now, soaring in arms above the mountains and bounding over the hills with his might, he has dispersed the clouds with his sun, whose light shines ever more brightly." Richard, it seemed, believed himself to be the radiant center around which his people's lives revolved. On holy days, wrote a monk of Canterbury, after the court had dined, the king would sit enthroned in his chamber silently surveying the assembled company, and anyone upon whom his gaze might fall, however high their rank, was expected in that instant to kneel before his majesty.[12]

The moon to his sun, the lesser light falling upon his subjects, was his little queen, who had just passed her ninth birthday. Isabella embodied the truce that bound the crowns of France and England, and Richard was delighted not only by her presence but by the parallels between his throne and that of his royal father-in-law. Like all his predecessors, Charles had been anointed at his coronation with oil from the Holy Ampulla, a miraculous vial sent from heaven to Clovis, the first Christian king of France 900 years before. Richard, who was fascinated by his own family's history and always concerned to demonstrate the greatness of his lineage, had recently been thrilled to discover an equivalent vial of his own. In a locked chest in a neglected corner of the Tower, he had unearthed a small crystal ampulla topped with a golden eagle that had apparently been given by the Virgin Mary to Saint Thomas Becket two centuries earlier. Somehow it had been mislaid in the intervening years, but a document preserved alongside it explained in the saint's own words that future kings of England must be anointed with the chrism it contained, and that "whenever a king wears the eagle on his breast he will be victorious over his enemies, and his kingdom will always increase." Richard had been wearing the vial around his neck ever since, and would have had himself re-anointed with the oil, had the new archbishop of Canterbury not managed to insist that the sacred rite should not be performed twice for the same person.[13]

It could hardly be denied that Richard and his father-in-law were the human incarnation in the two kingdoms of God's authority on earth. Unlike Charles, however, whose wife, Isabeau, had just given birth to their ninth child, Richard showed no concern to secure the embodiment of his crown in the next generation. He was full of affectionate gestures for his queen, but it would be four or five years before the earliest moment at which she could be expected to give him an heir. The lack of urgency apparent in his choice of bride was matched by his refusal to name an heir presumptive as a way of settling the succession while he waited for a son of his own. There were several possible claimants, but in recent years Richard had seemed more intent on whittling down their number than on clarifying their standing. Among the king's uncles and cousins, Woodstock was dead and his seventeen-year-old son, Humphrey, disinherited. Gaunt was desperately ill and Henry in exile. The earl of March, grandson of Richard's long-dead uncle Lionel of Antwerp, had gone back to Ireland as the king's lieutenant there after his brief appearance at the Shrewsbury parliament in January 1398; seven months later, news came that he had been killed in a skirmish with the Irish, leaving his six-year-old son to inherit his title. Meanwhile, Edmund of Langley, at fifty-seven, remained as ineffectual and politically irrelevant as ever.[14]

Langley's son Edward of Rutland, now duke of Aumale, was the only one of the royal cousins who currently basked in the glow of Richard's favor. Rutland was still routinely described in official documents as "the king's brother," even though his proposed match with the little queen's sister had long since been abandoned; in 1398, he had quietly married a woman he had known for years at court, Philippa Mohun, the widow of one of Richard's most trusted knights of the chamber. There were rumors that Richard intended to name Rutland as his heir, and certainly there were no other contenders who could rival the power the young man now held in England at the king's command. "Anything that he pleased he might have asked of the king," said Jean Creton, a French esquire who joined Richard's court in 1399, "for I solemnly declare there was no man alive, brother nor uncle, cousin, young nor old, whom he loved better." But Rutland's father, through whom he inherited his claim to the throne, was still alive. Even if Langley were not to survive much longer, it would be difficult to justify the proposition that his line should take precedence over those of his older brothers Lionel of Antwerp and John of Gaunt. In public, Richard met the question of the succession with evasion and silence. It appeared that the king wished to maintain his own sovereignty exactly as it was, unchanged through time as well as in the space of his court and his realm.[15]

But perfect stasis in a turbulent world was not so easy to achieve. The terms of the banishment that Richard had imposed on Henry and Mowbray, restricting where they could go and with whom they could communicate, presupposed that he could dictate his subjects' behavior even when they moved beyond the borders of his kingdom. It was true that both dukes had good reason to comply. Henry's eldest son was living in the king's household, and Mowbray's in that of the queen. Mowbray's estates were in the king's hands, and Henry's managed by his attorneys under royal license. Even so, Richard had apparently failed to anticipate the possibility that his decision to expel them from the realm might have unwelcome consequences. He was so disturbed by the warmth with which Henry was received in Paris, and especially by the offer of a marriage alliance with the duke of Berry's daughter, that he dispatched the earl of Salisbury to tell King Charles and his council that Henry was a traitor who deserved no marks of favor. The message was startling: Henry had never been formally charged with treason, let alone convicted. Salisbury was embarrassed when this obvious point was put to him by his French hosts, responding merely that he was doing as he was told. Henry was furious, but allowed himself to be reassured; in this case, Charles and his advisers were not inclined to listen to Richard. Henry was not breaching the terms of his exile. There was nothing his cousin could do.[16]

Nothing, that is, until everything changed. On February 3, 1399, four months after Henry's departure, John of Gaunt died, brokenhearted, at Leicester Castle. He had been a great prince, the son of a magnificent king, the father of remarkable queens. But he faced his end knowing that, after all he had achieved, he could be sure of very little beyond the loving presence of his wife, Katherine, at his bedside. At his nephew's command he had colluded in the arrest and death of his "well-beloved brother the duke of Gloucester, whom God absolve," as Gaunt called Woodstock when he dictated his will during his haunted final hours. For that decision, his soul might now face a terrible reckoning; yet this ultimate demonstration of loyalty to Richard had not been enough to protect Gaunt's son from an arbitrary banishment that left his family and his legacy exposed and vulnerable.[17]

Gaunt's fears were well-founded. While Katherine and their second son, Henry Beaufort, the twenty-four-year-old bishop of Lincoln, accompanied the duke's body on its final journey south, Richard was not mourning his uncle. Instead, he summoned the parliamentary commission to which the quarrel between Henry and Mowbray had originally been referred. Now that Gaunt was gone, he required a different decision. The commissioners were quick to fulfill his instructions. On March 16, 1399, Gaunt was finally laid to rest beside Henry's mother, Blanche, in their alabaster tomb near the high altar of St. Paul's Cathedral. Two days later, the lords of the realm gathered in Richard's presence at Westminster to hear the fate of the duchy Gaunt had left behind. There the chancellor announced that the royal letters confirming Henry's right to claim his inheritance on his father's death had been issued inadvertently, without due deliberation and in error, since they contravened the king's verdict given at Coventry, a judgment that allowed for no subsequent mitigation. The argument was tortuous and transparently flimsy, but the conclusion it was designed to reach was clear: Henry's right to claim his inheritance was revoked. For as long as he remained in exile, the greatest noble estate in the country would pass instead into Richard's hands.[18]

The about-face was staggering. Richard, it seemed, was never wrong until it suited him to be so, at which point royal promises might blow away like chaff in the breeze, to be replaced—for who knew how long—by entirely new royal truths. At a stroke he had annexed the vast Lancastrian patrimony—not, as Gaunt and Henry had feared, by reanimating judicial decisions taken during the reign of Edward II, but by seizing the opportunity to invent new ones of his own. Henry's banishment still had nine and a half years to run, but no one in the room at Westminster—or beyond, when the news raced around the country and across the Channel—believed Richard ever intended to let him return. The protections of law and precedent were gone, and Richard's retribution for 1388 was complete. He controlled the estates of all five lords who had taken up arms against him. He commanded a private army based in his principality of Chester, the inner citadel he had constructed in the northwest of his kingdom, and he enjoyed the obedient support of a new noble elite raised high by his own authority, among whom he distributed custody of the Lancastrian lands within days of their confiscation. To John Holand went the keeping of Gaunt's estates in Wales; to Thomas Holand, those in the northwest and north midlands; to Rutland, those in Lincolnshire and the east midlands; to Scrope and Salisbury, estates in Yorkshire and Wiltshire. The territories of England and Wales were Richard's to rule in exactly the way he believed they always should have been.[19]

And, with that settled, his lords would sail with him again to Ireland. To the king's surprise, his policy of receiving the homage of the Irish lords and then leaving, before disputes had been arbitrated or settlements enforced, had failed to bring peace to the island. The competition for power in Ulster between the earls of March and the Ó Néills had never been properly addressed, and could not be, for as long as March himself remained the king's representative in the lordship. Meanwhile, the Dublin administration over which March presided had failed to honor the agreement made at Christmas 1394 with Art Mac Murchadha, so that Leinster too spiraled into the violence that, in the end, had claimed the earl's life. Evidently, the king's presence was required once more. Thomas Holand, the young duke of Surrey, had been sent ahead to replace March as the lieutenant of the crown, and by late May 1399 royal forces were mustering to join him: about 5,000 men in total, including Richard's Cheshire archers and contingents led by Rutland, John Holand, Despenser, Salisbury, and Thomas Percy, the new earl of Worcester, as well as a handful of clerics including the bishops of St. David's and Carlisle, both former clerks of Richard's household, and Gaunt's son Henry Beaufort of Lincoln.[20]

In his brittle magnificence, Richard too was ready. Unlikely though it seemed that he would come to any harm, given his familiar place behind rather than at the head of his army, he made his will, a document set apart from the conventional royal compound of religious offerings and family bequests by its grandiose solipsism. The intricate instructions for his funeral included the outfit in which he wished to be buried—a robe of white velvet or satin with a golden crown and scepter and a ring with a precious stone on his finger—and he ordered that a gift of a golden cup should be sent in his name to every Christian king in Europe. But its most arresting section concerned his attempt from beyond the grave to maintain the precise form of the "peace" he had achieved in his realm. His still-unnamed successor—whoever next shouldered what Richard here called "the burden of the government of the English"—should inherit the contents of his treasury, he said, so long as every one of the judgments given in the last eighteen months against the five former Appellants was upheld. If his successor refused to fulfill his wishes, then the gold should pass instead to Rutland, Scrope, and John and Thomas Holand, who should defend the judgments "even to the death, if need be." It was a remarkable legacy to his kingdom: the threat of civil war as a means of enforcing eternal obedience to his will.[21]

Richard was wearing the Holy Ampulla with its golden eagle round his neck every day. He had his crowns and his jewels packed into strongboxes to take with him to Ireland. At Windsor he said farewell to his little queen, picking her up in his arms and showering her with kisses when she cried at his leaving, promising that in time she could join him there. He appointed his uncle Langley to watch over the realm with the assistance of John Beaufort as admiral of England, and William Scrope with the ubiquitous trio of Bushy, Bagot, and Green, all skilled practitioners at turning royal wishes into administrative reality, to lead the work of the privy council. When he sailed with his army from Milford Haven on May 29, 1399, Richard left his frightened subjects to contemplate the fall of the house of Lancaster, and to wonder where their king might turn the threat of his attention next.[22]

"He will do with us what he did with the others," Mowbray had told Henry in their fateful conversation about Richard's intentions back in December 1397. "He wants to wipe that slate clean." So it had proved. Little more than a year later, Woodstock and Arundel were dead, Warwick in prison, Mowbray banished, and the assurances on which Henry had depended were dust. Richard had taken his lands, his son, his family, his home.[23]

The king had made some small attempt to soften the blow. Henry would receive an allowance in exile of £2,000 a year, and the terms by which the Lancastrian estates had been parceled out to the noblemen around the throne explicitly allowed for the possibility that Richard might one day choose to grant them back to Henry, or perhaps to his son. It was a doubled attempt to ensure Henry's compliance, an olive branch in the shape of an imaginable future for his heir, even while the king continued to treat the boy as political insurance in human form. Only weeks earlier, the disinherited son of the earl of Arundel, seventeen-year-old Thomas, had managed to escape from John Holand's household to join his exiled uncle, Archbishop Arundel, on the Continent. Richard was not about to make the same mistake with twelve-year-old Henry, who traveled with the king and his army to Waterford, along with Woodstock's son, Humphrey.[24]

But political insurance would only work if its terms were reliable beyond doubt or hesitation, and Richard had demonstrated again and again that his word could not be trusted. Henry had spent the last two years obeying his cousin's every command. He carried the guilt of his own complicity in Woodstock's death and his participation in Arundel's trial and execution. He had accepted that he must leave England for a decade, a sentence that left him unable to comfort his dying father or to receive his last blessing. And now—without cause or process, and in contravention of the king's explicit promise—his rights as his father's heir had been ripped from his hands. Richard was insisting that, from moment to moment, the law was his to define. What hope remained that mute acceptance might achieve restitution, or even physical safety, for Henry's son? Nor could their destiny be separated from that of the country. If the king could seize the greatest estate in the kingdom at will, were any of England's people secure in possession of their property, or their lives?

Clearly, birth and wealth provided no protection. Nor did closeness to Richard. Other than Rutland, no one had been more publicly favored by the king in recent years than Mowbray, a fact that had done precisely nothing to lessen his panic when crisis approached, or to rescue him from political destruction. Distance from the throne offered no shelter either. Despite the French gold heaped in Richard's treasury, the "loans" made to the crown by so many of his subjects in 1397 remained overdue and irretrievable. In preparation for his departure to Ireland, the king had made meticulous arrangements for the safekeeping of the blank charters that put London and the southeast at his mercy, and the lists of names of those who had come forward to sue for individual pardons. Then he proclaimed that the general pardon granted at Shrewsbury to all his loyal subjects—all, of course, except those who had ridden with the Appellants at Harringay and Radcot Bridge—would by his grace be "continued" until November. There had been no previous mention of its impermanence. Richard's vision of his own security as king, it seemed, required permanent insecurity for the people of his kingdom.[25]

Henry, however, was no longer in England. He had lost almost everything, but he still had friends. Old friends, some of them: the able, fiercely loyal men who had spent years in Lancastrian service and were now either with him in France or doing whatever they could to protect his interests at home. Others were newer, their support less tangible but significant nonetheless. The warmth with which Louis of Orléans had welcomed Henry to Paris was fueled not only by their shared connection with Gian Galeazzo Visconti, but also by Orléans's frustration at the ongoing domination of his brother's government by the dukes of Burgundy and Berry. The French alliance with Richard was Burgundy and Berry's peace, and if Richard and Henry were now at odds, then Orléans would offer Henry his support. In May, the balance of power at the French court suddenly shifted when Burgundy and Berry retreated from Paris during an outbreak of plague, leaving Orléans with a chance to seize political control for the first time in years—and in

June, he and Henry signed a treaty of personal alliance. Whatever Henry might choose to do, his French hosts would not, now, stand in his way.[26]

Then there were friends who were both new and surprising. Archbishop Arundel had spent the eighteen months of his exile so far in Rome, Florence ("an earthly paradise," he thought), Cologne, and Utrecht, where his nephew, the young Arundel heir, had tracked him down after escaping from England. By the beginning of June, however, both the archbishop and his nephew had left the Low Countries to join Henry in Paris. Discretion was the watchword at the Hôtel de Clisson, but this meeting—arranged in direct contravention of Richard's orders—was the first public sign that resistance, not acceptance, was Henry's plan. It was neither a joyous nor an easy reunion, given the part Henry and his father had played in condemning the earl of Arundel to a traitor's death. Thomas Walsingham reported that, on the night Gaunt died, the duke's tormented spirit had appeared to the archbishop in Utrecht to beg his forgiveness. Whether or not ghostly intervention was required, the archbishop's willingness to join forces with Henry confirmed quite how dangerous Richard's behavior in the intervening two years had been, and how high the stakes now were.[27]

Many back in England felt the same. William Bagot—not long ago suspected of plotting to murder Gaunt, but always one to hedge his bets as extravagantly as he could—dispatched a private message of warning to Henry, his former Lancastrian lord, in Paris. The king, he said, was Henry's sworn enemy. If Henry hoped to reverse his disinheritance, he must do it himself by force. Meanwhile, others at the heart of Richard's government—Henry's brothers John and Henry Beaufort and his sister Elizabeth's husband, John Holand—had intensely personal reasons to feel disturbed by the evisceration of Gaunt's legacy, even while they benefited, for now, from the king's goodwill.[28]

The risks of expressing any form of dissent were greater than ever. Before leaving for Ireland Richard had given the sheriffs of Cheshire and Lancashire, two of the knights of his military retinue, wide-ranging powers during his absence to deal with anyone who might do or say anything "to the scandal, dishonour, prejudice or hurt of the king or realm." Doing or saying was dangerous, but Richard could not outlaw thinking. One poet, a midlander living in London, eventually dared put his thoughts, if not his name, in writing to lament the king's corruption of the rule of law, including his creation of his own personal army and his endorsement of their reign of terror. Every badge of the white hart Richard bestowed, the poet said, had cost him 200 loyal hearts—and "allegiance without love little thing availeth." It was a baffling and needless tragedy that the king should have turned on his subjects so viciously, "for first, at your anointing, all were your own."[29]

But those once-loyal hearts knew where to look for salvation. It was the "eagle duke"—Henry, inheriting a badge his dead father had used—who would defend England's people from Richard and his antlered harts, another poem declared: "Henry of Lancaster, our light, our glory." He was a noble knight, a soldier, a king's grandson, the only hope left; and in the four and a half months since his father's death—three since his disinheritance—Henry had made his plans. Now, in his sorrow and his anger, he was ready to try.[30]

His first steps were taken quickly and quietly. It was crucial to Henry, as a loyal Englishman, that his return to England should neither be, nor be seen as, a French invasion—and Louis of Orléans's ambition to undermine the power of his uncles stopped short of contemplating an immediate return to war. Their discussions therefore took place behind locked doors before Henry left Paris, pausing on the road at Saint-Denis to let it be known that he would be traveling south to his sisters in Spain. The misdirection bought him enough time to board an English merchant ship at Boulogne without any attempt from either side of the Channel to stop him. He was accompanied by the men of his household-in-exile, his eleven-year-old son, Thomas, wide-eyed and silent among them, along with Archbishop Arundel and the young heir to the Arundel earldom. The voyage was obvious insubordination, outright defiance of Richard's commands, but in no sense the mobilization of an army.[31]

Instead, it was an opening move, a statement of undefined intent. Every precedent in English law said that Henry had right on his side: he had been convicted of no crime, yet his lands and his home had been taken from him. By returning to challenge the king's decision, Henry would stand for all of

Richard's subjects who were suffering from the mounting injustices and outrageous depredations of the last two years. The questions that remained concerned the support he could muster and the remedy he might seek. If Richard were to reverse his banishment and restore his inheritance, would it be enough to secure his future and that of the realm? Even that scenario, optimistic as it was, solved nothing. Richard would never agree to overturn his own judgments without his hand being forced, and if his hand were forced, he would not rest until he was free once more to punish those responsible. It was a vicious circle from which there was no escape unless the king were removed from his throne. But if the king were removed from his throne, could Henry replace him? And if he tried, would he still have right—or England's people—on his side?

All he could do was roll the dice and play the odds with as much skill as he could muster. He already knew that Richard had raised an army and sailed away to Ireland. Henry's best chance of rallying support for his cause was to reach England before the king could return, to proclaim his right to the duchy of Lancaster, and to summon his own and his father's retainers to follow him. The duchy's lands and retinue were spread across the country, and the deep roots of Lancastrian service had not yet been destroyed or supplanted by Richard's redistribution of estates and offices in the few months since Gaunt's death. Fair winds brought Henry's ship to the harbor at Pevensey on the Sussex coast, beneath the massive walls and circular towers of the castle that had belonged for so long to his father. Beside him on deck stood John Pelham, Gaunt's constable of Pevensey, who had risen from humble beginnings in Lancastrian service before joining Henry in his French exile. They had surprise on their side as well as old loyalties; and when Pelham was put ashore with a handful of men, he took command of the castle in Henry's name.[32]

The ship sailed east and then north, hugging the shoreline to scout local defenses and pick up news and supplies from Lancastrian manors along the north Norfolk coast. At the end of June, Henry made landfall, first at Ravenspur at the mouth of the Humber in East Yorkshire, then forty miles farther north so that he could pray once again at the tomb of John of Bridlington. As soon as his feet touched English soil, Henry sent men riding across the country carrying letters to his Lancastrian retainers and to towns, cities, religious houses, and powerful landowners, including his uncle Langley as keeper of the realm. To the people, he wrote of his right to his inheritance and Richard's abuse of the law. To Langley—who knew better than most how little chance there was of Richard reacting calmly or constructively to Henry's challenge—he said he would explain his intentions when they met in person. The knights and esquires of the Lancastrian affinity were already responding to his call as he moved cautiously inland from castle to castle through his Yorkshire estates, first westward to Pickering and Knaresborough, then south to Pontefract. And not only his own knights and esquires: Henry Percy, the veteran earl of Northumberland, and Ralph Neville, the new earl of Westmorland, were rivals for power in the Scottish marches but united now in opposition to Richard's interference in the north and his annexation of the duchy of Lancaster. They joined Henry at Doncaster in south Yorkshire on July 15, along with Northumberland's formidable son Hotspur, whose military and diplomatic talents made him a leader to be reckoned with just as much as his father. By July 20, Henry and his new allies were in the midlands, at Leicester Castle with several thousand men. Of the other Lancastrian fortresses, nearby Kenilworth had already declared for him; so had Dunstanburgh on the Northumbrian coast. "An eagle is up and has taken his flight," another poet wrote, flush with the elation of hope. This was no invasion, but an uprising at the heart of Richard's kingdom.[33]

Four days earlier, on July 16, Langley had reached Oxford, where he and Henry's brother John Beaufort, England's admiral, were attempting to raise money and troops to counter this groundswell of revolt. But they were struggling, not least because it was still not clear to them or anyone else what exactly Henry planned to do. If he had returned to claim his inheritance, who—other than Richard—could blame him? And if he intended to protect England's people from the depredations of Richard's most indulged followers, would that not be a righteous mission? When Henry reached Warwick Castle on July 24, he found a carved white hart with a crown around its neck shining in the sun above the gate, along with the white hind that was the badge of Thomas Holand, the castle's master since the earl of Warwick's fall. Henry took one look and ordered his men to tear the emblems down.[34]

Perhaps he was taking aim only at the retainers who wore the king's badge, and the *duketti* who surrounded his throne; but Richard's subjects knew that the white hart represented the authority of the sovereign himself. With every command Henry uttered, with every moment that passed, it was harder to avoid the conclusion that his mission to rescue the kingdom must mean overthrowing the king. That thought did nothing to stem the hemorrhage of support from Richard's regime. At Oxford, Langley was discovering that the soldiers to whom he was distributing royal wages were melting away, many of them pocketing the king's money before going directly to join Henry at Warwick. Richard's well-stocked treasury could not buy their obedience, it turned out, if his name no longer commanded their loyalty.[35]

Even had they not found their forces disintegrating around them, Langley and Beaufort too were unwilling to raise their swords in defense of the king's actions. Langley had never been a decisive leader at the best of times; now, Walsingham alleged, "he did not wish to attack a man who had come in a just cause to regain his rightful inheritance." After that came the dawning comprehension that, if they were not prepared to fight Henry, their only other option was to join him. Richard had already made it plain that even those who obeyed him were not safe from his arbitrary judgments. What future security could there be for a keeper of the realm who had not kept the realm as the king wished?[36]

When Langley and Henry finally met on July 27 in a church outside the walls of Berkeley Castle in Gloucestershire, the outcome was a foregone conclusion: an agreement, "because the duke of York did not have the strength to resist him," one chronicler reported. Langley, Beaufort, and their forces, such as they were, joined Henry and his growing army and moved on to the port of Bristol in the west, where Scrope, Bagot, Bushy, and Green had taken up position in the hope of making the quickest possible contact with the king whenever he might return from Ireland. But the four men found they could not hold out for Richard's arrival. As the administrative architects of his tyranny, they were notorious and widely hated. On July 28, the castle garrison laid down its arms without a blow being struck. By that time Bagot, with his supreme talent for self-preservation, had already fled. The soldiers handed Scrope, Bushy, and Green over to Henry. The next day, on Henry's orders, the three men were brought before the earls of Northumberland and Westmorland, formally accused of the "evil government of both the king and the kingdom," summarily convicted as traitors, and dragged immediately to the block.[37]

Their deaths—for which the crowds massing in Henry's support had been clamoring—were remorselessly inevitable given that he needed to decapitate any potential resistance as swiftly and clinically as he could. They also marked the point of no possible return. William Scrope was earl of Wiltshire, a peer of the realm. Since 1397 he, Bushy, and Green had been among the most active lieutenants of Richard's reconfigured government, a regime built in revenge for the killing of other royal servants a decade earlier. Even before the three men died, a future accommodation between Henry as a restored duke of Lancaster and Richard as his sovereign had been functionally unimaginable. In that sense, the very act of crossing the Channel had been Henry's Rubicon. But this shedding of blood in the name of justice marked the moment at which Henry staked his claim to wield public authority as the champion of the kingdom against the misgovernment of the king. Four days later, on August 2, he used his duchy of Lancaster seal to appoint the earl of Northumberland as warden of the West March of Scotland, a royal office that was the king's to fill. Henry had chosen his path. There was no going back.[38]

The road might be clear, but he had not yet explicitly acknowledged where it led. So far, he had said nothing more than that he was seeking what was rightfully his; but neither he nor any of England's people could be made safe in possession of what was rightfully theirs while Richard still wore the crown. When the prospect of deposition had reared its head more than a decade earlier, it had been dismissed. Then the king had been twenty, a boy who would—surely, given time—learn his lesson, while the idea of replacing him had promised only chaos and danger. But eleven years had passed and Richard had learned nothing. For all his magnificence, his relentless self-assertion, at thirty-two he seemed frozen in time: a sovereign who had fathered no children and fought no battles, no longer a boy but, in the eyes of his subjects, not fully a man. He had chosen this confrontation—and this time he faced a cousin who, at exactly the same age, embodied every quality Richard lacked.

With the destruction of his enemies and the creation of his principality of Chester, with his private army and his new nobility, with the oaths, pardons, and blank charters, and then, at last, the annexation of the duchy of Lancaster, Richard believed he had placed his power beyond challenge. Instead, he had dismantled the foundations of his own rule. His glittering edifice was a house of cards, and he was not even there to watch it fall.

Fourteen

1399–1400

mine empty chair

Richard was in Dublin when the messengers arrived. His mood was petulant. Reality in Ireland was failing to conform to his will, and in almost
six weeks his campaign in Leinster had achieved very little. In the field, his
troops found themselves extended and under pressure, harried by Irish raids,
at one point running so short of supplies that they came close to starvation.
The king had retreated to his capital, sending Thomas Despenser to negotiate with Mac Murchadha, but Mac Murchadha's refusal to submit to Richard's sovereign authority left him white with anger, the French squire Jean
Creton reported, and swearing by the Confessor that he would never leave
Ireland "until, alive or dead, he had him in his power."[1]

Immersed in his outrage at this Irish resistance, he was unprepared for
what the frightened men kneeling before him had to report. Henry had
landed in Yorkshire, and reality in England was running out of control. In
an instant, Richard forgot Mac Murchadha and his own royal oath to the
Confessor. Through waves of rage and fear, his decision was obvious: king
and army must leave for England immediately. The question was how. His
men were deployed throughout Leinster, and most of the fleet in which they
had arrived had already dispersed. There was nothing for it but to divide
his forces. While vessels were mustered and troops recalled, a small advance
guard—the soldiers who could be marshaled immediately—would sail
from Dublin under the command of the earl of Salisbury, one of the more

experienced military leaders among the lords around the king. On landing in the northwest they would rally the great principality of Chester to the royal standard. Meanwhile, Richard would set out south to the port of Waterford, from where he and his reassembled army would make the crossing to south Wales. The two royal boys in the king's household, Henry's son and Woodstock's heir, would stay behind in Ireland, sent under guard to the fortress of Trim in the Mortimer lordship of Meath, their status as hostages now stark.[2]

In desperate circumstances, it was a rational plan. But as it unfolded, everything, step-by-step, went wrong. The struggle first to find ships and then to navigate through storms at sea left the king's laboriously reconstituted fleet scattered around the ports of southwestern England. When his royal flagship put in at Milford Haven in Pembrokeshire around July 24— the day on which Henry pulled down the white hart from Warwick Castle's gate—Richard hesitated to march on until he could do so at the head of a greater host. Another week passed while Rutland and Despenser rode east in an attempt to raise fresh troops, while the king waited thirty miles inland at the great fortress of Carmarthen. There he heard that Henry had taken Bristol, that Langley and Beaufort had joined him, and that Scrope, Bushy, and Green were dead. The chance of massing a royal army in south Wales was gone.[3]

All Richard's hopes now lay with Salisbury and the forces the earl had been sent to muster in Cheshire. It was imperative the king should reach them before Henry could track him down. On the night of July 31, leaving Rutland and the earl of Worcester in command at Carmarthen, Richard set out under cover of darkness, disguised for the journey as a poor priest, attended by John and Thomas Holand, Thomas Despenser, the bishops of St. David's and Carlisle, and Henry Beaufort of Lincoln, with a handful of guards. The little band moved north, hugging the coast as far as Harlech before striking out across the country to reach the castle of Conwy, forty miles west of Chester, on August 6.[4]

But when Richard rode through the castle gate under its looming circular towers, he found Salisbury there to meet him. The earl *had* been at Chester. He had raised an army, and they had waited for the coming of the king. Every day had brought news of Henry's advance and no word from Richard.

Soon the troops had begun to slip away, heading for the safety of home, or to join Henry before it was too late. In the end, Salisbury had seen no option but to retreat to Conwy with the hundred men who had sailed with him from Dublin. They were all that remained of Richard's imperial might.

Worse was to come. While the king had been making his way north along the coast, Henry and his forces had moved in parallel, northward from Bristol through the Welsh marches to Shrewsbury, thirty miles south of Chester. There on August 5, the day before the royal party reached Conwy, a delegation led by the sheriff of Cheshire had knelt before Henry to surrender the principality into his hands. And, back in Carmarthen with the rump of the king's household, Rutland and Worcester had begun to understand the hopelessness of their own position. They too rode north, not to stand with Richard at Conwy but to join Rutland's father, Langley, and Worcester's brother Northumberland in offering their service to Henry.

Of the defectors now gathering at Shrewsbury, Adam Usk—a cleric and ecclesiastical lawyer who had raced to rejoin his former master Archbishop Arundel in Henry's entourage—was most impressed by the strangest, rather than the most eminent. For two years, Usk wrote, the king had been accompanied night and day by a greyhound that had once belonged to his brother Thomas Holand, the old earl of Kent. When the earl died, the dog had found its way to Richard, and would not leave his side. But when the king had left his household at Carmarthen, the dog had deserted him. Once again, it had set off alone, this time to find Henry at Shrewsbury, where it lay down obediently at his feet. Before he returned to England as the avenging eagle, Henry had used a greyhound as one of his badges. Now, Usk wrote, the dog's presence gave him such pleasure that he let it sleep on his bed.[5]

Politic tales were matched by political assertion. On August 9, Henry and his army marched through Chester's open gates in triumph to take possession of the city and its castle. Richard's gold-stuffed treasury at Holt, seven miles south, was quickly seized on Henry's orders. He had promised that surrender would guarantee safety for the principality, but it was a promise he was unable or unwilling to keep. Among his followers, hatred for the thugs who wore the badge of the white hart mixed intoxicatingly with elation that they were no longer untouchable, and for the next two weeks Henry's men embarked on a campaign of looting and destruction, wasting crops in the fields and ransacking homes and churches. Chester, Usk said, "had become a nest of criminals, so that the whole kingdom cried vengeance upon them." The head of one of the most loathed of Richard's retainers, a man named Peter Leigh, was set on a spike over the east gate of the city.[6]

At Conwy, Richard was close to despair. Before leaving Ireland he had been galvanized by anger. "Good lord," Creton heard him say, "this man plans to deprive me of my country!" Now, in shock and distress at the speed with which his country had abandoned him, he seemed disoriented, at such a loss that he could only look to the lords around him for direction. It was John Holand who took the lead. Henry should be reminded of his noble father's lifelong loyalty, Holand said, and warned that if he sought to destroy the king he would bring eternal shame upon his name and family. But he should also be offered a way out. If he would agree to sue for pardon, to submit publicly to Richard's authority, the restoration of his inheritance should be his reward. Richard himself had no better ideas, and dispatched both Holands to Chester to open negotiations. After they set out, the king found it difficult to contain his own fear. He moved restlessly between the bleak and empty castles of Beaumaris and Caernarfon and then back to Conwy, short of food, shorn of his glory, clinging to the hope that his crown might yet be saved.[7]

But the Holands did not return. In their place came the earl of Northumberland, an envoy from Henry, with troops at his back. In tense exchanges, both Richard and Northumberland made promises: reciprocal pledges that the king would not be deposed if Henry were restored to his duchy and confirmed in his hereditary office as steward of England, a role that would allow him to preside over parliamentary trials of the men around the king for their part in the deaths of Woodstock and Arundel. But on both sides trust and truth were in short supply. The stark fact of the matter was that Richard was in no position to hold out. By the night of August 15 Northumberland had brought the king under guard to Flint Castle, overlooking the wide estuary of the river Dee just ten miles from Chester. The next day, Richard watched from the battlements as Henry and his army marched along the shore toward him.[8]

The cousins came face-to-face inside the fortress. Henry, fully armed but for his helmet, bowed low. Richard kept his composure. "Fair cousin of Lancaster, you are right welcome." "My lord," Henry replied, "I have come sooner than you sent for me, and I shall tell you why: it is commonly said among your people that for the last twenty or twenty-two years you have governed them very badly, and far too harshly, with the result that they are most discontented. But if it please our Lord, I will help you to govern them better than they have been governed in the past." "If it please you, fair cousin, it pleases us well." So Creton, standing nearby, noted their formal exchange. But the idea that Henry might "help" Richard govern was as much a fiction as the king's personal rule had been when he was a child. When they reached Chester that afternoon—with Richard mounted for the journey on a wretched little horse among heavily armed soldiers—he was immediately locked away in the castle's keep under the watch of the young earl of Arundel. The king had worn the eagle ampulla at his neck, but it was the eagle duke who had triumphed. However low he might bow, Henry now ruled England.

That was the necessary reality, if the principles of law and the constitutional relationship between crown and people were to be rescued from Richard's tyranny. But, according to these same principles, Henry—for all his royal blood, and all his qualities as a leader, a soldier, and a man—had no right to rule in his cousin's place. Richard was the king anointed by God, a sacred rite that could not be annulled or undone. In England's recent past, the three centuries since the Conquest of 1066, only one king, Edward II, had lost his crown, and he had been required to resign the throne to his son, a fourteen-year-old boy who bore no personal responsibility for his father's fall. Even if Richard could be compelled to take the same course, there would be nothing unequivocal about Henry's standing as his heir. But the circle had to be squared. To secure England's future, necessary reality and the principles of law must be made to meet in two places: first, to justify the removal of the crown from Richard's head, and second, to vindicate Henry's claim to wear it in his place.

In Richard's name, Henry summoned a parliament to meet at Westminster at the end of September. Whatever moves he was about to make, he would need the legitimizing presence of the representatives of the realm. In the meantime, he knew that, after all the chaos and uncertainty of the last month and the violence and looting that had marred his arrival in Cheshire, he needed to reimpose order on the country as a marker of the good government he had come to champion. First at Chester and then at Lichfield as he rode south with the captive king, instructions were sent to the justices and sheriffs in all counties that they must resume their work of keeping the peace and enforcing the law. The writs were issued under Richard's seal, on the advice (their text carefully explained) of the great men of England, and especially the king's well-beloved cousin Henry, duke of Lancaster, who had recently returned to amend the rule and governance of the kingdom.[9]

It was true that Henry was surrounded by the other great men of England, although some names were more prominent than others in the nascent regime's public announcements. Besides Henry himself, the writs mentioned Archbishop Arundel, now acting as de facto chancellor, as well as Henry's brother-in-law Ralph Neville, earl of Westmorland, and Henry Percy, earl of Northumberland. The commitment of all three men to Henry's cause since the moment of his return was clear and unblemished. Keeping a much lower profile in his entourage were the nobles who had worn the badge of the white hart until they found the ground shifting beneath their feet: Langley and his son Edward of Rutland, Thomas Percy of Worcester, Thomas Despenser, Henry's brothers John and Henry Beaufort, and his brother-in-law John Holand. The earl of Salisbury—whom Henry had not forgiven for declaring him a traitor in Paris—and Holand's nephew Thomas were under lock and key alongside the king. Messengers had been dispatched to retrieve the two royal boys, Henry's son Henry and Woodstock's son Humphrey, from Trim Castle in Ireland, and another to free the earl of Warwick from his prison on the Isle of Man. Warwick had already arrived to join the cavalcade by the time it advanced on the capital, where the severed head of his former jailer, William Scrope, was rotting on a spike above London Bridge.[10]

On the first day of September, the city threw wide its gates in welcome. Henry was no longer accompanied by an army; he had sent most of his troops home now that uncontested power lay in his hands. The challenge ahead was one of legitimacy, how to translate the control he currently enjoyed into permanent authority, and that was a context in which soldiers on the streets of the capital would undermine rather than strengthen his position. From now on, law and counsel would be his weapons. London's relationship with Richard had been fraught for years, despite Richard Whittington's canny attempts to protect the city's interests during his term as mayor. Now Whittington's successor in office came with the capital's leading citizens to greet Henry on the road as he approached, hailing him as a hero and a liberator, with trumpets blowing and cries of, "Long live the good duke of Lancaster!" Richard was quietly escorted away from the procession by Thomas Rempston, Henry's new constable of the Tower of London. Henry himself rode the length of Cheapside past cheering crowds to St. Paul's Cathedral. There he prayed at the high altar before turning, in tears, to the tomb where his father lay newly buried at his mother's side. It was a release of emotion he knew he could not afford to repeat in the days that lay ahead.[11]

In the Tower, Richard's feelings were all he had left. His rule had always meant uttering commands and then seeing his words shape the reality around him. Whenever this assertion of his royal will had not worked as he wished, his response had been fury. Now it had failed entirely. He had no strategy, no understanding of what had gone wrong, no resources, internal or external, with which to fight. Since Conwy he had cycled between rage at those who had betrayed him, grief at the losses he had endured, and appeals to heaven for divine intervention. His own actions, he believed, were beyond reproach. A king must always punish the wicked and hold fast to the truth, Creton recalled him saying, and that was what he had done. But since no fault lay with him, he had no idea, now that his words had lost all power, how to help himself. On September 21, two years to the day since the earl of Arundel's execution, Archbishop Arundel's man Adam Usk was sent to visit the imprisoned king to assess his state of mind. He found him passive and resigned, ruminating despondently on the fate that had befallen him. "My God," Richard said, "this is a strange and fickle land, which has exiled, slain, destroyed and ruined so many kings, so many rulers and great men. . . ." Over dinner he expanded on his theme, recounting such stories from the earliest times in England's past, and Usk found himself deeply affected by the isolation of a once-magnificent king brought low: "seeing then the troubles of his spirit . . . I departed much moved at heart."[12]

Henry had no time to contemplate his country's history unless it could serve his immediate needs. He appointed a group of churchmen, lawyers, and nobles—men including Adam Usk, and led by the recently appointed archbishop of York, William Scrope's cousin Richard, the former bishop of Lichfield—to examine all possible precedents for the deposition and replacement of a king. It was a sign of the speed with which the regime had collapsed that Archbishop Scrope, who had spent much of the last two years in Rome arguing on the king's behalf for the canonization of Edward II, now found himself analyzing the example of Edward's fall to justify Richard's overthrow. The commissioners also looked to the terms of a papal bull of 1245 by which Innocent IV had formally pronounced a sentence of deposition against the Holy Roman Emperor Frederick II, for what Usk described as "perjuries, sacrileges, sodomitical acts, dispossession of his subjects, the reduction of his people to servitude, lack of reason, and incapacity to rule." Religious houses around the country were ordered to send to Westminster the chronicles they kept that touched on the government of England since the time of the Conqueror, while Usk himself was thinking as far back as the legendary Arthgallus, king of the Britons, who had "debased the noble and exalted the ignoble, seizing the goods of the wealthy and amassing indescribable treasures."[13]

Out of these scholarly inquiries came thirty-three articles of accusation against Richard, a list that, step-by-step, traced an incriminating path through the events of the past twelve years. Here were the king's questions to the judges in 1387 and de Vere's raising of an army; here were the loans, the oaths, the pardons and blank charters; here too were the crimes of the king's Cheshiremen, the destruction of Woodstock, Arundel, and Warwick, the banishments of Archbishop Arundel and Henry himself, and the seizing of Henry's inheritance. The king's actions, the commissioners said, had been wicked, malicious, cunning, deceitful, and cruel; but the charge to which they came back again and again was his perjury in breaking the oath he had sworn at his coronation to uphold the law and do justice within his realm. Richard had declared "that his laws were in his own mouth, or sometimes in his breast"; he believed that the lives and property of his people "were his, and subject to his will"; and he had proved himself "so variable and dissimulating in both word and writings, and so inconstant in his behaviour . . . that almost no living person who came to know him could or would trust him."[14]

The portrait of his kingship was damning—but still, if a king was made by God, by what earthly authority could he be deposed? The example of 1327 offered a solution. As in the case of Edward II, the charges against Richard were such that, for the good of the kingdom, he must voluntarily resign his crown. He would be deposed, then, only to confirm his own abdication. When the representatives of the realm met at Westminster on Tuesday, September 30, the formal record of their proceedings asserted blandly that Richard had already freely agreed to abdicate back in August at Conwy Castle. He now wished—or so the record said—to confirm his decision, and had done so "with a cheerful expression" the previous afternoon, when Henry and Archbishop Arundel had visited him in the Tower. He had signed a formal renunciation—"I was and am utterly inadequate and unequal to the task of ruling and governing the said realm"—before nominating Henry as his successor and placing his golden ring, the royal signet, on his cousin's finger.[15]

The formal record of the proceedings, however, was economical with the truth. The visit from Henry and Archbishop Arundel was not the first Richard had received. The day before, Sunday, September 28, a deputation of lords had arrived at his rooms in the Tower, led by the earls of Northumberland and Westmorland and Archbishop Scrope. At that point, Richard had acknowledged no agreement at Conwy. He asked to see the written statement they wanted him to sign, and told them to come back in the morning. When they did, they found him furious, and refusing entirely to cooperate. "He declared," an eyewitness wrote, "that he would like to have it explained to him how it was that he could resign the crown, and to whom." He demanded to see his "dear cousin of Lancaster"; but when Henry came to the Tower with Archbishop Arundel and an imposing company of lords spiritual and temporal, the answers to the king's questions became brutally obvious. How: because he had no alternative. To whom: to the cousin he had tried to destroy. Richard read the statement of abdication aloud, and the lords signed their names as witnesses.[16]

England no longer had a king. As a result, the assembly that gathered at

Westminster on Tuesday, September 30, was no longer technically a parliament, since the authority that had summoned it had dissolved at the moment of Richard's abdication. Whatever its status, this was the first meeting of the realm since his craftsmen had finished their labors in Westminster Hall. His white harts were everywhere in finely chiseled stone, under the impassive gaze of exquisite wooden angels carved into the hammer beams, each one holding his coat of arms; but Richard was not there to see them. The throne, draped in cloth of gold, sat empty. Archbishop Scrope gave a brief sermon on a text from Isaiah—"I have put my words in thy mouth"—to explain the reasons for the king's resignation. The statement of abdication and the lengthy articles of deposition were recited in turn, and greeted by the lords and Commons with shouts of acclamation and approval. Then the assembly made a formal declaration that Richard was "deservedly deposed from every royal dignity and honour, if any of this dignity and honour should remain in him." There must be no doubt, no loophole through which his sovereignty could be revived or restored.

When silence fell, Henry rose from the place where he sat as duke of Lancaster. He made the sign of the cross on his forehead and chest, and spoke: "In the name of the Father, Son and Holy Ghost, I, Henry of Lancaster, challenge this realm of England, and the crown with all the members and appurtenances, as I that am descended by right line of the blood coming from the good lord King Henry the third, and through that right that God of his grace has sent me, with help of my kin and of my friends, to recover it; the which realm was in point to be undone for default of governance and undoing of the good laws." In one way, it was plain speaking: unadorned English, intended to reach the ears of all the people of England, and noted in full within the clerical Latin and French of the official record. In another way, it was not plain at all. Was he claiming the throne by blood? Or by conquest? Or by the acclamation of the people? The last could not stand, since it would imply that his sovereignty somehow derived *from* the people, rather than directly from God. Nor could a claim by conquest, which might mean that he was free to rewrite England's existing laws at will, rather than protect and uphold them. And blood had its own complications. Henry, through his father, Gaunt, was Richard's nearest heir in the male line. But if the female line were counted, the superior claim belonged to Edmund Mortimer, the seven-year-old earl of March, great-grandson of Lionel of Antwerp. Henry's best option therefore rested in this delicately worded compound of all three, allusively cited in support of his role as an instrument of God's will to save England from Richard's misgovernment.[17]

Again the assembly voiced its approval, the lords one by one and then all together, with renewed shouts of acclamation. Archbishops Arundel of Canterbury and Scrope of York kissed Henry's hands and led him to the throne. As the new king sat in royal state for the first time, Archbishop Arundel preached a sermon on a verse from the book of Samuel: "A man shall rule over the people." Manhood, by the archbishop's analysis, was a matter not of chronological age—which was just as well, given that the new king was three months younger than the old—but of understanding, and Richard's had been that of a child: inconstant, unconcerned with the truth, easily swayed by whim and flattery. "When a boy reigns, wilfulness reigns, and reason is exiled. . . . From this danger we are now liberated, because a man is ruling; he, that is, who rules not as a child but as one perfect in reason." In its end, it seemed, Richard's reign had circled back to its beginning: a king who had once been temporarily incapable of ruling because he was a child was now declared permanently incapable of ruling because he had never grown out of the solipsistic irrationality of childhood. Henry spoke again, to demonstrate, by contrast, the maturity of judgment England could expect from its new sovereign. He intended to disinherit no one by right of conquest, he said, but only to punish those who had opposed "the good purpose and the common profit of the realm." Then came an announcement that, within a fortnight, the new king would be crowned and the assembly would reconvene as a parliament. Smiling with relief, Henry rose from his throne, and the celebrations began.

The next day, October 1, 1399, a delegation representing the estates of the realm visited Richard in the Tower with the news that his abdication and deposition had taken effect. From now on, they said, no one would offer him obedience as their king. He did not look for that, Richard replied, all fury and bravado gone; "but he said that, after all this, he hoped that his cousin would be good lord to him."[18]

Monday, October 13—a year to the day since Henry had sailed into exile at his cousin's command—was the feast of the translation of Saint Edward the Confessor, Richard's royal patron. Beside the saint's shrine in Westminster Abbey, the gilded tomb that Richard had commissioned for himself and his dead queen, Anne, glowed in the torchlight. On the paneled back of Richard's seat in the choir, his image remained gloriously enthroned with crown, orb, and scepter, under the unreadable eyes of the white hart on the gallery wall above. But on the throne itself, draped in cloth of gold on a crimson-covered platform raised high at the crossing of the transepts, it was Henry who sat in majesty.

The ceremonies had begun in the Tower two days before. Henry's need to harness the legitimizing power of tradition was married with a determination to bolster his authority with new ritual, wherever opportunity allowed. Custom dictated that a king should spend the night before his coronation awake and at prayer, before taking a ceremonial bath to symbolize his purification in the sight of God. This time, by innovative design, forty-six of Henry's most loyal supporters kept the same vigil a day beforehand, on Saturday, October 11, and were then knighted by the king during mass on Sunday morning. Henry's eldest son had already been made a knight in a moment of theatrical magnanimity by Richard in Ireland; but these new creations included his three younger boys, twelve-year-old Thomas, ten-year-old John, and Humphrey, who had just turned nine. Young Henry's companion in Ireland, Woodstock's son, Humphrey, had died on his journey back to England, followed shortly afterward by his heartbroken mother; but alongside the Lancastrian boys stood the teenage earls of Arundel and Stafford and the son and heir of the earl of Warwick. With them were more than three dozen older esquires and gentlemen, including John Pelham, the Sussex man who had been first ashore from Henry's ship to take back Pevensey Castle for his "dearest and best loved of all earthly lords." All now became "knights of the bath." If Richard's knights had been a byword for partisan brutality, Henry's were pledging themselves to the service of the realm under the kingship of a man who had already—as Richard never had—proved himself a chivalric hero.[19]

On Sunday afternoon, dressed in green robes with tasseled cords of white silk looped on their left shoulders, the new knights joined a magnificent procession that accompanied Henry from the Tower to the palace of Westminster through the heart of the city of London. Six weeks earlier, Richard had been taken under guard in the opposite direction to be met with jeers in the streets, curses lobbed at "this evil bastard who has ruled us so badly." It was a striking taunt, the first time in years that anyone had dared allude to his mother's colorful marital history. The sheaf of documents that demonstrated the technical legality of his parents' marriage still rested where Richard had placed them for safekeeping, in the archive of Westminster Abbey, but Henry was concerned with legitimacy of a different kind. He rode west along Cheapside on a white charger, dressed in finest cloth of gold, bareheaded in the rain, surrounded by the mayor and citizens in scarlet liveries and, in silks and furs, England's dukes and earls, lords and ladies, their hundreds of attendants jostling to keep their places in the parade. Brightly colored hangings fluttered in the damp air as the crowds whooped and cheered, keeping off the chill with the wine running in the city conduits. Henry was enveloped by the noise—*his* people, *his* capital—but his attention was already turning to the next day's ritual in the abbey, a ceremony of king making in the company of heaven as well as his jubilant subjects.[20]

After the prayers of his own night's vigil, after making confession and hearing mass, he was led across the palace yard under a canopy of blue silk raised on silvered poles, the procession shadowed by memories from when he and Richard were children: how his father had carried the sword Curtana before the little king, with their uncles Langley and Woodstock following behind; how he had taken the sword from his father and held it upright, a symbol of royal justice, during the long hours of the coronation feast, a solemn duty diligently fulfilled. Now his father and Woodstock were dead, and it was his own son Henry—taller and stronger than he remembered, but still only just thirteen—who carried Curtana. On his other side, his stalwart ally Northumberland held the newly named Lancaster sword, the one he had worn when he landed at Ravenspur, a symbol of God's will made manifest in his claim to sovereignty.[21]

Beside him in the abbey, as he climbed the steps to the golden throne,

was Archbishop Arundel. The pope had not yet formalized his reinstatement
to the seat of Canterbury, but that administrative detail was of little concern;
neither Henry nor the archbishop himself acknowledged the authority of
the pen-pushing yes-man Richard had fleetingly installed in his place. Their
differences were deep—it was no small matter, the part Henry had played
in the archbishop's exile and his brother's execution—but they had been set
aside in the greater cause of England's rescue from Richard's tyranny. At the
archbishop's prompting, the congregation gave a great shout, echoing against
stone and glass, to acclaim Henry as England's king, and he swore the coronation oath—the sovereign's promise to rule justly, lawfully, mercifully, and
truthfully—that Richard had been deposed for breaking.

Then, the most sacred part of this sacred ceremony. The anointing of a
sovereign was a spiritual distinction that could never be undone—a point
on which Richard had continued to insist from his quarters in the Tower,
even as he was forced to recognize the material fact of his deposition. But
Henry's anointing would supersede Richard's, and the chrism through which
it would take effect would be the oil of Saint Thomas Becket from the ampulla topped with a golden eagle. Henry, not Richard, would be the "greatest
among kings" of the Virgin's prophecy. He took his place before the high
altar. Slowly, delicately, as clerical voices sang, the archbishop touched the
holy oil to Henry's hands, his breast, his shoulders, his back, and his head. It
was done. A fine cap was placed over the site of unction before Henry was
ritually invested with the regalia of his kingdom: spurs, sword, ring, and at
last the crown of the royal saint Edward the Confessor. The hymn of praise
Te Deum laudamus rose high to the vaulted ceiling; the coronation mass was
sung, and King Henry was led back through the press of his subjects to feast
in Westminster's hall.[22]

He sat at the highest table, archbishops and bishops to his right and his
left. Richard's harts, frozen in stone, looked down at the bestiary presented
on the plates of the banquet: boar, heron, pheasant and sturgeon, venison,
pullet, bittern and crane, rabbit, egret, partridge and eagle. The rich dishes
were offered to the king by noble attendants: Edward of Rutland, duke of
Aumale; John Holand, duke of Exeter; Thomas Holand, duke of Surrey;
John Beaufort, marquis of Dorset; and Thomas Beauchamp, earl of Warwick.

Performing this solemn and honorable task, Warwick betrayed no flicker of resentment at being forced to keep company with men who had accused him of treason and watched him beg for his life. Three and a half months after Henry's return, it appeared, in public at least, as though the events of the last two years might be wholly forgotten.[23]

The meal was only half eaten when the great door swung open. Into the hall rode a knight on a warhorse, man and animal armed in shining steel. Sir Thomas Dymoke was one of Henry's newly created knights, the son of one of Gaunt's retainers, and by hereditary right the king's champion. He passed a scroll to one of the heralds, who read its contents aloud in both English and French. "If there be any man high or low, of whatsoever estate or condition he be, who will say that Henry, king of England that here is and was this day crowned, that he is not rightful king nor rightfully crowned, right anon or else at whatever day our lord the king will assign I will give battle with my body and prove that he lies falsely!" The ceremonial challenge was met with ceremonial silence, until the king himself raised his voice: "If the need should arise, Sir Thomas, I will personally relieve you of this task."

It was an elegant intervention from a chivalric hero, but Henry's improvised addition to the script contained a warning. The question was whether everyone present was listening.

Parliament reconvened the next day; and, when its discussions began, the veneer of willed amnesia that had so gracefully sustained the installation of the new king fractured within forty-eight hours.

The session had started well. The representatives of the realm acclaimed the investiture of Henry's eldest son as prince of Wales, duke of Cornwall, and earl of Chester, and his recognition as heir apparent—the first time the line of succession had been clear in twenty-two years, since Richard himself had inherited the throne. They unanimously agreed that the acts of the parliament of 1397 should be revoked and the lords who had been convicted as traitors in that assembly restored to their lands and titles, whether in life, in Warwick's case, or in death, for Woodstock and Arundel. The acts of the Merciless Parliament of 1388 were reinstated in law, Richard's blank charters annulled, and the definition of treason explicitly confirmed as that contained in Edward III's statute of 1352. Recent judgments, Henry declared, had meant "that there was no man there who knew how he ought to act, speak or talk, for fear of such penalties." As their sovereign, he "wished to act in a quite different manner."[24]

But on Thursday, October 16, the bitter divisions of 1397 erupted into the open once again. The most explosive issue, just as it had been then, was the murder of Thomas of Woodstock. Thomas Mowbray was not there to answer charges about his part in the killing. In exile, he had traveled as a pilgrim to the Holy Land, and on his return journey—though the news had not yet reached England—he had died of plague in Venice on September 22. But in Mowbray's absence it was his former steward William Bagot who once again set the cat among the pigeons. After fleeing Bristol and the summary executions that had claimed the lives of Bushy, Green, and Scrope, Bagot had been captured in Ireland. Brought into parliament at the Commons' request, he defended himself boldly against the accusation that, as one of Richard's closest counselors, he was complicit in the king's crimes. "What man is there among you all," he said, "if King Richard had wished to demand such assent and support from you, who would have dared contradict him or refuse to obey him?"[25]

Bagot's question was direct, and devastating in its implications. If he was guilty, how many others there present could say they were innocent? Above all, Bagot insisted, he was not responsible for Woodstock's death. Richard had ordered the murder, Mowbray had arranged it, and Rutland had been the prime mover behind the king's decision. If the assembly wanted to know more, he said, they should question a former valet of Mowbray's named John Hall, who was currently to be found in Newgate Prison.

Rutland was already on his feet in furious denial, but Henry told him to sit down. More than anything else in Richard's toxic rule, the murder of their uncle had poisoned England's body politic. The truth—or some version of it—would have to come out if the rot were ever to heal. Two days later, on Saturday, October 18, Hall was brought in chains before the assembly and his confession read aloud. In September 1397, he said, he had been in Mowbray's service in Calais. Late one night, his master had summoned him from his bed and ordered him to join a group of esquires and valets at an inn in the town, some of them Richard's servants, some Mowbray's, and some Rutland's. Woodstock was brought into the chamber where they had gathered. There he was told it was the king's will that he should die. The duke was permitted to make his last confession to a chaplain summoned for the purpose, and then—while Hall guarded the door, in terror, he claimed, for his own life—the men made Woodstock lie on a bed, placed a feather mattress on top of him, held it down over his face, and suffocated him until he was dead.[26]

Whatever the rumors, whatever the information circulating behind closed doors, it was a shock to hear in public the bald facts of the duke's end, without trial, without a hearing, just the extinguishing of a life as though he were not the son of the great King Edward and King Richard's own uncle. Once again, Rutland stood to defend himself. But Lord Fitzwalter— an Essex landowner whose family had a proud history of service to Woodstock, and whose widowed stepmother was now Rutland's wife—shouted that Rutland was guilty of the murder, and threw down his hood to challenge him to a duel. Rutland did the same to accept the contest, and in moments such violent argument had broken out among the lords, with gloves and hoods thrown down in challenge and counter-challenge, that Henry almost lost control of the assembly. Every single thing they did, he said when he could finally make himself heard, must take place with proper deliberation and according to the law—or else how would their actions be better than the crimes they were prosecuting? It had never been clearer that the attempt to seek a balance between justice, revenge, and reconciliation would, for a man who had himself been centrally involved in the bloody proceedings of 1397, be nightmarishly complex.[27]

The only thing on which all present could agree was the guilt of the unfortunate John Hall. As soon as the verdict was given, he was bundled out of the hall and dragged on a hurdle to Tyburn. There he was hanged and cut down, still living, from the gallows, to be disemboweled and, in his agony, made to watch as his entrails were burned before him. At last, he was beheaded and his corpse hacked into quarters. His head was sent to Calais, the place of the duke's murder. The section of his body that included his right hand was impaled on a stake for display on the south side of London Bridge.[28]

This bloodletting—the catharsis of judicial violence—allowed time for tempers to cool. The next steps, whatever they were, would have to be taken with extreme care. On Monday, October 20, five of the six surviving lords who had made the appeal of treason in 1397—Rutland, Thomas and John Holand, Salisbury, and Despenser, all bar Henry's brother John Beaufort— were arrested on the king's orders with the unanimous approval of their peers. Parliament did not meet that day because, a week after Henry's coronation, the king was to undergo the ceremonial removal of the cap that covered the site of his anointing, and the ritual washing of his head. The grim discovery that Becket's ancient oil had left his hair crawling with lice and falling out in handfuls did nothing to improve the king's mood.[29]

The next day, when the assembly gathered for the first time without the detained lords, their immediate dilemma concerned the ex-king: Should Richard himself stand trial? That, for Henry, was the most nightmarish prospect of all. As Richard would inevitably ask, on what authority could a man be tried for actions he took as an anointed sovereign? And then, for the anointed sovereign who had taken his place, what alarming precedent might such a trial set, and to what further conflict might it lead? There was no knowing what else Richard might say or do, given the greatest stage and audience in the kingdom. It took several days of discussion among the lords temporal and spiritual and the careful advice of royal lawyers, but on Monday, October 27, the representatives of the realm agreed that the man who had once been king—now, as Usk noted, "a private person, Richard of Bordeaux, a simple knight"—should be kept in perpetual imprisonment. He should be held in a place known only to the king and council, attended by men who had not served him before, and allowed no means of communication with the outside world. His life—"which the king wished to be preserved to him in all events"—would be safe, but there must be no hope of conspiracy or rescue. Thirty-six hours later, under cover of darkness, Richard was taken from the Tower on the first stage of his journey into what Henry devoutly hoped would be oblivion.[30]

There remained the problem of the six Appellants. It was already obvious that Rutland—a man who had been named for years in official documents as "the king's brother," or recently even his "foster-child"—could not simply resume his place among the peers of the realm as though nothing had ever happened. All six must be given a right of reply, since the law, as Henry had said, must be scrupulously observed; but since the law must be scrupulously observed, all six must face charges for what they had done. On Wednesday, October 29, they were brought into parliament, where the records of the sessions of 1397–98 were read out. What responsibility did they acknowledge for these heinous acts?[31]

All denied any part in Woodstock's murder. All disclaimed any hand in drawing up the appeal of treason; they had known nothing of what Richard planned against Woodstock, Arundel, and Warwick in August 1397, they said, until they were called from their dinner to the gate of Nottingham Castle to be shown a document that had already been written. Beaufort and Despenser implied that some responsibility for its contents might lie with William Scrope, now dead. Thomas Holand humbly asked the king to consider "that he was very young at that time, and of little reputation." All impressed upon their listeners time and time again that they had acted only in fear of their lives on the express orders of the king, "a person," Beaufort noted, "who did not in any way wish to be answered with the truth." It was Rutland who found a way to turn defense into attack. The names of all the lords who had sat in judgment in the parliament of 1397 should be recited, he said, so that they could be asked one by one whether they had been coerced by Rutland himself or by anyone in his name to return the verdicts they did. And if any of them said yes, he stood ready to meet them on the field of combat at King Henry's command.

His logic was undeniable, but the lords in question—all of whom sat listening to him now, including King Henry himself—proved reluctant to take up his suggestion. As Rutland was showing to unanswerable effect, there were no clean hands when it came to Richard's tyranny. Even the earl of Warwick found himself humiliated by the record of his own abject confession of treason in 1397, now that those proceedings were being publicly reversed. Instead, Henry took the charges against the Appellants under careful advisement. The verdict, when it came on November 3, was merciful. Rutland, the Holands, Beaufort, and Despenser were stripped of their new titles— the dukedoms of Aumale, Exeter, and Surrey, the marquisate of Dorset, and

the earldom of Gloucester—as well as all royal gifts they had received in
the past two years. From now on, they were forbidden to distribute liveries
to anyone but their household servants. If they made any move to restore
Richard to the throne or to help him in any way, they would immediately be
punished as traitors. Salisbury was left aside only because he had accepted a
challenge to a duel from Thomas, Lord Morley, a man who had once served
both Woodstock and Mowbray; that case was therefore referred to the court
of Chivalry. William Bagot remained in custody. The Commons, who had
learned the lessons of recent history well, secured formal confirmation that
the judgments were nothing to do with them but belonged "solely to the
king and the lords." And when parliament finally closed on November 19,
they "thanked the king for his just judgement, and that God had sent them
such a king and ruler."[32]

Some of Henry's subjects wanted more. There was murmuring among
the people against the leniency of the king and council, Walsingham reported, and even rumors of revolt if the Appellants did not forfeit their lives.
But that way lay no kind of settlement. The six lords had offered their coop-
eration, supported Richard's deposition, participated in Henry's coronation,
and sworn allegiance to his authority as king. What he desperately needed
was to turn the page; to find them a place within his regime that might enable their loyalty to grow without alienating others who were outraged by
their actions. The parliament had been a balancing act, and the wretched
John Hall its only casualty. Would it be enough?

The answer was not long in coming. After a quiet Christmas spent recovering from a bout of food poisoning that laid the whole court low, Henry
intended to celebrate the feast of the Epiphany—January 6, 1400, Richard's
thirty-third birthday—with jousting and masques at Windsor Castle. But
two days beforehand, he heard that his life was in danger. An ambush was
planned to strike him down during the festivities, along with his sons, and
then to proclaim Richard king once again.[33]

Rumors of the conspiracy had been circulating in London, but the loudest of the loose tongues belonged to Rutland. His role in the events of the

previous months had been deeply ambivalent. For years, no one had stood higher in Richard's affection, and he had done whatever the king required, right up to the point at which it became clear that Henry's challenge to his cousin's authority was irresistible. But as Rutland himself had pointed out, he was not alone in that; plenty of other lords had manifestly done the same. And he was Henry's cousin just as much as Richard's. He claimed during his trial that he had taken not one penny from his share of the confiscated Lancastrian estates nor changed a single Lancastrian officeholder, except to give a new appointment to Robert Waterton, one of Henry's closest and most trusted friends. Yet he found himself denounced as Richard's darling by supporters of Henry's coup, and by Richard's loyalists as the Judas who had betrayed his sovereign. In January 1400, faced with the imminent need to take up arms for one or the other, he committed himself to Henry.[34]

Among the other Appellants, John Beaufort had already made his peace with his brother the king. The plot was the work of the remaining four: the Holands, Despenser, and Salisbury. John Holand's debt to Gaunt for saving him after he murdered Ralph Stafford had long been outweighed by the preferment his brother Richard had offered him. Despenser, Salisbury, and Holand's nephew Thomas, along with the executed William Scrope, were the men who had been accused by Mowbray in 1397 of plotting to murder Gaunt and Henry. All four felt themselves to be scapegoats for the destruction of Woodstock and Arundel; none could conceive of finding a place in the new regime with any kind of security, let alone the degree of privilege they had enjoyed under Richard's rule. If they had heard Henry's quiet warning at the coronation feast, they were choosing to ignore it. On the evening of January 4, Thomas Holand, Despenser, and Salisbury mustered their retinues at Kingston-upon-Thames, muffled against the cold, and rode fifteen miles in the icy dark to spring their trap at Windsor. But when they reached the castle, their target was already gone.[35]

Henry had fought in colder terrain than this. Just as in the marshes of Lithuania, he could rely on unstintingly loyal support from the men who had always served his family. He made for the capital, summoning his Lancastrian retainers to meet him there, while London's mayor raised forces in the city itself. The conspirators found themselves stranded and at a dangerous loss.

They made a half-hearted attempt to rally support at Sonning in Berkshire, the manor house where Richard's bewildered little queen was being cared for on Henry's orders. When that failed, the rebel lords fled. But the people's anger at the toppled regime ran so deep that when they were found—Holand and Salisbury in Cirencester, Despenser in Bristol—all were lynched, their heads crudely hacked from their bodies. John Holand, who had stayed behind in London, tried to escape in the opposite direction through Essex to the coast. He was captured and taken to Woodstock's castle of Pleshey, where Henry's mother-in-law, the countess of Hereford, had been living since the deaths of Woodstock's widow and his heir, her daughter Eleanor and grandson Humphrey. There, on the spot outside the castle gate where Richard had ordered Woodstock's arrest, Holand too was beheaded by the mob.

Henry and his troops had set out from London in pursuit of the rebel lords, but by the time they reached Oxford on January 11 the threat was over. All that remained was to deal with the men who had followed the dead lords into rebellion. Ninety were tried at Oxford Castle on January 12, but most were pardoned; Henry had no wish to condemn as traitors those of the lowest rank who had no choice but to follow orders. Twenty-seven were executed, of whom two knights and two esquires suffered the full penalties for treason. Adam Usk saw their remains brought back to London to be salted for display, "chopped up like the carcasses of beasts killed in the chase . . . partly in sacks and partly on poles slung between men's shoulders." One of the accused, however, received a special pardon because of his involvement long ago in a different revolt: a smallholder from Kent named John Ferrour who, as a rebel in 1381, had saved Henry's life when he was a frightened fourteen-year-old hiding in the Tower.[36]

Back then, Richard had been tasting the heady possibilities of his royal authority for the first time. Now he was the one trapped behind the walls of a fortress. When he was taken in secret from the Tower—weeping, and wishing he had never been born, Usk said—his destination, by boat to the Yorkshire coast and then inland via Pickering and Knaresborough, was the great Lancastrian castle of Pontefract. The king who had believed himself chosen by God, who had pinned his own badge of the white hart to the ranks of the angels in heaven, no longer controlled the smallest detail of his own existence. He posed no threat to his cousin except by continuing to breathe. While he did so, as a once and potentially future king, he would always be a focus for resistance and treachery. The issue, then, was his life, and it was an issue too fraught and too destabilizing to be contained by Henry's commitment to the law. When the king and his council met in early February, their minutes noted that if Richard were still alive—"as it is supposed that he is"—he should be securely guarded for the safety of the king and the kingdom. If, on the other hand, he had died, he should be shown to the people so that they might know that he was no longer living. The formulation was strikingly odd. A week later, news came that Richard was dead.[37]

His corpse was brought south slowly, to allow the cortège to stop along the way so that the ex-king's face could be displayed to his former subjects, just as the council had ordered with such arresting foresight. When it arrived in London, requiem masses were sung at St. Paul's Cathedral on March 6 and 7 in the presence of King Henry himself. But the body was not laid to rest next to Queen Anne in the exquisite tomb beside the Confessor's shrine in Westminster Abbey. Instead, "in the dead of night," Walsingham reported, it was taken twenty miles northwest of the capital for burial in the priory church at Langley. The fact of his death was as evident as Henry's government could make it, the place of his interment as quiet. In the matter of his end, when and where were clear, but not how. The story spread that Richard had been so devastated, thrown into "such grief, languor and weakness" by the failure of the Epiphany rising, that he had refused to eat or drink—but not everyone believed it. "Others say," reported the same chronicler, "that he was miserably put to death by starvation."[38]

At thirty-three—the age of Christ's passion, the perfect age at which all good Christians would be reborn on the dreadful day of judgment—Richard was gone. Approaching his own thirty-third birthday, Henry faced the beginning of an uncertain future. The people of England had united under his command to reject a tyrant. Only time would tell whether they would continue to obey a usurper and regicide.

PART FOUR
GRACE

Fifteen

1400-1403

so shaken as we are

In the summer and autumn of 1399, Henry's ascent to the throne had been irresistible. Getting rid of Richard was a desperate necessity, and the practical fact that Henry was his only possible replacement meant that the new king's claim to the crown—studiedly vague though it was—carried all before it.

But from the spring of 1400, with Richard dead and buried, the inexorable complications of Henry's position began to emerge. Every argument that seemed to vindicate his sovereignty had its own destabilizing shadow. So intense was popular anger at the old regime that the leaders of the Epiphany rising had been killed before Henry could reach them, an outcome that spared him the need to stage more trials in parliament, more aristocratic executions—but, as Henry and his council then fretted, for the people to believe they could take the law into their own hands was a grave danger to the kingdom. The new king had come to the throne to defend the rule of law—but he had imprisoned his predecessor without trial, and allowed him to die in custody. No one could dispute his claim to be Richard's heir in the male line of succession—but the English claim to the French throne, which Henry had no intention of renouncing, came through the female line, a principle of inheritance that, if applied in England, would hand the crown to the young earl of March. God's will had been made triumphantly manifest in Henry's victory—but if in time he too faced a contender for his throne, might God change His mind?

For now, the sacred rite of his anointing offered reassurance. "Henry the eagle has captured the oil by which he has received the rule of the realm," wrote the London poet John Gower, confident and jubilant, in one of three Latin poems he composed to celebrate the new king's accession. When French ambassadors arrived at Westminster shortly after the coronation to establish exactly what was happening in England and check on the well-being of the little queen, Henry welcomed them warmly, renewing his thanks to their king for the hospitality he had enjoyed during his exile. Reverently, he showed them the eagle ampulla, which he now carried with him always, telling them of the Virgin's gift to Thomas Becket and its heavenly guarantee of victory over his enemies. In their dispatches home, the envoys could not resist commenting on the English propensity for superstition, but they refrained from mentioning the fact that the king was still having to cover his head to hide the patches where Becket's oil had left his hair thinning and damaged. If it was an omen, it was one Henry was determined to ignore.[1]

Much harder to disregard was the scale of the task that confronted him. Henry's life so far had been spent preparing to succeed his father as duke of Lancaster. The role was immense, the responsibilities huge, but he knew everything Gaunt could teach him about the people and places that made up his duchy and the duties and powers they conferred on its duke. There had been no way of knowing that he would take up this precious, familiar inheritance at the same time as the exceptional duties and powers of a crown to which his claim had only ever been speculative. He had always been close to the throne, but observation and experience were not the same. Meanwhile, the consuming intensity of Richard's presence as king—the claustrophobic terror generated by his diktats and demands—had been so overwhelming for so long that his sudden absence was disorienting, almost baffling, in the un-moored liberation it brought. Henry would be required to shape England's new reality, to command this dislocated realm, despite the questions that remained about his right to rule in Richard's place. He was both a realist and, despite the losses he had faced, an optimist; and his hope was to demonstrate God's blessing on the legitimacy of his throne by uniting England's people under the good government he intended to provide, in which case the ongoing fact of his kingship would become its own justification.

Even that plan—the search for peace through justice, rather than subjection to the king's will—was not as straightforward as it seemed. Henry the
eagle had triumphed over Richard and his white harts, the favored friends
and military retainers who had undermined the dead king's duty to protect
and defend all of his subjects. But Richard had built himself a private affinity precisely to rival the followings his lords already had. Henry, as duke of
Lancaster, came to the throne in possession not only of vast estates but of the
greatest private affinity in the country. Would his own favored friends and
military retainers—able, trusted men as they were—be embraced as impar-
tial royal servants rather than partisan Lancastrian ones?

It would help if, as his supporters hoped, the massive revenues of the
duchy of Lancaster could contribute to the funding of the new king's government and obviate the need to ask his hard-pressed subjects for new grants of
taxation. In theory, the idea was a good one. In practice, its execution posed
insurmountable challenges. Almost all of Henry's income from his estates
was already being spent, not only on the administrative costs of running the
duchy but on the annuities paid to his retainers. They were the most devoted
servants of his family, his dynasty, and now his sovereignty; he had relied
on their support in regaining his duchy and gaining his crown, and would
rely on them now against threats to his throne or his kingdom. How could
he deprive them of money they had already been granted to recognize and
reward their service? Henry was determined not to put at risk their loyalty or
his own control over this private power base. The day after his coronation, he
publicly declared his intentions: the duchy of Lancaster, he said, should "in
all things be managed, governed and treated as . . . if we had never assumed
the ensign of royal dignity." The legal separation between his private possessions and the public responsibilities of his crown was underlined by the
creation of his eldest son as duke of Lancaster, as well as prince of Wales, but
the Lancastrian title was a fiction: both lands and retinue remained under
the direct command of the king.[2]

It was clear too that he needed them. There was no calm after the storm,
no breathing space in which Henry could test the air from his newly exalted
position. Relations with France had deteriorated rapidly during the winter of 1399 and the spring of 1400. Neither side wanted war, and Louis of

Orléans remained characteristically equivocal, concerned as always for his own advantage, but the hostility of King Charles, in his lucid moments, and of his uncles was explicit. Many Frenchmen believed that the English had rejected Richard because of his love for their country; "evil and unreasonable people as they are, they mortally hate the French," wrote Jean Creton. They were appalled by the deposition and death of an anointed king—nothing of the sort had ever been contemplated in France, even during the worst of Charles's madness—and by the insult to Charles's daughter Queen Isabella, left stranded in England along with the large dowry that Henry could not afford to repay. While this French antagonism toward Henry ("he who calls himself king of England") was expressed through diplomatic channels, their allies the Scots lost no time in sending raiding parties over the border. For Henry, this was both threat and opportunity: the urgent task of defending England offered him a chance to assert his new royal authority in action rather than words, and to demonstrate that he—unlike Richard—was a king ready to fight for his people. "He would never refrain from committing his body and his blood to this expedition," the rolls of parliament reported him saying, "or to any other for the salvation of his realm, if God gave him life."[3]

There was relief, as well as challenge, in the practical realities of war. By the time Henry marched into Scotland on August 14, 1400, he did so at the head of an army of more than 13,000 troops, with his Lancastrian retinue at its core. He had been here before, as an eighteen-year-old serving on campaign for the first time alongside his father within the host that Richard had so reluctantly led into enemy territory. Fifteen years had passed; now the royal command was his, and his own sons, thirteen-year-old Henry and twelve-year-old Thomas, were learning what it meant to ride with soldiers. But the military script remained the same. The English spent eight days camped in intimidating force at Leith, the port on the Firth of Forth just outside Edinburgh. There they found that the Scots would not meet them in the field. The castle on its rock remained impregnable. As in 1385, supplies began to run short. As in 1385, retreat proved the only viable option. Henry had demonstrated that he could muster the support of his kingdom: Richard's retainers as well as his own Lancastrians; the rival lords of the north, Percy of Northumberland and Neville of Westmorland; Edward of

Rutland alongside the young heirs of Arundel and Warwick. But in concrete terms, military or political, the mobilization and the money achieved nothing. And when he moved south again it was to discover that, while his back was turned, violence had erupted elsewhere in his kingdom.[4]

On September 16, 1400, a Welsh landowner named Owain Glyn Dŵr, a descendant of the native princes of Powys and Deheubarth, had declared himself prince of an independent Wales and raised a rebellion that was looting and burning its way through English-dominated towns in the north of the principality. The revolt blazed only briefly: by the time the king and his troops arrived in the border town of Shrewsbury on September 26, local forces had already dispersed the rebels and driven Glyn Dŵr into hiding. Henry was shaken, but determined to offer a route to redemption from what seemed little more than an opportunistic attempt to exploit the political turmoil of the previous twelve months. Wales, after all, had been ruled by the English for more than a century, ever since its conquest by his great-great-grandfather Edward I, and it was impossible to imagine that reality crumbling. Executions were matched with pardons for those who submitted to the authority of the crown, and garrisons installed to hold the fortresses of Beaumaris, Caernarfon, Criccieth, and Harlech on the north Welsh coast. By late October, the king had returned, in a somber mood, to Windsor Castle.[5]

His meeting there with a new French embassy was less good-tempered than the first genial encounter in the heady days after his coronation. The envoy, Jean de Hengest, had arrived without diplomatic credentials acceptable to the English, since the French government was refusing formally to acknowledge Henry as king. Meanwhile, Henry could not agree to hand back Richard's nine-year-old widow and her dowry, as required by the Anglo-French treaty, because the cash had already been spent. He had hoped to get round that difficulty by marrying Isabella to one of his sons, but her father's regime would not countenance offering her up to a usurper, and the little girl cried as she told de Hengest that she herself would never agree. It was the greatest desire she had in the world, she said, to see her parents and her siblings again.[6]

The Byzantine emperor Manuel II Palaeologus, landing at Dover in

December with a household of fifty, was a much more welcome visitor. He was an emperor fallen on hard times, touring the courts of Europe—so far, Venice, Pavia, Milan, and Paris—in the hope of raising men and money to save his capital, Constantinople, from the grip of a Turkish blockade that had already lasted more than five years. But an emperor fallen on hard times was an emperor still. Boucicaut, ever the heroic knight, had gone to the defense of the city in 1399, and brought Manuel back with him to Venice. Gian Galeazzo Visconti had accompanied the emperor through Italy to the borders of France. In Paris the palace of the Louvre had been specially decorated in preparation to receive him. Now Henry met him at Blackheath, south of the Thames, and escorted him with all honor to the nearby palace of Eltham, where they spent Christmas and the New Year in lavish style.[7]

In place of Richard's nine-year-old wife, Henry's eight-year-old daughter, Blanche, was the first lady of the English court, presiding over the jousts and masques devised for the emperor's amusement. The participants adopted allegorical disguises derived from classical myth, biblical tales, and chivalric romance, producing ornately written letters of recommendation from Nature and Virtue, Venus, Penelope, and Cleopatra, all addressed to the little girl as "the most excellent and most noble princess, lady Blanche, daughter to the most puissant prince, king of Albion." For Henry, it was a moment that combined magnificent fun with political self-assertion, a bright contrast to the darkness and danger of the revolt that had shaken his fledgling regime exactly a year before. The emperor—a striking figure in his long white robes—saw no difficulty in recognizing Henry as England's king, and presented him with a priceless relic, a piece of the seamless tunic of Christ that the Virgin herself had woven. In return, Henry proffered a contribution to Constantinople's defenses of £2,000 from the Exchequer, to fulfill a royal promise Richard had made that donations for that purpose would be collected from the English people.[8]

But by the time the imperial party left England in February 1401 after eight weeks of expensive entertainment, another parliament was already in session at Westminster. Sixteen months into his reign, Henry had to face the fact that he would not, for the foreseeable future, have either men or money to spare.

The mood in parliament was jumpy. It was an assembly packed with Henry's loyal supporters, but, precisely because of that fact, the vicious circle in which he was beginning to find himself trapped—as a usurper who had justified his usurpation with the promise of good government—was disconcertingly exposed. The representatives of his realm wanted to know that he had used every penny of his royal and Lancastrian revenues to defend his people, as a good king should, before he requested a grant of taxation. A monarch who could simply command the service of his subjects as an unquestioned right might have been able to do as they asked, but Henry was not in that fortunate position. He needed to reward the loyalty of his own men by continuing to pay their annuities, avoid alienating the men Richard had retained by continuing to pay theirs, and attempt to win over the previously uncommitted by rewarding and retaining even more. Already the annual bill came to £24,000 at the Exchequer and £8,000 from the duchy of Lancaster. The military and political upheavals of 1399 had cost more than £35,000; the Scottish campaign the following summer around £10,000 in loans that would need to be repaid. Ongoing defensive commitments in Calais, Aquitaine, Ireland, Wales, at sea, and on the Scottish border required funds of at least £50,000 a year. The growing total, piece by piece, was staggering.[9]

Parliament also wanted to know that every penny was properly accounted for; that, in Henry's brave new world, his regime was one of fiscal transparency and cast-iron competence. This too presented problems. The experienced officials who had run Richard's administration had been dismissed from their posts as soon as Henry reached Westminster, their loyalty under suspicion. In their place he appointed the men who ran his father's duchy. Everyone, in other words, found themselves suddenly in a new job. Before the autumn of 1399, Henry had no hands-on experience of being anything more than his father's deputy in the duchy of Lancaster, let alone king. The administrators now managing the vast responsibilities of his government had previously had charge only of Gaunt's duchy, while the officials Henry appointed to manage the duchy were also, in turn, new to their posts. The unsettling combination of rapidly increasing royal debt with questionable organizational competence drew such criticism from his loyal Commons that, six weeks into the parliament, Henry was forced to undo his own appointments to key offices and reinstate men who had served under Richard. At the head of his administration, his chancellor—John Scarle, a former chancellor of Gaunt's palatinate of Lancaster—was replaced by the bishop of Exeter, the man who had held office during the last two scarifying years of Richard's rule. The management of the royal household was also overhauled. Henry's steward, his friend Thomas Rempston, could not be faulted on questions of military proficiency or personal loyalty, but in sixteen months the household had run up debts of £10,000. Now, along with Henry's controller and treasurer, Rempston was relieved of his role. He was replaced by Thomas Percy, earl of Worcester, who had followed his brother, Northumberland, and nephew Hotspur into support for Henry's regime but before that had spent six years as steward of Richard's household.[10]

These were practical, not political, measures driven by pressure from those who supported Henry's rule and wanted him to get on with the job as effectively as possible, in circumstances where government spending was threatening to spiral out of control. Henry's difficulty in responding was twofold. He had never in his life faced the need to economize. Gaunt had been the richest nobleman in England even before he returned from Spain laden with Castilian gold; though his son had learned many things at his knee, cost cutting was not one of them. Magnificence was required as an expression of sovereignty, but a king who spent more than £450 on jewels and silver plate on the same day as asking his people for loans to pay his army— as Henry had done on his way to Scotland the previous summer—had not mastered the necessary art of balancing economy with display.

At the same time, his fundamental problem went deeper: Henry could not be sure that all his subjects would prove as loyal as the men currently representing his realm in parliament. It was becoming apparent that the task of turning himself from a nobleman at the head of a retinue into a king at the head of a kingdom required the resolution of infinitely regressive contradictions. A king had no need of a private retinue to uphold and enforce his authority, since the whole kingdom was his to command—and the presence of a private retinue would, as in Richard's case, raise alarming questions not simply about his spending, but about the nature of his commitment to his people as a whole. A nobleman who took the throne, on the other hand, urgently needed a constant source of support, both military and political, to quash challenges to his crown. The presence of that support in the form of Henry's private retinue, however, meant that the same alarming questions that had helped to undermine Richard's rule were in play from the very moment he became king.

Still, Henry was demonstrating at least that issues of financial policy could now be addressed without the king's rage precipitating the country into constitutional crisis. He had listened to the requests of his Commons, and they listened to his requests in return. Once the changes were made within his administration, the Commons granted Henry a fifteenth and tenth, the first direct taxation of the reign—even if, before they did so, they had to ask him to stop paying annuities out of the customs duties they had granted in his first parliament. ("This plea seemed just and reasonable to our lord the king," noted the parliamentary clerk, "and he agreed to it.")[11]

And, concerned though they were about the growing deficit in crown finances, the Commons were as anxious as Henry himself about active threats to the stability and the security of the regime. They joined the clergy in petitioning for stricter repression of Lollardy, an underground heresy sprung from the teachings of the Oxford theologian John Wycliffe that, in its criticism of ecclesiastical wealth and power, appeared frighteningly close to sedition. If men and women meeting in secret were prepared to defy the God-given authority of the Church, would they do the same to the God-given authority of the crown? During the parliament the first public burning of a relapsed heretic in decades took place before a huge crowd at Smithfield—a form of punishment that was ratified in English statute law for the first time a week later, along with a ban on unlicensed preaching and teaching. Profoundly unnerved by the aggression of Glyn Dŵr and his rebels, the Commons also sought and won a raft of restrictions on the rights of "full-blooded Welshmen" in the marches of Wales and in English towns along the border. In doing so, they intensified the grievances of people who already lived under legal and tenurial disadvantages in their own land as second-class subjects of the English crown.[12]

Henry's peculiar difficulty was that the contingent nature of his sovereignty—that uneasy compound of vagueness and realpolitik—encouraged anyone who felt dissatisfied with his decisions as king to consider whether there could be another, better option still to come. And dissatisfaction might come in many forms: there were those who thought him too harsh, those who thought him too lenient, those who thought themselves insufficiently rewarded for the service they had offered him. After all, what would constitute sufficient reward for men who believed they had put the crown on Henry's head? Prime candidates for the title of kingmaker were the Percies—the earl of Northumberland, his brother Worcester, and his son Hotspur—who had moved decisively in Henry's favor in the summer of 1399 and had been showered with grants and offices ever since. But the responsibilities conferred by grants and offices could be a burden as well as a reward, and the Percies were finding that balance shifting into unhappy deficit amid the disturbances of the reign's first years.

Hotspur in particular was entrusted by Henry with enormous military and judicial power across northern England and north Wales. In England, his appointments as warden of the East March, sheriff of Northumberland, and keeper of Bamburgh Castle reinforced his family's dominance in the northeast and the key role he had played for years in defense against the Scots. Other new grants vastly extended his territorial remit. In October 1399, Henry named Hotspur justiciar of north Wales and Chester, sheriff of Flint, and keeper of the lordship of Anglesey and the castles of Chester, Flint, Conwy, Caernarfon, and Beaumaris. In part this demonstration of royal favor reflected Hotspur's abilities and reputation. At thirty-seven, he was said to be "the best knight in England," Jean Creton reported: a soldier and diplomat whose career had taken him from the marches of Scotland to Prussia, Calais, Ireland, and Aquitaine. Henry understood, admired, and valued Hotspur's talents. But he was also giving him command in Wales because there was no one else to do it. In theory, the defense of Wales belonged to its prince, but in practice young Henry, at fourteen, was Hotspur's royal apprentice rather than his master. Of the other lords with lands in Wales and the marches, the earl of Arundel and the new earl of Warwick, who inherited his title when his father died that April, were not yet twenty; Thomas Mowbray's son was a teenager whose estates, after the death of his father in exile, lay in the hands of the king; and the earl of March was not yet ten. Hotspur, whose family had custody of March's estates and who was married to the boy's aunt, was the obvious candidate to step in.[13]

Obvious, that is, if the principality had remained quiet after Glyn Dŵr's fleeting revolt in September 1400, leaving Hotspur with time and resources to focus on the renewed threat from Scotland. Instead, on April 1, 1401, three weeks after parliament closed at Westminster, Glyn Dŵr's cousins Gwilym and Rhys ap Tudur launched a daring and impeccably planned raid to seize control of the great royal fortress at Conwy, forty miles west of Chester on the north Welsh coast. Hotspur was left to besiege the castle at his own expense for four weeks before Prince Henry arrived with reinforcements, and the ap Tudur brothers were able to negotiate wholesale pardons for themselves as their price for handing it back. Their success helped stir up the embers of revolt. Armed resistance spread again during the summer and autumn, reaching this time all the way from the north through mid-Wales to the south. Glyn Dŵr's guerrilla tactics—raising his standard of the golden dragon, sacking and burning English settlements, then melting back into the hills whenever English troops appeared on the horizon—were proving desperately difficult to counter.[14]

As a result, English tempers began to fray, and fault lines to emerge between Hotspur and the king. Hotspur, with greater experience as a soldier in the field, could see that the uncompromising suppression of Welsh rights from Westminster was lobbing fuel onto the fire of rebellion in the principality. Henry, with greater experience in the central corridors of power, believed that negotiating terms with individual rebels—as Hotspur just had with the Tudurs—risked encouraging more of their countrymen into direct action. This strategic rift became further entrenched with every passing week because of Hotspur's mounting resentment over money. His costs were mushrooming, while Henry—whose government had already borrowed more than £20,000 in the previous twelve months from lenders including Richard Whittington and other London merchants—was fighting an uphill battle, month after month after month, to reimburse even a fraction of his expenses.[15]

It was not only Hotspur whose disillusionment with England's new government was growing. Just as the king and his council had feared, the violent dislocation of established authority through which Henry had taken the
throne had precipitated a wave of disorder around the country that local officials were struggling to contain. In May 1401, Philip Repingdon, the abbot
of Leicester and one of Henry's close friends, was moved to write to the king
to warn him of the need to act. "Law and justice are exiles from the realm,"
he said. Henry's accession to the throne had been a miracle, a sign of God's
grace, but now "it is the wise who weep, and the depraved who laugh." The
king should bear in mind the lessons of Richard's unhappy example, as well
as his own promise, made when he returned to England in 1399, to protect
each and every one of his subjects, "and if you find the scales of justice to
be on the debit side, consider swiftly, for fear of retribution, how you might
balance them." It was exactly the kind of admonition that would have left
Richard incandescent with fury, but Henry knew his friend was right. It was
just that, buffeted as both king and kingdom were, there was nothing simple
about taking his advice.[16]

The sense that something was wrong—that heaven might no longer be
smiling on Henry's rule—found an echo from the heavens themselves. Harvests in the autumn of 1400 had been poor, and when bad weather continued,
some of Henry's subjects believed they knew where to pin the blame for
high prices and shortages of grain. Relentless rain in March 1402 prompted
a tailor's wife in Hertfordshire to declare that there had not been good or
seasonable weather for even a week since Henry took the throne—a sign,
she said, that he was not the rightful king, and that his reign would not
last half a year more. In the same month, a comet blazed high across the
sky, "spreading terror throughout the world," Adam Usk reported, and in
May and June—by which time floods were wrecking the wool production
on which England's trade with the Continent depended—violent thunder-
storms damaged churches in Essex and Hertfordshire. It was clearly, Thomas
Walsingham noted, the work of the devil.[17]

And if Henry's rule was not righteous, if he had not brought peace
and prosperity to England's people, might God's verdict on Richard yet
be reversed? Rumors were spreading that the former king had not died at

Pontefract but lived still, biding his time until he could reclaim his kingdom. Over the winter, tales of his imminent return had taken concrete shape north of the border in the person of an impostor named Thomas Ward, a kitchen boy newly "recognized" as Richard and welcomed with opportunistic alacrity at the Scots court. There he joined William Serle, a fugitive esquire of Richard's household and one of the small group of men named in the parliament of 1399 as the murderers of Thomas of Woodstock. Serle had forged a copy of the royal signet and was busy dispatching letters announcing the king's resurrection. Jean Creton, sent from Paris to investigate in April 1402, soon confirmed that this rediscovered Richard was a sham, but in England talk of the ex-king's survival continued to grow, carried from place to place by the preaching of itinerant friars. Those who wanted to believe—their numbers inflated, as memories of the old regime faded, by those bitterly disappointed in the new—were emboldened by the groundswell of gossip and speculation.[18]

England's new king, who had seized the throne with such charismatic confidence almost three years earlier, was unmistakably rattled. In May, Henry appointed commissioners in all counties to stamp out lies being told "in taverns and other gatherings of the people" that he had broken his promise to uphold the laws and customs of the kingdom. He did not mention Richard, but the elliptical language his government always used to describe the events of 1399—his promise had been made, the commission said, at "his coming into the realm"—told its own story. During the following weeks, more than a dozen friars were arrested and imprisoned in the Tower. Under interrogation, one of them succinctly articulated the vulnerability of Henry's position: "I do not say that Richard is alive, but I say that *if* he is, he is the rightful king of England." In early June, the friars and a handful of other unfortunates were found guilty of treasonable sedition and dragged to the gallows at Tyburn to be hanged and beheaded. Henry sought to draw a line under the crackdown on June 18 by proclaiming an amnesty for those who had heard the rumors and "innocently" passed them on without intending any treason, but the gesture did little to calm the atmosphere of panic and suspicion.[19]

While Henry tried to pacify England, the crisis in Wales was deepening. Glyn Dŵr was becoming bolder. In April 1402, he ambushed and captured

Reginald Grey, an English nobleman visiting his northern Welsh lordship of Ruthin near the castles of Conwy and Flint. Grey immediately set about negotiating his freedom for the huge sum of 10,000 marks; once he had paid the ransom in full, the rebels would have deep pockets to go with their implacable determination. On June 22, in a brutal engagement in the central Welsh lordship of Powys, Glyn Dŵr took a bigger prize: Hotspur's brother-in-law Edmund Mortimer, uncle of the little earl of March. But to Hotspur's enraged frustration, the king refused to allow Mortimer to be ransomed. What was required, Henry believed, was not a further transfer of resources from the crown to its mutinous Welsh subjects, but a royal campaign to strike down the growing insurrection. He would take command himself, with Prince Henry and the earl of Arundel as his young lieutenants.[20]

It took weeks to muster an army. By the time his troops were finally ready at the end of August, Henry found himself facing the elements rather than the elusive Glyn Dŵr. "From the day he entered the territory of Wales up to the time he left those regions behind, no bright weather ever favored the king," Walsingham reported, "but every single day and night rain mingling with snow and hail so afflicted his army that the men could not endure the rigor of the extreme cold." On September 7, the beleaguered English camp was battered so violently by a storm of wind and a torrential downpour that Henry's tent collapsed on top of him, knocking down his lance, point first, onto his bed. Only the fact that he was sleeping in his armor saved him from serious injury. The campaign had become a humiliating debacle even before the king was forced, yet again, to retreat without having encountered the enemy. Henry's military reputation, burnished in the Lithuanian wilderness, was tarnishing rapidly in the Welsh rain. To his own shock, the golden boy of Saint-Inglevert, the crusading ally of the Teutonic Knights, the man who swept to victory without raising his sword in battle when he landed on England's shores in 1399, had become a harried king in vain pursuit of a rebel leader who seemed capable of vanishing into thin air.

As Henry struggled in the west, Hotspur was in the north showing exactly how formidable a soldier he could be. Now that Scotland housed an unquiet ghost, Richard's looming shadow lent an uncanny edge to Scottish military maneuvers: they were not only joining French attacks on English shipping and attempting to help the Welsh rebels, but sending soldiers of their own deep into northern England. In early September, a Scots army of 10,000 men ranged across Northumberland, plundering the countryside at will right up to the walls of Newcastle. For Hotspur, this was not just English soil ravaged by Scottish troops; it was Percy territory under assault by the forces of the earl of Douglas, his family's greatest rival across the contested frontier. And when Douglas turned his men back toward the river Tweed and home, he found Hotspur waiting for him.[21]

On September 14, on the sweeping rise of Humbleton Hill in the Cheviots fifteen miles south of Berwick, Douglas drew up his troops in defensive phalanxes, hoping to use the high ground to his advantage. But nothing could save them from the English longbows. Hotspur's archers loosed a hail of arrows, a lethal, relentless assault that pinned the Scots in place, piercing helmets and breastplates until they "bristled like hedgehogs," one chronicler reported. Within an hour the Scottish lines gave way, and in minutes the pursuit became an overwhelming rout. Hundreds drowned in the Tweed as they tried to flee. The earl of Douglas took an arrow in the eye before he was seized by the English. Captured too were the earls of Angus, Moray, and Orkney and the son of the duke of Albany, along with a thousand of their men. It was an astonishing victory: not only personal revenge for Hotspur after his own capture by the Scots at Otterburn back in 1388, but—in a kingdom struggling on every front, internal and external—a decisive reversal in the balance of power between England and Scotland.

Under the laws of war, Hotspur was looking forward to collecting large ransoms for these powerful prisoners. At last, he saw a chance to recoup some of the multiplying costs he had so far been unable to retrieve from a government teetering on the edge of insolvency. But Henry—who had abandoned the damp fiasco of his Welsh campaign just as Hotspur triumphed at Humbleton—was more concerned with the Scottish lords' political value as bargaining chips with the regime in Edinburgh, and as collateral to bolster his own credit with the parliament summoned to meet in Westminster at the end of the month. The captives, he said, must not be ransomed, but brought south and handed over to him. For Hotspur, this was both insult and injury. Henry, who had achieved nothing, wished to appropriate his victory and the spoils it had brought. He would comply, but only up to a point. When the most eminent prisoners rode into London under close guard, neither the earl of Douglas nor Hotspur himself was with them.

Waiting in his palace at Westminster, Henry was uneasily aware that the blistering certainties of the summer of 1399—the golden moment at which God had taken the crown from Richard's head and placed it on his own— had been reduced, little by little, to ashes.

Enemies threatened his kingdom within and without. The truce with France was holding, but only just. Privateering in the Channel and the North Sea had become a proxy war between English and French ships. The dukes of Burgundy and Berry were grimly determined not to throw over the entirety of a peace they had worked so hard to construct, but that in turn meant that Louis of Orléans, intent on undermining his uncles' position in his brother's government, had worked his way round to declaring himself France's champion against the English usurper. A letter from Orléans had arrived in London in August challenging his former friend to personal combat with a hundred knights on either side, the loser to become the winner's prisoner. It was a calculated insult, engaging Henry's honor while refusing to recognize his status as king; but in such fraught diplomatic circumstances, the potential for insults to become international incidents could not easily be set aside.[22]

Meanwhile, Wales was a place of devastation, of burned towns and plundered harvests. Unrest was stirring again in Ireland, where Henry had sent his second son, fourteen-year-old Thomas, as lieutenant in November 1401, and in Aquitaine, where Rutland was now serving as the king's deputy. Every front required money, which Henry did not have. Income from these disordered territories had vanished while the costs of defending them soared. In just three months during the summer of 1402, the Exchequer was forced to borrow another £16,000, much of it from London merchants to whom royal plate and jewels were surrendered in pledge for the loans' promised repayment. The king could not cut his vast spending on annuities without compromising the military and political support for which his need remained acute. But, over and over, royal officers tried to explain that they could not do their jobs without adequate funds. Fifteen-year-old Prince Henry—taking command in Wales when his mentor Hotspur marched north—had told his father in May that he would soon be forced into shameful retreat if his troops were not paid. By the autumn, complaints were growing in England about the royal household's habit, on its travels around the kingdom, of taking the provisions it needed and failing to pay for them.[23]

Parliament met at the beginning of October 1402. Anxiety, on all sides, was palpable. The Commons were worried about money, seeking assurances about the king's intention to economize, to prioritize, to repay what he owed. Henry tried to impress them by producing the Scottish prisoners, who knelt before his throne in the White Chamber while the lords and Commons looked on. But the ceremony only served to underscore his debt to the Percies, and to raise uneasy questions about the absence of the greatest captive, Douglas, and his captor Hotspur. It took another month, and a change of treasurer—again, from a trusted friend of Henry's to an experienced servant of Richard's—before the grant of a fifteenth and tenth was forthcoming. Given the depth of the hole in the royal accounts, it was a drop in the ocean; but, given the urgent need to keep troops in the field and sustain royal borrowing, every drop was worth having.[24]

Henry was trying to shore up England's political credit in other ways. After tetchily protracted negotiations, the little ex-queen Isabella had finally been returned to France in July 1401, with her jewels but without her dowry. Dressed all in mourning black, she "scowled with deep hatred for King Henry" when she left London, Adam Usk reported. She was given back to the count of St. Pol in the diplomatic no-man's-land at Leulinghem, while her English ladies—led by Henry's cousin, Robert de Vere's first wife, Philippa de Coucy, and Henry's mother-in-law, the countess of Hereford—wept to see her go. The handover was conducted with extravagant ceremony in a lavish pavilion beside Leulinghem's modest church: a sour reenactment in reverse of the wedding summit that had brought Isabella to England, designed to prevent relations between Paris and London from deteriorating more disastrously than they already had. And while Henry fought to stabilize the truce she had represented, he was seeking out new marriage alliances to reinforce the legitimacy of his regime on the international stage.[25]

It helped that his sisters wore crowns in Portugal and Castile, and farther north Henry found another ruler as much in need of diplomatic recognition as he was. A year after Richard's fall, his hapless former brother-in-law Wenzel of Bohemia had at last been deposed as Holy Roman Emperor, to be replaced by the man Richard had hoped might mastermind his own imperial ambitions, Ruprecht, Count Palatine. In January 1401, Ruprecht wrote to Henry to propose a dynastic alliance between their freshly acquired crowns, and within weeks their envoys had come to terms: the new emperor's son Louis would marry the new king's elder daughter, Blanche. It was not easy to raise the 8,000 marks that made up the first installment of her dowry, but in June 1402, not long after her tenth birthday, the little girl set out for Cologne to meet her twenty-three-year-old husband, taking in her trousseau a crown that had once belonged to Richard's Queen Anne, a delicately wrought golden circlet set with pale sapphires, balas rubies, and clusters of pearls. Henry's family had endured many partings. His reunion with his children in 1399 was a joy on which he had not been able to depend until he took the decision to defy Richard and claim the throne for himself. Now Blanche, facing the future as the daughter of an embattled king, accepted her royal duty with a grace and composure that delighted the imperial court. "Most serene prince," Louis wrote to Henry after the wedding, "I know not how to thank you fully for so rich and rare a gift."[26]

Blanche had been first in order of precedence among the ladies of her father's kingdom. She left behind a younger sister to take her place, but Philippa, who turned eight just as Blanche said her goodbyes, would spend much less time sitting at Henry's left hand. Before the end of 1402, the little girl was betrothed to Eric, heir to the thrones of Denmark, Norway, and Sweden, although it was agreed that she would stay with her father until she was nearer the age at which the marriage could take effect. And by the time the diplomatic deal was done, it was clear that she would shortly acquire a new stepmother, and England a new queen. Henry had decided to marry again.[27]

Since the confrontations of 1399, amid ongoing war in Wales and the marches of Scotland, and in contrast to the fastidious style of Richard's court, Henry's household had been soldierly in its culture. It did not lack sophistication or recreation: Henry had always lived in luxury, and had no intention of compromising the splendor of his crown, however empty his treasury might become. Building was under way at Eltham to provide the king with new royal apartments, including a chamber filled with colored light from stained-glass windows in which crowns were scattered among birds, exotic beasts, and the forget-me-nots of his youth. He commissioned a private study to house his books. His musicians were in constant attendance. But, as had been the case in Prussia, Jerusalem, and Paris, Henry spent most of his time in the company of his Lancastrian friends and retainers, men he knew he could trust with his life.[28]

He was a good judge of character. Despite the constant parliamentary tensions over his finances, there was no public criticism of his friends in terms of their motives, their integrity, their influence on the king, or their service to the crown. Their comradeship and advice sustained him both personally and politically. Hugh Waterton, Henry's chamberlain of the duchy of Lancaster, still oversaw the upbringing of his younger children. Gaunt's old friend Thomas Erpingham, the under-chamberlain of the royal household, was constable of Dover Castle, warden of the Cinque Ports, and a knight of the Garter along with Thomas Rempston, the constable of the Tower and of Nottingham Castle, who also served as admiral in the west. The devoted John Pelham was not only a knight of Henry's chamber, but appointed sword-bearer to the king. These were able, levelheaded servants of both dynasty and realm, who were required to give Henry the benefit of their experience rather than telling him what they thought he wanted to hear. Philip Repingdon, the abbot of Leicester, had become even closer to the king since writing his excoriating letter about the state of the realm in 1401, so much so that Henry appointed him his confessor. And men who had served Richard were not excluded from Henry's favor, if they too were prepared to offer him their loyalty and their talents. Former knights of Richard's chamber such as Arnold Savage, a landowner from Kent whose father had served the Black Prince, or the Cheshire soldier John Stanley, had decades of military and diplomatic experience between them, and were rapidly finding a foothold within the new regime. Henry placed the two men in the household of his son the prince of Wales. It was possible that, from the time they had shared in Richard's household, Savage and Stanley by now knew the prince better than his father did.[29]

In private, the king was not without some discreetly managed female company. He took care to provide for an illegitimate son, Edmund, born to an unmarried woman in London in 1401, directing that the boy should be educated for a career in the Church. He had no need of more legitimate children: his four sons and three Beaufort brothers were already a royal throng at the head of what he hoped would become a new Lancastrian nobility. But for years his environment had been overwhelmingly male. Since Mary's death in 1394, Lucia Visconti in Milan had been the only serious candidate to become his wife, and after his exile in 1398 she had been promised elsewhere. With one daughter gone to Germany, the other betrothed to a husband across the North Sea, and Henry's stepmother, Katherine Swynford, living out her widowhood in luxurious retirement at Lincoln, England's court lacked a queen—and Henry, it turned out, had a bride in mind.[30]

Joan of Navarre was the widow of John de Montfort, the duke of Brittany who had long ago grown up in England with Gaunt, and who died three weeks after Henry's coronation. Her father and brother were rulers of the Pyrenean kingdom of Navarre. Through her mother she was the French king's first cousin, and niece of the dukes of Burgundy and Berry. Her royal blood made her a worthy consort, and her role as regent for her young son offered the tantalizing hope that the old alliance between England and Brittany might be revived, even if it also meant that French opposition to the match would be all but inevitable. But Henry's choice was not just a matter of strategy. He had had a home with Mary, and he had seen the support Katherine Swynford brought to his father's life; he had learned the value of loving companionship. At thirty-three, Joan was intelligent, cultured, and warm, with an extraordinary breadth of political experience. She and Henry had met several times during her years as Brittany's duchess, most recently on a brief visit to England with her husband in 1398, and evidently enjoyed each other's company. In February 1400, the new widow wrote to the king in strikingly affectionate terms, asking after the well-being of her "dearest and most honoured lord and cousin, that it may very often please you to let me know the certainty thereof, for the greatest comfort and gladness of my heart."[31]

The delicacy of political relations between Brittany and France, and between France and England, meant that when Henry sent envoys to open negotiations for the match in December 1401, he did so in secret. Joan, meanwhile, set about reaching a settlement in Brittany by which her twelve-year-old son was crowned as duke on March 23, 1402. Ten days later, she and Henry were married by proxy in a ceremony that took place behind closed doors at Eltham. The news could not be contained much longer: during that febrile summer, one of the rumors circulating in England claimed that Henry was taking treasure from his subjects in order to leave for a new life with the duchess in Brittany. There was nothing speculative, however, about the response from Paris. The duke of Burgundy arrived in Nantes in October to take guardianship of both the regency of the duchy and Joan's three sons. If Henry had hoped to extend English influence in Brittany, the great lords of France were determined to block his path.

But Joan was free to leave, and in January 1403, after a storm-lashed voyage from the Breton coast, she landed at Falmouth with her two young daughters. At their lavish wedding in Winchester Cathedral three weeks later, Henry's gift to his bride was a golden collar of *S*s, worked with forget-me-nots and studded with diamonds, rubies, sapphires, and pearls. The intricately spiced courses of the feast that followed were punctuated by elaborate sugar sculptures, including one in the form of a crowned eagle. When the royal couple approached the capital, the citizens of London came to welcome their new queen at Blackheath with minstrels and pageants, and on February 26 Joan was crowned in Westminster Abbey, attended by the nobles of England in a blaze of cloth of gold and candlelight. The money to pay for the gorgeous ceremonies had somehow been found. The crown might be almost bankrupt, but the magnificent style of the king's court, reflecting as it did the earthly authority entrusted to him by God, could not be allowed to falter.[32]

The magnificent personnel of the king's court, on the other hand—the nobility of England gathered around their sovereign—were a noticeably diminished band after the traumas of the past six years. Henry's lone remaining uncle, Edmund of Langley, the last of Edward III's sons, had died in August

1402 at the age of sixty-one. The only surviving peers of Langley's generation, men with political memories reaching back into the reign of Henry's grand-father, were the Percy brothers, the earls of Northumberland and Worcester. In Henry's own generation, the relationship between Northumberland's heir Hotspur—who did not accompany his father to the queen's coronation—and the king's brother-in-law Ralph Neville, earl of Westmorland, was freighted with their rivalry on the northern border. Edward of Rutland, the new duke of York in succession to his father, Langley, was a few years younger and hundreds of miles away, demonstrating his loyalty as Henry's lieutenant in Aquitaine.[33]

Otherwise, most of England's earls were young men, barely tested or completely untried. Some—the heirs of the rebels John and Thomas Holand and the earl of Salisbury—would need to prove their allegiance as they grew, if their forfeited estates were one day to be restored. But others were begin-ning to show promise in royal service: the earl of Arundel, who had been at Henry's side since Paris; the earl of Stafford, husband of Woodstock's daughter and heir; and the dashing new earl of Warwick, twenty-one-year-old Richard Beauchamp, who fought with flair as the queen's champion at the coronation jousts. And while they gained experience, Henry could look to the support of his brothers—John and Thomas Beaufort as soldiers and courtiers, Henry Beaufort as a man of the Church—and his four growing sons.[34]

There were some grounds for hope, then, as Henry and Joan spent the first weeks of their marriage among the books and gardens of Eltham, sur-rounded by the music they both loved. But the king's rift with Hotspur over the fate of the Scottish prisoners had not yet been mended, and Henry was preoccupied with finding a resolution that would sustain both Hotspur's loy-alty and his own authority. Four days after his wife's coronation, he made an audacious move, claiming possession of the Scottish earldom of Douglas for the English crown and granting it to Hotspur's father, Northumberland, as a reward for their labors in the north. The Percies would have to fight to annex these Scottish lands, but the plan that they should do so for themselves in the name of their king had a great deal to recommend it. South of the border, however, Henry's need to look to his kingdom's future meant that, while he gave to the Percies with one hand, he was taking away with the other. On April 1, he removed Hotspur and Worcester as his royal lieutenants in north and south Wales, giving command of the whole principality to his eldest son, Prince Henry, who had turned sixteen the previous autumn.[35]

Hotspur had struggled for three and a half years to defend Henry's authority in Wales without adequate support or resources, only to be demoted and replaced by a teenager. It remained to be seen whether title to the not-yet-conquered Scottish lands of the captured earl of Douglas would be sufficient compensation. Henry's relationship with the Percy heir was trapped, it seemed, in an acute iteration of the vicious circle with which he had struggled from the start of his rule: he was forced to lean on Hotspur more heavily than he would have chosen, had he had more widespread support or faced less widespread resistance; but, given the extent of that reliance, what reward for Hotspur's service could ever be enough?

Behind those questions lay a deeper unease. Edmund Mortimer, uncle of the earl of March, had been a prisoner of Owain Glyn Dŵr since June 1402. Since then, Henry's Welsh campaign had been a sodden failure, and by October the king and council had come to believe rumors that Mortimer had colluded in his own capture. Whether or not that was true, Henry's refusal to approve his ransom produced the same outcome. At the end of November 1402, Mortimer married Glyn Dŵr's daughter Catherine. Two weeks later, he wrote to his followers in the mid-Welsh marches announcing the withdrawal of his allegiance to Henry and support for his new father-in-law's cause: "if King Richard is alive, to restore him to his crown, and if not, that my honoured nephew, who is the right heir to the said crown, should be king of England, and that the said Owain should have his right in Wales." Not only was Mortimer now Glyn Dŵr's son-in-law, but his sister was Hotspur's wife. Could Mortimer's defection pave the way to a greater betrayal?[36]

Sixteen

1403-1406

meteors of a troubled heaven

Trust—or the lack of it—was the heart of the issue. Henry and Hotspur were intelligent men who recognized each other's talents and capabilities, but they did not know each other well. They had been comrades and competitors in the jousts at Saint-Inglevert, but in the decade since then they had barely been in each other's company. Henry had left England for Prussia and the Holy Land, and by the time he came home, Hotspur was serving in Aquitaine, then Ireland and Calais, before returning to the marches of Scotland. They had joined forces in 1399, but their new responsibilities thereafter meant that their physical separation continued. One English chronicler invented a face-to-face altercation over Henry's refusal to ransom Hotspur's brother-in-law Mortimer from the rebels who had taken him prisoner in Wales. "Shall a man spend his good, and put himself in peril for you and your realm," Hotspur angrily demands, "and you will not help him in his need?" "Thou art a traitor!" Henry responds. "Wilt thou that I should succour my enemies, and enemies of the realm?" The scene neatly encapsulated the essence of a bitter argument that—in fact rather than dramatic imagination—might have been easier to resolve had they not spent most of their time hundreds of miles apart.[1]

As it was, the distance between them left Henry hearing Hotspur's complaints as the simplistic response of a soldier to the intractable complexities with which he was dealing at Westminster, and Hotspur dismissing Henry's orders as the evasions of a king too busy luxuriating in the company of his new wife to understand the implacable realities of war. All the same, Henry had good reason not to reach for rash accusations of treachery. A usurper could never take loyalty for granted, but suspicion of his nobles was a luxury he could not afford to indulge. He knew that Richard's toxic paranoia had ended up consuming his kingship, and Henry was facing too many threats with the support of too few powerful lieutenants to sideline any of them on the basis of unproven fears. Hotspur had not come south with his father, Northumberland, for the last parliament or for the queen's coronation, but in the spring of 1403 Henry knew that he was heading north, riding with his men across the Scottish border in a bid to take possession of the earldom of Douglas. It was a mission in which the interests of the Percy family coincided entirely with those of the Lancastrian crown, and in such circumstances there was no advantage in openly doubting the allegiance of a man who had so far been an indispensable prop of Henry's regime.[2]

In Wales, meanwhile, there was a new lieutenant to step into the breach, one whose loyalty was beyond question. At sixteen, Prince Henry was emerging from Hotspur's shadow as a precociously able commander, a leader shaped by an upbringing that was dramatically different from Henry's own. As heir to the duchy of Lancaster, the king had had a chance to be young. He had traveled for pleasure, and for his own education; he had made his name on the tournament field long before his military skills had been tested on campaign; and by the time he was sixteen he had already married the girl who would become his son's mother. But the prince's childhood had been cut short by Mary's sudden death. In the wake of that loss, the peculiarities of Richard's relationship with the Lancastrian dynasty had left young Henry isolated from his siblings, detached not only by the weight of his future responsibilities, but because during his father's exile he had been taken from under his family's wing into the tense, rarefied, and increasingly unpredictable surroundings of Richard's royal household.

Then, in 1399, his future had changed out of all recognition. Now his responsibilities as heir to the Lancastrian throne weighed heavy on his present. Like his mentor Hotspur, who had first seen battle in the Scottish marches at the age of fourteen, the prince was by training and temperament a soldier:

a fighter, not a jouster, with no time for leisurely amusements or carefree extravagance. He was focused and fiercely independent, already profoundly frustrated with a regime hamstrung by its structural lack of financial and political credit, but determined to bring the utmost rigor to the war against Glyn Dŵr, the traitor who dared lay claim to his own title as prince of Wales.[3]

That spring he made some headway, relieving pressure on Harlech and Aberystwyth in the west and burning Glyn Dŵr's estates in the north of the principality at Glyndyfrdwy and at Sycharth, "where we thought we should have found him," the prince reported, ". . . but on our arrival there we found nobody." But if Glyn Dŵr could not be found, he could not be stopped. By the beginning of July, his rebels were on the move again, tearing through south Wales, occupying Carmarthen Castle and besieging the fortresses of Kidwelly and Brecon. While the prince desperately tried to raise funds from his base at Shrewsbury, the presence of the king was needed urgently, one of Henry's most trusted servants wrote in anguish from Hereford on July 8: "For God's love, my liege lord, think on yourself and your estate, or by my troth all is lost else."[4]

The king was thinking hard, but for now the prince would have to hold Wales by himself. Henry's anxieties were focused on the north of England. As ever, he did not have the money Hotspur and his father needed to pay their troops there; what he had instead were nagging doubts about the nature of Hotspur's maneuvers on the border. He knew that Percy forces were besieging Cocklaw near Hawick in Teviotdale—a garrisoned tower but by no means a target of crucial strategic significance. He also knew that in Hotspur's company on this campaign to seize Douglas lands was the captive earl of Douglas himself. Something did not add up.[5]

In the short term, however, there was little Henry could do to intervene or even investigate, since his presence was required in the south while bad-tempered talks with France took place at Leulinghem over the precarious state of the Anglo-French truce. As the king waited, the earl of Northumberland sent word that Hotspur had come to an arrangement with Cocklaw's defenders under the chivalric laws of war. Given that the siege had reached a stalemate, he had suspended his attack until August 1 to allow the garrison to appeal for help from their king. If, by that date, a Scots army did not arrive to confront the English, Cocklaw would be surrendered into Hotspur's hands. It was an agreement that engaged the honor, as well as the security, of both kingdoms, and the government in Edinburgh was already raising troops; it seemed the forces of Scotland might meet the forces of England in pitched battle at last. As soon as the truce with France was formally reconfirmed on June 27, Henry made hurried preparations to ride north.

On July 12, he was at Nottingham, a hundred miles into his journey, when news came that changed everything. Henry's instincts had been right. Hotspur was no longer in Scotland. The siege of Cocklaw had been a cover for military operations that he planned to unleash on a different target. He had won his name because his decisions were always bold, his movements swift, his instinct always to attack—and now, with the earl of Douglas still at his side, he had marched his men more than 150 miles south to Chester, the loyalist heartland of the old regime. There Richard was a living ghost, and Hotspur had declared for this dead king walking. The same English chronicler gave him a speech to sum up his alienation from Henry: "We brought thee in against King Richard, and now thou rulest worse than did he. Thou spoilest yearly the realm with taxes and tallages, thou payest no man, thou holdest no house, thou art not heir of the realm; and therefore, as I have hurt the realm by bringing in of thee, I will help to reform it."[6]

Thousands were rallying to his banner, many of them Cheshire archers wearing their old badges of the white hart—a reanimation of the past through which Hotspur intended to make his nephew the little earl of March into a king for England's future. For Henry, that prospect raised a worse terror still: that he might be in league with Glyn Dŵr and Edmund Mortimer, planning an assault on the realm from the north and the west simultaneously. Already certain was the treachery of Hotspur's uncle Thomas Percy, earl of Worcester, a former steward of the royal household to both Richard and Henry, and now, as tutor of the prince of Wales, serving in young Henry's army. When Hotspur and his troops began to march south from Chester toward Shrewsbury, aiming to eliminate the heir to the throne and the soldiers he commanded there before the king could react, Worcester and his retinue deserted the prince's camp to join them.

Worcester's defection was a shattering blow—but Henry had in store an ambush of his own. In 1399, he had won the kingdom by raising his standard, not his sword, and since then his reputation as a soldier had taken a hammering in the mists and mountains of Wales. But he was still the leader he had always been. His son and his crown were under attack by traitors, men who believed that they had made a king once and could do so again. But Henry had faith, even if the Percies did not, in the legitimacy of his kingship, in the irretrievable choice he had made in 1399. Since hearing of Hotspur's betrayal, Henry had not wasted a moment, moving west at speed from Nottingham through Derbyshire and Staffordshire to Shropshire. When Hotspur made his rendezvous with Worcester outside the walls of Shrewsbury on July 20 they discovered, in shock, that the king and his men were already there.[7]

There would be no confrontation that night. Both armies withdrew, Hotspur's to the northwest of Shrewsbury, Henry's to the northeast, to make camp and wait for day. The next morning, in the haze of the early sun, the two sides drew up their positions in open country a couple of miles north of the town. An attempt at parleying for peace came to nothing. Henry knew he had to crush this assault from within his own regime if his kingship was to survive. Hotspur, fighting in the name of a dead king to take the crown for his own nephew, knew his life depended on ending Henry's. Never had the years of struggle with Richard come to this: to pitched battle inside the realm of England. Back in 1387, Radcot Bridge had been a skirmish that became a rout. Otherwise, that conflict had played itself out as a lethal form of political theater in court and parliament, on the scaffold and in the lists. Now two English armies, matched like-for-like in weapons, skills, and tactics, confronted each other in the field. There would be no ransoms, no intervention of the laws of chivalry. This was a fight for survival: victory for one side, obliteration for the other. Henry and Hotspur led the central divisions. Ahead of them in command of the van, the young earl of Stafford faced the earl of Douglas, Hotspur's prisoner-turned-ally, fighting one-eyed after his injury at Humbleton almost a year earlier. Prince Henry—at sixteen, a decade younger even than Stafford—led the rear guard for his father. His opponent, the sixty-year-old earl of Worcester, had been his tutor until just forty-eight hours before.

From both sides there was silence, then a shout; arms readied, bows

raised. Another moment and the arrows came, shadowing the sun, scream-
ing in flight, death unleashed in two directions, wave after wave of steel that
sliced through metal, leather, flesh, and bone. Stafford tried to urge his soldiers on, but the fields ahead were thickly sown with peas, the plants ready for
harvest, stems and tendrils intertwined, coiling round limbs, snaring feet and
hands. His men were faltering even before Stafford himself fell dead. As the
front lines of the royal army broke and scattered, Douglas pushed his troops
forward, Hotspur leading his soldiers close behind. Their target was the king.
Henry's veteran standard-bearer, his father's close friend Walter Blount,
was one of two doppelgängers wearing the royal arms as a decoy. Both were
hacked down in the mêlée. After the deadly assault of the longbows, the
close fighting was brutal: exhausted men gasping for air, the wounded falling
among hundreds of corpses piled high on the darkened earth. Douglas took
the sharp edge of a blade in the soft place where the plates of his armor met
at his groin, severing part of his scrotum. Prince Henry, raising his visor at an
unlucky moment, caught the staggering impact of an arrow full in the face. It
lodged under his eye, six inches deep, but adrenaline and the brute force of his
will kept the boy on his feet: he snapped off the shaft and refused to leave his
father or his men. The king had dropped back in an attempt to draw Hotspur
on, and with nerveless self-control the wounded prince led a counterattack
to surround the enemy position. "Harry Percy king!" the rebels shouted, until,
in response, came a different cry: "Harry Percy's dead!" Hotspur's military
prowess had not saved him in the murderous press. Worcester and the injured
Douglas were taken. The revolt was over.[8]

Henry wept when he saw Hotspur's corpse. His grief was real, for the
death of a fine soldier, and the shattering blow to his own hopes that England might unite around his crown. There was gratitude too, that in this
trial by combat God had vindicated his kingship. But vindication did not
mean the danger was over. On Henry's orders, Hotspur's body was propped
between two millstones in Shrewsbury's market square to forestall rumors
of his survival. Worcester—who shed tears of a different kind when he saw
his dead nephew—was executed as a traitor and his head sent south to be
set upon London Bridge. Three weeks later at York, where Hotspur's rotting head now stared down from the city gate, his father, Northumberland,

met the king to submit to Henry's royal mercy. In a fraught exchange, the earl disclaimed any knowledge of the entire conspiracy: his son's treason, his brother's betrayal, or the suggestion that both had been in covert communication with Glyn Dŵr and Mortimer in Wales. Henry did not believe him—but, all the same, Northumberland was not so easily dispensed with. The Percies held the north. If the Percies were removed, would the north fall?[9]

For the moment, the king chose to reserve his royal judgment. Northumberland would be tried when parliament met. In the meantime, his estates would be administered by the steward of Henry's household, and his castles in the north taken into the king's hands. In case further warning were needed, a hermit named William Norham, who had once been imprisoned by Richard for his ill-advised prophecies, offered new observations to Henry at York, saying that he was not lawfully king and should give up the crown. Norham's head soon joined Hotspur's on the city walls. While Northumberland was taken under guard to the midlands, Henry turned west, marching into Wales in September to relieve Carmarthen Castle and make yet another attempt to hunt down Glyn Dŵr. But the truth was that the principality was slipping through his fingers. Civilian government was collapsing; no revenues could be collected or courts held. The revolt had become a hydra-headed threat that Henry, his resources stretched to breaking point, could not contain. Even worse, reports were surfacing of the presence in south Wales of a company of 200 French troops, come to lend their support to the rebels. By the time the king withdrew again to Hereford on October 3, it was chillingly clear that his project of demonstrating the legitimacy of his rule through the peace and justice it brought had run into the ground.[10]

God had blessed him on the battlefield, but even that verdict had been tainted by fear. Prince Henry had been taken from Shrewsbury to the Lancastrian castle at Kenilworth for treatment of his injury. He was lucky not just to be alive, but still to be able to see and speak. The broken end of the arrow's shaft had been pulled carefully out of his face, but the barbed arrowhead was lodged in the bone at the back of his skull. If he were to survive, it would somehow have to be removed without causing catastrophic damage or infection. Skilled physicians tried to extract it with medicines and ointments, but soon it was obvious that the king's surgeon, John Bradmore, would have to be summoned from London.[11]

At Kenilworth, Bradmore devised an extraordinary treatment. First, he dilated the wound using pads of elderwood pith covered with linen and dipped in rose honey, a substance that served both to prevent infection and to delay the healing process. Once the space was enlarged to the full width of the buried arrowhead, Bradmore inserted an implement he had designed and made specially for the purpose: narrow metal tongs, curved from side to side so that, when closed together, they formed a hollow tube to fit into the arrowhead's empty socket where the shaft had once been. Through this tube he passed a screw that pushed the sides of the tongs outward against the socket with enough purchase to give him a chance of loosening the metal from the bone. "Then," he wrote later in his notes on the case, "by moving it to and fro, little by little, with the help of God I extracted the arrowhead."

Even then, the prince's salvation was not assured. It took twenty more days for the open wound to heal. Bradmore was meticulous in his care, using wine to rinse out the lesion and more pads—of decreasing size this time, made antiseptic with honey and turpentine oil—to ensure that it closed slowly and safely, upward from the bottom to the surface. His patient's courage was astonishing. The prince's capacity to endure agonizing pain and to wait for the long weeks of treatment to take their course would have been extraordinary in a hardened soldier, let alone a sixteen-year-old in the aftermath of his first pitched battle. When Bradmore pronounced himself satisfied, God's judgment was clear. The Lancastrian crown might have received heaven's blessing, but the heir to the Lancastrian throne, his face now scarred forever, had been marked for a very special destiny indeed.

The young prince was not the only one who saw God's hand at work in the world. In Paris, Louis of Orléans had spent the first months of 1403 maneuvering to take control of his brother's government from their aging uncles. As the periods of Charles's lucidity grew briefer and his incoherence more overwhelming, Orléans believed it was his own God-given birthright to rule France in the king's place—and, in so doing, to restore the kingdom's honor by reopening the war with England. He was now convinced that the duke of Burgundy's commitment to peace stemmed from a determination at all costs to protect his private interests in Flanders rather than the good of France itself. Orléans, on the other hand, was eager to strike at a divided England in both Calais and Aquitaine—the latter a region where he was seeking to build up his own territorial power—while distancing himself once and for all from the allegation that he had colluded in Henry's usurpation. By the end of June, even as the Anglo-French truce was republished after the ill-tempered negotiations at Leulinghem, Orléans was making concerted preparations for a major military campaign the following spring. In the meantime, ships from French-dominated Brittany were pulling at the ragged edges of the peace by harrying English vessels in the Channel and subjecting England's southwestern coast to the worst raids for more than two decades. In August, while Henry was dealing with the earl of Northumberland in the north, the Bretons burned and looted Plymouth before disappearing back to sea, stopping off to plunder the islands of Guernsey and Jersey on their way home.[12]

As his power grew, Orléans was becoming more bombastic and more extravagantly unpredictable. Yet another provocative missive arrived in London in October, this one so bizarre in its rhetoric—the duke defying Henry by declaring himself the champion not only of his niece, Richard's little queen, but of all Frenchwomen—that even the clerk of the Paris *parlement* was moved to note that it was "prolix and windy, without profit or judgement." But Henry could afford neither to dismiss Orléans's posturing, nor to respond intemperately to his gibes. As the king sought to defend the coast by unleashing English privateers against the Breton fleet, a second letter of defiance arrived, this time from the count of St. Pol, Richard's former brother-in-law, who was now captain of the French forces permanently stationed outside Calais. St. Pol had already ordered a blockade of the town; in November, he sailed south to impose another cordon around the English city of Bordeaux in Aquitaine, before returning to launch an attack on the Isle of Wight in December.[13]

Henry's Christmas was frantic with planning against imminent threats that could not be seen from Westminster with any kind of clarity. His parliament, meeting there in the middle of January 1404, was not impressed by his efforts. When the chancellor, his brother Henry Beaufort, asked for a tax from his loyal subjects with which to confront these massing dangers, the response of the Commons was sharp. Their Speaker, Arnold Savage, did not hold back. The king had income enough, Savage said, from the revenues of the crown and the duchy of Lancaster and the duties on the wool trade. He should therefore not expect a subsidy "until we know how the king's wealth has been spent, and in what manner." Henry replied that he was "greatly amazed" at their recalcitrance—an amazement fueled by the fact that Savage himself now sat on the royal council and Henry had therefore hoped that he might help represent the king to the Commons rather than the other way round. But the Speaker was uncowed. The king's subjects were much harassed by royal expenses and financial demands, he declared, "and for this reason may it please you . . . to order your affairs in the way that your Commons outline to your council, and then you will enjoy peace and quiet within your realm."[14]

This was exactly the kind of exchange that Richard had seen as a full-blown threat to his sovereignty: the Commons daring to suppose that they might dictate the way money they supplied should be spent. Even Henry, hard-pressed as he was, found it difficult to take with any equanimity. He did not appear at the assembly for the next five or six days, instead sending his chancellor and treasurer to explain, yet again, his acute need for funds. But his absence was the result of an intense and careworn frustration, not Richard's murderous rage. He knew that to focus his anger on his critics in parliament—loyalists asking, however troublesomely, that their king should rule them well—would be to mistake his enemy. With stiff formality he returned on January 28 to take his throne among his lords. It took almost five weeks of strained negotiation, but by March 1 a deal was reached.[15]

The grant of taxation, when it came, was of a novel kind—on landed income as well as property—that must leave no trace in the records of parliament or exchequer, the Commons said, so that it should set no precedent for the future. The proceeds would be handed to four war treasurers, to be spent only on the defense of the realm. The royal household, meanwhile, would receive a set payment of just over £12,000 for each of the next two years—not even a third of its annual running costs of £42,000, but all that the Commons would sanction. In return, the king agreed that for the first time he would nominate the members of his council formally in parliament—a new form of scrutiny rather than control, but a significant concession nonetheless—and that the size of his household should be reduced and its composition over-hauled. Crisis in parliament was averted, albeit at the price of continuing uncertainty. The new form of the tax made its revenues impossible to predict, but they were unlikely to scratch the surface of royal debts, which included months of unpaid wages to front-line troops in Wales and the beleaguered garrison at Calais.

Not only that, but fears of military disintegration were magnified by the complex fractures in the body politic exposed by Hotspur's treason. The Commons, anxious about security in the north, petitioned for the earl of Northumberland's rehabilitation, despite the questions that hung over his complicity in his son's revolt. At the same time, disturbing rumors were cir-culating that other lords might have known of Hotspur's conspiracy, includ-ing both Archbishop Arundel and Edward of Rutland, who had returned from Aquitaine in time to serve in Wales the previous autumn. Here too Henry managed to find a way to paper over the cracks. In parliament on February 8 Northumberland was found guilty only of minor offenses against the statute of liveries, and the king immediately pardoned him the fine for that trespass. In turn the earl then declared "in peril of his soul" that, to his knowledge, Rutland and the archbishop—who had already protested fiercely at this "malevolent slander"—were loyal and true. Why exactly the earl might be a key witness to the personnel of a plot in which he had not been involved remained delicately unexamined.[16]

The next day, for the third time in recent months, the lords spiritual and temporal knelt before Henry one by one to renew their oath of allegiance to him and to the heirs of the Lancastrian succession, "to live and die against all persons in the world." They did so in honor of the Trinity, the rolls of parlia-ment explained, and "although there was no need"—words that did nothing to dispel the sense that Henry was hoping a tripled oath might somehow bring him greater security once the assembly was done. The same day, the king oversaw a formal reconciliation between Northumberland and the man who had displaced him as the crown's lieutenant in the north, Ralph Neville, earl of Westmorland, the husband of Henry's sister Joan Beaufort and the new warden of the West March alongside the king's fourteen-year-old son, John, in the east. The two earls took hands and exchanged the kiss of peace three times, "expelling all malice and rancor from their hearts, if there were any," the clerks noted with bright and implausible optimism.

If this was performance without conviction, it was still better than the alternative. Shortly after the parliament ended, Robert de Vere's fifty-nine-year-old mother, the dowager countess of Oxford, was arrested for her part in a recently discovered conspiracy of Ricardian loyalists. They had spent the winter planning to greet the invading fleet of the count of St. Pol on the beaches of Essex, and to reinstate the former king, who, they believed, was still living in exile at the Scottish court. Richard, of course, had not arrived, nor had St. Pol and his ships. For now, Henry was prepared to see the countess and her accomplices, three local abbots, as dupes of the white hart rather than irreconcilable traitors. But in June 1404 the man who had drawn them into this bungled plot—William Serle, the former esquire of Richard's household now resident at the Scottish court—ventured south of the border, hoping for support from Percy retainers holding out in the frontier town of Berwick who had not yet reconciled themselves to Hotspur's fall. It was a mistake. Serle found himself a prisoner, handed over to the king by the Percy diehards in exchange for a royal amnesty. Under interrogation he admitted that the "Richard" for whom the countess of Oxford had been waiting, thanks to his own letters written from Scotland under the forged royal signet, was an impostor. That confession would have been enough to seal his fate, even without his previously established guilt in the murder of Thomas of Woodstock. Brought by long-drawn-out stages from Yorkshire through Lincolnshire, East Anglia, Essex, and Hertfordshire to London, Serle was publicly hanged in every major town along the way and cut down again while still alive, to face the same torture in the next market square, and the next. Not until he reached the capital's public gallows at Tyburn did he finally meet the horrors of a traitor's end: hanging, evisceration, and only then death by decapitation.[17]

This hideously extended execution—"pains more severe than other traitors heretofore," as Henry acknowledged—was designed to impress upon his people's minds not only the fate of rebels but the fact that the king Serle had claimed to serve was no more than a phantom. Any relief at the prospect that Richard might now lie quieter in his grave, however, was short-lived. By the end of August, when Serle's head at last looked sightlessly down from London Bridge, the threat from a dead king had once again been overtaken by that of a live Welsh prince—or so Glyn Dŵr had called himself when he sent an embassy to Paris in May to propose a formal alliance between France and Wales. The French—who were now led without challenge by Louis of Orléans, after the death of the duke of Burgundy in April—greeted the Welsh envoys with magnificent honor, and wasted no time in drawing up a bond of friendship, sealed on June 14, by which both sides would do their utmost to destroy "Henry of Lancaster" and all who followed him.[18]

Since then, intensifying raids on England's south coast had been driven off with significant French losses, and English freebooters were returning their attacks in kind, descending on the shores of Brittany, Normandy, and Picardy "like a swarm of insects," reported the chronicler at Saint-Denis. But in Wales Glyn Dŵr seemed unstoppable. The besieged English garrison at Caernarfon in the north, reduced now to fewer than thirty men, was holding on by a thread. The same was true at Cardiff in the south. In between, as the year wore on, Harlech and Aberystwyth fell, and Kidwelly was looted and burned. The incursions of Glyn Dŵr's men across the border into Shropshire became so devastating that in August Henry was forced to give the county permission to negotiate directly with the rebels for a three-month local truce. Meanwhile, Glyn Dŵr himself—"Owain, by the grace of God prince of Wales," as he told the French—summoned his own parliament to meet at Machynlleth, fifteen miles northeast of Aberystwyth. For Henry, these were humiliations as well as dangers: manifestations of his failure to defend his people while the rebel upstart impersonated his majesty. And his capacity to respond was profoundly constrained, in part by the fact that his son, the prince whose title Glyn Dŵr was usurping, had only just returned to Wales after his long and difficult convalescence, but also—as always—by lack of money. Prince Henry had barely set foot in the principality before he wrote to tell his father he was having to pledge his own silver plate in the attempt to pay his soldiers, while the council, given urgent instructions by the king to send the prince some cash, explained in anxious detail that they had no idea how to raise any more.[19]

There was no choice but to call another English parliament, this time to Coventry in October 1404. The king did what he could to ensure a more cooperative meeting. The city was surrounded by the midland estates of Henry's duchy of Lancaster and of his son's earldom of Chester: for those who cared to see, there were faint and distant echoes of the parliament of 1397 sitting encircled by Richard's Cheshire archers. Not only that, but the king had forbidden the election of any lawyers to the Commons, ostensibly because they took up parliamentary time with their clients' private business, but also in the unspoken hope that a less forensically educated assembly might prove more politically tractable.[20]

This time too, it rapidly became apparent that Henry had come prepared to say what they wanted to hear. Their point, as always, was that the king had financial resources of his own, if only he were prepared to use them to the full. Now Henry agreed that all royal grants of land and revenue belonging to the crown that had been made since 1366, the year before his birth, should be examined by a specially appointed commission to see if they could be taken back into the king's hands. He also put his seal to an order that everyone receiving an annuity from the king should waive the current year of that income. The latter was the formalization of a measure already forced on Henry by his empty treasury, since the payment of annuities at the Exchequer had been stopped for lack of money in July—a dangerous circumstance, given how much he was currently having to rely on his retainers for military service, but one that, if it could not be avoided, might at least be turned to political advantage. The strategy worked. In return, the representatives of his realm at last agreed to open their purses. Since March, the new subsidy granted at Westminster had produced less than £10,000, a sum that had disappeared as fast as it was collected. Now they offered two fifteenths and tenths, two more years of the wool subsidy, and a tax of 5 percent on landed incomes above £333 a year, grants that came to a hefty total, and all reserved for the defense of the realm.

Henry's promises were easier to make than they would be to keep. Whatever the review of almost forty years of crown grants might conclude, he still could not afford to maximize his revenues at the expense of political and military support among his lords and retainers by taking money, land, and office out of their hands. He therefore began to issue exemptions from the proposed clawback as soon as the first documents were produced for inspection. But the Commons—free of suspicious legal minds as this "Unlearned Parliament" was—had given him the benefit of the doubt. The tax began to roll in, while his impressive and implacable son took a firm grip on military operations in Wales. Ambitious plans were under way for the defense of the Channel and the relief of Bordeaux. For Henry, spending Christmas with his queen in the comfort of the royal apartments at Eltham, it was a chance to wonder whether the rising tide that had threatened to drown him might finally be about to turn.[21]

Instead, the new year arrived and the floodwaters kept coming. This time, the wellspring lay within the royal family itself. The extraordinary conflict of 1399—the deposition of one cousin by another—had been a dynastic trauma as well as a political one, with unpredictable personal results. Some members of the family had proved remarkably resilient. Henry's glamorous, willful sister Elizabeth had lost her husband, John Holand, when he was killed outside the gates of Pleshey Castle after rebelling against her brother in January 1400—but the king made it clear that Holand's treason cast no shadow on his widowed countess. At Elizabeth's request, Henry allowed Holand's severed head to be retrieved for burial from its spike on London Bridge, and granted her custody of their three children and the bulk of their valuable estates. That summer, he gave his blessing when she chose as her next husband Sir John Cornwall, a handsome knight ten years her junior whose valor at a royal tournament caught her appreciative attention. On February 15, 1405, the new Lady Cornwall gave birth to a boy, and her brother the king agreed to stand godfather to his new nephew.[22]

Not all of their close relatives shared Elizabeth's capacity to make the best of changing times. Their cousin Constance, daughter of their uncle Langley and sister of Edward of Rutland, also lost her husband during the rebellion of January 1400: Thomas Despenser's death at the hands of a Bristol mob left her a widow with two small children and pregnant with a third. Like Elizabeth, Constance was granted custody of her little son and enough of the family's estates to maintain her household and income—but in her case, there was less of the gilded entitlement that seemed to cocoon Elizabeth from danger. In her reckless independence, Constance was much more like her mother, Isabel of Castile, whose long-ago affair with John Holand was rumored to have resulted in the birth of Isabel's youngest child, Richard. And in the years after her husband's death, Constance too became entangled with the Holands, in the dashing person of Edmund, brother and heir of Thomas Holand, earl of Kent, another of the rebels of 1400.[23]

Eight years younger than Constance, Edmund Holand was making his way as best he could in the new Lancastrian world. He proved his loyalty by fighting for Henry against Hotspur's rebels at Shrewsbury at the age of just twenty, and received his brother's forfeited lands from the king when he came of age less than six months later, in January 1404. At some point in his clandestine relationship with Constance, she became pregnant and gave birth to a baby girl—perhaps before the end of that year, when Henry ordered that her two daughters by her dead husband should be taken into royal custody "for certain causes." In January 1405, Edmund secured the king's formal permission to marry whomever he wished; but if the bride he had in mind was Constance, his gesture did not prove enough to offset the compound of new grievance and old loyalties with which she was wrestling.

At the beginning of the year, Constance was staying at Windsor Castle, where the thirteen-year-old earl of March and his younger brother were being brought up under careful royal supervision. Somehow she got hold of the keys to the castle and had duplicates made in secret by a locksmith. During the night of February 13, 1405, she took the boys from their beds and rode westward through the dark, making for the Despenser estates in south Wales. Her plan was to take them to their uncle Edmund Mortimer and his father-in-law, Glyn Dŵr, as claimants to the English throne who might rally resistance to Henry in place of Richard's ghostly presence. A scrambled pursuit from Windsor overtook them in woodland outside Cheltenham seventy miles away, before they reached the Welsh border—but the breach of security was alarming, and became more so once Constance began to talk.

The boys were Edmund Holand's nephews, sons of his sister Eleanor, but she did not implicate her lover. Instead, she accused her brother Rutland of masterminding the conspiracy. He, she declared, had even planned to scale the walls of Eltham Palace to kill the king.[24]

It seemed a wild allegation. Rutland had no need to go climbing to secure access to Henry, and had spent the last four years serving the king loyally in Aquitaine and Wales, for much of the time at his own expense. But on further investigation, reassurance was not forthcoming. With vanishingly little prospect of reimbursement from the crown, the costs of Rutland's military duties had become so crushing that he had already pawned his collection of silver plate, and now faced the need to mortgage the estates on which his income and regional influence depended. It began to appear as though desperation might have brought him to contemplate other ways of avoiding ruin. Under interrogation, Rutland insisted that he had never conspired against Henry's life and was innocent in the matter of the kidnapping—but he was forced to admit that he had known of his sister's plans, while attempting to claim that he had warned the king of what was to come. It was a sloppy defense, and did nothing to stop Henry from ordering his arrest and the confiscation of his lands and property. But the rot seemed to have spread further still. Young Thomas Mowbray—an heir seeking the restitution of his dead father's lands, whose wife was the daughter of John Holand and Henry's sister Elizabeth—admitted that he had also known about the plot, while protesting that he had never agreed with its intentions.[25]

This sprawling trail of conspiracy was deeply unnerving, but in response, as always, Henry was forced to tread the finest of political lines. A public example could at least be made of the locksmith: the man lost his offending hand and then his head in rapid succession. But the ranks of the nobility were already too thin, and Henry's need for support too great, for the axe to fall among them precipitately or irreversibly. Rutland was imprisoned at the Lancastrian castle of Pevensey on the south coast, and Constance at Kenilworth in the midlands, while the Mortimer boys were placed under redoubled guard. Mowbray was allowed to go free. Less than two weeks later, however, the king ruled against him in a precedence dispute with the earl of Warwick. The nineteen-year-old, it seemed, would have to watch his step.[26]

With the immediate crisis over and its details kept as much as possible out of the public eye, Henry turned his attention to the military plans that he and his council had drawn up over the winter. His second son, seventeen-year-old Thomas, was about to take command of a fleet intended to reassert English control in the Channel before sailing to the relief of Aquitaine. In Wales, Prince Henry, now eighteen, was beginning to inflict significant losses on the rebels, his forces getting the better of fierce engagements in Monmouthshire in March and April in which Glyn Dŵr's brother was killed and his son Gruffydd captured. The king himself was on his way to join his son's Welsh campaign, moving west to muster troops at Hereford and summoning lords including young Mowbray to his side. But then, in the first week of May 1405, the earl of Northumberland—the last survivor of his generation among England's lords, a man bruised and brooding over the loss of his son and of the territorial power in the north to which he had devoted his six decades—raised his banners in revolt.[27]

His rebellion, when it came, was difficult to read, not least because his initial move—an attempt to seize the earl of Westmorland, his own greatest rival and Henry's lieutenant in the north—was a first step intended to clear the path for the insurrection proper. It failed. Westmorland evaded his grasp, and Northumberland lost his nerve before he had issued any kind of explicit public defiance, retreating to barricade himself and his men within the walls of Berwick, the northernmost stronghold in England. In doing so, he left his allies and sympathizers farther south in Yorkshire stranded without support, under the improbable leadership of a pair of mismatched captains: Thomas Mowbray, a teenager so utterly unwilling to watch his step, it turned out, that he had chosen to ride north into rebellion instead of west to join the king in Wales; and the archbishop of York, fifty-five-year-old Richard Scrope.[28]

To all outward appearances, the archbishop had spent the last six years serving Henry as faithfully as he had once served Richard. In 1399, Scrope had put his scholarly training to work to help justify Henry's claim to the crown, and, with Archbishop Arundel, had stepped forward before the assembled lords to lead the new king to the empty throne. Since then, he had devoted himself above all else to his spiritual duties in his diocese. Now his resistance began with a sermon from the pulpit of York Minster in which

Scrope denounced the "bad governance in the kingdom," with its "harsh regulations and unmanageable taxes," and called, in the name of truth and justice, for redress of the realm's grievances. Yorkshire was Percy country, and York's people were stirred by a manifesto so rousingly vague as to be all-encompassing. The archbishop found the city in uproar around him.

By May 27, Mowbray and Scrope had assembled more than 8,000 men outside the city walls on the open land of Shipton Moor. Scrope's complaint about the oppressions of Henry's government remained their rallying cry, but—given that the people were gathering with weapons in hand—it was far from clear that they were seeking reform rather than, as Walsingham put it, being "enticed by a desire for revolution." The archbishop himself had been galvanized by the success of his message. He was "delighted to be seen in arms among them," Walsingham said, and promised the remission of sins for any of his followers who might lose their lives for the cause. Their motley company spent two days on the moor before troops were sighted in the distance. The rebels strained their eyes, searching for the standard of the earl of Northumberland, the leader for whose arrival they were keeping an anxious watch. Instead, riding at the head of the approaching army they saw the earl of Westmorland and the king's young son John.[29]

Mowbray and Archbishop Scrope knew their options were few, the dangers many. Even so, their naivety made itself plain. Westmorland admired their petition for reform, he told them when a meeting of the commanders was arranged between the two camps, and would do all he could to press their case with the king. Should they not therefore drink to their shared aims—and, while they did so, would the archbishop tell his men they could return to their homes? Congratulating himself on his handling of this tricky confrontation, Scrope gave the order. As soon as the moor had cleared, Westmorland's bonhomie vanished. Within moments, Mowbray and the archbishop found themselves under arrest.

Henry was already on his way, marching from Hereford toward York with the troops he had raised to fight the rebels in Wales. This time, his patience was gone. For six years, he had tried to contain the fallout of revolt by tempering his justice with mercy. He had given his lords chance after chance to prove their loyalty, to support his crown against the Welsh, the Scots, and the French. Whatever he did, revolt kept coming. Now he had to march in the opposite direction from the threat of Glyn Dŵr to deal with a reckless teenager and a fool of an archbishop playing politics for stakes they did not understand. When he appeared before York's city walls on Saturday, June 6, the people streamed through the open gates in desperate supplication, Walsingham reported, "barefooted and bareheaded, wearing filthy rags," weeping miserably as they begged for their lives. But the king had no time for their pleas. They should go home and wait for his judgment, he told them with peremptory ferocity. He would deal first with Mowbray and Scrope.[30]

What exactly that might mean was not yet clear by dawn on Monday, when Archbishop Arundel arrived without fanfare or warning, unslept and unkempt after riding through the night to beg Henry not to raise his royal hand against Archbishop Scrope. It could not be denied that the crown had the right to charge a man of the Church with treason, and three years earlier the friars who had spread stories of Richard's return had faced the gallows for their crimes. But the archbishop of York was the second spiritual peer in the kingdom. He should be brought to justice, Archbishop Arundel insisted, only in parliament, or by submitting his case to the judgment of the pope. Henry should think of the danger to his own soul, and let due process take its course.

Henry calmed and reassured him. The archbishop of Canterbury should sleep and hear mass, he said, and then they would breakfast together. About that, he did not lie. But Henry had a different kind of process in mind, from which he would not be deflected—and Archbishop Arundel's attempt at intervention sealed Scrope's fate. The king had already appointed a commission led by his brother Thomas Beaufort and the young earl of Arundel as temporary constable and marshal of England to hear all charges relating to the rebels at York. Now he told Beaufort and Arundel to convene a summary trial. The chief justice of King's Bench, William Gascoigne—who had been one of Henry's attorneys during his exile, and was as loyal a Lancastrian as any lawyer in England—refused to participate in the hearing, warning that the commission had no authority to sentence an archbishop to death. But Beaufort and Arundel had their orders, and they were as determined as Henry that the traitors should die. While the unsuspecting Archbishop

Arundel breakfasted with the king, Mowbray and Scrope were found guilty of treason. They were bundled onto horses and taken to a barley field outside the city, where their heads were cut from their bodies.[31]

Henry had laid down a marker that his mercy was not without limit, to serve as a warning of the terrible consequences that awaited anyone who might resist his rule in the future. But the warning brought consequences of its own. The king could attempt to argue that, by assembling in arms on Shipton Moor, Mowbray and Scrope had been as explicit in their treason as if they, like Hotspur and Worcester before them, had ridden into battle against him. The fact remained that the process by which they had been so quickly condemned was rickety at best, and in Scrope's case shockingly deficient. Another King Henry, more than two centuries before, had provoked the murder of another archbishop, Thomas Becket, with some hot-tempered words during a bitter dispute; but no king in England's history had ever executed an archbishop in cold blood. When Archbishop Arundel himself had been condemned as a traitor among the swingeing judgments of Richard's parliament of 1397, his punishment had been exile, not death. Not only Henry's mercy but his justice—the justice that distinguished his rule from Richard's tyranny—was now in question.[32]

But Henry did not stop. This was a pitiless, implacable anger he had not shown before. Within a day of the executions he had moved his army on, taking with them not only siege engines but cannons, which they ranged against the Percy fortresses of the northeast. He was fascinated by this new military technology, naming one of his great guns the "King's Daughter," and developing a detailed technical interest in their design. Now pieces of artillery were deployed in earnest for the first time on English soil. At the sight of them—and, at Warkworth and Berwick, a demonstration of the ruinous damage they could do to curtain walls—one by one the castles surrendered. By the time Berwick was taken, the earl of Northumberland had already fled across the border into Scotland. In his absence he too was found guilty of treason and his estates declared forfeit. The revolt was over, piecemeal and half-baked as it had been, but the cost was heavy. Brutal reprisals left heads on spikes across the north. The city of York lost its liberties. The Percies— Henry's most powerful allies in 1399, and the bulwark of the frontier against

the Scots—were gone. Of the two archbishops who had led him to Richard's empty throne, the king had killed one and alienated the other. And for
that, as Archbishop Arundel had warned, Henry would face the judgment
of heaven.[33]

The miracles began within days, and grew in the telling. Before its burial
in York Minster, Scrope's severed head had smiled with holy serenity, witnesses swore. The trampled field in which his blood had been shed was not
destroyed but blessed, producing a bountiful crop of barley with seven ears
to each stalk, the smallholder who farmed the land testified in wonder. Soon
the archbishop's grave became so popular a site of pilgrimage that on royal
orders it was boarded off to restrict access. Still the people came.[34]

But Henry had no time to brood over what he had done. In August,
a French fleet carrying more than 2,500 men landed at Milford Haven in
southwest Wales under the command of the marshal and the admiral of
France, along with Jean de Hengest, the former ambassador who had sparred
with Henry over his diplomatic credentials five years earlier. While they
and their Welsh allies set about forcing the surrender of the English garrison at Carmarthen Castle, Henry called a great council to Worcester, near
the Welsh border, to confront the fact that, yet again, the English treasury
was empty. Not for the first time, the king and his council leaned on the
clergy to open the coffers of the Church. Not for the first time, Archbishop
Arundel—still deeply distressed by what had happened at York—refused to
comply. When Henry pressed on into Wales in September, he found neither
the French, who had retreated back to the far southwest, nor the spectral
Glyn Dŵr. Instead, the weather again proved a formidable enemy. On the
king's mud-bound return journey, flash floods overwhelmed the royal convoy. Among the wagons swept away were those that carried his jewels and
crowns—but if the loss appeared to be a portent, no one was brave enough
to say so.[35]

By the time Henry returned to Westminster in early December, he was
faced with the unavoidable need to call another parliament. The fleet commanded by his son Thomas had spent several weeks of the summer burning

its way along the northern coast of France but had subsequently been re-called for lack of funds before it could sail to the rescue of Aquitaine. Rumors were flying of an imminent Scottish invasion in the north and a French naval assault in the south. With so little to show for the huge sums granted by the loyal Commons in Coventry sixteen months earlier, it was small wonder that their successors, meeting at the beginning of March 1406, approached their king with a skepticism bordering on mistrust. When the assembly broke for Easter almost five weeks later, nothing had been achieved except an agree-ment to return on April 26 and try again.

Henry marked his thirty-ninth birthday five days after parliament was prorogued. The pace of his life was relentless. He had been ill for a few days during the last summer's violent drama in Yorkshire, but it was a brief in-disposition in what had been seven years and more of unremitting political, physical, and psychological strain. The hopes of 1399 were a faded memory, along with the belief that the glory of his rule would serve to justify his possession of the crown. There was no choice but to go on. On Sunday, April 25, he presided over the magnificent annual gathering of the Order of the Garter at Windsor Castle. In the wake of the celebrations, the reopening of parliament was postponed for a few days until the king and his lords could more easily reconvene at Westminster.[36]

And then, without warning, Henry's health gave way.

Seventeen

1406–1410

will fortune never come with both hands full

The king had leprosy, they said. They were wrong, but that did nothing to dissuade those who said so from believing that Henry had been punished by God for killing his archbishop. He had been struck down within hours of Scrope's execution—or so the story went, retrospectively folding the short illness he had suffered in Yorkshire in the summer of 1405 into a narrative of the baleful consequences of royal sin.[1]

In fact, the crisis began on April 27, 1406, with what Henry described to his council as a "sudden malady" in his leg. He wrote from Windsor Castle early the following morning to tell them he would not be able to ride the twenty miles to Westminster that day as planned. For the time being his physicians had forbidden it, but he would join them there in three or four days. By that afternoon, when he wrote urgently for a second time, it was already clear that he had spoken too soon, and his condition was worsening. He was eventually able to travel by river in short stages to London, and took up residence on May 1 in the bishop of Durham's lavish town house on the Strand, a retreat offering more privacy than the royal apartments in his own palace of Westminster, where his parliament was by now in session again without him. This "severe attack," as he called it, may have been caused by a blood clot in his leg, or possibly even a rectal prolapse (a condition for which the copyist of a text by a master surgeon later noted the king had been treated). Although he struggled through a handful of days in parliament

during May and June, Henry's illness was so overwhelming that he was unable to take a regular part in the processes of government for several months.
The king's golden youth was well and truly over, his debilitated body unhap-
pily close to a living metaphor for the compromised state of the body politic
as it struggled to function under the strain of his usurpation.[2]

Yet the crown was still Henry's. The questionable legitimacy of his kingship had exposed his regime to repeated attack from inside and out, but all
the qualities, besides his royal blood, that had made him the only possible
contender for the throne in 1399—his ability to command, his sense of duty,
his capacity for both fine and savage judgment—meant that he also continued to inspire loyalty. As had been the case since the start of his reign, the
ways in which this loyalty was expressed could be uncomfortable for Henry.
In the reconvened session of parliament, the Commons declared their concern at the threats to Calais and Aquitaine, in Wales, the Scottish march,
and Ireland, but would not grant the king a tax without further commitments to financial and administrative efficiency. Their plan, following the
lead of previous parliaments, was to ensure fiscal competence in government
through scrutiny and accountability: they wanted greater formalization of
Henry's council and further reduction in the size of his household, which,
the Speaker curtly told him, remained far too expensive. It was characteristic
of this friendly fire that the man who delivered the reproof, John Tiptoft,
was himself a knight of the king's chamber who, at twenty-eight, had already
served Henry faithfully for a decade.[3]

Meanwhile, the lords refused simply to wave through confirmation of
the verdicts of treason against the executed Scrope and Mowbray and the
fugitive earl of Northumberland. It was one thing to have beheaded the earl's
brother after the fighting at Shrewsbury in 1403 when he had led troops into
battle against the king himself, quite another to pass summary judgment
on a hotheaded teenager and an archbishop who had allowed himself to
be swept away by the popular response to his calls for reform. Neither they
nor the missing earl had been tried by their peers in parliament as precedent required, while in Rome Pope Innocent VII had pronounced a sentence of excommunication on all those who were complicit in Scrope's death.
Henry tried to argue that the archbishop had forfeited the protections of

the priesthood and betrayed his own ordination by riding in arms against his sovereign, and sent Scrope's coat of mail to Rome to make his point; but the pope was unmoved. Although the papal bull took care to retain some diplomatic leeway by naming no names, it was impossible to imagine, given the circumstances of Scrope's beheading, that the king was not included in the anathema.[4]

However, by the time parliament was adjourned again on June 19—because, the clerks noted, the time for harvest was approaching, and it was very hot, and the realm's defenses needed attention—there were reasons for Henry to hope that God had not abandoned him. A year earlier, Archbishop Arundel had been so shattered by his own failure to save Scrope from the headsman's sword and the king from the sin of ordering his execution that he too had fallen ill immediately afterward, the chroniclers reported. But in the wake of the crisis, Henry had treated Archbishop Arundel with "extraordinary respect," Walsingham said; and now the archbishop quietly chose not to publish the papal bull of excommunication in England. In his service to the kingdom so far, and in his attempt to read God's purpose at work in the world, the archbishop had always combined faith, hope, and pragmatism. In 1399, his decision to forgive Henry's part in the trial of his brother, the earl of Arundel, had been vindicated by Henry's rule as a king who, unlike Richard, was capable of acknowledging his mistakes and seeking to put them right. Seven years later, despite Scrope's death and the physical affliction with which the king was struggling, the archbishop was not yet certain that Henry and his regime were beyond salvation.[5]

Other signs of heaven's grace could be added to the ledger. Back in March, the eleven-year-old heir to the Scottish throne had been captured at sea by English privateers on his way to France for a courtly education in Paris. ("The Scots could have sent him to me," Henry said dryly when he heard the news. "I speak French too.") Two weeks later, the boy's father, King Robert III, died—of grief, it was said—meaning that the young prisoner kept securely in the Tower was now James I, king of Scotland. From here on, any leverage the Scots might hope to exercise through the supposed presence of the dead king Richard in Edinburgh would be outweighed by the actual presence of their own king under lock and key in London.[6]

There was more. In Wales on Saint George's Day, April 23, the prince's troops emerged victorious from a bloody encounter with the rebels. One of Glyn Dŵr's sons was already a captive in the Tower alongside the little Scottish king; now another was dead on the battlefield with a thousand of his men. Meanwhile, the contingent of French soldiers who had arrived in Wales the previous autumn sailed for home that spring. Like their predecessors in Scotland in 1385, they had found themselves confounded by the landscape and the weather, and by the fact that the back door through which they planned to launch an assault on England had resolutely refused to open.[7]

Also heading to France was the earl of Northumberland. That February, he had fled from his refuge in Scotland, having caught wind of a proposal that his hosts might hand him over to Henry in an exchange of hostages. Arriving in Wales, he had sealed an alliance by which he, Glyn Dŵr, and Edmund Mortimer agreed to join forces against their common enemy, and one day, when their glorious victory was achieved, to divide the rule of "Greater Britain" between them, Glyn Dŵr as prince of an expanded Wales, Northumberland taking the English midlands and north, and Mortimer the south. In May, the earl set off for Paris in the hope of enlisting French support for their plans.[8]

There, however, he found the court struggling to contain a rekindled rivalry between Louis of Orléans and the house of Burgundy, this time in the person of the new duke, Philip's son John, who at thirty-five was already a more pugnacious politician than his elegantly assertive father. Northumberland did his utmost to rouse the French princes to action against the English usurper, but his lengthy denunciation of Henry's "execrable perfidy" was received with cool skepticism by those who remembered the earl's own part in Richard's fall. All he managed to secure, in the end, was a letter in the name of King Charles promising that France stood ready to help the English throw off the tyrant's yoke whenever they felt ready to help themselves. As endorsements went, it was barely lukewarm. And Northumberland's damp squib of a visit came just after the French royal family celebrated a wedding that carried political weight on both sides of the Channel. In June 1406, the king's eldest daughter, Richard's sixteen-year-old widow, Isabella, married her cousin, the eleven-year-old son of Louis of Orléans. For Orléans, the ceremony reinforced his position at the heart of his brother's regime. For Henry, following developments intently from his sickbed in London, it offered reassurance that France no longer proposed even to go through the motions of suggesting that Richard might still be alive.[9]

These were small mercies, for which there was every reason to be grateful—as was the fact that, by the middle of July, Henry had recovered enough to travel slowly from London into East Anglia. In August, he was in north Norfolk, praying as a pilgrim at the famous shrine of the Virgin at Walsingham, before moving another twenty miles west to the port of Lynn. There he and his queen and his sons Henry, Thomas, and Humphrey—John being occupied with his lieutenancy in the north—gathered to say good-bye to twelve-year-old Philippa, Henry's youngest child. Her marriage to the king of Denmark, Sweden, and Norway had taken place by proxy eight months before, and it was therefore as a queen that she sailed to join the husband she had never met, her cabin in the flagship of the little fleet hung with fine red worsted and cloth of gold. For now, her retinue, splendid in scarlet and green livery, still included familiar faces, among them Rutland's brother Richard representing the royal family, and Hugh Waterton's wife, Katherine, who had been Philippa's governess throughout her childhood. But they would return to England within weeks of her landing in Helsingborg; and her father and brothers knew they would not see her again.[10]

The year had brought Henry many sorts of loss: his health, his daughter, and in the autumn his friend Thomas Rempston. Henry's friends were—had always been—central to his life, and Rempston had been one of the closest, entrusted with military, administrative, and diplomatic responsibilities ranging from the command of the Tower of London, to managing local rule in the northeast midlands, to negotiating the king's marriage to Queen Joan. His death was a terrible accident, "all through foolishness," one chronicler noted in frustration. In London on October 31, 1406, this stubbornly forceful man decided he knew better than the Thames boatmen he had hired to row him to the Tower from Paul's Wharf in the west of the city. After the summer's heat there had been devastating floods across the country, and the river was running fast and strong against the tide; too strong, the boatmen said, to risk shooting the rapids through the narrow arches of London Bridge.

But Rempston told them to do their job if they wanted to keep their heads. Within minutes, the swollen current rammed the boat against one of the piles of the bridge, hurling him into the churning water. His body washed ashore the next morning at Dowgate, 300 yards upriver.[11]

Henry's sorrow was compounded by significant political cost. Even as he mourned Rempston, he would have to find a way to replace his experience and his ironclad loyalty. Henry had always relied heavily on men he knew well, men whose fidelity he could trust without question, men who, like Rempston, had spent their lives in the service of the duchy of Lancaster. They fought in his armies, kept order in his kingdom, sat in his parliaments, held office in his household and council. As individuals, their service was widely valued: the intelligent and vastly experienced Thomas Erpingham, for example, had twice been explicitly commended by the Commons in parliament, the first time alongside Rempston himself. Even so, the king would perhaps have been wise to make more concerted efforts to broaden the base of his regime; but the relentless firefighting of the last seven years had intensified his dependence on his Lancastrian core, while draining the wider pool of lords and lesser landowners from whom he might have hoped to recruit, all in circumstances that left him minimal time for strategic reflection.[12]

As it was, Henry had made it clear time and again that he would put his relationship with his Lancastrian retainers before financial retrenchment or administrative proficiency: after the stop on the payment of royal annuities in 1404, the king had exempted the retainers of his duchy from even that temporary measure. None were favorites in the mold of Robert de Vere, helping themselves from the public purse while contributing nothing to the public good, but the sense remained that Henry was allowing personal ties to compromise the effectiveness of his attempt to govern in the interests of his kingdom as a whole. When parliament reassembled in earnest in November 1406, not yet three weeks after Rempston's death, the king was in mourning and still not well. The treasury was empty again, and Calais and Aquitaine saved from renewed French attack only by the fact that the dukes of Orléans and Burgundy could not patch up their enmity long enough to sustain the campaign they had planned. The lords and Commons had already sat for a total of three months in the spring and early summer without agreement on a grant of taxation or the administrative reform the Commons sought in return. Something had to give.[13]

It took weeks of hard-fought negotiation, but a deal was finally done three days before Christmas: the Commons offered the king a tax of one fifteenth and tenth, and the king accepted that his administration should be reconfigured to new parliamentary specifications, drafted by the lords and approved by the Commons. The parameters of "good and abundant governance"—rules designed to ensure fiscal responsibility and official probity—were set out in detail in thirty-one articles, itemized in the parliamentary record, to which the members of a freshly appointed royal council were required to swear. These councillors, the king was told, were "pleasing to God and agreeable to his people," and until the end of the next parliament Henry would be required "to govern entirely in all cases with their advice."[14]

Enforcing restrictions of any sort on the sovereign was neither politically simple nor personally welcome to the king, but Henry was a realist, and he understood that this new framework of government was intended to sustain his rule, not undermine it. This was not—as it had been with Richard in the desperate crisis of 1386—an attempt to protect the realm from a dangerously loose royal cannon by elbowing the king aside completely. Henry's subjects did not doubt his understanding of the threats facing the kingdom, or his commitment to tackling them. What they questioned was his competence at handling the realm's revenues—and the articles sought to insist on the financial and administrative accountability that previous parliaments had failed to make stick. So serious was the attempt to make the reforms work that the Speaker of the Commons, the Lancastrian knight John Tiptoft, was required to put his money management where his mouth was, becoming treasurer of the royal household that he had criticized so robustly.

The composition of the council reinforced the supportive discomfort in which Henry now found himself held. Over the years, he had relied so heavily in government on the advice and service of his Lancastrian retainers not only because they were loyal, able men, but also because the ranks of the nobility had been drastically depleted. In any normal circumstances—a long-distant memory though normal circumstances were—the king's subjects expected that the great lords should be his natural advisers. Among the new councillors, therefore, there were only two knights: John Tiptoft, as trea-surer of the royal household, and the tough, plain-speaking John Stanley, a Cheshireman who had proved his loyalty by fighting for the king at Shrews-bury, and was now the household's steward. Otherwise, as best it could, par-liament filled the council with more "substantial" men. For his integrity, vast experience, and primacy among the spiritual lords, Archbishop Arundel's name was the first on the list. He was also persuaded in January to accept another term of office as England's chancellor, the first time he had served in that role since the earliest weeks of Henry's rule in 1399. Alongside him sat Henry's brothers John Beaufort, earl of Somerset, and Henry Beaufort, now bishop of Winchester, as well as the bishops of London and Durham, skilled administrators both. With them too was the duke of York, Henry's cousin Edward of Rutland, who, year on fraught year, was emerging as the greatest survivor in English politics. He had endured several months in custody after his sister Constance's conspiracy in 1405, before pleading his "trouble and heaviness" at the suspicions against him, and Henry—who could ill afford to lose the service of England's last remaining duke apart from his own eldest son—had given him one more chance to prove his loyalty as a free man. And when the councillors began their work, a prominent role in their delibera-tions was taken by the heir to the throne, Prince Henry, now twenty years old and a bracingly incisive political presence.[15]

The prince was, of course, his father's son, but the most striking feature of his new role in government was his distance from the king. Unlike Henry himself—who had spent his teenage years shadowing Gaunt's movements, surrounded by Gaunt's retainers and friends—Prince Henry had not lived with his father when he was a boy. He had not been at Henry's side on crusade in Lithuania or pilgrimage to Jerusalem, nor—unlike his brother Thomas—in exile in Paris. Since his father's accession to the throne, young Henry had been fighting to defeat Glyn Dŵr's rebels in his own principality of Wales, first under Hotspur's guidance, then with increasingly impressive degrees of inde-pendence. In the process, he was developing close working relationships with the new generation of nobles who campaigned alongside him, especially the earls of Arundel and Warwick and the youngest of his uncles, Thomas Beau-fort, all three men in their twenties, and all charismatic, talented captains.[16]

The appearance of the prince at Westminster—scarred, battle hardened, and intensely focused—together with the combined experience of the council, and its new powers of oversight, served to galvanize the administration. This group of spiritual and temporal peers led by the archbishop of Canterbury and the prince of Wales plausibly embodied a new Lancastrian establishment, one that represented the authority of the Lancastrian crown rather than the private power of the king's personal inheritance. The prince's central role in this reshaping of his father's rule was displayed that winter in the intricate new design of the royal seal. It showed Henry sitting in majesty, flanked by the saintly kings Edward the Confessor and Edmund the Martyr and the heavenly soldiers Saint Michael and Saint George—and on it, for the first time, his son's arms as prince of Wales, duke of Cornwall, and earl of Chester appeared alongside those of the English crown.[17]

Henry did not relish the restrictions on his prerogative that the council had been appointed to enforce. But his seat on the throne had never been comfortable; and if he could survive long enough—if he could see off every threat and every challenge, including the ill-health God now asked him to endure—it seemed that a new Lancastrian future might slowly be taking shape.

In January 1407, he was well enough to attend a wedding. Lucia Visconti had arrived at last in England, even if the stars had not smiled on her hopes of marrying Henry. Negotiations between Milan and London had been halted by his banishment in 1398, and in the spring of 1399, during the uncertainty of his exile, Lucia had reluctantly been persuaded to accept a match with a German princeling, the fifteen-year-old heir to the landgrave of Thuringia. She would never have stopped waiting for Henry, she said then, had she only been certain he would one day claim her hand. But certainty of any kind proved hard to find. When Henry took the English crown, Lucia's German betrothal remained in place, even though the relationship was neither formalized nor consummated. Three years later, after her cousin Gian Galeazzo died suddenly in the autumn of 1402, she took her chance to secure an annulment on the grounds that she had made her vows under duress. By the time she was free, Henry was newly married to Queen Joan.[18]

But the king had not forgotten her. If he could not make her his wife, he would find her another husband. The bridegroom he had in mind was Edmund Holand, the young earl of Kent. Holand's entanglement with Rutland's sister, Constance, the mother of his illegitimate daughter, was over: if he had ever intended to marry her, his plans had been halted by her kidnapping of the little earl of March and her subsequent arrest in 1405. By now Henry had released Constance from custody, but she was living quietly and carefully, her cards permanently marked by her conspiracy. Instead, Edmund and Lucia seemed the perfect match. At twenty-three, he had a noble title, a dazzling reputation on the tournament field, and a promising military career, though little in the way of land or money; a large proportion of his inheritance remained for now in the hands of his great-aunt, mother, and sister-in-law, the three dowager countesses of Kent. At twenty-six, Lucia was not only a member of the sprawling ruling dynasty of Milan and "an intelligent and beautiful woman," Walsingham noted, but came with the promise of a valuable dowry, to be paid by installments in golden florins. Henry conducted the negotiations with Gian Galeazzo's son and successor Gian Maria—out of the "deepest affection" he held for the noble lady, his letters explained—and on January 24, 1407, he gave her away at the church door of St. Mary Overy in Southwark, the great priory "over the river" from the capital. After the ceremony, king and court celebrated at a magnificent feast to welcome the new countess to her adopted home.[19]

A bittersweet moment for Lucia was leavened by the fact that Henry was no longer quite the glamorous figure she remembered meeting in Milan almost fifteen years before. At thirty-nine, the king was worn by the accumulating demands and sorrows of the last decade, and heavier and less mobile than he had been before his illness—a change that was as obvious to Henry as it was to Lucia. Still, he clung to the hope that his health might return, that his fighting days might not be done. When the wedding took place in January he was making plans to lead a campaign in France to defend either Calais or Bordeaux, but within weeks the muster was delayed until April, and then dropped altogether. On June 1 he announced his intention to march with his eldest son into Wales to recover the castles of Aberystwyth and Harlech from the rebels, but nine days later his retainers were told to postpone their arrival until further notice "as, for particular causes, the king does not purpose to be there so speedily." No more was said of the matter. The prince took sole command of the army, while Henry spent the summer traveling slowly north through the midlands and Yorkshire.[20]

Instead of military action, it was a time full of memories. At Nottingham on August 12, Henry took his seat in a specially built stand to preside at a trial by combat: a duel between two townsmen of Bordeaux, who had been summoned to resolve a bitter quarrel in which one accused the other of treason. Bertrand Ozanne was a merchant who had visited England before, as part of the delegation that had so stoutly defended Aquitaine's rights at Eltham long ago, when Richard was king and Henry still earl of Derby. A tailor named Jean Boulemer claimed that, in the first year of Henry's reign, Ozanne had told him in a Bordeaux street that the English were bad people who plundered the city's resources, that it would be better to leave their jurisdiction, and that anyone who disagreed would soon be run out of town. When Boulemer reported these treacherous words to the authorities, Ozanne furiously denied the accusation, and in 1406, with the case still unresolved, they were called to settle their dispute in person before the king.[21]

Boulemer and Ozanne were not even knights, let alone dukes, and Nottingham was not Coventry; but when Henry's eighteen-year-old son, John, stepped forward as constable of England to start the fight—"Let them go, let them go, let them go and do their duty!"—the echoes were overwhelming. In the stand, the king was surrounded by young men: his sons Thomas and Humphrey and the thirteen-year-old captive king of Scots, who had recently been moved under watchful guard from the Tower to Nottingham Castle. To them, this contest between a tailor and a merchant, old men not trained for battle, armed with a motley selection of weapons, seemed too much of an entertainment to end in killing. To Henry, there was nobility in the fact that the laboring combatants had come in arms to defend their lives and their reputations before their sovereign because of rash words spoken in a heated moment. And this time, the power of life and death lay in Henry's hands. He rose from his seat and told them to stop. They had both fought bravely and well, he said, and they should both go free, with nothing but honor attached to their names.

While Boulemer and Ozanne made arrangements to return to Aquitaine, to pick up their lives as best they could, Henry moved on from Nottingham into Yorkshire to pray at the shrine of John of Bridlington. He had
been there last after his landing at Ravenspur in the tumultuous summer of
1399. Two years after that, his envoys in Rome had secured the holy prior's
canonization. The six years since then had taken a heavy toll, but Henry had
no wish to live in the past: perhaps the new saint's intercession might work
another miracle.[22]

Incapacitated though Henry was, in Wales his son's growing stature as a
commander and stern commitment to the war were clawing back territory
and resources and, with them, momentum and political credibility. Anglesey
and Flintshire in the north and Cardiganshire in the west had already been
restored to English control, and the host the prince led into Wales in the
summer of 1407 was—despite the absence of the king—the greatest the principality had yet seen. Prince Henry was accompanied by Edward of Rutland
and the young earl of Warwick, and by other lords and knights including his
friends Richard Courtenay, an aristocrat, cleric, and scholar who was chancellor of the University of Oxford, and Sir John Oldcastle, a Herefordshire
landowner who had spent the last five years fighting in Wales under the
prince's command. With his troops, the prince brought a barrage of cannon
to bombard Aberystwyth, to mixed effect: the immense walls of the castle
could not be breached, and one of the guns, nicknamed the "Messenger,"
blew up when it was fired. But by September 12 the siege forced the struggling garrison into a deal: the castle would be surrendered on November 1 if
Glyn Dŵr did not come to its rescue.[23]

The agreement did not work quite as the prince had planned. He and the
lords left Wales for the opening of parliament on October 20—an assembly
that had been summoned to Gloucester, halfway between Aberystwyth and
London, to facilitate their attendance. In their absence, Glyn Dŵr materialized as quickly as he had so often vanished, briefly taking command of the
castle himself and nullifying the treaty of surrender. It was a brave stand, but
one made against an overwhelming English advance. At Gloucester in the

presence of the king, who had spent the last month riding by easy stages back from Yorkshire, the Commons' Speaker, Thomas Chaucer—son of the man whose first poem had been an elegy for Henry's mother—heaped praise on Henry's son for his "great labor and diligence" in resisting the rebels. The prince, in reply, seized the moment to show support for his comrade in arms Rutland, about whom derogatory whispers were still circulating. The duke, he declared, was a "loyal and valiant knight," who fought "as if he had been the poorest gentleman in the realm wishing to win honor through his service."[24]

The progress the prince was making as a commander in the field was mirrored in the corridors and chambers of government. The tightening of financial management instigated by the council under the leadership of the prince and Archbishop Arundel—stringency that they, at one remove from the complicated personal authority of the king, were better placed to enforce—was beginning to result in greater royal solvency. The process had not been pleasant either for Henry, who found himself a petitioner for funds at his own exchequer, or for the council itself. When the Commons inquired about how the tax granted at the last parliament had been spent, the archbishop responded with irritation: not only had he already explained at some length where the money had gone, he told Chaucer, but for the past year he and the other councillors had faithfully fulfilled their duties and personally underwritten large loans to the crown, "believing"—wrongly, it turned out—"that they would receive widespread agreement and gratitude." But, whatever the gripes on either side, progress had been made, and Henry reaped the reward of his patience. His councillors asked to be discharged from their oaths to uphold the formal articles of 1406, thus releasing the restrictions on his royal authority, while the Commons agreed to a tax of one and a half fifteenths and tenths. And, with his prerogative fully restored, Henry was content for the status quo to continue: for Archbishop Arundel to remain in office as chancellor and for the council under his direction to continue its work.[25]

A grudging kind of concord was breaking out in England. Across the Channel, the opposite was true. Two days after the Gloucester parliament ended, in Paris the simmering conflict between the dukes of Burgundy and

Orléans boiled into horror. On the evening of November 23, 1407, Louis of Orléans paid a visit to his sister-in-law Queen Isabeau. Despite the fact that King Charles's sanity was more elusive than ever, she had recently given birth to the royal couple's twelfth child, a boy who lived only a few hours. Orléans was in good spirits when he left the queen's lodging to ride home with five attendants along a street in the east of the city known as the Vieille-du-Temple. Without warning, masked figures stepped out of the shadows. There was a momentary flash of steel in the torchlight before swords and axes thudded into flesh and bone with such force that the duke's left hand was severed as he tried to shield himself from the blows. In seconds, his skull was split down to his teeth and the tissue of his brain spilled onto the paving stones. The men disappeared into the dark while a woman screamed for help from a window above. When news of the murder was brought to the royal council, the shock was visceral—to all, that is, except John of Burgundy. In one night, rivalry for control of government between the two greatest princes of France had become a blood feud.[26]

It was Westminster's turn to be appalled by events in Paris. The English might from time to time depose their kings, who might subsequently die, conveniently, behind closed doors, but—despite the variously ineffective plots against Gaunt in the 1380s and 1390s—barefaced assassination was not a political tactic with which England was familiar. Even Thomas of Woodstock, scrabbling desperately for breath as his mouth and nose were stopped by the suffocating weight of a feather-stuffed mattress, had been killed out of sight in Calais only to save Richard the difficulties that would otherwise have attended his uncle's public execution. For the French king's brother to be butchered on the streets of his capital by killers in the pay of his cousin represented a degree of political self-mutilation that England had rarely approached. Thomas Hoccleve, a poet and protégé of Geoffrey Chaucer who worked as a clerk in the royal office of the privy seal, spoke for many when he surveyed the destruction that followed in its wake: "France, no wonder though thy heart grow cold / And burn also, such is thy agony. . . ."

I am an English man and am thy foe;
For thou a foe art unto my ligeance;

And yet my heart stuffed is with woe
To see thy unkindly disseverance.[27]

The conflict unleashed by the murder ran hot during the bitterest winter anyone could remember. As he crossed the frozen Thames to spend Christmas with Joan at Eltham, Henry knew that the conflagration in Paris—lamentable though it might be to see princely blood spilled by princely hands—could only help him. Since 1399 the undeclared wars of attrition outside Calais, in Aquitaine, and along the coasts had become an unhappy and unaffordable way of life, from which escape had seemed impossible. But now his enemies had turned on each other, and at last there was hope of respite, perhaps even room to maneuver in international affairs.[28]

By the new year the reversal of fortunes was complete. France was teetering on the brink of civil war—and when resistance raised its weary head once more in England, it was swept aside with unaccustomed ease. In February 1408, with snow lying thick on the hard ground, the renegade earl of Northumberland made a last, desperate attempt to incite revolt in the north. The forces he gathered were little more than a rabble, but Henry, who felt physically stronger than he had for months, was determined to march against him in person. The king had not long left London when news came that the sixty-six-year-old earl was already dead, killed in the field at Bramham Moor near the Lancastrian castle of Knaresborough by local forces under the command of the sheriff. Northumberland's severed head, with its mane of white hair, was impaled on a lance and sent south to be carried in procession through the capital and set high on London Bridge.[29]

Henry stayed in Yorkshire until the snow began to melt in April, supervising judicial proceedings against those who had followed the earl into rebellion. By the middle of May when he rode the rutted roads, thick with mud, 150 miles south to Windsor Castle and on to the royal apartments at the Tower, he knew England was safer than it had been for years. The Percy heir was a fourteen-year-old boy, and Henry's own family held the kingdom. The north was in the hands of his son John and his brother-in-law Westmorland; his son Henry fought on in Wales, driving back Glyn Dŵr with ruthless determination; his son Thomas was preparing to return to Dublin for a new term as the crown's lieutenant in Ireland; his brother John Beaufort was captain of the garrison at Calais.

Still, there were reminders that at any moment God's plans might override his own—a lesson the new countess of Kent was forced to learn in the harshest of terms. That June, Edmund Holand took his first solo command at sea. His small fleet sailed for the Isle of Bréhat off the north coast of Brittany, on a mission to enforce payment of the inhabitants' share of Queen Joan's dower. The expedition was a brutal triumph—Bréhat's castle destroyed, the islanders put to the sword—except that it cost Holand his life. Riding without a helmet in the thick of the siege, he was hit in the head by a bolt from a crossbow. Like Prince Henry at Shrewsbury, he continued to fight despite the horror of his injury. But in the days afterward, without the expert care that had saved the prince, the wound festered. On September 15, Holand died. Twenty months after her wedding, Lucia mourned at her young husband's burial.[30]

Henry was not there to comfort her. At the beginning of June, after his return from Yorkshire to London, he had taken a boat upriver to stay with Archbishop Arundel at his palace of Mortlake on the south bank of the Thames. The interaction between the king and his archbishop had become intensely charged after the killing of Archbishop Scrope, but both men were prepared to acknowledge complexity and to recognize integrity, and over the past two challenging years their relationship had gradually deepened into one of genuine understanding and respect. "I thank you heartily of the great business that you do for me and for my realm," Henry had written during his journey south, "and trust plainly in your good counsel, and hoping to God to speak to you hastily and thank you with good heart. Your true friend and child in God, H.R."[31]

Although the news had not yet been published, the structural tension between them had also eased in April, when Gregory XII, Innocent VII's successor in Rome, lifted the sentence of excommunication on those responsible for Scrope's execution. The support of the king of England was too valuable for the Roman papacy to lose, given that the schism with Avignon was no nearer an effective resolution—and, almost three years after Scrope's death, both sides were willing to give ground in the search for a settlement.

Henry's envoys in Rome expressed the king's remorse and his desire for pardon, while the pope acknowledged the treachery of an archbishop whom the king had, until his rebellion, treated with honor. Papal absolution set the seal on the personal rapprochement between Henry and Archbishop Arundel, and at Mortlake the archbishop's company was a comfort as the king tried to recover from the exhaustion of his time in the north.[32]

But it was not just exhaustion. In late June 1408, Henry collapsed, losing consciousness for so long that his attendants thought he was dead. This time, there would be no hope of a quick recovery.

For several weeks, Henry remained in the care of the archbishop's household. When at last he was well enough to move, he did not go far. Traveling mainly by water—the river offering more privacy and fewer physical demands than the roads—he spent the rest of the year in and around London, including three lengthy stays at the home of his old friend Hugh Waterton. From September he was attended by a newly recruited Italian physician from Lucca. His appearances in public were few. Before Christmas the decision was made to call Prince Henry and his brother Thomas back from their posts in Wales and Dublin to Westminster. Neither had yet arrived when, in the new year, the king's health deteriorated again, to the point where Henry, resting now at his manor of Greenwich beside the Thames, felt moved to make his will.[33]

Royal wills were usually deeply formal texts. Richard's, drawn up as a precaution before his departure for Ireland in the spring of 1399, had been a lengthy Latin document, expressed, using the royal "we," with a rhetorically grandiose performance of humility. Invoking his personal patron saints, John the Baptist and "Edward the most glorious Confessor," it began with an elaborate preamble—"Since the sentence of inevitable death defers to no one at all, but rather judges nobility, power, strength, race, age and sex with a balanced scale"—before devoting most of its provisions to the king's wish for a spectacular funeral and his attempt to control his kingdom from beyond the grave. In the theater of sovereignty, Richard had intended to play the leading role in death just as much as in life.[34]

Henry's will was radically different. In part, the contrast reflected his admiration for the meditative, ascetic strain that was emerging within contemporary theology. But, written in English in the first person—a language and form not used in the will of a king of England in the three centuries since the Conquest—it was also an anguished plea for forgiveness and grace from a man who, facing the reality of death, could not rest easy in the knowledge that his actions had been righteous.[35]

> I Henry, sinful wretch, by the grace of God king of England and of France, and lord of Ireland ... bequeath to Almighty God my sinful soul, the which had never been worthy to be man but through His mercy and His grace; which life I have misspent, whereof I put me wholly in His grace and His mercy, with all my heart. . . . I thank all my lords and true people for the true service that they have done to me, and I ask them forgiveness if I have mistreated them in any wise. And as far as they have offended me in words or in deeds in any wise, I pray God forgive them it, and I do.

He felt no need for reassurance about the pomp that might attend his burial. The ceremony, whatever it was, could be left to Archbishop Arundel to arrange. He would not lie at Leicester with Mary, or at St. Paul's with his mother and father, or among his royal ancestors in Westminster Abbey, where Anne of Bohemia rested alone in Richard's magnificent tomb. Instead, he chose Canterbury, where a saintly archbishop had been murdered long ago as a consequence of another king's rage. But Henry did not invoke Thomas Becket. Archbishop Arundel had crowned him at Westminster. Now he would commit his body to the archbishop's care at Canterbury, trusting the man who was becoming his spiritual mentor to help him toward some kind of redemption.

Henry and his eldest son were not close, but the king had confidence too in the man who would succeed to his crown: "For great trust that I have in my son the prince, I ordain and make him my executor. . . . And to fulfil truly all things foresaid, I charge my foresaid son upon my blessing." His anxious concern lay with those to whom he owed material and personal debts. All annuities he had granted should continue to be paid after his death, he said, "in especial to all them that have been true servants to me and toward me always." Rewards should be given to the grooms of his chamber and other personal servants who now cared for him day and night, six of whom—William Wardell, John Warren, William Thorpe, Thomas Delacroix, Jacob Raysh, and John Halley—he commended by name. His wife, Queen Joan, who did not yet have all the estates she had been promised to support her own household, should be endowed from his duchy of Lancaster. And then a roll call of witnesses put their seal to the document, their names testifying to the unforeseen trajectory of his life. Among them were Lancastrian knights and esquires including Thomas Erpingham and Hugh Waterton's cousin Robert, who had been his second in 1398 at the abortive duel with Mowbray; Archbishop Arundel, his ally of 1399 and critic of 1405 turned friend and spiritual counselor; and his cousin Edward of Rutland, once duke of Aumale and Richard's "brother," now Henry's much-forgiven duke of York. The will's short text, dated January 21, 1409, reflected the intimate intensity of the sickroom, and the preoccupations of a king whose sovereignty had never escaped the troubling questions raised by its own creation.

But the men who gathered around his bed loved their king precisely because he knew he was a sinner. Henry understood, as Richard never had, that to be human—even for a man anointed by God to wear a crown—was to live an imperfect life, one that required resilience in the face of setbacks and contrition for one's own mistakes. Risk and uncertainty were intrinsic to Henry's rule from the beginning, apparent in everything from the circumlocutions required to draw a veil over the facts of Richard's deposition—Henry's return to England in 1399 as his "arrival" after "a certain journey," his duchy of Lancaster as the lands he had held "before his coronation"—to the spies and informers keeping ears to the ground in Paris, Calais, Bordeaux, Wales, Scotland, and within England itself. Yet Henry had not given in to paranoia. He knew that the experiences of the people around him and the choices they made were as complex, as fully real, as his own. He was prepared to listen, and to engage; his habit before his illness, a couple of times a week after dining in state in his chamber, had been to have a cushion laid on the sideboard, "and there he would lean by the space of an hour or more, to receive bills and complaints from whomsoever would come." The forms of art Henry loved best—the texts he read, the music he heard and played and composed—required communication and immersive participation, not the glitteringly self-referential images that had been Richard's aesthetic obsession. When the midland poet who had damned Richard for his tyranny in 1399 later turned his pen to England's grievances under Henry's regime, he took his alliterative aim at the greed and self-interest of those who would not speak the truth about the state of the realm; but Henry, he said, "trusteth on the Trinity that truth shall him help."[36]

It was possible that no writer would dare say otherwise, even anonymously, of a king who still wore the crown. The misdeeds of "evil counselors" were a well-worn trope for good political reason. And there were undoubtedly truths on which Henry was not prepared to act: any that might require him, for example, to compromise his commitment to his most faithful servants. Still, the last wishes he dictated from his sickbed corroborated the poet's judgment. Henry knew that he must see the world as it was, and account, in life and in death, for what he had chosen to do.

But hours became days and days became weeks, and Henry did not die. Hugh Waterton did, that summer. Waterton was more than a servant, more than a friend; a generation older with no sons of his own, he had been at Henry's side for thirty years, ever since Gaunt had first arranged for his heir to be attended by a household of his own. Waterton had traveled with Henry to Prussia and Lithuania and across Europe to Jerusalem, and had been a surrogate parent to Henry's children, just as he had once been to Henry himself. He was the safest of the safe pairs of hands into which the king had entrusted everything that was most precious or most necessary, and now he was gone. His death was a heavy blow, and it fell on an agonizing bruise. Less than a month before, a letter had reached London from the imperial court in Germany, the new home of Henry's seventeen-year-old daughter, Blanche, who had spent years of her childhood in Waterton's care. After a difficult pregnancy, she had given birth to a boy on May 22, and died later the same day. "Now that she is gone, the delight and joy of my life are gone too," wrote her heartbroken husband.[37]

Though grief compounded the physical strain under which Henry was already laboring, he put as brave a face as he could on his condition. "...you, next to God, I thank of the good health that I am in," he had told Archbishop

Arundel in April 1409 during his slow convalescence after January's desperate low. Since God had seen fit to spare him, he was also moved to atone for past wrongs. That summer, he finally made good a promise, given years before and neglected since, to build a chantry chapel on the field outside Shrewsbury where the bones of the men who had died in his battle with Hotspur lay heaped in a pit beneath the grass. By the time supplies of lead for the chapel roof were dispatched on his orders from Tutbury in August, Henry had recovered enough to take his place in public once again at the head of his court. In late July, he spent four days at Clerkenwell outside London's walls, accompanied by his eldest son and his nobles, to watch a cycle of plays telling the story of the world from the Creation to the Day of Judgment to come. From there he moved to neighboring Smithfield, staying at the priory of Saint Bartholomew, to preside over a week-long tournament in which eight knights led by Jean de Werchin, the steward of Hainaut and a new star of European chivalry, challenged an English team of eight representing the Order of the Garter. The king sat in comfort each day beneath cloth-of-gold hangings in the brilliantly painted stand, watching the Garter knights take the prize, by seven courses to one, under the elegantly skillful leadership of his brother John Beaufort and his brother-in-law John Cornwall.[38]

It was half a lifetime ago that Henry had made his own reputation in the lists against Boucicaut at Saint-Inglevert, with John Beaufort competing alongside him. Of his other companions then, John Holand, Thomas Mowbray, and Harry Hotspur—all of whom, one way or another, had become his enemies—and his friend Thomas Rempston were dead. Henry was forty-two, four years younger than his father had been when Gaunt took an army to Castile in 1386. Henry's sister Catalina still wore the crown Gaunt had won for her there, now as a widowed regent for her little son. But Henry could no longer fight. What remained was to hold the realm of England for his heir, and find some way to make peace with what he had done to become its king.

He faced the future in a state of chronic ill-health. He was struggling with a skin condition—Adam Usk called it a "festering of the flesh and dehydration of the eyes"—and debilitating circulatory or intestinal problems.

Within his suffering body, however, his mind was clear. There was no terrifying vacuum at the heart of government like that created by the absent
presence of King Charles in Paris. But there was an increasingly evident
vacancy when it came to the details of day-to-day command. In retrospect,
the wrangles over financial and administrative process in the long parliament
of 1406 had in some ways been a blessing; it was just as well, given Henry's
physical incapacity, that the council already had experience of managing the
kingdom around him.[39]

Their successes had continued after the financial and military campaigns
of 1407. Archbishop Arundel—with the help of the formidable John Tiptoft,
who had been promoted in July 1408 from treasurer of the king's household to treasurer of England—had made significant strides in stabilizing the
crown's finances. Greater rigor in planning and accounting had made good
use of the tax granted in 1407; greater security at sea had allowed wool exports to grow; greater economy in the royal household had reduced spending
and increased confidence in the regime. In Wales, Prince Henry finally took
Aberystwyth Castle in September 1408. Glyn Dŵr and his son Maredudd
slipped yet again through English hands, but when Harlech fell in February 1409 much of the rest of his family was captured: his wife, another of
their sons, two of their daughters, and three of their granddaughters. Edmund Mortimer, the little girls' father, died during the siege. The rebels were
now pinned back into the northwest of the principality where the revolt had
begun nine years before. Their Percy allies within England were dead and
their hopes of help from France and Scotland gone. Somewhere Glyn Dŵr
still lived, but his name was becoming, like Richard's, that of a ghost. By the
summer of 1409, as the officers of the principality set about reimposing royal
control and issuing pardons in return for heavy fines, the prince was back at
Westminster with Archbishop Arundel and the council.[40]

Behind the scenes, however, the council was not functioning as well as
it once had. John Beaufort's part in government was beginning to be limited by his health. At only thirty-eight, and despite his distinguished display in the jousts against the Hainauters, he was suffering from recurrent
bouts of illness. Meanwhile, Archbishop Arundel was less impressed by the
two younger Beaufort brothers. Henry Beaufort, bishop of Winchester, was

intelligent, politically ambitious, and worldly—too worldly, to the arch-bishop's taste, for a prelate. And Thomas, the youngest Beaufort—not yet a member of the council but a trusted lieutenant of Prince Henry—had over-seen the execution of Archbishop Scrope along with the earl of Arundel, Archbishop Arundel's nephew. Both had thereby incurred his displeasure. All three Beauforts were able men whose service to their brother the king was the basis of their power, but eight months after Scrope's death, when John secured confirmation of the act of parliament by which Richard had legitimized the Beaufort siblings, Archbishop Arundel's hostile influence could be detected in the insertion of a new clause specifying that their rights of inheritance must not include any claim to their brother's throne.[41]

These were tensions that might have been manageable had it not been for the fact that Prince Henry, who was close to the Beauforts, was not im-pressed by the archbishop. Having succeeded in driving Glyn Dŵr back into the Welsh hills, the prince turned his unsparing attention to the administra-tion at Westminster, and did not like what he saw. By the autumn of 1409, the final tranche of the tax granted two years earlier had come and gone, and, for all the improvements in financial efficiency, money was once again running short. The prince found particular fault with the inadequate funds supplied to the garrison at Calais, the bulwark of English defenses in France, of which his uncle and ally John Beaufort was captain, and where Thomas Beaufort held the command of the castle. In November, the council's deci-sion to halve the amount allocated to Calais from the proceeds of the wool subsidy proved the last straw. A parliament had already been summoned to meet after Christmas, but the prince, a man in perpetual motion, was un-willing to wait before acting on his dissatisfaction. On December 11, John Tiptoft, England's treasurer for the past seventeen months, resigned—or was pushed from—his office. Ten days later, his departure was followed by that of Archbishop Arundel himself as chancellor. They were not immediately replaced.[42]

The ailing king had not even been in London when Tiptoft left office: these were moves made by his eldest son to take over the running of his gov-ernment. The archbishop stepped down as chancellor on the day Henry ar-rived back in Westminster. The king knew exactly how much his son and his archbishop had contributed to his government, and how extraordinarily able both men were. He did not want to have to choose between them. But the prince was a young man, less than half the archbishop's age; he was forensic, he was remorseless, and one day he would be king of England. Henry did not have the strength—or in the end the will—to stand in his way.

Father and son were together at Eltham for the Christmas season, and the prince set about using his proximity to the king to consolidate his hold on the regime. On the feast of the Epiphany, January 6, 1410, a new treasurer was appointed: Henry, Lord Scrope of Masham, nephew of the dead archbishop, but in this context more importantly a man who had served the prince for years in the Welsh war. There was no chancellor yet in post by the time parliament opened on January 27; as a placeholder, the opening speech was given by a former chancellor, Henry Beaufort, bishop of Winchester. The next day, the Commons once again elected Thomas Chaucer as their Speaker, an experienced and able man who also happened to be the Beauforts' first cousin, since their mothers, Philippa Roët and Katherine Swynford, had been sisters. And when the king did finally appoint a new chancellor on January 31, it was Katherine Swynford's youngest son, Thomas Beaufort.[43]

Only days after the opening of parliament and despite Archbishop Arundel's long years of experience—his track record in Henry's service, and the fact that he had managed to survive Richard's—his defeat was obvious. The Beauforts were everywhere. They were the king's brothers, but, since Henry was physically unable to sustain his grip on the levers of government, what mattered was that they served his son. At twenty-three, the prince had already spent a decade on the military and political front line. He was confident in the purpose for which God had so painfully and miraculously marked him on Shrewsbury's bloody field. If there was a vacancy at the heart of his father's government, it was one that he, and no one else, would fill.

Eighteen

1410-1413

sorrows of the blood

Henry had been worrying about Lucia. If he did not, no one else would. Her dowry had not yet begun to arrive from her family in Milan, and there was vanishingly little chance of securing it now that her husband was dead. Edmund had left few lands and huge debts. Back in 1408, Henry had done what he could to make sure as much of the earldom's income as legally possible fell to Lucia. In November 1409, while the prince was picking over the inadequacies of the archbishop's financial administration, Henry issued an order under the privy seal pardoning any money she owed to the crown. He also paid £200 to reclaim a store of silver plate that her husband had pawned in Southampton to fund his fatal voyage to Brittany, some of it engraved with the arms of Kent and Milan, and gave it back to Lucia as a gift.[1]

They were small gestures. It was apparent that the king lacked the energy to tackle bigger questions, such as the conflict within his government between his eldest son and his archbishop of Canterbury. Henry was a closer, more indulgent father to his second son, Thomas, who had stayed on in the royal household with his entourage after his summons to Henry's sickbed, and was now irritating his older brother by refusing either to give up his title and income as the king's lieutenant in Ireland or to return to Dublin to do the job. But, more distant though his relationship with his firstborn might be, Henry recognized the remarkable qualities of the son who had never demanded his paternal tolerance. If the prince of Wales was taking a political lead while the king was incapacitated, that was an appropriate role for the heir to the throne—and, given the urgent need to secure a grant of taxation, Henry was prepared to let the prince handle the challenges of the parliament that assembled on January 27 under the gaze of the biblical kings and tyrants who ranged the walls of the Painted Chamber at Westminster.[2]

The king himself was present that day to hear Henry Beaufort, in his opening speech, explain that the duke of Burgundy—who had staged a coup in Paris in the autumn of 1409 to seize control of the government of France—was threatening an assault on Calais. Its defense would require immediate funding. But the financial request put to the Commons in the king's name was the prince's brainchild. Effective military and financial planning required budgets, which required reliable projections of income—and that would become possible if parliament would agree that a tax should be collected in every coming year of the reign, without the trouble and expense of having to call a new parliament for the purpose each time.

From the point of view of a prince attempting to whip his father's government into the kind of shape that might make it possible to defend the realm while simultaneously reducing the crown's debts, the plan made perfect sense. To the Commons, it made no sense at all. Their role in approving grants of taxation was what gave them a voice in government, a means of making the king accountable to his subjects for the resources he took from them. The prince's radical proposal would not fly. But it gave the Commons an opportunity, in response, to put forward a radical proposal of their own: that the finances of the crown should be transformed, and the need for taxation permanently removed, by confiscating the property of the Church.

The clergy already paid taxes as well as the laity, but in the eyes of many laymen their contribution was not enough. For decades, ideas had been circulating about the disendowment of the Church, the proposition being that a spiritual institution dedicated to Christ's teaching had been fundamentally corrupted by possession of the extraordinary wealth—lands, rents, offices, and treasure—that it had accrued over the centuries. Such arguments were associated with the underground sect known as the Lollards, whose beliefs—derived from the work of the Oxford theologian John Wycliffe—the Church loudly condemned as heretical. Some of their teachings were clearly and unequivocally so: most fundamentally, their rejection of transubstantiation, the doctrine at the heart of the Catholic faith according to which bread and wine were literally changed, through the sacrament of the Eucharist, into the body and blood of Christ. But the truth—unwilling though the Church was to acknowledge it—was that reformist proposals for ecclesiastical disendowment could be made without subscribing wholesale to doctrinal heresy, and that is what the Commons now did.[3]

The anonymous authors of the petition had thought through its contents in impressive detail. In enjoying their riches, the document argued, the clergy were "failing to live penitential and hard-working lives" and thereby setting an evil example for the laity, "with the result that scarcely any man fears God or the devil." Fortunately, a solution was at hand: if the king were to sequestrate the possessions of the Church, not only would he reform the spiritual life of the kingdom, but he could use this confiscated wealth to uphold and strengthen his crown, in ways the authors took the trouble to sketch out with some rough calculations. Totting up the estimated incomes of all the prelates, abbeys, and priories of England, they reckoned the king could support fifteen new earls, 1,500 knights, more than 6,000 esquires, a hundred new poorhouses, over 10,000 more priests, and fifteen new universities, on top of an annual sum of £20,000 for the royal treasury—all of which would also, of course, mean that he no longer needed to impoverish his loyal subjects by demanding taxes from them.

The calculations were hardly watertight, but still: to the Church, led in parliament by an alarmed Archbishop Arundel, the petition posed a multilayered threat. In principle, it offered the Commons and the crown the prospect of a win-win—financial relief through spiritual reform—without the explicit taint of heresy. At the same time, it had been shepherded into public view by a small handful of influential men, loyal servants of the king and prince, who were privately sympathetic to Lollard teachings on doctrinal matters and hoped that reform might one day go further. Among them was John Oldcastle, one of the prince's captains in the Welsh war, who was sitting among the lords in parliament for the first time as Lord Cobham, a baronial title recently inherited by his wife. Dabbling in heresy was a dangerous game, but Oldcastle had reason to hope that this was a moment to be seized: not only was his master, the prince, attempting a radical overhaul of royal finances from his position at the head of the king's government, but the new chancellor, Thomas Beaufort—the first layman to hold that office since Michael de la Pole a quarter of a century before—had been instrumental in the execution of Archbishop Scrope. Clearly, Beaufort was not a man to be cowed by ecclesiastical authority.

The Church's best line of defense against a proposition with obvious financial advantage to the laity had always been to insist that disendowment was inextricably linked with heresy, and heresy with sedition. The Lollards themselves maintained that they were not, and would never be, disloyal to the crown. Wycliffe had made the case that, while the secular power could correct the Church, only God could correct the secular power: a proposal for disendowment should never, therefore, lead to revolution in the state. But it was a distinction the Church rejected as both illegitimate and unrealistic. How could an attack on the Church's authority over its own property not spread, on the one hand, to its authority over doctrine, and on the other, to the authority and property of the laity?[4]

Archbishop Arundel's difficulty was that this argument landed with greater force in some political contexts than others. Back in 1401, the Commons had been so preoccupied with the threat of sedition—of subversive conspiracies, wherever they might be found—that they had joined the clergy in calling for harsher repression of unorthodox religious ideas. In the volatile aftermath of Richard's fall and the first months of the Welsh rebellion, the very thought of underground networks of dissenters seemed to loom as an existential danger to the English state as well as the English Church. But in early 1410, after nine years in which their king had survived wave after wave of enemies, pretenders, and rebels, the threats to the realm had ebbed to a manageable low. Rather than the danger within, the Commons had turned their attention back to the pressure on their own pockets, and the possibility that the wealth of the Church might offer a means to relieve it. The petition marked the first time a proposal for disendowment had been formally put forward in a parliament—and the month of debate it precipitated was so inflammatory that the clerks recorded none of it.

Archbishop Arundel knew that, if the Commons could not see the peril into which this attack on the Church might lead the kingdom and their own immortal souls, it was his duty to remind them. In 1401, for the first time in living memory, a relapsed heretic had been burned to death at Smithfield, in order to confirm that neither Church nor state would tolerate unauthorized preaching and teaching. It seemed a new public lesson was required. A Lollard named John Badby, a craftsman from Evesham, had been arrested more than a year earlier for his insistent denial of transubstantiation. "... he held the opinion," Walsingham reported in horror, "that it is not the body of Christ which is handled in the sacraments of the Church but an inanimate object, of less significance than a toad or a spider which are living creatures." In ordinary circumstances the Church saw no benefit in making martyrs of ordinary men, and in January 1409, when his guilt was first established, Badby had lost his freedom rather than his life. But at the beginning of March 1410, with the debate over disendowment not yet extinguished in parliament, Archbishop Arundel decided to make an example of him. Within a week the man was interrogated twice more, refused to recant, and was handed over to the secular authorities for execution.[5]

In this grim project, the archbishop found that he had powerful backing. The prince's differences with the archbishop ran deep, as deep as his determination to secure the revenues he needed in government, but the future king had no interest in ceding ground to heretics. He knew that he would one day be anointed and crowned by the archbishop of Canterbury, a day on which he would swear a solemn oath to be the protector of the English Church. He knew too that God had chosen him for that holy work, and had protected him in turn when his life hung in the balance after the battle at Shrewsbury. In the matter of defending God's word, he would stand shoulder to shoulder with the archbishop—or perhaps out in front. At Smithfield on March 5 the prince was there with the watching crowds when John Badby was enclosed in a wooden cask—a way of concentrating smoke and heat—before the fire was lit around him. Soon terrible cries were heard from the rising flames. The prince ordered that the kindling should be raked aside and the cask lifted, in the hope that Badby might at last be ready to save his own life by acknowledging his error. But the cries had been cries of agony, not contrition. The prince offered him three silver pennies for every day of the life he would regain by abjuring his heresy, but the man refused even as he retched and gulped for air. With a gesture, the prince directed that the cask should be put back and the pyre heaped up, until nothing was left but ashes.

Amid the horror, it was a masterful display: an expression of God's mercy—and a manifestation of its limits—performed in public with total command. In his twenty-three years, the prince had learned a great deal about control, of himself and of others. And what he had discovered during the last two months in parliament was that, for the moment at least, radical proposals—whether his own or anyone else's—would not serve his purpose. Ten days after Badby's execution, parliament was adjourned for Easter. When the assembly reconvened on April 7, there was no more talk of disendowment, or of annual taxes. Instead, a grant of taxation would depend, as it always had, on the "good and substantial governance" the Commons desired from the king. In return for one and a half fifteenths and tenths, to be paid in installments over the next two years, they asked for the provision of justice and the enforcement of order, especially in the midlands and the north where there had been recent disturbances; for restrictions on royal grants until the crown's debts were repaid; and for the effective defense of the realm, everywhere from Calais, Aquitaine, and Ireland to Wales and the frontier with Scotland.[6]

By now, it was clearer than ever that the prince himself would lead the response of the king's government to the Commons' requests. During the Easter break, John Beaufort's illness had suddenly worsened: he died on March 16 in the hospital of Saint Katharine by the Tower. Two days later, the prince succeeded him in office as captain of the town and garrison of Calais. And when the king formally named his council in parliament on May 2, it was a body unequivocally shaped in his eldest son's image. As well as the prince himself, along with the new chancellor, Thomas Beaufort, and the treasurer, Henry Scrope, its members included Henry Beaufort—who would almost certainly have become chancellor instead of his brother, had the Commons been in a kindlier mood toward bishops with a taste for luxury—and the prince's two closest noble allies: the earl of Arundel, now firmly in the prince's camp rather than that of his uncle the archbishop, and the earl of Warwick, who had just returned from two years traveling across Europe and the Holy Land.[7]

When parliament closed a week later, Archbishop Arundel welcomed the king to stay for a few days at his palace of Lambeth on the south side of the Thames. Over the river at Westminster, the prince made his plans to rule England without them.

The earl of Warwick's journey to Jerusalem and Lithuania had prompted vivid memories, but Henry was now struggling to move far even within the confines of his own kingdom. That summer, he made his way slowly into the midlands, where he spent the following six months, lingering particularly at the Lancastrian castles of Leicester and Kenilworth. He still had the consolations of music—the harp he had loved to play since he was a boy, and the entertainment provided by the minstrels he kept in constant attendance, as well as the haunting liturgical polyphony sung by the clerks and choristers of his chapel royal. He himself was "musically brilliant," the chronicler John Strecche would later note, and two motets ascribed to "King Henry," a *Gloria* and a *Sanctus*, found their way into a collection compiled for the chapel of his son Thomas in the years that followed.[8]

And if his body was betraying him, he could turn to the life of the mind. In 1398, despite the pressures of his exile, he had seized the opportunity to follow the debates of the expert theologians at the University of Paris. Now there was refuge to be found in his books, a collection containing histories, poetry, psalms, and scripture. He owned Bibles in both Latin and English, their pages rich with intricate illumination; a two-volume portable breviary, with silk and damask bags in which it could be carried when he traveled; and a book of poems by John Gower, who had died in 1408 and whose effigy in the church of Saint Mary Overy in Southwark proudly wore his Lancastrian collar of Ss, received from Henry in 1393 in return for the dedication of the *Confessio Amantis*. The king's library was kept in his new study at Eltham, where he had commissioned a great desk big enough to store a number of books inside its two levels. There he could read, using his silver bookmark

whenever he set a volume down, in the dancing light from windows filled
with images of the Virgin and the saints to whom he prayed: glazed figures
of Saint George, Saint Thomas Becket, and the name saints of his dead father, John the Baptist and John the Evangelist, whose symbol, like Henry's,
was the eagle.[9]

They were also the name saints of his brother John Beaufort, for whose
soul the king was offering heartfelt prayers. For Henry, the grief was profound, the loss one more among many. Others saw an opportunity. When
he died, John left four small sons and two infant daughters, all born over the
course of the last eight years to his young wife, Margaret Holand, sister of
Edmund, the dead earl of Kent. The new widow was in her mid-twenties,
not much older than the king's second son, Thomas; and now she controlled
her husband's estates on behalf of her eldest boy, as well as her own share
of her brother's earldom. Within five months—an alacrity of which he was
showing no sign in relation to his duties in Ireland—Thomas secured a papal
dispensation allowing him to take Margaret as his wife. Only the intervention of John's executor Henry Beaufort, who was concerned about the
wholesale diversion of his dead brother's estate into Thomas's hands, served
to postpone the consummation of this matrimonial coup.[10]

It was not clear what the king thought of Thomas's bid to become the
first of his sons to marry. Henry's health remained fragile, his attention fixed
on the fate of his own soul. He did not withdraw entirely from government.
In March 1411, he was present at a gathering of his lords spiritual and temporal at Lambeth, a meeting convened principally to consider the ongoing
deficit in the crown's finances. But his only contribution was to refuse to accept any cuts to his debt-ridden household, while instructing his council—a
body he no longer attended—to find some way of increasing revenues to the
point where current expenditure could be met. To Henry, the reality of death
was close, the demands of the next world more pressing than the practicalities of the one in which he still lived. A month later, he asked his archbishops
to arrange prayers and masses throughout the realm to beg God to continue
His grace to both king and kingdom. He knew, he said, what great favor
heaven had shown him since he took the throne, unworthy though he was,
and wanted to make sure that he could never be charged with ingratitude.

His intense preoccupation with forgiveness was given emotional voice again three weeks later, in a grant of pardon to two of his subjects:

> because the king sees clearly the graces poured upon him by the Most High King, not by his own merits but by His ineffable goodness, and wishes to expend on his subjects the gift of grace, and that his affection may have effect, and that mutual charity—without which other things are in vain—may flourish.[11]

It was Henry's eldest son, at the head of the council, who had to keep his eyes fixed on the bottom line. That, so far, had been the story of his life. The prince had learned young that he could rely on no one but God and himself. The men who had taken him into their care—first Richard, and then the Percies, his mentor Hotspur and his tutor Worcester—had turned out to be his enemies. And since his father's return to England in 1399, the king had needed to lean heavily on him rather than the other way around. In his twelve years as prince of Wales and England's heir, he had found allies and followers who would go where he led, but never enough time or money to shield him from the relentless need to make difficult choices.

What had been true on campaign in Wales was equally so in government at Westminster. The new council's task was not an easy one. On all sides, costs still outstripped income. The installments of the tax that had been granted in parliament in May 1410 were overcommitted long before the cash was collected; meanwhile, wool exports were slumping and, with them, the revenues from customs duties. In previous years, such pressures had been absorbed piecemeal, with inadequate funds parceled out wherever the need for defense seemed most urgent or creditors could least easily be palmed off with promises of future payment—the chaotic, precarious response of a violently buffeted regime led by a king who had never, in his previous life as heir to the duchy of Lancaster, had to pore over accounts or check the workings of those who did so on his behalf. Now, however, his son had a plan.[12]

The prince set detailed measures in motion to improve financial efficiency and stamp out fraud. Immediate cash flow was secured during the summer of 1410 by soliciting loans from the crown's loyal subjects county by county, a scheme that brought £8,000 into the Exchequer by the end of July, with more on the way. Public confidence in the council—essential to the success of this program of repayable borrowing—was underpinned by the fact that several of the councillors themselves, including Henry Beaufort, Henry Scrope, and the earl of Warwick, advanced substantial sums of money to the crown from their personal resources. At the beginning of August, the council put a stop on the payment of annuities, a measure the king had always been supremely reluctant to take, but which now remained in place for almost a year on the straightforward grounds that there was not enough money to cover them. And a clear order of priorities was set for the spending of revenues the government did receive, with the garrison and defenses at Calais at the head of the queue.[13]

The contrast with his father's improvised attempts at financial juggling demonstrated not only the prince's exacting character, but the changes that a decade had made to the crisis-torn realm. Against what had at times seemed nightmarishly steep odds, the kingdom itself was still intact, rebels defeated, royal control in Wales reasserted, enemy incursions held at bay. And Prince Henry, as the heir to the Lancastrian throne rather than a Lancastrian duke suddenly wearing a crown, felt no compulsion to indulge the closest sources of loyal support for the regime. In his view, all his father's subjects owed their allegiance and service equally to the crown, whether or not they received individual reward. Not only did his administration place annuities at the bottom of the list for payment, but it sought to rebalance the scales of royal justice away from any suggestion of Lancastrian partisanship.

It was becoming apparent that, in the years since the king had fallen ill, his oversight of his own retainers in the parts of the country dominated by his duchy of Lancaster had faltered. When the Commons in parliament complained of local disorder in the spring of 1410, the places they named included the north midland counties of Nottinghamshire, Derbyshire, and Staffordshire—and, in all three cases, men closely connected to Henry were involved in the disturbances. In Nottinghamshire, one of the king's retainers, a knight named Richard Stanhope, was exploiting the sudden vacuum of authority left by the drowning of Thomas Rempston in 1406 to throw his weight about in local affairs to such an intimidating extent that "no one dared say or do anything contrary to his will," a complaint against him later alleged. In Derbyshire, meanwhile, there was trouble within the Lancastrian retinue itself: a dispute between the duchy knights Roger Leche and John Cokayn escalated to the point of armed confrontation, backed by scores of their servants, at Ashbourne in the east of the shire in August 1410.[14]

But the worst of the disorder was in Staffordshire, where Henry had put too much local power in the hands of too few men, all of them his trusted retainers in the east of the shire where the duchy estates lay. During 1408 and 1409—by which time Henry's capacity to give complex problems his personal attention was profoundly hampered by his illness—landowners in the west of the shire had begun to respond to their exclusion from the government of their own region with a campaign of intimidation directed at Lancastrian officials, tenants, and properties. Their threats shut down the mill and the plow teams in the fields around the Lancastrian town of Uttoxeter; the homes they trashed included those of a poor widow and a carpenter who had worked for Gaunt and Henry for forty-six years; and their assaults killed two men and wounded several others. In the face of this violent provocation, the Lancastrians were quick to give as good as they got—although, as disorder spread, that fact was nowhere mentioned in the complaint they submitted to parliament in January 1410, an outraged litany of their opponents' crimes to which Henry offered a default response of uncompromising support. He ordered that the petition should be sent verbatim as an indictment into the court of King's Bench, with the extraordinary proviso that, if the accused men did not appear to answer the charges, they were to be declared guilty immediately, without further legal process.[15]

But the prince saw the risk his father was running. Backing the men of his duchy without question, however essential the safety net of their loyalty might seem, threatened to entrench division and heighten conflict to the point where they might become as hated as Richard's men of the white hart, with equal damage to Henry's already-vulnerable crown. Richard had narrowed his kingship from the universal to the partisan, with fatal results; Henry needed to move in the other direction. Violence could not be ignored, but its causes must be addressed. When the time came in November to appoint a new sheriff for the year in Staffordshire, the prince and council chose a landowner named John Delves, one of the men who had been summarily indicted on Henry's orders just ten months earlier. It was the first time since the start of the reign that this important office within local government had been held by anyone outside the small Lancastrian network in the county. Three months later, in February 1411, Delves and five of his local allies secured pardons for all previous offenses of which they had been accused; and later in the year, one of the duchy of Lancaster's local officials was charged with obstructing royal officers in the execution of their duties. Disputes and disorder in this part of the north midlands did not disappear at a stroke, but a corner had been turned, a principle underlined: the Lancastrian crown must offer access to justice to all of its subjects, whether or not they had a history of service to the Lancastrian duchy.

However, the prince was not yet king, which meant that his regime operated under constant pressure: every decision he took could in theory be countermanded at any time by his father. During the summer of 1411, that strain became more overt as the king's health began to improve a little, and with it, his capacity to intervene in government. For eighteen months, royal authority had been exercised on his behalf by the prince and the lords of the council led by Chancellor Thomas and Bishop Henry Beaufort, men who had devoted their intellects and energies—and, in several cases, significant amounts of their own money—to the task of stabilizing crown finances, imposing order on the realm, and reinforcing its defenses. But Henry had not agreed to give up control of his kingdom forever. And wherever differences of opinion arose, it was clear that two factions were now in play. In one camp stood the prince and council; in the other, depending on the issue, the lead might be taken by Archbishop Arundel, by the prince's brother Thomas, or by Henry himself during the lengthening moments of respite from his illness.

These were tensions over policy, played out inside the Lancastrian establishment rather than threatening its very existence. In that sense, the growing conflict represented an extraordinary victory: after years of rebellion within his kingdom and attack from without, the most significant opposition Henry now faced came from his eldest son and his two surviving brothers. Whatever else might happen, his dynasty was safer than ever before in possession of the crown. But some victories were happier and more comfortable than others. This one tore at the heart of the Lancastrian family, pitting father against son, and brother against brother, across two generations.

Some arenas of combat lay outside Westminster. In the summer of 1411, Archbishop Arundel's long-standing attempt to root out traces of heresy among the theologians of Oxford led to a showdown with the chancellor of the university, the prince's friend Richard Courtenay. That August, with Oxford in uproar—debates degenerating into riots, and Courtenay threatening to excommunicate the archbishop for interfering in a university that claimed to be exempt from his jurisdiction—the king summoned both sides to appear before him. It took until mid-November to find a settlement largely in favor of the archbishop's doughty defense of orthodoxy—although the prince was able to protect Courtenay's position as chancellor, even if not the full extent of the university's liberties.[16]

But the greatest fault line opening within the regime concerned the question of France. Three and a half years after the assassination of Louis of Orléans in the shadows of a Paris street, civil war had finally broken out between the man responsible for his murder, the duke of Burgundy, and supporters of the house of Orléans. Their new duke, Louis's teenage son Charles, had been left a widower in 1409 when his wife, Richard's widowed queen, Isabella, died at the age of nineteen after giving birth to their only child. Since then, as part of the formation of an anti-Burgundian league in 1410, Charles had married the daughter of the count of Armagnac, and it was this new father-in-law who lent his name to the coalition that sought to avenge Louis's death and destroy his murderer. By the spring of 1411, troops from both sides were in the field. Burgundian partisans controlled Paris and the distracted figure of the king, while the duke himself directed their operations from his territorial power base farther north in Flanders and Artois. The Armagnacs were mustering their forces in Picardy, the flatlands in between these two Burgundian strongholds, intending to blockade the capital and cut off the city's communication with the duke. Both sides were seeking advantage wherever they could find it; and by the end of April, envoys from both had arrived in England to solicit urgent military help against their opponents.[17]

It was an extraordinary moment. For decades, England's interactions with France, whether military or diplomatic, had been conditioned by the requirements of defense. Now two French armies were ranged on French soil with their sights set on each other. Back in 1390, Henry had not even been permitted to ride through France with a small company of men-at-arms to join a French-led crusade in North Africa; now he was invited to send soldiers to help the kingdom tear itself apart. After years on the back foot, dealing with crisis after crisis, threat after threat, Henry's government had the chance to act, rather than react: to pick its own path through a new world full of risk and opportunity. But in order to make that choice, Henry's government had first to look to itself. Who, in fact rather than name, ruled England?

There was no doubt in Henry's mind. During his illness, his son and the lords of his council had done a fine and necessary job of managing his revenues while maintaining the order and security of the realm. But this was a matter for the king as England's sovereign. He had a lifetime's experience of dealing with the French, and his queen—whose son the duke of Brittany was married to one of the French king's daughters, and whose brother the king of Navarre was currently in Paris—had a wealth of knowledge to supplement his own. He had been sick, but his mind was sharp; and he met both delegations, Armagnac and Burgundian, with barely disguised skepticism. For years, the great lords of France had called him a traitor and a usurper. Charles of Orléans's father had wanted to reopen the war with England; John of Burgundy was a murderer whose word could not be trusted. Both French armies—the Armagnacs in Picardy and the Burgundians in Flanders and Artois—stood within striking distance of Calais. It was a danger Henry did not intend to ignore. England would send soldiers, he decided, not to make common cause with any Frenchman, but to defend English territory. Any further choice could be made later, from a position of strength. And, with God's help, he would lead the campaign in person. On August 14, he summoned the retainers of his crown and his duchy to muster in London on September 23, from where they would sail with him to Calais "to resist the malice of certain enemies of France who are hastening there with their whole power, as he has learned."[18]

Meanwhile, the prince's answer to the question posed by the arrival of the French envoys was entirely different. It was blindingly obvious that his father was not well enough to fight. The king was barely able to ride, instead still moving by boat between his riverside manor houses of Beauregard at Chiswick, to the west of London, and Rotherhithe to the east, spending time with Archbishop Arundel at Lambeth along the way. As a result, the preparations the king set in motion in August—of ships and horses, weapons, pavilions, and pennons—were, by early September, looking increasingly fanciful, unless he could be convinced to let his son lead the army in his place. And that was exactly the prince's plan: not only to lead the army, but to direct its operations. He had defeated Glyn Dŵr in Wales, where his father had failed; he had taken control at Westminster, as his father never had. He had no intention of letting slip this sudden chance to assert the influence of the English crown within a war-torn kingdom it still claimed the right to rule.[19]

His assessment was clear: England's interests would best be served by a deal with the duke of Burgundy, who controlled King Charles in Paris, and whose county of Flanders was essential to the English wool trade. But such a deal could only be done if the prince could find a way of maneuvering round his father. John of Burgundy was offering a marriage alliance, the hand of his six-year-old daughter, Anne, as a bride for the heir to the English throne, if England would lend him troops to fight under the Burgundian banner. "The king would none men grant him," said a London chronicler; but by September 1 the prince had persuaded his father to let him send an exploratory embassy, led by his friend the earl of Arundel, to find out exactly what terms the duke was proposing. Henry made sure, in a document sealed at Rotherhithe, that the envoys' instructions were precisely delineated: the king wanted to know not only what lands the little girl might bring as her dowry, but who else might be associated in such an alliance, and whether the duke would commit himself to helping England recover lost territories in Aquitaine. England's king would decide nothing until the embassy returned.

But England's prince had other ideas. When his envoys took ship for Calais on September 26—by which time it was apparent to all, including the king himself, that Henry would not imminently be sailing in person to France—the earl of Arundel was accompanied by the earl of Warwick and the prince's captain John Oldcastle. With them were 200 men-at-arms and 800 archers, followed over the next few days by another 1,000 longbowmen. The whole expedition was funded out of the prince's own pocket. Silently, without the king's instruction or permission, the prince's embassy had become the army John of Burgundy had requested.[20]

The earls had no authority to agree to a treaty. Instead, they took the duke's pay to help him attack the Armagnacs, who had advanced on Paris from the north and west, capturing the town and abbey of Saint-Denis and the bridge over the Seine at Saint-Cloud. In a ferocious battle on November 10, Arundel and his archers played a decisive part in storming Saint-Cloud, retaking the bridge before forcing the Armagnacs to retreat in disarray from Saint-Denis. Four days later, the English earl and the Burgundian duke were dining with an oblivious King Charles—by now no more than a prop in the increasingly bloody drama of his kingdom— within the fortified palace of the Louvre. Nine days after that, weighed down with coin and silver plate, Arundel, Warwick, and Oldcastle marched their company back to Calais to sail for home.

It was an incisive display of English military capability in the French theater of war, and a tantalizing demonstration of the spoils to be won there. But, back in England, the campaign had precipitated political crisis. The prince's decision to override the king's explicit instructions was open insubordination, played out on an international stage. If he had hoped to force his father's hand by presenting him with a military fait accompli, he had miscalculated badly: Henry would not—could not—let it pass. The king had already summoned a parliament to meet at the beginning of November. In the weeks before its opening, as news reached England that the prince's envoys were marching under John of Burgundy's banner, it became clear that parliament would be the arena in which, one way or another, the conflict between the king and the prince would come to a head.

In the last week of October, the prince made his move. He and the council he led publicly staked their claim to be the guardians of good government in the kingdom. At Westminster on October 26—with the king twenty miles away at Windsor Castle—they appointed William Hankford, a judge in the court of Common Pleas, to investigate riots, unlawful gatherings, intimidation, and disorder in Yorkshire, Nottinghamshire, and Derbyshire, pointing out that they did so "in accordance with a petition of the Commons of the realm in the last parliament." It was a striking statement to make so explicitly, seventeen months after the last parliament had ended and just eight days before the start of the new one. Two days earlier, the prince and council had ordered the arrest of the king's knight Richard Stanhope, whose aggressive self-assertion had provoked a violent confrontation over a land dispute in Nottinghamshire that summer, and the duchy of Lancaster retainers Roger Leche and John Cokayn, who had clashed in a dangerous standoff in Derbyshire the previous year. They, along with three other knights involved in the Stanhope fracas, were sent to the Tower.[21]

The six men had connections with the prince as well as the king: Roger Leche, the steward of his household for the last four years, was particularly close. But the prince, it seemed, was positioning himself as a ruler who could be trusted to balance the scales of justice, to uphold the law and enforce order, no matter how powerful the men he was required to discipline. And, having laid the groundwork for his pitch to the Commons when they assembled at Westminster, he turned his attention to his father. This was a private and much more provocative message, delivered behind closed doors with the support of his uncle Bishop Henry Beaufort. The king was unwell, they said, and "no longer able to apply himself to the honour and profit of the realm." Henry should therefore abdicate his throne for the good of the crown and the kingdom, making way for his son to succeed him as King Henry V.[22]

For an heir to the throne who was impatient as well as implacable, and infinitely frustrated by his father's failure to grasp with both hands the opportunity presented by the political cataclysm unfolding in France, the proposal made perfect sense. The prince knew, just as well as Henry did, that Richard had resigned his crown because he was "unequal to the task of ruling." Though Henry's incapacity was different in kind, in the interests of the realm should the precedent still not apply? But that was exactly why Henry would not contemplate accepting what his son had to say. No matter the extent of his infirmity, he would not associate himself with the fate of the cousin he had deposed. He had not betrayed God and his people by breaking the sacred oath he had made at his coronation, and he would not compromise the sovereignty conferred on him by his anointing. He would rule, he retorted, for as long as breath remained in his body.

It was a case for which the prince had no answer. Sovereignty was his to inherit, not to take. And government was the king's to take back. Henry returned to Westminster to sit in state, surrounded by the representatives of his realm, when parliament opened on November 3. Two days later, he told Thomas Chaucer, newly elected once again as the Commons' Speaker, that he would not allow "any kind of novelty" in parliament's proceedings, or any restraint on his own royal liberties, which he intended to enjoy in exactly the same way his predecessors had. The day after that, he ordered that the six Nottinghamshire and Derbyshire knights held on the council's orders in the Tower should be brought immediately into the court of Chancery at Westminster, after which they were allowed to go free. The law of England was the king's law; the justice done to his subjects, his to determine. Then, on November 30, Henry summoned his eldest son and the other lords of the council to kneel before him in parliament to receive his gracious thanks for their diligence and care in discharge of their office over the last year and a half. The king was grateful; and they were dismissed.[23]

When parliament closed in the week before Christmas, Henry's resumption of power was complete. All restrictions on his prerogative dating back to the council's appointment in 1410 were annulled. Henry Scrope was removed as treasurer, to be replaced by the king's loyal servant and sword-bearer John Pelham, and Thomas Beaufort surrendered the chancellorship, which was restored in the new year to Archbishop Arundel. A new royal council would be appointed, and the king alone would decide on its composition. When he did so, there were no places for Prince Henry, the Beauforts, or the earls of Arundel and Warwick. On the last day of the parliamentary session, the Commons—clearly anxious about their own part in supporting the prince's defunct conciliar regime—asked their "most dread and most sovereign lord king" about a "great rumor" that he might harbor displeasure in his heart toward them or their predecessors in the last parliament. At their humble request, Henry was pleased to confirm that he recognized their loyalty. And when he issued a general pardon on December 22, there was no more talk of ineffable grace or mutual charity, only a terse reminder that all those who wished to take advantage of the grant should submit their paperwork by midsummer.[24]

Henry's illness was undeniable, but it was invigorating, after everything he had survived, to find a parliament begging his forgiveness rather than questioning his competence. His son, and the rest of his subjects, would do well to remember he was not dead yet.

In France, John of Burgundy appeared to be carrying all before him. With the Armagnacs in retreat, his forces swept through the regions around Paris as far north as Boulogne and as far south as the Loire. In England, from his new position outside the council chamber, the prince continued to lobby urgently for a formal Burgundian alliance. When the duke sent new envoys to London at the beginning of February 1412, they brought letters of accreditation addressed to the king, the queen, and the prince, but it was the prince who welcomed them as honored guests at his mansion on the waterfront at Coldharbour, upstream from London Bridge. There negotiations continued about his prospective marriage to the duke's daughter—a subject that was formally sanctioned for discussion by the king—and about the dispatch of more English troops in the duke's support, which was not.[25]

The Burgundians left London a month later in a buoyant mood. An agreement, they believed, was close. But their return to France was followed by the arrival in England of an Armagnac embassy, and neither the Burgundians nor their host the prince had bargained for what, in their desperation, the Armagnacs were prepared to put on the negotiating table. The Armagnac lords—the dukes of Orléans, Berry, and Bourbon and the counts of Armagnac and Alençon—authorized their envoys to confer with "Henry, by the grace of God king of England." This was formal French recognition, for the very first time, of Henry's right to wear the English crown. And what they were authorized to discuss was equally extraordinary. The duke of Burgundy was offering the hand in marriage of his small daughter. The Armagnacs offered England's king their political and military support in recovering the entire duchy of Aquitaine, "as fully and freely as any of his predecessors had ever held it." In return, all they asked was 1,000 men-at-arms and 3,000 archers, who would serve in France for three months under Armagnac command and at Armagnac wages.[26]

For Henry, this changed everything. For years, he had lived with the fear that the kingdom God had given him to rule might disintegrate in his hands: that the Scots might overrun the north, that Glyn Dŵr might take Wales, that Calais or what remained of English Aquitaine might fall to the French. So far, he had fought off every challenge, but the attritional toll had been devastating, on his kingdom, his government, his body, and his spirit. Here was vindication at last: the chance not merely to hold on to what he had, but to reclaim lost territories that rightfully belonged to his crown, with all the heavenly approval such success would signify. For the time being, the Armagnac proposal sidestepped the crucial issue of the claim he had inherited from his mighty grandfather to sovereignty over both Aquitaine and the kingdom of France itself—but that question could be addressed later, once the full extent of his ancestors' duchy was back in his hands. Walsingham's report of the Armagnac offer made clear Henry's delight. "Do you see how almighty God is making provision for us?" the king asked Archbishop Arundel. "See how welcome a time this is now, the day we have longed for!"[27]

He had just passed his forty-fifth birthday. After the far-flung travels of his youth, and harried as he had been by the ceaseless challenges in his own realm, Henry had become the first English king since the Conquest not to set foot on the Continent. Perhaps now was the time, and this the military triumph for which God had saved him. Already on April 10 he had forbidden any of his subjects to leave England for the war in France until he had raised an army to fight there. Then, two days before the Anglo-Armagnac treaty was formally sealed on May 18, he issued a summons to his retainers to muster in London on June 15, since "it is the king's intent to cross in person to the said duchy with what speed he may."

Henry's plans left his eldest son infuriated and humiliated in equal measure. Infuriated because he was convinced his father was making the wrong choice: the prince believed a treaty with John of Burgundy would protect both the garrison at Calais and English exports of wool to the Low

Countries, while the prospect of an Armagnac-assisted recovery of Aquitaine was no more than a mirage, guaranteeing only a Burgundian assault on the duchy sooner rather than later. And humiliated, because he faced the necessity of withdrawing from an alliance that had been all but concluded, an alliance in pursuit of which his retainer and friend the earl of Arundel had already fought with honor under the duke of Burgundy's command. At the end of May, both the prince and the earl wrote to the duke to offer their excuses and explanations, which—for all the chivalrous elegance of the Latin in which they were written—boiled down to the fact that the king had made his decision and they had no choice but to follow.[28]

Literally so, when it seemed that Henry would lead the campaign himself. On May 20, the prince and his three younger brothers all swore solemn oaths to join their father in defending the Armagnac cause; and if the king were to take personal command of the army, then the prince of Wales—who had been invested with the title of duke of Aquitaine as well as duke of Lancaster as his father's heir back in 1399—would naturally serve as his deputy. But, however buoyed the king was, his optimism about his own health could not long survive exposure to military reality. As the weeks went by, preparations for Henry's departure were increasingly noted in the conditional tense. And if the king were not to take personal command of the army, then political reality dictated one more inescapable conclusion: after the trick the prince had pulled in sending the earls of Arundel and Warwick to fight for the duke of Burgundy six months earlier, he could not be trusted to take his father's place.[29]

Instead, another candidate was being groomed for the role. In May, the prince's brother Thomas was finally allowed to marry Margaret Holand, widow of his uncle John Beaufort. The young couple were subsequently granted custody of her little son and the estates of the earldom of Somerset to which the boy was heir. Then on June 8, Henry appointed Thomas to lead the force of 4,000 troops promised to the Armagnac lords, with Edward of Rutland, duke of York, and Thomas Beaufort, the admiral of England, as his deputies. On July 9, with the soldiers mustering at Southampton, the king gave his second son the title of duke of Clarence, previously held by Henry's uncle Lionel of Antwerp, second surviving son of the great King Edward III.

Two days after that, Henry formally appointed Thomas his lieutenant in Aquitaine. A greater rebuff to the heir to the throne—who was nominally Aquitaine's duke, and Thomas's senior in both age and military experience—could hardly have been imagined.[30]

The prince made his unhappiness clear. In June, he left court for his estates in the midlands, from where he protested his loyalty in a lengthy open letter. He was too hardheaded to suppose that the question of command in Aquitaine might be reopened, now that the decision in favor of his brother had been made public. Instead, he was concerned with its wider ramifications: the possibility that Henry might intend to do still more to promote the son who had always been his favorite, or even that those around the throne might be whispering in the royal ear about his own place in the order of succession. Vicious rumors were circulating, the prince alleged in forensically sophisticated Latin, "saying that we, longing for the crown of England with murderous desire, were rising up against our own father with the violent support of the people, planning a heinous crime, and while our lord father lives were snatching the scepter and the royal insignia for ourself, his liegeman, by an unjust entitlement and by tyrannical force." In fact, he declared, his love and obedience were "as great as filial humility can express." He wanted nothing more than his father's happiness and the recovery of Aquitaine, while those who claimed otherwise were "children of iniquity, disciples of dissension, supporters of schism, instigators of wrath, and originators of strife."[31]

The prince sent copies of his letter to "almost every part of the realm," Walsingham noted, transcribing its text in full into his chronicle. But in both form and content it was a rhetorical salvo aimed at his father, with England's people as his witnesses, rather than a popular manifesto. He returned to the capital at the end of the month with a large and distinguished retinue—a move made "to strengthen the king's trust in his promises," Walsingham said, through a choreographed display of his rank and the loyalty of his following. When he was admitted to his father's presence, the king welcomed him with open arms. For all the last year's drama, Henry loved his son. And, for all the prince's suspicions, both the king and his chief counselor, Archbishop Arundel, were too pragmatic to mess with the legitimacy of the Lancastrian succession that had been established with such effort since 1399. Nor did they wish to deprive the kingdom of an heir of the prince's extraordinary caliber, however much he might chafe against his years in waiting.[32]

Although the thought went unspoken, it was also apparent that the wait might not go on much longer. Henry, Walsingham reported, could no longer ride or walk without pain. It might be wiser—as well as a suitable rebuke to his presumption—for the prince to remain on hand in England rather than lead an army on an unpredictable tour of duty in France. That the king had not turned his back completely on his son or his brothers was already clear from his commission to Thomas Beaufort, the former chancellor in the prince's toppled administration, to sail with the new duke of Clarence and his forces. Beaufort too received a new title, as earl of Dorset, before the fleet embarked. But the prince's estrangement from the campaign and the tension in his relationship with his father were manifest in the fact that he did not attend the ceremonies at which his brother and his uncle were so honored. It was a delicate peace that reigned in England by the time Clarence and his troops finally put to sea in the first week of August.[33]

They found an inconvenient peace waiting for them when they landed at Saint-Vaast-la-Hougue in Normandy. Over the previous two months, the conflict within France had shocked even its leading combatants in the speed and scale of its escalation. By the middle of June, John of Burgundy had brought the hapless King Charles with his army to besiege the Armagnac dukes of Berry and Bourbon in the walled city of Bourges, just south of the Loire. For the seventy-one-year-old duke of Berry, it was a matter of existential horror to find himself technically at war with his nephew the king, even if that war were intended to rescue the king from the duke of Burgundy. For both sides, the physical horrors of siege warfare were compounded by the summer's searing heat and, in the Burgundian camp, a deadly epidemic of dysentery. By July 12, John of Burgundy had made his decision. If he could not take Bourges by force, he would make peace with the Armagnac traitors before the English could arrive to rescue them. The duke of Berry agreed with relief; and on July 22 the Armagnac lords wrote to offer Henry their apologies that they would not, after all, be able to honor the treaty they had made, since their sovereign, King Charles, had forbidden it.[34]

Two could play at that game. The duke of Clarence and his troops had orders from their own sovereign and, as they began to move south toward the Loire, looting, killing, and burning everything in their path, they were determined to carry them out. The young duke explained with regret that he—not being his father or brother—could not accept any letters addressed to them, nor could he give credence to the suggestion that such noble lords of France might dishonor their word. Instead, he expected the payment he and his men had been promised. Their campaign of destruction was so brutally effective and so impossible to counter that the Armagnacs had no choice but to open negotiations in the attempt to buy them off. On November 14 at Buzançais, fifty miles west of Bourges, Clarence reached a settlement with the dukes of Berry, Bourbon, and Orléans: his army would leave the kingdom of France by January 1, 1413, in return for the sum of £40,000. As pledges while the lords attempted to raise the cash, Clarence accepted hostages including Orléans's thirteen-year-old brother, John, count of Angoulême, and exquisite pieces from the duke of Berry's treasury, including a jewel-studded golden cross housing a nail from the crucifixion.[35]

The agreement did not specify whether or not "the kingdom of France" Clarence was agreeing to leave included the duchy of Aquitaine. That was a question mired in more than half a century of cross-Channel conflict. But Clarence's reading of the terms became obvious as soon as his men were on the road once more. He had no intention of going home. They marched southwest, this time with impeccable discipline, to reach Bordeaux on December 11. As they settled into the city for Christmas, with the young duke and his captains Rutland and Thomas Beaufort making plans to reimpose effective English lordship in Aquitaine for the first time in a generation, they showed such imperious confidence, reported the monk of Saint-Denis, that they seemed "as secure as if they were in London, surrounded by their own countrymen."

If they had been in London, Henry's favorite son would have seen how badly his father was struggling with the demands of even his severely diminished days. The king was surrounded by as much magnificence as ever. One matching suite of his robes, a total of nine garments including two mantles and two warm hats, was furred with 80 skins of ermine and lined with nearly 12,000 pelts of softest gray-blue Baltic squirrel. Henry was ferried the short distances between his palaces and lodgings along the Thames in a gold and scarlet barge with a carved leopard—a royal echo of the cheetah he had once brought back from Cyprus—at its prow. But his body was failing. He was disfigured, increasingly immobile, in constant pain. In place of his abandoned dreams of fighting in France, his thoughts returned to those earlier travels. If he could not ride, perhaps the sea would carry him back to Jerusalem as a pilgrim. On October 1, 1412, he ordered the keeper of his ships to cut down 800 oaks in the park at Eltham for the building of three new galleys for his royal use. But with every passing day, the hope that he might live to see the vessels launched grew fainter.[36]

In November came cheering news of Thomas's military and diplomatic exploits, but money was, as always, in short supply. The prince, who had returned to the capital in late September "with an huge people," said one London chronicler, was lobbying hard for further funding of the defenses at Calais, which were now, as he had predicted, under threat from Burgundian forces. From his sickbed, Henry summoned a parliament to meet at the beginning of February 1413. He rallied enough to address the assembly, if only once and only briefly.[37]

On March 20, he left the palace of Westminster for the neighboring abbey to make an offering at the shrine of Saint Edward the Confessor, beside which stood the elaborate tomb Richard had commissioned, where his corpse did not lie. There Henry collapsed. He was carried to a room in the abbot's lodging and laid before the fire. On the timbers of the decorated ceiling high above his head, he could see the letter R repeated again and again and again, and over every one a delicately painted crown. He asked where he was. The Jerusalem Chamber, came the reply. A prophecy had foretold that he would die in Jerusalem, he said. He had hoped to set foot in the Holy Land once more, but his time had come. He would not see his forty-sixth birthday. He commended his soul to God's mercy. It was over.[38]

Nineteen

1413-1415

the balance and the sword

Many stories were told, by men who were not there, about the hours before Henry's death. Some of these tales looked to the past. The king's confessor, one chronicler claimed, urged him to repent and do penance for the deaths of King Richard and Archbishop Scrope, and for the "wrong title" of his crown. By this account, Henry responded that he had unburdened his conscience to the pope, who had absolved him; and "as for the third point, it is hard to set remedy, for my children will not suffer that the regality go out of our lineage."[1]

They certainly would not, as the stories looking to the future made clear. The Burgundian chronicler Enguerrand de Monstrelet put the prince at his father's bedside and had him pick up the crown, believing the king had died. But Henry regained consciousness, and asked where it was. "My lord," said the prince, "your attendants here assured me that you were dead, and because I am your eldest son, to whom your crown and your realm will belong after your death, I took it." "Good son," Monstrelet had Henry reply, "how will you have a right to it? For I never did, as you know well." "My lord, you held and kept it with your sword, and I intend to do the same for as long as I live." "Very well then," said the king. "The rest I leave to God, and I pray that He will have mercy on me."[2]

Whether heavily embroidered or spun out of thin air, these deathbed scenes spoke to an irrefutable and disturbing truth: that the events of 1399 lay

at the heart of Henry's legacy. Richard's right to the throne had been unquestioned, but his misrule had necessitated his violent removal. Henry's right
had been contested from the start, but the qualities he displayed in government had enabled him to hold on to power, white-knuckled though his grip
had often been. He had never been able to act with the freedom of a wholly
legitimate king, but he had survived to hand on the crown to his son. As a
result, King Henry V claimed England's throne by right of inheritance, even
if it was inheritance from a usurper. Had the deposition been a sin, for which
heaven might visit retribution on the usurper's heir? Or did the succession of
the usurper's heir mean that heaven had vindicated the deposition?

The new king—who spent the night after his father's death in prayer
with a holy recluse at Westminster—already knew that the political uncertainty caused by Henry's final illness had roused Richard's dormant ghost.
In the last days of Henry's life, notices had begun to appear on church doors
across the capital in the name of John Whitelock, a former groom in Richard's household, in which he swore by all manner of oaths that his royal
master was alive and well in Scotland. Henry's son, who was well aware that
the impostor Thomas Ward still lived in Stirling Castle under the protection
of the government in Edinburgh, immediately moved to strengthen his hand
against any conspiracy that might be forming north of the border: on the
first full day of his reign, he ordered that the captive king of Scots, eighteen-
year-old James I, should be returned to strict confinement in the Tower.[3]

He was determined that his own control of government in England
should be instant and total. That same day, March 21, he dismissed his father's chancellor and treasurer, Archbishop Arundel and John Pelham, and
replaced them in office with his uncle Bishop Beaufort and his military lieutenant the earl of Arundel. His administration, it appeared, would be the
conciliar regime of 1410 reborn, this time with the backing of his newly sovereign authority. He also issued a proclamation forbidding all disturbances
or unlawful gatherings on pain of immediate arrest, since "the king wills that
peace, quiet and tranquility shall be had within the borders of our realm."
But this peace secured through obedience to the king's will would be underpinned by his attention to law and justice. The following day, he summoned the first parliament of his reign to meet at Westminster in May; and

a week after that, he took the unusual step of replacing the chief justice of King's Bench with his own nominee, William Hankford, the judge he and the council had appointed to tackle disorder in the midlands back in 1411.[4]

The transfer of power from the old reign to the new required theological ritual as well as administrative change. The new king's first ceremonial task was to bury his father. The peculiarities of the last royal funeral, thirteen years before, offered no usable precedent: Richard's burial at Langley, like his death at Pontefract, had taken place in the shadows. But Henry's own last wishes meant that the lavish funeral of Edward III at Westminster almost four decades earlier could provide no direct template either. Henry had chosen Canterbury Cathedral as his resting place, not the Confessor's abbey, and he had been anxious about facing the judgment of heaven decked in the trappings of royal pomp. Instead, his spiritual mentor Archbishop Arundel took charge of a rite that, in its quiet reverence, reflected the dead king's unease about his chances of salvation.

With scrupulous care, Henry's body was embalmed, wrapped round five times in leather, and enclosed in molded lead with its lifeless hands raised together in prayer. Then the corpse in its leaden shroud was set in a roughly made elm-wood coffin, the space around it packed with ropes of twisted hay. A rudimentary cross formed of tied twigs was placed inside before the lid was nailed shut. Once the coffin was ready, the cortège made its way slowly by barge from Westminster more than twenty miles eastward along the river to the mouth of the Thames at Gravesend, and then by road another thirty miles to Canterbury, accompanied all the way by the new king with his brothers John and Humphrey and their noble attendants in torchlit procession. There Henry was interred, as he had wished, in the cathedral's Trinity Chapel beside the shrine of Saint Thomas Becket, with whose sacred oil he had been anointed at Westminster almost fourteen years earlier.[5]

Meanwhile, the oil and the abbey were prepared for another coronation. On Friday, April 7, not quite three weeks after his father's death, the new king rode with his attendants from Kingston-upon-Thames, southwest of the capital, to London Bridge, where he was met by a great company of lords, knights, clergy, and citizens, come to escort him in procession to the Tower. The next day, he created fifty new knights who, following the precedent of 1399, had kept vigil overnight in the Tower's chapel and then taken a purifying bath before receiving the honor. They included the twenty-one-year-old earl of March and his younger brother, Roger Mortimer, potential claimants to the crown who had lived in the prince's household for the last four years, after the drama of their attempted kidnapping by Rutland's sister, Constance, back in 1405. Alongside the Mortimer boys stood the heirs of two of the lords who had died in rebellion against the Lancastrian crown in 1400: Constance's sixteen-year-old son, Richard Despenser, and eighteen-year-old John Holand, son of the king's aunt Elizabeth by her first husband, the earl of Huntingdon. If the coronation of 1399 had focused on the legitimation by any means possible of a new Lancastrian regime, it seemed—if the inclusion of these young men was anything to go by—that the coronation of 1413 was predicated on a newly assertive claim to legitimacy by England's Lancastrian king.[6]

Later that day, the knights formed a guard of honor as the king rode through cheering crowds in the streets of his capital to his palace of West-minster, where he too spent a night at prayer. Then, on Passion Sunday, sur-rounded by the lords spiritual and temporal of his realm, he was anointed with Becket's sacred oil from the eagle ampulla, and crowned as England's sovereign. When he sat in state on the marble throne in Westminster Hall at the feast that followed, he looked, one observer reported breathlessly, like an angel—one more to add to the twenty-six who gazed down from the hall's magnificent hammer beams, impassively holding Richard's coat of arms in their heavenly hands.

The day was marked by a fierce snowstorm. Some of his people saw the unseasonable weather as a bad omen, foreshadowing harsh rule to come; others, as a happy indication that, in Walsingham's words, "the king would make the snows and frosts of vices in the kingdom disappear and the austere fruits of virtue appear." "Austere" was an apt choice of word, given how ap-parent it was that he intended righteously effective government to be the foundation of his rule. Within the duchy of Lancaster, the new king's ac-cession could be felt as a cold wind whistling through an institution that was used to basking in the warmth of privileged treatment. All its financial officers were to be closely monitored, he ordered, and contributions to royal

income given unquestioned priority over the payment of Lancastrian annuities, "so that the king shall be paid first from what belongs to him." That
was a refrain heard in public too, at the meeting of his first parliament. On
May 9, 1413, he sat enthroned in front of the representatives of his realm in
Westminster's Painted Chamber, listening to his chancellor, Bishop Beaufort, expound on the text "Consultation precedes every action." Three and
a half weeks of businesslike discussion later, agreement had been reached
that an annual sum of £10,000 from royal revenues should be assigned to the
king's own expenses before any crown annuities were paid. The Commons
then granted a tax of a fifteenth and tenth for the defense of the realm, and
were briskly dismissed with royal thanks for their loyal service.[7]

Eight days after that, on Friday, June 16, the king and his three brothers—
Clarence freshly returned from Aquitaine, leaving Thomas Beaufort in Bordeaux as his deputy—rode into Canterbury to honor their father's memory
and to pray for his soul. The quietness of Henry's burial had reflected his
private wishes; this, by contrast, would be the public commemoration of the
founder of a new royal dynasty. After a solemn feast the following evening,
on Trinity Sunday a requiem mass was sung, soaring notes in the cool air
of the cathedral, three months almost to the day since Henry's death. A
hearse—what the French called a "*chapelle ardente*," a "burning chapel"—had
been built to stand over the grave: a great rectangular frame of iron, draped
with pennons and decorated hangings, into which were set 120 torches and
row upon row of candles. Within this blaze of light the royal mourners
prayed, surrounded as they knelt by ninety banners painted with "the arms of
all the Christian kings and other noblemen of divers kingdoms of the world."
In his father's honor, the king offered a gold reliquary head, ornamented with
jewels and pearls, at Becket's shrine. Trinity Sunday had been the holy day on
which Richard's father, the Black Prince, had died nearly forty years before;
but these sacred and spectacular ceremonies, enacted only a few feet away
from the prince's magnificent tomb, demonstrated beyond question that the
new royal line of England enjoyed God's blessing.[8]

That, at least, was what the king fervently hoped. But during the hot
summer that followed the frozen spring, a challenge to his authority began
to unfold from an unexpected source. This time, the trouble did not lie in

Richard's unquiet grave. John Whitelock, his former groom, had been found and arrested in early June, and was charged with treason in July in an indictment that went to some effort to point out that Richard was "universally known" to be "a long time dead." To the king's fury, Whitelock then succeeded in escaping from the Tower, but he did not surface again. Instead, the king found himself buffeted by shock waves from a confrontation between two men at the very heart of his regime, both of whom were looking to him for support.[9]

Archbishop Arundel's removal from office as chancellor had enabled him, at the age of sixty, to devote all his remaining energies to the central vocation of his life: the spiritual health of the English Church and its defense against the threat of heresy. He knew that there were men close to the new king—principally John Oldcastle, his former captain from the war in Wales—who were privately sympathetic to the heretical beliefs of the Lollards, and the archbishop was determined to root out the danger before any public damage could be done. Oldcastle, meanwhile, saw the new reign as an opportunity to convince the king at last that he had a God-given duty to reform the Church, and that disendowment should be used as an instrument of spiritual discipline. It was a hope encouraged by the fact that, in his years as prince, the king had combined his own fierce orthodoxy with a willingness to leave the devotional lives of his servants uninterrogated, so long as their talents were valuable and their loyalty true. But the principle of "don't ask, don't tell" could not hold once Oldcastle was being formally examined by the archbishop—and neither as prince nor as king would Oldcastle's master give public comfort to heretics.[10]

In August, after a bruising conversation with the king at Windsor, Oldcastle retreated behind the walls of his castle at Cooling in Kent and refused to answer the archbishop's summons to trial. Without royal support, however, he could not hold out for long. By the end of September, he was a prisoner in the Tower. In October, after detailed interrogation before a distinguished ecclesiastical tribunal about the nature of the Eucharist and the authority of the Church, he was found guilty of heresy, excommunicated, and sent back to the Tower for forty days in the hope that he would recant. The hope was the king's: a less agonizing version of raking away the flames in which John

Badby burned at Smithfield, as an offer of mercy in return for public repentance. But Oldcastle, like Badby, was not prepared to submit. With the help of Lollard sympathizers in London, he escaped from his prison and vanished into hiding.[11]

The defiance of a renegade knight was not the backdrop the king wanted for what he had planned, that winter, as a symbolic denouement to the ceremonies that followed his accession. He had already offered one acknowledgment of past loss by commissioning a gilded metal effigy of his mother, Mary, for her tomb at Leicester, with graven royal arms to signify the destiny of the son she had not seen grow to adulthood. But he had another, greater and more public act of reverence in mind. In December, the rich heraldic banners that hung around his father's hearse in Canterbury Cathedral were sent to Westminster Abbey to be used in a second royal service of commemoration. Richard's body was exhumed from its grave at Langley, placed in a new elm-wood coffin, and carried in procession twenty miles back to London by the light of 120 torches on a horse-drawn bier draped in black velvet. There, with the borrowed banners displayed on a hearse newly built in Westminster Abbey, the corpse was interred at last beside the Confessor's shrine in the tomb on which Richard's own gilded effigy lay, holding hands with that of his queen. For the new king, the rite was one of atonement, the reuse of the Canterbury hangings not just a matter of canny economy, characteristic though that was, but of ceremonial repetition. He declared, Walsingham reported, "that he owed as much veneration to Richard as he did to the father of his own flesh." It was an implicit claim to be the heir of both kings, a sovereign uniquely placed to heal deep-seated fractures in the body politic.[12]

It was all the more unfortunate, then, that, while the court celebrated Christmas at Eltham, John Oldcastle was on the run with a bounty on his head, hoping to save his own skin and force religious change on his countrymen by raising a revolt. The rebels intended to capture the king on Twelfth Night, the feast of the Epiphany, when they planned to infiltrate the royal household disguised as mummers. The king knew, whether or not the rebels did, that the date marked what would have been Richard's forty-seventh birthday, and the anniversary of the revolt in 1400 that, in failing to kill

Henry, had precipitated Richard's death in custody. But this time the plot was betrayed before the conspirators even had a chance to assemble. Of the few hundred men who answered Oldcastle's call, thirty-eight were executed—seven hanged and then burned as traitors and heretics, thirty-one hanged as traitors—while Oldcastle himself fled into hiding once more.[13]

Insurrection was a shock to the regime, but there was reassurance in the speed with which it had been suppressed. The vast majority of England's people were faithful to the teachings of the Church and hostile to Lollard attacks on its doctrines—and the rebellion, born of desperation as it was, served to confirm what the Church had always sought to argue, that heresy and sedition walked hand in hand. The king had no intention of tolerating either one, or any other kind of insult to his God-given authority. He summoned a new parliament to meet at Leicester in the spring of 1414, where the assembly would sit alongside the court of King's Bench, relocated from Westminster under the supervision of his new chief justice to impose the king's peace across the disordered midlands. Bishop Beaufort's opening address to parliament on April 30 took as its text "He has set his heart to investigate the laws." In the sessions that followed, the king instituted a comprehensive overhaul of the systems by which laws would now be enforced, justice done, and order maintained in his realm.[14]

Almost fifteen years earlier, when Henry had taken the throne, Archbishop Arundel's text had been "A man shall rule over the people." "When a boy reigns, wilfulness reigns, and reason is exiled," he said. "From this danger we are now liberated, for a man is ruling." In 1399, the man—Henry—had been three months younger than the boy, his deposed cousin. The archbishop identified Richard's "youth" in his exercise of will without the restraint of reason, in his inconstancy and untrustworthiness, his preference for flattery over the truth. His self-conscious majesty had been glittering in its manifestation of the rights of kingship, but shallow in its understanding of the responsibilities they entailed. Henry's comprehension of the duties of sovereignty had been substantial, rather than decorative. Had he been born to inherit the throne, he might have been lauded, like his grandfather Edward III, as "a pattern for kings to come." But, in order to preserve the kingdom, he had had to undo the sacred authority of Richard's crown and then attempt, somehow, to refashion it in his own image—an attritional task that, year after exhausting year, had made him old before his time.[15]

In 1413, his successor was six years younger than either the boy or the man of 1399. Rather than Richard's brittle self-indulgence or Henry's intrinsic understanding of human frailty, there had always been a hard edge to the new king's conduct in every part of his life. Given the challenges he had endured and the duties he had faced, perhaps it was hardly surprising that everything he did, he did with uncompromising intensity. Rumor had it that he had sometimes played as hard as he fought; that he had been as relentless in his search for diversion behind closed doors as he was in pursuit of his enemies in the field. If that had ever been true, it did not survive the transformative moment of his accession. God had saved him when the arrow struck his face at Shrewsbury. Now that he was God's anointed, he dedicated himself to chastity for as long as he remained unmarried, and to virtue, under the guidance of his religious advisers; and he set himself to work.[16]

The task was to build on the foundations his father had laid. He wanted not just to resist rebellion as his father had done, but to bring order to his people, God's peace to his realm; not just to defend the kingdom as his father had done, but to vindicate the rights of his crown, riding into battle as God's own soldier. Both sides in France's brutal civil war, Burgundians and Armagnacs, were still seeking an accommodation with England, whether to enlist English help for themselves, to neutralize the threat of English help to their enemies, or to use as a bargaining chip in their political maneuvers within their own kingdom. But, preoccupied as they were with the horrors unfolding there, they did not recognize the extent of the danger they faced from across the Channel. While they fought among themselves, England's king— who had studied the history of England's military triumphs and disasters since the start of the Anglo-French conflict—intended to invade France to reclaim his rightful inheritance.[17]

Organization for war began in the autumn of 1414, with the same focus and intensity he was bringing to the administration of finance and justice. His plan for an invasion of northern France was ambitious and alarmingly costly, requiring him to mobilize the hearts and minds as well as the purses of his subjects. But the Commons were prepared to be persuaded by their severe and impressive king: a tax was granted, arms and armaments stockpiled, and ships requisitioned in ports from Bristol to Newcastle. The nobility were gathering under his banner, their ranks growing thanks to his new promotions and restorations. All three of the king's brothers were now dukes, Thomas confirmed in his title as duke of Clarence, and John and Humphrey created dukes of Bedford and Gloucester. The young earl of March had not only been knighted but allowed at last to take possession of his inherited estates. Rutland's younger brother, Richard, who had been married to March's sister until her death giving birth to their son in 1411, was given the title of earl of Cambridge. The descendants of Edward III were rallying to the Lancastrian crown, and all were deeply involved—along with every other Englishman of fighting age, it seemed—in plans for the campaign to come.[18]

And then in July 1415 at Southampton, amid final preparations for the departure for France—an extraordinary muster of 12,000 troops and twice that number of horses, along with support staff and supplies—the king learned that, like his father before him, he was facing betrayal by men close to him, men who had sworn loyalty to his crown and taken the rewards of his service, men who wanted to reanimate the past to destroy the Lancastrian future.

The conspiracy was led by the new earl of Cambridge. At thirty, the earl had led a dissatisfied life. The whispers about the circumstances of his birth—the possibility that he was the son not of Isabel of Castile's unhappy marriage to Edmund of Langley but of her reckless affair with John Holand, earl of Huntingdon—had never gone away. Langley had left him nothing in his will, and his brother, Rutland, had offered him no resources or preferment. In the unlikely event that his brother-in-law March and his brother, Rutland, remained childless, his three-year-old son, Richard, would one day inherit both the dukedom of York and March's earldom, along with their scattered estates; but for his own part, beyond his new and empty title, in his three decades the earl of Cambridge had acquired little and achieved less. If loyalty had not served him, perhaps treason would offer greater rewards.[19]

More difficult to comprehend was the complicity of Henry, Lord Scrope.

He was the nephew of the executed archbishop, but neither grief nor grievance had prevented him from working closely with both the old king and the new, as a soldier, councillor, and diplomat. There were signs that he too was disillusioned with the turns his life had taken: the king had not made him treasurer within the new administration, as he had been in the council of 1410; and his marriage to Joan Holand, Edmund of Langley's widow and Cambridge's former stepmother, was destructively unhappy. Now it seemed he had doubts both about the wisdom of the king's plans for war and about the incoherence of Cambridge's plans for rebellion: the earl was hoping for support from Scotland, if Richard's doppelgänger could be deployed, and from Percy partisans in the north, as well as men loyal to the fugitives Glyn Dŵr and John Oldcastle, in order to put the earl of March on the throne in place of the man he called "Harry of Lancaster, Usurper of England." But, trapped in the coils of his skepticism and despair, Scrope did not tell the king what Cambridge intended.

The fact of the plot, and its timing, were profoundly disturbing. The king had done everything he could to apply the lessons he had learned from Richard's reign, and from his father's, to establish his rule by right of inheritance and righteousness of government. He was about to leave the kingdom with the bulk of his military forces—something his father had not dared to do after the Scottish campaign of 1400, and never by sea—only to find treachery exposed in his closest counsels. And there were unnerving parallels in play with the traumatic events of his early life. When Richard and his army had left England for Ireland in the summer of 1399, the boy Henry had been with him. By the time young Henry returned home, Richard was no longer king.

But this time England was not waiting for liberation from the oppressions of a tyrant. It was the frightened earl of March himself who revealed the bungled conspiracy to the king. Scrope tried hopelessly to claim that he would have done the same, had March not got there first. Cambridge begged for mercy. On August 5, both Cambridge and Scrope were tried, convicted as traitors, and beheaded in front of staring crowds outside Southampton's fortified gate. March, who sat with his peers as one of their judges, was pardoned for his part in the plot. Edward of Rutland, duke of York, watched his brother die. It was Henry to whom he owed his loyalty: the king who, as prince, had accepted his service and vouched publicly for his courage and integrity. Once, long ago, King Richard had named him "brother," his royal "foster-child." Now—"of all sinners the most wretched and guilty," as Rutland called himself in his will—with thousands of his countrymen he would offer his sword arm and risk his life under the banners of the Lancastrian crown.[20]

Six days after the executions, the king and his fleet of 1,500 ships set sail for the port of Harfleur on the coast of Normandy. The crown of England was his. He would fight for the crown of France.

Henry knew he was special; and God would be his judge.

Ten years or so after the death of King Henry IV, his widow, Queen Joan, commissioned a monument for his resting place beside Becket's golden shrine in the cathedral at Canterbury. On the marble tomb, big enough to carry effigies of them both whenever she should follow him to the grave, alabaster angels held the royal arms of England and her birthplace of Navarre. Directly above, the same coats of arms were painted on an intricately carved wooden canopy, each encircled by a Lancastrian collar of *S*s with an eagle as its clasp. The decorated background was filled with diagonal lines of the couple's badges and mottoes. Joan's tag *À tempérance*—"Everything in moderation"—alternated with images of her ermines. For Henry, there were crowned eagles with the word *Souverain*—"Sovereign"—which since 1399 had taken the place of *Souvenez*—"Remember"—and the forget-me-nots of his youth.[1]

Becoming England's king had made sure that he would not be forgotten. The cost of what he had done could be traced in the alabaster face that gazed up at the heraldic stamps on the tester above: the cheekbones high and the nose long, a hint of a smile around the hooded eyes and small mouth, but the brow creased in concentration or pain, and the cheeks deeply lined above the weight of heavy jowls. Still, the prize he had gained was also there to be seen by future generations. Resting on the finely sculpted hair, cut round and fashionably high above the ears, the crown of England sat secure, the gilt and pigment of its painted jewels shining from the surface of the polished stone. Henry's effigy lay in majesty, and beside it, after her death in 1437, the marble figure of his slight and elegant wife.

Two and a half centuries later, however, questions were raised about whether the king's body truly lay beneath the magnificent tomb. In 1691, a clergyman and scholar named Henry Wharton published the text of a fifteenth-century manuscript he found in the library of Corpus Christi College, Cambridge. Written by a monk named Clement Maidstone, "A History of the Martyrdom of Richard Scrope, Archbishop of York" was a fervent defense of the archbishop and attack on the king who had executed him. Maidstone's account contained a story he claimed his own father had heard in 1413 from a man who had attended Henry's coffin on its final journey along the Thames. That day, he said, a storm had blown up with such violence that the little flotilla was scattered and everyone in it feared for their lives. While the wind raged and the barge was tossed on the towering waves, the three frightened men who were guarding the coffin opened its lid and threw the royal corpse into the water. Immediately there was calm. They closed the empty casket, replaced its cloth-of-gold covering, and continued to Canterbury, where it was buried as though nothing had happened.[2]

The moral of the story—the manifestation of God's damning judgment on Henry through the medium of a tempest—was so clear, so convenient to Maidstone's purpose, and so implausible as a confession supposedly made in the immediate aftermath of the king's death that it hardly stood as a serious historical proposition. But when another century and a half had passed, the curiosity of nineteenth-century antiquarians proved so overwhelming that the acting dean of Canterbury, Richard Bagot, bishop of Oxford, agreed that the tomb should be examined in the hope of settling the question. On August 21, 1832, a small group gathered in the Trinity Chapel: the bishop himself with his wife, Lady Harriet, and brother Sir Charles; the cathedral's surveyor and two prebendaries, including the Reverend John Spry, author of a subsequent account of the investigation; and two workmen, John Pedder and Thomas Laming, who set about removing a section of the marble pavement at the head of the monument.[3]

Once the stone and the rubble below had been cleared away, the party could see the lid of a large and roughly made wooden coffin projecting some way beyond the western end of the tomb. Just visible on top of it, but lying entirely underneath the paving on which the tomb chest stood, was a smaller shape of molded lead: the remains of Queen Joan, they surmised, laid upon her husband's coffin when she joined him in the grave. Given everything in place above it, the wooden coffin could not be opened. The party decided that the only way forward for their investigation was to saw through a section of the lid. It was elm wood, they discovered, about an inch and a half thick, very coarsely worked, but in a state of perfect preservation. Inside they found ropes of twisted hay used as packing, and a small cross of tied twigs, which fell apart as soon as it was moved. Underneath the packing lay another shroud of lead, molded into the approximate form of a human figure. Pedder and Laming were beckoned forward again with their tools. They removed an oval piece of lead, seven inches long and four inches wide, only to find wrappings of leather, five layers deep. Those too were cut through until—"to the astonishment of all present," Spry wrote—they found themselves staring at the lower part of Henry's face.

It was only a moment. Once the air was let in, the cartilage of the nose quickly sank away to nothing. But the embalmed skin was brown and moist, the preserved beard still thick and a deep russet in color. The king's teeth were all present in his jaw but for one at the front—probably lost during his lifetime, Spry thought—and although the opening cut into the lead was not big enough to reveal the eyes or forehead, the surveyor said that "when he introduced his finger under the wrappers to remove them, he distinctly felt the orbits of the eyes prominent in their sockets." Delighted at their conclusion that the king's body had indeed been buried in his grave—"and that it had never been disturbed," Spry added, with no hint of irony—the investigators replaced the layers of leather over the face, put back the excised sections of lead and elm, filled in the rubble, and relaid the marble slab in the chapel floor.

Becket's shrine was long gone, smashed into pieces in 1538 on the orders of Henry's great-great-great-nephew Henry VIII, its jewels seized, the saint's bones disappeared. But there had been no postmortem punishment for Henry's body. In death, if not in life, he lay at peace.

The opening of Richard's tomb in Westminster Abbey was an altogether more rigorous affair. In 1840, the scholar John Gough Nichols, writing a paper about the repeating designs of Richard's white hart and Anne's ostrich that were pricked into their effigies' cast-metal robes, lamented the dilapidated state of the monument. The very existence of these heraldic decorations, he said, had only recently been rediscovered thanks to an artist engaged to draw the figures for the Society of Antiquaries, who had had to spend four full days rubbing away a deep "crust of dirt" before he could pick up his pencil. ". . . for many generations," Nichols wrote, "both the gilding and the pounce-work have been obscured by a thick varnish of indurated dust, until at last they were entirely forgotten."[4]

Three decades later, his report was taken up by the new dean of Westminster, Arthur Penrhyn Stanley, a former Regius Professor of Ecclesiastical History at the University of Oxford, in consultation with the abbey's surveyor, the celebrated architect Sir Gilbert Scott, as part of a program to clean and restore all the Tudor and Plantagenet tombs. By the summer of 1871, with work already finished on the monuments to Henry's great-niece Margaret Beaufort and her son, Henry VII, they turned their attention to Richard's grave. An initial structural survey came to two immediate conclusions. The tomb was in a state of poor repair, but it had not been opened since Richard was reburied there in 1413. And, although the chest had been made airtight when Queen Anne was laid to rest, the same resinous cement had not been used in the marble joints when it was closed for the second time. Whatever the investigators might find inside would not be perfectly preserved.[5]

A hoist of pulleys and ropes was used to lift, first, the metal table on which the effigies lay, and then on August 3 the marble slab below. Beneath lay a chamber six and a half feet deep, two and a half feet lower than the floor of the tiny elevated chapel housing the Confessor's shrine on the edge of which the tomb had been built. The space into which the coffins had been placed therefore reached down almost as far as the pavement of the ambulatory that passed the tomb on its outer side, to the south. A stone arch running the length of the tomb's interior had been constructed to support the marble and metal above, and the coffins—or what remained of them— lay on the ground within. Everything was broken, rotten, in great disorder. "It was found that the contents had been subjected to much interference," Dean Stanley wrote. Over the years, five metal coats of arms that had once been fixed into the south side of the tomb at the lower level, directly beside the pavement of the ambulatory, had been stolen, leaving five holes in the marble. The holes had been sealed in the late eighteenth century, but until then visitors to the abbey had been able to reach their hands inside, "and thus the contents were felt and disturbed, and many portions abstracted and other objects introduced."

Now everything the tomb contained was taken out, piece by piece, for painstaking examination. There were coffin boards of rotting elm wood, and two sets of bones. Queen Anne's, lying on the side of the tomb where the holes had once been, were much depleted. Richard's skeleton was more nearly intact, although the jawbones of both were missing. A forensic report concluded that the king had been almost six feet tall, and that his frame, including his skull, showed no sign of violence or injury. Beside the bones of his legs lay a pair of plumber's shears stamped with a fleur-de-lis, apparently left by one of the workmen who had assisted at his reburial. There were two pairs of plain leather gloves, one large, one daintier, and some fragments of a spotted silk pall. Other objects had been added to the tomb much later, whether by tourists sightseeing in the abbey or by the boys of Westminster School for whom the abbey served as their chapel. These oddments included a handful of marbles; three tobacco-pipe bowls; seventy-two copper coins; a peach stone; an iron buckle; a copper-gilt button; the bones of a bird; a small broken table knife; the bell from a dog's collar; parts of a leather ball. When every item had been cataloged with care, the tomb was closed once again on September 18, its contents arranged inside in three meticulously labeled chests: "The Remains of Richard II and his Queen"; "Accompaniments of the Interment of Richard II and his Queen"; "Later Insertions into the Tomb of King Richard the Second."[6]

Two summers after that, by which time the monument's exquisite metalwork had been restored as closely as possible to the glory Richard had intended, Dean Stanley received a letter from a clergyman in Kent concerning a prized heirloom passed down in his family for a hundred years and more. Back in the 1760s, the clergyman explained, his grandfather had been a pupil at Westminster School. There, as a sixteen-year-old schoolboy, he had watched a friend "poke his hand into the tomb of Richard II" and "fish out the lower jaw-bone of the king." "My grandfather received the jaw-bone from the boy," the clergyman went on, "and it is now in my possession. I have often shown it to medical men, who say it is the jaw-bone of a man in the prime of life." The royal souvenir, he added, now bore a label in his grandfather's handwriting: "the jaw-bone of King Richard the Second taken out of his coffin by a Westminster scholar 1766."

It was a jaunty kind of correspondence. The dean, recording the results of the 1871 investigation for the Society of Antiquaries, relegated it to a footnote. His own thoughts drifted in a different direction:

In the case of none of the Plantagenet tombs have we a more complete account of its building and of its ornaments; in none did the sovereign himself take a keener interest during his lifetime. From none was any king kept away by such strange vicissitudes. . . . The tragedy of his life is centred in his grave.

ACKNOWLEDGMENTS

This book has been a long time in the making, and I owe deep thanks to those without whom it, and I, wouldn't have got here. My extraordinary agent, Patrick Walsh, has been both counsellor and champion, along with the PEW team past and present, especially Margaret Halton, Cora MacGregor, and John Ash. At Penguin, Tom Penn is simultaneously editor, friend, and formidable historian; the book has benefited immeasurably from his vision, as well as from the energy and expertise of Rosie Brown, Olivia Kumar, Corina Romonti, and Anna Wilson. Thank you to Neil Gower for the maps, and to Louisa Watson, with whom it was a pleasure to work so closely, for her care and precision with the text. Ben Loehnen and his team at Avid Reader—Carolyn Kelly, Jessica Chin, Alison Forner, Allison Green, Eva Kerins, Ruth Lee-Mui, Alexandra Primiani, Nicholas Rooney, Clay Smith—have been equally brilliant and fiercely supportive.

Thank you to the Royal Shakespeare Company of 2013, especially Greg Doran, David Tennant, and Elliot Barnes-Worrell, for an intensely inspiring day of thinking about Richard and Henry; and to my Booker comrades of 2022, Shahidha Bari, M. John Harrison, Alain Mabanckou, Neil MacGregor, and Gaby Wood, for an intensely inspiring year of thinking about writing and storytelling. It will be apparent how much I owe to other historians in the field: I should mention particularly Jonathan Sumption's magisterial volumes on the Hundred Years' War, and Chris Given-Wilson's remarkable body of work on these two kings, on which I've leaned with huge gratitude and from which I continue to learn. I'm grateful for the insight and friendship of Rowena Archer, Hugh Doherty, Gillian Kenny, and Dan Jones, who have variously read parts of the text and offered invaluable advice and information, and are responsible for exactly none of the errors that remain. Christine Carpenter has been and continues to be my teacher, mentor, and friend.

The roots of this book lie in her response to an undergraduate essay I wrote in the autumn of 1987, and in the inspiration of her profound understanding of the Middle Ages; I learn from every conversation we have, and hope I haven't let her down.

My friends and family make all the difference. Arabella Weir props me up and took me in when I was juggling book and builders. Thank you to Jo Marsh, Harriet Bell, Jane Morgan, Cathy Fehler, Robert Gordon, Barbara Placido, Anne Shewring, Russell Davies, Walter Donohue, and Declan Ryan. My sister Harriet Castor Jeffery is my example as a writer and a human being. I've drafted and deleted several sentences about my son, Luca Ferraro, in the attempt not to be an embarrassing mother, but I couldn't be prouder of the person he is. I'm so lucky to be able to claim Sam Babstock as my stepson. The greatest luck is to call Ken Babstock my husband.

The roots of everything lie with my mother and father, Gwyneth and Grahame. Words are not enough, but the book is for them, with my thanks and love.

DIRECTORY OF THE MAIN PLAYERS IN THE ROYAL AND NOBLE FAMILIES OF ENGLAND AND FRANCE

SONS OF EDWARD III OF ENGLAND:

Edward, the "**Black Prince**" (1330–76), earl of Chester (from 1333), duke of Cornwall (from 1337), **prince of Wales** (from 1343) and Aquitaine (from 1362)

Lionel of Antwerp (1338–68), earl of Ulster (by 1347), duke of Clarence (from 1362)

John of Gaunt (1340–99), earl of Richmond (1342–72), earl of Derby, Lincoln, and Leicester and duke of Lancaster (from 1362), duke of Aquitaine (from 1390), king of Castile and León (title claimed 1371–88)

Edmund of Langley (1341–1402), earl of Cambridge (from 1362), duke of York (from 1385)

Thomas of Woodstock (1355–97), earl of Buckingham (from 1377), duke of Gloucester (from 1385)

RICHARD AND HIS FAMILY:

Richard of Bordeaux (1367–1400), earl of Chester, duke of Cornwall, and prince of Wales (1376–99), king of England (1377–99)

Son of

Edward, the "**Black Prince**," and Joan [**Jeannette**] (c.1328–85), countess of Salisbury (1344–49), countess of Kent (from 1352), **princess of Wales** (from 1361) and Aquitaine (from 1362)

Half brother of

Thomas Holand (1350–97), earl of Kent (from 1380)

John Holand (c.1352–1400), earl of Huntingdon (from 1388), duke of Exeter (1397–99)

Maud Holand (d.1392), countess of St. Pol (from 1380)

Joan Holand (d.1384), duchess of Brittany (from 1366)

Uncle of

Thomas Holand (*c.*1374–1400), earl of Kent (from 1397), duke of Surrey
(1397–99)
Edmund Holand (1383–1408), earl of Kent (from 1403)

Cousin of

Edward of Langley (*c.*1373–1415), **earl of Rutland** (from 1390), duke of Aumale
(1397–99), duke of York (from 1402)

Husband of

Anne of Bohemia (1366–94), queen of England (from 1382)
Isabella of France (1389–1409), queen of England (1396–99), duchess of Orléans
(from 1407)

HENRY AND HIS FAMILY:

Henry of Bolingbroke (1367–1413), earl of Derby (from 1377), duke of Hereford
(from 1397), duke of Lancaster and king of England (from 1399)

Son of

John of Gaunt and **Blanche of Lancaster** (*c.*1342–68), countess of Derby,
Lincoln, and Leicester and duchess of Lancaster (from 1362)

Stepson of

Constanza of Castile (1354–94), duchess of Lancaster (from 1371), queen of
Castile and León (title claimed 1371–88)
Katherine [Roët] **Swynford** (*c.*1350–1403), duchess of Lancaster (from 1396)

Brother of

Philippa of Lancaster (1360–1415), queen of Portugal (from 1387)
Elizabeth of Lancaster (*c.*1364–1425), countess of Pembroke (1380–86), countess
of Huntingdon (1388–1400), duchess of Exeter (1397–99)

Half brother of

Catalina of Lancaster (1373–1418), queen of Castile (from 1388)
John Beaufort (1373–1410), earl of Somerset (from 1397), marquis of Dorset
(1397–99)
Henry Beaufort (*c.*1375–1447), bishop of Lincoln (1398–1404), bishop of
Winchester (from 1404), cardinal of England (from 1417)

Thomas Beaufort (*c.*1377–1426), earl of Dorset (from 1411), duke of Exeter (from 1416)

Joan Beaufort (*c.*1379–1440), countess of Westmorland (from 1396)

Husband of

Mary de Bohun (*c.*1369–94), countess of Derby (from 1381)

Joan of Navarre (1368–1437), duchess of Brittany (1386–99), queen of England (from 1403)

Father of

Henry of Monmouth (1386–1422), earl of Chester, duke of Cornwall, Lancaster, and Aquitaine, and **prince of Wales** (from 1399), king of England (from 1413)

Thomas of Lancaster (1387–1421), earl of Aumale and duke of Clarence (from 1411)

John of Lancaster (1389–1435), earl of Kendal and Richmond and duke of Bedford (from 1414)

Humphrey of Lancaster (1390–1447), earl of Pembroke and duke of Gloucester (from 1414)

Blanche of Lancaster (1392–1409), wife (from 1402) of Louis, son of Ruprecht, Count Palatine and Holy Roman Emperor

Philippa of Lancaster (1394–1430), queen of Norway, Denmark, and Sweden (from 1406)

ENGLISH LORDS:

(listed alphabetically by family name, chronologically by date of birth within families)

Beauchamp:

  Thomas (*c.*1338–1401), **earl of Warwick** (from 1369)

  Richard (1382–1439), **earl of Warwick** (from 1401)

Courtenay:

  William (1341/2–96), bishop of Hereford (1370–75), bishop of London (1375–81), **archbishop** of Canterbury (from 1381)

  Richard (*c.*1381–1415), bishop of Norwich (from 1413)

de la Pole, Michael (*c.*1330–89), earl of Suffolk (1385–88)

Despenser, Thomas (1373–1400), earl of Gloucester (1397–99)

de Vere:

  Aubrey (*c.*1349–1400), earl of Oxford (from 1393)

Robert (1362–92), earl of Oxford (1371–88), marquis of Dublin (1385–86), duke of Ireland (1386–88)

Fitzalan:

Richard (1346–97), **earl of Arundel** and Surrey (from 1376)

Thomas [known as Thomas **Arundel**] (1353–1414), bishop of Ely (1373–88), archbishop of York (1388–96), **archbishop** of Canterbury (1396–97 and from 1399)

Thomas (1381–1415), **earl of Arundel** and Surrey (from 1399)

Montagu:

William (1328–97), **earl of Salisbury** (from 1344)

John (c.1350–1400), **earl of Salisbury** (from 1397)

Mortimer:

Edmund (1352–81), **earl of March** (from 1360) and Ulster (from 1368)

Roger (1374–98), **earl of March** and Ulster (from 1381)

Edmund (1391–1425), **earl of March** and Ulster (from 1398)

Mowbray:

Thomas (1366–99), earl of Nottingham (from 1383), duke of Norfolk (from 1397)

Thomas (1385–1405), earl of Nottingham (from 1399)

Neville:

Alexander (c.1332–92), **archbishop** of York (1374–88)

Ralph (c.1364–1425), **earl of Westmorland** (from 1397)

Percy:

Henry (1341–1408), **earl of Northumberland** (from 1377)

Thomas (c.1343–1403), **earl of Worcester** (from 1397)

Henry [known as Harry "**Hotspur**"] (1364–1403), heir to the earldom of Northumberland (from 1377)

Scrope:

Richard (c.1327–1403), **Lord Scrope** of Bolton (from 1371)

Richard (c.1350–1405), bishop of Coventry and Lichfield (1386–98), **archbishop** of York (from 1398)

William (c.1351–99), earl of Wiltshire (from 1397)

Henry (c.1376–1415), Lord **Scrope** of Masham (from 1406)

Stafford, Hugh (c.1342–86), **earl of Stafford** (from 1372)

Ufford, William (c.1339–82), **earl of Suffolk** (from 1369)

THE FRENCH ROYAL FAMILY:
Charles VI (1368–1422), king of France (from 1380)

Son of
Charles V (1338–80), king of France (from 1364), and Jeanne of Bourbon (1338–78)

Husband of
Isabeau of Bavaria (*c.*1371–1435), queen of France (from 1385)

Father of
Isabella of France (1389–1409), queen of England (1396–99), duchess of Orléans (from 1407)

Brother of
Louis (1372–1407), duke of Touraine (1386–92), **duke of Orléans** (from 1392)

Nephew of
John (1340–1416), **duke of Berry** and Auvergne (from 1360)
Philip (1342–1404), **duke of Burgundy** (from 1363), count of Flanders, Artois, and Burgundy and duke of Brabant (from 1384)

Cousin of
John (1371–1419), count of Nevers (from 1384), **duke of Burgundy** (from 1404), count of Flanders, Artois, and Burgundy (from 1405)

LIST OF ABBREVIATIONS

Anon. Chron.	V. H. Galbraith (ed.), *The Anonimalle Chronicle, 1333 to 1381* (Manchester, 1970)
CChR	*Calendar of Charter Rolls, 1341–1417* (London, 1916)
CCR	*Calendar of Close Rolls, 1377–1419*, 11 vols. (London, 1914–32)
CFR	*Calendar of Fine Rolls, 1377–1422*, 6 vols. (London, 1926–34)
CPR	*Calendar of Patent Rolls, 1374–1416*, 12 vols. (London, 1895–1910)
Creton	J. Creton, "Metrical History of the Deposition of King Richard the Second," ed. and tr. J. Webb, *Archaeologia*, vol. 20 (1824), 1–423
Dobson, *Revolt*	R. B. Dobson (ed. and tr.), *The Peasants' Revolt of 1381* (London and Basingstoke, 1970)
EHR	*English Historical Review*
Eulogium	F. S. Haydon (ed.), *Eulogium historiarum sive temporis*, vol. 3 (London, 1863)
Foedera	T. Rymer (ed.), *Foedera, Conventiones, Litterae, Etc.*, 20 vols. (London, 1727–35)
Froissart	K. de Lettenhove (ed.), *Oeuvres de Froissart, Chroniques*, 25 vols. (Brussels, 1867–77)
Given-Wilson, *Chronicles*	C. Given-Wilson (ed. and tr.), *Chronicles of the Revolution, 1397–1400* (Manchester, 1993)
Hist. Parl.	J. S. Roskell, L. Clark, and C. Rawcliffe (eds.), *The History of Parliament: The House of Commons 1386–1421* (online resource)
Knighton	G. H. Martin (ed. and tr.), *Knighton's Chronicle, 1337–1396* (Oxford, 1995)
McHardy, *Reign*	A. K. McHardy (ed. and tr.), *The Reign of Richard II: From Minority to Tyranny, 1377–97* (Manchester, 2012)
ODNB	*Oxford Dictionary of National Biography* (online resource)
POPC	N. H. Nicolas (ed.), *Proceedings and Ordinances of the Privy Council of England*, 2 vols. (London, 1834)
PROME	P. Brand, A. Curry, C. Given-Wilson, R. Horrox, G. Martin, M. Ormrod, and S. Phillips (eds. and tr.), *Parliament Rolls of Medieval England* (online resource)
Religieux	M. L. Bellaguet (ed.), *Chronique du Religieux de Saint-Denys*, 6 vols. (Paris, 1839–52)
Traïson et Mort	B. Williams (ed. and tr.), *Chronicque de la Traïson et Mort de Richart Deux Roy Dengleterre* (London, 1846)
Usk	C. Given-Wilson (ed. and tr.), *The Chronicle of Adam Usk, 1377–1421* (Oxford, 1997)
Vitae et Regni	G. B. Stow (ed.), *Historia Vitae et Regni Ricardi Secundi* (Philadelphia, 1977)
Walsingham	J. Taylor, W. R. Childs, and L. Watkiss (eds. and tr.), *The St Albans Chronicle: The Chronica Maiora of Thomas Walsingham*, 2 vols. (Oxford, 2003, 2011)
Westm. Chron.	L. C. Hector and B. Harvey (eds. and tr.), *The Westminster Chronicle, 1381–1394* (Oxford, 1982)

NOTES

Introduction

1. S. Wells, introduction to W. Shakespeare, *Richard II* (Harmondsworth, 1969), pp. 7–14; G. Taylor, J. Jowett, T. Bourus, and G. Egan (eds.), *The New Oxford Shakespeare: Critical Reference Edition*, vol. 1 (Oxford, 2017), p. 357; J. J. Manning, introduction to *The First and Second Parts of John Hayward's The Life and Raigne of King Henrie IIII*, Camden Society, Fourth Series, vol. 42 (London, 1991), pp. 1–4, 17–34; B. Worden, "Which Play Was Performed at the Globe Theatre on 7 February 1601?," *London Review of Books*, vol. 25, no. 13 (2003); J. Scott-Warren, "Was Elizabeth I Richard II? The Authenticity of Lambarde's 'Conversation,'" *The Review of English Studies*, New Series, vol. 64, no. 264 (2013), pp. 208–30.

1. 1367–1377: by my scepter's awe

1. A. Gransden, "A Fourteenth-Century Chronicle from the Grey Friars at Lynn," *EHR*, vol. 72, no. 283 (1957), pp. 276–77.

2. For the life and career of the Black Prince, see M. Jones, *The Black Prince* (London, 2017); R. Barber, *Edward, Prince of Wales and Aquitaine* (London, 1978). The prince's decision to adopt the ostrich feather of John of Bohemia after the battle of Crécy was noted by John Arderne, a surgeon who accompanied him on campaign, in a treatise of 1376 about the treatment of anal fistulas: J. Arderne, *Treatises of Fistula in Ano*, ed. D. Power, Early English Text Society, original series, no. 139 (London, 1910), pp. xxvii–xxviii. The ostrich feather was also used as a badge in different forms by other members of the royal family, as detailed by N. H. Nicolas (who was convinced, partly on this account, that the badge instead derived from the family of the Black Prince's mother, Philippa of Hainaut): N. H. Nicolas, "Observations on the Origin and History of the Badges and Mottoes of Edward Prince of Wales," *Archaeologia*, vol. 31 (1845), pp. 350–84; N. H. Nicolas, "Contemporary Authority Adduced for the Popular Idea That the Ostrich Feathers of the Prince of Wales Were Derived from the Crest of the King of Bohemia," *Archaeologia*, vol. 32 (1847), pp. 332–34. For the ostrich feathers on a black field on the prince's shield of peace, pennons, and a set of tapestries (which he bequeathed to Canterbury Cathedral), see the prince's will: J. G. Nichols (ed.), *A Collection of All the Wills Now Known to Be Extant of the Kings and Queens of England* (London, 1780), pp. 68–69. Many arguments have been made about how and when he came to be called the "Black Prince," given that the name doesn't appear in extant written sources until the 1540s, but this association with the black field of his badge—which may also have been the livery color worn by his retainers—seems the most likely: cf. A. C. Fox-Davies, *A Complete Guide to Heraldry* (London, 1909), p. 459; Jones, *Black Prince*, pp. 3–4. For the chronicler Henry Knighton's comment on Nájera, see *Knighton*, pp. 194–95.

3. For the life and reign of Edward III, here and below, see W. M. Ormrod, *Edward III* (New Haven and London, 2011). Quotation from *PROME*, "Edward III: May 1366," item 1.

4. W. M. Ormrod, "Edward III and His Family," *Journal of British Studies*, vol. 26 (1987), pp. 402–3.

5. Ormrod, *Edward III*, pp. 288–89; J. Sumption, *The Hundred Years War*, vol. 1: *Trial by Battle*

(London, 1990), p. 564; M. A. E. Green, *Lives of the Princesses of England*, 6 vols. (London, 1849–55), vol. 3, pp. 180–86, 245–59; W. M. Ormrod, "The Royal Nursery: A Household for the Younger Children of Edward III," *EHR*, vol. 120, no. 486 (2005), pp. 412–13. For details of Joanna's clothes, plate, and chapel hangings, see the wardrobe accounts published in N. H. Nicolas, "Observations on the Institution of the Most Noble Order of the Garter," *Archaeologia*, vol. 31 (1845), pp. 52–56, 72–83, 145–46. For the letter Edward wrote to Pedro's father, King Alfonso, announcing her death, see R. Horrox (ed. and tr.), *The Black Death* (Manchester, 1994), p. 250.

6. J. Sumption, *The Hundred Years War*, vol. 2: *Trial by Fire* (London, 1999), pp. 8–10; for the Ordinance of Labourers of June 1349, which became the Statute of Labourers in 1351, see Ormrod, *Edward III*, pp. 359–62; A. R. Myers (ed.), *English Historical Documents, 1327–1485* (London, 1969), pp. 993–94. Edward's marriage policy is usually interpreted in purely political and strategic terms—which were clearly of crucial importance—but the cases of Isabella and the prince of Wales indicate that other factors were also in play.

7. Green, *Lives of the Princesses*, vol. 3, pp. 188–93, 198–207.

8. The duchy of Brittany was convulsed in conflict over the succession, and John de Montfort had been brought to England as a baby by his mother, who sought sanctuary and help from Edward. Even years after his daughters' deaths, the king continued to call Pembroke his "dear son." See Green, *Lives of the Princesses*, vol. 3, pp. 177, 271–94, 297–99.

9. For a reference to Joan as "Jeannette, my lord's cousin" in the Black Prince's treasurer's accounts for 1348–49, see Nicolas, "Observations on the Institution of the Most Noble Order of the Garter," p. 161. For her father, see S. L. Waugh "Edmund [Edmund of Woodstock], first earl of Kent (1301–1330)," *ODNB*; A. King, "The Death of Edward II Revisited," in J. Bothwell and G. Dodd (eds.), *Fourteenth Century England*, vol. 9 (Woodbridge, 2016), pp. 7–15. For Jeannette and the Salisburys, see M. W. Warner, "The Montagu Earls of Salisbury circa 1300–1428: A Study in Warfare, Politics and Political Culture," PhD thesis, University College London (1991), pp. 22, 39–40; A. Goodman, *Joan, the Fair Maid of Kent: A Fourteenth-Century Princess and Her World* (Woodbridge, 2017), pp. 27–29, 31.

10. For this paragraph and the next, see Jones, *Black Prince*, pp. 130–34; K. P. Wentersdorf, "The Clandestine Marriages of the Fair Maid of Kent," *Journal of Medieval History*, vol. 5, no. 3 (1979), pp. 203–31. For Thomas Holand's eye, see N. Bryant (ed. and tr.), *The True Chronicles of Jean le Bel* (Woodbridge, 2013), p. 173. Like Michael Jones, and unlike Karl Wentersdorf, I'm skeptical about the story of Jeannette's pre-contract with Thomas Holand: see, for example, the account of the chronicler Henry Knighton, who says that she "had previously been married to the earl of Salisbury, and having secured a divorce from him had married Sir Thomas Holand, for whose desire for her it was said the divorce had been made": *Knighton*, p. 185.

11. Goodman, *Joan, the Fair Maid of Kent*, pp. 42–45, 49–63, 69–73.

12. "*unde de isto matrimonio a multis plurimum fuerat admiratum*": J. R. Lumby (ed.), *Polychronicon Ranulphi Higden Monachi Cestrensis*, vol. 8 (London, 1882), p. 360; and for Jeannette as the "*virginem Cancie*," see "A Wigmore Chronicle, 1355–1377," in J. Taylor, *English Historical Literature in the Fourteenth Century* (Oxford, 1987), p. 292.

13. Ormrod, *Edward III*, pp. 450–51; Jones, *Black Prince*, p. 260. For Jeannette's wedding dress, see M. F. Bond (ed.), *The Inventories of St George's Chapel, Windsor: 1384–1667* (Windsor, 1947), pp. 40–41.

14. M. C. B. Dawes (ed.), *Register of Edward the Black Prince*, Part IV (London, 1933), pp. 401–3, 427, 475–76; Jones, *Black Prince*, pp. 265, 271.

15. *Froissart*, vol. 7, p. 258; A. E. Prince, "A Letter of Edward the Black Prince Describing the Battle of Nájera in 1367," *EHR*, vol. 41, no. 163 (1926), p. 418; M. K. Pope and E. C. Lodge (eds. and tr.), *Life of the Black Prince by the Herald of Sir John Chandos* (Oxford, 1910), pp. 63–65, 152–53.

16. A. H. Davis (ed. and tr.), *William Thorne's Chronicle of Saint Augustine's Abbey, Canterbury* (Oxford, 1934), p. 591; Goodman, *Joan, the Fair Maid of Kent*, pp. 95–96.

17. Pope and Lodge (eds. and tr.), *Life of the Black Prince*, pp. 116, 167.

18. P. E. Russell, *The English Intervention in Spain and Portugal in the Time of Edward III and Richard II* (Oxford, 1955), pp. 138–48.

19. For this paragraph and the next two, see Ormrod, *Edward III*, pp. 415–18; Jones, *Black Prince*, pp. 323–79; J. Sumption, *The Hundred Years War*, vol. 3: *Divided Houses* (London, 2009), pp. 14–16, 18–95; Pope and Lodge (eds. and tr.), *Life of the Black Prince*, pp. 126, 169. The magnificent state in which the prince lived did nothing to help persuade the lords of Aquitaine that his financial demands were reasonable: *Froissart*, vol. 7, pp. 258–59.

20. Not only was Perrers's portfolio of valuable estates growing prodigiously, but in 1373 she secured a grant of jewels and other property that had belonged to the dead queen: Ormrod, *Edward III*, pp. 511–12, 524–44. For an overview and analysis of the functioning of the fourteenth-century English constitution, see C. Carpenter and A. M. Spencer, "England in the Fourteenth Century," in P. Cane and H. Kumarasingham (eds.), *The Cambridge Constitutional History of the United Kingdom*, vol. 2: *The Changing Constitution* (Cambridge, 2023), pp. 84–107.

21. S. Armitage-Smith (ed.), *John of Gaunt's Register, Part I (1371–5)*, vol. 1, Camden Society, Third Series, vol. 20 (London, 1911), p. 47 [no. 63]; Sumption, *Divided Houses*, pp. 152–56.

22. W. M. Ormrod, "Lionel [Lionel of Antwerp], duke of Clarence (1338–1368)," *ODNB*; A. Tuck, "Edmund [Edmund of Langley], first duke of York (1341–1402)," and "Thomas [Thomas of Woodstock], duke of Gloucester (1355–1397)," *ODNB*. Cf. Sumption, *Divided Houses*, p. 229, on Edmund of Langley: "not a man to press his own view even if he had one."

23. A. Goodman, *John of Gaunt: The Exercise of Princely Power in Fourteenth-Century Europe* (London, 1992), pp. 30–35, 45–47; S. Walker, "John [John of Gaunt], duke of Aquitaine and duke of Lancaster, styled king of Castile and León (1340–1399)," *ODNB*. C. Given-Wilson, *Henry IV* (New Haven and London, 2016), p. 24, suggests that Blanche married Gaunt at twelve and died at twenty-one, but this seems too young—not least because, for reasons of physical safety, even girls of the highest status were not usually expected to face pregnancy so early. The juries who testified in the *inquisition post mortem* of her father, Henry of Grosmont, in 1361 offered a range of ages for both Blanche and her older sister, Maud, but those in Staffordshire and Derbyshire, the only two to specify the day and year of their births, gave the same dates: April 4, 1340, for Maud and March 25, 1342, for Blanche. Given the precision and consistency of these statements—and the fact that, if Blanche had been seventeen when she married, the immediate consummation of the relationship would be unremarkable by contemporary standards—this testimony seems the most convincing of the available evidence: *Calendar of Inquisitions Post Mortem, Edward III*, vol. 11 (London, 1935), pp. 92–107. The cause of Blanche's death is similarly uncertain, and it has been suggested that she died of plague: see, for example, L. Richmond, "Blanche of Lancaster (1340x1347–1368)," *ODNB*. But the timing of her death, seventeen months after the birth of her son, Henry, fits the pattern of her previous pregnancies, and I've followed Chris Given-Wilson in preferring that explanation: *Henry IV*, p. 24. For the date of Henry's birth, see I. Mortimer, *The Fears of Henry IV: The Life of England's Self-Made King* (London, 2007), Appendix 1.

24. For this paragraph and the following two, see Sumption, *Divided Houses*, pp. 108–10, 115–23, 171–252.

25. *Anon. Chron.*, pp. 81–83; Ormrod, *Edward III*, pp. 538–54.

26. *PROME*, "Edward III: April 1376," introduction and items 15, 24; Ormrod, *Edward III*, pp. 354–56.

27. Ormrod, *Edward III*, pp. 537, 554–57; G. Lambrick, "The Impeachment of the Abbot of Abingdon in 1368," *EHR*, vol. 82, no. 323 (1967), pp. 263–75.

28. Nichols (ed.), *Collection of All the Wills*, pp. 66–68; Pope and Lodge (eds. and tr.), *Life of the Black Prince*, pp. 129, 170.

29. Pope and Lodge (eds. and tr.), *Life of the Black Prince*, pp. 129, 170; Arderne, *Treatises of Fistula in Ano*, pp. xxvi–xxvii; *Walsingham*, vol. 1, pp. 36–39, 976–77; *PROME*, "Edward III: April 1376," item 50.

30. N. Saul, *Richard II* (New Haven and London, 1997), pp. 14–18; *PROME*, "Edward III: April 1376," item 50. Very little is known of the specifics of Richard's education, other than the standard schooling of a royal or aristocratic boy. I've therefore based my interpretation on an assessment of its context and its apparent effects as he grew to adulthood.

31. M. M. N. Stansfield, "Holland, Thomas, fifth earl of Kent (1350–1397)," and "Holland, John, first earl of Huntingdon and duke of Exeter (*c.*1352–1400)," *ODNB*; Goodman, *Joan, the Fair Maid of Kent*, pp. 90, 98. In 1372, Joan Holand was briefly captured by soldiers of the duke of Bourbon before being released because, the duke said, "we do not make war on women." In 1373, when her husband fled to England, she was left in command of a small garrison at Auray: Sumption, *Divided Houses*, pp. 7, 156–57, 182.

32. The princess's gift was so rich that Gaunt presented it to his father, the king, at New Year in 1373. She had not been in England at the New Year of 1371, so her gift to Gaunt is likely to have been made in 1372: S. Armitage-Smith (ed.), *John of Gaunt's Register, Part 1 (1371–5)*, vol. 2, Camden Society, Third Series, vol. 21 (London, 1911), pp. 22, 193; J. Stratford, *Richard II and the English Royal Treasure* (Woodbridge, 2012), p. 51; Jones, *Black Prince*, p. 374; Nichols (ed.), *Collection of All the Wills*, p. 75.

33. Ormrod, *Edward III*, pp. 565–67; *CPR 1374–7*, pp. 353–54, 364–65. For the "Good Parliament," see *Walsingham*, vol. 1, pp. lxxi, 1–2.

34. G. Holmes, "Mare, Sir Peter de la (*fl.c.*1365–1387)," *ODNB*; Ormrod, *Edward III*, pp. 567–72; *PROME*, "Edward III: January 1377," item 19; Sumption, *Divided Houses*, pp. 270–74, 276.

35. *PROME*, "Edward III: January 1377," introduction and items 1–2; P. Binski, "The Painted Chamber at Westminster, the Fall of Tyrants and the English Literary Model of Governance," *Journal of the Warburg and Courtauld Institutes*, vol. 74 (2011), pp. 122–42; C. Wilson, "A Monument to St Edward the Confessor: Henry III's Great Chamber at Westminster and Its Paintings," in W. Rodwell and T. Tatton-Brown (eds.), *Westminster, Part II: The Art, Architecture and Archaeology of the Royal Palace*, The British Archaeological Association Conference Transactions, vol. 39 (2015), pp. 153–86, esp. 169–75. The chamber was lost when the palace of Westminster was destroyed by fire in 1834; but for Charles Stothard's copies of the wall paintings, made when they were briefly uncovered from beneath layers of whitewash during repairs in 1819, see *Vetusta Monumenta*, Society of Antiquaries of London, vol. 6 (1885), plates XXVI–XXXIX.

36. *PROME*, "Edward III: January 1377," items 1–11.

37. J. Stow, *A Survey of London*, ed. C. L. Kingsford, 2 vols. (Oxford, 1908), vol. 1, pp. 96–97, a translation from the text of the *Anonimalle Chronicle*: *Anon. Chron.*, pp. 102–3. The date is given in the text as the Sunday before Candlemas, a feast day on February 2 that in 1377 fell on a Monday. The note in Galbraith's edition wrongly identifies the preceding Sunday as January 25: *Anon. Chron.*, p. 102n.

38. For Richard's interest in his family's history, see M. Bennett, "Richard II and the Wider Realm," in A. Goodman and J. L. Gillespie (eds.), *Richard II: The Art of Kingship* (Oxford, 1999), p. 190; W. M. Ormrod, "Richard II's Sense of English History," in G. Dodd (ed.), *The Reign of Richard II* (Stroud, 2000), pp. 100–2. For the rumors of Gaunt's ambitions in relation to the throne, see *Walsingham*, vol. 1, pp. 38–41; S. Armitage-Smith, *John of Gaunt* (London, 1904), pp. 142–43. For further rumors that Gaunt had poisoned Blanche of Lancaster's sister, Maud, in order to secure the whole Lancastrian inheritance, see *Knighton*, pp. 184–85. The duke, who was eating oysters with his friend Henry Percy, got up so quickly when he heard news of the approaching mob that he barked his shins on the table: *Walsingham*, vol. 1, pp. 88–93; Goodman, *Joan, the Fair Maid of Kent*, pp. 125–27; A. Goodman, "Vere, Aubrey de, tenth earl of Oxford (1338x40–1400)," *ODNB*; J. L. Leland, "Burley, Sir Simon (1336?–1388)," *ODNB*.

39. Sumption, *Divided Houses*, pp. 277–80.

40. For this paragraph and the next, see Ormrod, *Edward III*, pp. 573–54; G. F. Beltz, *Memorials of the Most Noble Order of the Garter* (London, 1841), p. 11.

41. Goodman, *John of Gaunt*, pp. 31, 63–64.
42. Ormrod, *Edward III*, p. 577; *Walsingham*, vol. 1, pp. 116–25.
43. For the raids on Rye, Hastings, and Lewes, see Sumption, *Divided Houses*, pp. 281–83. For all details of the funeral ceremonies and an exploration of their significance, see C. Given-Wilson, "The Exequies of Edward III and the Royal Funeral Ceremony in Late Medieval England," *EHR*, vol. 124, no. 507 (2009), pp. 257–82.
44. For all details in this paragraph and the following two, see *Anon. Chron.*, pp. 107–8; *Walsingham*, vol. 1, pp. 136–41; L. G. Wickham Legg (ed.), *English Coronation Records* (London, 1901), pp. 145–46, 164; G. Kipling, "Richard II's 'Sumptuous Pageants' and the Idea of the Civic Triumph," in D. M. Bergeron (ed.), *Pageantry in the Shakespearean Theatre* (Athens, Georgia, 1986), p. 88.
45. For all details of the coronation ceremony and its aftermath, in this and the following paragraphs, see Wickham Legg (ed.), *English Coronation Records*, pp. xxi–lvii, 146–50, 165–68; *Anon. Chron.*, pp. 108–15; *Walsingham*, vol. 1, pp. 141–55.
46. In 1390, Richard gave a replacement pair of shoes—made of red velvet embroidered with pearls in a pattern of fleurs-de-lis, blessed by the pope—to the abbey: *Westm. Chron.*, pp. 414–16; *Anon. Chron.*, pp. 114, 187. The eagle is noted in *Walsingham*, vol. 1, pp. 154–55.

2. 1377–1381: measure our confines

1. Richmond, "Blanche of Lancaster," *ODNB*; W. M. Ormrod, "Henry of Lancaster [Henry of Grosmont], first duke of Lancaster (*c.*1310–1361)," *ODNB*. See ch. 1, n. 23, above for Blanche's age.
2. J. Froissart, *Le joli Buisson de Jonece*, ed. A. Fourrier (Geneva, 1975), p. 55; for Blanche as fair and tall, see G. Chaucer, "The Book of the Duchess," in L. D. Benson (ed.), *The Riverside Chaucer* (Oxford, 1988), pp. 340 (ll. 855–88) and 342 (ll. 952–53); Ormrod, "Henry of Lancaster," *ODNB*; Richmond, "Blanche of Lancaster," *ODNB*; Given-Wilson, *Henry IV*, pp. 15–20.
3. Given-Wilson, *Henry IV*, p. 24; Armitage-Smith (ed.), *John of Gaunt's Register, Part I (1371–5)*, vol. 1, pp. 212–13 [no. 1394], 296–97 [no. 1659]; C. Wilson, "Yevele, Henry (d. 1400)," *ODNB*; D. Gray, "Chaucer, Geoffrey (*c.*1340–1400)," *ODNB*; Chaucer, "The Book of the Duchess," in Benson (ed.), *The Riverside Chaucer*, pp. 330–46, quotations from pp. 336 (l. 477) and 337 (l. 597); Goodman, *John of Gaunt*, pp. 46–47; M. Turner, *Chaucer: A European Life* (Princeton, 2019), pp. 126–44.
4. Given-Wilson, *Henry IV*, p. 24; S. Walker, "Katherine [*née* Katherine Roelt; *married name* Katherine Swynford], duchess of Lancaster (1350?–1403)," *ODNB*; Turner, *Chaucer*, pp. 50–51, 61–62, 118, 124–25; Goodman, *John of Gaunt*, pp. 48–49.
5. For this paragraph and the next, see Russell, *English Intervention*, pp. 68, 168–69, 173–77; *Anon. Chron.*, p. 69.
6. Being male, Edmund would remain in England with his family no matter whom he married, and his passivity made him much more biddable as a prospective husband than his elder brother the prince. Potential brides for whose hands serious negotiations had taken place during the previous decade were Margaret, daughter and heir of Louis de Mâle, count of Flanders—a match for which the pope, under pressure from France, refused a dispensation—and Violante Visconti, daughter of the lord of Milan, who in 1368 instead married Edmund's elder brother Lionel: Tuck, "Edmund [Edmund of Langley]," *ODNB*.
7. Walker, "Katherine [*née* Katherine Roelt . . .]," *ODNB*; Turner, *Chaucer*, pp. 61, 124–26, 155–56; Goodman, *John of Gaunt*, p. 50; F. Devon (ed.), *Issues of the Exchequer* (London, 1837), p. 195.
8. Armitage-Smith (ed.), *John of Gaunt's Register, Part I (1371–5)*, vol. 2, pp. 107 [nos. 1123–24], 191 [no. 1342]; for an example of King Edward's use of an eagle badge, see Ormrod, *Edward III*, p. 315n (a hood made of red wool embroidered with eagles and the letter *E* in gold, pearls, and silk); Goodman, *John of Gaunt*, pp. 49–51.

9. Given-Wilson, *Henry IV*, pp. 24–25, 29–31. No more is known about the specifics of Henry's education than of Richard's, and I've therefore assessed its context and effects in the same way: see above, ch. 1, n. 30.

10. Given-Wilson, *Henry IV*, pp. 25–26, 29–30; Ormrod, *Edward III*, pp. 575–76; see above, ch. 1.

11. *Anon. Chron.*, pp. 104–5. See also *Walsingham*, vol. 1, pp. 60–61, where the story goes that Gaunt was swapped in the cradle for a royal daughter to avoid the king's anger at the birth of a girl. For discussion of these rumors, including the connection between Gaunt's supposed ambition to take the throne for himself and speculation about his illegitimacy (which would help undermine any claim he might attempt to make), see W. M. Ormrod, "The DNA of Richard III: False Paternity and the Royal Succession in Later Medieval England," *Nottingham Medieval Studies*, vol. 60 (2016), pp. 191–99.

12. D. Crouch, "Marshal, William [*called* the Marshal], fourth earl of Pembroke (*c.*1146–1219)," *ODNB*; Saul, *Richard II*, pp. 27–28. For discussion of the whole question of the minority, see G. Dodd, "Richard II and the Fiction of Minority Rule," in C. Beem (ed.), *The Royal Minorities of Medieval and Early Modern England* (New York, 2008), pp. 103–60.

13. *Walsingham*, vol. 1, pp. 156–57; Goodman, *John of Gaunt*, pp. 71–73; *PROME*, "Richard II: October 1377," item 13.

14. *PROME*, "Richard II: October 1377," items 21–24.

15. Sumption, *Divided Houses*, pp. 291–304.

16. Sumption, *Divided Houses*, pp. 305–16, 322–27, 385–86, 405.

17. *Westm. Chron.*, pp. 122–23; Saul, *Richard II*, pp. 120–23; *PROME*, "Richard II: October 1377," item 19.

18. *PROME*, "Richard II: January 1380," item 12.

19. For all details in this paragraph and the next, see Sumption, *Divided Houses*, pp. 219, 231–36; *CPR 1377–81*, p. 485; *Walsingham*, vol. 1, pp. 356–65; Lumby (ed.), *Polychronicon Ranulphi Higden*, vol. 8, p. 403; J. G. Bellamy, "Sir John Annesley and the Chandos Inheritance," *Nottingham Medieval Studies*, vol. 10 (1966), pp. 94–105. Thomas of Woodstock later wrote a treatise, in his capacity as constable, setting out the rules and procedures by which trials by combat should be conducted: for the text in French, and a fifteenth-century text of a translation into English, see T. Twiss (ed.), *Monumenta Juridica: The Black Book of the Admiralty*, vol. 1 (London, 1871), pp. 300–29.

20. Goodman, *Joan, the Fair Maid of Kent*, pp. 146–47; Sumption, *Divided Houses*, pp. 366–67; E. C. Lodge and R. Somerville (eds.), *John of Gaunt's Register, 1379–1383*, vol. 1, Camden Society, Third Series, vol. 56 (London, 1937), p. 152 [no. 463], for the wedding gifts presented by Gaunt and Henry to Maud and Elizabeth, and the location of Elizabeth's marriage. For the little earl of Pembroke's age—he was born in November 1372—see *Calendar of Inquisitions Post Mortem, Edward III*, vol. 14 (London, 1952), pp. 143–64.

21. Given-Wilson, *Henry IV*, pp. 26–27; Tuck, "Thomas [Thomas of Woodstock]," *ODNB*; A. Goodman, *The Loyal Conspiracy: The Lords Appellant under Richard II* (London, 1971), pp. 88–90; Ormrod, *Edward III*, p. 489.

22. Armitage-Smith (ed.), *John of Gaunt's Register, Part I (1371–5)*, vol. 2, pp. 224–25 [no. 1431]; Sumption, *Divided Houses*, pp. 308–10, 385–90; *CCR 1377–81*, pp. 390–95, 439–40; *CPR 1377–81*, p. 502; Given-Wilson, *Henry IV*, pp. 26–27.

23. *CPR 1377–81*, p. 537; *CPR 1381–5*, p. 95; Given-Wilson, *Henry IV*, pp. 27–28, 78–80. For wedding gifts to Mary—a gold ring with a ruby from Gaunt, and silver-gilt cups and pitchers from Henry's sisters—see Lodge and Somerville (eds.), *John of Gaunt's Register, 1379–1383*, vol. 1, pp. 178–80 [no. 556].

24. Sumption, *Divided Houses*, pp. 390–412.

25. Goodman, *John of Gaunt*, pp. 76–78.

26. *PROME*, "Richard II: April 1379," item 13; *PROME*, "Richard II: November 1380," item 2. In January 1380, they had requested that no further parliament should be held to ask for a

subsidy before the end of September 1381: see *PROME*, "Richard II: January 1380," introduction and items 16–17; *Walsingham*, vol. 1, pp. 348–49.

27. For detailed accounts of the revolt, see D. Jones, *Summer of Blood: The Peasants' Revolt of 1381* (London, 2009); J. Barker, *England, Arise: The People, the King and the Great Revolt of 1381* (London, 2014); A. Dunn, *The Peasants' Revolt: England's Failed Revolution of 1381* (Stroud, 2004).

28. For initial evasion of the tax, see figures in C. Oman, *The Great Revolt of 1381* (Oxford, 1906), Appendix 2 (pp. 162–66). For the commission, see Oman, *The Great Revolt*, pp. 183–85 ("*ita quod aliqua persona laica ejusdem Comitatus contra formam dictae concessionis nullatenus pretermittatur*"); *Anon. Chron.*, p. 134 ("*les ditz gentz del comune leverount encontre eux and ne vodroient estre arrestez*"); Dobson, *Revolt*, pp. 119–22, 124.

29. *Froissart*, vol. 9, p. 390 ("*cils Wautres estoit uns couvrères de maisons de tieulle: mauvais gars et envenimés estoit*"). The chronology of the revolt isn't straightforward to establish, but see Barker, *England, Arise*, pp. 195–224; Dobson, *Revolt*, pp. 38–39, 153–54; Jones, *Summer of Blood*, pp. 57–75; Dunn, *England's Failed Revolution of 1381*, pp. 94–106; *Westm. Chron.*, pp. 2–5 ("the riotous and disorderly mob of peasants demanded that the king should meet them, since they intended to have conversations with him and to discuss affairs of state").

30. For Richard's itinerary, see W. H. B. Bird, "The Peasant Rising of 1381: The King's Itinerary," *EHR*, vol. 31, no. 121 (1916), pp. 124–26; Saul, *Richard II*, p. 469. Froissart gives details of the princess's narrow escape; she seems to have visited Canterbury Cathedral, where the Black Prince was buried, for the anniversary of his death on June 8: *Froissart*, vol. 9, p. 391 (transl. Dobson, *Revolt*, p. 139); Goodman, *Joan, the Fair Maid of Kent*, pp. 153–54. For the list of Richard's companions in the Tower, see C. Barron, "Froissart and the Great Revolt," in J. Lutkin and J. S. Hamilton (eds.), *Creativity, Contradictions and Commemoration in the Reign of Richard II* (Woodbridge, 2022), pp. 15–21; *Froissart*, vol. 9, pp. 391, 395 (transl. Dobson, *Revolt*, p. 142); *Knighton*, pp. 210–13. The *Anonimalle Chronicle* (*Anon. Chron.*, p. 138) says Thomas of Woodstock was also there, but Froissart—who seems to have been well-informed about the course of events—says he was in Wales, and that confusion arose because one of the rebels named Thomas looked very like him: *Froissart*, vol. 9, p. 397. (Both texts transl. in Dobson, *Revolt*, pp. 129, 143.)

31. "no king called John": *Walsingham*, vol. 1, pp. 412–13. For attacks on the property of Gaunt's controller Thomas Haselden, see *Anon. Chron.*, p. 138 (transl. Dobson, *Revolt*, p. 128); Barker, *England, Arise*, pp. 316–17. For the Kentish rebels' password, see *Anon. Chron.*, p. 139: "*Et les ditz comunes avoient entre eux une wache worde en Engleys, "With whome haldes yow?" et le respouns fuist, 'Wyth kynge Richarde and wyth the trew communes': et ceux qe ne savoient ne vodroient respondre, furount decolles et mys a la mort*" (transl. Dobson, *Revolt*, p. 130).

32. *Froissart*, vol. 9, pp. 395–96; *Anon. Chron.*, p. 138. (Both texts transl. in Dobson, *Revolt*, pp. 129, 142.)

33. *Froissart*, vol. 9, pp. 396, 398.

34. *Anon. Chron.*, p. 139: "*il respondist qil vodroit volunters, mes les ditz chanceller et tresorer luy conseillerount le reversee*" (transl. Dobson, *Revolt*, p. 130).

35. Walsingham says the rebels attacked the Savoy "to demonstrate their defiance of the duke, whom they called a traitor, and to strike fear into the hearts of the other traitors"—and gave an order not to take anything "in order to show the whole community of the realm that they were doing nothing out of greed": *Walsingham*, vol. 1, pp. 418–19; *Westm. Chron.*, pp. 4–5 (no one dared loot anything because "everybody caught in any act of theft was hauled away, without trial or judgement, to death by beheading"); *Knighton*, pp. 214–17.

36. *Froissart*, vol. 9, pp. 399–402; *Anon. Chron.*, pp. 143–44. (Both texts transl. in Dobson, *Revolt*, pp. 159–60, 189–90.)

37. *Froissart*, vol. 9, pp. 403–5; for the identification of Richard's companions at Mile End, see Barron, "Froissart and the Great Revolt," pp. 23–25.

38. Barker, *England, Arise*, pp. 248–50; *Anon. Chron.*, pp. 144–45 (transl. Dobson, *Revolt*, p. 161); *Westm. Chron.*, pp. 6–7. For the implausibility of the *Anonimalle Chronicle* placing Tyler at Mile End, see Jones, *Summer of Blood*, pp. 114, 223.

39. *Froissart*, vol. 9, pp. 403–6 (transl. Dobson, *Revolt*, pp. 192–93).

40. *Walsingham*, vol. 1, pp. 424–25; Goodman, *Joan, the Fair Maid of Kent*, pp. 155–57.

41. *Westm. Chron.*, pp. 6–7.

42. Barker, *England, Arise*, pp. 261–64; *Westm. Chron.*, pp. 6–7; *Anon. Chron.*, p. 145 (transl. Dobson, *Revolt*, p. 162); Given-Wilson, *Henry IV*, p. 29.

43. *Westm. Chron.*, pp. 8–11; for John Ball, see *Walsingham*, vol. 1, pp. 546–47.

44. *Anon. Chron.*, p. 147 (transl. Dobson, *Revolt*, pp. 164–65).

45. For this paragraph and the previous one, see *Froissart*, vol. 9, pp. 411–14 (transl. Dobson, *Revolt*, p. 196). *Westm. Chron.*, pp. 10–13, has "I am your king, your leader, your captain. Those among you who support me are to go out at once into the open country."

46. Barker, *England, Arise*, pp. 271–72; Jones, *Summer of Blood*, 154–55; *Walsingham*, vol. 1, pp. 500–1.

47. *Walsingham*, vol. 1, pp. 506–7; Saul, *Richard II*, pp. 74–75. For the disturbances in other parts of the country and their suppression, see Barker, *England, Arise*, chs. 11–15.

48. Barker, *England, Arise*, pp. 372, 377–79; *Knighton*, pp. 240–41; *Westm. Chron.*, pp. 14–15; *Walsingham*, vol. 1, pp. 516–19.

49. *PROME*, "Richard II: November 1381," item 8; J. L. Leland, "Seagrave [Segrave], Sir Hugh (*d.* 1387)," *ODNB*.

50. *PROME*, "Richard II: November 1381," items 11–13. The fact that they first requested to hear the instructions put to them for a second time suggests surprise or confusion about what they were being asked. See Barker, *England, Arise*, pp. 373–76, 385–86, for the alternative argument that Richard believed the rebels "had genuine grievances."

51. *PROME*, "Richard II: November 1381," items 17–18.

52. *PROME*, "Richard II: November 1381," items 19, 38; A. Tuck, "Pole, Michael de la, first earl of Suffolk (*c.*1330–1389)," *ODNB*.

3. 1381–1384: be rul'd by me

1. "… *scrutantibus verum videbatur non dari set pocius emi, nam non modicam pecuniam refundebat rex Anglie pro tantilla carnis porcione*": *Westm. Chron.*, pp. 24–25; see also *Walsingham*, vol. 1, pp. 572–73 ("she was bought for a considerable sum of money and only after difficult negotiation. This was despite the fact that the daughter of Bernabo, the duke of Milan, had been offered to him along with an enormous sum of gold"). The total loan promised to Wenzel was £12,000, of which £7,500 was handed over: Saul, *Richard II*, pp. 86, 90–91.

2. J. U. Nef, "Mining and Metallurgy in Medieval Civilisation," in M. M. Postan and E. Miller (eds.), *The Cambridge Economic History of Europe*, vol. 2 (second ed., Cambridge, 1987), pp. 721–23; Sumption, *Divided Houses*, pp. 340–50; C. Wickham, *Medieval Europe* (New Haven and London, 2016), pp. 212–13; Saul, *Richard II*, pp. 83–87.

3. Saul, *Richard II*, pp. 83–88; *Foedera*, vol. 7, pp. 290–95.

4. *Walsingham*, vol. 1, pp. 572–75: "*Accidit illo die mirabile cunctis auspicium, iuxta multorum opinionum, fauorem Dei.*" He went on: "Different interpretations from that above were put upon this, some thinking that she would cause the kingdom trouble, others, that some misfortune would come upon the country. However, the events that follow will show the difficulty of resolving these differences." For Henry jousting at Smithfield and the purchase of the gilded copper sequins, see Given-Wilson, *Henry IV*, pp. 30–31. For Anne's journey to England and reception in London, see *Froissart*, vol. 9, pp. 459–62; F. W. D. Brie (ed.), *The Brut or The Chronicles of England* (London, 1906), pp. 338–39; Kipling, "Richard II's 'Sumptuous Pageants,'" p. 88; *Westm. Chron.*, pp. 22–25.

5. Goodman, *John of Gaunt*, pp. 79–83; S. Walker, "Letters to the Dukes of Lancaster in 1381 and 1399," *EHR*, vol. 106, no. 418 (1991), pp. 68–71; K. Towson, "'Hearts Warped by Passion':

The Percy–Gaunt Dispute of 1381," in W. M. Ormrod (ed.), *Fourteenth Century England*, vol. 3 (Woodbridge, 2004), pp. 143–49; for Katherine, *Anon. Chron.*, pp. 152–54; for Constanza, *Knighton*, pp. 230–31.

6. *Anon. Chron.*, pp. 153–54; Walker, "Katherine [*née* Katherine Roelt . . .]," *ODNB*.

7. For this paragraph and the next, see Towson, "'Hearts Warped by Passion,'" pp. 150–51; Goodman, *John of Gaunt*, pp. 89–90; *Westm. Chron.*, pp. 20–23; *Walsingham*, vol. 1, pp. 568–71.

8. For this paragraph and the next, see *Anon. Chron.*, pp. 154–56; Towson, "'Hearts Warped by Passion,'" pp. 151–52; E. C. Lodge and R. Somerville (eds.), *John of Gaunt's Register, 1379–1383*, vol. 2, Camden Society, Third Series, vol. 57 (London, 1937), pp. 410–11 [no. 1243]; Goodman, *John of Gaunt*, pp. 89–91. The rolls of parliament recorded the bare minimum of this difficult moment: *PROME*, "Richard II: November 1381," introduction and item 1.

9. *PROME*, "Richard II: November 1381," items 37, 64–65; Goodman, *John of Gaunt*, pp. 91–92; Lodge and Somerville (eds.), *John of Gaunt's Register, 1379–1383*, vol. 1, p. 230 [no. 714].

10. *PROME*, "Richard II: November 1381," items 25, 35–36.

11. For this paragraph and the next, see Sumption, *Divided Houses*, pp. 379–84, 431–32.

12. Sumption, *Divided Houses*, pp. 434–37.

13. For this paragraph and the next, see *PROME*, "Richard II: November 1381," items 65–66 (from the adjourned session held on January 27, 1382).

14. *Westm. Chron.*, pp. 24–25; *Walsingham*, vol. 1, pp. 412–13; Goodman, *John of Gaunt*, p. 93; *PROME*, "Richard II: November 1391," items 67–70.

15. See, for example, *PROME*, "Richard II: November 1381," item 5.

16. Saul, *Richard II*, pp. 112–23.

17. M. King, "Richard II, the Mortimer Inheritance and the March of Wales, 1381–84," in J. S. Hamilton (ed.), *Fourteenth Century England*, vol. 8 (Woodbridge, 2014), pp. 95–106.

18. King, "Richard II, the Mortimer Inheritance and the March of Wales," pp. 96–97, 104, 106–15; *CPR 1381–5*, pp. 88–94, 96; Nichols (ed.), *Collection of All the Wills*, pp. 115–16; *Walsingham*, vol. 1, pp. 620–21 (where Walsingham alleges that the king was granting out the lands of the Mortimer inheritance, but see discussion in King, "Richard II, the Mortimer Inheritance and the March of Wales," n. 17 above); M. McKisack, *The Fourteenth Century 1307–1399* (Oxford, 1959), p. 428. Noting Scrope's appointment as chancellor—which he says was "at the request of the lords and the commons"—Walsingham calls him "a man of exceptional knowledge who was resolutely just": pp. 578–79.

19. *Walsingham*, vol. 1, pp. 622–23.

20. *CCR 1381–5*, pp. 214–15; *Walsingham*, vol. 1, pp. 622–23; Saul, *Richard II*, p. 469.

21. Goodman, *John of Gaunt*, pp. 93–94; Tuck, "Thomas [Thomas of Woodstock]," *ODNB*.

22. *Walsingham*, vol. 1, pp. 578–79; *Westm. Chron.*, pp. 22–23; R. Brooke, *A Catalogue and Succession of the Kings, Princes, Dukes, Marquesses, Earles, and Viscounts of This Realme of England, since the Norman Conquest, to This Present Yeare, 1619* (London, 1619), p. 203; J. L. Leland, "Montagu, William [William de Montacute], second earl of Salisbury (1328–1397)," *ODNB*.

23. A. Tuck, "Beauchamp, Thomas, twelfth earl of Warwick (1337x9–1401)," *ODNB*; C. Rawcliffe, "Stafford, Hugh, second earl of Stafford (*c*.1342–1386)," *ODNB*; C. Given-Wilson, "Fitzalan, Richard, fourth earl of Arundel and ninth earl of Surrey (1346–1397)," *ODNB*.

24. *Anon. Chron.*, p. 143; Dobson, *Revolt*, p. 159 (although Froissart suggests that at least the earl of Salisbury spoke up then: see ch. 2, pp. 52–53).

25. *PROME*, "Richard II: October 1382," items 11–12, 23; Sumption, *Divided Houses*, pp. 462–70, 475.

26. *PROME*, "Richard II: October 1382," item 11; Sumption, *Divided Houses*, pp. 413–18, 449–62.

27. Sumption, *Divided Houses*, pp. 413–14; Saul, *Richard II*, pp. 99–101.

28. Sumption, *Divided Houses*, pp. 434, 458–59, 470–71.

29. For this paragraph and the next, see *Walsingham*, vol. 1, pp. 380–81; Saul, *Richard II*, pp. 102–3; *Westm. Chron.*, pp. 30–31; M. Jurkowski, C. L. Smith, and D. Crook (eds.), *Lay Taxes*

in England and Wales, 1188–1688 (London, 1998), pp. xxix–xxxiv; *PROME*, "Richard II: October 1382," items 15, 46–47.

30. Sumption, *Divided Houses*, pp. 478–89.

31. Sumption, *Divided Houses*, pp. 487–89; Saul, *Richard II*, p. 103; *Westm. Chron.*, pp. 32–33; Goodman, *John of Gaunt*, pp. 94–95; *PROME*, "Richard II: February 1383," item 3; *Eulogium*, p. 356. By the late fourteenth century, "*laborare*" had the sense of both "to work" and "to travel": J. H. Baxter and C. Johnson (eds.), *Medieval Latin Word-List* (London, 1934), under *labor/*.

32. *PROME*, "Richard II: February 1383," items 9–11; *Westm. Chron.*, pp. 34–37; *Walsingham*, vol. 1, pp. 662–67; *Vitae et Regni*, p. 76.

33. For this paragraph and the next, see Sumption, *Divided Houses*, pp. 493, 495–506.

34. *Westm. Chron.*, pp. 48–49.

35. *Walsingham*, vol. 1, pp. 702–3; *Foedera*, vol. 7, pp. 408–11.

36. Sumption, *Divided Houses*, pp. 507–10; *PROME*, "Richard II: October 1383," items 18–20.

37. Among Richard's extensive improvements at Eltham Palace in the 1380s were a new bathhouse and dancing chamber, and he refurbished the bathhouse at Langley: Devon (ed.), *Issues of the Exchequer*, pp. 213, 221; *CPR 1381–5*, pp. 161–62; G. Mathew, *The Court of Richard II* (London, 1968), pp. 22–23, 33–34; R. A. Brown, H. M. Colvin, and A. J. Taylor (eds.), *The History of the King's Works: The Middle Ages*, 2 vols. (London, 1963), vol. 1, p. 550; vol. 2, pp. 934–35, 975–76, 997–98.

38. Saul, *Richard II*, pp. 455–56; K. L. Geaman, "A Personal Letter Written by Anne of Bohemia," *EHR*, vol. 128, no. 534 (2013), pp. 1088–89, 1091–94 (though I'm not as convinced as Dr. Geaman that Richard was actively committed to fathering an heir).

39. Parliament ended on March 10, and de la Pole was appointed chancellor three days later: *PROME*, "Richard II: February 1383," introduction and item 18; *Westm. Chron.*, pp. 54–55; McHardy, *Reign*, p. 113; E. B. Fryde, D. E. Greenway, S. Porter, and I. Roy (eds.), *Handbook of British Chronology* (third ed., London, 1986), p. 87.

40. Leland, "Burley, Sir Simon," *ODNB*; Goodman, "Vere, Aubrey de," *ODNB*; Tuck, "Pole, Michael de la," *ODNB*; J. Taylor (ed. and tr.), *The Kirkstall Abbey Chronicles*, Thoresby Society, vol. 42 (Leeds, 1952), pp. 71, 116. For the clothes among Burley's possessions by 1388, which also included a tabard of scarlet lined with white silk and embroidered with the sun and golden letters, see M. V. Clarke, *Fourteenth-Century Studies* (Oxford, 1937), p. 120.

41. King, "Richard II, the Mortimer Inheritance and the March of Wales," p. 96; *CFR 1383–91*, pp. 22–23 (grant to the trustees made "by advice of the council"); *CPR 1381–5*, pp. 161–2, 366–7, 370–71; C. Given-Wilson, "Richard II and His Grandfather's Will," *EHR*, vol. 93, no. 367 (1978), pp. 320–22, 327–30.

42. For this paragraph and the next, see J. Ross, "Vere [*née* Ufford], Maud de, countess of Oxford (1345?–1413), *ODNB*; M. H. Keen, "Coucy, Enguerrand [Ingelram] de, earl of Bedford (*c.*1340–1397)," *ODNB*; *CPR 1381–5*, pp. 177, 314.

4. 1384–1386: the blood is hot

1. *PROME*, "Richard II: October 1383," item 4.

2. Goodman, *John of Gaunt*, pp. 98–99; Sumption, *Divided Houses*, pp. 514–19; Stansfield, "Holland, John," *ODNB*.

3. C. Given-Wilson, "Fitzalan, Richard, third earl of Arundel and eighth earl of Surrey (*c.*1313–1376)," and "Fitzalan, Richard, fourth earl of Arundel," *ODNB*; A. Goodman, *The Loyal Conspiracy: The Lords Appellant under Richard II* (London, 1971), pp. 108–9; *PROME*, "Richard II: October 1383," item 20; *Westm. Chron.*, pp. 40–41.

4. *Westm. Chron.*, pp. 66–69 (transl. McHardy, *Reign*, pp. 117–18); *PROME*, "Richard II: April 1384," introduction.

5. For this paragraph and the following two, see Sumption, *Divided Houses*, p. 325; *Walsingham*, vol. 1, pp. 722–77; *Westm. Chron.*, pp. 68–81; *Vitae et Regni*, pp. 81–82 (transl. McHardy, *Reign*,

pp. 116–17). I've mainly used Walsingham's account; some details vary in the *Vitae* and *The Westminster Chronicle*.

6. *PROME*, "Richard II: April 1384," items 3, 16–18. The proposals for a settlement don't survive, and there has been argument about what they might have contained, but it seems certain—not least from both the logic of the situation and this exchange in parliament—that some concession of sovereignty and lost territory was required.

7. *PROME*, "Richard II: April 1384," item 10; *PROME*, "Richard II: November 1384," item 2; Sumption, *Divided Houses*, pp. 523–30.

8. *PROME*, "Richard II: November 1384," items 2–3, 10; *Walsingham*, vol. 1, pp. 733–37; Sumption, *Divided Houses*, pp. 530–31.

9. *Walsingham*, vol. 1, pp. 752–53; *Westm. Chron.*, pp. 110–13; Sumption, *Divided Houses*, pp. 536–37; Goodman, *John of Gaunt*, p. 102.

10. *Westm. Chron.*, pp. 110–15; Goodman, *John of Gaunt*, pp. 102–3; Sumption, *Divided Houses*, p. 537.

11. *Walsingham*, vol. 1, pp. 750–51; *Westm. Chron.*, pp. 114–15; *Vitae et Regni*, pp. 85–86.

12. *CPR 1381–5*, p. 542; Ormrod, *Edward III*, pp. 451–52; Given-Wilson, "Richard II and His Grandfather's Will," p. 327. For Burley at Dover, see ch. 3, p. 83.

13. *Westm. Chron.*, pp. 116–17; *Walsingham*, vol. 1, pp. 754–57; *Vitae et Regni*, pp. 85–86; Sumption, *Divided Houses*, p. 537; Goodman, *John of Gaunt*, p. 103.

14. *Foedera*, vol. 7, pp. 473–75; Sumption, *Divided Houses*, pp. 535–39, 543–44.

15. For this paragraph and the next, see N. B. Lewis, "The Last Medieval Summons of the English Feudal Levy, 13 June 1385," *EHR*, vol. 73, no. 286 (1958), Appendix 2; *Foedera*, vol. 7, pp. 481–84; *Knighton*, pp. 334–39; Sumption, *Divided Houses*, p. 548; C. Given-Wilson, "Richard II and the Higher Nobility," in Goodman and Gillespie (eds.), *Richard II: The Art of Kingship*, pp. 117–18. For the "excessive heat" of the summer, lasting from May to September, see *Westm. Chron.*, pp. 120–21.

16. For the argument, on a balance of probabilities, that John Holand was Richard of Conisbrough's father, see Ormrod, "The DNA of Richard III," pp. 200–6; T. B. Pugh, *Henry V and the Southampton Plot of 1415*, Southampton Records Series, vol. 30 (1988), pp. 89–91; G. L. Harriss, "Richard [Richard of Conisbrough], earl of Cambridge (1385–1415)," *ODNB*. For a carefully considered counterargument, see J. Stratford, "The Bequests of Isabel of Castile, First duchess of York, and Chaucer's 'Complaint of Mars,'" in Lutkin and Hamilton (eds.), *Creativity, Contradictions and Commemoration*, pp. 75–96. However, this account offers no explanation beyond Walsingham's general misogyny for his specific assertion that Isabel was "a lady of sensual and self-indulgent disposition" who had been "worldly and lustful" but "in the end by the grace of Christ repented and was converted." That trajectory would allow Jenny Stratford's analysis of Isabel's will in 1392—a document that confirms a close association with John Holand—to stand alongside the circumstantial evidence suggesting an earlier liaison between the two: *Walsingham*, vol. 1, pp. 962–63.

17. *Walsingham*, vol. 1, pp. 756–59; *Knighton*, pp. 338–39; *Froissart*, vol. 10, pp. 383–87; *Westm. Chron.*, pp. 122–23.

18. *Walsingham*, vol. 1, pp. 758–59; *Vitae et Regni*, pp. 88–90; Nichols (ed.), *Collection of All the Wills*, pp. 78–81.

19. *Vitae et Regni*, pp. 88–90; Sumption, *Divided Houses*, pp. 548–49.

20. *Walsingham*, vol. 1, pp. 762–63: "*semper tuis marsupiis consulens, meis nichil; et nunc, iuxta morem tuum, me cogis ad transitum maris Scotici, ut ego cum hominibus meis, fame peream, et inopia, et fiam hostibus meis preda . . . Ego enim et mei homines reuertemur. Ad hec respondente duce, 'Et ego homo uester sum,' 'nequaquam,' inquit rex, 'non apparet ita.'*"

21. Given-Wilson, *Henry IV*, pp. 38–39; Sumption, *Divided Houses*, pp. 549–50.

22. For this paragraph and the next, see Sumption, *Divided Houses*, pp. 547, 550–57.

23. *PROME*, "Richard II: October 1385," items 2–3 ("what kind of war should be waged for the defence of the realm, and . . . to provide the means of supporting such a war").

24. *PROME*, "Richard II: October 1385," introduction and item 14.
25. *PROME*, "Richard II: October 1385," items 14–17; *Walsingham*, vol. 1, pp. 782–83.
26. *PROME*, "Richard II: October 1385," items 17, 32.
27. J. J. N. Palmer, "The Parliament of 1385 and the Constitutional Crisis of 1386," *Speculum*, vol. 46, no. 3 (1971), pp. 478–86; *Westm. Chron.*, pp. 144–47; *PROME*, "Richard II: October 1385," introduction, items 42–43, Appendices 1 and 2.
28. *PROME*, "Richard II: October 1385," items 2–5.
29. Sumption, *Divided Houses*, pp. 496–97, 519–23, 531–33, 558–68; *Froissart*, vol. 9, pp. 265–66.
30. *PROME*, "Richard II: October 1385," item 10; Sumption, *Divided Houses*, pp. 569, 572–73.
31. *PROME*, "Richard II: October 1385," item 10; Given-Wilson, *Henry IV*, p. 39; *CCR 1381–5*, pp. 511–16.
32. For legal proceedings against Holand, see A. Gundy, *Richard II and the Rebel Earl* (Cambridge, 2013), pp. 119–20; for the confiscation of his lands on September 14, 1385, see *CFR 1383–91*, pp. 123–24. The precise chronology of Elizabeth's relationship with Holand, and of her pregnancy, is difficult to establish. The monk of Westminster says that Holand "fell violently in love with her, and pursued her day and night," until "by the time her father the duke left for the coast" she was pregnant. Gaunt set out for Plymouth in late March; so, for example, if she conceived in December and carried the baby to term, she would have given birth in Castile in September. In that context, it may be significant that the monk of Saint-Denis believed that Duchess Constanza was heavily pregnant when Gaunt's fleet sailed, and gave birth to a son when they arrived in Galicia. Given that Constanza was not in fact pregnant, this may be a garbled version of Elizabeth's story: *Westm. Chron.*, pp. 164–65, 192–93; *Religieux*, vol. 1, pp. 442–43; Armitage-Smith, *John of Gaunt*, pp. 459–60. If so, and if the baby born (probably) in the autumn of 1386 was a boy—their oldest son, Richard—then Elizabeth must have become pregnant again almost immediately, since their daughter Constance was four years old when she was betrothed to Thomas Mowbray's small son and heir in 1391: R. E. Archer, "Mowbray, Thomas, second earl of Nottingham (1385–1405)," *ODNB*.
33. *Westm. Chron.*, pp. 158–61, 192–93; Rawcliffe, "Stafford, Hugh, second earl of Stafford," *ODNB*.
34. *CPR 1385–9*, p. 110; *Foedera*, vol. 7, pp. 491–94; *Religieux*, vol. 1, pp. 320–27, 418–27; *Westm. Chron.*, pp. 154–57; Sumption, *Divided Houses*, pp. 575–76.
35. Walsingham says that the nobles thought Leo an "*illusor*," a con man, who "desired gifts more than peace, loved money more than he loved the people, and the gold of a kingdom more than the king": *Walsingham*, vol. 1, pp. 784–85, 804–5. For Richard and Arundel—an incident recorded without further detail in a chronicle written at Clerkenwell Priory in London, covering just seven months in 1385–86—see C. Given-Wilson, "The Earl of Arundel, the War with France, and the Anger of King Richard II," in R. F. Yeager and R. Takamiya (eds.), *The Medieval Python* (New York, 2012), pp. 27–29 and note on p. 36; for Richard's grant and curse, see *CPR 1381–5*, p. 110.
36. Sumption, *Divided Houses*, pp. 576–77; *Knighton*, pp. 340–41.
37. Sumption, *Divided Houses*, pp. 577, 582; A. Goodman, "Elizabeth of Lancaster (1364?–1425)" and "Philippa [Philippa of Lancaster] (1360–1415)," *ODNB*. Walsingham doesn't mention Elizabeth, while Henry Knighton, the chronicler closest to the house of Lancaster, elegantly glosses (over) the whole affair: "The lady Elizabeth, countess of Pembroke, left her young husband in England. The which earl obtained a divorce after his wife left, and married the earl of March's sister. Sir John Holand first took the said lady Elizabeth to wife": *Knighton*, pp. 342–43.
38. Given-Wilson, *Henry IV*, pp. 39–41.
39. Sumption, *Divided Houses*, p. 582; Given-Wilson, *Henry IV*, pp. 39–40; *Knighton*, pp. 340–41.

5. 1386–1387: am I not king?

1. *Froissart*, vol. 11, p. 359; Sumption, *Divided Houses*, pp. 578, 584–85.
2. For this paragraph and the next, see Sumption, *Divided Houses*, pp. 578–85; Saul, *Richard II*, pp. 152–53.

3. *CPR 1385–9*, pp. 175–76; McHardy, *Reign*, pp. 141, 146–49; Sumption, *Divided Houses*, p. 580; Saul, *Richard II*, p. 154.

4. See ch. 4, pp. 93, 100–2, 104–5; *CPR 1385–9*, pp. 123, 125, 132, 136, 175; Palmer, "Parliament of 1385," pp. 486–87; Sumption, *Divided Houses*, p. 580; Saul, *Richard II*, pp. 154–55.

5. Sumption, *Divided Houses*, pp. 583–84; Saul, *Richard II*, pp. 155–56.

6. Sumption, *Divided Houses*, pp. 585–86; *Walsingham*, vol. 1, pp. 792–93; R. R. Sharpe (ed.), *Calendar of Letter Books of the City of London: Letter Book H* (London, 1907), pp. 285–86.

7. *PROME*, "Richard II: October 1386," item 1.

8. The scale of the request for taxation is not recorded in the very minimal formal record of the rolls of parliament but given in the chronicle of Henry Knighton, the best informed of the contemporary observers: *Knighton*, pp. 354–55.

9. *Knighton*, pp. 352–55; *PROME*, "Richard II: October 1386," introduction. This parliament has come to be known as the "Wonderful Parliament," but that name was probably originally intended to refer to the parliament of February 1388, otherwise known as the "Merciless Parliament." "Wonderful"—*mirabilis*—to contemporaries meant "to be wondered at," and the Merciless Parliament was more extraordinary in its purpose and actions than that of 1386. See *PROME*, "Richard II: October 1386," introduction, n. 1: "The name comes from the tract written in 1388 by Thomas Favent, which opens with the words, 'Here begins the history or narration of the manner and form of the wonderful parliament (*mirabilis parliamenti*) at Westminster in the year of Our Lord 1386, the tenth year of the reign of King Richard the second since the conquest.' This sounds fairly unequivocal, but the title of Favent's tract is probably not contemporary, and in fact it deals very largely with the parliament of February 1388, barely mentioning that of 1386. It is also worth noting that it was the parliament of February 1388 which was described in *Knighton's Chronicle* (p. 353) as 'wonderful.'" For the Merciless Parliament, see ch. 6, n. 25.

10. The precise chronology and location of events isn't clear, but I've preferred the suggestion that Richard withdrew to Eltham *after* making his outrage clear with his provocative message to parliament. *Knighton*, pp. 354–55 ("*dicens se nolle pro ipsis nec minimum garcionem de coquina sua ammouere de officio suo*"); *PROME*, "Richard II: October 1386," introduction.

11. For this paragraph and the next, see *Knighton*, pp. 352–55; *PROME*, "Richard II: October 1386," introduction; *Walsingham*, vol. 1, pp. 800–3.

12. Sumption, *Divided Houses*, pp. 586–87; Tuck, "Vere, Robert de," *ODNB*.

13. J. Hughes, "Arundel [Fitzalan], Thomas (1353–1414)," *ODNB* (and for his name as "Thomas of Arundel" rather than Thomas Fitzalan, see, for example, *Walsingham*, vol. 1, p. 782); *Knighton*, pp. 354–59 ("*et nos eis submittere pocius quam succumbere subditis nostris*").

14. Sumption, *Divided Houses*, p. 588.

15. *Knighton*, pp. 358–61.

16. C. Given-Wilson, "Richard II, Edward II, and the Lancastrian Inheritance," *EHR*, vol. 109, no. 432 (1994), pp. 567–68; E. Perroy (ed.), *The Diplomatic Correspondence of Richard II*, Camden Society, Third Series, vol. 48 (London, 1933), pp. 62–63; J. M. Theilmann, "Political Canonization and Political Symbolism in Medieval England," *Journal of British Studies*, vol. 29, no. 3 (1990), p. 257; *Knighton*, pp. 360–61; *PROME*, "Richard II: October 1386," introduction.

17. For the list of peers summoned to the parliament, see *Reports from the Lords' Committees Touching the Dignity of a Peer of the Realm*, vol. 4 (London, 1829), pp. 721–23; for the birth of Henry's son, and Henry's movements, see Mortimer, *Fears of Henry IV*, pp. 64–65.

18. *PROME*, "Richard II: October 1386," introduction and items 6–17.

19. Sumption, *Divided Houses*, p. 590; *Foedera*, vol. 7, p. 549; *PROME*, "Richard II: October 1386," item 18.

20. *PROME*, "Richard II: October 1386," item 18.

21. *PROME*, "Richard II: October 1386," introduction and item 35; *Statutes of the Realm*, vol. 2 (London, 1816), pp. 39–43; McHardy, *Reign*, pp. 157–62; *Knighton*, pp. 370–71 (which says

that such repeat offenders should be punished "as a public traitor to the king and the kingdom"); *Westm. Chron.*, pp. 174–77.

22. Sumption, *Divided Houses*, pp. 590–93.

23. Sumption, *Divided Houses*, p. 594; Mortimer, *Fears of Henry IV*, p. 69; Geaman, "A Personal Letter," pp. 1086–94; *Walsingham*, vol. 1, pp. 800–1.

24. J. L. Kirby (ed.), *Calendar of Signet Letters of Henry IV and Henry V (1399–1422)* (London, 1978), pp. 1–2; Saul, *Richard II*, pp. 109–10, 117, 126, 171–72, 471; A. Tuck, *Richard II and the English Nobility* (London, 1973), pp. 65–70. Tuck points out (p. 70) that not a single patent letter was authorized by the signet while Bishop Arundel held office as chancellor, but that Richard was still using the signet to send instructions to officials (such as the chamberlain of Chester and the chief justices of King's Bench and Common Pleas) who would accept them directly from the king.

25. *Walsingham*, vol. 1, pp. 810–15 ("*rex nullum bonum uultum faceret, set omnino demissum*"); Sumption, *Divided Houses*, pp. 603–5; Given-Wilson, "Mowbray, Thomas," *ODNB*. Mowbray presumably saw Richard at the Garter celebrations at Windsor on April 23, which was the only time the king returned south and a date that fell in the interval between Arundel's maneuvers at sea. Mowbray and de Vere had been made Garter knights before Arundel (Mowbray and de Vere in 1383–84, Arundel only in 1386): Beltz, *Memorials of the Most Noble Order of the Garter*, pp. cliii–cliv.

26. *Froissart*, vol. 12, p. 239; *Walsingham*, vol. 1, pp. 822–23.

27. *Walsingham*, vol. 1, pp. 798–99 ("*familiaritatis obscene*"), 822–23, 826–29; *Froissart*, vol. 10, pp. 395, 397; *Froissart*, vol. 12, pp. 239, 262.

28. *Walsingham*, vol. 1, pp. 814–15; Mathew, *The Court of Richard II*, pp. 32–34; G. B. Stow, "Richard II and the Invention of the Pocket Handkerchief," *Albion*, vol. 27, no. 2 (1995), pp. 228–33; K. L. Geaman, "Anne of Bohemia and Her Struggle to Conceive," *Social History of Medicine*, vol. 29, no. 2 (2016), pp. 235–38.

29. C. Carpenter, "The Beauchamp Affinity: A Study of Bastard Feudalism at Work," *EHR*, vol. 95, no. 376 (1980), pp. 514–32; H. Castor, *The King, the Crown, and the Duchy of Lancaster: Public Authority and Private Power, 1399–1461* (Oxford, 2000), pp. 5–10 (and references at p. 7n).

30. *Westm. Chron.*, pp. 186–87 (transl. McHardy, *Reign*, pp. 165–66); C. Given-Wilson, *The Royal Household and the King's Affinity: Service, Politics and Finance in England, 1360–1413* (New Haven and London, 1986), pp. 213–14; Tuck, "Thomas [Thomas of Woodstock]," *ODNB*.

31. P. Morgan, *War and Society in Medieval Cheshire, 1277–1403*, Chetham Society, Third Series, vol. 34 (1987), chs. 1–3; *Westm. Chron.*, pp. 186–87; Saul, *Richard II*, p. 172; G. E. Cockayne, *The Complete Peerage*, ed. V. Gibbs, 12 vols. (London, 1910–59), vol. 10, p. 229; *CPR 1385–9*, p. 357.

32. Sumption, *Divided Houses*, p. 633; Saul, *Richard II*, p. 175; *Knighton*, pp. 392–93; *Westm. Chron.*, pp. 196–97.

33. For this paragraph and the following two, see *Statutes of the Realm*, vol. 2, pp. 102–4; McHardy, *Reign*, pp. 175–81; S. B. Chrimes, "Richard II's Questions to the Judges," *Law Quarterly Review*, vol. 72 (1956), pp. 365–90; D. Clementi, "Richard II's Ninth Question to the Judges," *EHR*, vol. 86, no. 338 (1971), pp. 96–113; Tuck, *Richard II and the English Nobility*, pp. 63–64; A. Prescott, "Brembre, Sir Nicholas (d. 1388)," *ODNB*; J. L. Leland, "Tresilian, Sir Robert (d. 1388)," *ODNB*.

34. Saul, *Richard II*, p. 175; *Knighton*, pp. 392–99; J. Tait, review of A. Steel, *Richard II*, *EHR*, vol. 57, no. 227 (1942), pp. 379–80. As Tait points out, Fulthorp's son explained his father's actions in a petition to parliament during the reign of Henry VI: *Rotuli Parliamentorum*, vol. 5, p. 393. The monk of Westminster, however, believed that the archbishop of Dublin told Thomas of Woodstock about what the king had been doing: *Westm. Chron.*, pp. 206–7.

35. F. Palgrave (ed.), *Antient Kalendars and Inventories of the Treasury of His Majesty's Exchequer*, 3 vols. (London, 1836), vol. 3, pp. 298–99 (loan November 26, 1386); Stratford, *Richard II and*

the English Royal Treasure, p. 48; Saul, *Richard II*, pp. 164–66; Sumption, *Divided Houses*, pp. 600–6, 624–31.

6. 1387–1389: come I appellant

1. *Westm. Chron.*, pp. 204–7; *Walsingham*, vol. 1, pp. 830–31; Sumption, *Divided Houses*, pp. 634–35; see ch. 5, pp. 115, 118.

2. For this paragraph and the next, see Sumption, *Divided Houses*, pp. 635–36; *Westm. Chron.*, pp. 206–9; *Walsingham*, vol. 1, pp. 828–31; *Knighton*, pp. 400–3; Gundy, *Richard II and the Rebel Earl*, pp. 125–29; Given-Wilson, *The Royal Household and the King's Affinity*, pp. 213–14.

3. For this paragraph and the next, see *Walsingham*, vol. 1, pp. 830–33; *Westm. Chron.*, pp. 208–11; *Knighton*, pp. 406–9; Sumption, *Divided Houses*, pp. 635–36; A. P. Baggs, D. K. Bolton, M. A. Hicks, and R. B. Pugh, "Hornsey, including Highgate: Communications," in T. F. T. Baker and C. R. Elrington (eds.), *A History of the County of Middlesex*, vol. 6 (London, 1980), p. 103.

4. For this paragraph and the next, see *Knighton*, pp. 408–13; *Westm. Chron.*, pp. 210–13; *Walsingham*, vol. 1, pp. 830–35.

5. For this paragraph and the following two, see *Walsingham*, vol. 1, pp. 834–37; *Westm. Chron.*, pp. 212–15; *Knighton*, pp. 412–17; *Calendar of Letter Books: H*, p. 321. In the different chronicle accounts, there is some variation in the order of the speeches.

6. For this paragraph and the next, see *Knighton*, pp. 416–21; *Westm. Chron.*, pp. 214–21; *Walsingham*, vol. 1, pp. 836–37; Tuck, "Pole, Michael de la," *ODNB*; Leland, "Burley, Sir Simon," *ODNB*; Tuck, "Vere, Robert de," *ODNB*; Sumption, *Divided Houses*, pp. 637–38.

7. Mortimer, *Fears of Henry IV*, p. 69; S. Walker, *The Lancastrian Affinity, 1361–99* (Oxford, 1990), pp. 167–71; Given-Wilson, *Henry IV*, pp. 44–45.

8. G. L. Harriss, "Thomas [Thomas of Lancaster], duke of Clarence (1387–1421)," *ODNB*; for Mary in London, and the 40 shillings Henry gave to the "*obstetrix*," a woman named Joanna, who attended the birth, see C. Barron, "Centres of Conspicuous Consumption: The Aristocratic Townhouse in London, 1200–1550," in M. Carlin and J. T. Rosenthal (eds.), *Medieval London: Collected Papers of Caroline M. Barron* (Kalamazoo, 2017), p. 437.

9. J. R. Maddicott, "Thomas of Lancaster, second earl of Lancaster, second earl of Leicester, and earl of Lincoln (c.1278–1322)," *ODNB*; Given-Wilson, *Henry IV*, pp. 48–49, 50n; Mortimer, *Fears of Henry IV*, pp. 396–97, nn. 28, 30. Years later, Henry would present a set of vestments embroidered with scenes from the life of Thomas of Lancaster to St. George's Chapel, Windsor: Bond (ed.), *Inventories of St George's Chapel*, pp. 4–5, 44–45.

10. For this paragraph and the next, see *Westm. Chron.*, pp. 218–19; Gundy, *Richard II and the Rebel Earl*, pp. 130–31; Given-Wilson, *Henry IV*, pp. 44–48.

11. McHardy, *Reign*, pp. 189–90, 195; *Knighton*, pp. 410–13; R. G. Davies, "Some Notes from the Register of Henry de Wakefield, Bishop of Worcester, on the Political Crisis of 1386–1388," *EHR*, vol. 86, no. 340 (1971), pp. 550, 556.

12. *Westm. Chron.*, pp. 218–25; *Knighton*, pp. 420–25; *Walsingham*, vol. 1, pp. 838–41; Given-Wilson, *Henry IV*, pp. 49–50.

13. The lords insisted on extensive checks for traps and ambushes before they agreed to enter the Tower. Given-Wilson, *Henry IV*, pp. 50–51; *Walsingham*, vol. 1, pp. 842–47; *Westm. Chron.*, pp. 224–27; *Knighton*, pp. 424–27.

14. *Walsingham*, vol. 1, pp. 840–41; *Knighton*, pp. 416–19; *Westm. Chron.*, pp. 222–25; McHardy, *Reign*, pp. 198, 200, 202; Tuck, "Vere, Robert de," and "Pole, Michael de la," *ODNB*; R. B. Dobson, "Neville, Alexander (c.1332–1392)," *ODNB*; Leland, "Tresilian, Sir Robert," *ODNB*; Prescott, "Brembre, Sir Nicholas," *ODNB*.

15. M. V. Clarke and V. H. Galbraith (eds.), "The Deposition of Richard II," *Bulletin of the John Rylands Library*, vol. 14, no. 1 (1930), pp. 157–61; Given-Wilson, *Henry IV*, p. 51.

16. M. Bennett, "Edward III's Entail and the Succession to the Crown, 1376–1471," *EHR*, vol. 113, no. 452 (1998), pp. 580–609; but see also Ormrod, "The DNA of Richard III," pp. 194–98: "The entail proposed in the previous autumn was abandoned and apparently suppressed

[in 1377], since there is no evidence of knowledge of it beyond court circles before the mid-fifteenth century. Edward III's death and Richard II's succession later in 1377 therefore wiped clean the slate of precedent, and once more left open the whole question of who was next in line to the throne."

17. Given-Wilson, *Henry IV*, p. 51; Saul, *Richard II*, p. 190; *Westm. Chron.*, pp. 228–33.

18. For this paragraph and the next, see Saul, *Richard II*, pp. 189–90; Given-Wilson, *Henry IV*, pp. 50–51; *Walsingham*, vol. 1, pp. 846–51; *Westm. Chron.*, pp. 232–35; *Knighton*, pp. 426–27; M. McKisack (ed.), "*Historia siue narracio de modo et forma mirabilis parliamenti*," Camden Society, Third Series, vol. 37 (London, 1926), pp. 14–15 (transl. McHardy, *Reign*, pp. 212–13).

19. *PROME*, "Richard II: February 1388," Part 1, items 6–8; Part 2, articles 1–4; Part 3; Saul, *Richard II*, p. 192; Given-Wilson, *Henry IV*, pp. 52–53.

20. *PROME*, "Richard II: February 1388," Part 2; Saul, *Richard II*, p. 191.

21. *PROME*, "Richard II: February 1388," Part 3.

22. McKisack (ed.), "*Historia siue narracio*," p. 17 (transl. McHardy, *Reign*, pp. 220–21); *Knighton*, pp. 498–99; Given-Wilson, *Henry IV*, p. 53.

23. *Westm. Chron.*, pp. 312–17 ("*. . . ut ipsi deponerent super credulitate eorum, scilicet an credebant ipsum scire de predictis prodicionibus supra specificatis vel non; qui dierunt ipsum putantes pocius de hujusmodi scire quam nescire*"); *PROME*, "Richard II: February 1388," Part 3; *Knighton*, pp. 500–1; *Walsingham*, vol. 1, pp. 852–53; McKisack (ed.), "*Historia siue narracio*," pp. 19–20 (transl. McHardy, *Reign*, p. 223). John Blake had drafted the questions to the judges for Tresilian: Saul, *Richard II*, p. 193. For the career and family of Thomas Usk, sergeant at arms and author of *The Testament of Love*, see R. Waldron, "Usk, Thomas (*c.*1354–1388)," *ODNB*.

24. For this paragraph and the next, see *Westm. Chron.*, pp. 286–93, 318–19, 328–33; *Knighton*, pp. 500–3; *Walsingham*, vol. 1, pp. 852–53; McKisack (ed.), "*Historia siue narracio*," pp. 20–21 (transl. McHardy, *Reign*, pp. 223–24). For Richard Burley, see Walker, *The Lancastrian Affinity*, pp. 25, 79, 102; Leland, "Burley, Sir Simon," *ODNB*.

25. *PROME*, "Richard II: February 1388," Part 1, items 35, 38–40, 48–51; *Westm. Chron.*, pp. 342–43. For Henry Knighton saying that the parliament came to be known as the Merciless Parliament, see *Knighton*, pp. 414–15.

26. *PROME*, "Richard II: February 1388," Part 1, item 16; *CPR 1385–9*, p. 479; Goodman, *The Loyal Conspiracy*, pp. 47–48; Sumption, *Divided Houses*, pp. 615–16. Holand and his wife, Elizabeth, left Gaunt's army in June 1387 and crossed the Pyrenees into Aquitaine but did not arrive back in England until April 1388. The timing supports the suggestion that Elizabeth gave birth to their second child, a daughter, Constance, in the latter part of 1387: see ch. 4, n. 32.

27. *PROME*, "Richard II: February 1388, Part 1, item 46; *Westm. Chron.*, pp. 342–43.

28. *PROME*, "Richard II: February 1388," Part 3.

29. *Westm. Chron.*, pp. 290–91.

30. Given-Wilson, *Henry IV*, p. 58.

31. For this paragraph and the following two, see Sumption, *Divided Houses*, pp. 594–600, 606–17; *Walsingham*, vol. 1, pp. 892–93.

32. For this paragraph and the following two, see Sumption, *Divided Houses*, pp. 617–23, 648–56, 660.

33. Sumption, *Divided Houses*, pp. 656–60; W. Bower, *Scotichronicon*, vol. 7, ed. A. B. Scott, D. E. R. Watt, U. Moret, and N. F. Shead (Aberdeen, 1996), pp. 414–19; *Knighton*, pp. 504–7.

34. *Westm. Chron.*, pp. 354–57; *PROME*, "Richard II: September 1388," introduction.

35. Given-Wilson, *Henry IV*, p. 59; Mortimer, *Fears of Henry IV*, pp. 82, 399nn. 65–66; Tuck, "Vere, Robert de," *ODNB*; Gundy, *Richard II and the Rebel Earl*, pp. 134–36.

36. Sumption, *Divided Houses*, pp. 649–52, 662–67.

37. *Westm. Chron.*, pp. 390–93; *Walsingham*, vol. 1, pp. 864–67; *Knighton*, pp. 528–31; L. Slater, "Imagining Place and Moralizing Space: Jerusalem at Medieval Westminster," *British Art Studies*, 6 (2017); N. M. Bradbury and S. Bradbury (eds.), *The Dialogue of Solomon and Marcolf*, TEAMS Middle English Texts (online resource, 2012), introduction.

38. *CCR 1385–9*, p. 671.
39. Given-Wilson, *Henry IV*, pp. 59–60; J. Stratford, "John [John of Lancaster], duke of Bedford (1389–1435)," *ODNB*; Sumption, *Divided Houses*, pp. 674–76; *Westm. Chron.*, pp. 406–9; *Walsingham*, vol. 1, pp. 894–95; Goodman, *John of Gaunt*, p. 144. The significance of the letter *S* in the Lancastrian collar is not clear. Suggestions include a link with Gaunt's mother, Queen Philippa, who owned clothes and wall hangings decorated with the letter for reasons unknown, or with Henry's motto "*Souvenez*": see D. Fletcher, "The Lancastrian Collar of Esses: Its Origins and Transformations down the Centuries," in J. L. Gillespie (ed.), *The Age of Richard II* (Stroud, 1997), pp. 191–204; Mortimer, *Fears of Henry IV*, Appendix 7.

7. 1389–1393: this little world

1. For Charles's physical energy, see P. de Mézières, *Le Songe du vieil Pelerin*, ed. G. W. Coopland (Cambridge, 1969), vol. 2, pp. 15, 212–13. For the celebrations at Saint-Denis, see *Religieux*, vol. 1, pp. 586–601; Sumption, *Divided Houses*, pp. 668–69.
2. *Religieux*, vol. 1, pp. 496–99, 594–95; Sumption, *Divided Houses*, p. 669.
3. *Religieux*, vol. 1, pp. 584–93, 598–605; Sumption, *Divided Houses*, pp. 610–11, 617, 668–89; R. E. Whitbread, "Tournaments, Jousts and Duels: Formal Combats in England and France, circa 1380–1440," PhD thesis, University of York (2013), p. 61; *Walsingham*, vol. 1, pp. 892–93.
4. C. Taylor and J. M. H. Taylor (eds. and tr.), *The Chivalric Biography of Boucicaut, Jean II le Meingre* (Woodbridge, 2016), pp. 28–31, 35–48; Given-Wilson, *Henry IV*, pp. 61–62. For detailed discussion of the chivalric biography, see C. Taylor, *A Virtuous Knight: Defending Marshal Boucicaut (Jean II Le Meingre, 1366–1421)* (Woodbridge, 2019).
5. Taylor and Taylor (eds. and tr.), *Chivalric Biography*, pp. 49–51. For John Beaufort as the Bastard of Lancaster, see *Religieux*, vol. 1, pp. 680–81, and an anonymous poem transcribed in *Froissart*, vol. 14, p. 416. For Harry Percy's ransom, see *Westm. Chron.*, pp. 400–1.
6. In the months between the issue of Boucicaut's challenge and the date on which the knights were to meet, Gaunt's former son-in-law, the seventeen-year-old earl of Pembroke, died in training for the lists when he was accidentally impaled on a lance. Henry was a much more experienced fighter, but accidents could always happen: Whitbread, "Tournaments, Jousts and Duels," pp. 64–65; *Westm. Chron.*, pp. 408–11; *Walsingham*, vol. 1, pp. 896–97. For the arrangements at Saint-Inglevert, see Taylor and Taylor (eds. and tr.), *Chivalric Biography*, pp. 49–50. The motto "*Ce que vous vouldrez*" can be variously translated, but the effect is always of a graceful bow to an opponent, combined with a confidence in meeting all demands.
7. For Boucicaut's training regime and his exploits, see Taylor and Taylor (eds. and tr.), *Chivalric Biography*, pp. 30–31; for his height, p. 36. For Henry and his companions as the bravest of the challengers, see *Religieux*, vol. 1, pp. 678–81. For Henry's largesse, see H. Moranvillé (ed.), *Chronographia Regum Francorum*, vol. 3 (Paris, 1897), p. 99. For accounts of the fighting (which differ in some details), see Moranvillé (ed.), *Chronographia*, vol. 3, pp. 97–100; *Religieux*, vol. 1, pp. 673–83; Taylor and Taylor (eds. and tr.), *Chivalric Biography*, pp. 49–52; *Froissart*, vol. 14, pp. 105–51, and for the text of a poem celebrating the jousts, pp. 406–19.
8. Taylor and Taylor (eds. and tr.), *Chivalric Biography*, p. 49. For Swynford and Rempston, see *Religieux*, vol. 1, pp. 680–81 ("*Thomas de Souviforde*" and "*Thomelin de Fanteston*"); *Froissart*, vol. 14, pp. 415–16 ("*Thomas Subincorde*" and "*Thomelin Nosenton*"); and for French difficulties with the English names, see Given-Wilson, *Henry IV*, pp. 62–3n. Rempston had first sat in parliament in 1381, which indicates that he was several years older than Henry; see C. Rawcliffe, "Rempston, Sir Thomas I (d. 1406), of Rempstone, Notts," *Hist. Parl.*
9. For this paragraph and the next, see Taylor and Taylor (eds. and tr.), *Chivalric Biography*, pp. 50, 52; Given-Wilson, *Henry IV*, p. 63; L. Toulmin-Smith (ed.), *Expeditions to Prussia and the Holy Land Made by Henry, Earl of Derby*, Camden Society, New Series, vol. 52 (London, 1894), pp. xxvi–xxvii.
10. E. Christiansen, *The Northern Crusades: The Baltic and the Catholic Frontier 1100–1525* (London and Basingstoke, 1980), chs. 3–6; S. Walker, "Percy, Sir Henry [*called* Henry Hotspur]

(1364–1403)," *ODNB*; F. R. H. Du Boulay, "Henry of Derby's Expeditions to Prussia 1390–1 and 1392," in F. R. H. Du Boulay and C. Barron (eds.), *The Reign of Richard II* (London, 1971), pp. 154–55.

11. For this paragraph and the next, see Toulmin-Smith (ed.), *Expeditions*, pp. 1, 5–38; Given-Wilson, *Henry IV*, p. 64; Mortimer, *Fears of Henry IV*, pp. 91–93.

12. Herman, the skipper of Henry's ship, was paid the very substantial sum of £26; Hankyn, steering the second ship, £13: Toulmin-Smith (ed.), *Expeditions*, pp. xliii–xlv, 37, 128–33.

13. *PROME*, "Richard II: January 1390," items 1, 6.

14. *Westm. Chron.*, pp. 412–15; *PROME*, "Richard II: January 1390," paragraphs 21–23, 27; *Walsingham*, vol. 1, pp. 898–99.

15. *Statutes of the Realm*, vol. 2, pp. 74–75; Saul, *Richard II*, p. 264. For the functioning of noble affinities, see Carpenter, "The Beauchamp Affinity," pp. 514–32.

16. See above, chs. 5 and 6; Tuck, "Pole, Michael de la," *ODNB*. For Richard biding his time about de Vere's return, see an exchange with Gaunt in the summer of 1390 reported by the Westminster chronicler. At a lavish hunting party he hosted at Leicester that July, Gaunt asked his nephew to pardon a former mayor of London who had been banished from the capital in 1384. "It is not in my power," Richard replied. "On the contrary, Gaunt said, '... you could do that and more. God forbid that your power should be so cramped that you could not extend grace to your liege subjects when the circumstances call for such action.'" "If I can do what you say," the king retorted, "there are others who have suffered great hardship; so that I know what to do for my own friends who are now overseas." See *Westm. Chron.*, pp. 440–41.

17. For Richard's mother and her badge of a white hind, see above, ch. 1, p. 21, and J. G. Nichols, "Observations on the Heraldic Devices Discovered on the Effigies of Richard the Second and His Queen in Westminster Abbey," *Archaeologia*, vol. 14, no. 1 (1841–42), p. 37. For King Charles and the "*cerf volant*," see C. de Mérindol, "De l'emblématique de Charles VI et de Jean de Berry: À propos d'un Plafond peint et armoré récemment publié," *Bulletin de la Société Nationale des Antiquaires de France, 2006* (2012), pp. 123, 125–29. For Richard's hart, see E. Scheifele, "Richard II and the Visual Arts," in Goodman and Gillespie (eds.), *Richard II: The Art of Kingship*, pp. 257–59.

18. *Religieux*, vol. 1, pp. 608–17, 614–15; *Froissart*, vol. 14, pp. 5–25, 253–54; *Westm. Chron.*, pp. 436–37. For the text of the "*criee des joustes*," see R. D. Moffat, "The Medieval Tournament: Chivalry, Heraldry and Reality," two vols., PhD thesis, University of Leeds (2010), vol. 2, pp. 117–19, and discussion in vol. 1, pp. 64–72.

19. *Froissart*, vol. 14, pp. 20–23; *Religieux*, vol. 1, pp. 614–15. Richard's proclamation talked of one knight bearing the white hart on his shield, but the *English Chronicle* describes all the knights and ladies of the "home team" wearing the badge: Moffat, "The Medieval Tournament," vol. 2, p. 117; J. S. Davies (ed.), *An English Chronicle of the Reigns of Richard II, Henry IV, Henry V, and Henry VI*, Camden Society, Old Series, vol. 64 (London, 1856), p. 6: "The xij yeer of king Richard, duryng this same parlement, he leet crie and ordeyne general justis at Londoun, in Smythfeld, for alle maner straungers, and othir that thider wolde come; and thay of the kyngis side were alle in on sute, thair cotearmuriȝ, sheldis, hors-trappuris, and alle, was white hertis, with cronneȝ aboute thair neckis, and cheynes of gold hangyng ther upon, and the cronne hangyng lowe befor the hertis bodye, the whiche hert was the kyngis liverey, that he gaf to knyghtis and squiers and othir. And atte firste comyng to thair justis, xxiiij ladieȝ ladde xxiiij knyȝtis of the gartir, with cheyneȝ of gold, and alle in the same sute her of hertis as before is said, from the tour of Londoun, on horsbak, thorouȝ the cite of Londoun in to Smythfeld."

20. Different writers give different numbers for the knights and ladies. Froissart says sixty, the original "*cri*" says twenty, the *English Chronicle* says twenty-four knights of the Garter: *Froissart*, vol. 14, pp. 260–62; Moffat, "The Medieval Tournament," vol. 2, p. 117; Davies (ed.), *English Chronicle*, p. 6. Ladies leading knights to the arena by a silver chain were a well-established tradition: see, for example, the jousts at Saint-Denis in 1389 (this chapter, pp. 157–58), or Edward III's jousts at Cheapside in 1331 (Ormrod, *Edward III*, p. 142).

21. *Froissart*, vol. 14, pp. 22, 262–63; *Westm. Chron.*, pp. 450–51; *Vitae et Regni*, pp. 131–32 (transl. McHardy, *Reign*, p. 258). For Richard's appearance in armour, see *Froissart*, vol. 14, p. 262 ("*Aprés nonne s'en vint le roy d'Angleterre sure la place armé et bien accompaignie de ducs, de contes et de seigneurs, car il estoit de ceulx de dedans*"). The queen arrived separately and went to the stands, but Richard isn't described as taking part in the jousts, and the prize among the English knights for that day went to Hugh Despenser. It's unthinkable that the king wouldn't have won had he fought. The monk of Westminster is the only chronicler to imply that the king *did* fight, saying that he was awarded the prize for the first day; but he gives no other details. The suggestion doesn't fit either with other accounts of the event or with the fact that Richard isn't known to have taken part in jousts at any point in his life before or after this: *Westm. Chron.*, pp. 450–51.

22. Sumption, *Divided Houses*, pp. 788, 793–4; *Froissart*, vol. 14, pp. 263, 314–15.

23. For de Vere in France and at Louvain, see *Froissart*, vol. 14, pp. 32–34 ("*Or n'est-il riens dont on ne se tanne*"); Keen, "Coucy, Enguerrand [Ingelram] de," *ODNB*; *CPR 1388–92*, p. 407. For Richard's geomantic handbook, see P. J. Eberle, "Richard II and the Literary Arts," in Goodman and Gillespie (eds.), *Richard II: The Art of Kingship*, pp. 241–44; Saul, *Richard II*, pp. 357–58; Mathew, *The Court of Richard II*, pp. 40–41; J-P. Genet (ed.), *Four English Political Tracts of the Later Middle Ages*, Camden Society, Fourth Series, vol. 18 (1977), pp. 22–23, 31. Genet discusses the possible identity of the volume's compiler, who describes himself as "the most humble servant of the Treasurers in Ireland," which seems, Genet argues, "to point to a Treasurer of Ireland during the reign of Richard II." He does not take March 1391 as a decisive date for the compilation of the whole manuscript, and therefore proposes the candidacy of John Thorpe, who held that office in 1393–94. Much more likely, I would argue—given both the specific dating of the geomantic treatise and the allusion in the preface of the whole compilation to the "innocent exile" (who, in Thorpe's case, would have to be identified not as de Vere in 1391 but Thomas Mowbray in 1398)—is his secondary suggestion of Richard White, the prior of the Order of St. John of Jerusalem in Ireland, who had been appointed as justiciar of Ireland by de Vere in April 1386, and served as treasurer there from 1388 to 1391: see Genet (ed.), *Four Lancastrian Political Tracts*, pp. 24–30; P. Crooks, "'The Calculus of Faction' and Richard II's Duchy of Ireland, *c.*1382–9," in N. Saul (ed.), *Fourteenth Century England*, vol. 5 (Woodbridge, 2008), pp. 108n, 112n; Tuck, *Richard II and the English Nobility*, p. 82. The manuscript is Bodleian Library MS Bodl. 581, and images of a selection of pages can be seen on the Bodleian Library website, including fos. 1r (preface to the compilation, referring to the "innocent exile" and the compiler's role in the Irish treasury), 9r (introduction to the geomantic treatise, including an illuminated portrait of Richard in the initial capital), and 15v–25v (geomantic tables).

24. Given-Wilson, *Henry IV*, pp. 64–68; Christiansen, *The Northern Crusades*, pp. 158–59.

25. Toulmin-Smith (ed.), *Expeditions*, pp. xxix–xxxi, 105 (payment of 40 shillings to a valet of Lord "Bourser" [Bourchier] for raising the standard); Given-Wilson, *Henry IV*, pp. 66–68; *Westm. Chron.*, pp. 448–49; Christiansen, *The Northern Crusades*, pp. 161–65 for the difficulties of campaigning in the wilderness in the autumn and winter.

26. Toulmin-Smith (ed.), *Expeditions*, pp. 88–93. The total cost of the expedition was £4,360, of which £3,542 came from Gaunt: Given-Wilson, *Henry IV*, p. 71.

27. Given-Wilson, *Henry IV*, pp. 68–70; Toulmin-Smith (ed.), *Expeditions*, pp. 52, 65, 68, 88–90, 92, 107–9, 113, 115–17.

28. Toulmin-Smith (ed.), *Expeditions*, pp. 98, 117, 143; M. J. Curley, "John of Bridlington [St. John of Bridlington, John Thwing] (*c.*1320–1379)," *ODNB*; *Vitae et Regni*, pp. 126–27. For Henry's birthday, see I. Mortimer, "Henry IV's Date of Birth and the Royal Maundy," *Historical Research*, vol. 80, no. 210 (2007), pp. 567–76; Mortimer, *Fears of Henry IV*, Appendix 1. Mortimer demonstrates that Henry celebrated his birthday on the movable feast of Maundy Thursday, which in 1391 was March 23.

29. Given-Wilson, *Henry IV*, p. 70; and for Henry's new pair of plates, see J. Anstis, *The Register*

of the Most Noble Order of the Garter (London, 1724), vol. 1, p. 114n (dated 14 Richard II, i.e., June 22, 1390–June 21,1391; the plates must therefore have been ordered soon after Henry's return from Prussia at the end of April). For "pair of plates," see J. Barker, *The Tournament in England, 1100–1400* (Woodbridge, 2003), p. 169. For Henry's wardrobe, see Given-Wilson, *Henry IV*, pp. 71–72, who interprets "*Soveyne Vous de Moy*" as a written motto; but it was the French name for the flower as well as Henry's tag, and it's clear that the flower and leaves are meant in this context: J. H. Wylie, *History of England under Henry the Fourth*, 4 vols. (London, 1884–98), vol. 4, pp. 161, 163; Mortimer, *Fears of Henry IV*, pp. 385–86.

30. Juan of Castile had died in October 1390 after a fall from his horse, leaving his son Enrique to succeed to the throne at the age of eleven with Catalina as his seventeen-year-old consort: Russell, *English Intervention*, pp. 532–33; Taylor and Taylor (eds. and tr.), *Chivalric Biography*, pp. 36, 38, 43, 52–53; *CPR 1388–92*, pp. 363, 413; *Westm. Chron.*, pp. 454–55, 474–81.

31. *Westm. Chron.*, pp. 478–79; Given-Wilson, *Henry IV*, pp. 77, 81–83. Edmund Mortimer, the son and heir of seventeen-year-old Roger Mortimer, earl of March, and Eleanor Holand, daughter of Thomas Holand, earl of Kent, was born on November 6, 1391: R. A. Griffiths, "Mortimer, Edmund, fifth earl of March and seventh earl of Ulster (1391–1425)," *ODNB*.

32. *Westm. Chron.*, pp. 478–85; *Walsingham*, vol. 1, pp. 912–13; *Foedera*, vol. 7, pp. 705–6; Tuck, "Thomas [Thomas of Woodstock]," *ODNB*.

33. Given-Wilson, *Henry IV*, pp. 72, 77; Toulmin-Smith (ed.), *Expeditions*, pp. xlvii–xlix, lxxii, 151–62, 278–79; Du Boulay, "Henry of Derby's Expeditions to Prussia," pp. 165–67. Mortimer, *Fears of Henry IV*, pp. 102–4, suggests that Henry was at Amiens with Gaunt for negotiations with the French in February, but the only brief mention of this is in *Froissart*, whereas the monk of Saint-Denis and Henry Knighton—both of whom were likely to be better informed about Gaunt's mission—say instead that Gaunt's nephew, the earl of Rutland was there: *Froissart*, vol. 14, pp. 377, 379; *Religieux*, vol. 1, pp. 738–41; *Knighton*, pp. 542–45. J. Baldwin, *The King's Council in England during the Middle Ages* (Oxford, 1913), p. 493, gives the minutes of the full council meeting on February 12, 1392, where it was decided that the embassy to France would consist of Gaunt, Langley, and John Holand with three other lords, not including Henry or Rutland.

34. For this paragraph and the next, see Toulmin-Smith (ed.), *Expeditions*, pp. l–lxiii, lxxiii–lxxvi, 179, 190–91, 194–95, 198, 201–2, 206–7, 211, 218–24, 257, 264–72, 274–76, 279–81; Given-Wilson, *Henry IV*, pp. 72–75; Mortimer, *Fears of Henry IV*, pp. 105–10.

35. Toulmin-Smith (ed.), *Expeditions*, pp. lxii–lxv, lxxvi, 226, 277–78; Mortimer, *Fears of Henry IV*, pp. 110–12; Given-Wilson, *Henry IV*, p. 388; P. Palladino, *Treasures of a Lost Art: Italian Manuscript Painting of the Middle Ages and Renaissance* (New Haven and London, 2003), pp. 58–59; E. Gordon-Duff (ed.), *Information for Pilgrims unto the Holy Land* (London, 1893).

36. Toulmin-Smith (ed.), *Expeditions*, pp. lxv–lxxi, lxxvii–lxxix, 227–30, 234, 236–38, 241–43, 254, 275–77, 284–88; Given-Wilson, *Henry IV*, pp. 74–75; Mortimer, *Fears of Henry IV*, pp. 112–15; *Calendar of State Papers, Milan, 1385–1618*, ed. A. B. Hinds (London, 1912), pp. 1–2. Saint Augustine, Boethius, and Lionel of Antwerp were all buried in the church of San Pietro in Ciel D'Oro. Lionel's body was later brought back to England to be buried at Clare in Suffolk: J. Capgrave, *Liber de Illustribus Henricis*, ed. F. C. Hingeston (London, 1858), pp. 100–1.

37. Given-Wilson, *Henry IV*, pp. 73–74; Toulmin-Smith (ed.), *Expeditions*, pp. lxv, 194, 229–33, 240, 256–57, 283, 286. See Wylie, *Henry the Fourth*, vol. 4, p. 179, for Mary buying 6 lbs of "popynjaysed" in the spring of 1394. The word used in the accounts is "*leopardus*," which could refer to a number of big cats; this one was almost certainly a hunting cheetah, probably a gift from the king of Cyprus. The practice of hunting with cheetahs came from the Arab world, but it was well established in Cyprus by this time. Royal hunts with "*domestici leopardi*" were described by two different travelers in 1335; sixty years after that, James I of Cyprus was said to keep twenty-four hunting cheetahs in Famagusta, and in 1391 Gian Galeazzo Visconti organized a cheetah hunt in Pavia in honor of the ambassadors of the duke of Burgundy. Henry's animal came with its own expert handler, a man named Mark, and the "matte" bought

for it was probably a "horse carpet," used to allow the cheetah to ride behind its handler on horseback until the moment in the hunt when it was loosed. See T. Buquet, "Hunting with Cheetahs at European Courts, from the Origins to the End of a Fashion," in N. Weber and M. Hengerer (eds.), *Animals and Court (Europe, c.1200–1800)* (Berlin, 2020), pp. 17–42; M. Masseti, "Pictorial Evidence from Medieval Italy of Cheetahs and Caracals, and Their Use in Hunting," *Archives of Natural History*, vol. 36 (2009), pp. 37–39, 45. See Wylie, *Henry the Fourth*, vol. 4, pp. 164–65, for supplies bought for the cheetah in the year after Henry's return from the Holy Land, although the purchase from an apothecary might suggest that by then it was ailing, and it makes no more appearances in the household accounts.

38. Given-Wilson, *Henry IV*, pp. 77–80, 387–88.

8. 1391–1394: to be a make–peace

1. *Knighton*, pp. 536–39; see also *Westm. Chron.*, pp. 452–53, 474–77; *Walsingham*, vol. 1, pp. 900–1; *Eulogium*, p. 369 ("Nothing is written here for the year of Our Lord 1391, because the kingdom of England was in a bad state"). For London, see N. H. Nicolas (ed.), *A Chronicle of London, from 1089 to 1483* (London, 1827), p. 79. The funds were taken from the Orphan Fund—that is, the inheritances of wealthy underage orphans being managed by the city: see *Calendar of Letter Books: H*, pp. 361–62; E. Clark, "City Orphans and Custody Law in Medieval England," *American Journal of Legal History*, vol. 34 (1990), p. 184.

2. *PROME*, "Richard II: November 1390," introduction and item 15; *PROME*, "Richard II: November 1391," introduction and item 13. Richard had commissioned a compilation of such statutes in *c.*1389–90: Saul, *Richard II*, p. 237; Eberle, "Richard II and the Literary Arts," pp. 240–41.

3. C. Barron, "The Quarrel of Richard II with London, 1392–7," in Carlin and Rosenthal (eds.), *Medieval London*, p. 30 and details in n. 16; cf. McKisack, *The Fourteenth Century*, pp. 467–68.

4. Loans: C. Barron, "Richard II and London," in Carlin and Rosenthal (eds.), *Medieval London*, pp. 111, 127n; Barron, "Quarrel of Richard II," p. 30; see above, ch. 5, pp. 126–27; *Westm. Chron.*, pp. 496–97. The Mildenhall case concerned William's father, Peter, a skinner and former alderman of London, who had been arrested on charges of felony and treason and taken to Nottingham Castle on the king's orders in August 1387: *CCR 1389–92*, p. 527; *Calendar of Letter Books: H*, p. 312; A. H. Thomas (ed.), *Calendar of Select Pleas and Memoranda of the City of London*: vol. 3: *1381–1422* (London, 1932), p. 151; M. Bennett, "'Defenders of truth': Lord Cobham, John Gower, and the Political Crisis of 1387–88," in Lutkin and Hamilton (eds.), *Creativity, Contradictions and Commemoration*, p. 35; Barron, "Quarrel of Richard II," p. 31. Orders about illegal assembly: *CCR 1389–92*, p. 530; Barron, "Quarrel of Richard II," p. 31.

5. Sumption, *Divided Houses*, pp. 787–88; Baldwin, *The King's Council*, pp. 494–96.

6. For this paragraph and the next two, see *Westm. Chron.*, pp. 484–87; Baldwin, *The King's Council*, pp. 494–95; Saul, *Richard II*, pp. 236, 255.

7. Barron, "Quarrel of Richard II," pp. 29–32.

8. Barron, "Quarrel of Richard II," pp. 32–33; *Calendar of Letter Books: H*, pp. 375, 378; *CPR 1391–6*, pp. 65, 67, 100; *CCR 1389–92*, pp. 466–67, 565–66.

9. Barron, "Quarrel of Richard II," pp. 33–37; *CFR 1391–9*, p. 49; *Statutes of the Realm*, vol. 1, pp. 346–47.

10. R. Maidstone, *Concordia (The Reconciliation of Richard II with London)*, ed. D. R. Carlson, with a verse translation by A. G. Rigg, TEAMS Middle English Texts (online resource, 2003), introduction 3.1 and 3.2, ll. 45–372; H. Suggett, "A Letter Describing Richard II's Reconciliation with the City of London, 1392," *EHR*, vol. 62, no. 243 (1947), pp. 209–13; *Westm. Chron.*, pp. 506–9; *Knighton*, pp. 546–49; Kipling, "Richard II's 'Sumptuous Pageants,'" pp. 85–98; Barron, "Richard II and London," pp. 123–24.

11. Maidstone, *Concordia*, ll. 373–545; *Westm. Chron.*, pp. 502–3; *CPR 1391–6*, pp. 171, 173, 226; Barron, "Quarrel of Richard II," pp. 38–42 (see n. 99 for the crucial wording from NA C66 333 m. 31, not transcribed in *CPR 1391–6*, p. 173: "*quousque aliter ordinandum que eisdem in*

cuius etc"); *CCR 1392–6*, pp. 21, 75–76; Barron, "Richard II and London," p. 125; J. H. Harvey, "The Wilton Diptych—a Re-examination," *Archaeologia*, vol. 98 (1959), p. 5.

12. Maidstone, *Concordia*, introduction 2 and 3, ll. 37–38; 112–17, 136–37, 203–18, 419–28.

13. L. Staley, "Gower, Richard II, Henry of Derby, and the Business of Making Culture," *Speculum*, vol. 75, no. 1 (2000), pp. 78–79; G. C. Macaulay (ed.), *The Complete Works of John Gower*, vol. 2 (Oxford, 1901), pp. xxi–xxiii, 2–6; D. Gray, "Gower, John (*d.* 1408)," *ODNB*.

14. Tuck, "Vere, Robert de," *ODNB*; *Westm. Chron.*, pp. 510–11; T. Hearne (ed.), *Duo Rerum Anglicarum Scriptores Veteres, viz. Thomas Otterbourne et Johannes Whethamstede*, vol. 1 (Oxford, 1732), p. 181; J. Leland, *Collectanea*, vol. 1 (London, 1770), p. 186; *PROME*, "Richard II: January 1393," items 15–16. Sixty-year-old Alexander Neville, the former archbishop of York, had died before de Vere, in May 1392 (see *Westm. Chron.*, pp. 492–93). Of the five "traitors" accused by the Appellants in 1388, de Vere had been the last, and now none remained.

15. *Religieux*, vol. 2, pp. 18–21; *Froissart*, vol. 15, pp. 35–43; F. Autrand, *Charles VI* (Paris, 1986), pp. 290–95; Sumption, *Divided Houses*, pp. 793–98.

16. Sumption, *Divided Houses*, pp. 783–84, 787, 793, 799–802; Autrand, *Charles VI*, pp. 268, 295–98; *Religieux*, vol. 2, pp. 22–23.

17. *Religieux*, vol. 2, pp. 74–77; *Walsingham*, vol. 1, pp. 940–41; Sumption, *Divided Houses*, pp. 805–6.

18. Sumption, *Divided Houses*, pp. 774–75, 777–78, 805–6; *Froissart*, vol. 15, pp. 110–22; Autrand, *Charles VI*, pp. 299–303; J. J. N. Palmer, "The Anglo-French Peace Negotiations, 1390–1396," *Transactions of the Royal Historical Society*, vol. 16 (1966), pp. 83–84.

19. *Westm. Chron.*, pp. 456–57, 490–91; Sumption, *Divided Houses*, pp. 774–78, 787–90, 792–93, 805–7.

20. Sumption, *Divided Houses*, pp. 788–93, 804–7; *Religieux*, vol. 2, pp. 78–79; *Froissart*, vol. 15, p. 109. The current truce, due to expire in September 1393, was extended for another twelve months to allow this process to be pursued: *Foedera*, vol. 7, p. 748.

21. Sumption, *Divided Houses*, pp. 806–8; Palmer, "Anglo-French Peace Negotiations," pp. 82–84; McHardy, *Reign*, pp. 276–78.

22. *Froissart*, vol. 15, p. 120 (Woodstock told Froissart about the conversation when Froissart visited England in the following year); Sumption, *Divided Houses*, pp. 807–8.

23. Sumption, *Divided Houses*, p. 805; Walker, *The Lancastrian Affinity*, pp. 171–72. For previous parliamentary complaints about armed violence in the palatinate of Cheshire, see *PROME*, "Richard II: October 1382," item 44; *PROME*, "Richard II: November 1390," item 23.

24. *Walsingham, vol.* 1, pp. 944–47; McHardy, *Reign*, p. 281; J. G. Bellamy, "The Northern Rebellions in the Later Years of Richard II," *Bulletin of the John Rylands Library*, vol. 47 (1964–65), pp. 263–64.

25. For Talbot, Clifton, and Massy, see Walker, *The Lancastrian Affinity*, pp. 171–74; for Richard's retaining in these years, see Given-Wilson, *The Royal Household and the King's Affinity*, pp. 214–22.

26. See above, chs. 5–7; *CPR 1385–9*, p. 450.

27. For this paragraph and the next, see *Foedera*, vol. 7, p. 746; Walker, *The Lancastrian Affinity*, pp. 173–74; *Walsingham*, vol. 1, pp. 944–49; Given-Wilson, *Henry IV*, pp. 73, 89; Bellamy, "The Northern Rebellions," pp. 264–65; Morgan, *War and Society in Medieval Cheshire*, pp. 196–97.

28. *CPR 1388–92*, p. 506; G. Holmes, "Mortimer, Edmund, third earl of March and earl of Ulster (1352–1381)," *ODNB*; Given-Wilson, "Fitzalan, Richard, fourth earl of Arundel," *ODNB*; Sumption, *Divided Houses*, pp. 673–74, 778; *Foedera*, vol. 7, p. 707; *Walsingham*, vol. 1, pp. 948–49; Goodman, *The Loyal Conspiracy*, pp. 112–13; Bellamy, "The Northern Rebellions," pp. 265–66.

29. *Religieux*, vol. 2, pp. 86–89, 92–93; Moranvillé (ed.), *Chronographia*, vol. 3, p. 110; *Froissart*, vol. 15, pp. 127–28; Sumption, *Divided Houses*, pp. 810–11.

30. *Walsingham*, vol. 1, pp. 956–57; *PROME*, "Richard II: January 1394," item 11.

31. For this paragraph and the next, see *PROME*, "Richard II: January 1394," item 11 (where the earl's words are given in English within an otherwise French account); *Walsingham*, vol. 1, pp. 956–57; *CPR 1391–6*, pp. 405–6.

32. *PROME*, "Richard II: January 1394," introduction and items 16–17, 20–21; Bellamy, "Northern Rebellions," pp. 266–67.

33. *Westm. Chron.*, pp. 518–19.

34. *Foedera*, vol. 7, pp. 766, 769–76; Sumption, *Divided Houses*, pp. 810, 814; *Westm. Chron.*, pp. 520–21.

35. *Foedera*, vol. 7, p. 776; *Walsingham*, vol. 1, pp. 960–61; *Westm. Chron.*, pp. 520–21; Given-Wilson, *Henry IV*, pp. 86, 90. See Mortimer, *Fears of Henry IV*, p. 406n, for the difficulties of establishing the date of Mary's death in June or July.

9. 1394–1395: an immortal title

1. Walker, *The Lancastrian Affinity*, pp. 216–17; Goodman, *John of Gaunt*, p. 256; Given-Wilson, *Henry IV*, p. 86; Walker, "Katherine [*née* Katherine Roelt . . .]," *ODNB*.

2. The amounts that Mary had spent on clothes were a fraction of the cost of Henry's wardrobe, and although she and the family visited Gaunt's splendid homes, there is no trace of her in London or at court after Thomas's birth in 1387. Her mother, Joan, was Arundel's sister, but neither her relationship with the Lancastrian family, nor that of Archbishop Arundel, seems to have been adversely affected by the earl's breach with Gaunt: Wylie, *Henry the Fourth*, vol. 4, pp. 165, 170–72; Mortimer, *Fears of Henry IV*, pp. 99, 118; Given-Wilson, *Henry IV*, p. 80; C. Allmand, *Henry V* (New Haven and London, 1992), pp. 9–10; *Knighton*, pp. 548–51; *Westm. Chron.*, pp. 520–21; *Walsingham*, vol. 1, pp. 960–61.

3. For this paragraph and the next, see *Walsingham*, vol. 1, pp. 960–63; *Foedera*, vol. 7, pp. 776, 784 (cf. *CCR 1392–6*, p. 307).

4. *CCR 1392–6*, p. 368; *Foedera*, vol. 7, p. 785; *PROME*, "Richard II: January 1393," item 15.

5. Walsingham, at least, thought it a "trivial or insignificant" reason for offense ("*pro leui uel nulla causa offensus*"): *Walsingham*, vol. 1, pp. 960–61. For the previous assault in 1386 and the pardon in April, see above, ch. 4, p. 105, and ch. 8, p. 195. J. G. Bellamy thinks it possible that between the pardon in April and the funeral Richard might have "received information that led him to believe Arundel had indeed been involved in the Cheshire insurrection and regretted the earl's earlier pardon"—but no surviving evidence supports the suggestion: Bellamy, "Northern Rebellions," p. 270.

6. J. J. N. Palmer, *England, France and Christendom, 1377–99* (London, 1972), pp. 152–60. For the earlier conspiracies, see above, ch. 4. For the gathering and rumors at Pontefract, see Goodman, *John of Gaunt*, p. 155; M. D. Legge (ed.), *Anglo-Norman Letters and Petitions from All Souls MS 182* (Oxford, 1941), pp. 74–76 (where the letter is misdated to 1397). For early plans for the crusade, see Sumption, *Divided Houses*, p. 816; R. Vaughan, *Philip the Bold* (revised ed., Woodbridge, 2002), p. 62.

7. Legge (ed.), *Anglo-Norman Letters*, pp. 74–76 (quotation from p. 75): ". . . *dont je m'ose mettre en la tesmoignance de Dieu et de tous loialx créatures que unques ne pensoie ne avoie l'entencioun de riens faire encontre vostre treshonuré estat, ne autrement que un vraye lige ne deust par tout loialté faire devers son tressovereigne seignur lige, et je tiens et espoir vrament, monseignur, que vous m'avéz en tout temps tielment provéz par experience de tous mes faitz par devers vous, que vous ne vouldrés croire aucuns tielx paroles sonnantz au contraire de mes ditz faitz.*"

8. *Calendar of Letter Books: H*, p. 412 (writ dated June 16, 1394, ordering the sheriffs to proclaim that all Irishmen in London should return to Ireland by August 15): *Foedera*, vol. 7, p. 782; Saul, *Richard II*, p. 279; Goodman, *The Loyal Conspiracy*, p. 62. For further details of the military preparations, see *CCR 1392–6*, pp. 307–8; J. F. Lydon, "Richard II's Expeditions to Ireland," *Journal of the Royal Society of Antiquaries of Ireland*, vol. 93, no. 2 (1963), pp. 138–43.

9. Sumption, *Divided Houses*, p. 815; Given-Wilson, *Henry IV*, p. 90n; Wylie, *Henry the Fourth*, vol. 3, pp. 327–28, and vol. 4, pp. 168, 170–72, 179–80.

10. Letter to either Archbishop Arundel as chancellor or Bishop Waltham as treasurer: Legge (ed.), *Anglo-Norman Letters*, pp. 230–31 (transl. McHardy, *Reign*, p. 290).

11. J. Tait, "'Plantagenet,' Edward, . . . second Duke of York (1373?–1415)," and "Mowbray, Thomas (I), twelfth Baron Mowbray and first Duke of Norfolk (1366?–1399)," archive edition *ODNB*; R. R. Davies, "Mortimer, Roger, fourth earl of March and sixth earl of Ulster (1374–1398)," *ODNB*; J. L. Gillespie, "Holland [Holand], Thomas, sixth earl of Kent and duke of Surrey (*c.*1374–1400)," *ODNB*; Legge (ed.), *Anglo-Norman Letters*, p. 222 (transl. McHardy, *Reign*, p. 290). John Holand was traveling with a French embassy to Hungary; he therefore joined the expedition late, for six weeks in March–April 1395: see below, ch. 10, p. 220.

12. Perroy, *The Diplomatic Correspondence of Richard II*, p. 103 (*"cuique signum nostrum quo fruimur et quo nostri milites nostris lateribus assistentes utuntur, admodum cervi cubantis, tradidimus ubilibet deferendum"*); Harvey, "The Wilton Diptych," p. 7; Given-Wilson, *The Royal Household and the King's Affinity*, pp. 64, 214–15, 220–22. The figures given here for Richard's retinue do not wholly match, probably because of difficulties arising from a damaged document (see n. 81 on p. 311).

13. Legge (ed.), *Anglo-Norman Letters*, p. 48 (*"si bien au punissement et correccioun de noz rebelx illoeque, come pour bone governance et juste reule faire et establir de et sur noz foialx liges de nostre terre avantdite"*); Saul, *Richard II*, p. 277; McHardy, *Reign*, pp. 131–32.

14. For this paragraph and the following two, see R. Frame, *The Political Development of the British Isles, 1100–1400* (Oxford, 1990), pp. 179–87; G. L. Harriss, *Shaping the Nation: England 1360–1461* (Oxford, 2005), pp. 508–11; R. Frame, "'Les Engleys Nées en Irlande': The English Political Identity in Medieval Ireland," *Transactions of the Royal Historical Society*, vol. 3 (1993), pp. 83–103; Lydon, "Richard II's Expeditions to Ireland," pp. 3–4; J. F. Lydon, "Ireland and the English Crown, 1171–1541," *Irish Historical Studies*, vol. 29, no. 115 (1995), pp. 281–90, 292–94; D. Johnston, "Richard II and the Submissions of Gaelic Ireland," *Irish Historical Studies*, vol. 22, no. 85 (1980), pp. 1–4; Saul, *Richard II*, pp. 281–82; N. Saul, "Richard II and the Vocabulary of Kingship," *EHR*, vol. 110, no. 438 (1995), pp. 866–67.

15. For this paragraph and the next, see R. Frame, "Mac Murchadha, Art Caomhánach [Art Kavanagh MacMurrough; *called* Art Mór Mac Murchadha] (*d.* 1416/17)," *ODNB*; K. Simms, "Ó Néill, Niall Mór (*d.* 1397)," *ODNB*; Harriss, *Shaping the Nation*, pp. 511–12; Lydon, "Richard II's Expeditions to Ireland," pp. 145–46; Legge (ed.), *Anglo-Norman Letters*, pp. 207–8, 222–23 (transl. McHardy, *Reign*, pp. 290–91); Johnston, "Richard II and the Submissions of Gaelic Ireland," pp. 4–5.

16. Legge (ed.), *Anglo-Norman Letters*, p. 224 (transl. McHardy, *Reign*, p. 291); E. Curtis (ed. and tr.), *Richard II in Ireland, 1394–5, and Submissions of the Irish Chiefs* (Oxford, 1927), pp. 80–85 (transl. 169–73).

17. Curtis (ed. and tr.), *Richard II in Ireland*, pp. 33–35, 39–41, 48, 62–63 (transl. 154–55), 67–68 (transl. 158–59), 71–72 (transl. 161–62), 74–75 (transl. 163–64), 87–90 (transl. 175–79), 95–97 (transl. 182–84).

18. Legge (ed.), *Anglo-Norman Letters*, pp. 210–11 (transl. McHardy, *Reign*, p. 295): *"nous quidons par la grace de Dieu d'avoir entiere obeissance en brief de toute nostre dit terre."* For Woodstock at the parliament of January–February 1395, see *PROME*, "Richard II: January 1395," introduction and item 1. For his antipathy toward the Irish campaign, see *Froissart*, vol. 16, p. 5 (claiming to quote the duke): *"Yrlande n'est pas terre de conqueste, ne de proufit. Yrlandois sont povres et meschans gens et ont ung très-povre pays et inhabitable."* In 1392, Gaunt had suggested that Woodstock should be sent to Ireland as royal lieutenant; enough preparations were made that Woodstock was in significant debt to the crown when the appointment was canceled only three months later: Tuck, "Thomas [Thomas of Woodstock]," *ODNB*; Baldwin, *The King's Council*, pp. 498, 500, 503.

19. Curtis (ed. and tr.), *Richard II in Ireland*, pp. 137–40 (transl. 217–19 and in McHardy, *Reign*, pp. 298–99); Johnston, "Richard II and the Submissions of Gaelic Ireland," pp. 5–8.

20. Johnston, "Richard II and the Submissions of Gaelic Ireland," pp. 8–12; J. L. Gillespie, "Richard II: Chivalry and Kingship," in Gillespie (ed.), *The Age of Richard II*, pp. 126–28; Harriss, *Shaping the Nation*, pp. 512–13; Curtis (ed. and tr.), *Richard II in Ireland*, pp. 131–32 (Ó Néill, transl. 211–12), and, for letters from many other lords, pp. 121–37, 140–42 (transl. 203–16, 219–20); Legge (ed.), *Anglo-Norman Letters*, pp. 132–33 (transl. McHardy, *Reign*, pp. 295–96).

21. Johnston, "Richard II and the Submissions of Gaelic Ireland," pp. 12–20; Frame, *Political Development of the British Isles*, pp. 212–17; Saul, *Richard II*, pp. 285–87; Curtis (ed. and tr.), *Richard II in Ireland*, pp. 48, 99–100 (transl. 186–87); Davies, "Mortimer, Roger, fourth earl of March," *ODNB* (March was appointed lieutenant on April 28, 1395).

22. McHardy (ed. and transl.), *Reign of Richard II*, p. 304; M. Bennett, *Richard II and the Revolution of 1399* (Sutton, 1999), pp. 217–18 and n. 90 for Henry Yeveley and Hugh Herland sending a carpenter to Ireland with a model of the new building to show the king; *Vitae et Regni*, p. 134 (transl. McHardy, *Reign*, p. 285); Saul, *Richard II*, pp. 472–73.

23. *Foedera*, vol. 7, pp. 795–96, 797–98; Nichols, "Observations on the Heraldic Devices," pp. 52–53; Devon (ed.), *Issues of the Exchequer*, pp. 258, 264. The Latin text of Richard's epitaph reads: "*Prudens et Mundus—Ricardus jure Secundus, per fatum victus—jacet hic sub marmore pictus. Verax sermone—fuit, et plenus ratione: Corpore procerus—animo prudens ut Omerus. Ecclesie favit—elatos suppeditavit, Quemvis prostravit—regalia qui violavit*": see *An Inventory of the Historical Monuments in London*, vol. 1: *Westminster Abbey* (London, 1924), p. 31.

24. Sumption, *Divided Houses*, pp. 822–23; McHardy, *Reign*, pp. 299–300; Palmer, *England, France and Christendom*, pp. 166–68.

25. Sumption, *Divided Houses*, pp. 823–24; Legge (ed.), *Anglo-Norman Letters*, pp. 158–60 (first offer) and 242–45 (Charles's letter to Richard).

26. Depending on the diagnosis, and among other uses, *trifera magna* could be drunk with wine, or used on a cotton pessary inserted into the vagina: see M. H. Green (ed. and tr.), *The Trotula: A Medieval Compendium of Women's Medicine* (Philadelphia, 2001), pp. 41, 112–13, and appendix, pp. 201–2; Geaman, "Anne of Bohemia and Her Struggle to Conceive," pp. 234–35. For the grant to Mowbray, see *Foedera*, vol. 7, p. 763.

27. The "Confessor's arms" were not used by Edward the Confessor in the eleventh century but had been attributed to him later: Froissart, vol. 15, p. 180; Harvey, "The Wilton Diptych," pp. 5–6; Scheifele, "Richard II and the Visual Arts," p. 259; Bennett, *Richard II and the Revolution of 1399*, p. 71. For the messengers to Rome, see Devon (ed.), *Issues of the Exchequer*, p. 259. For the investigation of the miracles and earlier requests for Edward II's canonization, see *Westm. Chron.*, pp. 436–39; Perroy, *Diplomatic Correspondence of Richard II*, p. 301; Theilmann, "Political Canonization and Political Symbolism in Medieval England," p. 257.

28. For French hopes of peace, see Bennett, *Richard II and the Revolution of 1399*, pp. 72–73; *Religieux*, vol. 2, pp. 414–15.

29. Froissart, vol. 15, pp. 155–56.

30. *Foedera*, vol. 7, pp. 802–5; Palmer, *England, France and Christendom*, pp. 169–70, 256–57 (transl. McHardy, *Reign*, pp. 305–7); Froissart, vol. 15, p. 187.

31. Froissart, vol. 15, pp. 142, 146, 156, 183–87; *Religieux*, vol. 2, pp. 328–29; Sumption, *Divided Houses*, pp. 826–27.

32. The date and location of the full-length portrait are not completely certain, but for best estimates dating it to 1395 and placing it in the choir, see W. R. Lethaby, "The Westminster Portrait of Richard II," *The Burlington Magazine*, vol. 65 (1934), pp. 220–21, quoting the issue roll of 1395 ("*Pro pictura unius ymaginis ad similitudinem unius Regis contrafacte in choro ecclesie predicte*"); Scheifele, "Richard II and the Visual Arts," pp. 264–65. For an account of the enormous amount of overpainting and "restoration" of the portrait in subsequent centuries, see G. Scharf, "The Westminster Portrait of Richard II," *Fine Arts Quarterly Review*, vol. 2 (1867), pp. 27–63. For the painting of the white hart in the mezzanine gallery, see J. Spooner, "The Virgin Mary and White Harts Great and Small: The 14th-Century Wall-Paintings in

the Chapel of Our Lady of the Pew and the Muniment Room," in W. Rodwell and T. Tatton-Brown (eds.), *Westminster, Part I: The Art, Architecture and Archaeology of the Royal Abbey*, The British Archaeological Association Conference Transactions, vol. 39 (2015), pp. 263, 278–86. For the coronation portrait of Edward the Confessor on the wall of the Painted Chamber in the palace of Westminster, see above, ch. 1, pp. 22–23, and Wilson, "A Monument to St Edward the Confessor," pp. 162, 169.

33. Scheifele, "Richard II and the Visual Arts," pp. 260–61; Bennett, *Richard II and the Revolution of 1399*, pp. 60–61; Brown, Colvin, and Taylor (eds.), *History of the King's Works*, vol. 1, pp. 528–33; L. T. Courtenay and R. Mark, "The Westminster Hall Roof: A Historiographic and Structural Study," *Journal of the Society of Architectural Historians*, vol. 46, no. 4 (1987), pp. 374–93. For instructions "to cause the great hall in the palace of Westminster to be repaired," see *CPR 1391–6*, pp. 348–49.

34. For this paragraph and the next, see Palmer, *England, France and Christendom*, p. 171; *Walsingham*, vol. 2, pp. 30–31; Beltz, *Memorials of the Most Noble Order of the Garter*, p. 302; Devon (ed.), *Issues of the Exchequer*, p. 262; Saul, *Richard II*, pp. 461, 473.

10. 1395–1396: conclude and be agreed

1. Curtis (ed. and tr.), *Richard II in Ireland*, pp. 139–40 (transl. 219); Given-Wilson, *Henry IV*, pp. 92–93.

2. For Holand's embassy, which seems to have taken him via Venice to negotiate for ships, involved a visit to Vienna, and was coordinated with a French embassy concerned with the same issue, see Palmer, *England, France and Christendom*, pp. 200, 202–4, 240–42; *Foedera*, vol. 7, p. 764; *CPR 1391–6*, p. 594; and for him joining the Irish campaign in March–April 1395, see M. M. N. Stansfield, "The Holland Family, Dukes of Exeter, Earls of Kent and Huntingdon, 1352–1475," DPhil thesis, University of Oxford (1987), pp. 88–89, 91–92. For Scrope, whose mother was Michael de la Pole's sister Blanche, see B. Vale, "Scrope, William, earl of Wiltshire (1351?–1399)," *ODNB*; Palmer, *England, France and Christendom*, p. 169; *Foedera*, vol. 7, pp. 802–5.

3. Richard was recruiting widely at this stage, including in Lancashire, Cheshire, Staffordshire, and Yorkshire: Given-Wilson, *The Royal Household and the King's Affinity*, pp. 219–20; Given-Wilson, *Henry IV*, pp. 93–94. For Talbot, and a pardon on April 14, 1395, to Thomas Holand, earl of Kent, and his lieutenant for allowing Talbot to escape, see Bellamy, "The Northern Rebellions," pp. 268, 271; *CPR 1391–6*, p. 560. Talbot's associates Massy and Clifton were both already free. Massy had been released on the king's orders on July 7, 1394, and Clifton "made his peace" that same summer: *CCR 1392–6*, p. 305; Bellamy, "The Northern Rebellions," p. 268.

4. Given-Wilson, *Henry IV*, pp. 93–96; Given-Wilson, "Richard II, Edward II, and the Lancastrian Inheritance," pp. 567–70; Theilmann, "Political Canonization and Political Symbolism in Medieval England," pp. 249–58.

5. *Livre des Bouillons*, Archives Municipales de Bordeaux (Bordeaux, 1867), pp. 257–67; *Froissart*, vol. 15, pp. 147–51, 158–59; Palmer, *England, France and Christendom*, pp. 152–62. Henry in Leicester: Given-Wilson, *Henry IV*, p. 92n. Henry at Eltham: Baldwin, *The King's Council*, p. 504.

6. Baldwin, *The King's Council*, pp. 135–36, 504; *Froissart*, vol. 15, pp. 156–57, 160–62. Froissart arrived in England on July 12 and visited the Black Prince's tomb in Canterbury Cathedral before attaching himself to the royal household to make his way via Leeds Castle and Rochester to Eltham: *Froissart*, vol. 15, pp. 142–48.

7. Palmer, *England, France and Christendom*, pp. 159–62; *Froissart*, vol. 15, pp. 161–62.

8. The Gascons and Gaunt's representatives left the chamber while the council discussed the issue: Baldwin, *The King's Council*, pp. 136, 505; *Froissart*, vol. 15, pp. 160, 162; Palmer, *England, France and Christendom*, p. 156.

9. Froissart's informant about the council meeting—which took more than four hours, he was

told—was Sir Richard Sturry, an elderly knight of the king's chamber whom Froissart had met twice in the reign of Edward III, and who agreed to speak to him in confidence since the substance of the meeting would soon be public. Another contact, Jean de Grailly, agreed with Sturry about Woodstock's likely motives for supporting Gaunt: *Froissart*, vol. 15, pp. 154, 162–63, 165–66; Baldwin, *The King's Council*, pp. 137, 505.

10. *Froissart*, vol. 15, pp. 163–66. Isabel of Castile had died in 1392, by which time she seems to have been reconciled with her husband after the earlier breach between them: see above, ch. 4, n. 16, and J. Stratford, "Isabel [Isabella] of Castile, first duchess of York (1355–1392)," *ODNB*.

11. *Froissart*, vol. 15, pp. 164, 166–67, 171; Palmer, *England, France and Christendom*, pp. 162–63.

12. For the terms of Gaunt's agreement with John de Montfort, see G-A. Lobineau, *Histoire de Bretagne*, vol. 2 (Paris, 1707), pp. 791–93. For Henry and Gaunt's movements, see Given-Wilson, *Henry IV*, p. 91; Mortimer, *Fears of Henry IV*, p. 129; Goodman, *John of Gaunt*, p. 200, and for Gaunt's health, p. 355. For Gaunt and Richard, see *Walsingham*, vol. 2, pp. 38–39. For the palace of "Chiltern Langley," see, e.g., *Foedera*, vol. 7, pp. 812, 817.

13. *Walsingham*, vol. 2, pp. 38–39; *Froissart*, vol. 15, pp. 238–40 (although he thinks the couple had only three children and conflates Henry Beaufort with Thomas).

14. The overwhelming balance of probability is that John Beaufort went on the Nicopolis campaign, along with Sir Ralph Percy: Palmer, *England, France and Christendom*, pp. 204, 239–40. For John of Nevers, see Vaughan, *Philip the Bold*, pp. 63–68.

15. *Froissart*, vol. 15, pp. 226–69, 269–71; Given-Wilson, *Henry IV*, p. 97–98.

16. Sumption, *Divided Houses*, pp. 826–88; Palmer, *England, France and Christendom*, pp. 171–74; *Religieux*, vol. 2, pp. 328–87, 412–15; *Froissart*, vol. 15, p. 237; *Foedera*, vol. 7, pp. 811–23.

17. *Religieux*, vol. 2, pp. 414–15; *Foedera*, vol. 7, p. 811 ("... que le Roy, son Friere, et les Uncles soient aliez ovec lui, encountre toutes maneres de Gentz, queux deussent en aucune manere obeir a lui. Et auxi de lui aider et susteigner ovec tout leur Povair encontre aucune de ses subgiz").

18. *Froissart*, vol. 15, pp. 196–98, 238; vol. 16, pp. 2–6, 9.

19. *Froissart*, vol. 15, pp. 188–202; Sumption, *Divided Houses*, pp. 828–29.

20. Richard's sister Maud Holand had died in 1392 and St. Pol remarried, but the connection remained: *Froissart*, vol. 15, pp. 272–73.

21. Palmer, *England, France and Christendom*, pp. 175–76; *Religieux*, vol. 2, pp. 402–9, 414–15, 444–45; *Foedera*, vol. 7, pp. 834–35.

22. *Religieux*, vol. 2, pp. 444–47; Sumption, *Divided Houses*, p. 830.

23. For this paragraph and the next, see *Religieux*, vol. 2, pp. 444–51; *Froissart*, vol. 15, pp. 274–76; Sumption, *Divided Houses*, p. 830.

24. The abbot of Westminster was sent with letters to both popes instructing them to follow the advice of "our father of France" in choosing the "*voie de cession*." The pope in Avignon would not see him, given that the letter did not address him as pontiff, and in the circumstances the abbot decided there was no point traveling on to Rome: *Religieux*, vol. 2, pp. 448–51.

25. *Religieux*, vol. 2, pp. 452–53; *Froissart*, vol. 15, pp. 298, 306; Sumption, *Divided Houses*, p. 831.

26. *Religieux*, vol. 2, pp. 452–59; *Walsingham*, vol. 2, pp. 38–39; Sumption, *Divided Houses*, p. 831; M. P. Meyer, M. M. Meyer, and S. Luce, "L'Entrevue d'Ardres, 1396," *Annuaire-Bulletin de la Société de l'histoire de France*, vol. 18, no. 2 (1881), pp. 212–13, 219–22; *Froissart*, vol. 15, pp. 298, 304–5, and vol. 18, p. 583; Given-Wilson, *Henry IV*, p. 98.

27. *Froissart*, vol. 15, pp. 299–300.

28. For the kings' outfits at their first meetings on October 26 and 27, see *Walsingham*, vol. 2, pp. 40–47; *Religieux*, vol. 2, pp. 456–59. For Charles as "a broken reed by now, even when he was lucid," see Sumption, *Divided Houses*, p. 820; *Religieux*, vol. 2, pp. 458–62; *Walsingham*, vol. 2, pp. 44–49; Meyer, Meyer, and Luce, "Entrevue," pp. 212–15; *Froissart*, vol. 15, pp. 302–4, and for the text of the oath, see vol. 18, pp. 582–83 (also *Walsingham*, vol. 2, pp. 38–41).

29. Sumption, *Divided Houses*, pp. 832–33. For Henry and Visconti, see above, ch. 7, p. 175, and ch. 9, p. 203. For Richard's decision, see also *PROME*, "Richard II: January 1397," items 9–10, and below, ch. 11, pp. 241–42.

30. Meyer, Meyer, and Luce, "Entrevue," pp. 217–20; *Religieux*, vol. 2, pp. 466–73; *Froissart*, vol. 15, pp. 305–7; *Walsingham*, vol. 2, pp. 48–51; Sumption, *Divided Houses*, p. 831. For the full list of Isabella's trousseau, see L. Mirot, "Un Trousseau royal à la Fin du XIVe Siècle," *Mémoires de la Société de l'histoire de Paris et de l'Ile-de-France*, vol. 29 (1902), p. 142.

31. For the dowry, see *Foedera*, vol. 7, pp. 846–47. Woodstock gave Isabella a brooch in the shape of an eagle made of gold and white enamel adorned with gemstones; Henry's gift was an enameled golden greyhound set with a balas ruby and a huge pearl: *Traison et Mort*, pp. 108, 110; Stratford, *Richard II and the English Royal Treasure*, pp. 65, 292. Isabella's seventh birthday was November 9 and her ceremonial entry into London November 23.

32. Very little has been conclusively resolved about the symbolism and resonances of the diptych, but the combination of broom-cods and white harts does strongly indicate an association, both chronological and symbolic, with the royal summit: Scheifele, "Richard II and the Visual Arts," pp. 265–70. For full discussion of this "tantalisingly cryptic" painting (p. 30), see D. Gordon, *The Wilton Diptych* (London, 2015).

11. 1396–1397: on ancient malice

1. *PROME*, "Richard II: January 1397," introduction and items 1–2, 7. For John Bushy, see C. Rawcliffe, "Bussy, Sir John (exec. 1399), of Hougham, Lincs. and Cottesmore, Rutland," *Hist. Parl.*

2. *PROME*, "Richard II: January 1397," introduction and items 8–9. William Courtenay, archbishop of Canterbury since 1381, died on July 31, 1396. Arundel was appointed to succeed him on September 25 and resigned the chancellorship two days later: R. N. Swanson, "Courtenay, William, archbishop of Canterbury (1341/2–1396)," and Hughes, "Arundel [Fitzalan], Thomas," *ODNB*.

3. *PROME*, "Richard II: January 1397," introduction and items 9–10 ("*Et dist outre nostre seignour le roy q'il voet estre a large et liberte de comander ses gentz, pur eux envoier en aide de ses amys, et pur disposer de ses biens propres a sa volentee, ou, et a tant des foitz, qe luy plerra*").

4. *PROME*, "Richard II: January 1397," introduction.

5. *PROME*, "Richard II: January 1397," introduction and items 8–10, 12–15; Sumption, *Divided Houses*, p. 835. Three other issues are mentioned as under discussion by the Commons—the qualifications and terms of office of sheriffs and escheators, the defense of the Scottish marches, and the giving of badges to men who were not lords' servants—but Richard's response indicates he was not angered by those.

6. Given-Wilson, *Royal Household*, p. 79. Waldby had previously been archbishop of Dublin, though had only visited Ireland with the king in 1394–95. He was translated to the bishopric of Chichester in November 1395, and then became archbishop of York in October 1396, less than a year later. Merks's predecessor as bishop of Carlisle, Robert Reade, who was also a household cleric, had only been appointed in January 1396, and was then promoted to the bishopric of Chichester nine months later: A. Tuck, "Stafford, Edmund (1344–1419)," *ODNB*; R. N. Swanson, "Burghill [Burghull], John (*c*.1330–1414)" and "Waldby, Robert (*c*.1335–1397)," *ODNB*; R. G. Davies, "Merk [Merke], Thomas (*d*. 1409/10)" and "Rede [Reade], Robert (*d*. 1415)," *ODNB*; A. K. McHardy, "Haxey's Case, 1397: The Petition and Its Presenter Reconsidered," in Gillespie (ed.), *The Age of Richard II*, p. 108.

7. *PROME*, "Richard II: January 1397," introduction, items 16–17 and 23, and Appendix 1; *Rotuli Parliamentorum*, vol. 3, pp. 407–8; Given-Wilson, *The Royal Household and the King's Affinity*, pp. 79, 81–83, 86–87, 89–90, 94.

8. The decree had immediate effects: at seventeen, Joan Beaufort was already the widowed mother of two girls from her early marriage to a Warwickshire knight, but shortly after the court returned from Calais in November she was snapped up as a bride by Ralph, Lord Neville, a landowner as powerful in the far northwest of England as the earl of Northumberland in the northeast: A. Tuck, "Beaufort [*married names* Ferrers, Neville], Joan, countess of

Westmorland (1379?–1440)," *ODNB; Calendar of Papal Registers Relating to Great Britain and Ireland*, vol. 4, *1362–1404* (London, 1902), p. 545; *CCR 1396–9*, pp. 74–75.

9. Sumption, *Divided Houses*, pp. 834–35; *Froissart*, vol. 16, pp. 1–2; *PROME*, "Richard II: January 1397," items 28–32. The first date is said here to be February 4 but must correctly be February 6 because it was a Tuesday (whereas February 4 fell on Sunday in 1397). Soon afterward John Beaufort married Margaret, daughter of Thomas Holand, earl of Kent, and was made a knight of the Garter: G. L. Harriss, "Beaufort, John, marquess of Dorset and marquess of Somerset (*c.*1371–1410)," *ODNB*.

10. For this paragraph and the next, see above, ch. 4, p. 100, and ch. 9, pp. 208, 212; *PROME*, "Richard II: October 1385," item 16; *PROME*, "Richard II: January 1397," items 28–29 ("*come entier emperour de son roialme d'Engleterre*"); Saul, "Richard II and the Vocabulary of Kingship," pp. 857–59, 865–67, 869–75.

11. For this paragraph and the next, see *PROME*, "Richard II: January 1397," introduction and items 29, 42; *Walsingham*, vol. 2, pp. 54–55.

12. *PROME*, "Richard II: January 1397," introduction and items 5, 24, 32.

13. For this paragraph and the next, see Sumption, *Divided Houses*, p. 836; *Religieux*, vol. 2, pp. 532–33; *Calendar of Papal Registers*, vol. 4: *1362–1404*, pp. 294–95, 300; *Walsingham*, vol. 2, pp. 62–63.

14. See above, ch. 2, p. 41; Stansfield, "The Holland Family," pp. 83, 86–87, 282–83; M. C. E. Jones, *Ducal Brittany, 1364–1399* (Oxford, 1970), pp. 137–39 and nn.; Sumption, *Divided Houses*, p. 836; *Foedera*, vol. 7, pp. 850–53.

15. For this paragraph and the next, see P. H. Wilson, *The Holy Roman Empire* (London, 2016), pp. 393–95; *Walsingham*, vol. 2, pp. 60–61; D. M. Bueno de Mesquita, "The Foreign Policy of Richard II in 1397: Some Italian Letters," *EHR*, vol. 56, no. 224 (1941), pp. 632–33; C. Holdsworth, "Langton, Stephen, archbishop of Canterbury (*c.*1150–1228)" and N. Vincent, "Richard, first earl of Cornwall and king of Germany (1209–1272)," *ODNB*.

16. Bueno de Mesquita, "Foreign Policy of Richard II," pp. 631–33; *Walsingham*, vol. 2, pp. 60–61; *Foedera*, vol. 7, pp. 854–56, 858–59 and vol. 8, pp. 2–4.

17. *Rotuli Parliamentorum*, vol. 3, pp. 407–8; *CPR 1391–6*, pp. 109, 141; *PROME*, "Richard II: January 1397," items 7, 11; see above, ch. 8, pp. 190–92. For obedience, see S. Walker, "Richard II's Views on Kingship," in R. E. Archer and S. Walker (eds.), *Rulers and Ruled in Late Medieval England* (London, 1995), pp. 51–53; for the suggestion that there was concern among the imperial electors about Richard's capacity to manage his own kingdom, see *Walsingham*, vol. 2, pp. 60–61.

18. *CCR 1396–9*, pp. 123–25; R. Mott, "Richard II and the Crisis of July 1397," in I. Wood and G. A. Loud (eds.), *Church and Chronicle in the Middle Ages* (London, 1991), p. 168 and n.

19. *CPR 1396–9*, pp. 10 (Scrope, Caernarfon, July 6, 1397), 16 (Scrope, Beaumaris, July 8, 1397), 24 (Rutland, Dover and Cinque Ports, September 11, 1396), 36 (Scrope, Pembroke, November 28, 1396), 82 (Scrope, Anglesey and Beaumaris, February 22, 1397), 150 (Rutland, Isle of Wight and Carisbrooke, June 4, 1397), 153 (Scrope, Queenborough, June 15, 1397, grant for life to replace grant during the king's pleasure of June 5, 1396, for which see *CPR 1391–6*, p. 715); Mott, "Richard II and the Crisis of July 1397," p. 168 and n. Kent died on April 25 and Salisbury on June 3: Stansfield, "Holland, Thomas, fifth earl of Kent," and Leland, "Montagu, William," *ODNB*; Given-Wilson, *The Royal Household and the King's Affinity*, pp. 214–16, 220–23.

20. *Religieux*, vol. 2, pp. 476–77; *Traïson et Mort*, pp. 1–2 (transl. 117–20); Sumption, *Divided Houses*, pp. 837–38; Jones, *Ducal Brittany*, pp. 138–39 and nn.

21. Sumption, *Divided Houses*, pp. 306–11; Goodman, *The Loyal Conspiracy*, p. 6. Froissart, the monk of Saint-Denis, and the author of the *Traïson et Mort* were all convinced that Woodstock was actively plotting against Richard, but the details of their narratives—dates, personnel, et cetera—do not add up: *Froissart*, vol. 16, pp. 7–9, 15–19; *Religieux*, vol. 2, pp. 478–79; *Traïson et Mort*, pp. 3–6 (transl. 121–26).

22. See above, ch. 6, pp. 129–30; *Walsingham*, vol. 2, pp. 64–67; *Eulogium*, pp. 371–72 (transl. Given-Wilson, *Chronicles*, pp. 64–65); *Traïson et Mort*, p. 7 (transl. 127); *CCR 1391–6*, p. 140.

23. For this paragraph and the next, see *Walsingham*, vol. 2, pp. 66–73; *Eulogium*, pp. 371–72 (transl. Given-Wilson, *Chronicles*, pp. 64–65).

24. In this paragraph and the next, for the Cheshire archers, see Mott, "Richard II and the Crisis of July 1397," p. 172 (*"a tout le haste que vous purrez pur aucune voie de monde"*); Saul, *Richard II*, p. 375. The proclamations were to be made by the sheriffs: *CCR 1396–9*, pp. 197, 204–5, 208; *Foedera*, vol. 8, pp. 6–7; *Calendar of Letter Books: H*, p. 437; *Walsingham*, vol. 2, pp. 72–73. The sheriffs were also instructed on July 15 to arrest servants of the three detained lords if they were found in arms or unlawfully gathering in London, Middlesex, Essex, Hertfordshire, Surrey, Sussex, Kent, Shropshire, Warwick, Leicestershire, Gloucestershire, and Worcestershire: *CCR 1396–9*, p. 137. On the same day, the mayor and sheriffs of London were ordered to arrest any adherents of the three lords in the city who were inciting the people against the king: *CPR 1396–9*, p. 241. For the embassy to Cologne, and gifts (of white harts made of silver, and cloth worth £405) "for the honour of us and our realm" to the archbishops of Cologne and Trier, the duke of Saxony, and the Count Palatine, see Given-Wilson, *Chronicles*, p. 70n; Bennett, *Richard II and the Revolution of 1399*, p. 84.

25. *CCR 1396–9*, p. 197; T. B. Pugh, "Despenser, Thomas, second Lord Despenser (1373–1400)," and R. L. J. Shaw, "Holland [*married name* Beaufort], Margaret, duchess of Clarence (*b.* in or before 1388, *d.* 1439)," *ODNB*. Margaret's date of birth is not certain, but twelve was the canonical age at which girls could marry and she would therefore have been fifteen or sixteen when she started having children in 1400–1.

26. Given-Wilson, *Henry IV*, p. 102 and n; Mott, "Richard II and the Crisis of July 1397," p. 172; Given-Wilson, *The Royal Household and the King's Affinity*, p. 284; *CPR 1396–9*, p. 171.

27. *CPR 1396–9*, pp. 190–91, 241; *CCR 1396–9*, p. 208; *Foedera*, vol. 8, pp. 6–7.

28. For loans, see *CPR 1396–9*, pp. 178–92; C. Barron, "The Tyranny of Richard II," in Carlin and Rosenthal (eds.), *Medieval London*, pp. 4–6. For the Londoners, see above, ch. 8, p. 182.

29. Stansfield, "Holland, John," Vale, "Scrope, William," and A. Goodman, "Montagu [Montacute], John, third earl of Salisbury (*c.*1350–1400)," *ODNB*; *PROME*, "Richard II: September 1397," Part 2, item 2.

30. C. Barron, "Richard Whittington: The Man Behind the Myth," in Carlin and Rosenthal (eds.), *Medieval London*, pp. 269–70, 273, and Appendix 1; Barron, "Tyranny of Richard II," p. 7; Barron, "The Quarrel of Richard II with London," p. 43.

31. *CCR 1396–9*, pp. 137, 177, 210; J. L. Gillespie, "Richard II's Cheshire Archers," *Transactions of the Historic Society of Lancashire and Cheshire*, vol. 75 (1974), p. 2; *Walsingham*, vol. 2, pp. 76–77; *CPR 1396–9*, p. 192; Bennett, *Richard II and the Revolution of 1399*, p. 97; *Foedera*, vol. 8, p. 7.

32. Given-Wilson, *Henry IV*, pp. 104–5n; for the king and his soldiers riding *"terribiliter"* through the city, see *Eulogium*, p. 373 (transl. Given-Wilson, *Chronicles*, pp. 65–66); J. Gairdner (ed.), *The Historical Collections of a Citizen of London in the Fifteenth Century*, Camden Society, New Series, vol. 17 (1876), p. 96; C. T. Allmand, "Henry V, king of England and lord of Ireland, and duke of Aquitaine (1386–1422)," and Harriss, "Thomas [Thomas of Lancaster]," *ODNB*. For the houses Henry rented at various times on Fleet Street, one the inn of the bishop of St. David's on the west bank of the Fleet River just south of Fleet Bridge and another described as "John Roetis Place," see Barron, "Centres of Conspicuous Consumption," p. 437; Gairdner (ed.), *Historical Collections*, p. 96.

33. The *Eulogium* describes the temporary structure in which the parliament took place as a tent (*"tentorium"*); another account calls it "a long and large hous of tymber . . . couered with tileȝ, and open on bothe sideȝ and atte endis." Either way, it's clear how intimidating the surrounding presence of Richard's archers was intended to be. See *Eulogium*, p. 373 (transl. Given-Wilson, *Chronicles*, p. 66), and Davies (ed.), *An English Chronicle*, p. 9. See also *Walsingham*, vol. 2, pp. 76–79; *Vitae et Regni*, pp. 137–38 (transl. Given-Wilson, *Chronicles*, p. 55); *Usk*, pp.

20–25. Westminster's half-refurbished hall had been used for Queen Isabella's coronation feast in January 1397: M. Collins, P. Emery, C. Phillpotts, M. Samuel, and C. Thomas, "The King's High Table at the Palace of Westminster," *The Antiquaries Journal*, vol. 92 (2012), p. 207.

34. For this paragraph and the following two, see *PROME*, "Richard II: September 1397," Part 1, items 1–3; *Vitae et Regni*, pp. 137–40 (partly transl. Given-Wilson, *Chronicles*, pp. 55–56).

35. Rawcliffe, "Bussy, Sir John," *Hist. Parl.*; L. S. Woodger, "Green, Sir Henry (*c.*1347–1399), of Drayton, Northants," and "Bagot, Sir William (bef. 1354–1407), of Baginton, Warws," *Hist. Parl.*

36. *PROME*, "Richard II: September 1397," introduction and Part 1, items 11–13. Archbishop Arundel was not named in item 11, but it was immediately clear to whom Bushy was referring.

37. *Usk*, pp. 22–23; *Walsingham*, vol. 2, pp. 80–81.

38. See above, chs. 5 and 6.

39. *PROME*, "Richard II: September 1397," Part 1, items 11–13, 15; *Walsingham*, vol. 2, pp. 82–83, 86–87; *Usk*, p. 22–27.

40. For this paragraph and the next, see *Vitae et Regni*, p. 142 (transl. Given-Wilson, *Chronicles*, p. 58); *Usk*, pp. 26–29; *Walsingham*, vol. 2, pp. 86–89; *PROME*, "Richard II: September 1397," Part 2, items 1–7. For Ralph Neville's appointment as constable of the Tower, see *CPR 1396–9*, p. 194.

41. *Usk*, pp. 26–29; *Walsingham*, vol. 2, pp. 86–89; *Vitae et Regni*, pp. 142–43 (transl. Given-Wilson, *Chronicles*, pp. 58–59); *Eulogium*, pp. 374–75; *PROME*, "Richard II: September 1397," Part 2, "Concerning Richard earl of Arundel."

42. For this paragraph and the next two, see *Vitae et Regni*, pp. 143–44 (transl. Given-Wilson, *Chronicles*, pp. 59–60); *Usk*, pp. 28–31; *Walsingham*, vol. 2, pp. 90–95; *PROME*, "Richard II: September 1397," Part 2, "Concerning Richard earl of Arundel."

43. For this paragraph and the next, see *PROME*, "Richard II: September 1397," Part 2, "Concerning Thomas, duke of Gloucester"; M. Giancarlo, "Murder, Lies, and Storytelling: The Manipulation of Justice(s) in the Parliaments of 1397 and 1399," *Speculum*, vol. 77, no. 1 (2002), pp. 79–92.

44. For this paragraph and the next, see *Walsingham*, vol. 2, pp. 96–99; *Usk*, pp. 34–35; *Vitae et Regni*, pp. 144–45 (transl. Given-Wilson, *Chronicles*, pp. 60–62); *PROME*, "Richard II: September 1397," Part 2, item 8. The Isle of Man was Scrope's own lordship, bought in 1392 from the earl of Salisbury: Vale, "Scrope, William," *ODNB*.

45. *PROME*, "Richard II: September 1397," Part 1, item 28; *Usk*, pp. 32–33; *Walsingham*, vol. 2, pp. 76–77, 102–3.

46. *CPR 1396–9*, pp. 196 (Scrope, Bushy, Green), 198 (Bushy, Green, including the barge and kitchen), 200–1 (Scrope, Thomas Holand, Rutland), 205 (Rutland), 207 (Scrope), 210–11 (Bagot, Beaufort), 215–16 (Thomas Holand), 218–21 (Bushy, Despenser, Mowbray, Green), 224 (Despenser), 226 (Green), 280–81 (John Holand, Rutland).

47. *PROME*, "Richard II: September 1397," Part 1, items 20, 22, 26; *Usk*, pp. 32–33.

48. *PROME*, "Richard II: September 1397," Part 1, item 27.

49. For this paragraph and the next, see *PROME*, "Richard II: September 1397," Part 1, item 35; *Walsingham*, vol. 2, pp. 102–3; *Vitae et Regni*, pp. 145–46 (transl. Given-Wilson, *Chronicles*, p. 62). Mowbray's grandmother Margaret of Brotherton, from whom he inherited his claim to the earldom of Norfolk, was created duchess of Norfolk in her own right on the same day as he became duke: R. E. Archer, "Brotherton [Marshal], Margaret, *suo jure* duchess of Norfolk (*c.*1320–1399)," *ODNB*.

50. *Walsingham*, vol. 2, pp. 102–3; *PROME*, "Richard II: September 1397," Part 1, items 36–43.

51. For this paragraph and the next, see *Traïson et Mort*, p. 11 (transl. 140); Bueno de Mesquita, "Foreign Policy of Richard II," pp. 632–34; letter to the duke of Bavaria printed and translated in Harvey, "The Wilton Diptych," Appendix 2.

12. 1397–1398: to stand upon my kingdom

1. *CPR 1396–9*, p. 427; G. Dodd, "Getting Away with Murder: Sir John Haukeston and Richard II's Cheshire Archers," *Nottingham Medieval Studies*, vol. 46 (2002), pp. 102–18; W. Thornbury, *Old and New London*, vol. 1 (London, 1873), p. 32.

2. Given-Wilson, *Henry IV*, p. 107; Barron, "Centres of Conspicuous Consumption," p. 437.

3. *Walsingham*, vol. 2, pp. 94–97; *Usk*, pp. 30–31; Clarke and Galbraith (eds.), "The Deposition of Richard II," pp. 168–69 (transl. Given-Wilson, *Chronicles*, p. 97); Theilmann, "Political Canonization," pp. 261–62.

4. *CCR 1396–9*, pp. 149–50, 157; H. A. Dillon and W. H. St J. Hope, "Inventory of the Goods and Chattels Belonging to Thomas, Duke of Gloucester, and Seized in His Castle at Pleshy, Co. Essex, 21 Richard II (1397); with Their Values, as Shown in the Escheator's Accounts," *Archaeological Journal*, vol. 54 (1897), pp. 275–308. For Woodstock's later burial in Westminster Abbey, see J. Tait, "Thomas of Woodstock, Earl of Buckingham and Duke of Gloucester (1395–1397)," archive edition *ODNB*.

5. For the mission to Rome in June 1397 of Richard Scrope, bishop of Coventry and Lichfield, see Theilmann, "Political Canonization," p. 257; Devon (ed.), *Issues of the Exchequer*, p. 264. For Richard's possible intentions and Henry's movements, see Given-Wilson, *Henry IV*, p. 108; Bennett, *Richard II and the Revolution of 1399*, p. 114.

6. C. L. Kingsford (ed.), *Chronicles of London* (Oxford, 1905), pp. 51–53; *PROME*, "Henry IV: October 1399," Appendix 1; Woodger, "Bagot, Sir William," *Hist. Parl.*

7. For this paragraph and the next, see *PROME*, "Richard II: September 1397," Part 1, item 53.

8. Given-Wilson, *Henry IV*, pp. 109–10; Mortimer, *Fears of Henry IV*, p. 147.

9. *Usk*, pp. 48–49; *Traïson et Mort*, pp. 16–17 (transl. 148); Given-Wilson, *Henry IV*, p. 110 and n.

10. See Bennett, *Richard II and the Revolution of 1399*, p. 118, for a fight in Shrewsbury on Sunday, January 27, in which two of Richard's Cheshire guard were killed by men of the town.

11. *PROME*, "Richard II: September 1397," Part 1, items 44–52.

12. For this paragraph and the next, see *PROME*, "Richard II: September 1397," Part 1, items 53–54; Part 2, item 11.

13. *PROME*, "Richard II: September 1397," Part 1, items 75–78; see above, ch. 11, pp. 255, 262.

14. For this paragraph and the next, see Barron, "Tyranny of Richard II," pp. 6–10; *POPC*, vol. 1 (London, 1834), pp. 75–76; *CPR 1396–9*, pp. 317, 331.

15. Barron, "Tyranny of Richard II," pp. 11–13 and appendix; Nicolas (ed.), *A Chronicle of London*, pp. 155–56.

16. Gairdner (ed.), *Historical Collections*, p. 101; *Foedera*, vol. 8, p. 32 (pardon granted to Henry, January 25, 1398, at Lilleshall; *PROME*, "Richard II: September 1397," Part 1, item 67 (second pardon, January 31, 1398).

17. *PROME*, "Richard II: September 1397," Part 1, items 55–66, 71–72.

18. *CPR 1396–9*, pp. 285, 317 (pardon to Bagot for all offenses before January 6, 1398); *CCR 1396–9*, pp. 291–92. Gaunt kept a copy of Richard's charter in his own archive: Given-Wilson, *Henry IV*, p. 111n.

19. Both men were initially held at Windsor, before Henry was released on bail (according to the author of the *Traïson et Mort*, on sureties provided by Gaunt, Langley, Rutland, and Thomas Holand); Mowbray was kept in custody at the Great Wardrobe in London. For this paragraph and the next, see *Traïson et Mort*, pp. 12–13 (transl. 142–43); *PROME*, "Richard II: September 1397," Part 1, item 79, and Part 2, item 11; *Foedera*, vol. 8, pp. 32, 35–36; Given-Wilson, "Richard II, Edward II, and the Lancastrian Inheritance," pp. 564–65. For Gaunt in Scotland, see Goodman, *John of Gaunt*, p. 164; *Rotuli Scotiae*, vol. 2 (London, 1819), pp. 142–43.

20. *Traïson et Mort*, pp. 13–15 (transl. 145–47).

21. For this paragraph and the next, see *Traïson et Mort*, pp. 15–17 (transl. 147–49); *PROME*, "Richard II: September 1397," Part 2, item 11; Given-Wilson, *Henry IV*, p. 112.

22. See above, ch. 11, pp. 241–42; Bueno de Mesquita, "Foreign Policy of Richard II," pp. 634–35.

23. Given-Wilson, *Henry IV*, pp. 113–14 (where, as on p. 71, he takes "*Soveyne Vous de Moy*" to be the motto rather than the flower); *Froissart*, vol. 16, pp. 95–96; Bueno de Mesquita, "Foreign Policy of Richard II," pp. 635–36. For Gaunt's movements, see Goodman, *John of Gaunt*, p. 165.

24. Bueno de Mesquita, "Foreign Policy of Richard II," p. 633; Sumption, *Divided Houses*, pp. 844–45; *Foedera*, vol. 8, pp. 22–24, 36–38; Myers (ed.), *English Historical Documents*, vol. 4, pp. 174–75.

25. The commissions to Rutland and Holand were issued in March and May: Bennett, *Richard II and the Revolution of 1399*, pp. 123, 127–28; *CPR 1396–9*, pp. 365, 368; *CCR 1396–9*, pp. 277, 288.

26. Bennett, *Richard II and the Revolution of 1399*, pp. 123–24, 127–28; E. G. Kimball (ed.), *Oxfordshire Sessions of the Peace in the Reign of Richard II*, Oxfordshire Record Society, vol. 53 (1979–80), pp. 82–86; Legge (ed.), *Anglo-Norman Letters*, p. 271.

27. Bennett, *Richard II and the Revolution of 1399*, p. 130; *CCR 1396–9*, p. 392; Davies, "Richard II and the Principality of Chester," p. 261.

28. *Traïson et Mort*, pp. 17–18 (transl. 149–50); Bennett, *Richard II and the Revolution of 1399*, p. 132; Given-Wilson, *Henry IV*, pp. 113–14. For Roper's remains, see Kimball (ed.), *Oxfordshire Sessions of the Peace*, pp. 87–89.

29. *Traïson et Mort*, pp. 18–21 (transl. 150–56), where Rutland's and Holand's outfits—"*courtes houpelandez de cendal rouge*"—are translated as "kendal" (wool), but given the magnificence of the court they must have been made from "sendal" (silk).

13. 1398–1399: the hollow crown

1. *Traïson et Mort*, p. 21 (transl. 156).

2. For this paragraph and the next, see *Traïson et Mort*, pp. 21–23 (transl. 156–58); *PROME*, "Richard II: September 1397," Part 2, item 11.

3. *PROME*, "Richard II: September 1397," Part 2, item 11.

4. *CPR 1396–9*, pp. 417, 425; *PROME*, "Richard II: September 1397," Part 2, item 11; Given-Wilson, *Henry IV*, pp. 116–17. Mowbray secured the same provision about the right to take possession of an inheritance—which mattered as much to him as it did to Henry, because Mowbray's elderly grandmother would soon leave him her dukedom (previously earldom) of Norfolk—although his situation was even more precarious, since his exile was for life: *CPR 1396–9*, p. 487.

5. Given-Wilson, *Henry IV*, pp. 117–18; *Foedera*, vol. 8, pp. 47–52; Given-Wilson, "Mowbray, Thomas," *ODNB*.

6. For a portrait of Paris in (almost) the moment of Henry's exile, see J. Sumption, *The Hundred Years War*, vol. 4: *Cursed Kings* (London, 2015), ch. 1; for the aristocratic *hôtels*, pp. 7–9.

7. *Froissart*, vol. 16, pp. 132–33, 136; Given-Wilson, *Henry IV*, p. 121n.

8. *Froissart*, vol. 16, pp. 141–42; Given-Wilson, *Henry IV*, pp. 119–20.

9. Goodman, *John of Gaunt*, pp. 166–68; *CPR 1396–9*, p. 427; Dodd, "Getting Away with Murder," pp. 102–18.

10. See William Bagot's later account of Richard declaring that he wanted "never longer to live than that he might see the crown of England in all so high prosperity, and so lowly be obeyed of all his lieges, as it had been in any other king's time, having consideration how he had been oppressed and disobeyed as well by his lords as by his commons, so that it might be chronicled perpetually that with wit and wisdom and manhood he had recovered his dignity, regality, and honourable estate": Kingsford (ed.), *Chronicles of London*, p. 52; *PROME*, "Henry IV: October 1399," appendix.

11. *Usk*, pp. 48–49; *Creton*, p. 68n. See also *Walsingham*, vol. 2, pp. 76–77 ("they became so impudent that they began to regard the king as a comrade, and to have contempt for all others, be they men in authority or lords"), pp. 130–31; Gairdner (ed.), *Historical Collections*, p. 98.

12. Taylor (ed. and tr.), *The Kirkstall Abbey Chronicles*, p. 119 (transl. 75); *Eulogium*, p. 378. Both texts are translated in Given-Wilson, *Chronicles*, pp. 68, 96.

13. *Walsingham*, vol. 2, pp. 237–41; *Eulogium*, p. 380. Details differ between these two accounts, but they agree that Richard did find the ampulla.

14. For the earl of March, see Davies, "Mortimer, Roger," *ODNB*. On October 18, 1398, Richard rewarded a French messenger bringing news of the birth of his queen's new baby brother, Jean: Bennett, *Richard II and the Revolution of 1399*, p. 137.

15. R. Horrox, "Edward [Edward of Langley, Edward of York], second duke of York (*c*.1373–1415)," *ODNB*; *Creton*, p. 309 (transl. 45).

16. Archer, "Mowbray, Thomas," *ODNB*; *Foedera*, vol. 8, pp. 49–50; *Froissart*, vol. 16, pp. 143–50; *Religieux*, vol. 2, pp. 674–75; Bennett, *Richard II and the Revolution of 1399*, p. 137.

17. Nichols (ed.), *Collection of All the Wills*, pp. 145, 156; Taylor (ed. and tr.), *The Kirkstall Abbey Chronicles*, p. 120 (transl. 76).

18. *PROME*, "Richard II: September 1397," Part 1, item 87, and Part 2, item 14. This decision was not outright confiscation, but a refusal to allow Henry's attorneys to take possession of Gaunt's estates during his exile, as Richard had previously promised they could; nor was Henry's exile explicitly extended from ten years to life. But it was enough to shatter any remaining confidence that Richard's word could be trusted, on a matter—inheritance rights—that struck at the heart of the king's relationship with his subjects: for discussion, see C. Fletcher, "Narrative and Political Strategies at the Deposition of Richard II," *Journal of Medieval History*, vol. 30 (2004), pp. 323–41. Richard gave the same order in relation to the rich lands Mowbray had hoped to inherit from his elderly grandmother, who died just six days later: *PROME*, "Richard II: September 1397," Part 1, item 88.

19. For the assertion that Richard had extended, or intended to extend, Henry's banishment for life, see *Walsingham*, vol. 2, pp. 120–23; Clarke and Galbraith (eds.), "The Deposition of Richard II," p. 170 (transl. Given-Wilson, *Chronicles*, pp. 97–98); and for William Bagot's later statement that he had heard Richard swear that he would never let Henry return to England, see Kingsford, *Chronicles of London*, p. 53. For grants of custody of the Lancastrian estates, see *CFR 1391–9*, pp. 293–97.

20. Saul, *Richard II*, pp. 285–89; Bennett, *Richard II and the Revolution of 1399*, pp. 146–49; Harriss, *Shaping the Nation*, p. 513.

21. The will is printed in Nichols (ed.), *Collection of All the Wills*, pp. 191–201, and *Foedera*, vol. 8, pp. 75–77. The author of the *Eulogium* said it was a "will exceedingly prejudicial to the realm, as those who saw it said" ("*testimonium suum regno valde præjudiciale, ut dixerunt qui viderunt*"): *Eulogium*, pp. 380–81.

22. *Traison et Mort*, pp. 26–27 (transl. 166–67); *Eulogium*, p. 380; *Walsingham*, vol. 2, pp. 134–37.

23. *PROME*, "Richard II: September 1397," Part 1, item 53.

24. Given-Wilson, *Henry IV*, pp. 116–17, 123–24; Gairdner (ed.), *Historical Collections*, p. 101; Tuck, "Thomas [Thomas of Woodstock]," *ODNB*. For the terms by which the Lancastrian estates were granted out, see *CFR 1391–9*, pp. 293–97.

25. Barron, "Tyranny of Richard II," pp. 7, 13; *CCR 1396–9*, pp. 438, 503; *Foedera*, vol. 8, pp. 66–67.

26. L. Douët-d'Arcq (ed.), *Choix de Pièces inédites relatives au Règne de Charles VI*, vol. 1 (Paris, 1863), pp. 157–60 (transl. Given-Wilson, *Chronicles*, pp. 112–14); Given-Wilson, *Henry IV*, p. 125; Sumption, *Divided Houses*, pp. 856–57.

27. Given-Wilson, *Henry IV*, p. 124 and n; *Walsingham*, vol. 2, pp. 122–23.

28. Kingsford, *Chronicles of London*, p. 53.

29. *CCR 1396–9*, p. 505. The poem, now known as *Richard the Redeless* ("redeless" meaning uncounseled or foolish), seems to have been written during the second half of 1399 and the beginning of 1400: H. Barr (ed.), *The Piers Plowman Tradition* (London, 1993), pp. 16–19, 105 (l. 111), 110 (passus 2, ll. 42–43, 47), and for the poet's background and location, so far as they can be gleaned from the text, pp. 16n and 17; see also J. M. Dean (ed.), *Richard the Redeless and*

Mum and the Sothsegger, TEAMS Middle English Texts (online resource, 2000), "*Richard the Redeless*: Introduction."

30. This Latin poem was written by an unknown poet in June–July 1399: T. Wright (ed.), *Political Poems and Songs Relating to English History*, vol. 1 (London, 1859), pp. 366–68. The author of *Richard the Redeless* also refers to Henry, within an extended metaphor, as an eagle: Barr (ed.), *The Piers Plowman Tradition*, pp. 113, 115, 118–19 (passus 2, ll. 145, 176, 190; passus 3, ll. 70, 91).

31. Given-Wilson, *Henry IV*, pp. 124–27; *Religieux*, vol. 2, pp. 704–9 (transl. Given-Wilson, *Chronicles*, pp. 110–11).

32. *CPR 1396–9*, p. 596; A. Dunn, *The Politics of Magnate Power: England and Wales 1389–1413* (Oxford, 2003), p. 173; L. S. Woodger and J. S. Roskell, "Pelham, John (d. 1429), of Pevensey Castle and Laughton, Suss," *Hist. Parl.*

33. Given-Wilson, *Henry IV*, pp. 127–29; Bennett, *Richard II and the Revolution of 1399*, pp. 155–58; *Walsingham*, vol. 2, pp. 140–47. None of Henry's letters survive, but see *Traison et Mort*, pp. 35–37 (transl. 180–83). For the poem, see Wright (ed.), *Political Poems and Songs*, vol. 1, p. 365 (where "erne" is an Old and Middle English word meaning eagle).

34. Given-Wilson, *Henry IV*, pp. 129–30; Given-Wilson, *Chronicles*, pp. 135–36.

35. Given-Wilson, *Henry IV*, pp. 129–30; *Walsingham*, vol. 2, pp. 144–45; *Vitae et Regni*, pp. 153–54 (transl. Given-Wilson, *Chronicles*, p. 127).

36. *Walsingham*, vol. 2, pp. 142–45.

37. *Vitae et Regni*, p. 154 (transl. Given-Wilson, *Chronicles*, pp. 127–28); *Walsingham*, vol. 2, pp. 146–51; Given-Wilson, *Henry IV*, pp. 130–31.

38. *Walsingham*, vol. 2, pp. 148–49; Given-Wilson, *Henry IV*, p. 131. Richard had appointed Rutland warden of the West March in February 1398, the latest in a series of moves to insert his own candidates into the rule of the north, and a key reason for the Percies' support of Henry when he returned: Horrox, "Edward [Edward of Langley]," *ODNB*; J. M. W. Bean, "Percy, Henry, first earl of Northumberland (1341–1408)," *ODNB*.

14. 1399–1400: mine empty chair

1. *Creton*, p. 307 (transl. 43–44), and for the whole campaign in Ireland, pp. 297–308 (transl. 22–45); Bennett, *Richard II and the Revolution of 1399*, pp. 149–50.

2. The precise chronology of the messengers' arrival and Richard's departure is difficult to establish, but it seems likely that the king left Ireland in the week beginning July 20: D. Johnston, "Richard II's Departure from Ireland, July 1399," *EHR*, vol. 98, no. 389 (1983), pp. 785, 789–94; *Creton*, pp. 309–15 (transl. 46–61), where Rutland's advice is alleged to be treacherous.

3. Richard's movements after he reached Wales are also difficult to decipher: Johnston, "Richard II's Departure from Ireland," pp. 794–97; Bennett, *Richard II and the Revolution of 1399*, p. 160.

4. For this paragraph and the next, see Given-Wilson, *Henry IV*, pp. 131–34; *Creton*, pp. 321–25 (transl. 76–98).

5. *Usk*, pp. 86–87.

6. *Usk*, pp. 54–59.

7. *Creton*, pp. 312, 329–41 (transl. 55, 106–19).

8. Northumberland's negotiations with Richard: according to Creton, Henry demanded that John and Thomas Holand, Salisbury, and the bishop of Carlisle should be tried for the wrongful death of Thomas of Woodstock; Richard agreed but then privately promised Salisbury and Carlisle that he would not allow the trials to proceed and that Henry would be put to death for his actions. For this paragraph and the next, see *Creton*, pp. 349–75 (transl. 129–75), quotation in the next paragraph from pp. 373–74 (transl. 167–68).

9. *Foedera*, vol. 8, pp. 84–85; *CCR 1396–9*, pp. 512, 520–22.

10. *CCR 1396–9*, p. 512; *Creton*, pp. 374–77 (transl. 170–78); *Walsingham*, vol. 2, pp. 154–59; *Usk*, pp. 60–61; Given-Wilson, *Henry IV*, pp. 137–39. For Scrope's head on London Bridge, John

Bushy's on the bridge at York, and Henry Green's on the bridge at Bristol, see Taylor (ed. and tr.), *The Kirkstall Abbey Chronicles*, p. 122 (transl. 78 and Given-Wilson, *Chronicles*, p. 134).

11. *Creton*, pp. 377–78 (transl. 178–81); Rawcliffe, "Rempston, Sir Thomas," *Hist. Parl.*; Given-Wilson, *Henry IV*, p. 140. Walsingham says that Richard was taken first to the palace of Westminster, "because he had asked that he should not be seen by the citizens of London, who he believed would be especially delighted about his overthrow," and then the following day by boat along the river to the Tower, but the author of the *Traïson et Mort* says that he rode through London's streets and was jeered by the people: *Walsingham*, vol. 2, pp. 156–57; *Traïson et Mort*, pp. 63–64 (transl. 215), and see this chapter, p. 323.

12. *Creton*, p. 325 (transl. 97–98); *Usk*, pp. 64–65.

13. *Usk*, pp. 62–63; *Walsingham*, vol. 2, pp. 158–59.

14. *PROME*, "Henry IV: October 1399," Part 1, items 17–50 (quotations from 33, 34, 42, 43).

15. *PROME*, "Henry IV: October 1399," Part 1, items 10–14 (and for the translation used here, see Given-Wilson, *Chronicles*, pp. 169–72).

16. For this paragraph and the next, see G. O. Sayles, "The Deposition of Richard II: Three Lancastrian Narratives," *Bulletin of the Institute of Historical Research*, vol. 54, no. 130 (1981), pp. 257–70; Given-Wilson, *Chronicles*, pp. 162–67; *PROME*, "Henry IV: October 1399," Part 1, items 51–52; C. Given-Wilson, "The Manner of King Richard's Renunciation: A 'Lancastrian Narrative'?," *EHR*, vol. 108, no. 427 (1993), pp. 365–70; Giancarlo, "Murder, Lies, and Storytelling," pp. 92–104.

17. For this paragraph and the next, see *PROME*, "Henry IV: October 1399," Part 1, items 53–57 (at the end of which Henry is described as "*populum vultu hillari et benigno respiciens*," "looking at the people with a cheerful and kindly face"); *Walsingham*, vol. 2, pp. 206–9; Given-Wilson, *Chronicles*, pp. 164–67; Given-Wilson, *Henry IV*, pp. 144–46.

18. *PROME*, "Henry IV, October 1399," Part 1, items 58–60; Giancarlo, "Murder, Lies, and Storytelling," pp. 92–104.

19. Given-Wilson, *Henry IV*, pp. 147–48. The new "knights of the bath" were not a formal and numerically limited order equivalent to the Order of the Garter, but a group of knights all dubbed into knighthood through the same ceremonies: F. Pilbrow, "The Knights of the Bath: Dubbing to Knighthood in Lancastrian and Yorkist England," in P. Coss and M. Keen (eds.), *Heraldry, Pageantry and Social Display in Medieval England* (Woodbridge, 2002), pp. 196, 199–213. The devotion expressed in John Pelham's letter, written to Henry from Pevensey Castle after the landing of 1399, meant that for a long time it was assumed to be a letter from the (nonexistent) "Lady Joan Pelham" to her husband: Walker, "Letters to the Dukes of Lancaster," pp. 75–79.

20. "*le mauvais bastart qui nous a si mauvaisement gouvernez*": *Traïson et Mort*, p. 64 (transl. 215); *Religieux*, vol. 2, pp. 722–73. For Richard giving the documents to the abbot of Westminster in 1394, see A. K. McHardy, "Richard II: A Personal Portrait," in Dodd (ed.), *The Reign of Richard II*, pp. 11–12. For the procession, see *Froissart*, vol. 16, p. 205; *Walsingham*, vol. 2, pp. 224–25.

21. For this paragraph and the next, see above, chs. 1 and 11; *Froissart*, vol. 16, pp. 206–7; *Usk*, pp. 70–73; Given-Wilson, *Henry IV*, pp. 149–50. For Richard's coronation oath, see *PROME*, "Henry IV: October 1399," Part 1, item 17.

22. *Froissart*, vol. 16, pp. 207–8; *Walsingham*, vol. 2, pp. 216–17, 236–39; *Religieux*, vol. 2, pp. 726–31.

23. For this paragraph and the next, see *Froissart*, vol. 16, pp. 208–9; *Usk*, pp. 72–73; Kingsford (ed.), *Chronicles of London*, pp. 49–50; Given-Wilson, *Henry IV*, pp. 152–53; A. J. Musson, "Dymoke [Dymmok] family (*per. c.*1340–*c.*1580)," *ODNB*.

24. *PROME*, "Henry IV: October 1399," Part 1, items 66–72; *Walsingham*, vol. 2, pp. 242–47. Cf. Kingsford (ed.), *Chronicles of London*, pp. 50–51: "the kyng him sylff seyd that at the forseyd shrewed parlement there were meny tresons ordeyned that were nat aforehand, and euery

worde that was ayens the crovne was holde ffor treson, wher herfore we wole ffro this day fforth that ther be held no moo tresons but thoo that weren in tyme off oure noble progenytours, and thoo that ben ordeyned by the olde statutes."

25. For this paragraph and the next, see *Walsingham*, vol. 2, pp. 246–51; *PROME*, "Henry IV: October 1399," introduction and Appendix 1; Kingsford (ed.), *Chronicles of London*, pp. 51–54; Given-Wilson, "Mowbray, Thomas," *ODNB*.

26. *PROME*, "Henry IV: October 1399," Part 2, items 11–15; Kingsford (ed.), *Chronicles of London*, p. 54.

27. *Walsingham*, vol. 2, pp. 258–61; Kingsford (ed.), *Chronicles of London*, pp. 54–55; C. Starr, "Fitzwalter family (*per. c.*1200–*c.*1500)," *ODNB*.

28. *PROME*, "Henry IV: October 1399," Part 2, item 16; *Usk*, pp. 78–79; *Walsingham*, vol. 2, pp. 260–61; Kingsford (ed.), *Chronicles of London*, p. 55.

29. *Usk*, pp. 242–43; *PROME*, "Henry IV: October 1399," introduction; *CCR 1399–1402*, p. 28.

30. *PROME*, "Henry IV: October 1399," introduction and Part 1, items 73–74, 76; *Walsingham*, vol. 2, pp. 264–65; *Usk*, pp. 68–69; Kingsford (ed.), *Chronicles of London*, pp. 56–57.

31. For this paragraph and the next, see *PROME*, "Henry IV: October 1399," introduction and Part 2, items 1–8; Kingsford (ed.), *Chronicles of London*, p. 57. For Rutland as Richard's brother, see above, ch. 11, pp. 255–56; as his foster child ("*nurri*"), see R. L. Atkinson, "Richard II and the Death of the Duke of Gloucester," *EHR*, vol. 38, no. 152 (1923), p. 564.

32. For this paragraph and the next, see *PROME*, "Henry IV: October 1399," introduction and Part 2, items 9–10, 17; *Walsingham*, vol. 2, pp. 266–79; Kingsford (ed.), *Chronicles of London*, pp. 57–62. For Morley, see Cockayne, *Complete Peerage*, vol. 9, pp. 216–17.

33. *Walsingham*, vol. 2, pp. 282–85.

34. See above, this chapter, pp. 328–29; *PROME*, "Henry IV: October 1399," Part 2, item 3; *Creton*, pp. 309–11 (transl. 55–59).

35. For this paragraph and the next, see *Walsingham*, vol. 2, pp. 284–97; *Usk*, pp. 88–89; Given-Wilson, *Henry IV*, pp. 161–62.

36. Given-Wilson, *Henry IV*, pp. 29, 162–63, 442–43; *Usk*, pp. 88–89; *Walsingham*, vol. 2, pp. 296–99; see above, ch. 2, p. 55. For Ferrour's pardon, dated the Monday after Epiphany, see J. E. Tyler, *Henry of Monmouth: or, Memoirs of the Life and Character of Henry the Fifth, as Prince of Wales and King of England*, vol. 1 (London, 1838), p. 7n ("our lord the king remembering that in the reign of Richard the second, during the insurrection of the counties of Essex and Kent, the said John saved the king's life in the midst of that commonalty, in a wonderful and kind manner, whence the king happily remains alive unto this day. For since every good whatever naturally and of right requires another good in return, the king of his especial grace freely pardons the said John").

37. The council met on February 8–9; it was known by February 17 that Richard was dead: *POPC*, vol. 1, pp. 107, 111–12; Given-Wilson, *Henry IV*, p. 164 and n.

38. "*in tantam deuenit tristiciam, languorem ac infirmitatem, sine spe euadendi, quod decidit in lectum, nolensque in cibo, potu uel aliquo releuari seu confortari* [. . .] *Aliter tamen dicitur et uerius, quod ibidem fame miserabiliter interiit*": *Vitae et Regni*, p. 166 (transl. Given-Wilson, *Chronicles*, p. 241). Walsingham recounts the story that Richard starved himself; Usk says both that he pined away in grief and that he was starved of food: *Walsingham*, vol. 2, pp. 298–99; *Usk*, pp. 88–91. Jean Creton heard that Richard, in despair, died because he stopped eating and drinking, but didn't believe it; he suggested that another corpse had been displayed in Richard's place, and that the king was still alive: *Creton*, p. 408 (translation pp. 219–21). The author of the *Traïson et Mort* alleges that Richard was killed on Henry's orders with an axe to the head by "Sir Piers Exton" (perhaps meaning the Lancastrian knight Peter Buckton), but when Richard's skull was examined in the nineteenth century it showed no injury: *Traïson et Mort*, pp. 94–96 (transl. 248–50); A. P. Stanley, "On an Examination of the Tombs of Richard II and Henry III in Westminster Abbey," *Archaeologia*, vol. 45 (1880), pp. 315, 323–25.

15. 1400–1403: so shaken as we are

1. J. Gower, *The Minor Latin Works with In Praise of Peace*, ed. R. F. Yeager and M. Livingston, TEAMS Middle English Texts (online resource, 2005), 9: "*H. aquile pullus*," l. 3 ("*H. aquile cepit oleum, quo regna recepit*"); *Religieux*, vol. 2, pp. 730–73.

2. W. Hardy (ed. and tr.), *The Charters of the Duchy of Lancaster* (London, 1845), pp. 137–38. The prince was also given the title of duke of Aquitaine: *PROME*, "Henry IV: October 1399," Part 1, items 75, 81. Henry promised in parliament not to ask for taxation except when there was a clear and demonstrable necessity to do so—a restatement of the established financial relationship between the crown and its subjects. However, in the circumstances of 1399, many people came to believe that he had promised not to levy taxes at all: Given-Wilson, *Henry IV*, p. 174; *Walsingham*, vol. 2, pp. 222–23.

3. *Creton*, p. 410 (transl. 221–22); Sumption, *Cursed Kings*, pp. 43–45, 47–52, 54; Given-Wilson, *Henry IV*, pp. 165–69; A. Tuck, "Henry IV and Europe: A Dynasty's Search for Recognition," in R. H. Britnell and A. J. Pollard (eds.), *The McFarlane Legacy: Studies in Late Medieval Politics and Society* (Stroud, 1995), pp. 106–9; *PROME*, "Henry IV: October 1399," Part 1, item 80. The relationships Henry had previously built in Paris had been warm—"the earl of Derby was loved by all" ("*le conte d'Erby estoit bien amé de tous*"), Froissart had written, adding that Henry was "gracious, good-natured, courteous and easy to deal with" ("*gracieux, doux, courtois, et traittable*")—but personal warmth could not survive the political upheavals of 1399: *Froissart*, vol. 16, pp. 139–41.

4. A. Curry, A. R. Bell, A. King, and D. Simpkin, "New Regime, New Army? Henry IV's Scottish Expedition of 1400," *EHR*, vol. 125, no. 517 (2010), pp. 1382–1413; Given-Wilson, *Henry IV*, pp. 168–70; Sumption, *Cursed Kings*, pp. 52–56.

5. R. R. Davies, *The Revolt of Owain Glyn Dŵr* (Oxford, 1995), Part 1 and pp. 102–3; Given-Wilson, *Henry IV*, pp. 170–71; Sumption, *Cursed Kings*, pp. 56–61.

6. Given-Wilson, *Henry IV*, pp. 171–73; for Jean de Hengest's account of his embassy, see *Froissart*, vol. 16, pp. 366–77.

7. Wylie, *Henry the Fourth*, vol. 1, pp. 158–64; Given-Wilson, *Henry IV*, pp. 179–80; *Usk*, pp. 118–21; *Walsingham*, vol. 2, pp. 306–13.

8. No detailed description of the jousts survives, but these letters give some sense of how elaborately theatrical they were: P. E. Bennett, S. Carpenter, and L. Gardiner, "Chivalric Games at the Court of Edward III," *Medium Ævum*, vol. 87, no 2 (2018), pp. 304–5, 310–11; Green, *Lives of the Princesses*, vol. 3, pp. 313–15; Devon (ed.), *Issues of the Exchequer*, p. 282.

9. Given-Wilson, *Henry IV*, pp. 174–78; Sumption, *Cursed Kings*, pp. 67–70; *POPC*, vol. 1, p. 254; Castor, *The King, the Crown, and the Duchy of Lancaster*, pp. 28–30; Curry, Bell, King, and Simpkin, "New Regime, New Army?," pp. 1391–92.

10. Three months later, Henry's close friend John Norbury was also replaced as treasurer of England by Laurence Allerthorpe, an experienced officer of the Exchequer. For this paragraph and the next, see *PROME*, "Henry IV: January 1401," introduction; A. Rogers, "The Political Crisis of 1401," *Nottingham Medieval Studies*, vol. 12 (1968), pp. 85–96; Given-Wilson, *The Royal Household and the King's Affinity*, pp. 107–8, 115, 135–36, 190–92; Given-Wilson, *Henry IV*, pp. 178–82.

11. *PROME*, "Henry IV: January 1401," items 9, 17, 47.

12. *PROME*, "Henry IV: January 1401," introduction and items 15–16, 29, 48, 77, 91, 94, 101–7; Given-Wilson, *Henry IV*, pp. 183–89; M. Aston, "Lollardy and Sedition," in M. Aston, *Lollards and Reformers: Images and Literacy in Late Medieval Religion* (London, 1984), pp. 1–18, 20–23, 38–42; Davies, *Revolt of Owain Glyn Dŵr*, Part 1 and pp. 103, 281–90.

13. *CPR 1399–1401*, pp. 31, 37, 155, 158; *Creton*, p. 371 (transl. 159); Walker, "Percy, Sir Henry," *ODNB*; G. L. Harriss, "Fitzalan, Thomas, fifth earl of Arundel and tenth earl of Surrey (1381–1415)," *ODNB*; C. Carpenter, "Beauchamp, Richard, thirteenth earl of Warwick (1382–1439)," *ODNB*; Archer, "Mowbray, Thomas," *ODNB*; R. A. Griffiths, "Mortimer, Edmund, fifth earl of March and seventh earl of Ulster (1391–1425)," *ODNB*.

14. *Usk*, pp. 128–29, 146–47; Davies, *Revolt of Owain Glyn Dŵr*, pp. 103–4; Given-Wilson, *Henry IV*, pp. 190–94.

15. Given-Wilson, *Henry IV*, pp. 177, 195–96.

16. For the letter in full, see *Usk*, pp. 136–43; see also Given-Wilson, *Henry IV*, pp. 206–8; S. Forde, "Repyndon [Repington, Repingdon], Philip (*c.*1345–1424)," *ODNB*.

17. I. D. Thornley, "Treason by Words in the Fifteenth Century," *EHR*, vol. 32, no. 128 (1917), pp. 558–59; *Usk*, pp. 154–55; *Walsingham*, vol. 2, pp. 316–17, 320–25; Given-Wilson, *Henry IV*, pp. 208–9; H. Bradley, "The Datini Factors in London," in D. Clayton, R. Davies, and P. McNiven (eds.), *Trade, Devotion and Governance* (Stroud, 1994), pp. 60–61. Welsh bards called the comet "Owain's star": Wylie, *Henry the Fourth*, vol. 4, p. 280.

18. P. Morgan, "Henry IV and the Shadow of Richard II," in R. E. Archer (ed.), *Crown, Government and People in the Fifteenth Century* (Stroud, 1995), pp. 3, 9–11; Given-Wilson, *Henry IV*, pp. 209–11; *Foedera*, vol. 8, pp. 261–62; *CCR 1399–1402*, pp. 548–49. For Serle's part in the murder of Woodstock (he was one of two men supposed to have taken the most active part in pressing down on the duke's face beneath the feather mattress), see *PROME*, "Henry IV: October 1399," Part 2, items 11–12.

19. *CPR 1401–5*, pp. 126–30; *Foedera*, vol. 8, pp. 255, 261–62; Wylie, *Henry the Fourth*, vol. 1, pp. 269–79; Given-Wilson, *Henry IV*, pp. 209–11; Morgan, "Henry IV and the Shadow of Richard II," pp. 12–13.

20. For this paragraph and the next, see Davies, *Revolt of Owain Glyn Dŵr*, pp. 106–9; *POPC*, vol. 1, pp. 185–86; *Walsingham*, vol. 2, pp. 324–27; Given-Wilson, *Henry IV*, pp. 194–97.

21. For this paragraph and the following two, see *Walsingham*, vol. 2, pp. 328–33; Sumption, *Cursed Kings*, pp. 85–88; Given-Wilson, *Henry IV*, pp. 197–201, 214–15; W. Bower, *Scotichronicon*, vol. 8, ed. D. E. R. Watt (Aberdeen, 1987), vol. 8, pp. 46–47 ("*ad Scotos procedentes architenentes Angli ipsos sagittis consuerunt et ad modum erinacii hispidos reddiderunt*").

22. Sumption, *Cursed Kings*, pp. 73–75, 78–83, 89–98; Given-Wilson, *Henry IV*, pp. 202–4. For the text of Orléans's letter, see L. Douët-d'Arcq (ed.), *Chronique d'Enguerran de Monstrelet, 1400–1444*, vol. 1 (Paris, 1857), pp. 43–45.

23. *POPC*, vol. 1, pp. 151–52, and vol. 2, pp. 57–59, 62–63; *Walsingham*, vol. 2, pp. 314–15; Given-Wilson, *Henry IV*, pp. 177–79, 205–6, 247–51, 253–56. In Ireland in August 1401, Henry's second son, Thomas, was "so destitute of money that he has not a penny in the world, nor can borrow a single penny, because all his jewels and his plate that he can spare of those which he must of necessity keep are spent and sunk in wages," his desperate council reported: F. C. Hingeston (ed.), *Royal and Historical Letters during the Reign of Henry the Fourth*, vol. 1 (London, 1860), pp. 73–76.

24. *PROME*, "Henry IV: September 1402," introduction and items 14–16, 28, 31, 81, 86, 111; *Eulogium*, p. 395; *Vitae et Regni*, p. 175; Given-Wilson, *Henry IV*, pp. 211–12, 214–15. Henry Bowet, who had served Gaunt and Henry since the early 1390s and had gone into exile with Henry in 1398, was appointed bishop of Bath and Wells in 1401 and treasurer of England in February 1402; in October 1402, he was replaced by Guy Mohun, bishop of St. David's, one of Richard's household clerks who had been with the king when he returned from Ireland in 1399: T. F. Tout, revised by J. J. N. Palmer, "Bowet, Henry (*d.* 1423), archbishop of York," *ODNB*; R. G. Davies, "Mohun [Mone], Guy (*d.* 1407), administrator and bishop of St David's," *ODNB*.

25. All of Isabella's finery—clothes, bed hangings, the outfits of her attendants—was black, including saddles of black leather and reins covered with black velvet: *Religieux*, vol. 3, pp. 2–7; *POPC*, vol. 1, pp. 136–42, 154; *Usk* pp. 132–33, 142–43; Wylie, *Henry the Fourth*, vol. 1, pp. 205–11, and vol. 4, pp. 199–200.

26. Green, *Lives of the Princesses*, vol. 3, pp. 316–28; Stratford, *Richard II and the English Royal Treasure*, pp. 13–14, 258–62; Wylie, *Henry the Fourth*, vol. 1, pp. 252–55, and vol. 3, pp. 248–51; Tuck, "Henry IV and Europe," pp. 115–19, 120–21.

27. Green, *Lives of the Princesses*, vol. 3, pp. 313–15, 344–51; Tuck, "Henry IV and Europe," pp. 119–21; Given-Wilson, *Henry IV*, pp. 235–36.

28. Brown, Colvin, and Taylor (eds.), *The History of the King's Works*, vol. 2, pp. 935–36; Given-Wilson, *Henry IV*, pp. 385–86, 389–90.

29. Given-Wilson, *The Royal Household and the King's Affinity*, pp. 188–93, 195–96. For Repingdon as Henry's confessor by June 1404, see *CPR 1401–5*, pp. 412, 441, although he may have been acting in that capacity as early as 1401: Given-Wilson, *Henry IV*, p. 208n. For Savage and Stanley, see J. S. Roskell and L. S. Woodger, "Savage, Sir Arnold I (1358–1410), of Bobbing, Kent," *Hist. Parl.*; M. J. Bennett, "Stanley, Sir John (*c.*1350–1414)," *ODNB*.

30. For Lucia Visconti, see above, ch. 13, p. 294, and below, ch. 17, p. 391. For Henry's son, see *Calendar of Papal Registers Relating to Great Britain and Ireland*, vol. 6, *1404–1415* (London, 1904), p. 314: papal dispensation of February 1412 allowing "Edmund Leboorde, son of Henry, King of England, scholar, of the diocese of London," a boy in his eleventh year, to be promoted to holy orders despite his illegitimate birth, "the pope being induced thereto by the devotion which Edmund's father King Henry and Edmund's other ancestors have shown toward the Roman Church, and which his said father shows to the pope and the same Church." Nothing more is known of Edmund or his mother.

31. For this paragraph and the next, see Hingeston (ed.), *Royal and Historical Letters*, vol. 1, pp. 19–20; Sumption, *Cursed Kings*, pp. 100–2; Given-Wilson, *Henry IV*, pp. 216, 234–35; Wylie, *Henry the Fourth*, vol. 1, pp. 260–64, 306–9.

32. Devon (ed.), *Issues of the Exchequer*, p. 305; Wylie, *Henry the Fourth*, vol. 1, pp. 309–10, and vol. 2, p. 288n; W. Herbert, *The History of the Twelve Great Livery Companies of London* (London, 1834), p. 91; Given-Wilson, *Henry IV*, p. 216. The menu for the wedding feast, including the subtlety of the crowned eagle, is in T. Austin (ed.), *Two Fifteenth-Century Cookery-Books* (London, 1888), pp. 58–59.

33. Tuck, "Edmund [Edmund of Langley]"; Bean, "Percy, Henry"; A. L. Brown, "Percy, Thomas, earl of Worcester (*c.*1343–1403)"; Walker, "Percy, Sir Henry"; A. Tuck, "Neville, Ralph, first earl of Westmorland (*c.*1364–1425)"; Horrox, "Edward [Edward of Langley]"; all in *ODNB*.

34. Given-Wilson, *Henry IV*, pp. 446–47; Harriss, "Fitzalan, Thomas," *ODNB*; Cockayne, *Complete Peerage*, vol. 12, Part 1, pp. 180–81 (Stafford); Carpenter, "Beauchamp, Richard," *ODNB*; Wylie, *Henry the Fourth*, vol. 1, p. 310; Harriss, "Beaufort, John," "Beaufort, Henry [*called* the Cardinal of England] (1375?–1447)," and "Beaufort, Thomas, duke of Exeter (1377?–1426)," *ODNB*.

35. Given-Wilson, *Henry IV*, pp. 216–17, 385–90, 421n. Joan would later be a patron of the influential English composer John Dunstaple: M. Bent, "Dunstaple [Dunstable], John (*d.* 1453)," *ODNB*.

36. H. Ellis (ed.), *Original Letters Illustrative of English History*, vol. 1 (London, 1824), pp. 24–26; Given-Wilson, *Henry IV*, p. 195.

16. 1403–1406: meteors of a troubled heaven

1. Walker, "Percy, Sir Henry," *ODNB*; Davies (ed.), *An English Chronicle*, p. 27.

2. Given-Wilson, *Henry IV*, pp. 216–17; Sumption, *Cursed Kings*, pp. 110–11.

3. Allmand, "Henry V," *ODNB*; Walker, "Percy, Sir Henry," *ODNB*.

4. Given-Wilson, *Henry IV*, pp. 218–19; Davies, *Revolt of Owain Glyn Dŵr*, pp. 111–12; Ellis (ed.), *Original Letters*, pp. 11–13 (the prince's letter) and 14–20 (quotation from p. 19, letter of Richard Kingston, archdeacon of Hereford, for whose service to Henry see Given-Wilson, *Henry IV*, pp. 64n, 75, 76n, and *The Royal Household and the King's Affinity*, p. 198).

5. For this paragraph and the next, see Sumption, *Cursed Kings*, pp. 106–7, 110–11; Given-Wilson, *Henry IV*, pp. 218, 220–21.

6. For this paragraph and the next, see Given-Wilson, *Henry IV*, pp. 218–21; Sumption, *Cursed Kings*, pp. 112–14; *POPC*, vol. 1, pp. 203–9; *Foedera*, vol. 8, pp. 312–13; Morgan, *War and Society in Medieval Cheshire*, pp. 212–18; Davies (ed.), *An English Chronicle*, pp. 27–28.

7. For this paragraph and the next, see *Walsingham*, vol. 2, pp. 362–69; Given-Wilson, *Henry IV*, pp. 221–25.

8. *Walsingham*, vol. 2, pp. 364–65, 368–77; *Usk*, pp. 170–71; Given-Wilson, *Henry IV*, pp. 225–27.

9. *Walsingham*, vol. 2, pp. 376–81; Nicolas (ed.), *A Chronicle of London*, p. 88; Given-Wilson, *Henry IV*, pp. 228–29; Wylie, *Henry the Fourth*, vol. 1, p. 364. For the heads of Thomas Percy in London and Hotspur at York and the quarters of Hotspur's body sent to Chester, London, Bristol, and Newcastle, see *CPR 1401–5*, pp. 293, 299.

10. Given-Wilson, *Henry IV*, pp. 229–30, 233–34; Davies, *Revolt of Owain Glyn Dŵr*, pp. 112–15; Sumption, *Cursed Kings*, pp. 118–19; Hingeston (ed.), *Royal and Historical Letters*, vol. 1, pp. 160–62. For William Norham, see *Walsingham*, vol. 2, pp. 118–21, 380–81; Bower, *Scotichronicon*, vol. 8, pp. 29, 161; Morgan, "Henry IV and the Shadow of Richard II," pp. 27–28.

11. For this paragraph and the following two, see S. J. Lang, "The 'Philomena' of John Bradmore and Its Middle English Derivative: A Perspective on Surgery in Late Medieval England," PhD thesis, University of St. Andrews (1998), pp. 65–71; C. Rawcliffe, *Medicine and Society in Later Medieval England* (Stroud, 1995), pp. 76, 140–41; S. J. Lang, "Bradmore, John (*d.* 1412), surgeon," *ODNB*.

12. Sumption, *Cursed Kings*, pp. 102–9; *Walsingham*, vol. 2, pp. 384–85.

13. Sumption, *Cursed Kings*, pp. 117–22; Given-Wilson, *Henry IV*, pp. 236–38; A. Tuetey (ed.), *Journal de Nicolas de Baye, Greffier du Parlement de Paris, 1400–1417*, vol. 1 (Paris, 1885), p. 75n ("*verbose et ventoso, absque fructu et discretione*"); Moranvillé (ed.), *Chronographia Regum Francorum*, vol. 3, pp. 228–29.

14. *PROME*, "Henry IV: January 1404," introduction, items 1–3, and Appendix 1; *Eulogium*, pp. 399–400; Given-Wilson, *Henry IV*, pp. 281–82.

15. For this paragraph and the next, see *PROME*, "Henry IV: January 1404," introduction and items 16, 19, 26–33, 37, 49; *Walsingham*, vol. 2, pp. 392–97; Given-Wilson, *Henry IV*, pp. 282–87; Roskell and Woodger, "Savage, Sir Arnold I," *Hist. Parl.* The average annual cost of Richard's household in the last four years of his reign had been £53,000: Given-Wilson, *The Royal Household and the King's Affinity*, p. 94.

16. For this paragraph and the next, see *PROME*, "Henry IV: January 1404," items 11–14, 17–18; Horrox, "Edward [Edward of Langley]," *ODNB*; Tuck, "Neville, Ralph," *ODNB*.

17. *Walsingham*, vol. 2, pp. 414–17; Given-Wilson, *Henry IV*, pp. 262–64; *CCR 1402–5*, pp. 203, 357; *CPR 1401–5*, p. 441; J. Ross, "Seditious Activities: The Conspiracy of Maud de Vere, Countess of Oxford, 1403–4," in L. Clark (ed.), *The Fifteenth Century*, vol. 3: *Authority and Submission* (Woodbridge, 2003), 25–41.

18. Quotation about Serle's execution from *CCR 1402–5*, p. 357; *Eulogium*, pp. 402–3; Given-Wilson, *Henry IV*, pp. 238–39, 263–64; *Foedera*, vol. 8, pp. 365–67; *Religieux*, vol. 3, pp. 164–67.

19. *Religieux*, vol. 3, pp. 196–97; Ellis (ed.), *Original Letters*, pp. 33–38; for Glyn Dŵr described as "aping or mimicking" parliaments, see *Usk*, pp. 176–77; Davies, *Revolt of Owain Glyn Dŵr*, pp. 115–16, 162–66; Given-Wilson, *Henry IV*, pp. 239–41, 285–86; *PROME*, "Henry IV: October 1404," introduction; *POPC*, vol. 1, pp. 265–70.

20. For this paragraph and the next, see *PROME*, "Henry IV: October 1404," introduction and items 3, 9–10, 14–23; Given-Wilson, *Henry IV*, pp. 287–90.

21. *Walsingham*, vol. 2, pp. 418–19; Sumption, *Cursed Kings*, pp. 151–52; Given-Wilson, *Henry IV*, pp. 241–42, 543; E. Wright, "Henry IV, the Commons and the Recovery of Royal Finance in 1407," in Archer and Walker (eds.), *Rulers and Ruled in Late Medieval England*, pp. 69–70.

22. See above, ch. 14, pp. 331–32; *CCR 1399–1402*, pp. 49, 56; *Walsingham*, vol. 2, pp. 302–5, 430–31.

23. For this paragraph and the next, see above, ch. 14, p. 332, and ch. 4, p. 96; R. Horrox, "Despenser, Constance, Lady Despenser (*c.*1375–1416)," *ODNB*; M. M. N. Stansfield, "Holland, Edmund, seventh earl of Kent," *ODNB*; *CPR 1401–5*, pp. 260–61; Cockayne, *Complete Peerage*, vol. 4, p. 281, and vol. 7, p. 161; Devon (ed.), *Issues of the Exchequer*, p. 300.

24. *Walsingham*, vol. 2, pp. 430–31; W. Dugdale (ed.), *Monasticon Anglicanum*, vol. 6, Part 1 (London, 1849), p. 355; Given-Wilson, *Henry IV*, pp. 264–65; Wylie, *Henry the Fourth*, vol. 2, pp. 37–43.

25. Horrox, "Edward [Edward of Langley]," *ODNB*; *Eulogium*, p. 402; *Walsingham*, vol. 2, pp. 432–33; *Foedera*, vol. 8, pp. 386–87.

26. Wylie, *Henry the Fourth*, vol. 2, pp. 31–33, 43; Given-Wilson, *Henry IV*, p. 265; *POPC*, vol. 2, pp. 104–5.

27. *Walsingham*, vol. 2, pp. 434–35; Sumption, *Cursed Kings*, pp. 152, 161, 166–67; Given-Wilson, *Henry IV*, pp. 241–42, 266–67.

28. For this paragraph and the next, see *Walsingham*, vol. 2, pp. 440–45; *PROME*, "Henry IV: March 1406," Part II, items 5–6; P. McNiven, "The Betrayal of Archbishop Scrope," *Bulletin of the John Rylands Library*, vol. 54 (1971), pp. 174–208; P. McNiven, "Scrope, Richard (c.1350–1405), archbishop of York," *ODNB*; Given-Wilson, *Henry IV*, pp. 267–68, 272–76.

29. For this paragraph and the next, see *Walsingham*, vol. 2, pp. 444–49; *Eulogium*, p. 406; McNiven, "The Betrayal of Archbishop Scrope," pp. 208–13.

30. For this paragraph and the next, see *Walsingham*, vol. 2, pp. 448–51; *Eulogium*, p. 407; Given-Wilson, *Henry IV*, pp. 268–69.

31. *Walsingham*, vol. 2, pp. 450–55; for the commission to deal with traitors, and the temporary appointment of the earl of Arundel and Thomas Beaufort to act as constable and marshal of England while the earl of Westmorland and Henry's son John were occupied farther north, see *CPR 1405–8*, p. 65; Wylie, *Henry the Fourth*, vol. 2, pp. 233–40; E. Powell, "Gascoigne, Sir William (c.1350–1419)," *ODNB*.

32. R. G. Davies, "After the Execution of Archbishop Scrope: Henry IV, the Papacy and the English Episcopate, 1405–8," *Bulletin of the John Rylands Library*, vol. 59, no 1 (1976), pp. 44–45; for Henry II and Thomas Becket in 1170, see F. Barlow, "Becket, Thomas [St Thomas of Canterbury, Thomas of London] (1120?–1170)," *ODNB*.

33. *POPC*, vol. 1, p. 275, and vol. 2, pp. 339–41; *Walsingham*, vol. 2, pp. 456–63; Given-Wilson, *Henry IV*, pp. 270–71, 276–77, 455; Sumption, *Cursed Kings*, p. 170; *PROME*, "Henry IV: March 1406," Part 2, items 6–11.

34. *Walsingham*, vol. 2, pp. 454–55; S. Walker, "Political Saints in Later Medieval England," in Britnell and Pollard (eds.), *The McFarlane Legacy: Studies in Late Medieval Politics and Society*, pp. 84–85.

35. For this paragraph and the next, see *Walsingham*, vol. 2, pp. 462–65; Given-Wilson, *Henry IV*, pp. 242, 261, 290–92; Sumption, *Cursed Kings*, pp. 162–64, 189–91; *PROME*, "Henry IV: March 1406," introduction.

36. For Henry's birthday on Maundy Thursday, see Mortimer, *Fears of Henry IV*, Appendix 1; for the Garter celebrations and the postponement of the reopening, see *PROME*, "Henry IV: March 1406," Part 1, item 28; for Henry's illness in 1405, see P. McNiven, "The Problem of Henry IV's Health, 1405–1413," *EHR*, vol. 100, no. 397 (1985), pp. 759–60.

17. 1406–1410: will fortune never come with both hands full

1. J. E. Thorold Rogers, *Loci e Libro Veritatum* (Oxford, 1881), pp. 225–29; *Eulogium*, pp. 405, 408; McNiven, "The Problem of Henry IV's Health," pp. 747–48, 751–52, 758–59. The diagnosis of leprosy was disproved when Henry's grave was opened in the nineteenth century and his nasal cartilage found to be intact: J. Spry, "A Brief Account of the Examination of the Tomb of King Henry IV, in the Cathedral of Canterbury, August 21, 1832," included within A. J. Kempe, "Some Account of the Jerusalem Chamber in the Abbey of Westminster, and of the Painted Glass Remaining Therein," *Archaeologia*, vol. 26 (1836), p. 444.

2. For Henry's letters, see *POPC*, vol. 1, pp. 290–92 (describing "*une grande accesse*" when "*une maladie soudeinement nous survint en nostre jambe*"). For John Arderne's treatise, see Arderne, *Treatises of Fistula in Ano*, pp. xii, 74 ("with this medicine was King Henry of England cured of the going out of the lure"); T. McW. Millar, "John of Arderne, the Father of British Proctology," *Proceedings of the Royal Society of Medicine*, vol. 47 (1953), pp. 75–84; Given-Wilson, *Henry IV*, pp. 293–34. For the suggestion of thrombosis, see McNiven, "The Problem of Henry IV's Health," p. 769.

3. *PROME*, "Henry IV: March 1406," introduction and Part 1, items 31–34, 39–41, 51–52; J. S. Roskell and L. S. Woodger, "Tiptoft, Sir John (d. 1443), of Burwell, Cambs," *Hist. Parl.*

4. *PROME*, "Henry IV: March 1406," introduction and Part 2, items 1–2, 5–15; *Eulogium*, p. 408; Davies (ed.), *An English Chronicle*, pp. 32–34; *Walsingham*, vol. 2, pp. 470–71. It's not clear exactly when Henry sent the mail coat to Rome.

5. *PROME*, "Henry IV: March 1406," item 53; *Walsingham*, vol. 2, pp. 456–57; Davies, "After the Execution of Archbishop Scrope," p. 52.

6. *Walsingham*, vol. 2, pp. 472–73 ("*michi misissent hunc iuuenem docendum et alendum, nam et linguam Gallicam ego noui*"); Bower, *Scotichronicon*, vol. 8, pp. 60–63; Given-Wilson, *Henry IV*, pp. 292–93.

7. Sumption, *Cursed Kings*, pp. 191–93.

8. For the text of the "tripartite indenture," see J. A. Giles (ed.), *Incerti Scriptoris Chronicon Angliae* (London, 1848), pp. 39–42; for its dating to February 1406 rather than 1405, see Given-Wilson, *Henry IV*, p. 317; Sumption, *Cursed Kings*, pp. 171, 197.

9. For Northumberland's speech and the French response, see *Religieux*, vol. 3, pp. 426–31; for the full text of Charles's letter, see *Traison et Mort*, pp. 299–302; for the French court, Orléans, and Burgundy, see Sumption, *Cursed Kings*, pp. 154–59, 171–83, 193–97; Mortimer, *Fears of Henry IV*, p. 285.

10. *Walsingham*, vol. 2, pp. 476–77; Wylie, *Henry the Fourth*, vol. 2, pp. 441–51. For Philippa's trousseau, which included a gown embroidered with forget-me-nots and another with golden eagles, see W. P. Baildon (ed.), "The Trousseaux of Princess Philippa, Wife of Eric, King of Denmark, Norway and Sweden," *Archaeologia*, vol. 67 (1916), pp. 163–88.

11. Given-Wilson, *The Royal Household and the King's Affinity*, pp. 190–91; S. J. Payling, *Political Society in Lancastrian England: The Greater Gentry of Nottinghamshire* (Oxford, 1991), pp. 121–24; Wylie, *Henry the Fourth*, vol. 2, pp. 470–72, 480; N. H. Nicolas, *The Controversy between Sir Richard Scrope and Sir Robert Grosvenor*, vol. 2 (London, 1832), pp. 200–1; Brie (ed.), *The Brut*, p. 367 (Rempston "was dreynt yn Themys at London Brygge as he com fro Westmynstre towarde þe Tour yn a barge, and al þrouȝ lewdenesse [foolishness, ignorance]").

12. For the parliamentary commendations of Erpingham, see *PROME*, "Henry IV: October 1404," item 36 (with Rempston), and "Henry IV: March 1406," item 43 ("who has performed much good service for our said lord the king, and who has on many an occasion placed himself at risk for the honour and benefit of the king and his kingdom").

13. Castor, *The King, the Crown, and the Duchy of Lancaster*, p. 31; Given-Wilson, *Henry IV*, pp. 296–98; Sumption, *Cursed Kings*, pp. 201–21.

14. For this paragraph and the next, see *PROME*, "Henry IV: March 1406," introduction and Part 1, items 66–91 (quotations from 67–68).

15. *PROME*, "Henry IV: March 1406," Part 1, item 66; Given-Wilson, *Henry IV*, pp. 298–300; Bennett, "Stanley, Sir John," *ODNB*; and see *Foedera*, vol. 8, pp. 387–88, for petitions from Rutland and his wife asking for his freedom after the "*disaise et pesantrie*" of seventeen weeks' imprisonment.

16. Harriss, "Fitzalan, Thomas," and "Beaufort, Thomas," *ODNB*; Carpenter, "Beauchamp, Richard," *ODNB*.

17. J. Cherry, "Some Lancastrian Seals," in J. Stratford (ed.), *The Lancastrian Court* (Donington, 2003), pp. 20–22; Given-Wilson, *Henry IV*, p. 405.

18. H. Bradley, "Lucia Visconti, Countess of Kent (d. 1424)," in C. Barron and A. F. Sutton (eds.), *Medieval London Widows* (London, 1994), pp. 77–78; J. Tait, review of K. Wenck, *Eine mailändisch-thüringische Heiratsgeschichte aus der Zeit König Wenzels*, *EHR*, vol. 10, no. 40 (1895), p. 791; *Calendar of State Papers, Milan, 1385–1618*, pp. 1–2.

19. It's not clear exactly when the proposal for the marriage was first made, but it seems to have been in 1405, in other words once it was clear that Edmund would not, after her kidnapping of the Mortimer boys, be marrying Constance Despenser. M. M. N. Stansfield, "Holland, Edmund, seventh earl of Kent (1383–1408)," *ODNB*; Bradley, "Lucia Visconti," pp. 78–79;

Walsingham, vol. 2, pp. 516–17; *Foedera*, vol. 10, pp. 136–42 ("*ob affectionis intimae puritatem*"); *Calendar of State Papers, Milan, 1385–1618*, pp. 275–76; Horrox, "Despenser, Constance," *ODNB*. The glamorous wedding seems to have made a splash, and was reported by almost all the chroniclers: see, for example, Brie (ed.), *The Brut*, p. 367 ("And yn þe vij yere of King Henryeȝ regne come Dame Luce, þe Dukeȝ sistir of Millane, yn-to Engelond, and so vnto London, and þere was weddid to Ser Edmunde Helond, Erle of Kent, yn þe priory of Saint Mary Ouerey yn Southwerke, with moche solempnite and grete worschip; and þere was the King hym selfe, and yaf hir at þe churche dore").

20. For Henry's weight, I'm extrapolating from his funeral effigy—with a presumption that the stoutness apparent there must have increased gradually over the years—and for his mobility, from the nature of his "attack" in 1406: *CCR 1405–9*, pp. 259, 261, 286 (from where the quotation in the text is taken); McNiven, "The Problem of Henry IV's Health," pp. 761–62; Given-Wilson, *Henry IV*, pp. 302–3, 318, 544.

21. For this paragraph and the next, see *Foedera*, vol. 8, pp. 538–40; *Calendar of Gascon Rolls*, The Gascon Roll Project, 1317–1468 (online resource), C61/104, items 70–71; C61/111, item 27; C61/112, items 23, 25. Henry had "his sons" with him at Nottingham—plausibly Thomas and Humphrey as well as John, who was there in his capacity as constable—and the thirteen-year-old king of Scots, an honored prisoner being moved under careful guard to Nottingham Castle: see *POPC*, vol. 1, p. 304n; *Foedera*, vol. 8, p. 484. At the beginning of June 1408, Henry issued letters patent declaring the vindication of the good name of both Boulemer and Ozanne but granted to Boulemer "because of his good service" the keeping for life of two houses in the street where the quarrel had taken place: *Calendar of Gascon Rolls*, C61/112, items 23, 25.

22. Curley, "John of Bridlington," *ODNB*.

23. *Foedera*, vol. 8, pp. 419 (misdated to 1406), 496–99; *Walsingham*, vol. 2, pp. 520–29; Davies, *Revolt of Owain Glyn Dŵr*, pp. 123–25; Given-Wilson, *Henry IV*, p. 318; R. G. Davies, "Courtenay, Richard (*c.*1381–1415), bishop of Norwich," *ODNB*; J. A. F. Thomson, "Oldcastle, John, Baron Cobham (*d.* 1417)," *ODNB*.

24. Given-Wilson, *Henry IV*, pp. 303, 318; *PROME*, "Henry IV: October 1407," item 24. Thomas Chaucer's mother, Philippa, was the sister of Katherine Swynford: see above, ch. 2, p. 35, and C. Rawcliffe, "Chaucer, Thomas (*c.*1367–1434)," *ODNB*.

25. *PROME*, "Henry IV: October 1407," items 13–14, 21–22, 27; Given-Wilson, *Henry IV*, pp. 302–3.

26. *Religieux*, vol. 3, pp. 730–43; for the eyewitness testimony, see R. Vaughan, *John the Fearless* (Woodbridge, 2002), pp. 44–47; P. Cochon, *Chronique Normande*, ed. C. de R. de Beaurepaire (Rouen, 1870), p. 221 (skull "cleft down to the teeth"). The witness at the window was Jaquette, a shoemaker's wife, who was bringing in her washing from a pole outside the window and then putting her child to bed.

27. T. Hoccleve, *The Regiment of Princes*, TEAMS Middle English Texts (online resource, 1999), ll. 5290–91, 5307–10; J. A. Burrow, "Hoccleve [Occleve], Thomas (*c.*1367–1426)," *ODNB*.

28. *Walsingham*, vol. 2, pp. 530–31; Wylie, *Henry the Fourth*, vol. 3, pp. 149–52; Given-Wilson, *Henry IV*, p. 544; Kingsford (ed.), *Chronicles of London*, p. 68 ("In the same yeer was a gret froste, and longe durynge, ffor men myht gone ouer Temese vpon the yse").

29. For this paragraph and the next, see *Walsingham*, vol. 2, pp. 530–35; Wylie, *Henry the Fourth*, vol. 3, pp. 153–58; Given-Wilson, *Henry IV*, pp. 303–4, 544; Sumption, *Cursed Kings*, pp. 234–45; Harriss, "Thomas [Thomas of Lancaster]," and "Beaufort, John," *ODNB*.

30. *Religieux*, vol. 4, pp. 314–17; *Walsingham*, vol. 2, pp. 538–39; Nicolas (ed.), *A Chronicle of London*, p. 91 ("the erle of Kent was sclayn thorugh his owne folye, at Bryak in Bretayne, for he rood withoughte basnet [bascinet]"); Cockayne, *Complete Peerage*, vol. 7, pp. 161–62 (for Holand's burial at Bourne Abbey in Lincolnshire).

31. For Henry's note, written in English, see Kirby (ed.), *Calendar of Signet Letters*, p. 148, and *Foedera*, vol. 8, p. 584. Henry had divided into two the piece of Christ's seamless tunic with which

he had been presented by the Byzantine emperor, giving one half to Westminster Abbey and the other to the archbishop "because of his great trust and close friendship": Given-Wilson, *Henry IV*, p. 179n, and for Henry's movements, p. 304.

32. For this paragraph and the next, see M. Archer (ed.), *The Register of Bishop Philip Repingdon, 1405–1419*, vol. 1, Lincoln Record Society, vol. 57 (Hereford, 1963), pp. 135–40 (papal decree, April 12, 1408); Davies, "After the Execution of Archbishop Scrope," pp. 69–70; M. Bennett, "Henry IV, the Royal Succession and the Crisis of 1406," in G. Dodd and D. Biggs (eds.), *The Reign of Henry IV: Rebellion and Survival, 1403–1413* (Woodbridge, 2008), pp. 22, 24; *Walsingham*, vol. 2, pp. 534–37; Given-Wilson, *Henry IV*, p. 304.

33. Wylie, *Henry the Fourth*, vol. 3, pp. 231–33; Given-Wilson, *Henry IV*, pp. 304–5, 544. For Henry's doctors, including the Lucchese David Nigarellis, see Mortimer, *Fears of Henry IV*, Appendix 6.

34. Nichols (ed.), *Collection of All the Wills*, pp. 191–201, and see above, ch. 13, p. 301.

35. For the will and what follows, see Nichols (ed.), *Collection of All the Wills*, pp. 203–7. For the names of Henry's servants, see p. 204. I'm assuming the "Wilkin" named in the will may plausibly be identified with the William Wardell listed (with Halley, Warren, and Thorpe) in the 1408–9 Great Wardrobe account among the grooms who kept watch around the king's bed at night ("*garciones vigilatores circa lectam domini in noctibus*"): Given-Wilson, *Henry IV*, p. 305n. Henry had sent Thomas Delacroix to Milan in 1406 to negotiate Lucia Visconti's marriage: *Foedera*, vol. 10, pp. 136–42; *Calendar of State Papers, Milan, 1385–1618*, pp. 275–76.

36. Given-Wilson, *Henry IV*, pp. 385–88, 401, 411–14; F. Grose and T. Astle (eds.), *Antiquarian Repertory*, vol. 1 (London, 1807), p. 314; G. Dodd, "Patronage, Petitions and Grace: The 'Chamberlains' Bills' of Henry IV's Reign," in Dodd and Biggs (eds.), *The Reign of Henry IV*, p. 105; for the poem *Mum and the Sothsegger*, see Barr (ed.), *The Piers Plowman Tradition*, pp. 22–30, 137–202 (quotation at l. 216).

37. H. Castor, "Waterton, Sir Hugh (*d.* 1409)," *ODNB*; Green, *Lives of the Princesses*, vol. 3, pp. 335–38, 449–50 ("*ea abeunte, [vitae] simul deliciae et leticiae abiere*").

38. Kirby (ed.), *Calendar of Signet Letters*, p. 152 (note in Henry's own hand, April 6, 1409); Wylie, *Henry the Fourth*, vol. 3, pp. 239–43, 246–48, and vol. 4, pp. 212–13; L. M. Clopper, "London and the Problem of the Clerkenwell Plays," *Comparative Drama*, vol. 34, no. 3 (2000), pp. 291–303; Given-Wilson, *Henry IV*, pp. 396–97, 400; Beltz, *Memorials of the Most Noble Order of the Garter*, Appendix 15, pp. 403–7; Nicolas (ed.), *A Chronicle of London*, pp. 91–92.

39. *Usk*, pp. 243–44; Given-Wilson, *Henry IV*, pp. 304–5; Mortimer, *Fears of Henry IV*, pp. 300–3.

40. Given-Wilson, *Henry IV*, pp. 308–14, 318–19, 465; Davies, *Revolt of Owain Glyn Dŵr*, pp. 124–26.

41. Harriss, "Beaufort, John," *ODNB*; G. L. Harriss, *Cardinal Beaufort: A Study of Lancastrian Ascendancy and Decline* (Oxford, 1988), pp. 39–43; Given-Wilson, *Henry IV*, p. 306; S. Bentley (ed.), *Excerpta Historica* (London, 1831), pp. 152–54. Archbishop Arundel and his nephew the earl of Arundel also became involved in a dispute in the autumn of 1409 about rights to hunt and fish on their adjoining estates in Sussex: Given-Wilson, *Henry IV*, p. 466.

42. For this paragraph and the next, see Harriss, *Cardinal Beaufort*, pp. 48–49; K. B. McFarlane, *Lancastrian Kings and Lollard Knights* (Oxford, 1972), pp. 107–8; Given-Wilson, *Henry IV*, pp. 465–66, 545.

43. For this paragraph and the next, see Harriss, *Cardinal Beaufort*, pp. 50–51; Given-Wilson, *Henry IV*, pp. 466–67; B. Vale, "Scrope, Henry, third Baron Scrope of Masham (*c.*1376–1415)," *ODNB*; *PROME*, "Henry IV: January 1410," introduction and items 1–5.

18. 1410–1413: sorrows of the blood

1. For Lucia's dower, lands, debts, and silver, see *CCR 1405–9*, pp. 422–23; *CPR 1408–13*, pp. 35–36, 147; Bradley, "Lucia Visconti," p. 80. For the dowager countesses, see Stansfield, "The Holland Family," pp. 151–61.

2. For this paragraph and the next, see Given-Wilson, *Henry IV*, pp. 465–67; *POPC*, vol. 1, pp.

319–20; *PROME*, "Henry IV: January 1410," items 1–5; Sumption, *Cursed Kings*, pp. 255–60; *Walsingham*, vol. 2, pp. 590–91; Harriss, *Cardinal Beaufort*, p. 50.

3. For this paragraph and the following two, see *Walsingham*, vol. 2, pp. 582–89; *PROME*, "Henry IV: January 1410," introduction; Aston, "Lollardy and Sedition," pp. 10–13, 20–24; Given-Wilson, *Henry IV*, pp. 367–71, 374, 376–77; Thomson, "Oldcastle, John," *ODNB*.

4. For this paragraph and the next, see Aston, "Lollardy and Sedition," pp. 2–17, 38–42; *PROME*, "Henry IV: January 1410," introduction.

5. For this paragraph and the next, see *Walsingham*, vol. 2, pp. 580–85; Nicolas (ed.), *A Chronicle of London*, p. 92; *Eulogium*, pp. 416–17; *PROME*, "Henry IV: January 1410," introduction; P. McNiven, *Heresy and Politics in the Reign of Henry IV: The Burning of John Badby* (Woodbridge, 1987), pp. 199–219.

6. *PROME*, "Henry IV: January 1410," items 15–33.

7. For this paragraph and the next, see Harriss, "Beaufort, John," *ODNB*; *PROME*, "Henry IV: January 1410," introduction and items 14, 39, 44–45; Harriss, *Cardinal Beaufort*, pp. 51–52; Given-Wilson, *Henry IV*, pp. 467–68, 471, 545. Arundel and Warwick were both now retained by Prince Henry: Harriss, "Fitzalan, Thomas," and Carpenter, "Beauchamp, Richard," *ODNB*.

8. It isn't clear whether the "*Roy Henry*" mentioned in the manuscript is Henry IV or Henry V, but I've followed Chris Given-Wilson's argument for the plausibility of the former identification: Given-Wilson, *Henry IV*, pp. 385–87, 545.

9. J. Gerson, *Opera Omnia*, vol. 2 (1728), p. 149; Wylie, *Henry the Fourth*, vol. 3, pp. 232–33, and vol. 4, pp. 138–39; H. Summerson, "An English Bible and Other Books Belonging to Henry IV," *Bulletin of the John Rylands Library*, vol. 79 (1997), pp. 111–15; Gray, "Gower, John," *ODNB*; Brown, Colvin, and Taylor (eds.), *History of the King's Works*, vol. 2, pp. 935–36; Given-Wilson, *Henry IV*, pp. 387–90. In the summer of 1406, when Henry visited Bardney Abbey in Lincolnshire after saying goodbye to his daughter Philippa at Lynn, he spent all morning reading in the abbey's library: Wylie, *Henry the Fourth*, vol. 2, p. 460.

10. Harriss, *Cardinal Beaufort*, pp. 63–64; Shaw, "Holland [*married name* Beaufort], Margaret," *ODNB*.

11. *POPC*, vol. 2, pp. 6–13; *Foedera*, vol. 8, p. 679; *CCR 1409–13*, p. 150; *CPR 1408–13*, p. 286; Given-Wilson, *Henry IV*, pp. 469, 473–74.

12. For this paragraph and the next, see Given-Wilson, *Henry IV*, pp. 470–75.

13. Given-Wilson, *Henry IV*, pp. 470–75; Harriss, *Cardinal Beaufort*, pp. 52–55; for the councillors' loans, see *POPC*, vol. 1, pp. 347–49.

14. *PROME*, "Henry IV: January 1410," item 17; Payling, *Political Society*, pp. 130–31, 189, 191–93; Castor, *The King, the Crown, and the Duchy of Lancaster*, pp. 222–23.

15. For this paragraph and the next, see Castor, *The King, the Crown, and the Duchy of Lancaster*, pp. 207–18; *PROME*, "Henry IV: January 1410," items 37–38; *CPR 1408–13*, pp. 275–76.

16. Given-Wilson, *Henry IV*, pp. 488–90; Davies, "Courtenay, Richard," *ODNB*; *PROME*, "Henry IV: November 1411," items 15–17.

17. Sumption, *Cursed Kings*, pp. 250–73, 281–82.

18. Given-Wilson, *Henry IV*, pp. 493–94; *Walsingham*, vol. 2, pp. 598–601; *CCR 1409–13*, pp. 240–41. Jonathan Sumption argues (*Cursed Kings*, pp. 282–84) that Henry initially committed himself to the pro-Burgundian policy favored by his son but then changed his mind; I would argue, with Chris Given-Wilson, that Henry's position was consistent, and that the disagreement with his son took time to break into the open.

19. For this paragraph and the next, see Given-Wilson, *Henry IV*, pp. 493–94, 545; Wylie, *Henry the Fourth*, pp. 37–39; Sumption, *Cursed Kings*, pp. 283–84; A. H. Thomas and I. D. Thornley (eds.), *The Great Chronicle of London* (London, 1938), p. 90; *POPC*, vol. 2, pp. 19–24; *Foedera*, vol. 8, pp. 668–69.

20. For this paragraph and the following two, see Sumption, *Cursed Kings*, pp. 284–98; Given-Wilson, *Henry IV*, pp. 494–95; *Walsingham*, vol. 2, pp. 600–3; L. Douët-d'Arcq (ed.), *Chronique*

d'Enguerran de Monstrelet, vol. 2 (Paris, 1858), pp. 210–11; *PROME*, "Henry IV: November 1411," introduction.

21. The arrest of the six knights has sometimes been argued to be a move made by King Henry against the prince, since several of them were members of the prince's household (see next paragraph); but the order was given on the authority of the council at Westminster, to which the king had not yet returned: *CPR 1408–13*, p. 374; R. Virgoe, "Hankeford [Hankford], Sir William (*c.*1350–1423)," *ODNB*; *CCR 1409–13*, p. 243; Payling, *Political Society*, pp. 130–31, 192–93, 214; see above, this chapter, pp. 416–17.

22. For this paragraph and the next, see Giles (ed.), *Incerti Scriptoris Chronicon Angliae*, pp. 62–63 ("*non poterat circa honorem sit utilitatem regni ulterius laborare*"); *Eulogium*, pp. 420–21 (which places the episode, less plausibly, at the end of the reign); *PROME*, "Henry IV: November 1411," introduction; and for Richard's "abdication," above, ch. 14, p. 319.

23. *PROME*, "Henry IV: November 1411," introduction and items 1, 9, 11; *CCR 1409–13*, p. 244 (order recorded as given by the king).

24. *PROME*, "Henry IV: November 1411," introduction and items 25–26; J. L. Kirby, "Councils and Councillors of Henry IV, 1399–1413," *Transactions of the Royal Historical Society*, vol. 14 (1964), pp. 58–59; Given-Wilson, *Henry IV*, p. 496; *CCR 1409–13*, p. 311.

25. Sumption, *Cursed Kings*, pp. 298–309; for the terms of the negotiation and appointment of representatives for the king and prince, see *Foedera*, vol. 8, p. 721. Henry had granted Coldharbour to the prince for life in March 1410, when it was clear that he would step up to lead the council during the king's illness: *Foedera*, vol. 8, p. 628.

26. The Armagnac embassy was explosive in many ways: the envoys only just managed to reach England—Henry had to send armed ships to collect them from Brittany—and the capture of their baggage on their way through France meant that the Burgundians learned of the terms they were offering the English king, causing horror and outrage in Paris: Sumption, *Cursed Kings*, pp. 307–11; Given-Wilson, *Henry IV*, pp. 497–98; Foedera, vol. 8, pp. 712–13, 715–19, 721, 726, 738–42; *CCR 1409–13*, pp. 350–52.

27. For this paragraph and the next, see *Walsingham*, vol. 2, pp. 602–11 (quotation from pp. 608–9); *Foedera*, vol. 8, p. 728; *CCR 1409–13*, p. 339; *Calendar of Letter Books of the City of London: Letter Book I*, ed. R. R. Sharpe (London, 1909), p. 102; Given-Wilson, *Henry IV*, pp. 499–500.

28. For the texts of the letters, see B.-A. Pocquet du Haut-Jussé, "La Renaissance litteraire autour de Henri V, Roi d'Angleterre (deux Lettres inédites, 1412)," *Révue Historique*, vol. 224, no. 2 (1960), pp. 329–38; Given-Wilson, *Henry IV*, pp. 502–3; P. McNiven, "Prince Henry and the English Political Crisis of 1412," *History*, vol. 65, no. 213 (1980), pp. 3–4.

29. For the oath taken by the prince and his brothers, see *Foedera*, vol. 8, p. 743. The details of the plans made for the prince to go on campaign with his father are not clear from the surviving evidence, but for what can be reconstructed, see Sumption, *Cursed Kings*, p. 318 and n. 51 on pp. 806–7; *POPC*, vol. 2, p. 34 (dated probably late May rather than July, as listed here: see Given-Wilson, *Henry IV*, p. 503n).

30. Harriss, *Cardinal Beaufort*, p. 64; *CPR 1408–13*, p. 422; *Foedera*, vol. 8, pp. 745–47, 749–51, 757–60; *CChR 1341–1417*, p. 447.

31. The prince's letter was dated June 17 at Coventry: *Walsingham*, vol. 2, pp. 610–15. Information reaching the Burgundian administration in Paris alleged that the prince tried for several days to stop his brother's departure but had to back down in the face of his father's will: *Religieux*, vol. 4, pp. 658–59.

32. *Walsingham*, vol. 2, pp. 614–15; Given-Wilson, *Henry IV*, pp. 503–5. For the prince returning to London on June 30 "with moche peple of lordes and gentyles," see Nicolas (ed.), *A Chronicle of London*, p. 94.

33. *Walsingham*, vol. 2, pp. 608–9, 614–15; Given-Wilson, *Henry IV*, pp. 504–8; *CChR 1341–1417*, p. 447.

34. Given-Wilson, *Henry IV*, pp. 508–9; Sumption, *Cursed Kings*, pp. 312–23.

35. For this paragraph and the next, see Given-Wilson, *Henry IV*, pp. 509–11; Sumption, *Cursed Kings*, pp. 323–39; *Religieux*, vol. 4, pp. 732–33.

36. For Henry's robes, see E. M. Veale, *The English Fur Trade in the Later Middle Ages* (Oxford, 1966), p. 20; for Baltic squirrel, see J. Martin, *Treasure of the Land of Darkness: The Fur Trade and Its Significance for Medieval Russia* (Cambridge, 1986), pp. 64–65. For the king's barge, see Given-Wilson, *Henry IV*, p. 456; for the commission to the keeper of the king's ships, see *CPR 1408–13*, p. 476.

37. Nicolas (ed.), *A Chronicle of London*, p. 95; Given-Wilson, *Henry IV*, pp. 514–16.

38. Given-Wilson, *Henry IV*, p. 517; Kempe, "Some Account of the Jerusalem Chamber," pp. 434–35; Lumby (ed.), *Polychronicon Ranulphi Higden*, vol. 8, p. 547; *Eulogium*, p. 421.

19. 1413–1415: the balance and the sword

1. J. Capgrave, *The Chronicle of England*, ed. F. C. Hingeston (London, 1858), pp. 302–3.

2. Douët-d'Arcq (ed.), *Chronique d'Enguerran de Monstrelet*, vol. 2, pp. 338–39.

3. T. Hearne (ed.), *Thomæ de Elmham, Vita et Gesta Henrici Quinti* (Oxford, 1727), p. 15; G. Sayles (ed.), *Select Cases in the Court of King's Bench*, vol. 7 (London, 1971), pp. 212–15; E. Powell, *Kingship, Law, and Society: Criminal Justice in the Reign of Henry V* (Oxford, 1989), p. 137; *Foedera*, vol. 9, p. 2; *CCR 1413–19*, p. 1.

4. *CPR 1413–19*, p. 1; Fryde, Greenway, Porter, and Roy (eds.), *Handbook of British Chronology*, p. 87; *Foedera*, vol. 9, p. 1; *PROME*, "Henry V: May 1413," introduction; *CCR 1413–19*, pp. 10, 60–61, 63–64; above, ch. 18, pp. 422–23.

5. Spry, "A Brief Account of the Examination of the Tomb of King Henry IV," pp. 443–44; Given-Wilson, *Henry IV*, pp. 519–20.

6. For this paragraph and the next, see Hearne (ed.), *Thomæ de Elmham, Vita et Gesta Henrici Quinti*, pp. 17–24; J. H. Wylie, *The Reign of Henry the Fifth*, vol. 1 (Cambridge, 1914) pp. 3–4; C. A. Cole, *Memorials of Henry the Fifth, King of England* (London, 1858), p. 65 (a Latin poem about the coronation, addressed to the king: "*angelus in specie residebas*"). For the young lords, see Griffiths, "Mortimer, Edmund," *ODNB*; Richard Despenser in Horrox, "Despenser, Constance," *ODNB*; R. A. Griffiths, "Holland [Holand], John, first duke of Exeter (1395–1447)," *ODNB*.

7. *Walsingham*, vol. 2, pp. 618–21 ("*rex uidelicet niues et frigora uiciorum faceret in regno cadere et seueros uirtutum fructus emergere*"); *Usk*, pp. 242–43; Nicolas (ed.), *A Chronicle of London*, p. 95 ("a ful trobly wet day"); Wylie, *Henry the Fifth*, vol. 1, pp. 8–9; *PROME*, "Henry V: May 1413," introduction and items 2, 12, 17. The reforms Henry imposed within the administration of the duchy of Lancaster were not finally codified until 1417, but the overhaul of its systems began at the very start of the reign, and the increase in income was apparent straightaway: Castor, *The King, the Crown, and the Duchy of Lancaster*, pp. 33–34.

8. Wylie, *Henry the Fourth*, vol. 4, pp. 113–14; Wylie, *Henry the Fifth*, vol. 1, pp. 47–48; Devon (ed.), *Issues of the Exchequer*, pp. 321–22, 325–26; Given-Wilson, *Henry IV*, pp. 520–21; above, ch. 1, p. 19.

9. Sayles (ed.), *Select Cases in the Court of King's Bench*, pp. 212–15; Powell, *Kingship, Law, and Society*, pp. 137–38.

10. Given-Wilson, *Henry IV*, pp. 371–76; Thomson, "Oldcastle, John," *ODNB*; Powell, *Kingship, Law, and Society*, pp. 145–48.

11. W. T. Waugh, "Sir John Oldcastle," *EHR*, vol. 20, no. 79 (1905), pp. 445–56; W. T. Waugh, "Sir John Oldcastle (Continued)," *EHR*, vol. 20, no. 80 (1905), pp. 637–38; *Calendar of Letter Books: I*, p. 166; *Walsingham*, vol. 2, pp. 622–35.

12. Devon (ed.), *Issues of the Exchequer*, pp. 321, 325–28, 332; Brie (ed.), *The Brut*, p. 373; Wylie, *Henry the Fifth*, vol. 1, pp. 209–11; Given-Wilson, *Henry IV*, p. 521; *Walsingham*, vol. 2, pp. 634–37 ("*fatebatur se tantum sibi uenerationis debere quantum patri suo carnali*").

13. Waugh, "Sir John Oldcastle (Continued)," pp. 638–52; *Walsingham*, vol. 2, pp. 636–43; Powell, *Kingship, Law, and Society*, pp. 150–61.

14. *PROME*, "Henry V: April 1414," introduction and items 1, 16–26; "*Posuit cor suum ad investigandum leges*," Ezra 7:10; Powell, *Kingship, Law, and Society*, pp. 168–94.
15. See above, ch. 14, p. 321; Ormrod, *Edward III*, p. 583 and n.
16. *Walsingham*, vol. 2, pp. 620–21; for the legends of his riotous youth, see, for example, C. L. Kingsford, *Henry V: The Typical Medieval Hero* (London, 1901), pp. 80–93. Two years into his reign, a French observer claimed that Henry's close friend Richard Courtenay, now bishop of Norwich, had said not only that the king was great and virtuous, but that Courtenay "did not believe he had known a woman carnally after he had become king." The Frenchman himself thought that Henry was more suited to a life in the Church than he was to war: L. Mirot (ed.), "Le Procès de Maitre Jean Fusoris, Chanoine de Notre-Dame de Paris (1415–1416): Épisode des Négociations franco-anglaises durant la Guerre de Cent Ans," *Mémoires de la Société de l'histoire de Paris et de l'Ile de France*, vol. 27 (1900), pp. 175, 244.
17. Sumption, *Cursed Kings*, chs. 9 and 10.
18. For this paragraph and the next, see Sumption, *Cursed Kings*, pp. 402–3, 412–21; *PROME*, "Henry V: April 1414," items 8, 10; *PROME*, "Henry V: November 1414," items 1–5; Griffiths, "Mortimer, Edmund," *ODNB*; Harriss, "Richard [Richard of Conisbrough]," *ODNB*; Pugh, *Henry V and the Southampton Plot*, pp. 59–61.
19. For this paragraph and the next, see Pugh, *Henry V and the Southampton Plot*, pp. 81–82, 88–102, 109–17, 166–73; *Walsingham*, vol. 2, pp. 658–63; Sumption, *Cursed Kings*, pp. 428–29. Pugh points out that Scrope had lent the earl of March large sums of money, and that, if Scrope betrayed the conspiracy to the king and March was therefore condemned as a traitor, any prospect of March repaying the loans would be gone.
20. Neither Cambridge nor Scrope confessed to planning to kill the king; that had to be inferred in order to find them guilty of treason under the developing interpretation of the statute of 1352. For this paragraph and the next, see Pugh, *Henry V and the Southampton Plot*, pp. 61–62, 80–82, 122–31; Horrox, "Edward [Edward of Langley]," *ODNB*; Sumption, *Cursed Kings*, pp. 430–31.

Epilogue

1. For this paragraph and the next, see C. Wilson, "The Tomb of Henry IV and the Holy Oil of St Thomas at Canterbury," in E. Fernie and P. Crossley (eds.), *Medieval Architecture in Its Intellectual Context* (London, 1990), pp. 181–90; C. Wilson, "The Medieval Monuments," in P. Collinson, N. Ramsay, and M. Sparks (eds.), *A History of Canterbury Cathedral* (Oxford, 1995), pp. 498–506; Given-Wilson, *Henry IV*, pp. 521–22.
2. C. Maidstone, "Historia de Martyrio Ricardi Scrope, Archiepiscopi Eboracensis," in H. Wharton (ed.), *Anglia Sacra*, vol. 2 (London, 1691), p. 372; Given-Wilson, *Henry IV*, pp. 523–24; S. Walker, "Maidstone [Maydestone], Clement (c.1389–1456)," *ODNB*.
3. For this paragraph and the following two, see Spry, "A Brief Account of the Examination of the Tomb of King Henry IV," pp. 440–45; P. B. Nockles, "Bagot, Richard (1782–1854), bishop of Bath and Wells," *ODNB*; Barlow, "Becket, Thomas," *ODNB*.
4. J. G. Nichols, "Observations on the Heraldic Devices Discovered on the Effigies of Richard the Second and His Queen in Westminster Abbey," *Archaeologia*, vol. 29 (1842), pp. 54–59.
5. Stanley, "On an Examination of the Tombs of Richard II and Henry III," pp. 311–14; P. C. Hammond, "Stanley, Arthur Penrhyn (1815–1881), dean of Westminster," *ODNB*; G. Stamp, "Scott, Sir George Gilbert (1811–1878), architect," *ODNB*; J. Dart, *Westmonasterium, or The History and Antiquities of the Abbey Church of St Peter's Westminster*, vol. 2 (London, 1742), p. 45 ("the Arms stolen, from the side next the Area, in the holes of which putting my Hands, I could turn the Boards of his Coffin").
6. For this paragraph and the following two, see Stanley, "On an Examination of the Tombs of Richard II and Henry III," pp. 309–10, 314–17, 323–27.

BIBLIOGRAPHY

Primary Sources

Archer, M. (ed.), *The Register of Bishop Philip Repingdon, 1405–1419*, vol. 1, Lincoln Record Society, vol. 57 (Hereford, 1963)

Arderne, J., *Treatises of Fistula in Ano, Haemorrhoids, and Clysters*, ed. D. Power (London, 1910)

Armitage-Smith, S. (ed.), *John of Gaunt's Register, Part I (1371–5)*, vols. 1 and 2, Camden Society, Third Series, vols. 20–21 (London, 1911)

Atkinson, R. L., "Richard II and the Death of the Duke of Gloucester," *EHR*, vol. 38, no. 152 (1923), 563–64

Austin, T. (ed.), *Two Fifteenth-Century Cookery-Books* (London, 1888)

Barr, H. (ed.), *The Piers Plowman Tradition* (London, 1993)

Bellaguet, M. L. (ed.), *Chronique du Religieux de Saint-Denys 1380–1422*, 6 vols. (Paris, 1839–52)

Benson, L. D. (ed.), *The Riverside Chaucer* (Oxford, 1988)

Bentley, S. (ed.), *Excerpta Historica* (London, 1831)

Bond, M. F. (ed.), *The Inventories of St George's Chapel, Windsor, 1384–1667* (Windsor, 1947)

Bower, W., *Scotichronicon*, vol. 7, ed. A. B. Scott, D. E. R. Watt, U. Moret, and N. F. Shead (Aberdeen, 1996)

Bower, W., *Scotichronicon*, vol. 8, ed. D. E. R. Watt (Aberdeen, 1987)

Bradbury, N. M., and Bradbury, S. (eds.), *The Dialogue of Solomon and Marcolf*, TEAMS Middle English Texts (online resource, 2012)

Brand, P., Curry, A., Given-Wilson, C., Horrox, R., Martin, G., Ormrod, M., and Phillips, S. (eds. and tr.), *Parliament Rolls of Medieval England* (online resource)

Brie, F. W. D. (ed.), *The Brut or The Chronicles of England* (London, 1906)

Bryant, N. (ed. and tr.), *The True Chronicles of Jean le Bel* (Woodbridge, 2013)

Calendar of Charter Rolls, 1341–1417 (London, 1916)

Calendar of Close Rolls, 1377–1419, 11 vols. (London, 1914–32)

Calendar of Fine Rolls, 1377–1422, 6 vols. (London, 1926–34)

Calendar of Gascon Rolls, The Gascon Roll Project, 1317–1468 (online resource)

Calendar of Inquisitions Post Mortem, Edward III, vols. 11 and 14 (London, 1935, 1952)

Calendar of Letter Books of the City of London: Letter Book H, ed. R. R. Sharpe (London, 1907)

Calendar of Letter Books of the City of London: Letter Book I, ed. R. R. Sharpe (London, 1909)

Calendar of Papal Registers Relating to Great Britain and Ireland, vols. 4 and 6 (London, 1902, 1904)

Calendar of Patent Rolls, 1374–1416, 12 vols. (London, 1895–1910)

Calendar of State Papers, Milan, 1385–1618, ed. A. B. Hinds (London, 1912)

Capgrave, J., *The Chronicle of England*, ed. F. C. Hingeston (London, 1858)

Capgrave, J., *Liber de Illustribus Henricis*, ed. F. C. Hingeston (London, 1858)

Chaucer, G., "The Book of the Duchess," in Benson (ed.), *The Riverside Chaucer*, 329–46

Clarke, M. V., and Galbraith, V. H. (eds.), "The Deposition of Richard II," *Bulletin of the John Rylands Library*, vol. 14, no. 1 (1930), 125–81

Cochon, P., *Chronique Normande*, ed. C. de R. de Beaurepaire (Rouen, 1870)

Cole, C. A. (ed.), *Memorials of Henry the Fifth, King of England* (London, 1858)

Creton, J., "Metrical History of the Deposition of King Richard the Second," ed. and tr. J. Webb, *Archaeologia*, vol. 20 (1824), 1–423

Curtis, E. (ed. and tr.), *Richard II in Ireland, 1394–5, and Submissions of the Irish Chiefs* (Oxford, 1927)

Davies, J. S. (ed.), *An English Chronicle of the Reigns of Richard II, Henry IV, Henry V, and Henry VI*, Camden Society (London, 1856)

Davis, A. H. (ed. and tr.), *William Thorne's Chronicle of Saint Augustine's Abbey, Canterbury* (Oxford, 1934)

Dawes, M. C. B. (ed.), *Register of Edward the Black Prince, Part IV* (London, 1933)

Dean, J. M. (ed.), *Richard the Redeless and Mum and the Sothsegger*, TEAMS Middle English Texts (online resource, 2000)

Devon, F. (ed.), *Issues of the Exchequer, Henry III to Henry VI* (London, 1837)

Dillon, H. A., and Hope, W. H. St J., "Inventory of the Goods and Chattels Belonging to Thomas, Duke of Gloucester, and Seized in His Castle at Pleshy, Co. Essex, 21 Richard II (1397); with Their Values, as Shown in the Escheator's Accounts," *Archaeological Journal*, vol. 54 (1897), 275–308

Dobson, R. B. (ed. and tr.), *The Peasants' Revolt of 1381* (London and Basingstoke, 1970)

Douët-d'Arcq, L. (ed.), *Choix de Pièces inédites relatives au Règne de Charles VI*, 2 vols. (Paris, 1863)

Douët-d'Arcq, L. (ed.), *Chronique d'Enguerran de Monstrelet, 1400–1444*, 6 vols. (Paris, 1857–62)

Dugdale, W. (ed.), *Monasticon Anglicanum*, vol. 6, part 1 (London, 1849)

Ellis, H. (ed.), *Original Letters Illustrative of English History*, 4 vols. (London, 1824–27)

Froissart, J., *Le joli Buisson de Jonece*, ed. A. Fourrier (Geneva, 1975)

Fryde, E. B., Greenway, D. E., Porter, S., and Roy, I. (eds.), *Handbook of British Chronology* (3rd ed., London, 1986)

Gairdner, J. (ed.), *The Historical Collections of a Citizen of London in the Fifteenth Century*, Camden Society, New Series, vol. 17 (London, 1876)

Galbraith, V. H. (ed.), *The Anonimalle Chronicle, 1333 to 1381* (Manchester, 1970)

Geaman, K. L., "A Personal Letter Written by Anne of Bohemia," *EHR*, vol. 128, no. 534 (2013), 1086–94

Genet, J-P. (ed.), *Four English Political Tracts of the Later Middle Ages*, Camden Society, Fourth Series, vol. 18 (London, 1977)

Giles, J. A. (ed.), *Incerti Scriptoris Chronicon Angliae* (London, 1848)

Given-Wilson, C. (ed. and tr.), *The Chronicle of Adam Usk, 1377–1421* (Oxford, 1997)

Given-Wilson, C. (ed. and tr.), *Chronicles of the Revolution, 1397–1400* (Manchester, 1993)

Gordon-Duff, E. (ed.), *Information for Pilgrims unto the Holy Land* (London, 1893)

Gower, J., *The Minor Latin Works with In Praise of Peace*, ed. R. F. Yeager and M. Livingston, TEAMS Middle English Texts (online resource, 2005)

Gransden, A., "A Fourteenth-Century Chronicle from the Grey Friars at Lynn," *EHR*, vol. 72, no. 283 (1957), 270–78

Green, M. H. (ed. and tr.), *The Trotula: A Medieval Compendium of Women's Medicine* (Philadelphia, 2001)

Grose, F., and Astle, T. (eds.), *Antiquarian Repertory*, vol. 1 (London, 1807)

Hardy, W. (ed. and tr.), *The Charters of the Duchy of Lancaster* (London, 1845)

Haydon, F. S. (ed.), *Eulogium historiarum sive temporis*, vol. 3 (London, 1863)

Hearne, T. (ed.), *Duo Rerum Anglicarum Scriptores Veteres, viz. Thomas Otterbourne et Johannes Whethamstede*, vol. 1 (Oxford, 1732)

Hearne, T. (ed.), *Thomæ de Elmham, Vita et Gesta Henrici Quinti* (Oxford, 1727)

Hector, L. C., and Harvey, B. (eds. and tr.), *The Westminster Chronicle, 1381–1394* (Oxford, 1982)

Hingeston, F. C. (ed.), *Royal and Historical Letters during the Reign of Henry the Fourth*, vol. 1 (London, 1860)

Hoccleve, T., *The Regiment of Princes*, ed. C. R. Blyth, TEAMS Middle English Texts (online resource, 1999)

Horrox, R. (ed. and tr.), *The Black Death* (Manchester, 1994)

An Inventory of the Historical Monuments in London, vol. 1: *Westminster Abbey* (London, 1924)

Kimball, E. G. (ed.), *Oxfordshire Sessions of the Peace in the Reign of Richard II*, Oxfordshire Record Society, vol. 53 (1979–80), 82–86

Kingsford, C. L. (ed.), *Chronicles of London* (Oxford, 1905)

Kirby, J. L. (ed.), *Calendar of Signet Letters of Henry IV and Henry V (1399–1422)* (London, 1978)

Legge, M. (ed.), *Anglo-Norman Letters and Petitions from All Souls MS 182* (Oxford, 1941)

Leland, J. (ed.), *Collectanea*, vol. 1 (London, 1770)

Lettenhove, K. de (ed.), *Oeuvres de Froissart, Chroniques*, 25 vols. (Brussels, 1867–77)

Livre des Bouillons, Archives Municipales de Bordeaux (Bordeaux, 1867)

Lobineau, G-A., *Histoire de Bretagne*, vol. 2 (Paris, 1707)

Lodge, E. C., and Somerville, R. (eds.), *John of Gaunt's Register, 1379–1383*, vols. 1 and 2, Camden Society, Third Series, vols. 56–57 (London, 1937)

Lumby, J. L. (ed.), *Polychronicon Ranulphi Higden Monachi Cestrensis*, vol. 8 (London, 1882)

Macaulay, G. C. (ed.), *The Complete Works of John Gower*, vol. 2 (Oxford, 1901)

Maidstone, C., "Historia de Martyrio Ricardi Scrope, Archiepiscopi Eboracensis," in Wharton (ed.), *Anglia Sacra*, vol. 2, 369–72

Maidstone, R., *Concordia (The Reconciliation of Richard II with London)*, ed. D. R. Carlson, with a verse translation by A. G. Rigg, TEAMS Middle English Texts (online resource, 2003)

Martin, G. H. (ed. and tr.), *Knighton's Chronicle, 1337–1396* (Oxford, 1995)

McHardy, A. K. (ed. and tr.), *The Reign of Richard II: From Minority to Tyranny, 1377–97* (Manchester, 2012)

McKisack, M. (ed.), "Historia siue narracio de modo et forma mirabilis parliamenti," Camden Society, Third Series, vol. 37 (London, 1926), i–viii, 1–27

Meyer, M. P., Meyer, M. M., and Luce, S., "L'Entrevue d'Ardres, 1396," *Annuaire-Bulletin de la Société de l'histoire de France*, vol. 18, no. 2 (1881), 209–24

Mézières, P. de, *Le Songe du vieil Pelerin*, ed. G. W. Coopland (Cambridge, 1969)

Mirot, L. (ed.), "Le Procès de Maitre Jean Fusoris, Chanoine de Notre-Dame de Paris (1415–1416): Épisode des Négociations franco-anglaises durant la Guerre de Cent Ans," *Mémoires de la Société de l'histoire de Paris et de l'Ile de France*, vol. 27 (1900), 137–287

Mirot, L. (ed.), "Un Trousseau royal à la Fin du XIVe Siècle," *Mémoires de la Société de l'histoire de Paris et de l'Ile-de-France*, vol. 29 (1902), 125–58

Moranvillé, H. (ed.), *Chronographia Regum Francorum*, 3 vols. (Paris, 1891–97)

Myers, A. R. (ed.), *English Historical Documents, 1327–1485* (London, 1969)

Nichols, J. G. (ed.), *A Collection of All the Wills Now Known to Be Extant of the Kings and Queens of England* (London, 1780)

Nicolas, N. H. (ed.), *A Chronicle of London, from 1089 to 1483* (London, 1827)

Nicolas, N. H. (ed.), *Proceedings and Ordinances of the Privy Council of England*, 2 vols. (London, 1834)

Palgrave, F. (ed.), *Antient Kalendars and Inventories of the Treasury of His Majesty's Exchequer*, 3 vols. (London, 1836)

Perroy, E. (ed.), *The Diplomatic Correspondence of Richard II*, Camden Society, Third Series, vol. 48 (London, 1933)

Pope, M. K., and Lodge, E. C. (eds. and tr.), *Life of the Black Prince by the Herald of Sir John Chandos* (Oxford, 1910)

Prince, A. E., "A Letter of Edward the Black Prince Describing the Battle of Nájera in 1367," *EHR*, vol. 41, no. 163 (1926), 415–18

Reports from the Lords' Committees Touching the Dignity of a Peer of the Realm, vol. 4 (London, 1829)

Roskell, J. S., Clark, L., and Rawcliffe, C. (eds.), *The History of Parliament: The House of Commons 1386–1421* (online resource)

Rotuli Parliamentorum, 6 vols. (London, 1767–77)

Rotuli Scotiae, vol. 2 (1819)

Rymer, T. (ed.), *Foedera, Conventiones, Litterae, Etc.*, 20 vols. (London, 1727–35)

Sayles, G. (ed.), *Select Cases in the Court of King's Bench*, vol. 7 (London, 1971)

Sayles, G. O., "The Deposition of Richard II: Three Lancastrian Narratives," *Bulletin of the Institute of Historical Research*, vol. 54, no. 130 (1981), 257–70

Shakespeare, W., *King Henry IV, Part I*, ed. A. R. Humphreys (London, 1960)

Shakespeare, W., *King Henry IV, Part II*, ed. A. R. Humphreys (London, 1966)

Shakespeare, W., *King Richard II*, ed. P. Ure (London, 1956)

Statutes of the Realm, 11 vols. (London, 1810–28)

Stow, G. B. (ed.), *Historia Vitae et Regni Ricardi Secundi* (Philadelphia, 1977)

Stow, J., *A Survey of London*, ed. C. L. Kingsford, 2 vols. (Oxford, 1908)

Stratford, J., *Richard II and the English Royal Treasure* (Woodbridge, 2012)

Suggett, H., "A Letter Describing Richard II's Reconciliation with the City of London, 1392," *EHR*, vol. 62, no. 243 (1947), 209–13

Taylor, C., and Taylor, J. M. H. (eds. and tr.), *The Chivalric Biography of Boucicaut, Jean II le Meingre* (Woodbridge, 2016)

Taylor, J. (ed. and tr.), *The Kirkstall Abbey Chronicles*, Thoresby Society, vol. 42 (Leeds, 1952)

Thomas, A. H. (ed.), *Calendar of Select Pleas and Memoranda of the City of London*, vol. 3: *1381–1422* (London, 1932)

Thomas, A. H., and Thornley, I. D. (eds.), *The Great Chronicle of London* (London, 1938)

Thornley, I. D., "Treason by Words in the Fifteenth Century," *EHR*, vol. 32, no. 128 (1917), 556–61

Thorold Rogers, J. E. (ed.), *Loci et Libro Veritatum* (Oxford, 1881)

Toulmin-Smith, L. (ed.), *Expeditions to Prussia and the Holy Land Made by Henry, Earl of Derby*, Camden Society (London,1894)

Tuetey, A. (ed.), *Journal de Nicolas de Baye, Greffier du Parlement de Paris, 1400–1417*, vol. 1 (Paris, 1885)

Twiss, T. (ed.), *Monumenta Juridica: The Black Book of the Admiralty*, vol. 1 (London, 1871)

Wickham Legg, L. G. (ed.), *English Coronation Records* (London, 1901)

Williams, B. (ed.), *Chronicque de la Traïson et Mort de Richart Deux Roy Dengleterre* (London, 1846)

Wright, T. (ed.), *Political Poems and Songs Relating to English History*, vol. 1 (London, 1859)

Secondary Sources

Allmand, C., *Henry V* (New Haven and London, 1992)

Allmand, C., "Henry V, king of England and lord of Ireland, and duke of Aquitaine (1386–1422)," *ODNB*

Ambühl, R., Bothwell, J., and Tompkins, L. (eds.), *Ruling Fourteenth-Century England* (Woodbridge, 2019)

Amin, N., *The House of Beaufort: The Bastard Line That Captured the Crown* (Stroud, 2017)

Anstis, J., *The Register of the Most Noble Order of the Garter*, vol. 1 (London, 1724)

Archer, R. E., "Brotherton [Marshal], Margaret, *suo jure* duchess of Norfolk (*c.*1320–1399)," *ODNB*

Archer, R. E. (ed.), *Crown, Government and People in the Fifteenth Century* (Stroud, 1995)

Archer, R. E., "Mowbray, Thomas, second earl of Nottingham (1385–1405)," *ODNB*

Archer, R. E., and Walker, S. (eds.), *Rulers and Ruled in Late Medieval England* (London, 1995)

Armitage-Smith, S., *John of Gaunt* (London, 1904)

Arvanigian, M., "Henry IV, the Northern Nobility and the Consolidation of the North," in Dodd and Biggs (eds.), *Henry IV: The Establishment of the Regime*, 117–38

Ashe, L, *Richard II: A Brittle Glory* (London, 2016)

Aston, M., *Lollards and Reformers: Images and Literacy in Late Medieval Religion* (London, 1984)

Aston, M., "Lollardy and Sedition, 1381–1431," in Aston, *Lollards and Reformers: Images and Literacy in Late Medieval Religion*, 1–47

Aston, M., *Thomas Arundel* (Oxford, 1967)

Autrand, F., *Charles VI* (Paris, 1986)

Baggs, A. P., Bolton, D. K., Hicks, M. A., and Pugh, R. B., "Hornsey, including Highgate: Communications," in Baker and Elrington (eds.), *A History of the County of Middlesex*, vol. 6, 103–7

Baker, T. F. T., and Elrington, C. R. (eds.), *A History of the County of Middlesex*, vol. 6 (London, 1980)

Baldwin, J., *The King's Council in England during the Middle Ages* (Oxford, 1913)

Barber, R., "Edward [Edward of Woodstock; known as the Black Prince], prince of Wales and Aquitaine (1330–1376)," *ODNB*

Barber, R., *Edward, Prince of Wales and Aquitaine* (London, 1978)

Barker, J., *England, Arise: The People, the King and the Great Revolt of 1381* (London, 2014)

Barker, J., *The Tournament in England, 1100–1400* (Woodbridge, 2003)

Barker, J. W., *Manuel II Palaeologus (1391–1425): A Study in Late Byzantine Statesmanship* (New Brunswick, 1969)

Barron, C., "Centres of Conspicuous Consumption: The Aristocratic Townhouse in London, 1200–1550," in Carlin and Rosenthal (eds.), *Medieval London: Collected Papers of Caroline M. Barron*, 421–47

Barron, C., "Froissart and the Great Revolt," in Lutkin and Hamilton (eds.), *Creativity, Contradictions and Commemoration in the Reign of Richard II*, 11–34

Barron, C., "The Quarrel of Richard II with London, 1392–7," in Carlin and Rosenthal (eds.), *Medieval London: Collected Papers of Caroline M. Barron*, 27–55

Barron, C., "Richard II and London," in Carlin and Rosenthal (eds.), *Medieval London: Collected Papers of Caroline M. Barron*, 105–32

Barron, C., "Richard II: Image and Reality," in Gordon, *The Wilton Diptych*, 15–25

Barron, C., "Richard Whittington: The Man behind the Myth," in Carlin and Rosenthal (eds.), *Medieval London: Collected Papers of Caroline M. Barron*, 267–33

Barron, C., "The Tyranny of Richard II," in Carlin and Rosenthal (eds.), *Medieval London: Collected Papers of Caroline M. Barron*, 3–25

Barron, C., and Sutton, A. F. (eds.), *Medieval London Widows, 1300–1500* (London, 1994)

Bean, J. M. W., "Percy, Henry, first earl of Northumberland (1341–1408)," *ODNB*

Beem, C. (ed.), *The Royal Minorities of Medieval and Early Modern England* (New York, 2008)

Bellamy, J. G., "The Northern Rebellions in the Later Years of Richard II," *Bulletin of the John Rylands Library*, vol. 47 (1964–5), 254–74

Bellamy, J. G., "Sir John Annesley and the Chandos Inheritance," *Nottingham Medieval Studies*, vol. 10 (1966), 94–105

Beltz, G. F., *Memorials of the Most Noble Order of the Garter* (London, 1841)

Bennett, M., "'Defenders of truth': Lord Cobham, John Gower, and the Political Crisis of 1387–88," in Lutkin and Hamilton (eds.), *Creativity, Contradictions and Commemoration in the Reign of Richard II*, 35–52

Bennett, M., "Edward III's Entail and the Succession to the Crown, 1376–1471," *EHR*, vol. 113, no. 452 (1998), 580–609

Bennett, M., "Henry of Bolingbroke and the Revolution of 1399," in Dodd and Biggs (eds.), *Henry IV: The Establishment of the Regime*, 9–34

Bennett, M., "Henry IV, the Royal Succession and the Crisis of 1406," in Dodd and Biggs (eds.), *The Reign of Henry IV: Rebellion and Survival*, 9–27

Bennett, M., *Richard II and the Revolution of 1399* (Sutton, 1999)

Bennett, M., "Richard II and the Wider Realm," in Goodman and Gillespie (eds.), *Richard II: The Art of Kingship*, 187–204

Bennett, M., "Richard II in the Mirror of Christendom," in Ambühl, Bothwell, and Tompkins (eds.), *Ruling Fourteenth-Century England*, 263–88

Bennett, M., "Stanley, Sir John (c.1350–1414)," *ODNB*

Bennett, P. E., Carpenter, S., and Gardiner, L., "Chivalric Games at the Court of Edward III," *Medium Ævum*, vol. 87, no 2 (2018), 304–42

Bent, M., "Dunstaple [Dunstable], John (d. 1453)," *ODNB*

Bergeron, D. M. (ed.), *Pageantry in the Shakespearean Theatre* (Athens, Georgia, 1986)

Biggs, D., "The Commission to Ensure Good Governance of 11 May 1402: A Case Study of Lancastrian Counter-Propaganda," in Clark and Fleming (eds.), *The Fifteenth Century*, vol. 18, *Rulers, Regions and Retinues*, 17–26

Biggs, D., "An Ill and Infirm King: Henry IV, Health, and the Gloucester Parliament of 1407," in Dodd and Biggs (eds.), *The Reign of Henry IV: Rebellion and Survival*, 180–209

Biggs, D., "The Politics of Health: Henry IV and the Long Parliament of 1406," in Dodd and Biggs (eds.), *Henry IV: The Establishment of the Regime*, 185–206

Binski, P., "The Painted Chamber at Westminster, the Fall of Tyrants and the English Literary Model of Governance," *Journal of the Warburg and Courtauld Institutes*, vol. 74 (2011), 121–54

Binski, P., and Guerry, E., "Seats, Relics and the Rationale of Images in Westminster Abbey, Henry III to Edward II," in Rodwell and Tatton-Brown (eds.), *Westminster, Part I: The Art, Architecture and Archaeology of the Royal Abbey*, 180–204

Bird, W. H. B., "The Peasant Rising of 1381: The King's Itinerary," *EHR*, vol. 31, no. 121 (1916), 124–26

Boffey, J., and Davis, V. (eds.), *Recording Medieval Lives* (Donington, 2009)

Bothwell, J., "Edward III and the 'New Nobility': Largesse and Limitation in Fourteenth-Century England," *EHR*, vol. 112, no. 449 (1997), 1111–40

Bothwell, J., and Dodd, G. (eds.), *Fourteenth Century England*, vol. 9 (Woodbridge, 2016)

Bothwell, J., and Hamilton, J. S. (eds.), *Fourteenth Century England*, vol. 12 (Woodbridge, 2022)

Bradley, H., "The Datini Factors in London," in Clayton, Davies, and McNiven (eds.), *Trade, Devotion and Governance*, 55–79

Bradley, H., "Lucia Visconti, Countess of Kent (d. 1424)," in Barron and Sutton (eds.), *Medieval London Widows*, 77–84

Britnell, R. H., and Pollard, A. J. (eds.), *The McFarlane Legacy: Studies in Late Medieval Politics and Society* (Stroud, 1995)

Brooke, R., *A Catalogue and Succession of the Kings, Princes, Dukes, Marquesses, Earles, and Viscounts of this Realme of England, since the Norman Conquest, to This Present Yeare, 1619* (London, 1619)

Brown, A. L., "The Commons and the Council in the Reign of Henry IV," *EHR*, vol. 79, no. 310 (1964), 1–30

Brown, A. L., "Percy, Thomas, earl of Worcester (c.1343–1403)," *ODNB*

Brown, A. L., "The Reign of Henry IV: The Establishment of the Lancastrian Regime," in Chrimes, Ross, and Griffiths (eds.), *Fifteenth-Century England, 1399–1509*, 1–28

Brown, R. A., Colvin, H. M., and Taylor, A. J. (eds.), *The History of the King's Works: The Middle Ages*, 2 vols. (London, 1963)

Bueno de Mesquita, D. M., "The Foreign Policy of Richard II in 1397: Some Italian Letters," *EHR*, vol. 56, no. 224 (1941), 628–37

Buquet, T., "Hunting with Cheetahs at European Courts, from the Origins to the End of a Fashion," in Weber and Hengerer (eds.), *Animals and Court (Europe, c. 1200–1800)*, 17–42

Burden, J., "How Do You Bury a Deposed King? The Funeral of Richard II and the Establishment of Lancastrian Royal Authority in 1400," in Dodd and Biggs (eds.), *Henry IV: The Establishment of the Regime*, 35–54

Burrow, J. A., "Hoccleve [Occleve], Thomas (c.1367–1426)," *ODNB*

Burt, C., and Partington, R., *Arise, England: Six Kings and the Making of the English State* (London, 2024)

Cane, P., and Kumarasingham, H. (eds.), *The Cambridge Constitutional History of the United Kingdom*, vol. 2: *The Changing Constitution* (Cambridge, 2023)

Carlin, M., and Rosenthal, J. (eds.), *Medieval London: Collected Papers of Caroline M. Barron* (Kalamazoo, 2017)

Carpenter, C., "The Beauchamp Affinity: A Study of Bastard Feudalism at Work," *EHR*, vol. 95, no. 376 (1980), 514–32

Carpenter, C., "Beauchamp, Richard, thirteenth earl of Warwick (1382–1439)," *ODNB*

Carpenter, C., and Spencer, A. M., "England in the Fourteenth Century," in Cane and Kumaras-ingham (eds.), *The Cambridge Constitutional History of the United Kingdom*, vol. 2: *The Changing Constitution*, 84–107

Carr, H., *The Red Prince: John of Gaunt, Duke of Lancaster* (London, 2021)

Castor, H., *The King, the Crown, and the Duchy of Lancaster: Public Authority and Private Power, 1399–1461* (Oxford, 2000)

Castor, H., "Waterton, Sir Hugh (*d.* 1409)," *ODNB*

Catto, J., "The King's Servants," in Harriss (ed.), *Henry V: The Practice of Kingship*, 75–95

Catto, J., "Religious Change under Henry V," in Harriss (ed.), *Henry V: The Practice of Kingship*, 97–115

Cherry, J., "Some Lancastrian Seals," in Stratford (ed.), *The Lancastrian Court*, 19–28

Chrimes, S. B., "Richard II's Questions to the Judges," *Law Quarterly Review*, vol. 72 (1956), 365–90

Chrimes, S. B., Ross, C. D., and Griffiths, R. A. (eds.), *Fifteenth-Century England, 1399–1509* (Manchester, 1972)

Christiansen, E., *The Northern Crusades: The Baltic and the Catholic Frontier, 1100–1525* (London and Basingstoke, 1980)

Clark, E., "City Orphans and Custody Law in Medieval England," *American Journal of Legal History*, vol. 34 (1990), 168–87

Clark, L., "Bagot, Sir William (*d.* 1407)," *ODNB*

Clark, L. (ed.), *The Fifteenth Century*, vol. 3: *Authority and Submission* (Woodbridge, 2003)

Clark, L., and Fleming, P. (eds.), *The Fifteenth Century*, vol. 18: *Rulers, Regions and Retinues* (Woodbridge, 2020)

Clarke, M. V., *Fourteenth-Century Studies* (Oxford, 1937)

Clayton, D., Davies, R., and McNiven, P. (eds.), *Trade, Devotion and Governance* (Stroud, 1994)

Clementi, D., "Richard II's Ninth Question to the Judges," *EHR*, vol. 86, no. 338 (1971), 96–113

Clopper, L. M., "London and the Problem of the Clerkenwell Plays," *Comparative Drama*, vol. 34, no. 3 (2000), 291–303

Cockayne, G. E., *The Complete Peerage*, ed. V. Gibbs, 12 vols. (London, 1910–59)

Collins, M., "The Heraldry and Badges of King Richard II at Westminster Hall, Palace of Westminster," *The Coat of Arms: The Journal of the Heraldry Society*, Fourth Series, vol. 1 (2018), 1–17

Collins, M., Emery, P., Phillpotts, C., Samuel, M., and Thomas, C., "The King's High Table at the Palace of Westminster," *The Antiquaries Journal*, vol. 92 (2012), 197–243

Collinson, P., Ramsay, N., and Sparks, M. (eds.), *A History of Canterbury Cathedral* (Oxford, 1995)

Coss, P., and Keen, M. (eds.), *Heraldry, Pageantry and Social Display in Medieval England* (Woodbridge, 2002)

Courtenay, L. T., and Mark, R., "The Westminster Hall Roof: A Historiographic and Structural Study," *Journal of the Society of Architectural Historians*, vol. 46, no. 4 (1987), 374–93

Crooks, P., "'The Calculus of Faction' and Richard II's Duchy of Ireland, *c.* 1382–9," in Saul (ed.), *Fourteenth Century England*, vol. 5, 94–115

Crouch, D., "Marshal, William [*called* the Marshal], fourth earl of Pembroke (*c.*1146–1219)," *ODNB*

Curley, M. J., "John of Bridlington [St John of Bridlington, John Thwing] (*c.*1320–1379)," *ODNB*

Curry, A., *Henry V: Playboy Prince to Warrior King* (London, 2015)

Curry, A., "The Making of a Prince: The Finances of 'the Young Lord Henry,' 1386–1400," in Dodd (ed.), *Henry V: New Interpretations*, 11–34

Curry, A., "Richard II and the War with France," in Dodd (ed.), *The Reign of Richard II*, 33–50

Curry, A., Bell, A. R., King, A., and Simpkin, D., "New Regime, New Army? Henry IV's Scottish Expedition of 1400," *EHR*, vol. 125, no. 517 (2010), 1382–1413

Davies, R. G., "After the Execution of Archbishop Scrope: Henry IV, the Papacy and the English Episcopate, 1405–8," *Bulletin of the John Rylands Library*, vol. 59, no 1 (1976), 40–74

Davies, R. G., "Courtenay, Richard (c.1381–1415), bishop of Norwich," *ODNB*

Davies, R. G., "Merk [Merke], Thomas (d. 1409/10), bishop of Carlisle," *ODNB*

Davies, R. G., "Mohun [Mone], Guy (d. 1407), administrator and bishop of St David's," *ODNB*

Davies, R. G., "Rede [Reade], Robert (d. 1415), bishop of Chichester," *ODNB*

Davies, R. G., "Some Notes from the Register of Henry de Wakefield, Bishop of Worcester, on the Political Crisis of 1386–1388," *EHR*, vol. 86, no. 340 (1971), 547–58

Davies, R. R., "Mortimer, Roger, fourth earl of March and sixth earl of Ulster (1374–1398)," *ODNB*

Davies, R. R., *The Revolt of Owain Glyn Dŵr* (Oxford, 1995)

Davies, R. R., "Richard II and the Principality of Chester, 1397–9," in Du Boulay and Barron (eds.), *The Reign of Richard II*, 256–79

Dobson, R. B., "Neville, Alexander (c.1332–1392), archbishop of York," *ODNB*

Dodd, G., "Getting Away with Murder: Sir John Haukeston and Richard II's Cheshire Archers," *Nottingham Medieval Studies*, vol. 46 (2002), 102–18

Dodd, G. (ed.), *Henry V: New Interpretations* (Woodbridge, 2013)

Dodd, G., "Henry IV's Council, 1399–1405," in Dodd and Biggs (eds.), *Henry IV: The Establishment of the Regime*, 95–115

Dodd, G., "Henry V's Establishment: Service, Loyalty and Reward in 1413," in Dodd (ed.), *Henry V: New Interpretations*, 35–76

Dodd, G., "Patronage, Petitions and Grace: The 'Chamberlains' Bills' of Henry IV's Reign," in Dodd and Biggs (eds.), *The Reign of Henry IV: Rebellion and Survival*, 105–35

Dodd, G. (ed.), *The Reign of Richard II* (Stroud, 2000)

Dodd, G., "Richard II and the Fiction of Minority Rule," in Beem (ed.), *The Royal Minorities of Medieval and Early Modern England*, 103–60

Dodd, G., "Richard II and the Transformation of Parliament," in Dodd (ed.), *The Reign of Richard II*, 71–84

Dodd, G., "Tyranny and Affinity: The Public and Private Authority of Richard II and Richard III," in Clark and Fleming (eds.), *The Fifteenth Century*, vol. 18: *Rulers, Regions and Retinues*, 1–16

Dodd, G., and Biggs, D. (eds.), *Henry IV: The Establishment of the Regime, 1399–1406* (Woodbridge, 2003)

Dodd, G., and Biggs, D. (eds.), *The Reign of Henry IV: Rebellion and Survival, 1403–1413* (Woodbridge, 2008)

Du Boulay, F. R. H., "Henry of Derby's Expeditions to Prussia 1390–1 and 1392," in Du Boulay and Barron (eds.), *The Reign of Richard II*, 153–172

Du Boulay, F. R. H., and Barron, C. (eds.), *The Reign of Richard II* (London, 1971)

Duffy, M., *Royal Tombs of Medieval England* (reprint, Stroud, 2011)

Dunn, A., *The Peasants' Revolt: England's Failed Revolution of 1381* (Stroud, 2004)

Dunn, A., *The Politics of Magnate Power: England and Wales 1389–1413* (Oxford, 2003)

Eberle, P. J., "Richard II and the Literary Arts," in Goodman and Gillespie (eds.), *Richard II: The Art of Kingship*, 231–53

Fernie, E., and Crossley, P. (eds.), *Medieval Architecture and Its Intellectual Context* (London, 1990)

Fletcher, C., "Charles VI and Richard II: Inconstant Youths," in Boffey and Davis (eds.), *Recording Medieval Lives*, 85–101

Fletcher C., "Manhood and Politics in the Reign of Richard II," *Past and Present*, vol. 189 (2005), 3–39

Fletcher, C., "Narrative and Political Strategies at the Deposition of Richard II," *Journal of Medieval History*, vol. 30 (2004), 323–41

Fletcher, C., *Richard II: Manhood, Youth, and Politics, 1377–99* (Oxford, 2008)

Fletcher, D., "The Lancastrian Collar of Esses: Its Origins and Transformations down the Centuries," in Gillespie (ed.), *The Age of Richard II*, 191–204

Forde, S., "Repyndon [Repington, Repingdon], Philip (c.1345–1424)," *ODNB*

Fox-Davies, A. C., *A Complete Guide to Heraldry* (London, 1909)

Frame, R., "'Les Engleys Nées en Irlande': The English Political Identity in Medieval Ireland," *Transactions of the Royal Historical Society*, vol. 3 (1993), 83–103

Frame, R., "Mac Murchadha, Art Caomhánach [Art Kavanagh MacMurrough; *called* Art Mór Mac Murchadha] (*d*. 1416/17)," *ODNB*

Frame, R., *The Political Development of the British Isles, 1100–1400* (Oxford, 1990)

Geaman, K. L., "Anne of Bohemia and Her Struggle to Conceive," *Social History of Medicine*, vol. 29, no. 2 (2016), 224–44

Geaman, K. L., "Anne of Bohemia: Overcoming Infertility," in Norrie, Harris, Laynesmith, Messer, and Woodacre (eds.), *Later Plantagenet and the Wars of the Roses Consorts: Power, Influence and Dynasty*, 67–86

Geaman, K. L, "Beyond Good Queen Anne: Anne of Bohemia, Patronage, and Politics," in Tanner (ed.), *Medieval Elite Women and the Exercise of Power*, 67–90

Giancarlo, M., "Murder, Lies, and Storytelling: The Manipulation of Justice(s) in the Parliaments of 1397 and 1399," *Speculum*, vol. 77, no. 1 (2002), 76–112

Gillespie, J. L. (ed.), *The Age of Richard II* (Stroud, 1997)

Gillespie, J. L., "Holland [Holand], Thomas, sixth earl of Kent and duke of Surrey (*c.*1374–1400)," *ODNB*

Gillespie, J. L., "Richard II: Chivalry and Kingship," in Gillespie (ed.), *The Age of Richard II*, 115–38

Gillespie, J. L., "Richard II: King of Battles?," in Gillespie (ed.), *The Age of Richard II*, 139–64

Gillespie, J. L., "Richard II's Cheshire Archers," *Transactions of the Historic Society of Lancashire and Cheshire*, vol. 75 (1974), 1–39

Given-Wilson, C., "The Earl of Arundel, the War with France, and the Anger of King Richard II," in Yeager and Takamiya (eds.), *The Medieval Python*, 27–38

Given-Wilson, C., "The Exequies of Edward III and the Royal Funeral Ceremony in Late Medieval England," *EHR*, vol. 124, no. 507 (2009), 257–82

Given-Wilson, C., "Fitzalan, Richard, fourth earl of Arundel and ninth earl of Surrey (1346–1397), *ODNB*

Given-Wilson C., "Fitzalan, Richard, third earl of Arundel and eighth earl of Surrey (*c.*1313–1376), *ODNB*

Given-Wilson, C. (ed.), *Fourteenth-Century England*, vol. 6 (Woodbridge, 2010)

Given-Wilson, C., *Henry IV* (New Haven and London, 2016)

Given-Wilson, C., "The Manner of King Richard's Renunciation: A 'Lancastrian Narrative'?," *EHR*, vol. 108, no. 427 (1993), 365–70

Given-Wilson, C., "'The Quarrels of Old Women': Henry IV, Louis of Orléans, and Anglo-French Chivalry in the Early Fifteenth Century," in Dodd and Biggs (eds.), *The Reign of Henry IV: Rebellion and Survival*, 28–47

Given-Wilson, C., "Richard II and His Grandfather's Will," *EHR*, vol. 93, no. 367 (1978), 320–37

Given-Wilson, C., "Richard II and the Higher Nobility," in Goodman and Gillespie (eds.), *Richard II: The Art of Kingship*, 107–28

Given-Wilson, C., "Richard II, Edward II, and the Lancastrian Inheritance," *EHR*, vol. 109, no. 432 (1994), 553–71

Given-Wilson, C., "Royal Charter Witness Lists, 1327–1399," *Medieval Prosopography*, vol. 12, no. 2 (1991), 35–93

Given-Wilson, C., *The Royal Household and the King's Affinity: Service, Politics and Finance in England, 1360–1413* (New Haven and London, 1986)

Goodman, A., "Elizabeth of Lancaster (1364?–1425)," *ODNB*

Goodman, A., *Joan, the Fair Maid of Kent: A Fourteenth-Century Princess and Her World* (Woodbridge, 2017)

Goodman, A., *John of Gaunt: The Exercise of Princely Power in Fourteenth-Century Europe* (London, 1992)

Goodman, A., *The Loyal Conspiracy: The Lords Appellant under Richard II* (London, 1971)

Goodman, A., "Montagu [Montacute], John, third earl of Salisbury (*c.*1350–1400)," *ODNB*

Goodman, A., "Philippa [Philippa of Lancaster] (1360–1415)," *ODNB*

Goodman, A., "Vere, Aubrey de, tenth earl of Oxford (1338x40–1400)," *ODNB*

Goodman, A., and Gillespie, J. L. (eds.), *Richard II: The Art of Kingship* (Oxford, 1999)

Gordon, D., *The Wilton Diptych* (London, 2015)

Grady, F., "Gower's Boat, Richard's Barge, and the True Story of the *Confessio Amantis*: Text and Gloss," *Texas Studies in Literature and Language*, vol. 44, no. 1 (2002), 1–15

Gray, D., "Chaucer, Geoffrey (*c.*1340–1400)," *ODNB*

Gray, D., "Gower, John (*d.* 1408)," *ODNB*

Green, M. A. E., *Lives of the Princesses of England*, 6 vols. (London, 1849–55)

Griffiths, R. A., "Holland [Holand], John, first duke of Exeter (1395–1447)," *ODNB*

Griffiths, R. A., "Mortimer, Edmund, fifth earl of March and seventh earl of Ulster (1391–1425)," *ODNB*

Gundy, A., *Richard II and the Rebel Earl* (Cambridge, 2013)

Hamilton, J. S. (ed.), *Fourteenth Century England*, vol. 4 (Woodbridge, 2006)

Hamilton, J. S. (ed.), *Fourteenth Century England*, vol. 8 (Woodbridge, 2014)

Hammond, P. C., "Stanley, Arthur Penrhyn (1815–1881), dean of Westminster," *ODNB*

Hardman, P., "The 'Book of the Duchess' as a Memorial Monument," *The Chaucer Review*, vol. 28 (1994), 205–15

Harriss, G. L., "Beaufort, Henry [*called* the Cardinal of England] (1375?–1447)," *ODNB*

Harriss, G. L., "Beaufort, John, marquess of Dorset and marquess of Somerset (*c.*1371–1410)," *ODNB*

Harriss, G. L., "Beaufort, Thomas, duke of Exeter (1377?–1426), *ODNB*

Harriss, G. L., *Cardinal Beaufort: A Study of Lancastrian Ascendancy and Decline* (Oxford, 1988)

Harriss, G. L., "Financial Policy," in Harriss (ed.), *Henry V: The Practice of Kingship*, 159–79

Harriss, G. L., "Fitzalan, Thomas, fifth earl of Arundel and tenth earl of Surrey (1381–1415)," *ODNB*

Harriss, G. L. (ed.), *Henry V: The Practice of Kingship* (Oxford 1985)

Harriss, G. L., "Introduction: The Exemplar of Kingship," in Harriss (ed.), *Henry V: The Practice of Kingship*, 1–29

Harriss, G. L., "The King and His Magnates," in Harriss (ed.), *Henry V: The Practice of Kingship*, 31–51

Harriss, G. L., "The Management of Parliament," in Harriss (ed.), *Henry V: The Practice of Kingship*, 137–58

Harriss, G. L., "Richard [Richard of Conisbrough], earl of Cambridge (1385–1415)," *ODNB*

Harriss, G. L., *Shaping the Nation: England 1360–1461* (Oxford, 2005)

Harriss, G. L., "Thomas [Thomas of Lancaster], duke of Clarence (1387–1421)," *ODNB*

Harvey, J. H., "The Wilton Diptych—a Re-examination," *Archaeologia*, vol. 98 (1961), 1–28

Herbert, W., *The History of the Twelve Great Livery Companies of London* (London, 1834)

Holdsworth, C., "Langton, Stephen, archbishop of Canterbury (*c.*1150–1228)," *ODNB*

Holmes, G., "Fitzalan, Richard, fourth earl of Arundel," *ODNB*

Holmes, G., "Mare, Sir Peter de la (*fl.c.*1365–1387)," *ODNB*

Horrox, R., "Despenser, Constance, Lady Despenser (*c.*1375–1416)," *ODNB*

Horrox, R., "Edward [Edward of Langley, Edward of York], second duke of York (*c.*1373–1415)," *ODNB*

Hughes, J., "Arundel [Fitzalan], Thomas, administrator and archbishop of Canterbury (1353–1414)," *ODNB*

Johnston, D., "Richard II and the Submissions of Gaelic Ireland," *Irish Historical Studies*, vol. 22, no. 85 (1980), 1–20

Johnston, D., "Richard II's Departure from Ireland, July 1399," *EHR*, vol. 98, no. 389 (1983), 785–805

Jones, D., *The Plantagenets: The Kings Who Made England* (London, 2013)

Jones, D., *Summer of Blood: The Peasants' Revolt of 1381* (London, 2009)

Jones, M., *The Black Prince* (London, 2017)

Jones, M. C. E., *Ducal Brittany, 1364–1399* (Oxford, 1970)

Jurkowski, M., "Henry V's Suppression of the Oldcastle Revolt," in Dodd (ed.), *Henry V: New Interpretations*, 103–30

Jurkowski, M., Smith, C. L., and Crook, D. (eds.), *Lay Taxes in England and Wales, 1188–1688* (London, 1998)

Keen, M. H., "Coucy, Enguerrand [Ingelram] de, earl of Bedford (*c.*1340–1397)," *ODNB*

Kempe, A. J., "Some Account of the Jerusalem Chamber in the Abbey of Westminster, and of the Painted Glass Remaining Therein," *Archaeologia*, vol. 26 (1836), 432–45

King, A., "The Death of Edward II Revisited," in Bothwell and Dodd (eds.), *Fourteenth-Century England*, vol. 9, 1–22

King, A., "'They Have the Hertes of the People by North': Northumberland, the Percies and Henry IV, 1399–1408," in Dodd and Biggs (eds.), *Henry IV: The Establishment of the Regime*, 139–60

King, M., "Richard II, the Mortimer Inheritance and the March of Wales, 1381–84," in Hamilton (ed.), *Fourteenth Century England*, vol. 8, 95–118

Kingsford, C. L., *Henry V: The Typical Medieval Hero* (London, 1901)

Kipling, G., "Richard II's 'Sumptuous Pageants' and the Idea of the Civic Triumph," in Bergeron (ed.), *Pageantry in the Shakespearean Theatre*, 83–103

Kirby, J. L., "Councils and Councillors of Henry IV, 1399–1413," *Transactions of the Royal Historical Society*, vol. 14 (1964), 35–65

Kniphfer, T. C., "The Last of the Duketti? Richard II, Henry of Monmouth and the House of Lancaster," in Bothwell and Hamilton (eds.), *Fourteenth Century England*, vol. 12, 151–78

Krochalis, J. E., "The Books and Reading of Henry V and His Circle," *The Chaucer Review*, vol. 23, no. 1 (1988), 50–77

Lacey, H., "'Mercy and Truth Preserve the King': Richard II's Use of the Royal Pardon in 1397 and 1398," in Hamilton (ed.), *Fourteenth Century England*, vol. 4, 124–35

Lambrick, G., "The Impeachment of the Abbot of Abingdon in 1368," *EHR*, vol. 82, no. 323 (1967), 250–76

Lancashire, A., "Multi-day Performance and the Clerkenwell Play," *Early Theatre*, vol. 9, no. 2 (2006), 114–29

Lang, S. J., "Bradmore, John (*d.* 1412), surgeon," *ODNB*

Lang, S. J., "The 'Philomena' of John Bradmore and Its Middle English Derivative: A Perspective on Surgery in Late Medieval England," PhD thesis, University of St. Andrews (1998)

Leland, J. L., "Burley, Sir Simon (1336?–1388)," *ODNB*

Leland, J. L., "Montagu, William [William de Montacute], second earl of Salisbury (1328–1397)," *ODNB*

Leland, J. L., "Seagrave [Segrave], Sir Hugh (*d.* 1387)," *ODNB*

Leland, J. L., "Tresilian, Sir Robert (*d.* 1388)," *ODNB*

Lethaby, W. R., "The Westminster Portrait of Richard II," *The Burlington Magazine*, vol. 65, no. 380 (1934), 220–22

Lewis, N. B., "The 'Continual Council' in the Early Years of Richard II, 1377–80," *EHR*, vol. 41, no. 162 (1926), 246–51

Lewis, N. B., "The Last Medieval Summons of the English Feudal Levy, 13 June 1385," *EHR*, vol. 73, no. 286 (1958), 1–26

Lutkin, J., "Isabella de Coucy, Daughter of Edward III: The Exception Who Proves the Rule," in Given-Wilson (ed.), *Fourteenth Century England*, vol. 6, 131–48

Lutkin, J., and Hamilton, J. S. (eds.), *Creativity, Contradictions and Commemoration in the Reign of Richard II* (Woodbridge, 2022)

Lydon, J., "Ireland and the English Crown, 1171–1541," *Irish Historical Studies*, vol. 29, no. 115 (1995), 281–94

Lydon, J., "Richard II's Expeditions to Ireland," *Journal of the Royal Society of Antiquaries of Ireland*, vol. 93, no. 2 (1963), 135–49

Maddicott, J. R., "Thomas of Lancaster, second earl of Lancaster, second earl of Leicester, and earl of Lincoln (*c*.1278–1322)," *ODNB*

Maginn, C., "Gaelic Ireland's English Frontiers in the Late Middle Ages," *Proceedings of the Royal Irish Academy*, vol. 110C (2010), 173–90

Manning, J. J., introduction to *The First and Second Parts of John Hayward's The Life and Raigne of King Henrie IIII*, Camden Society, Fourth Series, vol. 42 (London, 1991)

Martin, G. H., "Narrative Sources for the Reign of Richard II," in Gillespie (ed.), *The Age of Richard II*, 51–69

Martin, J., *Treasure of the Land of Darkness: The Fur Trade and Its Significance for Medieval Russia* (Cambridge, 1986)

Masseti, M., "Pictorial Evidence from Medieval Italy of Cheetahs and Caracals, and Their Use in Hunting," *Archives of Natural History*, vol. 36 (2009), 37–47

Mathew, G., *The Court of Richard II* (London, 1968)

McFarlane, K. B., *Lancastrian Kings and Lollard Knights* (Oxford, 1972)

McHardy, A. K., "Haxey's Case, 1397: The Petition and Its Presenter Reconsidered," in Gillespie (ed.), *The Age of Richard II*, 93–114

McHardy, A. K., "Richard II: A Personal Portrait," in Dodd (ed.), *The Reign of Richard II*, 11–32

McKisack, M., *The Fourteenth Century, 1307–1399* (Oxford, 1959)

McNiven, P., "The Betrayal of Archbishop Scrope," *Bulletin of the John Rylands Library*, vol. 54 (1971), 173–213

McNiven, P., *Heresy and Politics in the Reign of Henry IV: The Burning of John Badby* (Woodbridge, 1987)

McNiven, P., "Prince Henry and the English Political Crisis of 1412," *History*, vol. 65, no. 213 (1980), 1–16

McNiven, P., "The Problem of Henry IV's Health, 1405–1413," *EHR*, vol. 100, no. 397 (1985), 747–72

McNiven, P., "Scrope, Richard (*c*.1350–1405), archbishop of York," *ODNB*

Mérindol, C. de, "De l'Emblématique de Charles VI et de Jean de Berry: À propos d'un Plafond peint et armoré récemment publié," *Bulletin de la Société Nationale des Antiquaires de France, 2006* (2012), 120–35

Millar, T. McW., "John of Arderne, the Father of British Proctology," *Proceedings of the Royal Society of Medicine*, vol. 47 (1953), 75–84

Mitchell, S. M., "Some Aspects of the Knightly Household of Richard II," PhD thesis, University of London (1998)

Moffat, R. D., "The Medieval Tournament: Chivalry, Heraldry and Reality," 2 vols., PhD thesis, University of Leeds (2010)

Morgan, P., "Henry IV and the Shadow of Richard II," in Archer (ed.), *Crown, Government and People*, 1–31

Morgan, P., *War and Society in Medieval Cheshire, 1277–1403*, Chetham Society, Third Series, vol. 34 (1987)

Mortimer, I., *The Fears of Henry IV: The Life of England's Self-Made King* (London, 2007)

Mortimer, I., "Henry IV's Date of Birth and the Royal Maundy," *Historical Research*, vol. 80, no. 210 (2007), 567–76

Mortimer, I., "Richard II and the Succession to the Crown," *History*, vol. 91, no. 3 (2006), 320–36

Mott, R., "Richard II and the Crisis of July 1397," in Wood and Loud (eds.), *Church and Chronicle in the Middle Ages*, 165–77

Musson, A. J., "Dymoke [Dymmok] family (*per. c*.1340–*c*.1580)," *ODNB*

Nef, J. U., "Mining and Metallurgy in Medieval Civilisation," in Postan and Miller (eds.), *The Cambridge Economic History of Europe*, vol. 2, 691–761

Neville, C. J., "Scotland, the Percies and the Law in 1400," in Dodd and Biggs (eds.), *Henry IV: The Establishment of the Regime*, 73–94

Nichols, J., "Observations on the Heraldic Devices discovered on the effigies of Richard the Second and His Queen in Westminster Abbey," *Archaeologia*, vol. 29 (1842), 32–59

Nicolas, N. H., "Contemporary Authority Adduced for the Popular Idea That the Ostrich Feathers of the Prince of Wales Were Derived from the Crest of the King of Bohemia," *Archaeologia*, vol. 32 (1847), 332–34

Nicolas, N. H., *The Controversy between Sir Richard Scrope and Sir Robert Grosvenor*, vol. 2 (London, 1832)

Nicolas, N. H., "Observations on the Institution of the Most Noble Order of the Garter," *Archaeologia*, vol. 31 (1845), 1–163

Nicolas, N. H., "Observations on the Origin and History of the Badges and Mottoes of Edward Prince of Wales," *Archaeologia*, vol. 31 (1845), 350–84

Nockles, P. B., "Bagot, Richard (1782–1854), bishop of Bath and Wells," *ODNB*

Norrie, A., Harris, C., Laynesmith, J. L., Messer, D. R., and Woodacre, E. (eds.), *Later Plantagenet and the Wars of the Roses Consorts: Power, Influence and Dynasty* (Cham, Switzerland, 2023)

Nuttall, J., *The Creation of Lancastrian Kingship: Literature, Language and Politics in Late Medieval England* (Cambridge, 2007)

Oman, C., *The Great Revolt of 1381* (Oxford, 1906)

Ormrod, W. M., "The DNA of Richard III: False Paternity and the Royal Succession in Later Medieval England," *Nottingham Medieval Studies*, vol. 60 (2016), 187–226

Ormrod, W. M., *Edward III* (New Haven and London, 2011)

Ormrod, W. M., "Edward III and His Family," *Journal of British Studies*, vol. 26, no. 4 (1987), 398–422

Ormrod, W. M. (ed.), *Fourteenth-Century England*, vol. 3 (Woodbridge, 2004)

Ormrod, W. M., "Henry of Lancaster [Henry of Grosmont], first duke of Lancaster (c.1310–1361)," *ODNB*

Ormrod, W. M., "Lionel [Lionel of Antwerp], duke of Clarence (1338–1368)," *ODNB*

Ormrod, W. M., "The Rebellion of Archbishop Scrope and the Tradition of Opposition to Royal Taxation," in Dodd and Biggs (eds.), *The Reign of Henry IV: Rebellion and Survival*, 162–79

Ormrod, W. M., "Richard II's Sense of English History," in Dodd (ed.), *The Reign of Richard II*, 97–110

Ormrod, W. M., "The Royal Nursery: A Household for the Younger Children of Edward III," *EHR*, vol. 120, no. 486 (2005), 398–415

Oxford Dictionary of National Biography (online resource)

Palladino, P., *Treasures of a Lost Art: Italian Manuscript Painting of the Middle Ages and Renaissance* (New Haven and London, 2003)

Palmer, J. J. N., "The Anglo-French Peace Negotiations, 1390–1396," *Transactions of the Royal Historical Society*, vol. 16 (1966), 81–94

Palmer, J. J. N., *England, France and Christendom, 1377–99* (London, 1972)

Palmer, J. J. N., "The Historical Context of the 'Book of the Duchess': A Revision," *The Chaucer Review*, vol. 8, no. 4 (1974), 253–61

Palmer, J. J. N., "The Parliament of 1385 and the Constitutional Crisis of 1386," *Speculum*, vol. 46, no. 3 (1971), 477–90

Payling, S., *Political Society in Lancastrian England: The Greater Gentry of Nottinghamshire* (Oxford, 1991)

Pilbrow, F., "The Knights of the Bath: Dubbing to Knighthood in Lancastrian and Yorkist England," in Coss and Keen (eds.), *Heraldry, Pageantry and Social Display in Medieval England*, 195–218

Postan, M. M., and Miller, E. (eds.), *The Cambridge Economic History of Europe*, vol. 2 (2nd ed., Cambridge, 1987)

Powell, E., "Gascoigne, Sir William (c.1350–1419), justice," *ODNB*

Powell, E., *Kingship, Law, and Society: Criminal Justice in the Reign of Henry V* (Oxford, 1989)

Powell, E., "The Restoration of Law and Order," in Harriss (ed.), *Henry V: The Practice of Kingship*, 53–74

Prescott, A., "Brembre, Sir Nicholas (*d.* 1388), merchant and mayor of London," *ODNB*

Pugh, T. B., "Despenser, Thomas, second Lord Despenser (1373–1400)," *ODNB*

Pugh, T. B., *Henry V and the Southampton Plot of 1415*, Southampton Records Series, vol. 30 (1988)

Rawcliffe, C., "Bussy, Sir John (exec. 1399), of Hougham, Lincs. and Cottesmore, Rutland," *Hist. Parl.*

Rawcliffe, C., "Chaucer, Thomas (*c.*1367–1434)," *ODNB*

Rawcliffe, C., *Medicine and Society in Later Medieval England* (Stroud, 1995)

Rawcliffe, C., "Rempston, Sir Thomas I (d. 1406), of Rempstone, Notts," *Hist. Parl.*

Rawcliffe, C., "Stafford, Hugh, second earl of Stafford (*c.*1342–1386)," *ODNB*

Richmond, L., "Blanche of Lancaster (1340x1347–1368)," *ODNB*

Rodwell, W., and Tatton-Brown, T. (eds.), *Westminster, Part I: The Art, Architecture and Archaeology of the Royal Abbey*, The British Archaeological Association Conference Transactions, vol. 39 (2015)

Rodwell, W., and Tatton-Brown, T. (eds.), *Westminster, Part II: The Art, Architecture and Archaeology of the Royal Palace*, The British Archaeological Association Conference Transactions, vol. 39 (2015)

Roskell, J. S., Clark, L., and Rawcliffe, C. (eds.), *The History of Parliament: The House of Commons 1386–1421* (online resource)

Roskell, J. S., and Woodger, L. S., "Savage, Sir Arnold I (1358–1410), of Bobbing, Kent," *Hist. Parl.*

Roskell, J. S., and Woodger, L. S., "Tiptoft, Sir John (d. 1443), of Burwell, Cambs," *Hist. Parl.*

Ross, J., "Seditious Activities: The Conspiracy of Maud de Vere, Countess of Oxford, 1403–4," in Clark (ed.), *The Fifteenth Century*, vol. 3: *Authority and Submission*, 25–41

Ross, J., "Vere [*née* Ufford], Maud de, countess of Oxford (1345?–1413)," *ODNB*

Russell, P. E., *The English Intervention in Spain and Portugal in the Time of Edward III and Richard II* (Oxford, 1955)

Saul, N. (ed.), *Fourteenth-Century England*, vol. 5 (Woodbridge, 2008)

Saul, N., *Richard II* (New Haven and London, 1997)

Saul, N., "Richard II and the Vocabulary of Kingship," *EHR*, vol. 110, no. 438 (1995), 854–77

Saul, N., "Richard II, York, and the Evidence of the King's Itinerary," in Gillespie (ed.), *The Age of Richard II*, 71–92

Scharf, G., "The Westminster Portrait of Richard II," *Fine Arts Quarterly Review*, vol. 2 (1867), 27–63

Scheifele, E., "Richard II and the Visual Arts," in Goodman and Gillespie (eds.), *Richard II: The Art of Kingship*, 255–71

Scott-Warren, J., "Was Elizabeth I Richard II? The Authenticity of Lambarde's 'Conversation,'" *The Review of English Studies*, New Series, vol. 64, no. 264 (2013), 208–30

Shaw, R. L. J., "Holland [*married name* Beaufort], Margaret, duchess of Clarence (*b.* in or before 1388, *d.* 1439)," *ODNB*

Simms, K., "Ó Néill, Niall Mór (*d.* 1397)," *ODNB*

Slater, L., "Imagining Place and Moralizing Space: Jerusalem at Medieval Westminster," *British Art Studies*, 6 (2017)

Spooner, J., "The Virgin Mary and White Harts Great and Small: The 14th-Century Wall-Paintings in the Chapel of Our Lady of the Pew and the Muniment Room," in Rodwell and Tatton-Brown (eds.), *Westminster, Part I: The Art, Architecture and Archaeology of the Royal Abbey*, 262–90

Spry, J., "A Brief Account of the Examination of the Tomb of King Henry IV, in the Cathedral of Canterbury, August 21, 1832," included within A. J. Kempe, "Some Account of the Jerusalem Chamber in the Abbey of Westminster, and of the Painted Glass Remaining Therein," *Archaeologia*, vol. 26 (1836), 432–45 (Spry: 440–45)

Staley, L., "Gower, Richard II, Henry of Derby, and the Business of Making Culture," *Speculum*, vol. 75, no. 1 (2000), 68–96

Stamp, A. E., "Richard II and the Death of the Duke of Gloucester," *EHR*, vol. 38, no. 150 (1923), 249–51

Stamp, A. E., "Richard II and the Death of the Duke of Gloucester," *EHR*, vol. 47, no. 187 (1932), 453

Stamp, G., "Scott, Sir George Gilbert (1811–1878), architect," *ODNB*

Stanley, A.P., "On an Examination of the Tombs of Richard II and Henry III in Westminster Abbey," *Archaeologia*, vol. 45 (1880), 309–27

Stansfield, M. M. N., "Holland, Edmund, seventh earl of Kent (1383–1408)," *ODNB*

Stansfield, M. M. N., "The Holland Family, Dukes of Exeter, Earls of Kent and Huntingdon, 1352–1475," DPhil thesis, University of Oxford (1987)

Stansfield, M. M. N., "Holland, John, first earl of Huntingdon and duke of Exeter (*c*.1352–1400)," *ODNB*

Stansfield, M. M. N., "Holland, Thomas, fifth earl of Kent (1350–1397)," *ODNB*

Starr, C., "Fitzwalter family (*per. c.*1200–*c.*1500)," *ODNB*

Steel, A., *Richard II* (Cambridge, 1941)

Stow, G. B., "Richard II and the Invention of the Pocket Handkerchief," *Albion*, vol. 27, no. 2 (1995), 221–35

Stow, G. B., "Richard II in the *Continuatio Eulogii*: Yet Another Alleged Historical Incident?," in Saul (ed.), *Fourteenth Century England*, vol. 5, 116–29

Stratford, J., "The Bequests of Isabel of Castile, first duchess of York, and Chaucer's 'Complaint of Mars,'" in Lutkin and Hamilton (eds.), *Creativity, Contradictions and Commemoration in the Reign of Richard II*, 75–96

Stratford, J., "Isabel [Isabella] of Castile, first duchess of York (1355–1392)," *ODNB*

Stratford, J. (ed.), *The Lancastrian Court* (Donington, 2003)

Stratford, J., *Richard II and the English Royal Treasure* (Woodbridge, 2012)

Strohm, P., *England's Empty Throne: Usurpation and the Language of Legitimation, 1399–1422* (New Haven and London, 1998)

Strohm, P., "The Trouble with Richard: The Reburial of Richard II and Lancastrian Symbolic Strategy," *Speculum*, vol. 71, no. 1 (1996), 87–111

Summerson, H., "An English Bible and Other Books Belonging to Henry IV," *Bulletin of the John Rylands Library*, vol. 79 (1997), 109–15

Sumption, J., *The Hundred Years War*, vol. 1: *Trial by Battle* (London, 1990)

Sumption, J., *The Hundred Years War*, vol. 2: *Trial by Fire* (London, 1999)

Sumption, J., *The Hundred Years War*, vol. 3: *Divided Houses* (London, 2009)

Sumption, J., *The Hundred Years War*, vol. 4: *Cursed Kings* (London, 2015)

Swanson, R. N., "Burghill [Burghull], John (*c.*1330–1414), bishop of Coventry and Lichfield," *ODNB*

Swanson, R. N., "Courtenay, William, archbishop of Canterbury (1341/2–1396)," *ODNB*

Swanson, R. N., "Waldby, Robert (*c.*1335–1397), archbishop of York," *ODNB*

Tait, J., "Mowbray, Thomas (I), twelfth Baron Mowbray and first Duke of Norfolk (1366?–1399)," archive edition *ODNB*

Tait, J., "'Plantagenet,' Edward, more correctly Edward of Norwich, second Duke of York (1373?–1415)," archive edition *ODNB*

Tait, J., review of A. Steel, *Richard II*, *EHR*, vol. 57, no. 227 (1942), 379–83

Tait, J., review of K. Wenck, *Eine mailändisch-thüringische Heiratsgeschichte aus der Zeit König Wenzels*, *EHR*, vol. 10, no. 40 (1895), 791

Tait, J., "Thomas of Woodstock, Earl of Buckingham and Duke of Gloucester (1395–1397)," archive edition *ODNB*

Tanner, H. J. (ed.), *Medieval Elite Women and the Exercise of Power, 1100–1400* (Cham, Switzerland, 2019)

Taylor, C., *A Virtuous Knight: Defending Marshal Boucicaut (Jean II Le Meingre, 1366–1421)* (Woodbridge, 2019)

Taylor, C., "'Weep Thou for Me in France': French Views of the Deposition of Richard II," in Ormrod (ed.), *Fourteenth Century England*, vol. 3, 207–22

Taylor, G., Jowett, J., Bourus, T., and Egan, G. (eds.), *The New Oxford Shakespeare: Critical Reference Edition*, vol. 1 (Oxford, 2017)

Taylor, J., *English Historical Literature in the Fourteenth Century* (Oxford, 1987)

Theilmann, J. M., "Political Canonization and Political Symbolism in Medieval England," *Journal of British Studies*, vol. 29, no. 3 (1990), 241–66

Thomson, J. A. F., "Oldcastle, John, Baron Cobham (*d.* 1417)," *ODNB*

Thornbury, W., *Old and New London*, vol. 1 (London, 1873)

Thornton, T., "Cheshire: The Inner Citadel of Richard II's Kingdom?," in Dodd (ed.), *The Reign of Richard II*, 85–96

Thurley, S., *Houses of Power: The Places That Shaped the Tudor World* (London, 2017)

Tingle, L., "Isabella of Valois: Child Queen," in Norrie, Harris, Laynesmith, Messer, and Woodacre (eds.), *Later Plantagenet and the Wars of the Roses Consorts: Power, Influence and Dynasty*, 87–104

Tout, T. F., revised by J. J. N. Palmer, "Bowet, Henry (*d.* 1423), archbishop of York," *ODNB*

Towson, K., "'Hearts Warped by Passion': The Percy–Gaunt Dispute of 1381," in Ormrod (ed.), *Fourteenth Century England*, vol. 3, 143–54

Tuck, A., "Beauchamp, Thomas, twelfth earl of Warwick (1337x9–1401)," *ODNB*

Tuck, A., "Beaufort [*married names* Ferrers, Neville], Joan, countess of Westmorland (1379?–1440)," *ODNB*

Tuck, A., "The Earl of Arundel's Expedition to France, 1411," in Dodd and Biggs (eds.), *The Reign of Henry IV: Rebellion and Survival*, 228–40

Tuck, A., "Edmund [Edmund of Langley], first duke of York (1341–1402)," *ODNB*

Tuck, A., "Henry IV and Chivalry," in Dodd and Biggs (eds.), *Henry IV: The Establishment of the Regime*, 55–72

Tuck, A., "Henry IV and Europe: A Dynasty's Search for Recognition," in Britnell and Pollard (eds.), *The McFarlane Legacy: Studies in Late Medieval Politics and Society*, 107–25

Tuck, A., "Neville, Ralph, first earl of Westmorland (*c.*1364–1425)," *ODNB*

Tuck, A., "Pole, Michael de la, first earl of Suffolk (*c.*1330–1389)," *ODNB*

Tuck, A., *Richard II and the English Nobility* (London, 1973)

Tuck, A., "Stafford, Edmund (1344–1419)," *ODNB*

Tuck, A., "Thomas [Thomas of Woodstock], duke of Gloucester (1355–1397)," *ODNB*

Tuck, A., "Vere, Robert de, ninth earl of Oxford, marquess of Dublin, and duke of Ireland (1362–1392)," *ODNB*

Tudor-Craig, P., "The Painted Chamber at Westminster," *Archaeological Journal*, vol. 114, no. 1 (1957), 92–105

Turner, M., *Chaucer: A European Life* (Princeton, 2019)

Tyler, J. E., *Henry of Monmouth: or, Memoirs of the Life and Character of Henry the Fifth, as Prince of Wales and King of England*, vol. 1 (London, 1838)

Vale, B., "Scrope, William, earl of Wiltshire (1351?–1399)," *ODNB*

Vale, M., *Henry V: The Conscience of a King* (New Haven and London, 2016)

Vaughan, R., *John the Fearless* (revised ed., Woodbridge, 2002)

Vaughan, R., *Philip the Bold* (revised ed., Woodbridge, 2002)

Veale, E. M., *The English Fur Trade in the Later Middle Ages* (Oxford, 1966)

Vetusta Monumenta, Society of Antiquaries of London, vol. 6 (1885)

Vincent, N., "Richard, first earl of Cornwall and king of Germany (1209–1272)," *ODNB*

Virgoe, R., "Hankeford [Hankford], Sir William (*c.*1350–1423)," *ODNB*

Waddell, G., "The Design of the Westminster Hall Roof," *Architectural History*, vol. 42 (1999), 47–67

Waldron, R., "Usk, Thomas (*c.*1354–1388)," *ODNB*

Walker, S., "John [John of Gaunt], duke of Aquitaine and duke of Lancaster, styled king of Castile and Léon (1340–1399)," *ODNB*

Walker, S., "Katherine [*née* Katherine Roelt; *married name* Katherine Swynford], duchess of Lancaster (1350?–1403)," *ODNB*

Walker, S., *The Lancastrian Affinity, 1361–99* (Oxford, 1990)

Walker, S., "Letters to the Dukes of Lancaster in 1381 and 1399," *EHR*, vol. 106, no. 418 (1991), 68–79

Walker, S., "Maidstone [Maydestone], Clement (*c.*1389–1456)," *ODNB*

Walker, S., "Political Saints in Later Medieval England," in Britnell and Pollard (eds.), *The McFarlane Legacy: Studies in Late Medieval Politics and Society*, 77–106

Walker, S., "Richard II's Reputation," in Dodd (ed.), *The Reign of Richard II*, 119–28

Walker, S., "Richard II's Views on Kingship," in Archer and Walker (eds.), *Rulers and Ruled in Late Medieval England*, 49–63

Walker, S., "The Yorkshire Risings of 1405: Texts and Contexts," in Dodd and Biggs (eds.), *Henry IV: The Establishment of the Regime*, 161–84

Warner, K., *Richard II: A True King's Fall* (Stroud, 2017)

Warner, M. W., "The Montagu Earls of Salisbury *circa* 1300–1428: A Study in Warfare, Politics and Political Culture," PhD thesis, University College London (1991)

Waugh, S. L., "Edmund [Edmund of Woodstock], first earl of Kent (1301–1330)," *ODNB*

Waugh, W. T., "Sir John Oldcastle," *EHR*, vol. 20, no 79 (1905), 434–56

Waugh, W. T., "Sir John Oldcastle (Continued)," *EHR*, vol. 20, no. 80 (1905), 637–58

Weber, N., and Hengerer, M. (eds.), *Animals and Court (Europe, c. 1200–1800)* (Berlin, 2020)

Wells, S., introduction to W. Shakespeare, *Richard II* (Harmondsworth, 1969)

Wentersdorf, K. P., "The Clandestine Marriages of the Fair Maid of Kent," *Journal of Medieval History*, vol. 5, no. 3 (1979), 203–31

Whitbread, R. E., "Tournaments, Jousts and Duels: Formal Combats in England and France, circa 1380–1440," PhD thesis, University of York (2013)

Wickham, C., *Medieval Europe* (New Haven and London, 2016)

Wilson, C., "The Medieval Monuments," in Collinson, Ramsay, and Sparks (eds.), *A History of Canterbury Cathedral*, 451–510

Wilson, C., "A Monument to St Edward the Confessor: Henry III's Great Chamber at Westminster and Its Paintings," in Rodwell and Tatton-Brown (eds.), *Westminster, Part II: The Art, Architecture and Archaeology of the Royal Palace*, 152–86

Wilson, C., "The Tomb of Henry IV and the Holy Oil of St Thomas at Canterbury," in Fernie and Crossley (eds.), *Medieval Architecture and Its Intellectual Context*, 181–90

Wilson, C., "Yevele, Henry (d. 1400), master mason," *ODNB*

Wilson, P. H., *The Holy Roman Empire* (London, 2016)

Wiswall, F. L., "Politics, Procedure and the 'Non-minority' of Edward III: Some Comparisons," in Gillespie (ed.), *The Age of Richard II*, 7–25

Wood, I., and Loud, G. A. (eds.), *Church and Chronicle in the Middle Ages* (London, 1991)

Woodacre, E., "Joan of Navarre: Beloved Queen and (Step)Mother or Unbeloved Witch?," in Norrie, Harris, Laynesmith, Messer, and Woodacre (eds.), *Later Plantagenet and the Wars of the Roses Consorts: Power, Influence and Dynasty*, 105–22

Woodger, L. S., "Bagot, Sir William (bef. 1354–1407), of Baginton, Warws," *Hist. Parl.*

Woodger, L. S., "Green, Sir Henry (*c.*1347–1399), of Drayton, Northants," *Hist. Parl.*

Woodger, L. S., and J. S. Roskell, "Pelham, John (d. 1429), of Pevensey Castle and Laughton, Suss," *Hist. Parl.*

Worden, B., "Which Play Was Performed at the Globe Theatre on 7 February 1601?," *London Review of Books*, vol. 25, no. 13 (2003)

Wright, E., "Henry IV, the Commons and the Recovery of Royal Finance in 1407," in Archer and Walker (eds.), *Rulers and Ruled in Late Medieval England*, 65–81

Wylie, J. H., *History of England under Henry the Fourth*, 4 vols. (1884–98)

Wylie, J. H., *The Reign of Henry the Fifth*, vol. 1 (Cambridge, 1914)

Yeager, R. F., and Takamiya, R. (eds.), *The Medieval Python* (New York, 2012)

LIST OF ILLUSTRATIONS

Art Insert Credits
1. Portrait of Richard II, Westminster Abbey.
2. Tomb of Richard II and Anne of Bohemia, Westminster Abbey: copyright, Dean and Chapter of Westminster.
3. White hart painting on the wall of the Muniment Room, Westminster Abbey: copyright, Dean and Chapter of Westminster.
4. Illumination of Charles VI by the Boucicaut Master from the *Dialogues de Pierre Salmon*, Bibliothèque de Genève, Ms. fr. 165, fol. 4r.
5. Left interior panel of the Wilton Diptych, National Gallery, London.
6. Right interior panel of the Wilton Diptych, National Gallery, London.
7. Folio from a handbook of geomancy, Bodleian Library, MS Bodl. 581, fol. 017v.
8. Westminster Hall: *An Inventory of the Historical Monuments in London*, vol. 2 (London, 1925), plate 175.
9. Hammerbeam angel, Westminster Hall: *An Inventory of the Historical Monuments in London*, vol. 2 (London, 1925), plate 180.
10. Tomb of Henry IV and Joan of Navarre, Canterbury Cathedral: Bridgeman Images.

INDEX